M000191143

O'BRIEN'S

Collecting

TOY CARS & TRUCKS

IDENTIFICATION & VALUE GUIDE

3rd Edition

EDITED BY ELIZABETH A. STEPHAN

On The Cover

All values are for toys on the cover are listed in C10 condition.

Front Cover

Buddy "L" Tank and Sprinkler Truck, 1924 .... $2,000
Ideal's Talking Police Car.. $120
Lansing Slik-Toy Pickup Truck, No. 9601 .... $50
Marx "Old Jalopy" tin wind-up, college boys, post WWII .. $300
Texaco Jet Fuel Truck, possibly a gas station premium .... NPF

Back Cover

Auburn Rubber Fire Truck $70
Banner Ambulance $40

Corgi 310 Corvette Sting Ray $80
Manoil Rocket.. $120
Marx Pet Shop Delivery truck $110
Matchbox No. 25 Petrol Tanker BP.................................... $20
Matchbox No. 42 Studebaker Lark Wagonaire.................. $19
Matchbox No. 48 Studebacker Lark Wagonaire $19
Matchbox No. 68 Mercedes Coach $418
Matchbox Y-11 1912 Packard Landaulet $42
Midgetoy Cadillac $20
Tootsietoy Greyhound Bus $45

© 2000 by
Krause Publications

All rights reserved.
No portion of this publication may be reproduced or transmitted in any form or by any means,
electronic or mechanical, including photocopy, recording, or any information storage and retrieval system, without permission in
writing from the publisher, except by a reviewer who may quote brief passages in a critical article or review to be printed in a
magazine or newspaper, or electronically transmitted on radio or television.

Published by

krause publications

700 E. State Street • Iola, WI 54990-0001
Telephone: 715/445-2214

Please call or write for our free catalog.
Our toll-free number to place an order or obtain a free catalog is 800-258-0929
or please use our regular business telephone 715-445-2214
for editorial comment and further information.

Library of Congress: 99-68143
ISBN: 0-87341-580-9

Printed in the United States of America

CONTENTS

Introduction

Toy vehicles are one of the most popular collectibles on today's toy market. Who doesn't want to find those cars and trucks they played with as a child? Attend any toy show and you will find all varieties of toy vehicles — old and new. It is my hope that this book will help clear up any mysteries surrounding the sometimes confusing world of collecting toy cars and trucks.

Since 1994, *Collecting Toy Cars & Trucks* has been the most comprehensive toy vehicle identification and price guide on the market. Together with a group of expert contributors, Richard O'Brien provided information about toy vehicle manufacturers that no other book had ever covered before. Now that Richard O'Brien has retired, I hope to carry on that tradition.

In this, the third edition of *O'Brien's Collecting Toy Cars & Trucks*, the collector and toy car enthusiast should find more information than before. Prices have been updated, photos have been added and manufacturers such as Johnny Lightning/Topper have been included.

The more things change, the more they stay the same

The basic layout of O'Brien's has stayed the same. Some manufacturers have been split into subcategories, others have been slightly reorganized. I did this hoping it would make the book easier to use. A Miscellaneous chapter was created for the toy companies with only a few listings; the individual manufacturers can be found alphabetically in the table of contents.

In the past, distinct numbers were used to identify some items in this book. These numbers, also known as O'Brien's Numbers, were not manufacturer marks, but were meant to help collectors catalog and organize their collections. Considered by some collectors as useful, these numbers often confused others. Because of this, the O'Brien Numbers can now be found in parentheses at the end of the listing. **Please be aware, these numbers cannot be found on the toy, they are only meant to aid in the identification of certain toys**.

I would like to thank everyone who contributed to this edition — Kent Comstock, Reid Covey, Don and Barb DeSalle, Perry Eichor, John Gibson, Dave Leopard, Jack Matthews, Fred Maxwell, Randy Prasse, Mark Rich, Vincent Rosa, Brian Seligman, Bob Smith, Ron Smith and John Taylor. Mark Rich, Ken Boyer, Brent Frankenhoff and Tom Michael donated the items shown on the cover. Ross Hubbard photographed the cover and Tom Dupuis designed it. *O'Brien's Collecting Toy Cars & Trucks* was paginated by Shelly Johnson; Mike Jacquart was photo editor. My appreciation also goes out to *Toy Shop* editor Sharon Korbeck, *Toy Cars & Vehicles* associate editor Merry Dudley and *Warman's Today's Collector* associate editor Lisa Jacobsen for their help when I needed it most. To all the others who lent their advice, opinions and expertise, thank you.

A Guide is Just a Guide

Values in this book come from outside contributors, from advertisements in toy magazines, and from observations at toy shows — be aware that a toy which is valued at $1,000 in C10 may not bring that amount on the secondary market. A dealer will give you a percentage of the value of a toy. Remember that a dealer must mark up the item to market value in order to make a profit.

Because a price guide is just that — a guide — it is best to use this book as a way to gauge the collectibility and desirability of your toy. The price offered for a toy can vary from dealer to dealer due to geographical differences, economic factors and time of year.

Contributors are always needed for a book like this. If you feel you can assist in any way, I would love to hear from you. Thank you for picking up *O'Brien's Collecting Toy Cars & Trucks*. I hope you find it helpful.

Elizabeth A. Stephan, editor
700 E. State St.
Iola, WI 54990
stephane@krause.com

Abbreviations

NPF = No Price Found; this means that a value was never found for this item. It could mean the toy is rare or rare and valuable (the two do not always go hand in hand).

n/a = not applicable; this is used when an item must be Mint in Pack or Mint in Box to have any value.

C6 = Good; there is overall wear, and the item has been played with but still carried some value.

C8 = Very Good; minor wear but the item is clean.

C10 = Mint in Box, Mint in Pack, Mint on Card; like new. With items that are almost impossible to find with the original box, C10 stands for Mint without box.

c. = circa; approximately, i.e., c.1950.

Reproduction Alert

By Mark Rich

Collecting toys seems to become more complicated, the more years that pass. Beginning collectors especially must be wary these days. Because of growing interest in vintage toy cars and trucks, increasing numbers of reproductions and outright fakes are appearing. Some are made with the intention of deceiving buyers into thinking they have obtained a rare and valuable antique toy. Others are made with the honest intent of lovingly re-creating a popular toy of bygone times, and then are sold by middlemen, or sometimes by ignorant dealers, as the Real McCoy. What stands between the collector and the unprincipled scoundrels hunting for a dishonest dollar? One thing, and one thing only — Knowledge.

This book exists for your education. Study it closely. Do not rely upon it exclusively, however. However expert the various authors are in their areas of specialty, none of them can convey to you, the reader, in a few notations, how to know the true from the fake.

The various collectors and dealers I have talked with agree on one thing — nothing replaces experience — not only direct experience with the toy itself, but indirect experience, which is readily available from fellow collectors and dealers who have been long active in the field. If you are a new collector, you can make no greater mistake than to enter with a spirit of competition. Most collectors and dealers (who are also usually collectors) act with a cooperative spirit. They are usually willing to share their experience with the novice, partly because the sharing of information is pleasurable, and partly because all serious toy hobbyists and historians welcome additions to their ranks. While what one collector told me is extreme — that against the fakes "the novice doesn't have a chance," he said — it is absolutely true that the unassisted novice hasn't a chance. That said, here are a few general tips to keep in mind on your collecting forays.

In tin-lithographed toys, according to long-time collector and toy dealer Chip Strode-Jackson of Sheboygan, Wisconsin, the main thing to keep in mind is that most vintage items are not going to be in Mint condition. The boxes are apt to be stressed and even disintegrating, most having been made of materials that normally would not last more than ten years. Since it is difficult to reproduce the antique look of the original tin litho, most reproductions have a shiny paint. Usually, too, they are made of a lighter tin than the originals. He also noted that modern printing seems to use more colors than were available years ago. "Always know where your toy came from," Strode-Jackson also recommended. The ideal — which is only occasionally possible — is to buy items that have been parts of a long-established collection. In any case, try to discover as much of the background of that particular toy as possible, and ask for the card of the person selling the item in case questions arise later. Also use a reasonable amount of caution if considering buying an item with a "rare paint scheme" or "rare color," since unscrupulous dealers have been known to "restore" items to a state that is simply wrong, as opposed to rare.

Similarly, in older pressed-steel vehicle toys, expect a certain amount of dullness and wear. "It's not going to be shiny, fresh, or new," Strode-Jackson said. "There are very few of those out there." In other words, if someone has an exceptional example of an authentic toy, they should know the history of that toy. There should be a reason the toy survived in that condition.

Even die-cast collectors can take some reasonable precautions. Corgi collector Joseph Hurd, of Arlington Heights, Illinois, outlined several important points. Some valuable die-cast toys came with various accessories, any of which might be either reproduced or replaced. Sometimes such parts as bumpers or windshields may be replaced, or shifted from another toy. Hurd noted that boxes should be examined carefully for signs of having been reproduced or patched together from incomplete boxes. Corgi boxes of the early 1970s are easily reproduced, he noted. Hurd, too, emphasized how important it is to establish the provenance of a toy before buying.

Cast-iron toys usually come first to mind at the thought of reproductions. Ray Lacktorin of Stillwater, Minnesota, who has over thirty years of experience with cast iron, told me that for serious collectors, reproductions have never been a significant problem. Beginning collectors, however, can get themselves into real difficulties if they do not take care. "Something an older dealer told me when I started in this business in 1966 has stayed with me," Lacktorin said. "He told me, 'If you're going to spend more than twenty dollars for anything, know what you're buying.' I've always kept this in mind." When I talked to him, Lacktorin had recently started looking at items available online, and was surprised, not pleasantly, by the number of reproductions being sold. With his experienced eye, he could detect the forgeries. When I asked him what tips he would give a novice in examining photos, he recommended that novices simply not buy from photos. "Photographs hide what's the matter," he said. Whenever possible, he said, pick up the cast-iron toy and look inside. "Ninety-nine percent of all cast-iron toys were dipped in paint," he said. "They're smooth as glass." In other words, both outside and inside received the usually thick paint. "Most of your nice old toys have decent and good workmanship," he said, adding that he had recently seen "a bunch of very crude Mack trucks, just like globs of metal," being passed off as old.

Many cast-iron toys made as decorator items from the 1970s through the 1990s have several tell-tale characteristics. Usually the parts are poorly matched, the large grain-size of the molds has left a rough surface texture, and screws hold the pieces together. Frequently the axles and rivets or screws remain shiny even after attempts to "antique" them.

As far as specific models Lacktorin had noticed recently, he pointed out a variety of roughly four-inch autos and race cars by Hubley and Arcade being copied, as well as Kenton fire-tuck toys, large "Utexico" emergency vehicles which may be Dent copies, and the Skoglund and Olson bus.

Collectors of plastic cars and trucks should be aware that some Marx vehicles, including a Coca Cola bottle truck, are being "re-popped," as Marx collectors put it. Keeping in contact with other collectors and major dealers will help keep you abreast of developments there.

Numerous slush-metal vehicles, including Barclays, are also being re-issued. Usually the freshness of paint and of the metal itself is a dead give-away. These are not being sold as anything but re-issues, and only occasionally are being offered as originals by the unscrupulous or ignorant.

Several collectors and dealers have told me they worry that new collectors shelling out for reproductions will give up the hobby in disgust, when they discover what they own. Sometimes we must simply swallow pride and take the fake for what it is: a hard-earned lesson.

Above all, persevere in your collecting, for the pleasures of collecting and spending time with other collectors are far greater than the pains of the mistakes.

Mark Rich is a collector, dealer and free-lance writer from Wisconsin. He can be reached at P.O. Box 971, Stevens Point, WI 54481-0971, mark.rich@sff.net.

A.C. WILLIAMS

A.C. Williams was founded in 1886 when Adam Clark Williams bought the J.W. Williams Company from his father. After a fire in 893, the firm moved from Chagrin Falls, Ohio, to Ravenna. Toy production began about this time. Small cast-iron toys were Williams' specialty, with banks, cars, and aircraft predominant. A.C. Williams retired in 1919, but the firm continued to make toys until 1938, after which it continued in business in a non-toy capacity. Williams marked few, if any, of its toys. Two clues to an A.C. Williams toy are turned steel hubs and starred axle peens.

	C6	C8	C10
Austin for Car Carrier	75	128	175
Auto Bank, early, 6" long..................	250	40	550
Bus, 5" long....................................	75	125	175
Bus, twin coach, 1936, 8-1/4" long...	300	425	650
Car Carrier, w/three Austins, 1920, 12-1/2" long..................................	350	550	775
Coast to Coast Cartage Co. Stake Trailer Truck, 10-1/8" long	150	250	375
Coast to Coast Co. Stake Truck, two-piece, 7" long	250	400	550
Coupe, 1930s, 7" long.....................	500	800	1100
Coupe, w/rumble seat, sidemounts, 1930, 6-3/4" long........................	150	250	375
Coupe, 1928, 6" long	120	175	250
Coupe, 4-1/2" long	90	140	200
Coupe, 3" long, two-piece body, 1936..	75	125	200
Coupe, 3-1/2" long	50	75	100
Delivery Van, 8" long......................	350	525	750
Doctor's Coupe, w/curtains, 5" long .	200	325	450
Double Decker Faegol Bus, blue with gold side stripes, 7-3/4" long...............................	500	700	900
Dump Truck, 7" long	100	150	225
Fageol Bus, stenciling on roof reads Wisconsin Motor Bus Lines, 7-3/4"	600	800	1400
Fire Pumper, interchangeable, 5" long..	80	120	175

	C6	C8	C10
Ford Opera Coupe, 5" long..............	150	225	350
Gasoline-Motor Oil Truck, cast iron, 10-1/4" long	400	600	750
Grader, 6" long...............................	200	300	425
Hook & Ladder, 7-1/2" long..............	125	200	300
Laundry Truck, 8" long	375	550	825
Lincoln Touring Car, 7" long............	175	275	400
Lincoln Touring Car, 9-1/4" long	450	675	950
Lincoln Touring Coupe, 8-3/4" long..	500	850	1250
Machinery Hauler, three lowboy trailers, roadscraper, roadroller, tractor, overall length 28-5/8" long	1500	2750	4500
Mack Gas Tank Truck, 7-1/4" long...	125	200	300

A.C. Williams Fageol Bus, stenciling on roof reads Wisconsin Motor Bus Lines, 7-3/4".

A.C. Williams Mack Gas Tank Truck, 10-1/4".

A.C. Williams Double Decker Bus, blue with gold side stripes, 7-3/4".

A.C. Williams Sedan, 1936, 6-3/4".

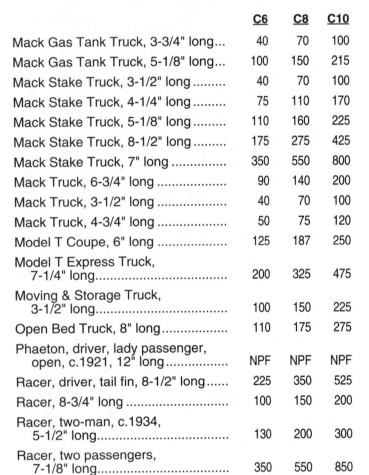

A.C. Williams Sedan, two-piece, 4-1/2". Photo from Mapes Auctioneers and Appraisers.

	C6	C8	C10
Mack Gas Tank Truck, 3-3/4" long...	40	70	100
Mack Gas Tank Truck, 5-1/8" long...	100	150	215
Mack Stake Truck, 3-1/2" long	40	70	100
Mack Stake Truck, 4-1/4" long	75	110	170
Mack Stake Truck, 5-1/8" long	110	160	225
Mack Stake Truck, 8-1/2" long	175	275	425
Mack Stake Truck, 7" long	350	550	800
Mack Truck, 6-3/4" long	90	140	200
Mack Truck, 3-1/2" long	40	70	100
Mack Truck, 4-3/4" long	50	75	120
Model T Coupe, 6" long	125	187	250
Model T Express Truck, 7-1/4" long..............................	200	325	475
Moving & Storage Truck, 3-1/2" long..............................	100	150	225
Open Bed Truck, 8" long..................	110	175	275
Phaeton, driver, lady passenger, open, c.1921, 12" long	NPF	NPF	NPF
Racer, driver, tail fin, 8-1/2" long......	225	350	525
Racer, 8-3/4" long	100	150	200
Racer, two-man, c.1934, 5-1/2" long.................................	130	200	300
Racer, two passengers, 7-1/8" long.................................	350	550	850

	C6	C8	C10
Racer, boat-tailed, 6-1/2" long	100	180	260
Radiator Car, four-casting, nickeled, approx 4" long..............................	75	110	150
Sedan, c.1931, cast-iron, interchangeable body, 6-3/4" long	300	450	625
Sedan, 5" long..............................	100	160	220
Sedan, two-piece, 4-1/2" long	100	160	230
Sedan, c.1920, 4" long....................	60	100	150
Sedan, 1936, 6-3/4" long	250	500	700
Sedan, approx 3-1/2" long	175	300	450
Sedan, c.1930, cast-iron, streamlined rear fender, 6-1/2" long...	200	325	475
Steamroller, 1930s, 5-1/2" long........	75	110	160
Streamline Sedan, 8" long	450	750	1250
Studebaker, two-tone sedan, c.1933-34, approx 4" long............	100	150	225
Tank, 4" long	60	100	140
Taxi, 1920s, 5-1/4" long	150	250	350
Touring Car, w/two riders, c.1917, 11-3/4" long	550	900	1300
Touring Car, 7" long	400	600	850
Touring Car, cast-iron, 9-1/2" long...	350	450	725
Tractor, w/driver, 5" long..................	100	150	225
Wrecker, 5" long.............................	75	125	175
Wrecker, 6-1/2" long	200	350	500
Wrecker, 7-3/4" long	350	500	750

ACME PLASTIC TOYS, INC.

Collectors may notice a strong similarity between Acme Plastic Toys' vehicles and Thomas Toys, and there is. With an address of 121 East 124th St., New York, New York, Acme handled the marketing of Thomas Toys from 1945 to 1950. Toys from this era bear the Acme Plastic Toys mark.

Islyn Thomas, owner of Thomas Toys, bought out Ben Shapiro of Acme in 1950. From that point on, all toys carried the Thomas Toys' mark.

Acme also made other toys—helicopters, planes, baby carriages and strollers and wagons.

Acme Transporter, green cab, red trailer, two cars, 1950s.

Acme Jeep with original box, yellow jeep with red wheels.

Top to Bottom: Acme Truck and Trailer, green, blue trailer, 9", 1947; Acme Truck Wrecker, red.

	C6	C8	C10
Aerocar PT 560, plastic, marked "Made in U.S.A. Plas-Tex," 7-1/2" long	125	175	200
Airline Limousine, No. 29, 1947, 4-1/2" long	23	25	27
Auto Carrier, No. ?, 9" long	20	25	30
Convertible Coupe, streamlined, No. 77, 4-1/2" long (Acme used the same number for sedan and convertible)	9	11	15
Coupe and House Trailer, No. 30, 1947, 8-1/4" long	20	22	24
Delivery Truck, No. 41, 1947, 4" long	16	18	20
Dump Truck, No. 42, 1947, 5" long	12	14	16
Esso Gas Truck, No. 43, 1947	NPF	NPF	NPF
Jeep, No. 17, movable windshield, 1947, 4-1/2" long	23	25	27
Jeep and Trailer, No. 19, 1947, 8-1/2" long	14	16	18
Limousine and Trailer, No. 55, 6-4" long	26	31	36
Merry-Go-Round Truck, No. 74, 4-3/4" long	20	25	30
Motorcycle, plastic, w/rider, No. 72, 4" long	45	50	55
Motorcycle, plated, No. 125, 4" long	NPF	NPF	NPF

	C6	C8	C10
Police-Fire Chief Radio Car, No. 67, 4-1/2" long	23	25	27
Sedan, No. 27, 1947, 4-5/16" long	18	20	22
Sedan, streamlined, No. 77, 4-1/2" long	11	13	15
Service Motorcycle, w/rider, No. 90, 4-7/16" long	25	30	35
Texaco Gas Truck, No. 40, 1947, 4" long	21	23	25
Transporter, green cab, red trailer, two cars, 1950s	NPF	NPF	NPF
Transporter, green cab w/red trailer and two cars, 1950s	20	35	50
Truck and Trailer, No. 16, 1947, 9" long	14	16	18
Truck Wrecker, No. 26, 5" long	35	40	45
Truck, streamlined, No. 18, 1947, 5" long	10	12	14
Utility Trailer, streamlined, No. 48, marked "fits items 27-29-40-41," 2-1/2" long	6	8	10

ALL AMERICAN TOY COMPANY (OREGON)

All American was founded by Clay Steinke in Salem, Oregon in 1948. It continued until 1955, with its location in the Jorgenson Building on Ferry Street. At its peak, it employed forty-two people. In total, it sold 26,000 toys. And despite formidable 1950 price of $20, All American's most popular toy was the Timber Toter. Collectors should note that toy vehicles made by All American had air-horn steering and Goodyear tires.

Patrick Russell purchased All American Toy Company in 1992. Available now are parts and new limited edition vehicles.

	C6	C8	C10		C6	C8	C10
Cargo Liner, model CL-8, 38" long...	275	400	600	Midget Skagit, model S-I, 16" long...	120	240	360
Cattle Liner, model C-5, 38" long..........................	400	650	925	Midget Skagit, model MS, battery-powered, 18" long......................	250	450	600
Dyna-Dump, model D-3, 20" long..........................	250	400	550	Play-Dozer, model HD-7, 9" long............................	300	500	700
Heavy Hauler, model HH-9, 38" long..........................	300	475	750	Play-Loader, model HD-6, 11" long...........................	300	500	700
Midget Skagit, model W/T-6.............	NPF	NPF	NPF	Timber Toter, model L-2, w/logs, 38" extended length	260	400	585
Midget Skagit, model U-1, Midget Skagit....................................	NPF	NPF	NPF	Timber Toter Jr., model LJ-4, 20" long......................................	100	200	300

The Cargo-Liner, Timber Toter and Utility truck were other new offerings from All-American in 1953. Photo from 1953 All-American catalog.

All-American Dyna-Dump, white cab with "All-American" insignia, red bed. Photo from Roy Bonjour.

A.C. Williams Double Decker Bus, blue with gold side stripes, 7-3/4".

The Timber Toter Jr., and an optional trailer. Photo from 1953 All-American catalog.

The Model S-1 Scoop-A-Veyor, the Model HD-6 Play-Loader, Model HD-7 Play-Dozer as shown in the 1953 All-American catalog.

ALLIED

Allied, of Corona, New York, only made plastic toys. They specialized in small, inexpensive items, including as cars trucks, and boats, to pistols, animals, and dollhouse furniture.

	C6	C8	C10		C6	C8	C10
Auto Sales and Station, w/five vehicles	65	100	130	Emergency Truck, 7" long, No. 129	NPF	NPF	NPF
Cement Mixer, No. 197, 4" long	NPF	NPF	NPF	Furniture Moving Van, large, No. 208, clear trailer ("Viso Box"), 5-1/2" long, price without original ten pieces of furniture	10	15	20
Construction Set, No. 620, included dump truck, cement truck and emergency truck w/ladder, 15" long box	NPF	NPF	NPF	Haulaway Truck and Trailer, w/two small cars and one large car, No. 122, 10" long	15	25	38
Delivery Service Truck	35	52	70				
Dump Truck, large, No. 174, 5-1/2" long	NPF	NPF	NPF	Old Fashioned Car, No. 218, 4-1/2" long	NPF	NPF	NPF
Dump Truck, small, No. 191, 4-1/2" long	10	15	20	Pick-up Truck, 3-1/2" long	8	10	15

	C6	C8	C10
Racer, No. 130, 4-5/8" long..............	15	25	33
Stake Truck, 4-1/2" long..................	10	15	20
Stake Truck, w/eight assorted farm animals and removable racks, No. 193, 9-1/2" long....................	NPF	NPF	NPF
Station Wagon, 3-1/2" long	8	10	15
Steam Shovel Truck, No. 134, 6" long...	NPF	NPF	NPF
Taxi, 3-1/2" long	8	10	15
Tractor, No. 30, 3" long	NPF	NPF	NPF
Van, enclosed, 6" long	10	15	20
Wrecker, 4-3/8" long	15	20	25

Allied Furniture Moving Van. Photo from Dave Leopard.

ALL-NU

	C6	C8	C10			C6	C8	C10
Field Kitchen, lead, marked "Made in USA," approx. 2-1/2" long (ANV001)	NPF	NPF	NPF	**Cardboard Vehicles**				
				Ambulance, No. Military 154		3	5	7
Searchlight, lead, marked "Made in USA," approx. 2-3/4" long (ANV002)	NPF	NPF	NPF	Army Troop Carrier, No. 155............		3	5	7
				Cannon, No. 151		3	5	7
Sound Detector, lead, marked "Made in USA," approx., 2-3/4" long (ANV003)	NPF	NPF	NPF	Jeep, No. 150.................................		3	5	7
				Tank, No. 153		3	5	7
Tank, lead, marked "Made in USA," "USA", 3" long (ANV004)	NPF	NPF	NPF	Wheeled AA Gun, No. 152..............		3	5	7

The All-Nu Searchlight, Field Kitchen, Tank and Sound Detector.

AMERICAN NATIONAL

Founded by the Diemer brothers—William, Walter and Harry—around 1894, American National, of Toledo, Ohio, produced a huge number of pedal cars and a line of pressed steel trucks in the 1920s and 1930s.

	C6	C8	C10
American Railway Express, 27" long..............................	1000	1600	2400
Army Truck, Mack "Giant," 26-1/2" long..	800	1400	2000
Chemical Fire Truck, 28" long..........	2000	3200	4500
Circus Truck, 27" long......................	800	1400	2000
Coal Truck..	1500	2500	4200
Duesenberg Bobtail Pedal Car, late 1920s..	3000	5500	7000
Dump Truck, 28" long	800	1400	2000
Fire Chief Pedal Truck, 66" long	3000	5000	7900
Fire Pedal Truck, c.late 1920s	4000	7500	13,000
Jordan Pedal Car, 40" long	1000	1700	2400

	C6	C8	C10
Juvenile Auto Dump Truck Pedal Car, 57" long.................................	2000	3500	5000
Lincoln Dual Cowl Pedal Car	4000	7500	12,000
Moving Van, 28" long	800	1400	2000
Packard, brown, extensive side trim, 28" long..	NPF	NPF	NPF
Packard Convertible, red, 28" long ..	NPF	NPF	NPF
Packard Coupe Pedal Car, 1928, 56" long..	2000	3200	4600
Packard Coupe Pedal Car, steerable front wheels, 54" long ..	1500	2500	3400
Packard Fire Chief Car, 27" long	3000	5500	10,000
Packard Pedal Car, 1923, 70" long..	3000	5500	10,000

**American National American Railway Express, 27",
black cab, red and silver tires, green bed.**

**American National Packard Convertible, 28", red.
Photo from Bill Bertoia Auctions.**

**American National Packard, 28", brown, extensive
side trim. Photo from Bill Bertoia Auctions.**

**American National Packard Coupe, 1928 pedal car,
56", red, red centers, white tires.**

	C6	C8	C10
Racing Car, 1927	2000	3200	4500
Richfield Gasoline Truck, 27" long ...	1500	2250	3100
Screenside Truck	1500	2500	3600
Sprinkler Truck	1400	2500	3500
Tanker	1400	2500	3500
Truck, open bed, 29" long	700	1150	1700

American National Packard Coupe, 1923 pedal car, 70", yellow, brown top.

ANDY GARD

	C6	C8	C10		C6	C8	C10
Bell Telephone Truck	22	33	45	Gee I Jeep, battery-operated	20	30	40
Brink's Armored Car, battery-operated	30	45	60	MG, motor-powered cable steering..	100	150	200
Crane, magnetic, battery-operated ..	62	93	125	Pickup Truck, 6" long, soft plastic	7	11	15
Fire Engine, battery-operated	37	56	75	Telephone Truck	30	45	60
				Touring Sedan, 19" long	37	56	75

ANIMATE TOY CO.

In 1918, this firm was located at East 17th St., in New York City, and its president was L.T. Savage. By 1931, it has moved to 30 North 15th Street in East Orange, NJ, and employed ten men and forty women. In 1934, the president-vice president was George V. Turnbull, and the secretary-treasurer was George H. Webb. Five men and eleven women made up the work force. See also "Woodhaven."

	C6	C8	C10
Baby Haymaker Push Toy Playset, tin, 1916	100	150	200
Baby Tractor, friction, marked "patented June 20, 1916"	85	130	175
Climbing Tractor, wind-up, 9" long, 1929	110	165	225
Toy Tractor, wind-up, 8-1/2" long.....	NPF	NPF	NPF
Toy Tractor and Dump Trailer, wind-up, 15-1/2" long.........................	NPF	NPF	NPF
Toy Tractor w/Snow Plow, 13" long, wind-up	NPF	NPF	NPF
Toy Tractor w/Sweeper, wind-up, 12-1/2" long...............................	NPF	NPF	NPF
U.S. Baby Tank, wind-up, pat. June 20, 1916 (new in 1918), 2-1/2" long, ...	37	56	75

Animate Toy Baby Tractor, friction.

ARCADE

In 1869, a foundry in Freeport, Illinois, was organized as a two-man partnership under the name of Novelty Iron and Brass Foundry. It was dissolved in 1885 when a new, larger factory was incorporated under the name of Arcade Manufacturing Co. Arcade made industrial castings and household items, but no toys. After a disastrous fire in 1892 and management changes in 1893, toys began to appear in its catalog, and by the early 1900s the line had become so extensive that a fifty-page catalog was issued showing a large line of notions and novelties, small stoves, banks and a few trains, including a unique pile-driver. But it was not until an enterprising young lawyer married the daughter of one of the officers and joined the firm in 1919 that the firm rapidly became one of the major makers of cast-iron toys. Struck by the large numbers of Yellow Cabs in the streets of Chicago, the young man approached the Yellow Cab Company with a novel proposition: in return for the sole right to make toy replicas of the cab, the Yellow Cab Company would have the exclusive right to use the toy in its advertising. Success was instantaneous.

Arcade went on to duplicate this pattern with miniature Buick, Chevrolet, Ford, Plymouth and Pontiac automobiles; and McCormack-Deering and International Harvester farm equipment; and several makes of trucks and buses.

In the booming 1920s, the company's sales swelled so much that a new and larger plant was built in 1927. Two years later, the stock market crash heralded the Great Depression, and hard times hit the small car business just as it did the large ones.

Cheap competition and dwindling demand for toys costing more than a dime had brought the company to the brink of bankruptcy by 1933. But once again the enterprising management gave the firm new life with an exclusive arrangement to provide souvenir replicas of the fairground buses made by G.M.C. for the Chicago Century of Progress. The Depression caused a cheapening of quality, but World War II gave the firm business in military material.

After the war, the company returned to making industrial and household hardware and a few toys, but cheaper toys of die-cast zamac, plastic, rubber and lithographed tin eclipsed the more expensive cast-iron toys. In 1946 the firm was sold to Rockwell Manufacturing Co. of Pittsburgh. Death and retirement soon finished the change of the old firm, and it followed its guiding directors into oblivion when Rockwell moved to Alabama.

Arcade toys were meant to be played with and are extremely rare in Mint condition. The year listed is the year the toy was introduced.

Contributor: Michael W. Curran, Illinois Antiques, P.O. Box 545, Hampton, IL 61256, 309-496-9426.

	C6	C8	C10
A.C.F. Bus, 1927, 11-1/2" long (AR001)	1700	2700	4100
Allis-Chalmers Tractor and Dump Trailer, No. 2657, 1937, 12-3/4" long w/trailer (AR003)	125	175	275
Allis-Chalmers Tractor and Dump Trailer, No. 2660, 1937, 8-1/4" long (AR003A)	75	125	180
Allis-Chalmers Tractor and Trailer, No. 2650, 1936, 13" long total length (AR002)	200	300	450
Allis-Chalmers Tractor Trailer, No. 2650, 1937, 13" long w/ trailer (AR004)	200	310	475
Allis-Chalmers WC Tractor, 1941, 7-3/4" long (AR005)	425	675	1000

Animate Toy Climbing Tractor, 9", driver, red wheels, 1929.

Left to Right: Arcade A.C.F. Bus, 11-1/2", 1927; Arcade Yellow Parlor Coach Bus, 13", 1926. Photo from Bill Bertoia Auctions.

Variations of numerous Arcade ambulances from the 1930s. Photo from Bill Bertoia Auctions.

Arcade Andy Gump Car, red and green, white tires, 1920s, 7-1/4". Photo from Bill Bertoia Auctions.

Arcade Austin Wrecker, 1932, 3-3/4".

Arcade Brinks Express Truck, red, red and white wheels, 1932, 11-3/4". Photo from Bill Bertoia Auctions.

	C6	C8	C10
Ambulance, No. 187, 1932, 7-3/4" long (AR006)	350	575	850
Ambulance, blue, No. 188, 1932, 6" long (AR007)	300	500	725
Ambulance, white, No. 188, 1932, 6" long (AR007A)	275	425	625
Ambulance, white-painted version of No. 2620X Chevrolet Panel Delivery Truck, 1936, 4" long (AR008)	350	575	800
American Gasoline Mack Tank Truck, 1925, 13-1/4" long (AR152)	1200	1850	2500
Andy Gump Car, 1920s, 7-1/4" long (AR263)	1250	2250	3500
Anthony Dump Truck, 1927, 8-1/8" long (AR009)	1000	1700	2750
Austin Autocrat Road Roller, No. 291, 1928, 7" long (AR010)	300	475	675
Austin Delivery Truck, No. 173, 1932, 3-3/4" long (AR011)	50	75	100
Austin Racer, No. 175X, 1932, 3-3/4" long (AR012)	50	75	100

	C6	C8	C10
Austin Roadster, No. 174, 1932, 3-3/4" long (AR013)	125	200	275
Austin Roll-A-Plane, 7-1/2" long (AR014)	500	900	1400
Austin Stake Truck, No. 176X, 1932, 3-3/4" long (AR015)	125	200	300
Austin Wrecker, No. 177X, 1932, 3-3/4" long (AR016)	125	200	300
Avery Tractor, stack, no hood, 1923, 4-/2" long (AR017)	30	45	60
Avery Tractor, has hood, no stack, 1926, 4-1/2" long (AR018)	110	170	250
Borden's Milk Bottle Truck, No. 2640X, 1936, 6-1/4" long (AR019)	1000	1600	2400
Brinks Express Truck, 1932, 11-3/4" long (AR020)	8000	15,000	20,000
Buick Coupe, 1927, 8-1/2" long (AR021)	2500	4400	6250

ARCADE CAST IRON TOYS

THE 25 LINE

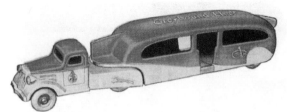

No. 4360 Great Lakes Expo Bus

An exact model in miniature of the Cleveland Exposition Transportation Bus.
Length 7¼ inches, width 1½ inches, height 1¾ inches.
Color: Bright blue, white and silver, as illustrated. White rubber wheels. Stencilled on top "Greyhound Lines." Trailer turns on pivot and is detachable.
Packed 6 in carton, 3 dozen in case.
Case net weight 22 lbs., case gross weight 27 lbs.
Case measurements: 10x12x14 inches.

No. 1440 Racer

Length 8 inches, width 3 inches, height 2 inches.
Color: Assorted red, silver and blue. Driver's head and number high lighted with gold bronze. White rubber wheels with red centers on the blue and silver toys, blue centers on the red toys.
Packed 6 in box, 3 dozen in case.
Case net weight 36 lbs., case gross weight 42 lbs.
Case measurements: 11x12x20 inches.

No. 1100X Pontiac Sedan

Length 6½ inches, width 2½ inches, height 2¼ inches.
Color: Assorted red, blue, green and silver. Nickeled radiator, hood center, lights and bumper. White rubber wheels with red centers on blue, green and silver toys, blue centers on red toys.
Packed 6 in box, 3 dozen in case.
Case net weight 38 lbs., case gross weight 42 lbs.
Case measurements: 11x11x22 inches.

No. 1680X Pierce Arrow Coupe

Length 7¼ inches, width 2¼ inches, height 2¼ inches.
Color: Assorted red, green, and blue. "Silver Arrow" on sides, and headlights gold bronze striped. Nickeled radiator and bumper. White rubber wheels with centers colored red or blue, in contrast to color of body.
This toy is also supplied in bright silver finish with red centered wheels, when ordered.
Packed 6 in carton, 3 dozen in case.
Case net weight 38 pounds, case gross weight 42 pounds.
Case measurements: 11x13x14 inches.

No. 1250X DeSoto Sedan

Length 6⅞ inches, width 2½ inches, height 2¼ inches.
Color: Assorted red, green, grey, and blue. Nickeled radiator, lights and bumper. White rubber wheels with red centers on blue, green and gray toys, blue centers on red toy.
Packed 4 assorted colors, 6 in carton, 3 dozen in case.
Case net weight 34 pounds, case gross weight 39 pounds.
Case measurements: 9x13x15 inches.

No. 2390X Pontiac Stake Truck

Length 6¼ inches, width 2½ inches, height 2¼ inches.
Color: Assorted red, blue and green. Nickeled radiator, hood center, lights and bumper. White rubber wheels with red centers on blue and green toys, blue centers on red toy.
Packed 6 in box, 3 dozen in case.
Case net weight 38 lbs., case gross weight 42 lbs.
Case measurements: 11x12x20 inches.

"THEY LOOK REAL"

Page 7 from the No. 51 Arcade catalog.

Arcade issued numerous buses in the 1930s-1940s. Photo from Bill Bertoia Auctions.

	C6	C8	C10
Buick Sedan, 1927, 8-1/2" long (AR022)	1500	2500	4000
Bullet Racer, No. 139X, 1931, 7-5/8" long (AR191)	900	1300	2300
Bus, Double-Decker, No. 316X, 1929, 8-1/2" long (AR023)	400	600	900
Bus, Double-Decker, No. 317, 1936, stamped "Chicago Motor Coach," 8-1/4" long (AR024)	400	675	950
Cab, brown and white, 1923, 9" long (AR020A)	1800	3000	4500
Cab, brown and white, 1923, 8" long (AR020B)	2200	3700	5500
Cab, green and white, c.1923, 9" long (AR111A)	1200	2000	3200

	C6	C8	C10
Car Carrier, cargo has four 25-cent cars or three 50-cent Arcade cars, No. 238, 1931, 24-1/2" long (AR025)	1500	2500	4000
Car Carrier, carries either two No. 114 Ford Sedans and one No. 113X Ford Arcade Coupe or one No. 213 Ford Stake and one each of the others; No. 296, 1932, 24-1/2" long (AR026)	1400	2400	3800
Car Transport, came w/two No. 1501 Sedans, No. 1502 Stake Truck and Wrecker No. 1503; 1937, No. 3107, 18-1/2" long (AR027)	800	1250	1800
Car Transport, holds two sedans, two trucks; No. 2977, 1937, 11-1/4" long (AR028)	425	600	900

Left to Right: Arcade Buick Coupe and Buick Sedan. Photo from Bill Bertoia Auctions.

Arcade Green and White Cab, 9", 1920s. Photo from Bill Bertoia Auctions.

Arcade Buick Sedan, 8-1/2", 1927. Photo from James S. Maxwell and Virginia Caputo.

Left to Right: Arcade Brown & White Cab, 9", 1923; Arcade Brown & White Cab, 8" 1923. Photo from Bill Bertoia Auctions.

	C6	C8	C10
Carry Car Truck and Trailer Set, carries Austin Coupe, Delivery and Stake; No. 2970, 1934, 14-1/4" long (AR029)	650	1000	1650
Caterpillar Tractor, No. 271, 1930, 7-1/2" long (AR030)	300	425	650
Caterpillar Tractor, No. 269X, 1931, 6-7/8" long (AR031)	650	1100	1550
Caterpillar Tractor, No. 268X, 1931, 5-5/8" long (AR031A)	500	800	1350
Caterpillar Tractor, No. 267X, 1931, 3-7/8" long (AR032)	225	325	500
Caterpillar Tractor, No. 266X, 1931, 3" long (AR033)	25	38	50
Caterpillar Tractor, No. 270Y (later became No. 2700Y) 1936, 7-3/4" long (AR034)	750	1250	1850
Century of Progress Bus, No. 3200 (became No. 3250 in 1934), 1933, 14-1/2" long (AR035)	250	375	500
Century of Progress Bus, No. 3210, 1933, 12" long (AR036)	200	325	450
Century of Progress Bus, No. 3220, 1933, 10-1/2" long (AR037)	175	275	425
Century of Progress Bus, No. 3230, 1933, 7-5/8" long (AR038)	100	160	225
Century of Progress Bus, does not pivot or detach, 1933, approx. 5-1/2" long (AR038A)	175	275	375
Century of Progress Yellow Cab, 6-1/2" long (AR038B)	1000	2000	3200
Checker Cab, with and without "Checker" on visor, 1932, 9-1/4" long	NPF	NPF	NPF

	C6	C8	C10
Checker Cab, paint variation of No. 1 Yellow Cab, 1923, 9" long (AR039)	2500	4000	6500
Checker Cab, marked "Checker" on visor, 1932, No. 157, 9-1/4" long (AR040)	15,000	20,000	62,000
Chevrolet Coupe, No. 121X, 1929, 8-1/4" long (AR041)	650	1100	1800
Chevrolet Coupe, w/rumble seat, No. 1150X, 1934, 4-3/8" long (AR042)	150	225	325
Chevrolet Panel Delivery Truck, No. 2620X, 1936, 4" long (AR043)	125	175	275
Chevrolet Sedan, single stripe, No. 122X, 1929, 8-1/4" long (AR044)	900	1500	2200
Chevrolet Sedan, double stripe, No. 122X, 1929, 8-1/4" long (AR044A)	1250	1750	3000
Chevrolet Sedan, No. 1170X, 1934, 4-1/4" long (AR045)	50	75	100
Chevrolet Stake Truck, 1925, 9" long (AR046)	950	1650	2500

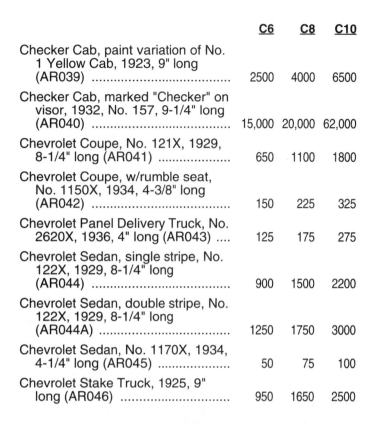

Arcade Checker Cab, 9-1/4", came with and without "Checker" on visor, 1932. Photo from Bill Bertoia Auctions.

Arcade made several variations of the Century of Progress Bus; because prices vary, make sure you know which is which. Photo from Mapes Auctioneers and Appraisers.

Arcade Century of Progress Bus, 1933, 10-1/2".

Arcade Chevrolet Coupe, 8-1/4", 1929. Photo from Virginia Caputo.

ARCADE CAST IRON TOYS

THE 10 LINE

No. 1350X Pontiac Sedan

Length 4¼ inches, width 1⅝ inches, height 1½ inches.

Color: Assorted blue, green, orchid and red. Nickeled radiator, hood center, lights and bumper, white rubber wheels with red centers on blue and green toys, blue centers on orchid and red toys.

Packed 1 dozen in box, 1 gross in case.

Case net weight 68 lbs., case gross weight 74 lbs.

Case measurements: 10x14x15 inches.

No. 1350Y Yellow Cab

Length 4¼ inches, width 1⅝ inches, height 1½ inches.

Color: Yellow, with "Yellow Cab" stencilled in black on the top. Nickeled radiator, lights, bumper and hood center. White rubber wheels with black centers.

Packed 1 dozen in box, 1 gross in case.

Case net weight 68 lbs., case gross weight 74 lbs.

Case measurements: 10x14x15 inches.

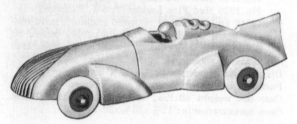

No. 3610X Boeing United Airplane

Length 3⅝ inches, width 5 inches, height 1½ inches.

Color: Assorted red, blue, green and silver. Nickeled under carriage. Nickeled propellors. White rubber wheels.

Packed 1 dozen in box, 1 gross in case.

Case net weight 45 lbs., case gross weight 50 lbs.

Case measurements: 9x11x13 inches.

No. 1450X Racer

Length 5¾ inches, width 2 inches, height 1⅜ inches.

Color: Assorted silver, green, red and blue. White rubber wheels with red centers on blue, green and silver toys, blue centers on red toy.

Packed 1 dozen in box, 1 gross in case.

Case net weight 70 lbs., case gross weight 76 lbs.

Case measurements: 11x12x17 inches.

No. 2000X Pontiac Wrecker

Length 4¼ inches, width 1⅝ inches, height 1¾ inches.

Color: Assorted red, blue and green. Nickeled radiator, hood center, lights and bumper, and nickeled steel wrecker hook. White rubber wheels with red centers on blue and green toys, blue centers on red toy.

Packed 1 dozen in box, 1 gross in case.

Case net weight 72 lbs., case gross weight 78 lbs.

Case measurements: 10x14x15 inches.

No. 2780X Pontiac Stake Truck

Length 4¼ inches, width 1⅝ inches, height 1½ inches.

Color: Assorted red, green and blue. Nickeled radiator, lights and bumper. White rubber wheels with red centers on blue and green toys, blue centers on red toy.

Packed 1 dozen in box, 1 gross in case.

Case net weight 70 lbs., case gross weight 76 lbs.

Case measurements: 10x14x15 inches.

"THEY LOOK REAL"

Page 4 from the No. 51 Arcade catalog.

Arcade Chevrolet Superior Sedan, 1925. Photo from Bill Bertoia Auctions.

Arcade Circus Wagon, horse-drawn, driver at top. Photo from Liz Isham Cory.

Arcade Chevrolet Superior Touring Car, 7", 1925. Photo from Bill Bertoia Auctions.

A pair of Arcade Coupes. Photo from Bill Bertoia Auctions.

	C6	C8	C10
Chevrolet Stake Truck, No. 2610, 1936, 4-1/4" long (AR047)	NPF	NPF	NPF
Chevrolet Superior Roadster, 1925, 7" long (AR048)	1000	1700	2500
Chevrolet Superior Sedan, 1925, 7" long (AR049)	450	700	1050
Chevrolet Superior Touring Car, 1925, 7" long (AR050)	700	1250	2000
Chevrolet Utility Coupe, 1925, 7" long (AR051)	750	1300	1950
Chevrolet Wrecker Truck, No. 2630X, 1936, 4-1/4" long (AR052)	150	225	325
Chief Fire Chief Coupe, No. 1230, 1934, 6-3/4" long (AR053)	1400	2400	3500
Chief Fire Chief Coupe, No. 1240, 1934, 5" long (AR054)	450	750	1100
Circus Wagon, horse-drawn, driver at top..........................	NPF	NPF	NPF
Coal Mack High Dump Truck, No. 244X, 1931, 12-3/8" long (AR141)	1000	1500	2200

	C6	C8	C10
Coast To Coast GMC Transcontinental Bus, No. 4378X, 1937, 9" long (AR055)	200	325	475
Coast To Coast Greyhound Cruiser Coach bus, No. 4400, 9-1/8" long (AR112A)	225	375	525
Coast To Coast Greyhound Lines Bus, 1937, No. 3850X (AR113A)	250	375	525
Corn Harvester, 1939, No. 702, 6-1/2" long (AR056)	175	275	400
Corn Harvester, 1939, No. 4180, 5" long (AR057)	130	200	300
Corn Planter, 1939, 4-1/2" long (AR058)	60	90	125
Coupe, marked "1922" on spare tire, 9" long (AR059)	1500	2500	4000
Coupe, like above w/o 1922 date on spare (AR060)	850	1250	1750
Coupe, no Arcade markings, rumble seat opens, No. 109, 1932, 6" long (AR061)	250	375	550
Deluxe Sedan, same as Yellow Cab No. 1590Y, but w/top lights and w/o sun roof; No. 1590X, 1941, 8-1/2" long (AR062)	475	800	1250

	C6	C8	C10
DeSoto Sedan, No. 1460X, 1936, 4" long (AR063)	150	225	325
Double Decker Bus, No. 3180, 1939, 8" long (AR064)	425	625	900
Dump Truck, No. 2320, 1936, 4-1/2" long (AR065)	50	80	120
Dump Truck, No. 3910X, 1941, 7" long (AR066)	275	425	625
Dump Truck, transitional, lighter metal, 1940s, 11-1/4" long (AR066A)	275	425	625
Dump Truck Trailer, No. 234, 1931, 12-/8" long (AR067)	850	1450	2250
Dump Wagon, w/driver, no cab, 1917, 7" long (AR068)	450	650	1000
Express Truck, No. 270X, 1929, 8" long (AR069)	450	650	1000
Express Truck, No. 209X, 1929, 8" long (AR070)	NPF	NPF	NPF
Express Truck, No. 214X, 1929, 5" long (AR071)	NPF	NPF	NPF
Fageol Bus, 1925, 12" long (AR072)	375	550	800

	C6	C8	C10
Fageol Bus, 12-1/2" long (AR073) ..	450	700	1000
Fageol Bus, 8" long (AR074)	325	525	750
Farm Mower, No. 4210X, 1939, 4" long (AR075)	60	90	125
Farm Wagon, horse-drawn, driver, reins, red wagon	NPF	NPF	NPF
Farmall A Tractor, No. 7050, 1941, 7-1/2" long (AR076)	600	1000	1500
Farmall M Tractor, No. 7070, 1941, 7-1/4" long (AR077)	225	325	500
Farmall Tractor, No. 279, 1929, 6" long (AR078)	500	750	1100
Fire Chief Car, 5-5/8" long, 1941 (AR078A)	150	225	300
Fire Engine, pumper, 1923, 7-1/2" long (AR079)	225	375	525
Fire Engine, pumper, No. 1740, 1936, 9" long (AR080)	475	775	1250
Fire Engine, No. 1810, 1936, 6-1/4" long (AR081)	NPF	NPF	NPF
Fire Engine, No. 2340, 1936, 4-1/2" long (AR082)	90	135	180
Fire Engine, No. 6990, 1941, 13-1/2" long (AR083)	700	1150	1650
Fire Ladder Truck, No. 1820, 1936, 7" long (AR084)	200	300	450
Fire Trailer Truck, ladder truck, No. 1940, 1934, 16-1/4" long (AR085)	450	700	950
Ford Carry Car Truck and Trailer, No. 2400, 1934 (AR086)	NPF	NPF	NPF

Arcade DeSoto Sedan, 4", 1936. Photo from Bill Bertoia Auctions.

Arcade Dump Wagon, driver, no cab, 1917, 7". Photo from Sotheby's New York.

Arcade Express Truck, 8", 1929. Photo from Bill Bertoia Auctions.

Arcade Chevrolet Coupe, 8-1/4", 1929. Photo from Virginia Caputo.

Arcade Farm Wagon, horse-drawn, driver, reins, red wagon. Photo from Liz Isham Cory.

Arcade Farmall Tractor, 6", 1929. Photo from Perry Eichor.

Arcade Fire Ladder Truck, 1936, 7".

Arcade Fire Engine, 13-1/2", 1941. Photo from Bill Bertoia Auctions.

Arcade Fire Trailer Truck, 16-1/4", 1934. Photo from Bill Bertoia Auctions.

Arcade Ford Dump Truck, 1929. Photo from Bill Bertoia Auctions.

Arcade Ford Fordor Sedan, 6-1/2", red, 1924. Photo from Bill Bertoia Auctions.

Arcade Ford Touring Car, 6-1/2", 1923. Photo from Bill Bertoia Auctions.

Arcade Greyhound Cruiser Coach, 1941, 9-1/8". Photo from Sotheby's.

	C6	C8	C10
Ford Coupe, 1923, 6" long (AR087)	150	250	375
Ford Coupe, 1924, 6-1/2" long (AR088)	275	400	600
Ford Coupe, rumble seat opens, No. 1610X, 1934, 6-3/4" long (AR089)	150	250	375
Ford Coupe, No. 1190X, 1930s, 4-3/4" long (AR090)	110	175	250
Ford Dump Truck, No. 219X, 1929, 7-1/2" long (AR091)	275	400	600
Ford Express Truck, No. 210X, 1929, 8-1/4" long (AR092)	1000	1650	2400
Ford Fordor Sedan, w/removable chauffeur, 1924, 6-1/2" long (AR093)	225	350	525
Ford Sedan, "Center Door," 1923, 6-1/2" long (AR094)	325	400	650
Ford Sedan, No. 1620X, 1934, 6-7/8" long (AR095)	NPF	NPF	NPF
Ford Sedan, "Century of Progress," 1934, 6-7/8" long (AR096)	1000	1750	2750
Ford Sedan, No. 1200, 1930s, 4-3/4" long (AR097)	175	275	400
Ford Sedan, "Century of Progress," 1934, 4-3/4" long (AR097A)	NPF	NPF	NPF
Ford Sedan with Trailer, No. 1970, 1937, sedan: 12" long, trailer: 5-1/2" long (AR098)	600	1000	1600
Ford Stake Truck, 1927, 9" long (AR100)	1000	1600	2250
Ford Stake Truck, No. 2010X, 1934, 4-3/4" long (AR101)	NPF	NPF	NPF
Ford Stake Truck, 1925, 8-3/4" long (AR99)	700	1250	1600
Ford Touring Car, 1923, 6-1/2" long (AR102)	450	650	900

	C6	C8	C10
Ford Touring Car Bank, 1923, 6-1/2" long (AR103)	1100	1800	2700
Ford Tractor and Plow, No. 7220, 1941, tractor: 6-1/2" long, overall length: 8-3/4" (AR104)	425	625	875
Ford Truck, One-Ton Pickup, C-Cab, 1923, 8-1/2" long (AR105)	900	1400	2200
Ford Wrecker, No. 215, 1929, 8-1/4" long to end of hoist (AR106)	500	750	1100
Ford Wrecker, No. 217, 1929 (AR106A)	300	450	650
Ford Wrecker, No. 218, 1930, 4-1/2" long (AR107)	125	175	250
Fordson Tractor, 1923, 5-3/8" long (AR108)	150	225	325
Fordson Tractor, No. 275, 1928, 6" long (AR108A)	125	175	275
Fordson Tractor, No. 274, 1928, 4-3/4" long (AR109)	100	150	225
Fordson Tractor, No. 273, 1928, 3-7/8" long (AR110)	50	75	110
Fordson Tractor, rubber wheels, No. 2730X, 1934, 3-1/2" long (AR111)	60	110	150
Greyhound Cruiser Coach bus, No. 4400, 1941, 9-1/8" long (AR112)	200	300	450

ARCADE CAST IRON TOYS

THE 10 LINE

No. 2340 Fire Engine

Length 4½ inches, width 1⅝ inches, height 1⅞ inches.
Color: Red with nickeled radiator, hood center, head lights and bumper. White rubber wheels with green centers.
Packed 1 dozen in box, 1 gross in case.
Case net weight 70 lbs., case gross weight 76 lbs.
Case measurements: 10x10x18 inches.

No. 2350 Fire Ladder Truck

Length 4¾ inches, width 1⅝ inches, height 1⅞ inches.
Color: Red with nickeled radiator, hood center, head lights and bumper. White rubber wheels with green centers.
Packed 1 dozen in box, 1 gross in case.
Case net weight 70 lbs., case gross weight 76 lbs.
Case measurements: 10x10x18 inches.

No. 2320 Dump Truck

Length 4½ inches, width 1¼ inches, height 1½ inches.
Color: Red chassis with green dump body. White rubber wheels with green centers.
Packed 1 dozen in box, 1 gross in case.
Case net weight 62 lbs., case gross weight 68 lbs.
Case measurements: 10x14x16 inches.

No. 2620X Chevrolet Panel Delivery Truck

Length 4 inches, width 1⅝ inches, height 1½ inches.
Color: Assorted red, green and blue bodies with chassis red and green, wheel centers red and blue. White rubber wheels with colored centers. Nickeled radiator, lights and bumper. The toys with red bodies have green chassis and red centered wheels. The toys with green bodies have red chassis and blue centered wheels. The toys with blue bodies have red chassis with blue centered wheels.
Packed 1 dozen in box, 1 gross in case.
Case net weight 60 lbs., case gross weight 66 lbs.
Case measurements: 9x14x14½ inches.

No. 1460X DeSoto Sedan

Length 4 inches, width 1⅝ inches, height 1⅜ inches.
Color: Assorted red, green, blue and gray. White rubber wheels with red centers on blue, green and gray toys, blue centers on red toy.
Packed 1 dozen in box, 1 gross in case.
Case net weight 60 lbs., case gross weight 66 lbs.
Case measurements: 10x14x15 inches.

No. 3790X Pullman Railplane

Length 5⅛ inches, width 1 inch, height 1¼ inches.
Color: Assorted red, green, brown, and blue. White rubber wheels.
Although illustration shows "Pullman Railplane" stencilled on sides, this is on the top of the toy.
Packed 1 dozen in carton, 1 gross in case.
Case net weight 45 lbs., case gross weight 50 lbs.
Case measurements: 11x12x18 inches.

"THEY LOOK REAL"

Page 5 from the No. 51 Arcade catalog.

	C6	C8	C10
Greyhound Lines Bus, No. 3850 SP, 1937, 7-3/4" long (AR113)	140	225	325
Greyhound Lines Great Lakes Exposition, No. 437, 1936, 11" long (AR114)	450	700	1000
Greyhound Lines Great Lakes Exposition, No. 436, 1936, 6-3/4" long (AR115)	350	475	725
Greyhound Super Coach, No. 4380, 1937, 9" long (AR116)	275	425	575
Ice Truck, No. 1933, c.1941, 6-3/4" long (AR117)	275	375	575
Ice Wagon, horse-drawn..................	NPF	NPF	NPF
International Delivery Truck, No. 226, 1932, 9-3/4" long (AR118) ..	500	800	1300

	C6	C8	C10
International Delivery Truck, No. 3020, 1936, 9-1/2" long (AR119)	1800	2900	4200
International Dump Truck, No. 236-0, 1931, 10-3/4" long (AR120)	750	1200	1850
International Dump Truck, No. 3030, 1936, 10-1/2" long (AR121)	1000	1600	2350
International Dump Truck, No. 3710, 1937, 9-1/2" long (AR122)	450	700	1000
International Dump Truck, steel chassis and dump box, No. 1670, 1940, 11-5/8" long (AR123)	650	1000	1650
International Dump Truck, No. 7100, 1941, 11-1/8" long (AR124)	600	900	1250

Arcade Greyhound Lines Bus, 6-3/4" 1936. Photo from John Gibson.

Arcade International Delivery Truck, green top, light blue and yellow bottom, yellow wheels, 1932, 9-3/4". Photo from Bill Bertoia Auctions.

Arcade Ice Truck, 6-3/4", 1940s. Photo from Bill Bertoia Auctions.

Arcade International Dump Truck, red, white bed, 1940, 11-5/8". Photo from Tim Oei.

Arcade Ice Wagon, horse-drawn. Photo from Liz Isham Cory.

Arcade International Stake Truck, yellow, 9-1/2", 1937. Photo from Bill Bertoia Auctions.

Arcade Mack 6 Bus, 13-1/4" white and red, 1929. Photo from Bill Bertoia Auctions.

Arcade Mack Chemical Truck, fire ladder truck, 15" 1929. Photo from Bill Bertoia Auctions.

Arcade Mack High Dump Truck, "Coal" on side, 12-3/8", 1931. Photo from Bill Bertoia Auctions.

Left to Right: Arcade Mack Ice Truck, 1932; Arcade Mack Ice Truck, 1930. Photo from Bill Bertoia Auctions.

	C6	C8	C10
International Harvester Company Public Utility Truck, No. 197, 1932, 11-1/4" long (AR125)	NPF	NPF	NPF
International Pickup Truck, No. 7000, 1941, 9-1/2" long (AR126)	500	750	1100
International Stake Truck, No. 237-0, 1931, 12" long (AR127)	700	1100	1700
International Stake Truck, 1935, 12" long (AR127A) ,...........................	900	1500	2250
International Stake Truck, No. 3090, 1936, 12" long (AR128)	900	1500	2300
International Stake Truck, No. 2600,1937, 9-1/2" long (AR129)	850	1450	2250
International Stake Truck, No. 7090, 1941, 11-1/2" long (AR130)	950	1450	2100
International Wrecker, steel body and crane, No. 1650, 1940, 13" long, (AR131)	500	800	1200
Ladder Truck, No. 1700, 1936, length w/ladders: 12-1/2" (AR132)	475	725	1000
Ladder Truck, No. 2350, 1936, 4-3/4" long (AR133)	75	110	150
Lubrite Mack Tank Truck, 1925, 13-1/4" long (AR153)	1200	2100	3250
Mack 6 Bus, No. 318, 1929, 13-1/4" long (AR134)	8000	15,000	24,200

	C6	C8	C10
Mack Cement Mixer, revolving drum, 1931, 6-11/16" long (AR135)	NPF	NPF	NPF
Mack Chemical Truck, fire engine w/ladders, No. 245R, 1928, 15" long (AR136)	2000	3500	5500
Mack Chemical Truck, fire truck w/ladders, 1929, 15" long (AR137)	800	1300	1900
Mack Chemical Truck, fire engine w/ladders, 1929, 10" long (AR138)	425	625	900
Mack Dump Truck, 1925, 12" long (AR139)	1000	1700	2750
Mack Dump Truck, No. 248X, 1929, 8-1/2" long (AR140)	600	950	1400
Mack Fire Apparatus Truck, ladder truck, 1929, No. 242, 21" long (AR143)	600	1000	1600
Mack High Dump Truck, No. 259X, 1931, 8-1/2" long (AR142)	675	1150	1600
Mack Hoist Truck, No. 198, 1932, body: 8" long (AR144)	900	1500	2200
Mack Ice Truck, No. 257, 1930, 10-5/8" long (AR145)	375	550	775
Mack Ice Truck, No. 226, 1931, 8-1/2" long (AR146)	450	675	950
Mack Ice Truck, w/driver, glass "ice" and tongs, No. 257, 1932, 10-3/4" (AR147)	1600	2800	4200

	C6	C8	C10
Mack Ladder Truck, c.1928, 17-3/4" long (AR147A)	1100	2000	3100
Mack Side Dump Truck, No. 1960, 1932, 9" long (AR148)	1100	1900	2800
Mack Stake Truck, No. 246X1929, 12" long (AR149)	1100	1900	2800
Mack Stake Truck, No. 253, 1929, 8-3/4" long (AR150)	950	1500	2250
Mack Tank Truck, sheet metal tank, marked "Gasoline" and "Mack," No. 241, 1930, 13" long (AR154)	1100	1900	2800
Mack Wrecker, No. 255, 1930, 12-1/2" long (AR155)	1900	3200	4700
McCormick-Deering Farmall Tractor, gray, yellow and red wheels, 1937, 6-1/4" long.........................	NPF	NPF	NPF
McCormick-Deering Farmall Tractor, 1937, 6-1/4" long (AR156)	325	500	750
McCormick-Deering Thresher, 1927, 12" long (AR157)	300	450	650
McCormick-Deering Thresher, 11" long (AR157A)	200	300	450
McCormick-Deering Thresher, 1930, 9-1/2" long (AR158)	200	275	385

	C6	C8	C10
McCormick-Deering Tractor, 10-20, 1925, 7-1/4" long (AR159)	400	600	850
Milk Truck, wood box, No. 256, 1931,13-5/8" long (AR160)	NPF	NPF	NPF
Model A Coupe, rumble seat, No. 116X, 1928, 5" long (AR161)	200	300	450
Model A Coupe, rumble seat, No. 106, 1928, 6-3/4" long (AR162) ..	500	850	1300
Model A Coupe, No. 113X, 1928, 4-1/8" long (AR163)	125	175	275
Model A Fordor, No. 207, 1928, 6-3/4" long (AR164)	325	475	675
Model A Tudor, No. 108, 1928, 6-3/4" long (AR165)	450	700	1150
Model T Stake Truck, 1927, 9" long (AR166)	575	925	1300
Model T Stake Truck, 1927, 5-3/4" long (AR167)	125	175	275

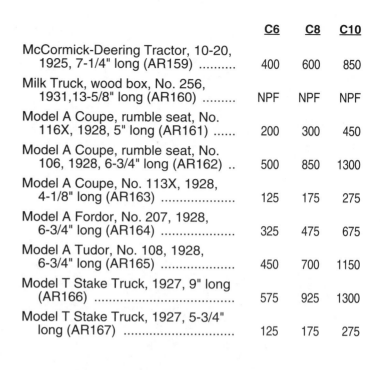

Arcade McCormick-Deering Thresher, 12", 1927. Photo from Liz Isham Cory.

Arcade Mack Tank Truck, 13-1/4", Lubrite marking, 1925. Photo from Bill Bertoia Auctions.

Arcade McCormick-Deering Farmall Tractor, 6-1/4", gray, yellow and red wheels, 1937. Photo from Liz Isham Cory.

Arcade Model A Coupe, 6-3/4", orange, rumble seat, 1928. Photo from Bill Bertoia Auctions.

ARCADE CAST IRON TOYS

No. 2230X Mack Dump Truck

Length 12¼ inches, width 4¼ inches, height 5¾ inches.

Color: Assorted red, green, and blue, trimmed in gold bronze. Nickeled hoist, pulleys and driver.

Wheels: Dual rear wheels. Real rubber wheels with colored centers,—red centers on blue and green toys, blue centers on red toys.

By pressing lever, the spring in a cylinder back of cab raises the hoist which in turn raises the dump box. End-gate opens and closes.

Packed 1 in carton, 1 dozen in case.

Case net weight 57 pounds, case gross weight 63 pounds.

Case measurements: 13½x17½x20 inches.

No. 2420 Mack Fire Apparatus Truck

Length 21 inches, width 4¾ inches, height 4¾ inches.

Color: Red trimmed in gold. Yellow extension ladders. Imitation hose wound on nickeled hose reel. Removable nickeled ladder racks, nickeled driver. Nickeled bell attached under truck rings when truck is in motion.

White rubber wheels with blue centers.

Packed 1 in carton, ½ dozen in case.

Case net weight 44 pounds, case gross weight 50 pounds.

Case measurements: 11x15x20 inches.

No. 2410X Mack Tank Truck

Length 13 inches, width 4½ inches, height 5¾ inches.

Color: Assorted red, green, and blue with gold trimmings. Nickeled driver. Dual rear wheels. White rubber wheels with red centers on blue and green trucks, blue centered wheels on red truck.

Tank holds water, rubber drain hose at rear, screw cap on top for filling. Drag chain hangs from rear end of truck.

Packed 1 in carton, 1 dozen in case.

Case net weight 65 pounds, case gross weight 73 pounds.

Case measurements: 13x18x20 inches.

No. 4490 Assorted Toys

Three assorted $1.50 toys in assorted colors, four of each in a case. Contains:

No. 2420 Mack Fire Truck, red, 21 inches.
No. 2230 Mack Dump Truck, blue, 12¼ inches.
No. 2410 Mack Tank Truck, green, 13 inches.

All toys equipped with rubber wheels with colored centers. See description of each individual item on this page.

Packed 1 each in carton, 4 each toy (12) in case.

Case net weight 70 pounds, case gross weight 80 pounds.

Case measurements: 12x15x20 inches.

"THEY LOOK REAL"

Page 14 from the No. 51 Arcade catalog.

Arcade National Trailways Bus, 9-1/4", 1937. Photo from Bob Smith.

Arcade Oliver Tractor, red, driver, white tires with blue centers, 1937, 7-1/2".

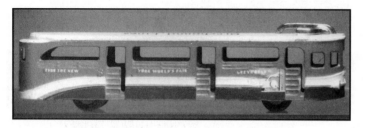

Arcade made several variations of the New York World's Fair Bus. The largest (10-1/2") from 1939, is also the most valuable.

	C6	C8	C10
Model T Wrecker, 1927, 11" long (AR168)	675	1150	1700
Nash Wrecker, 1936, 4-1/2" long (AR169)	225	400	575
National Trailways Bus, No. 3870, 1937, 9-1/4" long (AR170)	750	1300	1800
New York World's Fair Bus, No. 3780, 1939, 10-1/2" long (AR171)	400	625	925
New York World's Fair Bus, No. 3770, 1939, 8-1/2" long (AR172)	300	450	675
New York World's Fair Bus, No. 3750, 1939, 7" long (AR173)	125	200	325
New York World's Fair Tractor-Train, tractor and one car, No. 7270, 1939; tractor: 3-1/4" long, car: 4-1/4" long (AR174)	200	350	525
New York World's Fair Tractor-Train, w/three cars, No. 7290, 1939 (AR175)	450	675	900
Oliver Plow, 1923, 6-1/2" long (AR176)	225	375	550
Oliver Plow, No. 4230X, 1941, 6-1/4" long (AR177)	125	200	300
Oliver Superior Spreader, No. 7140, 1941, 9-1/2" long (AR178)	600	950	1400
Oliver Tractor, No. 356, 1937, 7-1/2" long (AR179)	325	500	700
Oliver Tractor, No. 359, 1937, 5-1/2" long (AR179A)	75	125	185

	C6	C8	C10
Oliver Tractor, No. 3560, 1941, 7-1/2" long (AR180)	500	800	1200
Panel Delivery Truck, 1925, 8-1/8" long (AR180A)	NPF	NPF	NPF
Pennsylvania Mack Stake Truck, No. 253, 1929, 8-3/4" long (AR151B)	1200	2000	3000
Plymouth Coupe, No. 1340X, 1934, 4-1/2" long (AR181)	400	800	1100
Plymouth Sedan, 4-3/4" long, 1934, No. 1330X (AR182)	350	550	775
Plymouth Stake Truck, No. 1840X, 1934, 4-3/4" long (AR183)	NPF	NPF	NPF
Plymouth Wrecker, No. 1830X, 1934, 4-3/4" long (AR184)	125	175	250
Pontiac Fire Pumper, 4-1/2" long (AR184A)	50	75	110
Pontiac Sedan, No. 1350X, 1934, 4-1/4" long (AR185)	150	225	325
Pontiac Sedan, 1935, 6-1/2" long (AR186)	325	500	700
Pontiac Stake Truck, No. 2390X, 1935, 6-1/4" long (AR187)	300	450	650
Pontiac Stake Truck, No. 2780X, 1936, 4-1/4" long (AR188)	NPF	NPF	NPF
Pontiac Wrecker, No. 2000X, 1936, 4-1/4" long (AR189)	125	175	275
Racer, pre-1923, 7-3/4" long (AR190)	400	600	850
Racer, No. 138X, 1931, 6-3/4" long (AR192)	150	225	300
Racer, w/plastic or celluloid windshield, 1932, No. 140X, 10-1/2" long (AR1930)	4000	9000	11,500
Racer, No. 137X, 1932, 5-5/8" long (AR194)	120	175	250

	C6	C8	C10
Racer, No. 1440X, 1937, 8" long (AR195)	NPF	NPF	NPF
Racer, No. 1457, 1937, 5-3/4" long (AR196)	60	90	135
Red Baby Dump Truck, No. 2, 1923, 10-3/8" long (AR197)	500	750	1200
Red Baby Truck, No. 1, 1923, 10-3/4" long (AR198)	500	750	1200
Red Baby Weaver Wrecker, 1929, 12" long (AR199)	900	1400	2200
Red Coupe, No. 1247, 1931, 9-3/8" long (AR200)	900	1700	2600
Red Coupe, No. 1247, 1931, 9-3/8" long (AR201)	900	1700	2400
REO Coupe, yellow, red, black, 1930s	NPF	NPF	NPF
Sand Loading Shovel, No. 298 (later became No. 299), 1932 (AR202)	500	800	1250
Scraper, No. 287, 1929, 8-1/4" long (AR203)	42	63	85
Sedan, No. 1501X, 1937, 4-3/4" long (AR204)	90	135	180

	C6	C8	C10
Sedan and Mullins Red Cap Trailer, No. 1497X, 1937; car: 5-5/8" long, trailer: 2-1/2" long (AR205)	400	600	900
Service Station, "Arcade Service" (AR205A)	500	750	1030
Shortline Greyhound Lines Bus, 1937 (AR113B)	1000	1650	2400
Showboat, green, yellow, red...........	NPF	NPF	NPF
Side Dump Trailer, fastens to trucks or tractors, 1932, No. 290, 7" long (AR206)	NPF	NPF	NPF

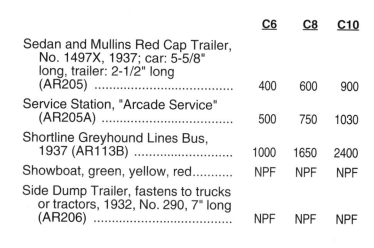

Arcade Showboat, green, yellow, red. Photo from Liz Isham Cory.

Arcade Red Baby Dump Truck, 10-3/8", 1923.

Arcade Red Coupe, 9-3/8", 1931. Photo from Bill Bertoia Auctions.

Arcade Red Baby "Weaver" Wrecker, red, 1929, 12". Photo from Bill Bertoia Auctions.

Arcade REO Coupe, yellow, red, black, 1930s. Photo from Harris Auctions.

Arcade Stake Trailer Truck, 11-5/16", 1931. Photo from Bill Bertoia Auctions.

Arcade Stake Truck, light blue, 1929, 7-1/2". Photo from Bill Bertoia Auctions.

Arcade Trac Tractor, 7-1/2", 1941. Photo from Thomas G. Nefos.

	C6	C8	C10
Silver Arrow, 1934, 7-1/4" long (AR207)	275	375	600
Stake Trailer Truck, No. 233, 1931, 11-5/16" long (AR208)	325	550	750
Stake Truck, No. 206, 7-1/4" long (AR208A)	1100	1700	2500
Stake Truck, No. 208X, 1929, 6" long (AR209)	220	325	475
Stake Truck, 1932, approx. 6" long (AR209A)	175	300	450
Stake Truck, No. 213X, 1929, 5" long (AR210)	125	188	250
Stake Truck, 1929, 7-1/2" long (AR210A)	325	475	675
Stake Truck, no Arcade markings, No. 208, 1932, 6" long (AR211)	275	425	600
Stake Truck, No. 1502X, 1937, 4-1/4" long (AR212)	125	175	275
Steam Shovel, Industrial Derrick, No. 292, 1932, body 6" long (AR213)	750	1125	1600
Tandem Disc Harrow, No. 704, 1939, 6-3/4" long (AR214)	60	90	125
Tank, Army, No. 400, 1937, 8" long (AR215)	600	950	1500
Tank, Army, No. 3960, shoots, 1941, 4" long (AR216)	200	300	450
Texas Centennial Bus, 1936, extremely rare, 10-3/4" long (AR217)	1500	2500	4000

	C6	C8	C10
Trac Tractor, No. 7120, 1941, 7-1/2" long (AR219)	1500	2500	3750
Tractor, No. 7200, 1941, 6-1/2" long (AR222)	175	275	400
Tractor, w/black rubber wheels, No. 4060X, 1941, 6-1/4" long (AR223)	325	500	700
Tractor, 1941, No. 7341X, 6-1/4" long, wood wheels (AR224)	400	600	850
Tractor, No. 7321X, 1941, 4-1/4" long (AR225)	NPF	NPF	NPF
Tractor, wooden wheels, No. 7260X, 1941, 3-1/8" long (AR226)	NPF	NPF	NPF
Tractor, rubber wheels, No. 7240X, 1941, 3-1/8" long (AR227)	100	140	225
Tractor and Dump Trailer, No. 7300, 1941, 15-1/2" long (AR228)	600	950	1400
Trac-Tractor, International Harvester, No. 277, 1937, 8-1/4" long (AR218)	800	1200	1700
Trailer, farm, No. 286, 1929, 6-3/8" long (AR229)	150	225	375
Trailer, farm, No. 288, 1929, 4-5/8" long (AR230)	35	52	75
Trailer, farm, No. 289, 1929, 3-3/4" long (AR231)	30	45	70
Transport Trailer Truck, No. 1800, 1934, 7-1/2" long (AR232)	385	550	775
Two-wheeled Jack, No. 216, 1932, 5-1/2" long (AR234)	30	45	60
W&K Truck Trailer, 1923, 8-1/2" long (AR233)	100	150	225
Webaco Fuel Co. Mack Stake Truck, No. 253, 1929, 8-3/4" long (AR151A)	1100	1900	2800

	C6	C8	C10
Webaco Oil Co. Truck, 13-1/4" long (AR234A see AR151A)			
White Bus, No. 319, 1928, 13-1/4" long (AR235)	2700	5000	7750
White Delivery Truck, No. 252X, 1929, 8-1/4" long (AR236)	2000	3800	6250
White Delivery Truck, side mounts, No. 252X, 8-1/4" long (AR236A)	1500	2600	4250
White Dump Truck, No. 249, 1929, 11-1/2" long (AR238)	8000	15,000	23,000
White Dump Truck, No. 258X, 1931, 13-1/2" long (AR239)	NPF	NPF	NPF
White Moving Van, No. 251, 1929, 13-1/2" long (AR237)	4000	9000	13,000
White Tank Truck, "Gasoline," No. 254X, 1931, 14-1/8" long (AR240)	1000	1500	2200
Whitehead and Kales Tractor, 1923, 5-3/4" long (AR240A)	160	240	350
Wrecker, No. 217, 1928, body: 8" long (AR241)	450	700	1100
Wrecker, no Arcade markings, No. 225, 1932 (AR242)	500	850	1350

	C6	C8	C10
Wrecker, No. 2020X, 1934, 7" long (AR243)	550	900	1400
Wrecker, No. 1493X, 1937, 6-1/2" long (AR244)	125	200	325
Wrecker, No. 1503X, 1937, 4-3/4" long (AR245)	75	125	180
Wrecker, No. 3900X, 1941, 8-1/2" long (AR246)	90	135	200
Yellow Baby Dump Truck, 1923, 10-1/2" long (AR246A)	600	1050	1650
Yellow Baby Wrecker, 1929, 12" long (AR247)	650	1100	1750
Yellow Cab, No. 1, 1922, 9-1/4" long (AR248)	550	900	1500
Yellow Cab, No. 2, 1923, 8" long (AR249)	500	800	1250
Yellow Cab, No. 1, 1927, 9" long (AR250)	600	900	1500
Yellow Cab, No. 05, 1927, 8-1/2" long (AR251)	425	650	950
Yellow Cab, No. 2, 1927, 8" long (AR252)	550	850	1300

Arcade White Bus, 1928, 13-1/4". Photo from Bill Bertoia Auctions.

Arcade Yellow Cab, 1927, 9". Photo from Sotheby's New York.

Arcade Webaco Oil Co. Truck, 13-1/4".

Arcade Yellow Cab, 1923, 8". Photo from Bill Bertoia Auctions.

Arcade Yellow Cab Bank, 1923, 8". Photo from Bill Bertoia Auctions.

Variation of Arcade Yellow Parlor Coach Bus, black roof, yellow, green body, "Pennsylvania Rapid Transit" marking. Photo from Bill Bertoia Auctions.

	C6	C8	C10
Yellow Cab, No. 3, 1927, 5-1/4" long (AR253)	500	800	1200
Yellow Cab, Ford Sedan, 1934, 6-7/8" long (AR254)	1300	2000	3000
Yellow Cab, No. 1580Y, 1936, 8-1/4" long (AR255)	1700	2800	4250

Arcade Yellow Cab Panel Delivery Truck, driver, 8-1/4", orange and black. Photo from Bill Bertoia Auctions.

	C6	C8	C10
Yellow Cab, No. 1590Y, 1941, 8-1/2" long (AR256)	175	263	350
Yellow Cab Bank, 1923, 8" long (AR257)	700	1200	1900
Yellow Cab Bank, 1927, 8-1/2" long, (AR258)	1800	4500	9200
Yellow Cab Panel Delivery Truck, w/driver, 1925, 8-1/4" long (AR259)	1000	1700	2700
Yellow Coach Double-Decker Bus, 1925, 14" long (AR260)	1750	3250	4800
Yellow Parlor Coach Bus, 1926, 13" long (AR261)	70	1250	1900
Yellow Parlor Coach Bus, 1926, 9-1/2" long (AR262)	325	475	675

ARCHER

	C6	C8	C10
Futuristic Auto Carrier, contains four of the 5" futuristic vehicles, No. 349, 14" long (A032A)	NPF	NPF	NPF
Futuristic Convertible, 10" long (A022)	42	63	85
Futuristic Convertible, 5" long (A028)	18	27	36
Futuristic Coupe, 10" long (A024)	42	63	85
Futuristic Coupe, 5" long (A025)	18	27	36
Futuristic Sedan, 5" long (A026)	18	27	36
Futuristic Truck, 10" long (A023)	55	83	110
Futuristic Truck, 5" long (A027)	18	27	36

From left: Archer Futuristic Coupe; Futuristic Sedan; Futuristic Truck; Gasoline Truck.

Archer Raymobile.

Top left to right: Archer Futuristic Convertible; Futuristic Truck; Futuristic Coupe. Bottom left to right: Futuristic Convertible, Sedan, Truck.

	C6	C8	C10
Raymobile (A029)	37	56	75
Rocket, red, yellow and black, 13" long (A021)	75	112	150

	C6	C8	C10
Scopemobile (A030)	NPF	NPF	NPF
Searchmobile (A031)	NPF	NPF	NPF
Steam Roller, non-space	32	48	65

ARGO

	C6	C8	C10
Ambulance, bell rings (AR001)	12	15	20
Armored Car, Army, w/cannon (AR008)	12	15	20
Armored Car, machine gun (AR009)	12	15	20
Chief Car, bell rings (AR002)	12	15	20
Chief Car, bell fixed in place (AR010)	12	15	20

	C6	C8	C10
Police Car, gun moves (AR003)	12	15	20
Sedan, windshield wipers work (AR006)	12	15	20
Sedan, windows roll up and down (AR007)	12	15	20
Taxi, meter in roof moves (AR004)	12	15	20
Taxi, meter in windshield moves (AR005)	12	15	20

Argo Ambulance, Chief Car. Photo from Dave Leopard.

Arcade Yellow Cab, 1923, 8". Photo from Bill Bertoia Auctions.

Cars Galore with accessories that work like real cars!

Fleet of Twelve Argo Steel Action Autos

2⁹⁸ set   **each 4 inches long**

32-6-3 A fleet of cars under his Christmas tree . . . to delight him! The windows on 3 sedans go up and down automatically! 2 Sedans have windshield wipers that really work! 2 Police cars have Rat-a-Tat guns! An ambulance with ringing bells! 2 Fire Chief Cars with bells! 2 Taxis with meters that actually register fares!

Argo autos, as shown in the Nov. 13, 1955 *St. Louis Globe-Democrat.*

	C6	C8	C10
A560 Motorcycle, wind-up, green, 7-3/4" long....................................	200	325	450
Arnold Jeep, three MP figures, rare white version with green stars	NPF	NPF	NPF
Arnold Jeep, three MP figures, radio...	NPF	NPF	NPF
Fire Chief Car, tin lithographed, friction, battery siren, 10" long	150	225	300

	C6	C8	C10
Jeep, w/United States Military Police crew, postwar	90	175	300
Jeep, white, w/remote control, postwar, rare..............................	175	275	550
Mac 700 Motorcycle, wind-up, black	325	488	650
Military Rider, No. A754 , w/rifle motorcycle	388	582	775
Motorcycle, No. A63, wind-up, orange, 8" long	200	325	450
Packard Convertible, 10" long..........	90	135	180
Police Car, friction, 10" long.............	250	375	500
Sparkling Fire Truck, U.S. Zone, 4-1/2" wind-up.............................	238	355	475

Arnold motorcycles, orange, 8"; green (right), 7-3/4".

Arnold Mac 700, wind-up, black.

Arnold jeep, three MP figures, rare white version with green stars.

Argo Taxis. Photo from Dave Leopard.

Arnold jeep, three MP figures, radio.

AUBURN RUBBER

For more than twenty years, American kids and moms loved rubber toys—children thought they were fun, and moms like the fact that these toys wouldn't scratch furniture and floors. Then, almost as suddenly as they appeared on the market, the toys disappeared.

The Auburn Rubber Company of Auburn, Indiana, was not the first to introduce rubber toys to the American market, but it was no doubt the largest and had the greatest impact on the toy market. After producing toy soldiers in 1935, Auburn introduced its first vehicle in 1936—a beautiful coffin-nosed Card Sedan. Today, the Auburn Cord in one of the most prized rubber toys and is seldom seen for sale.

Auburn followed the Cord with a wealth of vehicles, including trucks, farm tractors and implements, motorcycles, racers, fire engines, military vehicles, aircraft, ships and trains. The following listing consists of approximately ninety varieties of Auburn Rubber vehicles.

According to catalogs, 1952 was the final year Auburn Rubber exclusively marketed rubber vehicles. by 1955, Auburn's line was mostly vinyl with a few rubber toys left in the line. What appear to be the last rubber toys to be marketed by Auburn were two fire engines shown in the 1956 catalog.

Auburn continued in the toy business in Auburn, Indiana, and later Deming, New Mexico, until going out of business in 1969.

Note: the number is parenthesis coincide with the numbers in Dave Leopard's book *Rubber Toy Vehicles*.

Contributor: Dave Leopard, 2507 Feather Run Trail, West Columbia, SC 29169-4915. Leopard, a retired United States Air Force Colonel now employed by the State of South Carolina, is a collector of small, American-made toy cars and trucks. He is considered an expert in on the subject of rubber toys and self-published *Rubber Toy Vehicles*, a definitive work in this field.

	C6	C8	C10
'35 Ford, two-door slantback sedan, 4" long (AA009)	27	41	55
'35 Ford Coupe, 4" long (AA008)	27	41	55
'36 Cord, four-door, coffin-nose sedan, 6" long (AA001)	65	100	150
'37 International Cabover Stake Truck, "U.S. Army" decal, khaki	22	33	45
'37 International Cabover Stake Truck, 5-3/8" long (AT001)	22	33	45
'37 International Cabover Stake Truck, "U.S. Army" decal, khaki, minor variations (AT002)	22	33	45
'37 International Cabover Stake Truck, 4-1/4" long (AT003)	20	30	40
'37 International Cabover Stake Truck, 4-1/4" long, minor variations (AT004)	20	30	40
'37 International Cabover Stake Truck, 3-3/4" long (AT005)	20	30	40
'37 International Cabover Stake Truck, milk version, 4-1/4" long (AT006)	60	80	100

Auburn 1937 International Cabover Stake Truck, milk version, 4-1/4". Photo from Dave Leopard's book *Rubber Toy Vehicles*.

Left to right: Auburn 1937 Internaitonal Cabover Stake Truck, 5-3/8"; 1937 International Cabover Stake Truck, 4-1/4"; 1937 International Cabover Stake Truck, 3-3/4". Photo from Dave Leopard's book *Rubber Toy Vehicles*.

Auburn 1936 Cord, four-door sedan, 6".

Auburn 1937 Oldsmobile, four-door sedan, 4-1/2".
Photo from Dave Leopard's book *Rubber Toy Vehicles*.

Auburn 1937 International Cabover Stake Truck,
ambulance version. Photo from Dave Leopard's book
Rubber Toy Vehicles.

Auburn 1938 GMC Cab/Open Squared-Off Trailer, 9".
Photo from Dave Leopard's book *Rubber Toy Vehicles*.

Auburn 1938 GMC Carry Car Auto Transport, 11-1/2",
rubber on top to carry cars. Photo from Dave Leopard.

Auburn 1938 Oldsmobile, four-door sedan, 5-3/4".
Photo from Dave Leopard's book *Rubber Toy Vehicles*.

	C6	C8	C10
'37 International Cabover Stake Truck, ambulance version (AT007)	NPF	NPF	NPF
'37 International Cabover Stake Truck, ambulance version (AT007)	NPF	NPF	NPF
'37 Olds, four-door sedan, 4-1/2" long (AA002)	25	35	50
'38 GMC Cab/Open Squared-off Trailer, 9" long (AT015)	42	63	85
'38 GMC Carry Car Auto Transport, no top, 11-1/2" long (AT013)	45	65	95
'38 GMC Carry Car Auto Transport, w/rubber on top to carry cars, 11-1/2" long (AT014)	50	70	110

	C6	C8	C10
'38 GMC/Cab/Open Squared-off Trailer, no tailgate, 9" long (AT016)	42	63	85
'38 Olds, four-door sedan, 5-3/4" long (AA003)	30	50	70
'39 Buick, Y Job Experimental Roadster, 9-3/4" long (AA007)	NPF	NPF	NPF
'39 Plymouth, two-door trunkback sedan, 4-1/4" long (AA011)	25	35	50

	C6	C8	C10
'40 Olds, four-door sedan, open fenders, 6" long (AA004)	27	41	59
'40 Olds, four-door sedan, fender skirts, 6" long (AA005)	25	38	50
'40s Fire Engine, hose and ladders, 7-3/4" long (AE002)	35	52	70
'40s Fire Engine, ladders, no hose, 7-3/4" long (AE004)	40	55	80
'40s Pumper, boiler, 7-1/4" long (AE003)	35	52	70
'46 Lincoln Convertible, two-door, square headlights, 4-1/2" long (AA012)	20	30	40

	C6	C8	C10
'46 Lincoln Convertible, two-door, round headlights, 4-1/2" long (AA013)	20	30	40
'47 Chevy Cab Forward Box Truck, 5-3/4" long (AT010)	22	33	45
'48 Buick, two-door sedanette, fastback, 7-1/4" long (AA006)	40	70	100
'50 Cadillac, four-door sedan, 7-1/4" long (AA010)	40	60	80
'50 Pickup Truck, wheels inside fenders, 4-1/2" long (AT012)	20	30	40
'50s Pickup Truck, wheels outside fenders, 4-1/2" long (AT011)	20	30	40

Auburn 1939 Plymouth, two-door trunkback sedan, 4-1/4". Photo from Dave Leopard's book *Rubber Toy Vehicles*.

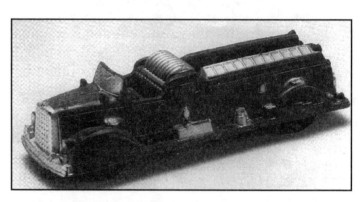

Auburn 1940s Fire Engine hose and ladders, 7-3/4". Photo from Dave Leopard's from his book *Rubber Toy Vehicles*.

Another look at the Auburn 1939 Plymouth.

Auburn 1940s Fire Engine, ladders, no hose, 7-3/4". Photo from Dave Leopard.

Left to right: Auburn 1940 Oldsmobile, fender skirts; Auburn 1940 Oldsmobile, open fenders. Photo from Dave Leopard's book *Rubber Toy Vehicles*.

Auburn 1940s Pumper, boiler, 7-1/4". Photo from Dave Leopard.

Left to right: Auburn 1946 Lincoln convertible, square headlights; 1946 Lincoln convertible, round headlights. Photo from Dave Leopard's book *Rubber Toy Vehicles*.

Auburn 1947 Chevy Cab Forward Box Truck, 5-3/4". Photo from Dave Leopard's book *Rubber Toy Vehicles*.

Auburn 1948 Buick, two-door sedanette, fastback, 7-1/4". Photo from Dave Leopard.

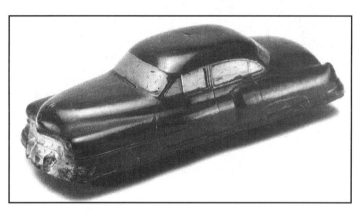

Auburn 1950 Cadillac, four-door sedan, 7-1/4". Photo from Dave Leopard's book *Rubber Toy Vehicles*.

Auburn Blade, 2-3/4" fits Graham-Bradley tractor. Photo from Dave Leopard's book *Rubber Toy Vehicles*.

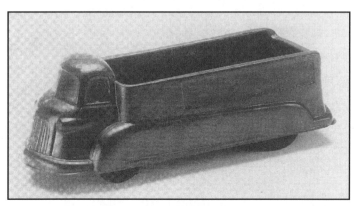

Auburn Cab-Forward Box Truck, futuristic, 5-1/2". Photo from Dave Leopard's book *Rubber Toy Vehicles*.

Auburn Cabover Box Truck, futuristic, 4-1/8". Photo from Dave Leopard's book *Rubber Toy Vehicles*.

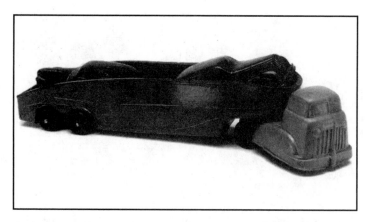

Auburn Updated Carry Car Transport, 11-3/4". Photo from Dave Leopard's book *Rubber Toy Vehicles*.

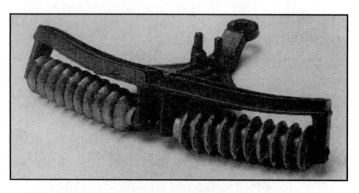

Auburn Disc Harrows, 4-1/2". Photo from Dave Leopard's book *Rubber Toy Vehicles*.

Auburn Farm Tractor, John Deere, 5". Photo from Dave Leopard's book *Rubber Toy Vehicles*.

	C6	C8	C10
Ahrens-Fox Fire Engine, 5-1/2" long (AE001)	75	112	150
Army Motor Scout on motorcycle (AC001)	30	40	60
Army Staff Car, '40 Olds w/"U.S. Army" label, sedan, open fenders, 6" long (AA016)	25	38	50
Blade, 2-3/4", fits Graham-Bradley tractor (AI014)	NPF	NPF	NPF
Cab-Forward Box Truck, smooth sides, futuristic, 5-1/2" long (AT008)	22	33	45
Cabover Box Truck, smooth sides, futuristic, 4-1/8" long (AT009)	20	30	40
Carry Car Transport, updated version of '38 GMC Cab, cab changed, trailer same, 11-3/4" long (AT017)	45	65	95
Cultipacker (Disc Harrows?), David Bradley, 4-3/8" long (AI010)	22	33	45
David Bradley Hay Wagon (AI015)	20	30	40
Disc Harrows, 4-1/2" long (AI012)	22	33	45
Farm Tractor, John Deere "A," 5" long (AF001)	22	33	45

	C6	C8	C10
Farm Tractor, Minneapolis-Moline "Z," 4" long (AF002)	22	33	45
Farm Tractor, Minneapolis-Moline "R," early style, 7-1/2" long (AF003)	40	60	85
Farm Tractor, Minneapolis-Moline "R," later style, 7-1/4" long (AF004)	40	60	85
Farm Tractor, Oliver Row Crop "70," 8" long (AF005)	40	60	85
Farm Tractor, McCormick-Deering IH Farmall "M," 4" long (AF007)	22	33	45
Farm Tractor, Graham-Bradley, 4-1/4" long (AF008)	25	38	50
Ford Stake Truck, 4-3/4" long (AT018)	35	45	60
Futuristic Sedan, fin down back, late 1940s, 5" long (AA014)	20	30	40

Auburn Farm Tractor, Minneapolis-Moline, 4". Photo from Dave Leopard's book *Rubber Toy Vehicles*.

Auburn Farm Tractor, Minneapolis-Moline, early style, 7-1/2". Photo courtesy Dave Leopard from his book *Rubber Toy Vehicles*.

Auburn Farm Tractor, Mineapolis-Moline, later style, 7-1/4". Photo courtesy Dave Leopard from his book *Rubber Toy Vehicles*.

Auburn Farm Tractor.

Auburn Farm Tractor, McCormick-Deering, 4". Photo from Dave Leopard's book *Rubber Toy Vehicles*.

Auburn Farm Tractor, Graham-Bradley, 4-1/4". Photo from Dave Leopard's book *Rubber Toy Vehicles*.

	C6	C8	C10
Harrow, 4-1/2" long (AI011)	20	30	40
Harvester, open top, 5-1/2" long (AI003)	30	45	65
Manure Spreader, David Bradley, 4-3/4" long (AI004)	20	30	40
Motorcycle Cop, small, 3-4/5" long (AC003)	25	40	70
Motorcycle Cop, large, 5" high (AC004)	35	45	75
Motorcycle Soldiers, w/sidecar (AC002)	30	40	60
Open Racer, high fin, 10-1/2" long (AR001)	55	82	110

	C6	C8	C10
Open Racer, V-6, low fin, 10-1/2" long (AR002)	45	65	90
Open Racer, short, tapered tail, large tires, 10-1/2" long (AR003)	40	60	80
Open Racer, short, boat tail 6-1/2" long (AR004)	30	45	60

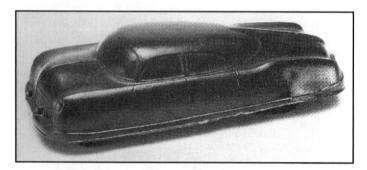

Auburn Late '40s Futuristic Sedan, fin down back, 5". Photo from Dave Leopard from his book *Rubber Toy Vehicles.*

Left to right: Auburn Manure Spreader, David Bradley, 4-3/4"; Spreader, 4-3/4". Photo courtesy Dave Leopard from his book *Rubber Toy Vehicles.*

Auburn Harrow, 4-1/2". Photo from Dave Leopard's book *Rubber Toy Vehicles.*

Auburn Open Racer, V-6, high fin, 10-1/2".

Auburn Harvester, open top, 5-1/2". Photo from Dave Leopard's book *Rubber Toy Vehicles.*

Auburn Open Racer, V-6, low fin, 10-1/2". Photo from Dave Leopard's book *Rubber Toy Vehicles.*

Auburn Open Racer, short, boat tail, 6-1/2". Photo from Dave Leopard.

Auburn Open Racer, boat tail, 4-3/4". Photo from Dave Leopard's book *Rubber Toy Vehicles*.

Auburn Open Racer, small fin, 6-1/4". Photo from Dave Leopard's book *Rubber Toy Vehicles*.

Auburn Open Racer, short, boat tail, early, 6-1/2". Photo from Dave Leopard's book *Rubber Toy Vehicles*.

Auburn Open Racer, no fenders, low fin, long back, 5-1/4". Photo from Dave Leopard's book *Rubber Toy Vehicles*.

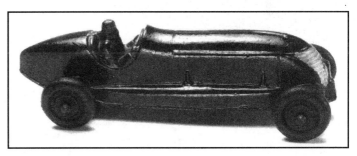

Auburn Open Racer, boat tail, no side pipes, 4-3/4". Photo from Dave Leopard's book *Rubber Toy Vehicles*.

	C6	C8	C10
Open Racer, boat tail, 4-3/4" long (AR005)	30	45	60
Open Racer, small fin, 6-1/4" long (AR006)	30	45	60
Open Racer, short, boat tail, early, 6-1/2" long (AR007)	40	60	80
Open Racer, no fenders, low fin, long back, 5-1/4" long (AR008)	20	30	40
Open Racer, boat tail, no side pipes, 4-3/4" long (AR009)	25	35	50
Open Racer, midget type, early, 5" long (AR010)	NPF	NPF	NPF
Plow, w/riding farmer (AI013)	NPF	NPF	NPF
Plow, updated (AI09)	20	30	40
Reliable Front-Lift Seeder, 5" long (AI006)	25	35	50

	C6	C8	C10
Side-Cutter Sickle Bar Mower, David Bradley, 3-3/4" long (AI007)	20	30	40
Spreader, 4-3/4" long (AI05)	20	30	40
Tank, Marmon-Harrington, 4-1/2" long (AM001)	25	35	50
Tank, Marmon-Harrington, 3-1/4" long (AM002)	15	25	35

Auburn Plow with riding farmer. Photo from Dave Leopard's book *Rubber Toy Vehicles*.

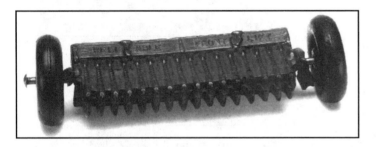

Auburn Reliable Front-Lift Seeder, 5". Photo from Dave Leopard's book *Rubber Toy Vehicles*.

Auburn Trailer, four-wheel, Graham-Bradley, 4-3/4". Photo from Dave Leopard's book *Rubber Toy Vehicles*.

Auburn Trailer, two-wheel, Graham-Bradley, 5-3/4". Photo from Dave Leopard's book *Rubber Toy Vehicles*.

Top row, left to right: Tank; Army Recon Car. Bottom row, left to right: Jeep with Cannon; Army Truck.

Left to right: Auburn Two-Furrow Plow, David Bradley, 4-3/4"; Cultipacker, David Bradley, 4-3/8". Photo from Dave Leopard's book *Rubber Toy Vehicles*.

	C6	C8	C10
Tractor and Cannon, olive green, 11-1/2" long (AM003)	NPF	NPF	NPF
Trailer, four-wheel, Graham-Bradley, 4-3/4" long	22	33	45
Tractor and Cannon, olive green, 11-1/2" long (AM003)	NPF	NPF	NPF
Trailer, four-wheel, Graham-Bradley, 4-3/4" long	22	33	45
Trailer, two-wheel, Graham-Bradley, 5-3/4" long (AI001)	22	33	45
Two-Furrow Plow, David Bradley, 3-3/4" long (AI008)	20	30	40

Vinyl

	C6	C8	C10
Airport Limousine, No. 504, 7-1/2" long	10	15	20
Army Recon Car, No. 652	8	12	16
Army Truck, No. 656	8	12	16
Bulldozer, No. 348, 8" long	30	45	60
Cadillac Convertible, 3-1/2" long	6	9	12
Cadillac Convertible, 5" long	12	18	25
Crane Shovel, No. 356	50	75	100
Delivery Truck	10	15	20

	C6	C8	C10
Dump Truck, No. 352, 10-1/2" long	35	52	70
Fire Truck, No. 614	10	15	20
Fire Truck Pumper, No. 500, 7-1/2" long	10	15	20
Fork Lift with driver, No. 538, 5" long	35	52	70
Hot Rod, No. 612, 4-1/4" long	10	15	20
Hot Rod Take-A-Part Kit, w/box	50	75	100
Jeep	7	11	15
Jeep, w/Cannon, No. 654	16	24	33
Krazy Tow Set: Hot Rod and Tow Truck	55	82	110
Motorcycle	32	48	65
Motorcycle Cop, No. 530, 6-1/4" long	35	52	70
Motorcycle Cop, three-wheel, No. 521, 4" long	15	22	30
Motorcycle Cop, No. 520, 3-7/8" long	25	38	50

Auburn Vinyl Fork Lift with driver, 5".

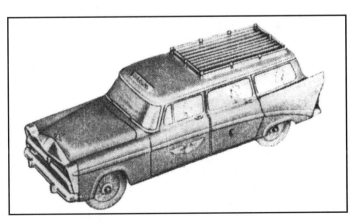

Auburn Vinyl Airport Limousine, 7-1/2".

Auburn Vinyl Police Set with original box.

	C6	C8	C10		C6	C8	C10
Police Set, No. 9 w/original box	150	225	300	Station Wagon, No. 577, 4 5/8" long..............................	12	18	25
Racer, No. 556, 10-1/2" long............	27	41	55	Steamroller, No. 362	17	25	35
Racer, 7" long	37	56	75	Streetsweeper, No. 360, 9" long	75	112	150
Ranchero, No. 610, 4-3/4" long........	10	15	20	Take-Apart Hot Rod	32	48	65
Road Scraper, No. 350, 10-1/2" long..............................	30	45	60	Tank, Army No. 650	7	11	15
Sedan..	20	30	40	Telephone Truck, No. 503, 7" long ..	15	22	30
Stake Bed Truck, No. 354, 10 5/8" long..............................	10	15	20	Tractor, w/plow, 8" overall...............	16	24	32
				Truck, No. 518, 5-1/2" long	14	21	28
				Utility Truck, No. 508......................	12	18	25

BANNER

Banner, founded by Emanuel m Pressner and Bernard Schiller in 1944. Pressner had been an toy importer, and in 1938, he bought interest in Columbia Protektosite, which cast Beton's plastic toy soldiers. Schiller was eventually edged out.

In 1950, Banner moved from 150 Buckner Blvd., Bronx, New York, to 80 Beckwith Ave., Paterson, New Jersey, where it remained.

Banner manufactured small plastic cars and trucks and specialized in plastic tea sets and metallic plastic forks, knives and spoons. Banner used "off-falls"—blanks formed when holes were cut in steel for car windows and television tubes—to produce their stamped-steel toys.

The company, which at its peak had up to 00 employees, went into Chapter 11 bankruptcy in 9165. They rebounded for a few years, only to be sold in 1967 to Tal-Cap, a toy conglomerate in Minnesota.

Contributor: John Taylor, P.O. Box 63, Nolensville, TN 37135-0063. Taylor has loved antiques his entire life, and is an avid collector of pressed-steel trucks. He became hopelessly hooked on toy trucks in 1994 when he inherited a 1930s Turner ladder truck from his grandmother's estate. Since that time he has amassed an extensive collection of Turner, Steelcraft, Marx, Wyandotte, Metalcraft, Buddy "L," Banner, and Canadian-made pressed-steel trucks. Even though he also rediscovered all of his early 1960s childhood Tonka trucks in his parents' attic, he sold them off because the older stuff was "cooler." When he's not hunting antique trucks, Taylor, a 17 year veteran law enforcement agent, is busy hunting criminals. Turner is married, has one daughter, and lives near Nashville, Tennessee.

	C6	C8	C10		C6	C8	C10
Ambulance, Army, tin and plastic, 6" long..............................	12	25	40	Clown Van, 4-1/2" long, 1950s.........	12	25	40
American Express Truck, 11-1/2" long..............................	150	225	300	Coronation Milk Van........................	162	243	325
American Express Truck, 11-1/4" long..............................	150	225	300	Cross Country Express, rubber tires, late 1940s-early 1950s, 12" long .	125	200	275
American Express Truck, tin, 10" long..............................	75	150	225	Delivery Van, 4-1/4" long	8	12	25
Aeriel Ladder Fire Truck, pressed metal wheels, No. 1143, 20" long	125	175	250	Dodge, 1950, plastic, 4" long	8	15	25
Army Truck, 12" long......................	37	56	75	Dump Truck, metal, 9" long..............	50	75	100
Auto Transport, wood wheels, 1940s, 16" long.........................	100	175	250	Dump Truck, plastic, 5-1/4" long	10	15	20
Buick Sedan, 4-1/2" long.................	7	11	14	Dump Truck, plastic, 4-1/2" long	9	14	19
Car Transport, lithographed trailer, w/two cars, 16" long....................	125	200	275	Express Truck, plastic, 7" long.........	22	33	45
Circus Train, pulled by tractor, c.1949	NPF	NPF	NPF	Fair-Lawn Dairy Truck, pressed metal wheels, 1940s, 11-1/2" long	125	175	250
				Garbage Truck, Ford, plastic, 1954, 4" long..............................	8	12	25
				Grocery Service Truck, pressed metal wheels, 13" long	125	200	275

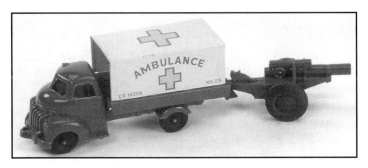

Banner Army Ambulance, tin and plastic, 6".

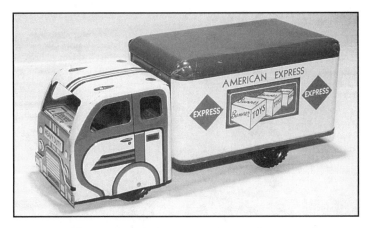

Banner American Express Truck, tin, 10". Photo from Bob Smith.

Left to Right: Banner Army Truck, 12"; Banner Army Ambulance. Photo from Roger Johnson and Charles Breslow.

Banner American Express Truck, 11-1/2". Photo from Ron Fink.

Banner Aerial Ladder Truck, metal wheels, 1940s, 20". Photo from John Taylor.

Banner Auto Transport, wood wheels, 1940s, 16". Photo from John Taylor.

Banner Car Transport, two cars, lithographed trailer, 12". Photo from John Taylor.

Banner Clown Van, 1950s, 4-1/2". Photo from Bob and Alice Wagner.

Banner Circus Train, pulled by tractor, late 1940s. Photo from Terry Sells.

Banner Cross Country Express, late 1940s, early 1950s, 10". Photo from John Taylor.

Banner Delivery Van, 4-1/4". Photo from Terry Sells.

Banner Fair-Lawn Dairy Truck, 1940s, 11-1/2". Photo from John Taylor.

Banner Garbage Truck, Ford, plastic, 1954, 4". Photo from Terry Sells.

Banner Hi-Way Emergency Truck, two spares, jack, late 1940s, 12". Photo from John Taylor.

Banner Grocery Service Truck, 13". Photo from John Taylor.

	C6	C8	C10
Grocery Service Truck, plastic wheels, 11-1/2" long	75	125	175
Hi-Way Emergency Tow Truck, w/tools and two spare tires, 1940s, 12" long	150	225	325
International Harvester Metro 1950 Van, plastic, 4" long	8	12	25
Jewel Tea Van	175	275	375
Kellogg's Express Truck, six wheels, pressed metal wheels, dual metal axles, 1940s, 13" long, very rare	250	400	550
LaFrance Fire Truck, plastic, 1950, 4" long	8	12	25
Livestock Truck, 5-1/2" long	12	18	25
Livestock Truck, plastic, 7" long	22	33	45
Lumber Truck, pressed metal wheels, No. 1140, 15" long	100	175	250

	C6	C8	C10
North American Van Lines Truck and Trailer, 15" long	100	175	225
Oil Truck, plastic, 4-3/8" long	9	14	18
Sand and Gravel Dump Truck, pressed metal wheels, No. 1142, 13" long	100	175	225
Sand and Gravel Truck, plastic, 7" long	25	38	50
Sedan, plastic, 1950s, 4-1/2" long	7	11	15
Service Station, cardboard w/three plastic trucks, late 1940s-early 1950s	22	35	50
Side Dump Truck, plastic, 1950s, 5-1/4" long	10	20	30
Stake Truck, pressed metal wheels, 13" long	75	100	125
Stake Truck, plastic, 8" long	25	38	50
Stake Truck, wood wheels, 1940s, 10" long	50	75	100
Stake Truck, wood wheels, 1940s, 8" long	50	75	100
Stake Truck, 4-1/2" long	9	14	19

Banner Kellogg's Express, dual rear axles, 1940s, 13". Photo from John Taylor.

Banner Lumber Truck, metal wheels, 1940s, 15". Photo from John Taylor.

Banner Stake Truck, metal wheels, 1940s, 13". Photo from John Taylor.

Banner Sand and Gravel Truck, plastic, 13". Photo from John Taylor.

Banner Stake Truck, wood wheels, 1940s, 8". Photo from John Taylor.

Banner Stake Truck, wood wheels, 1940s, 10". Photo from John Taylor.

Variants of the Barclay Oil Truck. Left to Right: a plain version, Yoo Hoo, Pepsi-Cola Truck and Coca-Cola. Photo from Stan Alekna.

	C6	C8	C10
Station Wagon, 1948 Oldsmobile, plastic, 4" long	16	24	32
Steamroller, plastic, 4" long	10	15	20
Steamshovel, plastic, 4" long	10	15	20
Tanker, plastic, 7" long	15	22	30
Toy Truck, pressed metal wheels, 13" long	100	175	225
Toy Truck Van, 9" long	75	112	150
Tractor, plastic, wheelhorse, 3" long	12	18	25
Trailer Steamshovel, 6-3/4" long	15	25	35
U.S. Army Truck, plastic and tin, 6" long	22	33	45
U.S. Mail Truck, 11" long	35	52	70
Whelan's Steel Truck, rare	150	225	325
Wonder Bread Truck, tin lithographed, 11" long	75	125	175

Barclay Tow Car, white rubber tires, red wood wheels, 3".

BARCLAY

Barclay, named after Barclay Street in West Hoboken, New Jersey, began in 1924 or late 1923, and was owned by partners Leon Donze (1865-1950) and by Michael Levy (c.1895-1964). In 1929, Levy took over the company and turned it into a major toy manufacturer. Under his guidance, it grew from five employees to a prewar peak of 400 workers and moved several times to increasingly larger quarters.

While known for its toy soldiers, Barclay was the largest producer of lead-alloy vehicles in the 1930s and early 1940s. The most popular vehicle being the tiny No. 53 racer.

World War II was a difficult time for all toy manufactures and Barclay was no exception. Forced to lay off all but four of its employees, Barlcay moved in the direction of subcontract work. Unfortunately, the firm was never able to regain its prewar success and closed its doors in 1971.

	C6	C8	C10		C6	C8	C10
Ambulance, w/small cross, No. 194, 3-1/2" long (BV001)	12	18	25	Ambulance, No. 50, 5" long (BV003)	70	105	140
Ambulance, w/large cross, No. 194, 3-1/2" long (BV002)	20	30	40	Anti-Aircraft Gun Truck, sown in 1931 Barclay catalog, No. 198, 3-1/8" long (BV016)	20	30	40

	C6	C8	C10
Anti-Aircraft Gun Truck, w/one man, No. 48, 4" long (BV019)	22	33	45
Anti-Aircraft Gun Truck, w/two men, No. 48, 4" long (BV020)	16	24	32
Armored Army Truck, No. 152, 2-7/8" long (BV006)	9	13	18
Armored Army Truck, w/variations, 2-7/8" long, (BV006A)	10	15	20
Army Car, w/two silver bullhorns, approx. 2-1/2" long (BV008 may be same as BV8)	22	33	44
Army Oil Truck, c.1968, approx. 2" long (BV106)	8	13	18
Army Tank Truck, No. 197, c.1935-36, 3-1/8" long (BV007)	15	22	30
Army Tractor, (Minneapolis-Moline "Jeep"), 2-3/4" long (BV009)	15	22	30
Army Truck, open bed, c.1968, approx. 2" long (BV105)	7	11	15
Army Truck w/Anti-Aircraft Gun, No. 151, 2-1/2" long (BV005)	12	18	25
Army Truck w/Gun, No. 151, 2-3/4" long (BV004)	10	15	20
Auburn Speedster, No. 58, c.1931 (BV139)	17	26	35
Austin Coupe, No. 43, c.1931, 2" long (BV010)	30	45	60
Auto Transport Set, w/two 1950s cars, No. 330, 4-1/2" long (BV011)	50	75	100
Beer Truck, w/wood barrels, No. 376, c.1940, 4" long (BV012)	26	39	52
Beer Truck, w/barrels, No. 377 (BV013)	35	52	70

	C6	C8	C10
Build and Paint Auto Set, No. 100/4, includes six vehicles, parts, paints, 1930s (BV089)	NPF	NPF	NPF
Build and Paint Auto Set, No. 5004, c.1934 (BV089A)	NPF	NPF	NPF
Build and Paint Set, No. 2004, includes truck, coupe, sedan, parts, paints (BV090)	180	270	360
Build and Paint Set, No. 2004, only inlcudes two vehicles (BV090A) .	NPF	NPF	NPF
Bus, futuristic, marked "Made U.S.A.," 3" long (BV014)	34	51	68
Cabover Truck, tailgate, updated, c.1937, 3-1/4" long......................	20	25	30
Cannon Car, gunner low, 3-5/16" long (BV015)	14	21	28
Cannon Car, slight casting differences from headlight version, 3-1/4" long (BV017)	25	38	55
Cannon Car, battery-powered headlight, shown in 1935 catalog, 3-1/2" long (BV018)	80	130	225
Cannon Car, no fitting for bulb, shown in 1935 catalog, 3-1/2" long (BV018A)	22	33	44
Cannon Truck, w/moveable cannon, 4" long (BV021)	20	30	40
Cannon Truck, moveable cannon, 4" long (BV083)	37	56	75
Car Carrier, w/two small cars, early 1930s (BV114)	25	38	50
Chief Police Car, approx. 2" long (BV097 like BV86 and BV96)	5	8	10
Chrysler Airflow, c.1936, 4" long (BV023)	30	45	60

Barclay Build and Paint Auto Set, 1930s. Photo from Perry Eichor.

Left to Right: Barclay Cord Front Drive Coupe; Parcel Delivery Truck, 1930s; Golden Arrow Racer.

Barclay Convertible with vacationers.

Barclay Coupe, 1930s, 3".

	C6	C8	C10
Chrysler Airflow Sedan, large, 1935, No. 1703 (BV127)	17	26	35
Coast To Coast Bus, die-cast, two-piece, marked "Barclay Toy," No. 405, 2-7/8" long (BV024)	40	50	85
Contractor Set, w/hole hitch for wire, No. 338, 1930s, approx. 6-1/4" long (BV142)	NPF	NPF	NPF
Convertible, w/vacationers (BV088)	50	75	100
Convertible Sports Car, driver and passenger, c.1960 (BV159)	9	13	18
Cord Front Drive Coupe, No. 40, c.1931, 3-5/8" long (BV031)	25	38	50
Coupe, 1930s, marked "Made in U.S.A.," 3" long (BV025)	10	20	25
Coupe, c.1935, 2-1/2" long (BV026)	40	70	100
Coupe, 1934, 4-1/2" long (BV027)	40	60	80
Coupe, two-piece, 1930s, "Barclay Toy," 2-7/8" long (BV028)	40	50	85
Coupe, 1934, 4-1/2" long (BV030)	40	60	80
Coupe, No. 51, c.1931, 2-3/16" long (BV132)	18	27	35
Coupe, cast rear tire, 200 series?, c.1935, 3-1/8" long (BV145)	21	31	42
Coupe, removable spare tire, shown in 1935 catalog, 4-1/2" long (BV146)	30	45	60
Coupe, open, w/driver in cap, early 1930s (BV110)	60	90	120
Delivery Truck, No. 309, 2-15/16" long (BV033)	14	21	28

Barclay Double Decker Auto Transport. Photo from Craig Clark.

	C6	C8	C10
Delivery Truck, marked "Bakery Fine Cake Pies," No. 206, c.1934, 3-1/8" long (BV131)	70	105	140
Delivery Truck, No. 309, c.1936, 3-1/2" long (BV136)	12	18	25
DeSoto AirFlow, 1935, 5-3/16" long (BV113)	17	26	35
Double Decker Bus, 4" long (BV034)	60	90	120
Double Transport Set, four cars on upper and lower racks, hinged for unloading, No. 44, 1963 on, 4-1/2" long (BV107)	72	108	145
Double Transport Set, four cars on upper and lower racks, truck has one side window, 1939-1963, No. 440 (BV157)	25	40	75

	C6	C8	C10
Double-Decker Bus, No. 56, c.1931, 3-1/4" long (BV138)	22	33	45
Dump Truck, approx. 2" (BV094)	7	11	15
Dump Truck, spring action, ratchet, shown in 1935 catalog, 4" long (BV147)	20	30	40
Esso Gas Truck, 1930s, 5" long (BV111)	20	30	40
Express stake Truck, 1930s, 2-15/16" long (BV037)	30	45	60
Field Kitchen, 2-1/4" long (BV039) ..	10	15	20
Fire Engine, moveable ladder, No. 390?, 1950s (BV038)	15	22	30

	C6	C8	C10
Fire Engine, two firemen, black metal wheels, No. 41, 1930s, 2-3/4" long (BV040)	17	26	35
Fire Engine, French-looking (Barclay often copied foreign toys), 4" long (BV041)	17	26	35
Fire Engine, No. 209, c.1934, 3-1/8" long (BV134)	25	38	50
Fire Truck, marked "Fire Dept. No. 99," No. 386, 1930s, 5-3/4" long (BV126)	20	30	40
Fire Truck, shown in "Fire Dept. No. 99," No. 368, 1930s, 5-3/4" long (BV127)	20	30	40
Fire Truck, No. 210, c.1934, 3-1/8" long (BV133)	25	38	50
Fire Truck, No. 50, c.1931, 2-3/8" long (BV137)	22	33	45
Fire Truck, but w/gold hydraulics on both sides, wood hubs, rubber tires, c.1931, 2-7/16" long (BV137A)	25	38	50
Ford, 1931, 2-1/4" long (BV042)	15	22	30
Fordson Tractor, white rubber tires, red wood wheels, 2-1/8"	NPF	NPF	NPF

Barclay Fordson Tractor, white rubber tires, red wood wheels, 2-1/8".

5c PEWTER TOYS... Big For The Money

F-6290—2 doz. in box.............Doz ▲39c
Tractor, 2¼ in.

F-6291—2 doz. in box...........Doz ▲39c
Hook & Ladder, 2¾ in.

F-6292—2 doz. in box...........Doz ▲39c
Fire engine, 2⅜ in.

F-6293—2 doz. in box.........Doz ▲39c
Gasoline trucks, 3⅜ in.

This September 1931 Butler Bros. catalog is the earliest catalog appearance known for Barclay vehicles. Note the metal wheels.

	C6	C8	C10
Gas Truck, four tank top, 200 series?, c.1935, 3" long (BV144A)	25	38	50
Gasoline Truck, small, three tank top, c.1931, 2-5/16" long (BV144)	30	45	60
Golden Arrow Racer, 4-1/2" long (BV043)	20	30	40
Hook and Ladder Truck, shown in 1935 catalog, No. 208, 3" long (BV122)	16	24	32
Hospital Truck, c.1968, approx. 2" long (BV104)	8	13	18
Hospital Truck, cab over, approx. 2" long (BV158)	8	13	18
Imperial Chrysler Coupe, No. 39, c.1931 (BV129)	15	22	30
Large Streamline Coupe, 1930s (BV143)	15	22	30
Large Streamline Racer, shown in 1935 catalog, No. 363, 6 7/8" long (BV065)	45	68	90
Log Truck, approx. 2" (BV093)	7	11	15
Mack Pickup Truck, 3-1/2" (BV044)	15	22	30
Milk and Cream Truck, white rubber tires, stamped "No. 377," 3 5/8" long (BV045)	32	48	65

	C6	C8	C10
Milk Truck, black rubber tires, No. 377, 3 5/8" long (BV045A)	22	33	45
Milk Truck, in shape of bottle, No. 567 (BV084)	145	217	290
Milk Van Truck, bottle on side, 2-7/8" long (BV085)	20	30	41
Motorcycle, w/flat rider, full-dimensional sidecar, No. 55, 2-3/4" long (BV046)	48	71	95
Moving Truck, approx. 2" (BV092)	8	12	16
Moving Truck, c.1960, approx. 2" long (BV161)	8	13	18
Officer's Car, w/megaphone on top, 2-1/2" long (BV086)	22	33	44
Oil Truck, approx. 2" long (BV099)	8	13	18
Oil-Fuel Truck, c.1936, 3-9/16" long (BV047)	12	18	25
Parcel Delivery, slush lead, No. 45, c.1931, 3-5/8" long (BV048)	100	150	200
Pepsi-Cola Truck, 1960s, approx. 2" long (BV100)	8	13	18
Pickup Truck, No. 319 (BV166)	NPF	NPF	NPF
Police Car, 1939 Packard, (Radio Police), slush mold, No. 317, approx. 3-5/8" long, 1930s (BV049)	34	51	68
Police Car, No. 317, die-cast, 3-5/8" long (BV049A)	17	26	35

Barclay Moving Truck, decal variants, 1960s, approximately 2". Photo from Stan Alekna.

Variants of the Barclay Oil Truck. Left to Right: a plain version, Yoo Hoo, Pepsi-Cola Truck and Coca-Cola. Photo from Stan Alekna.

Left to Right: Barclay Coupe, two-tone; Barclay Parcel Delivery Truck; Barlcay Golden Arrow Racer. Photo from Evelyn Besser and Bill Kauffman.

Left to right: Barclay Pickup Truck; Tow Truck. Photo from Richard MacNary.

Left to right: Barclay Racer, two passengers; Coupe, 1934, 4-1/2"; Wrecker, 1930s, 3-15/16". Photo from Bill Kauffman.

	C6	C8	C10		C6	C8	C10
Police Car, approx. 2" long (BV096 like BV86 and BV97)	5	8	10	Racer, w/two passengers, 4-1/4" long (BV054)	55	83	110
Race Car, 3" long (BV050)	12	18	24	Racer, w/tail fin, marked "Made U.S.A.," 3-1/2" long (BV055)	25	38	50
Race Car, open, w/driver, 4" long (BV150)	70	105	140	Racer, shown in 1936 catalog, No. 306 (BV120)	55	83	110
Racer, closed cockpit, 5-1/2" long (BV051)	17	26	35	Racer, Golden Arrow, shown in 1931 magazine, No. 5 (BV130) ..	15	22	30
Racer, closed cockpit, c.1939, 7" long (BV052)	30	45	60	Racing Car, c.1968, approx. 2" long (BV095)	5	8	10
Racer, No. 53, approx. 2" long (BV053)	40	60	80	Racing Car, no fenders, c.1968, approx. 2" long (BV101)	5	8	10

	C6	C8	C10
Racing Car, large, No. 37, 1930s, 14-1/4" long (BV115)	16	24	32
Racing Car, large, w/driver, raised exhaust pipe, shown in 1935 catalog (BV149)	17	26	35
Racing Car, large, w/driver, raised exhaust pipe, battery-powered headlight, shown in 1935 catalog, 4" long (BV149A)	NPF	NPF	NPF
Renault Tank, c.1937, No. 47, 4" long (BV056)	22	33	45
Roadster, open, w/driver, dummy spare tire on each side, shown in 1935 catalog, 4-1/2" long (BV154)	80	120	160
Rocket Ship, No. 610	NPF	NPF	NPF
Rocket Ship, No. 611	NPF	NPF	NPF
Searchlight Truck, white rubber tires, c.1940, 4-1/16" long (BV057)	87	130	175
Searchlight Truck, second version (BV057A)	87	130	175
Sedan, four-door, maybe Chrysler, c.1936, approx. 5" long (BV058) .	17	26	35
Sedan, slush lead, rubber wheels, two-door, c.1935, 3-1/8" long (BV059)	60	90	120

	C6	C8	C10
Sedan, die-cast, two-piece, two-door, marked "Barclay Toy," No. 401, 1930s, 2-7/8" long (BV060)	40	50	85
Sedan, two-door, 1960s, 1-5/8" long (BV108)	2	3	5
Sedan, No. 311, c.1936 (BV135)	21	32	43
Sedan, c.1934 (BV140)	17	26	35
Sedan and Tourist Trailer, marked "Made in U.S.A.," 1930s, 6-1/2" long (BV061)	62	93	125
Side Dump, approx. 1-1/2" long (BV087)	7	11	15
Silver Arrow Race Car, 5-1/2" long (BV062)	22	33	45
Sport Coupe, removable spare tire, shown in 1935 catalog, 2-7/8" long (BV148)	32	48	65
Stake Truck, shown in 1935 catalog, No. 207, 3-1/8" long (BV124)	50	75	100
Stake Truck, shown in 1935 catalog, 4-3/8" long (BV151)	36	54	72
Stake Truck, marked "Trucking," shown in 1936 catalog, 3-1/2" long (BV168)	NPF	NPF	NPF
Station Wagon, die-cast, two-piece "Barclay Toy," No. 404, 1930s, 2-15/16" long (BV063)	37	55	75

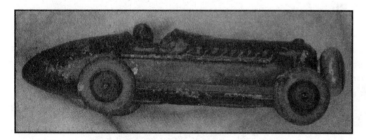

**Barclay Racing Car, battery-operated flashlight, 4".
Photo from Fred Maxwell.**

Barclay Sedan and Tourist Trailer, 6-1/2", 1930s.

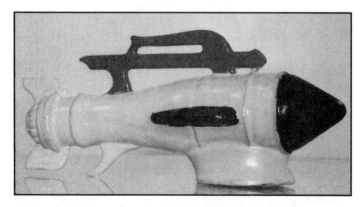

Barclay Rocket Ship No. 610. Photo from Stan Alekna.

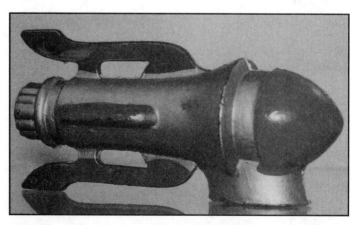

Barclay Rocket Ship No. 611. Photo from Stan Alekna.

Left to Right: Barclay Streamline Car, 1930s; Delivery Truck; Fire Engine. Photo from Evelyn Besser.

Barclay Stake Truck, 3-1/2". Photo from Craig Clark.

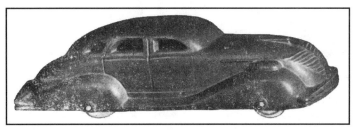

Barclay Streamline Sedan, large.

Barclay Army Tank, two men in turret, white rubber tires, 3-7/8".

	C6	C8	C10
Steam-Roller, slush lead w/tin roof, traction type, No. 44, 3-1/4" long (BV064)	30	45	60
Streamline Car, No. 302, 1936, 3-1/8" long? (BV032)	45	68	90
Streamline Coupe, large , No. 361 (BV112)	17	26	35
Streamline Coupe, No. 301, 3-1/4" long (BV123)	50	75	100
Streamline Coupe, shown in 1937 catalog, 5" long (BV155)	NPF	NPF	NPF
Streamline Racer, No. 303, 4-3/8" long (BV121)	60	90	120
Streamline Sedan Large, shown in 1935 catalog, No. 362 (BV125)	41	61	82
Tank, one man in turret , marked "4562," 3 7/8" long (BV066)	17	26	35
Tank, two men in turret, marked "4562," 3-7/8" long (BV067)	21	31	42
Tank, die-cast, man in turret, black rubber tires, 2-5/8" long (BV069)	12	18	25
Tank, base on US M2 light tank, 2-1/2" long (BV070)	12	18	25
Tank T41, 4-1/4" long (BV068)	17	26	35
Taxi, slush mold, 3-1/4" long (BV071)	14	21	28
Taxi, die-cast, No. 318, 3-1/4" long (BV071A)	25	38	50
Taxi, approx. 2" long (BV163)	5	8	10
Tow Car, white rubber tires, red wood wheels, 3" long	NPF	NPF	NPF

	C6	C8	C10
Tow Car, shown in 1935 catalog, No. 205, 3-1/16" long (BV141)	34	51	68
Tow Truck, No. 316 (BV167)	NPF	NPF	NPF
Towing Service Truck, large, No. 1105 (or 1705) (BV117)	82	124	175
Towing Truck, shown in 1936 catalog, No. 312, 3-3/8" long (BV119)	50	75	100
Tractor, slush lead, caterpillar type, approx. 2-5/8" long, (BV072)	17	26	35
Tractor, No. 203, peg hitch, 2-1/8" long (BV109)	11	16	22
Tractor, No. 7, c.late 1920s-early 1930s (BV116)	15	22	30

Barclay was the largest manufacturer of lead-alloy vehicles in the 1930s and 1940s. Photo from Craig Clark.

	C6	C8	C10
Tractor, small, shown in 1931 magazine, No. 42, 2-3/16" long (BV128)	12	18	25
Trailer Truck, marked "Railway Express" or w/other moving company name, 1950s (BV074)	5	8	10
Transport, Set No. 330, two cars, 1960s, 4-1/2" long (BV075)	25	40	75
Transport set, w/two cars, approx. 4-3/4" long (BV152)	42	63	85
Transport Set, open-cab Mack truck w/four 2-1/2" cars, shown in 1935 catalog, 10-1/4" long (BV153)	NPF	NPF	NPF
Truck U.S. Motor Unit, white rubber tires, came three ways, no hitch, c.1940 (BV078)	12	17	26
U.S. Army Sedan, approx. 2" long (BV162)	6	9	12
U.S. Army Truck, no hitch, red wood hubs, No. 204, 2-1/2" long (BV076)	11	16	22
U.S. Army Truck, white rubber wheels, wire or peg hitch, 2-1/2" long (BV077)	12	18	25
U.S. Army Truck, c.1968, approx. 2" long (BV103)	7	11	15
U.S. Mail Truck, 1960s, approx. 2" long (BV091)	10	17	24
Vintage Car, approx. 2" long (BV098)	15	22	30
Vintage Car, no windshield (BV165)	5	8	10
Volkswagen, 1960s, approx. 2" long (BV102)	10	17	24
Volkswagen, 1960s (BV160)	12	18	24

Barclay Tow Car, white rubber tires, red wood wheels, 3".

	C6	C8	C10
Volkswagen Hot Rod, approx. 2" long (BV164)	12	18	24
Wheel-A-Rific speedway track, two lead racers, black rubber wheels, sold for $1.00, c.1970, 10" of plastic track (BV079)	7	26	35
White Horse Van, some have sticker reading "Welcome I.C.M.A. compliments THE WHITE MOTOR CO.," approx. 3" long (BV156)	55	83	110
Wrecker, No. 46, c.1931, 3-1/2" (BV080)	45	68	90
Wrecker, c.1934, 3-15/16 long (BV081)	30	45	60
Wrecker, die-cast, two-piece, marked "Barclay Toy," No. 403, 1930s 2-7/8" long (BV082)	40	50	85

BEST TOY & NOVELTY FACTORY

Best Toy & Novelty was founded by John M. Best Sr. an entrepreneur and printer. Best had lived in Clifton, Kansas, the home of Kansas Toy & Novelty, so he was well-aware of the ups and downs of small toy companies. According to Dee Buchanan, Best's great-granddaughter, Best and his wife Rosanna purchased a company from Kansas Toy & Novelty Company in Vining, Kansas—a suburb of Clifton. The Bests moved the company to the back of their house in Manhattan, Kansas. Although contradictory, evidence from other family members suggests Best purchased of the assets of a Clifton toy company occurred about 1933.

It started as a family business for his children, relatives, friends and neighbors, according to Minnie Nelson, Best's daughter. Conrad Morsch was a molder for Best Toy. Items produced included farm implements, tractors, airplanes, buses and trains, as well as all types of cars. What began as a family hobby grew into a respectable business, supplying toy distributors and dime stores. After several years of operation, it was sold to Ralstoy, a Ralston, Nebraska company, in 1939.

It is not certain when Best started or what the first number used in the Best Toy & Novelty series. Nor do we know if he introduced any new patterns. (See history of "Kansas Toy" in this book).

Donated by Ms. Buchanan was a faded copy of a Best Toy brochure. This appears to be a pre-publication printer's mockup, and undated; but its forty-two illustrations were helpful in identifying many Best Toy and Kansas Toy items in collections. With no paper trail available, this was indeed a find. Many thanks to all who helped and continue to help.

Distinguishing Best Toy vehicles from other slush-mold toys can be very difficult. Molds were passed from one manufacturer to another. Best Toy products can usually be distinguished from other slush-mold toys because they usually have white rubber wheels and are embossed "Made in USA." However, some of the toys used the metal wheels of the Kansas Toy originals, or the later wood hubs with rubber tires. It is also possible that Best Toy modified or rebuilt molds to create variations.

Best molded a great number of designs. To reduce redundancy in this book, we list them here, but will not describe them in detail, if they are adequately covered in Kansas Toy or Ralstoy lists. The following numbered toys and some unnumbered duplicates were found—6, 10, 14, 17, 20, 25, 26, 27, 31, 32, 34, 35, 36, 37, 39, 40, 41, 42, 43, 45, 46, 47, 49, 51, 54, 55, 57, 58, 59, 60, 67, 70, 71, 72, 74, 76, 77, 78, 79, 80, 81, 85, 86, 87, 90, 91, 92, 93, 94, 95, 97, 99, 100, 101, 102.

Contributors: Fred Maxwell, 4722 N. 33 St., Arlington, VA 22207. Maxwell, a collector and occasional author, has been collecting antique aircraft and vehicle toys for over twenty-five years. He founded the Auto Collectors Club twenty-five years ago to promote interest in the central Atlantic states region. **Perry R. Eichor,** 703 North Almond Drive, Simpsonville, SC, 29681. Captain Eichor has been collecting aircraft toys since he was a young officer in the Air Force, his twenty-one years as an Air Force officer only served to deepen his interest in the subject. Today when he is not collecting, researching or writing about aeronautical toys, he works as a criminal justice administrator as well as an appraiser and auctioneer.

Abbreviations

The following abbreviations are for the details and variations useful in identification.

HG	horizontal grille pattern	SM	sidemounted spare
HL	horizontal hood louvers	SP	string-pull knob in handcrank area
HO	hood cap, Motometer or ornament	T	external trunk
L	lacquer finish	UV	unnumbered version
LI	landau irons on convertibles	VG	vertical grille pattern
MDW	metal disc wheels	VL	vertical hood louvers
MDSW	metal disc solid spokes	WS, W/S	windshield
MDWBT	wheels with black painted tires	WV	windshield visor
MSW	metal open spoke wheels	WHRT	wooden hubs, rubber tires
MWW	metal simulated wire wheels	WRDW	white hard rubber disc wheels
OW	open windows	WRW	white soft rubber wheels (balloon tires)
RM	rearmount spare tire/wheel		

Best Cab unit, No. 101, with a Best Oil Transport, No. 102.

Top row, left to right: Best Sedan, No. 95; Best Coupe, No. 93; Best Sedan, No. 90. Middle row, left to right: Best Large Sedan, No. 94; Best Record Race Car, No. 85. Bottom Row, left to right: Best Pontiac Sedan, No. 100; Best Large Racer, No. 97. Photo from Fred maxwell.

Top row from left: Best Coupe; Large Sedan, two-door airflow. Bottom row from left: Sedan, three headlamps, hard rubber wheels; Sedan, Police Dept. shield on doors. Photo from Fred Maxwell.

Best Record Race Car, No. 85. Photo from Perry Eichor.

	C6	C8	C10
Cab Unit, No. "101," International? sleeper cab, slanted grille, HO, two OW, rare; 3-1/4" long (BEV015)	40	60	80
Coupe, No. "92," Dodge?, chopped top, Brewster-like heart shaped grille, HO, long streamlined front fenders; 3-3/4" long (BEV006)	20	30	40
Coupe, No. "93," Cadillac?, streamlined, hood similar to No. 91, grid pattern grille, two OW; 3-5/8" long (BEV007)	20	30	45
Coupe, No. "96," apparently same car as No. 93; it is not known if both were produced; 3-1/2" long (BEV010)	20	45	50
Coupe, No. "98" (BEV012)	15	30	40
Coupe, No. "99," Pontiac?, streamlined, HO, rearmount; 4" long (BEV013)	25	45	70
Oil Transport, No. "102," streamlined "Gasoline" semi-trailer to No. 101, four tanks, four storage compartments; Total length of cab-trailer - 6-3/4" (BEV016)	50	75	100

	C6	C8	C10
Racer, No. "85," record car w/large square fin, driver, HO, VG, twelve exhaust ports, WHRT, 4" long (BEV001)	20	30	40
Racer, large, No. "97," Bluebird record car, driver, large fin, twelve exhaust ports, hard-rubber wheels, faired; 4-1/2" long (BEV011)	25	45	75
Sedan, No. "86," Lincoln? two-door fastback, slanted grille w/grid pattern, HL, divided w/s, rear wheel skirts, 4" long (BEV002) ...	20	30	50
Sedan, No. "87," Brewster? (BEV003)	15	25	35
Sedan, No. "90," two door, airflow, hood reaches front bumper w/no grille, four OW, hard rubber wheels, 3-1/2" long (BEV004)	25	40	70
Sedan, No. "91," Cadillac? two door airflow, high style vee grille, faired front fenders, 3-1/2" long (BEV005)	25	40	70
Sedan, No. "95," two-door, airflow similar to No. 94, w/three headlamps, four OW, trunk, hard-rubber wheels; Chrysler-Briggs show car?; 3-1/2" long (BEV009a)	30	40	55

	C6	C8	C10
Sedan, No. "95," two-door, airflow similar to No. 94, w/three headlamps, four OW, trunk, hard-rubber wheels; w/"Police Dept." shield on doors; centered headlamp may be a siren, one version has "Police" painted on roof; 3-1/2" long (BEV009b)	35	45	60
Sedan, No. "100," Pontiac, streamlined, two door, HO, HG, four OW, trunk, 4" long (BEV014)	20	30	40
Sedan, large, No. "94," two door, airflow, similar to No. 90, four OW, taxi lamp on roof; 4-1/2" long (BEV008)	35	45	70

Top row, left to right: Best Coupe; Best Pontiac Sedan, two-door. Middle row, left to right: Best Coupe and Sedan reproduction. Bottom row: Best Sedan reproduction. Photo from Perry Eichor.

BING TOY WORKS

Bing Toy Works started producing tin toys in the 1880s. By 1914, it employed more than 5,000 people. Business flourished through the 1920s until the Great Depression. In 1932, after falling to hard times, the company went into receivership. About two years later, it ceased production of tin toys entirely. Karl Bub, another German toy manufacturer, took over the company soon after.

Bing automobiles are difficult to find and are held in high regard by most collectors. The Model T series came in solid black, red, yellow, green and blue lithograph; the color lithographed versions are difficult to find.

Contributor: Bob Smith, The Village Smith, 62 West Ave., Fairport, NY 14450-2102.

	C6	C8	C10
Dog Cart, Live Steam, leather seats, 10" long......................................	3000	6000	9000
Double-Decker Bus, 10" long...........	650	1200	1800
Fire Ladder Truck, clockwork motor, composition figures, 13" long.......	2000	3500	5100
Fire Pumper, clockwork motor, composition figures, 11" long.......	1800	3200	4500

	C6	C8	C10
Garage, tin lithographed, clockwork motor, w/two open cars, c.1925, car length 5-1/2", garage 8" x 6-1/2"	450	750	1000
Garage, Raceabout and Limousine, tin lithographed, clockwork motor; cars 5-1/2" long, garage 8" x 6-1/2", c.1912	450	700	900

Bing Garage with two open cars, 1920s. Photo from Bob Smith.

Bing Garage, Raceabout and Limousine, autos 5-1/2", garage 8". Photo from Bob Smith.

Bing Limousine, circa 1908, maroon with yellow stripes, 14" long. Photo from Bill Bertoia.

Bing Limousine, 9-1/2", issued around 1915. Photo from Bob Smith.

A sampling of 1920s Bing Model T Fords—each measures 6-1/2". Photo from Bob Smith.

Bing Model T Ford Coupe, red, 6-1/2", 1920s. Photo from Bob Smith.

	C6	C8	C10
Limousine, clockwork motor, maroon and yellow striping, driver, c.1908, 14" long	1000	2000	4700
Limousine, blue and black lithographed, clockwork motor, c.1915, 9-1/2" long	900	1250	1800
Limousine, w/wind-up, driver, 15-1/4" long	700	1100	1700
Model T Doctor's Coupe, clockwork motor, black, 6-1/2" long	300	425	575
Model T Ford Coupe, clockwork motor, red, black and cream tin lithographed, c.1924, 6-1/2" long	500	750	1200
Model T Ford Roadster, clockwork moto, red, black and yellow tin lithographed, c.1924, 6-1/2" long	600	900	1300
Model T Ford Sedan, clockwork motor, blue, black and cream tin lithographed, c.1924, 6-1/2" long	450	650	1100
Model T Ford Touring Car, clockwork motor, color tin lithographed, c.1924, 6-1/2" long	450	650	1100

Bing Model T Ford Roadster, 6-1/2", 1920s, red, black and yellow tin. Photo from Bob Smith.

Bing Model T Ford Sedan, blue, 6-1/2", 1920s. Photo from Bob Smith.

A pair of Bing Model T Fords with their original boxes. Photo from Len Rosenberg.

Bing Touring Car, Type-I, spoked wheels, male driver, 6", 1920. Photo from Bob Smith.

Bing Touring Car, Type-II, with female driver, red and black, 6", 1920s. Photo from Bob Smith.

Bing Yellow Taxi, 9", 1920s, orange and black. Photo from Bob Smith.

Bing Vis a Vis, steam, 10", issued around 1902. Photo from Bill Bertoia Auctions.

	C6	C8	C10		C6	C8	C10
Model T Fords, sedan, roadster, touring, and coupe, painted black, c.1923, 6-1/2" long, each	350	450	675	Touring Car, wind-up, 13" long	600	1100	1650
				Two Seater, open, 9-1/2" long	1000	1700	2500
Touring Car, type-I spoked wheels, clockwork motor, red and black, male driver, c.1920, 6" long	250	400	600	Vis a Vis, steam, driver, c.1902, 10" long	3000	6000	9000
Touring Car, type-II, solid wheels, clockwork motor, red and black, female driver, c.1923, 6" long	250	400	600	Yellow Taxi, clockwork motor, orange and black lithographed, c.1924, 9" long	800	1500	2200

BRITAINS

Britains, of London, England, was originally owned by William Britain. In 1893, he introduced hollow-casting of toy soldiers. Britains is still in business and its soldiers are the most collected military figures. It made, and continues to make, a number of vehicles. Understandably, many, perhaps the majority, are military. (Except where noted, photos by K. Warren Mitchell).

	C6	C8	C10		C6	C8	C10
Armored Car (BR0027d)	NPF	NPF	NPF	Army Staff Car, officer and driver, third version: rectangular windshield, rubber tires; 1948-50 (RB1448b)	145	265	325
Armoured Car (BR1321)	150	325	400				
Army Ambulance, wounded man and stretcher, all doors open, 6" long (BR1512)	150	210	275	Army Staff Car, officer and driver, fourth version: lead tires, painted gray, split windshield; 1951-57 (RB1448c)	150	285	350
Army Staff Car, officer and driver, first version: smooth white tires, black fenders (BR1448)	175	310	385				
Army Staff Car, officer and driver, second version: white tires, all khaki body (RB1448a)	165	300	375	Army Staff Car, officer and driver, fifth version: black plastic tires; 1958-59 (RB1448d)	125	225	300
				Army Tender, covered, ten-wheel (BR1432)	125	200	325

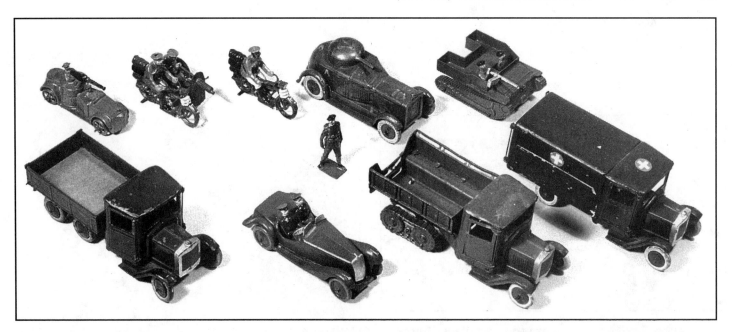

Prewar Britains vehicles include, back row from left: Armoured Car; Motorcycle Machine Gun; Dispatch Rider; Armoured Car; Tank (Carden Loyd type). Front row from left: Lorry, Army, six-wheeled type; Army Staff Car, officer and driver; Covered Lorry, R.A. Gun, drivers; Army Ambulance, wounded man and stretcher, 6".

Britains Farm, Lorry with driver, four-wheel.

Britains Centurion Tank.

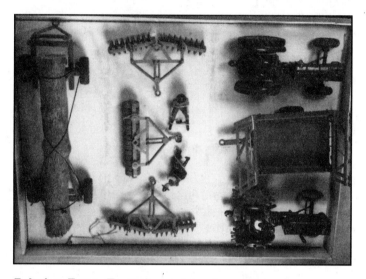

Britains Farm, Tractors and Implements.

	C6	C8	C10
Army Tender, covered, caterpillar type (BR1433)	95	150	200
Bren Gun Carrier (BR0876)	35	65	85
Covered Lorry, R.A. Gun, drivers (BR10462)	150	350	450
Dispatch Rider (BR0200)	20	30	50
Lorry, Army, Caterpillar type (BR1333)	125	200	300
Lorry, Army, four-wheeled type (BR1334)	105	130	210
Lorry, Army, w/driver (BR1335)	115	165	230
Motorcycle Machine Gun (BR0199)	40	75	110
Police Car, w/two officers (BR1413)	350	600	900
Speed Record Car, The Blubird (BR1400)	135	270	370
Tank, Carden Loyd Type (BR1203)	110	155	230

Farm

	C6	C8	C10
Acrobat Rake (BR0176F)	NPF	NPF	NPF
BP Gas Pump (BR0750)	10	17	22
Cultivator (BR0175F)	NPF	NPF	NPF

	C6	C8	C10
Fordson Major Tractor, driver, rubber tires (BR0128F)	60	80	150
Fordson Power Major Tractor, no driver (BR0172F)	50	75	100
Fordson Tractor, metal wheels, driver (BR0127F)	75	125	200
Lorry w/driver, four-wheel (BR0059F)	10	17	22
Motorcycle w/sidecar (BR0641)	500	700	1250
Muledozer (BR0174F)	NPF	NPF	NPF
Power Pump (BR07051)	10	17	22
Shell Gas Pump (BR0748)	11	19	25
Shellmax Gas Pump (BR0749)	10	17	22
Three Furrow Plough (BR0173F)	7	11	16
Timber Trailer, w/real log (BR0129F)	25	50	75
Tractors and implements (BR0134F)	200	350	500

Lilliput

	C6	C8	C10
Army Ambulance, measures 3" long (LV/618)	NPF	NPF	NPF
Army Covered Three-ton Truck, removable plastic top (LV/607)	25	38	50
Army Truck, 1-1/2 ton, w/spare wheel (LV/612)	NPF	NPF	NPF
Articulated Lorry (LV/603)	20	30	40
Articulated Truck w/Spare Wheel (LV/614)	NPF	NPF	NPF
Austin Champ, removable hood (LV/609)	NPF	NPF	NPF
Boxed Set, w/accessories and Carter as listed in the 1951 Catalog Supplement, includes: one LV/602, one LV/602; one LV/603; one LV/604; w/driver, one LV/605, w/Milkman, one LV/606 (LV/SA)	65	125	200
Centurion Tank (LV/610)	25	38	50
Covered Army Truck, 1-1/2 Ton, w/spare wheel (LV/613)	NPF	NPF	NPF

	C6	C8	C10
Farm Lorry, three ton (LV/608)	NPF	NPF	NPF
Farm or Civilian Truck, 1-1/2 ton, w/spare wheel, measures 2-13/16" long (LV/616)	NPF	NPF	NPF
Fordson Tractor with Driver (LV/604)	20	30	40
Lilliput Display Box, contains Saloon Car, tractor, tumbrel cart and milk float, farmer, farmer's wife, stable lad, farm girl and dog, horses, cows and calf, sheep and lamb, pig, geese, hurdles and tree, twenty-eight pieces (L7)	75	150	250
Lilliput Railway Personnel and Vehicles, includes: saloon car, lorry, sports car, articulated lorries, Austin "Champ," motorcyclists, station trollies, packing cases, barrels, hampers, porters w/trollies, guards, station master, porters w/luggage, newsvendor, general public asst., forty-three pieces (L11)	NPF	NPF	NPF
Local Authority Ambulance, cream, measures 3" long (LV/617)	8	15	20
Open Army Truck, three ton, w/spare wheel, measures 3-1/4" long (LV/620)	NPF	NPF	NPF
Open Sports Car (LV/601)	20	30	40
Post Office Royal Mail Van, measures 3" long (LV/619)	NPF	NPF	NPF
Saloon Car (LV/602)	20	30	40
Saracen Armoured Personnel Carrier (LV/615)	NPF	NPF	NPF
Sexton Self-Propelled Gun (LV/611)	27	41	55

Prewar

	C6	C8	C10
Beetle Lorry and Driver (BR1877) ...	60	95	135
Bren Gun Carrier, w/full crew (BR1876)	35	65	85

Postwar

	C6	C8	C10
155mm Gun mounted on Centurion Tank body (BR2175 (also 9748))	200	350	500

	C6	C8	C10
Austin Champ (BR2102)	30	50	65
Balloon Barrage Unit, (lorry, winch, balloon) (BR1757)	700	1000	1600
Batallion Anti-Tank Gun (BR2173 (also 9720))	10	14	18
Beetle Lorry and driver (BR1877b) .	50	85	125
Bren Gun Carrier, w/full crew (BR1876a)	30	55	75
Centurion Tank (BR2150 (also 9770))	150	275	375
Centurion Tank, painted for Desert Warfare (BR2154)	250	450	600
Complete Mobile Howitzer Unit, 4 pcs., w/limber and caterpillar trailer (BR1727)	300	550	750
Corporation Motor Ambulance, driver, wounded and stretcher (BR1514)	350	600	850
Dispatch Rider (BR1791)	30	50	65
Heavy Duty Lorry, underslung, w/driver (BR1643)	600	900	1200
Heavy-Duty Lorry, driver, searchlight, battery and lamp (BR1642)	300	500	700
Howitzer, 4-1/2" long (BR1725)	13	20	30
John Cobb's Railton Wonder Car (BR1656)	200	350	500
John Cobb's Railton Wonder Car, chromium-plated boyd, 10" long (BR1658)	125	200	325
Light Goods Van, w/driver (BR2024)	250	450	600

Britains Complete Mobile Howitzer Unit.

Britains Lorry, Army, four-wheeled type.

Britains Heavy Duty Lorry, underslung, with driver.

Postwar Britains vehicles include, back row from left: Bren Gun Carrier; Army Lorry, four-wheeled type; towing Mobile Unit; Army Lorry, six-wheeled type; Army Staff Car; Covered Army Tender; towing Mobile Searchlight. Front row from left: Army Ambulance; Beetle Lorry; towing 4-1/2" Howitzer and Regulation Timber; Dispatch Rider; Austin Champ; towing Batallion Anti-Tank Gun.

	C6	C8	C10		C6	C8	C10
Lorry and Trailer, w/hydrogen cylinders (BR1879)	115	165	210	Mobile Searchlight (BR1718)	30	50	70
Lorry, ten wheel, w/two pdr., AA gun on chassis (BR1832)	350	700	1000	Mobile Unit, two-pounder (BR1717)	30	50	70
Lorry, ten wheel, w/searchlight on chassis (BR1833)	200	450	675	Motor Ambulance, w/doctor, wounded, nurses, orderlies, eighteen pcs. (BR1897)	175	325	450
Miniature Balloon Barrage Unit, w/lorry, winch and balloon (BR1855)	125	250	350	Regulation Limber (BR1726)	15	22	27
				Underslung Heavy-Duty Lorry (BR1641)	200	350	550

BROOKLIN

The love of cars, both prototype and model, are the reasons John and Jenny Hall created Brooklin Models Ltd., a firm that makes 1:43-scale replicas of white-metal model cars. Many collectors say that Brooklin models are the standard of the industry—very similar to the "standard of the world" description for Lionel toy trains or Britains toy soldiers. Brooklins today are known worldwide. The new Brooklin Collection includes some of the greatest and most controversial American motor cars made by U.S. manufacturers in the past five decades.

John Hall began humbly in the basement of his Canadian home in the early 1970s, making models by hand with resin and no windows, using popsicle sticks, wood-burnt with the familiar early Brooklin Models logo to keep the resin casting from warping. Brooklin Models is named after a suburb of Ontario, Canada, called Brooklin.

Brooklin Codes

- **Code I**: All pieces built, assembled and decaled from the Brooklin factory in England. Also, those pieces produced in the factory, but partially assembled/partially or totally decaled outside, with total knowledge and approval of John Hall. These are considered 100-percent authentic Brooklin. For example, some CTCS, CPCTS and promotionals such as Mobil and City of Toronto, Bay State Lobster, Model Auto Review, Coca-Cola, et. al.

- **Code II**: Altered or modified Brooklin models outside the factory, done with full approval of the company. At present, there are only a few such models that fall into this category. The first is the series of convertibles produced by the Model Car Shop. Its first car was the Burgundy 1953 Skylark with wire wheels. The only other Code II piece presently is the plated (silver color) Edsel done by Danhausen.

- **Code III**: Altered or modified Brooklin models outside the factory done without the approval of the company. There are many beautiful models in this category that can enhance your collection, but cannot be considered true Brooklin pieces. The excellent convertibles done by Jerry Rettig, the Orange County Fire Dept. Dodge Pick-up done by TFC and the Yellow Corvette with wire wheels done by the Model Car Shop are some examples.

- **Prototypes**: These are pieces that may have been cast differently or paint-tested in color variation and were never intended for sale. These do not fall into any category above. There are many such models and the collector need not feel that his/her collection is incomplete without them. If, however, these pieces were put up for sale by the company or by an individual with permission of the company, then they would be Code I, such as the turquoise Mercury, and the eleven Tucker samples given to the Tucker Club (so it could choose three promotional colors).

Discontinued Color/Style

Only 1,253 Shelby American G.T. 500 Fastbacks were built in 1968, making it one of the rarest cars in its class. It was the undisputed King of the 1960s muscle cars.

Numbers 1, 16a, 17, 26a and 31 were discontinued from the Brooklin Collection during 1992.

When the Brooklin company was in its infancy, it experienced the greatest changes in technology and process. Therefore, the early Canadian models reflect many different changes since Hall, in an attempt to perfect his models, experimented with many forms of casting materials and color variations. The year 1974 was a pivotal one for Hall. It was early that year when he decided to leave his teaching position at Durham College and devote full-time to model-making and designing equipment to create finished scale-model cars. Most of the companies at this time were doing kits, not built-up models.

Meanwhile, back in the basement, Hall was dabbling in model-making and scratch-building models for himself and other collectors. He helped form the Canadian Toy Collector's Society (CTCS) with Ron Faithful and Tony Topley. Through the CTCS, Hall met many collectors from Canada and Buffalo, where he went to his first toy show called "Motoring in Miniatures." At the show, collectors persuaded him to make a Pierce Arrow. Thinking this was a good idea, Hall made two master models out of resin. He then cast eighty-six models at the laborious rate of ten models per week. The hand-painted Pierce Arrow with resin base became car No. 1. The Pierce Arrow was retired in 1993.

In 1975, Hall felt he could raise money at the Canadian Plowing Match held in Toronto, by selling a model of a plow commemorating the event. Two thousand were produced, but only 200 were sold. The remainder were melted down. To say the least, it was not a financial success. Today, it is a rare and sought-after piece, as many Brooklin collectors have never seen one. There is one pictured in the hardcover *Brooklin Collection Book*.

Initially, Hall did everything to create a Brooklin Model. He carved the master, made the mold, cast the piece and assembled the models. Two employees helped assemble and paint. As business improved, more people were hired. Today, the business supports twenty-five or more employees, including Jenny Hall, who runs the business office, and John, who overseas the entire operation.

In October of 1979, John and Jenny decided to move back to the United Kingdom. This ceased all future production of Brooklin Models stamped "Made in Canada." They settled in Bath, England. The first factory was located in the Huggett Electrical building in Bath. Many of Brooklin's No. 16 Dodger models carry the Huggett logo. In England, new markets opened up and orders began to pour in. American cars are quite popular in Europe, so are Brooklin models. They have always been popular in America.

Today, Hall continues his original idea—to manufacture only models of American cars. He has chosen some of the most controversial cars of the past five decades. Each is a legend or classic in its own right. When asked why he models only American cars, Hall replies, "I think being influenced by living and working in North America is the obvious reason. And, of course, the sheer outrageous design and ostentation of the American car calls out to be modeled."

At the new Brooklin factory in Bath, Brooklin manufacturers more than 50,000 models a year. Since 1988, the models were marketed in a new box, which includes the Statue of Liberty, the New York City skyline and an Edsel with an American flag banner. Gone are the old tan and brown logo boxes. These have been resurrected as of late for promotional issues, lending a nostalgic touch for the collector.

Prices are for items Mint in Box.

Contributor: Vincent Rosa, 28 Arthur Ave., Blue Point, NY 11715, (516) 363-2134. Rosa grew up in Brooklyn, New York, and moved to Long Island, where he attended Adelphi-Suffolk-Dowling College. Rosa holds a master's degree in history from Stony Brook University and looks forward to be working on his doctorate. His hobbies include collecting Lionel Trains, toy soldiers of the British Victorian period and Slingerland Radio-King Drums. Rosa and his wife Bonnie operate Model Cars and Trains Unlimited of Blue Point, New York, a firm specializing in the sale of collectible trains, die-cast model cars and toy soldiers of all types and varieties. In the past, Rosa has contributed to *Greenberg's Guide to Lionel H.O.* In addition to his books on Brooklin models, Rosa had his short story, "The Man with the Shopping Cart," published in the December 1994 issue of *O-Gauge Railroading*. He has published his own copyrighted work, *The Brooklin Collection* (1989) and *The Official Brooklin Models Collector Guide* (1989). **Source for Brooklin Models chapter:** Rosa, Vincent. *1974-1989 The Brooklin Collection*, 1989, 80 pgs. Hardcover with color photos. $49.95 postpaid, comes with free collector's guide. Send to: Model Cars & Trains Ultd., 28 Arthur Ave., Blue Point, NY 11715, (516) 363-2134.

KEY

Abbreviations can be found in parenthesis in the item's description.

1	Resin baseplate		**15**	Last 250 made came with certificate
2	No plastic windows		**16**	Gold trim
3	Rare (not plentiful, hard to find, in demand)		**App.**	Approximately
			C	Discontinued color
4	Detailed chassis		**CPCTS**	Canadian Pacific Coast Toy Show
5	One of a kind		**CTCI**	Classic Thunderbird Collectors International
6	First casting		national	
7	No gas cap		**CTCS**	Canadian Toy Collectors Society
8	With gas cap		**D**	Discontinued body style
9	Numbered on baseplate		**L**	Means No. 14 in Tucker Canadian
10	Smooth side		Issue	
11	Small decals		**M**	Metallic
12	Rim linted sides		**P**	Promotional; Limited run
13	No Window; van style		**PROTO**	Prototype
14	Large scale		**R**	Regular Issue

	C6	C8	C10		C6	C8	C10
Canadian Issues				No. 01 1933 Pierce Arrow, green/gray, (D-1-2-3), approx. thirty made, second issue	n/a	n/a	NPF
No. 01 1933 Pierce Arrow, medium blue, (M), third issue	n/a	n/a	350	No. 01 1933 Pierce Arrow, maroon/gray, (D-1-2-3), approx. thirty made, second issue	n/a	n/a	NPF
No. 01 1933 Pierce Arrow, blue/gray, (D-5-3), all resin, first issue	n/a	n/a	NPF	No. 01 1933 Pierce Arrow, blue/gray, (D-1-2-3), approx. thirty made, second issue	n/a	n/a	NPF
No. 01 1933 Pierce Arrow, silver gray, (M), third issue	n/a	n/a	350	No. 01 1933 Pierce Arrow, brown/cream, (D-5-3), all resin, first issue	n/a	n/a	NPF
No. 01 1933 Pierce Arrow, silver gray, (D-M-1-2-3), third issue	n/a	n/a	350	No. 01 1933 Pierce Arrow, champagne, (R), maroon interior, third issue	n/a	n/a	350
No. 01 1933 Pierce Arrow, white, (D-1-2-5-3)	n/a	n/a	NPF	No. 02 1949 Tucker, dark blue, (D-2-6-2-L), gray interior	n/a	n/a	200
No. 01 1933 Pierce Arrow, champagne, red interior, third issue	n/a	n/a	350	No. 02 1949 Tucker, dark blue, (D-R-M), gray interior	n/a	n/a	200
No. 01 1933 Pierce Arrow, brown/cream, (D-1-2-3), approx. thirty made, second issue	n/a	n/a	NPF				

	C6	C8	C10
No. 02 1949 Tucker, medium blue, (D-M)	n/a	n/a	200
No. 02 1949 Tucker, maroon, (D-3), fourteen made	n/a	n/a	NPF
No. 02 1949 Tucker, black, (D-2-3-6-L), light gray interior	n/a	n/a	200
No. 02 1949 Tucker, medium blue, (2-6-2-L), gray interior	n/a	n/a	200
No. 02 1949 Tucker, very dark blue, (D-2-6-2-L), gray interior	n/a	n/a	200
No. 02 1949 Tucker, black, (D-2-3-6-L), beige interior	n/a	n/a	200
No. 03 1930 Ford Victoria Two-door, beige/olive, (D-4), tan interior, white wheels	n/a	n/a	90
No. 03 1930 Ford Victoria Two-door, white top beige body, (D-M-2), tan interior, cream wheels	n/a	n/a	275
No. 03 1930 Ford Victoria Two-door, white/olive, (D-2), gray interior, white wheels	n/a	n/a	250
No. 03 1930 Ford Victoria Two-door, white/medium brown, (D-4), gray interior, white/wheels	n/a	n/a	105
No. 03 1930 Ford Victoria Two-door, white/olive, (D-4), tan interior, white wheels	n/a	n/a	250
No. 04 1937 Chevy Coupe, buff green, (D-R)	n/a	n/a	325
No. 04 1937 Chevy Coupe, medium green, (D)	n/a	n/a	325
No. 04 1937 Chevy Coupe, dark green, (D)	n/a	n/a	325
No. 04 1937 Chevy Coupe, dark green, (D-4)	n/a	n/a	325
No. 04 1937 Chevy Coupe, black, (D-4-3), approx. eighteen made	n/a	n/a	NPF
No. 05 1930 Model A Two-door Coupe, black top/brown body, (D), Tudor body, orange wheels	n/a	n/a	525
No. 05 1930 Model A Two-door Coupe, black top/brown body, (D-4), Tudor body, white wheels	n/a	n/a	500
No. 05 1930 Model A Two-door Coupe, black/black, (D-3), Tudor body, white wheels	n/a	n/a	500
No. 06 1932 Packard, light beige/maroon, gray interior	n/a	n/a	NPF
No. 06 1932 Packard, medium gray/medium gray, medium blue fenders	n/a	n/a	NPF
No. 06 1932 Packard, light gray/light gray, blue gray fenders	n/a	n/a	NPF
No. 06 1932 Packard, light gray/metallic gray, maroon fenders, gray interior	n/a	n/a	325

	C6	C8	C10
No. 06 1932 Packard, white/maroon, gray interior	n/a	n/a	NPF
No. 06 1932 Packard, dark beige top maroon body, gray interior	n/a	n/a	NPF
No. 06 1932 Packard, dark gray/maroon	n/a	n/a	325
No. 07 1934 Chrysler Airflow, cream (off white), (R)	n/a	n/a	190
No. 08 1940 Chrysler Newport Four-door, light green, (M-R), light brown interior	n/a	n/a	175
No. 08 1940 Chrysler Newport Four-door, medium green, (M-R), light brown interior	n/a	n/a	200
No. 08A 1941 Chrysler Newport Pace Car, white, Dearborn Nat. Car Convention, (3), red interior, 200 made	n/a	n/a	475
No. 09 1940 Ford Van, dark blue, (P-12-3), Marque, fifty made	n/a	n/a	600
No. 09 1940 Ford Van, tan, (P-3), Toledo Toy Show, 213 made	n/a	n/a	500
No. 09 1940 Ford Van, dark blue, (P-12-3, CTCS '79), sixty made	n/a	n/a	800

English Issues

	C6	C8	C10
Bk 02 Bx 1948 Tucker, light blue T.A.C.A. second issue, (P), Tucker Club	n/a	n/a	150
BK 15-1 1949 Mercury Pace Car, limited edition	n/a	n/a	99
BK 22-1 1958 Edsel Citation Brooklin No. 22 Video w/Edsel Convertible, complete set	n/a	n/a	150
BK 25 1948 Tucker, (P), metallic green, Tucker Club	n/a	n/a	350
No. 01 1933 Pierce Arrow, medium blue, (M), gray interior	n/a	n/a	NPF
No. 01 1933 Pierce Arrow, dark blue, (M), gray interior	n/a	n/a	NPF
No. 01 1933 Pierce Arrow, champagne, (M), 100 made	n/a	n/a	350
No. 01 1933 Pierce Arrow, light silver, (M), gray interior	n/a	n/a	350
No. 01 1933 Pierce Arrow, dark silver,(M), gray interior	n/a	n/a	350
No. 01 1933 Pierce Arrow, silver, (M-P), Harrah's, blue interior	n/a	n/a	200
No. 01 1933 Pierce Arrow, Light blue, (R-M), gray interior	n/a	n/a	65
No. 02 1948 Tucker, light maroon, (D-R-M-7)	n/a	n/a	195
No. 02 1948 Tucker, dark maroon, (D-R-M-8)	n/a	n/a	NPF
No. 02 1948 Tucker, light maroon, (D-R-M-8)	n/a	n/a	195

LANSDOWNE MODELS *Available now!*

❶ LDM 9	❷ LDM 7 X	❸ LDM 11	❹ LDM 10	❺ LDM 6B	❻ LDM 6A	❼ LDM 8
1953	1953	1963	1956	1961	1961	1954
AUSTIN	FORD ZEPHYR 6	SUNBEAM	HILLMAN	WOLSELEY	WOLSELEY	TRIUMPH
SOMERSET	MONTE CARLO	ALPINE III	MINX	6-110 POLICE	6-110	RENOWN

ROBEDDIE MODELS *Available now!*

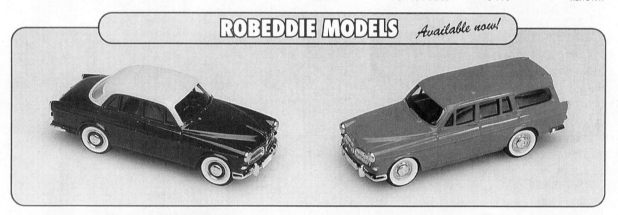

RE 9 1957 VOLVO AMAZON 120   RE 10 1969 VOLVO AMAZON ESTATE

NEW ROBEDDIE MODELS FOR RELEASE DURING 1996

RE 11 1972 VOLVO P1800 ES   RE 12 1935 VOLVO P36 CARIOCA

A page from Brooklin's 1996 Supplementary Catalog.

	C6	C8	C10
No. 02 1948 Tucker, maroon, (D-2-M)	n/a	n/a	195
No. 02A 1948 Tucker, green, (5 Proto)	n/a	n/a	NPF
No. 02A 1948 Tucker, Jaguar Coral, (5 Proto)	n/a	n/a	NPF
No. 02A 1948 Tucker, Zircon blue, (5 Proto)	n/a	n/a	NPF
No. 02A 1948 Tucker, champagne, (5 Proto)	n/a	n/a	NPF
No. 02A 1948 Tucker, Signa Amber, (5 Proto)	n/a	n/a	NPF
No. 02A 1948 Tucker, black, (5 Proto)	n/a	n/a	NPF
No. 02A 1948 Tucker, Sierra beige, (5 Proto)	n/a	n/a	NPF
No. 02A 1948 Tucker, gold, (R-M), tan interior	n/a	n/a	65
No. 02A 1948 Tucker, white, (5 Proto)	n/a	n/a	NPF
No. 02A 1948 Tucker, turquoise, (P-M), Paramount Pictures, semi-limited - 1000 made	n/a	n/a	200
No. 02A 1948 Tucker, dark gold, (R-M), tan interior	n/a	n/a	65
No. 02A 1948 Tucker, maroon, (P-M-3), tan interior, 500 made, Tucker Club	n/a	n/a	200
No. 02A 1948 Tucker, silver, (P-M), tan interior, Harrah's	n/a	n/a	175
No. 02A 1948 Tucker, light brown, (P-M), gray interior, Harrah's	n/a	n/a	175
No. 02A 1948 Tucker, gold, (P-M), beige interior, Harrah's	n/a	n/a	175
No. 02A 1948 Tucker, Lazer red, (P-M), Paramount Pictures, semi-limited - 1000 made	n/a	n/a	200
No. 02A 1948 Tucker, stratus silver, (P-M), Paramount Pictures, semi-limited - 1000 made	n/a	n/a	200
No. 03 1930 Ford Victoria Two-door, beige top/medium green body, (D-R-4-15), beige wheels, light brown interior	n/a	n/a	150
No. 03 1930 Ford Victoria Two-door, beige/light green, (D-C-4), beige wheels, light brown interior	n/a	n/a	150
No. 03 1930 Ford Victoria Two-door, beige/tan, (D-4), white wheels, light brown interior	n/a	n/a	175
No. 03 1930 Ford Victoria Two-door, beige/light olive, (D-4), beige wheels, light brown interior	n/a	n/a	150
No. 04 1937 Chevy Coupe, red, (D-P), James Leake 87, 150 made, 15th Auc.	n/a	n/a	NPF
No. 04 1937 Chevy Coupe, bright green, (P), Ill. Toy Show, 100 made	n/a	n/a	NPF
No. 04 1937 Chevy Coupe, Police, (P), Bay Brooklin Club	n/a	n/a	150
No. 04 1937 Chevy Coupe, blue, (D-P-3-9), Ill. Toy Show '86, 100 made	n/a	n/a	400
No. 04 1937 Chevy Coupe, dark green, (D-C-4), beige wheels	n/a	n/a	160
No. 04 1937 Chevy Coupe, dark green, (D-R-4-15), beige wheels	n/a	n/a	160
No. 04 1937 Chevy Coupe, beige, (D-P-3), Webers 87, seventy made	n/a	n/a	NPF
No. 04 1937 Chevy Coupe, blue, (P), Brooklin Club England, 275 made	n/a	n/a	NPF
No. 04 Model A Ford Two-door Coupe, black top/dark brown body, (D-3), Tudor body	n/a	n/a	150
No. 04 Model A Ford Two-door Coupe, black/green, (D-R-15)	n/a	n/a	100
No. 04 Model A Ford Two-door Coupe, black/light green, (D-C), New Orleans Fire, 100 made	n/a	n/a	325
No. 04 Model A Ford Two-door Coupe, black/red, (D-P), Philly Fire, 300 made	n/a	n/a	300
No. 04 Model A Ford Two-door Coupe, black, (D-P-3), Webers '86, sixty-nine made	n/a	n/a	NPF
No. 06 1932 Packard Standard 8, light brown top/cream body, (R), brown fenders, light brown interior	n/a	n/a	125
No. 06 1932 Packard Standard 8, tan/light gray, (3), brown fenders, red interior	n/a	n/a	200
No. 06 1932 Packard Standard 8, blue-gray top silver, (3), metallic light blue fenders, red interior	n/a	n/a	200
No. 06 1932 Packard Standard 8, gray light gray, (3), dark gray fenders, red interior	n/a	n/a	200
No. 07 1934 Chrysler Airflow, light blue, (R), black wall tires	n/a	n/a	65
No. 07 1934 Chrysler Airflow, medium blue, (R), white wall tires, all variants	n/a	n/a	90+
No. 07 1934 Chrysler Airflow, medium blue, (R), black wall tires	n/a	n/a	90+
No. 07 1934 Chrysler Airflow, dark blue, (R), white wall tires	n/a	n/a	90+
No. 07 1934 Chrysler Airflow, dark blue, (R), black wall tires	n/a	n/a	90+

	C6	C8	C10
No. 08 1940 Chrysler Newport, yellow, (R-D-15)	n/a	n/a	125
No. 08A 1941 Chrysler Pace Car, white, (P-3), Mtr. Sp. 60th Anv., sixty made	n/a	n/a	350
No. 08A 1941 Chrysler Pace Car, white, (P), Motor Sport, 140 made	n/a	n/a	225
No. 08A 1941 Chrysler Pace Car, white, (R), Chrysler logo	n/a	n/a	65
No. 09 1940 Ford Van, cream, (P), Spanish Armada, 150 made	n/a	n/a	200
No. 09 1940 Ford Van, dark blue, (P-3), BF Goodrich, fifty made	n/a	n/a	400-800
No. 09 1940 Ford Van, white, (P), Harrah's '85, 400 made	n/a	n/a	225
No. 09 1940 Ford Van, dark brown, (P), Hershey	n/a	n/a	375
No. 09 1940 Ford Van, maroon, (P-3-9), J.U.N.K., fifty made w/certificate	n/a	n/a	800
No. 09 1940 Ford Van, beige, (P-12-3), Lamberts, 100 made w/certificate	n/a	n/a	650
No. 09 1940 Ford Van, white, (P-3), Mobil Bk. Tires, twenty-six made	n/a	n/a	NPF
No. 09 1940 Ford Van, white, (P-3), Maidenhead, 150 made	n/a	n/a	500
No. 09 1940 Ford Van, black, (D-R-12), Ford	n/a	n/a	75
No. 09 1940 Ford Van, blue, (P), Deaf Child Society, 200 made	n/a	n/a	220
No. 09 1940 Ford Van, yellow, (P), Shell-Model Garage, 140 made	n/a	n/a	175
No. 09 1940 Ford Van, beige, (P-3), Model Auto, fifty made	n/a	n/a	450
No. 09 1940 Ford Van, green, (P-10), Toronto Works, fifty made	n/a	n/a	300
No. 09 1940 Ford Van, green, (P-12), Toronto Works, fifty made	n/a	n/a	300
No. 09 1940 Ford Van, beige, (P-3), Webers '84, sixty-seven made, rare	n/a	n/a	NPF
No. 09 1940 Ford Van, maroon, (P-3), Wessex Model, seventy-five made, rare	n/a	n/a	NPF
No. 09 1940 Ford Van, red, (P), Yateley, 150 made	n/a	n/a	225
No. 09 1940 Ford Van, green, (P), Huggett	n/a	n/a	110
No. 09 1940 Ford Van, red, (P), Weeties	n/a	n/a	150
No. 09 1940 Ford Van, green (P-3), Randalls, fifty made	n/a	n/a	390

	C6	C8	C10
No. 09 1940 Ford Van, red, (P-12-3, CTCS '80), beige interior, 125 made	n/a	n/a	550
No. 09 1940 Ford Van, brown, (P-3), Marque, fifty made	n/a	n/a	350
No. 09 1940 Ford Van, black, (R), Ford	n/a	n/a	550
No. 09 1940 Ford Van, red, (P), Old Toyland, 100 made	n/a	n/a	275
No. 09 1940 Ford Van, red, (P-3-10, CTCS '80), light brown interior 125 made	n/a	n/a	550
No. 09 1940 Ford Van, blue, (P, CPCTS '84), 100 made	n/a	n/a	350
No. 09 1940 Ford Van, light blue, (P, CPCTS '87), 150 made	n/a	n/a	250
No. 09 1940 Ford Van, yellow, (P-12-11), Coke, "Drink"	n/a	n/a	325
No. 09 1940 Ford Van, yellow, (P-11), Coke, marked "Drink"	n/a	n/a	325
No. 09 1940 Ford Van, yellow, (P), Coke, "Enjoy"	n/a	n/a	325
No. 09 1940 Ford Van, yellow, (P), Coke, marked "Drink"	n/a	n/a	325
No. 09 1940 Ford Van, orange, (P), James Leake '88, 150 made 16th Auc.	n/a	n/a	225
No. 09 1940 Ford Van, yellow, (P), Danhausen, 150 made first Issue	n/a	n/a	225
No. 09 1940 Ford Van, gray, (P), Danhausen, red wheels, 150 made, first issue	n/a	n/a	225
No. 09 1940 Ford Van, tan, (P), Danhausen, second issue	n/a	n/a	225
No. 09 1940 Ford Van, red, (P-3), Indian River Fire, fifty made	n/a	n/a	500
No. 09 1940 Ford Van, white, (P), Nutmeg Ambulance, 300 made	n/a	n/a	200
No. 09 1940 Ford Van, red, (P), Springfield Fire, 100 made	n/a	n/a	350
No. 09 1940 Ford Van, off white, (P), Philly Ambulance, 300 made	n/a	n/a	350
No. 09 1940 Ford Van, maroon, (P), Buchi Optik, sixty made	n/a	n/a	400
No. 09 1940 Ford Van, black, (P), James Leake '85, 250 made 13th Auc.	n/a	n/a	200
No. 10 1949 Buick Roadmaster, black, (3), Autosatisfaction, 100 made w/o hood ornnament	n/a	n/a	NPF
No. 10 1949 Buick Roadmaster, light silver gray, (R-C), beige interior, w/o hood ornament	n/a	n/a	65

	C6	C8	C10
No. 10 1949 Buick Roadmaster, black, (3), beige interior, w/hood ornament	n/a	n/a	200
No. 10 1949 Buick Roadmaster, medium gray, (R), beige interior, w/o hood ornament	n/a	n/a	75
No. 10 1949 Buick Roadmaster, maroon, (P), beige interior, Mini cars	n/a	n/a	70
No. 10 1949 Buick Roadmaster, dark gray, (R), beige interior, w/o hood ornment	n/a	n/a	75
No. 11 1956 Lincoln Continental Mark II, black, (P-9), Accent, first Issue, white interior	n/a	n/a	195
No. 11 1956 Lincoln Continental Mark II, gold, (P-3), Autosatisfaction, fifty made, rare	n/a	n/a	NPF
No. 11 1956 Lincoln Continental Mark II, black, (P-9), Accent, gray interior, 400 made	n/a	n/a	150
No. 11 1956 Lincoln Continental Mark II, black, (P), maroon interior, 500 made	n/a	n/a	125
No. 11 1956 Lincoln Continental Mark II, dark blue, (R-M-C), red interior	n/a	n/a	75
No. 11 1956 Lincoln Continental Mark II, medium blue, (R-M), gray interior	n/a	n/a	70
No. 11 1956 Lincoln Continental Mark II, light blue, (R-M), gray interior	n/a	n/a	65
No. 11 1956 Lincoln Continental Mark II, white, (5-Proto)	n/a	n/a	NPF
No. 12 1931 Hudson Boattail, orange/cream fenders, (R)	n/a	n/a	70
No. 12 1931 Hudson Boattail, beige top black body, (P, CTCS '81), red fenders, 250 made	n/a	n/a	550
No. 13 1956 Ford T-Bird, green, (P, CTCI '88), 200 made	n/a	n/a	200
No. 13 1956 Ford T-Bird, red, (R)	n/a	n/a	NPF
No. 13 1956 Ford T-Bird, dark red, (R)	n/a	n/a	NPF
No. 13 1956 Ford T-Bird, beige, (R, CTCI '82), 300 made	n/a	n/a	350
No. 13 1956 Ford T-Bird, white, (P-9), Ill. Toy Show '87, 100 made w/certificate, red interior	n/a	n/a	350
No. 13 1956 Ford T-Bird, white, (P), Mini Cars, black interior	n/a	n/a	80
No. 13 1956 Ford T-Bird, tan, (P, CTCI '82)	n/a	n/a	350
No. 14 1940 Cadillac V-16 Convertible, gold-bronze, (R-M)	n/a	n/a	65
No. 14 1940 Cadillac V-16 Convertible, dark bronze-brown, (R-M)	n/a	n/a	75
No. 14 1940 Cadillac V-16 Convertible, white top/red body, (P, CTCS '83), 400 made	n/a	n/a	375
No. 15 1949 Mercury, medium green, (R-M)	n/a	n/a	65
No. 15 1949 Mercury, turquoise blue, (Proto), six made	n/a	n/a	NPF
No. 15 1949 Mercury, dark green, (R-M)	n/a	n/a	75
No. 15 1949 Mercury, maroon, (P, CTCS)	n/a	n/a	175
No. 15 1949 Mercury, cream, (C-R), red or gray interior	n/a	n/a	200
No. 15 1949 Mercury, dark blue, (P-M-9), Ill. Toy Show '88, 100 made w/certificate	n/a	n/a	200
No. 16X 1935 Dodge Pick-up, orange/brown, (P), J. Leake '86, 150 made w/certificate 14th Auc.	n/a	n/a	300
No. 16X 1935 Dodge Pick-up, green/beige, (P, CTCS '84), 400 made	n/a	n/a	300
No. 16X 1935 Dodge Pick-up, Burgundy/cream, (P, CPCTS '86), 150 made	n/a	n/a	300
No. 16X 1935 Dodge Pick-up, green/green, (P), A.T.T. w/pole, 400 made	n/a	n/a	350
No. 16X 1935 Dodge Pick-up, green/green, (P-3), Huggetts, 100 made	n/a	n/a	300
No. 16X 1935 Dodge Pick-up, blue/black, (P), Markham, 500 made	n/a	n/a	200
No. 16X 1935 Dodge Pick-up, red/red, (P), Orange City Fire, 400 made	n/a	n/a	350
No. 16X 1935 Dodge Pick-up, red/brown, barrel seats, (P), McDonald's, Benefit No. 2	n/a	n/a	295
No. 16X 1935 Dodge Pick-up, olive green, (P), New Eng. Telephone & Pole Truck, 400 made	n/a	n/a	250
No. 16X 1935 Dodge Pick-up, orange body/brown fenders, (P), Avon, seventy-five made	n/a	n/a	400
No. 16X 1935 Dodge Pick-up, Yellow, (P), Brasilla Press, 700 made	n/a	n/a	75
No. 16X 1935 Dodge Pick-up, Yellow/blue, (P, CTCS '86), 450 made	n/a	n/a	290

	C6	C8	C10
No. 16X 1935 Dodge Pick-up, red/black, (P), Yateley's, 150 made	n/a	n/a	185
No. 16X 1935 Dodge Pick-up, red, (P), Yately, 150 made	n/a	n/a	285
No. 16X 1935 Dodge Pick-up, blue/cream, (P-3), B.F. Goodrich, fifty made	n/a	n/a	700
No. 17 1952 Studebaker Starlight, gray, (R), gray interior	n/a	n/a	65
No. 17 1952 Studebaker Starlight, gray, (R), red interior	n/a	n/a	70
No. 17 1952 Studebaker Starlight, black, (C-R), gray interior	n/a	n/a	110
No. 18 1941 Packard Clipper, gold/bronze, (P-M, CTCS '85), 400 made	n/a	n/a	350
No. 18 1941 Packard Clipper, Yellow, (P), American Taxi, 500 made	n/a	n/a	140
No. 18 1941 Packard Clipper, maroon, (R)	n/a	n/a	65
No. 18 1941 Packard Clipper, Khaki/white Stars, (P), Military Staff Car, 160 made	n/a	n/a	400
No. 19 1936 Dodge Van, gray body/red fenders, (R-C), Burma Shave, black run bds.	n/a	n/a	90
No. 19 1936 Dodge Van, blue/black, (P), Buchi Optik, 100 made	n/a	n/a	300
No. 19 1936 Dodge Van, brown/black, (P), Bimbo, 100 made	n/a	n/a	300
No. 19 1936 Dodge Van, white/red, (P), Dr. Bernardo's, 100 made	n/a	n/a	300
No. 19 1936 Dodge Van, cream/orange, (P), Bayview Model, fifty made	n/a	n/a	500
No. 19 1936 Dodge Van, blue, (P), Argus De LaMiniature, 100 made	n/a	n/a	295
No. 19 1936 Dodge Van, orange/brown, (P-3), Avon Club, seventy-five made	n/a	n/a	395
No. 19 1936 Dodge Van, light blue/dark blue, (R), City Ice	n/a	n/a	65
No. 19 1936 Dodge Van, white, (P), Bay St. Lobster, J. Leake redo, fifty made (?)	n/a	n/a	300
No. 19 1936 Dodge Van, pea green/green, (P-M), Calandre, 100 made	n/a	n/a	300
No. 19 1936 Dodge Van, gray body/red fenders, (R-C), Burma Shave, red run bds.	n/a	n/a	90
No. 19 1936 Dodge Van, beige/brown, (P), Gems & Cobwebs, 100 made	n/a	n/a	275

	C6	C8	C10
No. 19 1936 Dodge Van, silver/black, (P-M, CPCTS '85), w/logo 100 made	n/a	n/a	200
No. 19 1936 Dodge Van, Yellow/black, (P), Coca Cola	n/a	n/a	450
No. 19 1936 Dodge Van, maroon/black, (P, CPCTS '83), fifty made	n/a	n/a	400
No. 19 1936 Dodge Van, gray/black, (P, CPCTS '85), w/o logo (?)	n/a	n/a	200
No. 19 1936 Dodge Van, brown/black, (P), Hershey	n/a	n/a	300
No. 19 1936 Dodge Van, green/gray, (P-3), Huggett Elec. '83, 100 made w/certificate	n/a	n/a	325
No. 19 1936 Dodge Van, beige/brown, (P, CTCS '82), 250 made	n/a	n/a	225
No. 19 1936 Dodge Van, gold/red, (P-M-16), Collectors Gazette '86, 24k gold, 200 made	n/a	n/a	425
No. 19 1936 Dodge Van, gray body/black fenders, (3), Burma Shave, approx. fifty made	n/a	n/a	250
No. 19 1936 Dodge Van, dark blue/red, (P), Merley Museum, 100 made	n/a	n/a	300
No. 19 1936 Dodge Van, red/red, (P-3), Indian River, fifty made	n/a	n/a	495
No. 19 1936 Dodge Van, white/red, (P), ITT Kruse '87, 150 made	n/a	n/a	175
No. 19 1936 Dodge Van, white/red, (P), J. Leake '84, 12th Auction	n/a	n/a	275
No. 19 1936 Dodge Van, red, (P), Litchfield Fire, 200 made	n/a	n/a	275
No. 19 1936 Dodge Van, dark red, (P), Litchfield Fire, 200 made	n/a	n/a	275
No. 19 1936 Dodge Van, cream/brown, (P), Camel, seventy-five made	n/a	n/a	450
No. 19 1936 Dodge Van, dark blue, (P-3), Maidenhead, 100 made	n/a	n/a	300
No. 19 1936 Dodge Van, light blue/dark blue, (P), Mini Wheels of Midland, fifty made	n/a	n/a	395
No. 19 1936 Dodge Van, dark green/light green, Model Auto Review, 100 made	n/a	n/a	295
No. 19 1936 Dodge Van, Yellow/black, (P-3), Weber's '85, sixty-eight made	n/a	n/a	NPF
No. 19 1936 Dodge Van, white/blue, (P), London Mtr. Fair '85, 100 made	n/a	n/a	300
No. 19 1936 Dodge Van, maroon, (P), Wessex silver Key	n/a	n/a	120

	C6	C8	C10
No. 19 1936 Dodge Van, Yellow/red, (P), Old Toyland '87, 100 made ...	n/a	n/a	295
No. 19 1936 Dodge Van, gold/black, (P-M-16), Spielgoed Otten, 100 made..............................	n/a	n/a	250
No. 19 1936 Dodge Van, cream/green, (P, St), Martins, approx. 150 made......................	n/a	n/a	295
No. 19 1936 Dodge Van, black/black, (P-R), Sears, semi limited	n/a	n/a	70
No. 19 1936 Dodge Van, red/red, (P), Philly Fire, approx. 300 made	n/a	n/a	295
No. 19 1936 Dodge Van, maroon/black, (P-R), Dr. Pepper, semi limited........................	n/a	n/a	70
No. 19 1936 Dodge Van, goldish green/black, (P-M), Passport Transport, 150 made	n/a	n/a	275
No. 19 1936 Dodge Van, red/black, (P), classic and sport, 200 made .	n/a	n/a	200
No. 19 1955 Chrysler, red, (R), 500 made.............................	n/a	n/a	70
No. 19 1955 Chrysler, black/tan, (P), Mini Cars, 500 made.............	n/a	n/a	70
No. 19 1955 Chrysler C-300, (P), Brooklin Club Model, white	n/a	n/a	65
No. 20 1953 Buick Skylark, Aqua, (R-M).................................	n/a	n/a	NPF
No. 20 1953 Buick Skylark, white Convertible, (P), Ketchner Oct. Fest., 100 made......................	n/a	n/a	350
No. 20 1953 Buick Skylark, maroon convertible, Code II, Produced for Model Car Shop - New Model Cars and Trains unlimited blue, PT, NY, very rare, fifty pieces	n/a	n/a	450
No. 21 1963 Corvette, white, (R), red interior.................................	n/a	n/a	65
No. 21 1963 Corvette, red, (P)	n/a	n/a	400
No. 21 1963 Corvette, silver, (P-M-3), 350 made.............................	n/a	n/a	300
No. 21 1963 Corvette, red/gray interior, (P), Mini Cars.................	n/a	n/a	70
No. 21 1963 Corvette, blue, (C-R-M)	n/a	n/a	NPF
No. 21 1963 Corvette, red, (P), Ill. Toy Show '87, black interior, 100 made....................................	n/a	n/a	375
No. 21 1963 Corvette, red, (P), Ill. Toy Show, 100 made..................	n/a	n/a	NPF
No. 22 1958 Edsel Citation, green, (M-R), w/Cont. Kit	n/a	n/a	65
No. 22 1958 Edsel Citation, pink, (R), gold name decal	n/a	n/a	150
No. 22 1958 Edsel Citation, pink, (R), black name decal.................	n/a	n/a	75

	C6	C8	C10
No. 22 1958 Edsel Citation, lavender-pink, (R-C), gold name..	n/a	n/a	NPF
No. 23 1956 Ford Fairlane Victoria, white top/green body, (R), marked No. 22 in error................	n/a	n/a	90
No. 23 1956 Ford Fairlane Victoria, white top/green body, (R)	n/a	n/a	65
No. 24 1968 Shelby Mustang, blue, (D-R-M).............................	n/a	n/a	149
No. 24 1968 Shelby Mustang, green, (D-P-3), Model Expo, 250 made (?); How many are in the hands of collectors is not known..	n/a	n/a	NPF
No. 24A 1968 Ford Mustang, red, (R).................................	n/a	n/a	NPF
No. 25 1958 Pontiac Bonneville Conv., black, (R), gray interior	n/a	n/a	65
No. 25 1958 Pontiac Bonneville Convertible, black, (R-3), burgundy interior, forty made.......	n/a	n/a	150
No. 26 1956 Chevy Nomad, white top/light blue boyd, (R)	n/a	n/a	65
No. 26 1956 Chevy Nomad, white/Coral, (P, CTCS '87), 375 made...............................	n/a	n/a	275
No. 26X 1956 Chevy Nomad Van, black, (P, CPCTS '88), 150 made	n/a	n/a	195
No. 26X 1956 Chevy Nomad Van, black, (P), Webers '88, seventy-one made................................	n/a	n/a	NPF
No. 26X 1956 Chevy Nomad Van, black (P), Das Automobile, 200 made................................	n/a	n/a	250
No. 26X 1956 Chevy Nomad Van, dark blue, (P), cars only, 150 made................................	n/a	n/a	275
No. 26X 1956 Chevy Nomad Van, maroon, (P), Wessex.................	n/a	n/a	150
No. 26X 1956 Chevy Nomad Van, red, (P), Fire Chief	n/a	n/a	75
No. 27 1957 Caddy Eldorado Brougham, silver, (R-M)..............	n/a	n/a	NPF
No. 27-1 1957 Caddy Eldorado Brougham, (P), gold plating, Pacific Coast Toy Show..............	n/a	n/a	150
No. 28 1957 Mercury Turnpike Cruiser, bronze/tan, (R-M)..........	n/a	n/a	65
No. 28 1957 Mercury Turnpike Cruiser, monarch blue, (R-M, CTCS '88), 450 made	n/a	n/a	300
No. 29 1953 Kaiser Manhattan, standard Issue, 1989	n/a	n/a	65
No. 29 1953 Kaiser Manhattan, blue, (R), 500 Produced for Rotterdam Shoppe	n/a	n/a	275

BROOKLIN COLLECTION
NEW EDITIONS FOR RELEASE DURING 1996

Models shown as Brass Masters and castings

❶ BRK 60	❷ BRK 58	❸ BRK 59	❹ BRK 57	❺ BRK 50A
1963	1963½	1957	1960	1948
OLDSMOBILE STARFIRE	FORD FALCON SPRINT	RAMBLER REBEL	LINCOLN CONTINENTAL	CHEVROLET POLICE CAR

✳ BRK 53x & 62 CHEVROLET CAMEO AND HORSE TRAILER SET
(illustrated on front cover and available now)

Deletions from the Brooklin Collection as of January 1996 are BRK 18, BRK 21, BRK 23, BRK 34A, and BRK 35.
BRK 18a will be re-issued as 1947 Packard Super Clipper, June 1996; BRK 21a as 1964 Corvette Convertible, May 1996; BRK 35a Top Down Convertible, October 1996.

❻ **BRK 61** 1960 CHEVROLET IMPALA
Brass Master Shown

LANSDOWNE MODELS
NEW EDITIONS FOR RELEASE DURING 1996

Brass Master Shown

❶ LDM 13	❷ LDM 12	❸ LDM 14
1963	1958	1963
HILLMAN SUPER MINX	AUSTIN A105 WESTMINSTER	SINGER GAZELLE

A page from Brooklin's 1996 Supplementary Catalog.

The standard version of Brooklin's 1953 Kaiser Man-hattan.

Brooklin 1948 Chevy Police Car, black, white.

	C6	C8	C10
No. 29 1953 Kaiser Manhattan 29X, black, (P).............................	n/a	n/a	275
No. 29 1953 Kaiser Manhattan 30, standard issue, 1990	n/a	n/a	65
No. 30-1 1953 Dodge 500 Convertible, convertible, (R), Indianapolis Pace Car.................	n/a	n/a	95

New Releases

	C6	C8	C10
BK 31-12 1953 Pontiac Delivery, (P), "Vacheauirit," mid-1990s.......	n/a	n/a	95
BK 31-8 1953 Pontiac Delivery, (P), "Milano 43," mid-1990s................	n/a	n/a	95
BK 35-1 Ford Retractable, (P), Route 66, 1957, mid-1990s	n/a	n/a	95
BRK 50A 1948 Chevy Police Car, (R), black/white doors, 1996	n/a	n/a	69
BRK 53X and No. 62 Chevy Cameo and Horse Trailer Set, w/tools, haybales, green/silver trim...........	n/a	n/a	160
BRK 60 1963 Olds Starfire, (R), 1996...	n/a	n/a	69
No. 31A 1953 Pontiac Sedan Deliver, Mobil Gas, (R), 1952, 1992...	n/a	n/a	NPF

	C6	C8	C10
No. 31A 1953 Pontiac Sedan Deliver, Sunoco, (R), 1953, 1992	n/a	n/a	NPF
No. 31A 1953 Pontiac Sedan Deliver, (R), orange Gulf regular issue, 1990	n/a	n/a	NPF
No. 31X 1953 Pontiac Sedan Deliver, (P), part of boxed set Brooklin Video No. 1, silver w/tonneau cover, blue	n/a	n/a	NPF
No. 32 1953 Studebaker Commander, (R), light green, regular Issue, 1990	n/a	n/a	NPF
No. 33 1938 Phantom Corsair, (R), black body	n/a	n/a	NPF
No. 33A 1938 Phantom Corsair, tan, (D), original brochure color, mini grid....................................	n/a	n/a	NPF
No. 34 1938 Phantom Corsair, maroon, (R), regular issue, dark maroon, 1991	n/a	n/a	NPF
No. 34A 1954 Nash Lemans Coupe, (P)..	n/a	n/a	95
No. 35 1957 Ford Skyliner, (R), tan/gold chrome enhanced	n/a	n/a	NPF
No. 36 1953 Hudson Hornet, (R), green, tan Interior, 1992	n/a	n/a	NPF

The most variations and collectible items since 1989 have appeared on the No. 31 Pontiac Van. Since Brooklin models has changed its policy on the number of promotionals produced a pattern for value has yet to be determined. Values tend to be regional and varied. The average production for promotional tends to be 750 models. The higher the production runs, the lower the after-market prices tend to be. Lower prices attract more collectors since they have a chance to own at least one or more promotional items.

Changes for 1992

No. 17A—1952 Studebaker convertible replaced No. 17 Studebaker Champion Coupe.

No. 20—1953 Buick Skylark available in red (only) as of October 1991.

No. 22A—Reworked Edsel; improved casting replaced No. 22A Edsel Citation

No. 31B—1953 Pontiac Sedan Delivery "Gulf Oil" replaced by another Gas Co. livery, Mobilgas, and then Sunoco making for an attractive oil company series. Set ongoing, yearly promotionals for the collector and service station enthusiast.

Brooklin 1952-53 Nash Ambassador LeMans Coupe, yellow, white top.

Brooklin 1959 Chevy El Camino, black with red interior.

Brooklin 1954 Hudson Italia, silver.

	C6	C8	C10
No. 37 1960 Ford Sunliner, (R), purple metal flake, maroon top, convertible, 1992	n/a	n/a	NPF
No. 38 1938 Graham Sharknose, (R), khaki tan, 1992	n/a	n/a	NPF
No. 39 1952 Olds Fiesta, (R), blue and white two-tone - a first for Brooklin models, 1992	n/a	n/a	NPF
No. 40 1948 Cadillac, (R), dark Navy blue, red interior, 1992.................	n/a	n/a	NPF
No. 41 1959 Chrysler Convt., (R), gold, Regular Issue.....................	n/a	n/a	NPF
No. 41A Light Milky Gold, (R), mistake a Brooklin factory released	n/a	n/a	NPF
No. 42 1952 Ford F1, Alka Seltzer...	n/a	n/a	185
No. 42 1952 Ford F1 Ambulance, (R), Jasper County Hospital Services, white w/decals..............	n/a	n/a	69
No. 42 1952 Ford F1 Pavel Special Delivery, (CTCS) "1992," one of 500...	n/a	n/a	185
No. 42-2 1952 Ford F1, (P), Modelex 91	n/a	n/a	95
No. 43A 1948 Packard Station Wagon, (R), w/o rack	n/a	n/a	69
No. 44 1961 Chevy Impala, (R), red/white stripe	n/a	n/a	69
No. 45A 1948 Buick Roadmaster, (R), white/beige interior................	n/a	n/a	69
No. 46 1959 Chevy El Camino, (R), black/red interior	n/a	n/a	69
No. 46-2 El Camino Pickup, (P), "Modelex," 1994......................	n/a	n/a	95
No. 47 1965 Ford T-Bird, (R), red convertible	n/a	n/a	69
No. 48 1958 Chevy Impala, (R), Baley blue hardtop......................	n/a	n/a	69
No. 49 1954 Hudson Italia, (R), silver	n/a	n/a	69
No. 50 1948 Chevy Aero Sedan, (R), "Country Club Woody"	n/a	n/a	69

	C6	C8	C10
No. 51 1951 Ford Victora, (R), two-tone green	n/a	n/a	69
No. 51X Ford Victoria Hardtop, "Modelex 1995"...........................	n/a	n/a	95
No. 52 1941 Hupmobile Skylark, (R), maroon	n/a	n/a	69
No. 53 1955 Cameo Pick-up Truck, (R), red/white	n/a	n/a	69
No. 54 1953 Air Stream-Wonderer, (R), silver	n/a	n/a	69
No. 55 1951 Packard Mayfair, (R), maroon/beige top.......................	n/a	n/a	69
No. 56X Mustang Indy Pace Car, (P)	n/a	n/a	95
No. 57 1960 Lincoln Continental, (R), convertible, white.................	n/a	n/a	69

Quick General Tips For The Collector	
Type	Expect To Pay
1st Production (Canada)	$100+
Farley (UK)	$75+
Current Production	$70+
Current Production Specials	$900+
Rare, Limited Edition	
Less Than 50 Pcs.	$350-550
Less Than 10 units	$1,000+

Prices for rare models and promotionals tend to be higher in England and France. Prices have been rising in the United States where prices for new models vary from $69 to $79.

Brooklin 1954 Hudson Italia, silver.

Brooklin 1960 Chevy Impala, brown, white striping.

Brooklin 1957 Rambler Rebel, silver, brown stripe.

Brooklin 1952-53 Nash Ambassador LeMans Coupe, yellow, white top.

	C6	C8	C10
No. 58 1963-1/2 Ford Falcon Spirit, (R), light green metallic, 1996	n/a	n/a	69
No. 59 1957 Rambler Rebel, (R), four-door, silver, 1996	n/a	n/a	69
No. 61 1960 Chevy Impala, (R), bronze color	n/a	n/a	69
No. B Pale Gold, (R), variation of regular issue - color only	n/a	n/a	175

Special Dealer Programme

	C6	C8	C10
1946 Lincoln Continental Special Label, "Dealer Special," black/dark beige interior	n/a	n/a	NPF
BRK 45 D.S. 1948 Buick Roadmaster, D.S., red	n/a	n/a	NPF

	C6	C8	C10
No. 63 1956 Plymouth Fury, two-door hardtop, eggshell color, 1997-99	n/a	n/a	75
No. 65 1947 Wesley Slumber Coach, small wooden trailer, 1997-99	n/a	n/a	75
No. 66 1956 Packard Patrician, four-door sedan, metallic gray, 1997-99	n/a	n/a	75
No. 67 1961 Chrysler Imperial Southhamprton, two-door coupe, metallic green, 1997-99	n/a	n/a	75
No. 68 1954 Chevy Bel Air, two-door hard top, coral/ivory, 1997-99	n/a	n/a	75
No. 691946 Mercury Sportsman Convertible, maroon, 1997-99	n/a	n/a	75
No. 70 1950 Dodge Wayfarer Coupe, island green/dark red, 1997-99	n/a	n/a	75
No. 73 1949 Oldsmobile 98 Holiday Coupe, praline brown over tawnee buff w/beige interior, 1997-99	n/a	n/a	75

BUDDY "L"

Buddy "L" toys were first manufactured by the Moline Pressed Steel Company, Moline, Illinois, in 1921, and were named after Buddy Lundahl the son of the owner, Fred Lundahl. Lundahl started the company eight years earlier, manufacturing auto and truck parts. The toys, originally made as special items for his son, caught the attention of Buddy's playmates. Soon their fathers began asking Lundahl to make duplicate toys for their sons. Lundahl went into the toy business.

Typically twenty-one to twenty-four inches long for trucks and fire engines, the heavy steel construction was strong enough to support a man's weight. These were made until the early 1930s, when the line was modified and lighter weight materials were employed. Before this time, Fred Lundahl had died, having already lost control of the company. The company has changed names several times, being known as the Buddy "L" Corp. and Buddy "L" Toy Co. In recent years, the quotes were dropped from around the L.

Buddy "L," like most toy companies, stopped production of metal toys during World War II. Although main Buddy "L" plant made nothing but war-related items, a few wooden toys were produced during the war years.

The early Buddy "L" trains are also popular, and tend to be worth more than the vehicles. Buddy "L" vehicles from the pre-1932 period are almost indestructible; as a consequence, many of the pieces found are either very rusty or have been repainted at some point. The basic metal seems to hold up against time, but repainting and rust drops the price well below "good."

Contributors: Michael W. Curran, Illinois Antiques, P.O. Box 545, Hampton, IL 61256, 309-496-9426. John Taylor, P.O. Box 63, Nolensville, TN 37135-0063.

1932-on

	C6	C8	C10
Aerial Ladder Truck, 25" long..........	275	375	600
Aerial Ladder Truck, No. 947, 1940 .	250	375	500
Aerial Ladder Truck, wooden, 32" long..	800	1300	1800
Aerial Ladder Truck, 1933-34, 40" long..	500	850	1400
Air Force Truck, No. 5577	100	150	200
Airway Express Van, No. 563	150	225	325
Allied Van Lines Moving Van, No. 366, 31" long..............................	300	450	625
Ambulance Truck	130	195	260
Anti-Aircraft Air Force Blue Truck, GMC	45	65	100
Army Combat Car, wooden, w/cannon	150	225	325
Army Combination Set, No. 5560.....	200	300	400
Army Electric Searchlight Truck, No. 5545, 1957.................................	125	200	325
Army Half Track, w/cannon..............	125	200	325

	C6	C8	C10
Army Signal Corps Truck, 1941-42, 12" long....................................	140	225	300
Army Supply Corps, cloth top	100	175	250
Army Supply Corps Truck, 12" long .	45	70	110
Army Tank, wood, 1943, No. 362, 13" long....................................	45	75	125

Buddy "L" Army Supply Corps Truck, 12". Photo from Continental Hobby House.

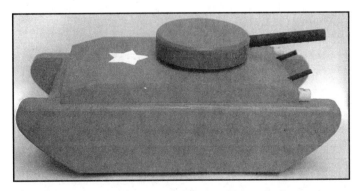

Buddy "L" Army Tank, 1943, 13". Photo from Jack Mathews.

Buddy "L" Aerial Ladder Truck, 1933-34. Photo from Bill Bertoia Auctions.

Buddy "L" Army Transport Truck, canvas missing, 19-1/2". Photo from Calvin L. Chaussee.

Buddy "L" Baby Ruth/Butterfinger Curtiss Candies Tandem Truck, late 1930s, early 1940s. Photo from John Taylor.

	C6	C8	C10
Army Transport, w/canvas-top trailer	225	350	475
Army Transport, six-spoke wheels, 27" w/towed cannon.....................	150	225	325
Army Transport Truck, 19-1/2" long .	150	250	350
Army Truck, wooden, canvas top, 13" long.................................	115	180	275
Army Truck, No. 506, 20-1/2" long...	125	170	250
Army Truck, wooden, canvas top, 16" long.................................	100	175	275
Army Truck, c.1940, cloth top, 21" long.................................	100	165	250
Atlas Van Lines	200	325	500
Automatic Tail-Gate Loader, w/steering handle, 25" long..........	200	325	475
Baby Ruth/Butterfinger Curtiss Candies Tandem Truck, International-style cab, late 1930s-1940s	750	1500	2000
Baggage Truck, No. 11, 1933, 26-1/2" long...............................	225	350	550
Baggage Truck, No. 203-B, 1930-32, 26" long............................	3000	5000	8800
Baggage Truck, wood wheels, 1940s, 17" long	95	150	200

Buddy "L" made several Army trucks made of wood. Photo from Richard MacNary.

Buddy "L" Big Show Circus Truck, wood, 1947, 25".

Buddy "L" Chemical Fire Truck, 22". Photo from John Taylor.

	C6	C8	C10
Bell Telephone Truck, GMC, three linemen	138	205	275
Big Show Circus Truck, wood, 1947, No. 484, 25-1/2" long	750	1000	1500
Brinks Armored Truck	230	345	460
Buick Convertible, wooden, 18" long	275	450	750
Bus, early 1930s, 23-1/2" long	300	475	750
Camper, 1961	75	125	175
Car Carrier, 1961	125	200	300
Car Lift, 1960s...............................	45	68	100
Cattle Truck....................................	70	105	150
Chain Dump, 1920s	450	679	1000
Chemical Fire Truck, marked "Fire and Chemical," 1949, 22" long	225	425	625

	C6	C8	C10
Circus Tractor Trailer, 1960s............	200	300	450
City Baggage Dray, No. 439, 1934, 19" long.............................	175	275	400
City Baggage Dray, No. 839, 1939, 20-3/4" long.............................	125	175	275
City Dray, 24" long	1500	2500	4000
Coca Cola Truck, wooden, c.WWII, only three known, 19" long...........	1500	2500	4200
Coca-Cola Truck, 1950s, 14" long ...	150	233	375
Concrete Mixer, 1930s	150	275	400
Concrete Mixer, No. 832, 1950-51 w/motor sound, 10-3/4" long........	250	400	575
Concrete Mixer, 1941, No. 932	100	150	225
Concrete Mixer, No. 5465, 1965	75	100	150
Concrete Mixer with Truck, No. 54, 1937, 34-1/2" long........................	100	150	250
Construction Truck, 1960s	50	75	100
Convertible, wooden, 18" long	400	700	1000
Cook Coffee Van, similar to Sunshine Biscuits and Ice Cream vans	200	300	400
Country Squire Station Wagon, 15" long	100	150	250
Curtic Candies Tandem, 1940s, 40" long	750	1500	2000

	C6	C8	C10
Curtis Candy Semi, 1950s, 29" long	275	500	650
Curtiss Candy Truck	200	325	450
Dandy Digger, No. 33	75	100	150
Delivery Truck Deluxe Rider, No. 803, 1945-48, 22-3/4" long	225	400	650
Desert Rats Colt Jeep.....................	75	100	150
Double Hydraulic Self-Loader-N-Dump Truck, No. 5892	75	125	225
Dump Truck, No. 434, 1936.............	212	318	425
Dump Truck, No. 634, 20-1/2" long..	125	200	320
Electric Emergency Unit Tow Truck.	100	150	250
Emergency Auto Wrecker, No. 3317	75	150	250
Emergency Unit Tow Truck, 1950s..	100	150	250

Buddy "L" Concrete Mixer, 1930s. Photo from Calvin L. Chaussee.

Buddy "L" Coca-Cola Truck, wooden, 19". Photo from Richard MacNary.

Buddy L Coca-Cola Truck, 1950s, 14", bottles missing. Photo from Calvin L. Chaussee.

Buddy "L" Concrete Mixer, 1950-51, 10-3/4". Photo from Bill Bertoia Auctions.

Buddy "L" Delivery Truck, Deluxe Rider, 22-3/4".
Photo from Joe and Sharon Freed.

Buddy "L" Double Hydraulic Self-Loader-N-Dump
Truck. Photo from Thomas G. Nefos.

Buddy "L" Fire Chief's Car, 1947, 19-1/2". Photo from
William G. Floyd.

Buddy "L" Fire Ladder Truck, semi-rounded trailer
fenders, 1960. Photo from Calvin L. Chaussee.

Buddy "L" Excavator Truck and Shovel Set, 1940.
Photo from John Taylor.

	C6	C8	C10
Engine, No. 29, 1933-34, 25-1/2" long	175	300	450
Excavation and Construction Truck and Shovel Set, 1940s, 30" long..	300	450	600
Excavator Truck and Shovel, Set No. 948, 1940, 27-1/2" long	275	400	600
Express Trailer Truck, No. 35, 1934	475	650	950
Express Truck, screenside, 1932	1200	2000	3000
Farm Machinery Hauler	65	80	130
Farm Supplies Hi-Lift Dump Truck, 1954, 20" long	100	175	275
Farm Supply Truck, No. 634, 1949	170	250	350
Fast Delivery Truck, No. 3313	75	100	150

	C6	C8	C10
Fast Freight, 20" long	100	175	225
Fire Chief's Car, w/siren, No. 483, wood, 1947, 19-1/2" long	475	750	1100
Fire Engine, wood, 13" long	100	140	220
Fire Hose Truck, 12" long	75	145	185
Fire Ladder Truck, semi, rounded trailer fenders, 1960	100	150	200
Fire Ladder Truck, No. 859, 15" long	85	128	170
Fire Ladder Truck, wooden, 20" long	90	130	190
Fire Pumper, 1960s	45	60	100
Fire Station, wooden, w/wooden chief car and ladder truck, 17" x 15"	1200	1500	2500
Firestone Service Wrecker	500	800	1100
Freight Hauler, GMC, 1957	200	300	400
Giraffe Truck	75	112	150
Greyhound Bus, 1950s, 7-1/2" long	40	60	80
Greyhound Bus, w/bell, No. 481, wooden, 18-1/2" long	450	675	1000

MADE OF
STYRON ®
475
A SUPER-IMPACT DOW PLASTIC!

BUDDY "L" HI-LIFT
FARM SUPPLIES DUMP TRUCK

Molded by Kiddie Brush and Toy Co., Jonesville, Michigan. Distributed by Mr. Harold Bettendorf, Moline Pressed Steel Corp., 1300 5th Street, East Moline, Illinois. Available in green and red; 20″ x 6″ x 5″.

APPROXIMATE RETAIL PRICE.......$3.98

Buddy "L" Farm Supplies Hi-Lift Dump Truck, 1954, 20". Note the original price!.

	C6	C8	C10
Greyhound Bus, winds up, 16" long .	300	325	500
Grocery Truck	150	225	375
Half Track..	75	100	150
Heavy Machinery Truck	120	180	250
High Lift Dumper, 1954	150	275	425
Highway Maintenance Dump	50	75	125
Hi-Lift Scoop-A-Dump	65	100	150
Hook and Ladder, 1961....................	75	125	200
Hook and Ladder Truck, No. 859, wooden, 21-1/2" long	250	375	550
Horse Van, 18" long	75	125	200

	C6	C8	C10
Hose Truck, No. 38, 1933, 21-3/4" long..	125	225	325
Hot Rod	50	75	100
Hot Rod Station Wagon	60	90	125
Husky Dumper, late 1950s...............	100	150	225
Hydraulic Aerial Truck, No. 27, 1933-34, 40" long w/ladders down	1200	1300	1500
Hydraulic Dump, No. 5859, 1949.....	275	400	700
Hydraulic Dump, 1938, 26" long	900	1400	2400
Hydraulic Dump, 1960s...................	150	225	400
Hydraulic Dump Truck, No. 10, 1933-34, 23-3/4" long	200	300	450
Hydraulic Dump Truck, 1932, 25" long...	1100	1700	2800
Hydraulic Highway Maintenance Truck, 17" long............................	125	175	275
Hydraulic Plow Truck	80	120	175
Hy-way Maintenance Mechanical Truck and Concrete Mixer, No. 822, 1949, 36" long.....................	350	525	700
Ice Cream Truck	65	100	140
Ice Truck, No. 12, 1933-34, 26-1/2" long..	600	1000	1750

Buddy "L" Hose Truck, 1933, 21-3/4". Photo from Joe and Sharon Freed.

Buddy "L" Fire Station, wooden, with wooden chief car and ladder truck. Photo from Bill Bertoia Auctions.

Buddy "L" Greyhound Bus, wooden. Photo from Bill Bertoia Auctions.

Buddy "L" Hydraulic Aerial Truck, 1930s. Photo from Bill Bertoia Auctions.

Buddy "L" Hydraulic Dump Truck, 1960s.

Buddy "L" Hydraulic Highway Maintenance Truck, 17". Photo from Calvin L. Chaussee.

Buddy "L" Hy-Way Maintenance Mechanical Truck and Concrete Mixer, 1949, 36". Photo from Tim Oei.

Buddy "L" Ice Truck, 1930s, 26-1/2". Photo from Tim Oei.

	C6	C8	C10
International Delivery Truck, No. 51, 1935, 24-1/2" long	200	300	475
International Ice Truck, 28" long, 1939	500	800	1200
International Wrecker	700	1100	1800
Kennel Truck, w/twelve dogs	75	125	175

Buddy "L" Ladder Truck, 1935. Photo from Heinz Mueller.

Buddy "L" Long Distance Moving Van, wooden. Photo from Bill Bertoia Auctions.

Buddy "L" Lumber Truck, wooden. Photo from Bill Bertoia Auctions.

	C6	C8	C10
Ladder Truck, 1935	375	563	750
Lift Gate Truck	65	100	150
Long Distance Moving Van, wooden	225	350	500
Lumber Truck, wooden, 30" long	400	600	900
Machinery Hauler	125	200	275
Mack 30-Ton Dump	75	125	190
Mack Quarry Dump	40	60	90
Mack Tandem, 1969	35	60	90
Marshall Field Company, 1966 Step Van	125	200	300
Merry-Go-Round Truck, No. 5429	75	125	175
Milk Delivery Truck, early, 24" long	1500	2500	4250
Milk Farms Truck, wooden	200	300	450
Missile Launcher, GMC	75	125	180
Mister Buddy Ice Cream Van	125	200	325

	C6	C8	C10
Mobile Repair-It, 1940s, 24" long.....	200	300	400
Motor Market, 1937, 22" long..........	175	275	425
Pepsi-Cola Truck, wooden...............	800	1000	1600
Pickup Truck, early 1960s...............	50	75	125
Popsicle Truck, wooden, 17" long....	400	600	900
Pure Ice Truck, wooden, 16" long....	125	175	300
Railroad Transfer Truck, 1945-48, 23" long.................................	250	400	550
Railway Express Truck, No. 480, wooden, 1947, 16-1/4" long.........	300	500	750
Railway Express Truck, "Baby Ruth," "Butterfinger" tandem, 1935..	1000	1750	2750

Buddy "L" Jr. Milk Delivery Truck. Photo from Bill Bertoia Auctions.

Buddy "L" Milk Farms Truck, wooden. Photo from Bill Bertoia Auctions.

Buddy "L" made several Repair-It trucks.

	C6	C8	C10
Railway Express Truck, 1953, milk ad...	125	200	325
Ranchero Stake Truck	100	150	225
Red Baby Pickup, doors open, 26" long..	1500	2500	4000
Red Baby Pickup, 24" long	500	800	1300
Repair-It, 15" long	125	200	300
Ride-Em Dump, No. 702, 20" long...	200	300	450
Ride-Em Fire Truck, electric lights, 1920s...	800	1600	2500
Riding Academy, No. 5455 truck, w/three horses	50	75	125
Rival Dog Food Truck, came w/either one or two banks shaped as dog food cans, 1950s, rare	175	325	475
Robotoy Dump Truck, w/driver, operates on remote control..........	500	1000	1250
Sand and Gravel Truck, No. 3312 ...	100	150	225
Sand and Gravel Truck, 1950s, 15" long...	75	100	150
Sanitation Truck, late	75	100	150
Scarab, No. 711, winds up..............	200	275	425

Buddy "L" Mister Buddy Ice Cream Van.

Buddy "L" Riding Academy Truck, three horses. Photo from Thomas G. Nefos.

Buddy "L" Sand and Gravel Truck. Photo from Bill Bertoia Auctions.

Buddy "L" Station Wagon, 19", wooden. Photo from Joe and Sharon Freed.

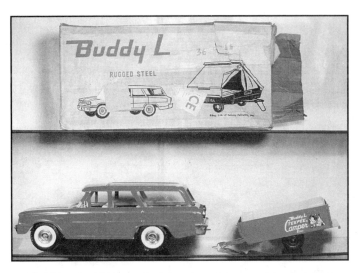

Left to Right: Buddy "L" Station Wagon, Ford, 1964; Camper, 1961.

Buddy "L" Sunshine Biscuits Van. Photo from Joe and Sharon Freed.

	C6	C8	C10
Scarab, No. 211, no wind-up mechanism	200	350	550
Scissors Dump	40	60	100
Scoop Conveyor	75	100	150
Scoop Dump	100	175	275
Searchlight Truck, GMC, 1950s	75	100	150
Service Truck, 1953	120	180	250
Shell Truck, 13-1/2" long	175	275	400
Shell Truck, 1941, 17-1/2" long	500	750	1250
Signal Corps Unit, 1957, 24" long	150	250	350
Siren Pull-n-Ride	100	160	240
Stake Truck, GMC, 1960s (?)	100	150	225
Standard Oil Truck, 1933-34, 26" long	850	1300	2200
Station Wagon, Ford, 1964, 14-1/2" long	60	100	160
Station Wagon, wooden, No. 371, 19" long	140	200	325
Steam Shovel, No. 944	200	275	425
Steam Shovel, 1938	100	150	225
Steam Shovel, mechanical, No. 30, 1935, 17-1/2" long, 13-1/2" high	150	275	450
Steam Shovel and International Truck, No. 16, 1937, 29-1/2" long, 13-1/2" high	150	275	350

	C6	C8	C10
Stepside Pickup Truck, 1950s	50	100	150
Store Delivery Truck	75	125	200
Sunshine Biscuits Van	150	250	350
Super Market Delivery Truck	80	125	175
Super Motor Market Truck	250	425	650
Supply Truck w/load	100	150	250
Surf Truck, 1953, 12" long	100	150	225
Tank Truck, No. 938, 1941, 21-1/2" long	200	300	450
Tank Truck, 1930s, 27" long	500	750	1200
Tank Truck, No. 438, 1935, 19-1/4" long	400	650	1000
Taxi, wooden	450	750	1250
Telephone Truck, w/trailer	75	125	175
Telephone Truck, GMC	125	175	250
Texaco Tanker, 27" long	125	200	325
Texaco Tanker, promo sold at gas stations, 25" long	75	125	200

(handwritten: 325)

BUDDY "L" TOYS

No. 4013 — BUDDY "L" DUMP TRUCK. Length 17⅜ inches, width 5 inches, height 5 3/16 inches. A sturdy, attractive item in the new popular price line. Made of steel finished in brilliant enamels. Quiet wood wheels. Dumping body fitted with hinged tail gate. Packed one dozen in a carton.....................................Per Doz. $8.00

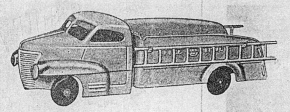

No. 4014 — BUDDY "L" LADDER TRUCK. Length 17½ inches, width 5 inches, height 5 inches. Sturdily made of steel finished in bright colors. Fitted with quiet wood wheels and two steel ladders. Packed one dozen in a carton.....................................Per Doz. $8.00

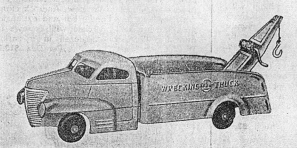

No. 4015 — BUDDY "L" WRECKING TRUCK. Length 19¼ inches, width 5 inches, height 5 inches. Sturdily made of steel finished in bright colors. Quiet wood wheels. Features a realistic working crane. Packed one dozen in a carton.....................................Per Doz. $8.00

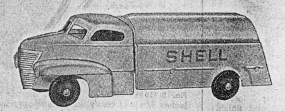

No. 4016 — BUDDY "L" SHELL TANK TRUCK. Length 17⅜ inches, width 5 inches, height 5¼ inches. A perfect duplicate of this famous oil company's truck. Sturdy steel construction which features quiet wood wheels, attractive finish and a hinged rear door. Packed one dozen in a carton.....................................Per Doz. $8.00

No. 4017 — BUDDY "L" STAKE TRUCK. Length 17⅜ inches, width inches, height 5 inches. An old favorite in new design and beau color combinations. Sturdily made of steel which features quiet w wheels and a small, sturdy hand truck. Packed one dozen in a car Per Doz. $

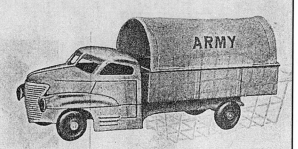

No. 4018 — BUDDY "L" ARMY TRUCK. Length 17⅛ inches, width inches, height 7 inches. A sturdy, perfect duplicate of the regular a unit. Features quiet wood wheels and a cloth body top. True in a and design. Packed one dozen in a carton.............Per Doz. $

No. 4050 — BUDDY "L" BAGGAGE DRAY. Length 20¾ inches, w 6 inches, height 5 5/16 inches. Made of steel in baked enamel fir Features rubber wheels and includes a small, sturdy hand truck. Per Doz. $1

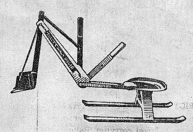

No. 4081 — BUDDY "L" DANDY DIGGER. Length 28 inches, width inches, height 17 inches. The seat and boom revolve. Shovel is contro by easily operated levers. By pulling the cord, the shovel dumps load. Finished in green and yellow baked enamel. Packed one i carton.....................................Per Doz. $1

PRICES SUBJECT TO CHANGE WITHOUT NOTICE

These are some original prices for various Buddy "L" vehicles.

Buddy "L" Jr. Milk Delivery Truck. Photo from Bill Bertoia Auctions.

Buddy "L" Texaco Tanker, 27". Photo from Calvin L. Chaussee.

Buddy "L" Trench Digger, yellow frame, red elevator and conveyor frames, 24". Photo from Bill Bertoia Auctions.

Buddy "L" U.S. Mail Truck, 1950s, green. Photo from Calvin L. Chaussee.

Buddy "L" Water Tower Truck, 1930s. Photo from Bill Bertoia Auctions.

	C6	C8	C10
Timber Truck, wood, 25" long	150	225	350
Towing Service Truck, 25" long	175	275	425
Town and Country Convertible, 1945, wood	300	500	750
Traveling Zoo, post WWII	80	110	150
Trench Digger, yellow frame, red elevator and conveyor frames, 24" long	850	1250	2750
Truck, open bed, wooden, 16" long	NPF	NPF	NPF
U.S. Mail Truck, "2582," c.1941, 21-3/4" long	325	500	750
U.S. Mail Truck, 1950s, green	NPF	NPF	NPF
U.S. Mail Truck, No. 5354, 1964	100	150	225
U.S. Mail Truck, early 1930s, 22" long	1000	1800	3200
Utility Delivery Truck, No. 946, 25" long, 1941-42	75	125	200
Utility Truck, GMC	75	110	165

	C6	C8	C10
Van Freight Carrier, 1940s, 20" long	150	225	300
Victory Jeep and Cannon, wood	100	150	250
Volkswagen Bus, 1960s	75	125	200
Water Tower, No. 28, 1936	1250	2250	3500
Wild Animal Circus Truck	100	175	300
Wrecker, Emergency Towing Rider, No. 903, 1949, 33" long	75	125	200
Wrecker, No. 937, 1939, 25-1/4" long	125	200	325

	C6	C8	C10
Wrecker, 1938, 26" long...................	800	1600	2500
Wrecker, No. 647, 1949, 26-1/4" long	150	250	375
Wrecker, wooden, 18" long	125	175	250
Wrecker, No. 937, 1941-42 version, 25" long..	125	175	300
Wrecker, 16" long.........................	100	150	250
Wrecker, No. 437, 1934, 24" long	350	500	850
Wrecker, No. W37, 1939, 25-1/4" long	100	150	250
Wrecker, No. 813, 1938, 32" long	75	125	225
Wrecker, No. 903, 1950, "Buddy L Emergency Towing," 33" long......	80	140	225

	C6	C8	C10
Wrecker, 1936-37, 27" long	500	900	1500
Wrecker, No. 37, 1933, 24" long	125	250	450
Wrecker, No. 13, 1933, 31" long	800	1500	3200
Wrecker, 1963, w/tools, No. 5427	75	125	225
Wrecker, No. 503, 1940, 1941-42, 19-1/4" long	175	275	375
Wrecker, 1940s, 22" long................	175	275	375
Wrecking Truck, wood wheels, 1940, scarce variation, 19" long ..	150	275	325
Wrigley's Spearmint, 1957	150	200	350
Wrigley's Spearmint Railway Express Agency Truck, No. 953, 1940	800	1350	2250
Wrigley's Spearmint Railway Express Truck, No. 835, 1938, 25" long..	750	1250	2000
Wrigley's Spearmint Railway Express Truck, 1935, headlights light up, 23-1/8" long....................	750	1250	2250

Buddy L Jr.

	C6	C8	C10
Airmail Truck, 22" long	1500	2500	3750
Baggage Truck, 22" long..................	1800	3000	4500
Cement Mixer...................................	300	450	600
Dairy Truck, No. 2002, 1930-32, 24" long...	350	525	700

Buddy "L" Wild Animal Circus Truck. Photo from Thomas G. Nefos.

Buddy "L" Wrecker, wooden, 18". Photo from Perry Eichor.

Buddy "L" Wrecker, 1940s. Photo from John Taylor.

Buddy "L" Wrecker, 1940s, wood wheels, scarce version, 19-1/2". Photo from John Taylor.

Buddy "L" Wrigley's Spearmint Railway Express Truck, 1935, with working headlights, 23-1/28".

BUDDY "L" TOYS

No. 4105 — BUDDY "L" DELIVERY TRUCK. Length 24⅝ inches, width 7¼ inches, height 9¾ inches. Made of heavy steel finished in yellow and red baked enamel. Fitted with two metal ladders, Pull-n-Ride feature and rubber wheels................................Per Doz. $48.00

No. 4101—BUDDY "L" FIRE TRUCK. Length 28½ inches, width 9¼ inches, height 10¼ inches. Pull-N-Ride feature with removable seat. Brilliant two-tone color combination. Finest steel construction. Quiet rubber wheels................................Each $7.50

No. 4112—BUDDY "L" RAILWAY EXPRESS TRUCK. Length 25 inches, width 7½ inches, height 10 inches. A true reproduction of the Railway Express Trucks. It has Buddy "L" Pull-n-Ride Feature, hinged doors in the rear and a removable top. Ideal for children to ride on and strong enough to take it. Brilliant two-tone colors and quiet rubber wheels. Per Doz. $54.00

No. 4102 — BUDDY "L" AUTO WRECKER. Length 32¼ inches, width 9⅛ inches, height 13¾ inches. Made of heavy steel finished in flash red and white baked enamel. Fitted with full swinging crane and cable windlass for hoisting and pulling. Complete with Pull-n-Ride feature and rubber wheels. Packed one in a carton....................Each $7.50

No. 4098 — BUDDY "L" HYDRAULIC DUMP TRUCK. Length 26½ inches, width 9½ inches, height 10 inches. Chassis and box finished in red and white enamel, equipped with rubber wheels, bumper, headlights, enclosed cab, Pull-n-Ride seat, pull handle and hydraulic cylinder unit. Packed one in carton................................Each $7.50

No. 4103—BUDDY "L" ICE TRUCK. Length 28½ inches, width 9⅛ inches, height 11¼ inches. Has Pull-n-Ride handle and seat. Comes equipped with a block of imitation ice, metal tongs and canvas body cover. Finished in brilliant two-tone enamel......................Each $7.5

PRICES SUBJECT TO CHANGE WITHOUT NOTICE

Buddy "L" Wrigley's Spearmint Railway Express trucks were only $54 per dozen in the 1930s. Likewise the Hydraulic Dump Truck was only $7.50 new.

Buddy "L" Jr. Dump Truck, 22". Photo from Bill Bertoia Auctions.

Buddy "L" Jr. Milk Delivery Truck. Photo from Bill Bertoia Auctions.

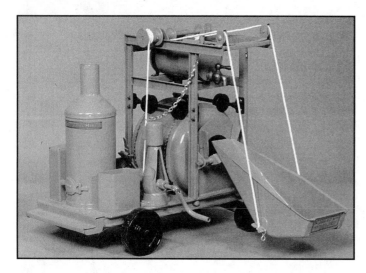

Buddy "L" Concrete Mixer, 1926-30. Photo from Bill Bertoia Auctions.

Buddy "L" pre-1932 Road Roller. Photo from Calvin L. Chaussee.

Buddy "L" Steam Shovel, 1920s. Photo from Calvin L. Chaussee.

	C6	C8	C10
Dairy Truck, late	105	158	210
Dairy Truck, 22" long	1000	1800	2750
Dump Truck, early, 24" long	1300	2500	4500
Dump Truck, 22" long	800	1200	1850
Milk Delivery Truck, No. 2002	2000	3500	5000
Oil Truck, 22" long	1200	2000	2800
Steam Shovel, treads, 24" long	800	1400	2000
Steam Shovel on Treads, No. 2005, 1930-32, 24" long	150	275	400

Construction Equipment

	C6	C8	C10
Aerial Tramway, 1929-30, No. 360	1500	240	3700
Concrete Mixer, 1926-30, No. 280	500	750	1000

	C6	C8	C10
Dredge (Clamshell), 1926-30, No. 270	800	1200	1600
Heavy Shovel (on Treads), 1929-30, No. 220AB	2500	4000	7000
Heavy Steam Shovel, 1929-30, No. 220A	400	600	800
Hoisting Tower, 1929-31, No. 350	500	900	1250
Large Derrick, 1922-31, No. 241	275	375	600
Mixer (on Treads), 1929-31, No. 280A	1100	1700	2600
Overhead Crane, 1924-27, No. 250	700	1100	1750
Pile Driver, 1926-28, No. 260	750	1125	1600
Road Roller, 1929-31, No. 290	2100	3700	5280
Sand Loader, 1925-31, No. 230	175	250	350
Sand Screener, 1929-30, No. 300	700	1100	1700
Small Derrick, 1922-31, No. 240	300	450	625
Steam Shovel, 1921-31, No. 220	250	375	600
Tractor Dredge (on Treads), 1929-30, No. 270A	2500	5000	8000
Traveling Crane, 1928-30, No. 250A	NPF	NPF	NPF
Trencher, 1928-31, No. 400	1800	2700	4200

BUDDY "L" TOYS

No. 4047 — BUDDY "L" LADDER TRUCK. Length 24 inches, width 7 inches, height 6¾ inches. Sturdy construction throughout. Fitted with rubber wheels. Complete with two adjustable ladders. Two-tone enamel finish. Packed one in a carton........................Per doz. $16.00

No. 4048 — BUDDY "L" AUTO WRECKER. Length 25¼ inches, width 6 inches, height 6⅞ inches. One of the most popular of all Buddy "L" trucks. Fitted with rubber wheels and realistic crane that really does the work. Flashy enamel colors. Packed one in a carton......Per doz. $16.00

No. 4085 — BUDDY "L" CITY DRAY. Length 20¾ inches, width 6 inches, height 6 5/16 inches. Made of steel. Finished in green and yellow baked enamel. Equipped with enclosed cab, hand truck made of metal finished in black enamel, rubber wheels. Packed one in a carton.
Per doz. $16.00

No. 4046 — BUDDY "L" JUNIOR DUMP TRUCK. Extreme length 22 5/16 inches, width 6¼ inches, height 8¾ inches. Made of steel in the usual Buddy "L" quality construction way. Streamline dump body with automatic end gate. Polished silver radiator grille and solid rubber wheels. Finished in a combination of bright enamels. Packed one in a carton.
Per doz. $16.00

No. 4082½ — BUDDY "L" DUMP TRUCK. Extreme length 22 5/16 inches, width 6¼ inches, height 8¾ inches. End gate on streamlined body is automatic in operation. Fitted with sturdy dumping device and rubber wheels. Packed one in a carton........................Per doz. $16.00

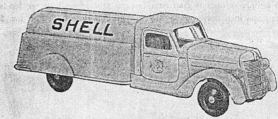

No. 4049 — BUDDY "L" SHELL TANK TRUCK. Length 21½ inches, width 6⅛ inches, height 6 5/16 inches. For added play appeal, the rear of the tank opens. Fitted with rubber wheels. Brilliant two-tone authentic colors. Packed one in a carton........................Per doz. $16.00

No. 4090 — BUDDY "L" SADDLE DUMP TRUCK. Extreme length 21 9/16 inches, height 9½ inches, width 8½ inches. Made of 20 gauge steel throughout and very sturdy. Fitted with Pull-n-Ride feature, and rubber wheels. Packed one in a carton........................Per doz. $24.00

No. 4088 — BUDDY "L" ARMY TRUCK. Length 34½ inches, width 5¾ inches, height 9 inches. A perfect duplicate of the large Army Transport. The added trailer gives this unit a special appeal. Features rubber wheels and cloth body and trailer tops. Finished in authentic colors.
Per doz. $24.00

No. 4082 — BUDDY "L" ARMY TRUCK. Truck only, less Trailer. Otherwise same as No. 4088........................Per doz. $16.00

PRICES SUBJECT TO CHANGE WITHOUT NOTICE

Many Buddy "L" vehicles that cost so little new are now priced in the hundreds or thousands today in Mint condition.

	C6	C8	C10
Fire Trucks			
Aerial Ladder, 1926-30, No. 205B....	750	1400	2200
Hook & Ladder, 1924-31, No. 205 ...	800	1250	1950
Insurance Patrol, 1926-30, No. 205C	1500	2500	3500
Pumper, 1925-30, No. 205A	1100	1800	2500
Pumper (Working), 1930-31, No. 205AB	1000	1800	3000
Water Tower Truck (Working), 1930-31, No. 205D.........................	2500	4500	7250
Large Trucks			
206B Street Sprinkler Truck, 1924-31, No. 206	1250	1750	2750
A Hydraulic Dump Truck, 1926-31, No. 201	600	1100	1700
Auto Wrecker, 1928-31 (Tow Truck), No. 209	1750	2750	4500
Baggage Truck, 1929-31, No. 203B.	1400	2300	3500
Coach, 1928-31, light green, No. 208..	2000	3300	4800

	C6	C8	C10
Coal Truck, 1926-31, No. 202..........	2500	4000	6500
Dump Truck (Ratchet), 1921-30, No. 201..	500	750	1250
Express Truck, 1921-31, No. 200	1000	1600	2500
Ice Truck, 1926-31, No. 207	600	750	1250
Lumber Truck, 1925-30, No. 203A...	1500	2500	4000
Moving Van, 1924-30, No. 204	750	1250	2000
Oil Truck, 1925-30, No. 206A	900	1500	2200
Railway Express, 1926-31, No. 204A	1000	1600	2500
Sand & Gravel Truck, 1926-31, No. 202A	1500	2500	3500
Stake Truck, 1921-24, 1926-28, No. 203..	750	1350	1900

Buddy "L" Street Sprinkler Truck, 1924-31. Photo from Bill Bertoia Auctions.

Buddy "L" pre-1932 Hook and Ladder. Photo from Calvin L. Chaussee.

Top to bottom: Buddy "L" Hydraulic Dump Truck, 1926-31; Dump Truck (Ratchet), 1921-30. Photo from Tim Oei.

Buddy "L" Pumper, 1925-30. Photo from Bill Bertoia Auctions.

Buddy "L" Baggage Truck, 1929-31. Photo from James S. Maxwell and Viginia Caputo.

Top to bottom: Buddy "L" Baggage Truck, 1929-31; Auto Wrecker, 1928-31. Photo from Bill Bertoia Auctions.

Buddy "L" pre-1932 Coach, light green motorbus. Photo from Bill Bertoia Auctions.

Buddy "L" Auto Wrecker, 1928-31. Photo from Bill Bertoia Auctions.

Buddy "L" Dump Truck (Ratchet), 1921-30. Photo from Joeseph and Sharon Freed.

Top to Bottom: Buddy "L" Coal truck, 1926-31; Sand and Gravel Truck, 1926-31. Photo from Bill Bertoia Auctions.

Buddy "L" Express Truck, 1921-31. Photo from Bill Bertoia Auctions.

Buddy "L" pre-1932 Oil Truck, yellow and black, Hill City inscription. Photo from Calvin L. Chaussee.

Buddy "L" pre-1932 Stake Truck. Photo from Bill Bertoia Auctions.

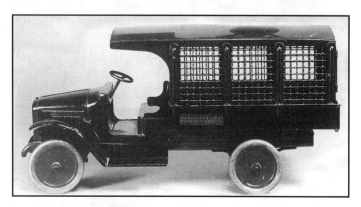

Buddy "L" Railway Express, 1926-31. Photo from Bill Bertoia Auctions.

Buddy "L" Flivver Roadster, 1925-27. Photo from Harry Wolf, Detroit Antique Museum.

	C6	C8	C10
Model T Series			
Flivver Coupe, 1925-30, No. 210B...	400	700	1200
Flivver Roadster, 1925-27, No. 210A	500	750	1250
Flivver Truck, 1925-30, No. 210.......	900	1400	1900
Ford Dump Cart, 1926-30, No. 211..	800	1550	2750

	C6	C8	C10
Ford Dump Truck, 1926-30, No. 211A	1100	1700	2650
Ford Express Truck, 1929-30, No. 212	1400	2300	3250
One-Ton Ford Delivery Truck, 1929-30, No. 212A	2000	3500	5000

BUILT-RITE

Built-Rite, of Lafayette, Indiana, began in 1922 as a cardboard box manufacturer. In 1934, it began to produce cardboard construction toys.

	C6	C8	C10
Armored Car, No. 84	NPF	NPF	NPF
Army Battery Set, No. 20	80	100	125
Army Raiders' Victory Unit, truck, tank, AA gun, jeep, semitrack truck, twenty soldiers, WWII, No. 50, twenty-eight pieces	65	75	85

	C6	C8	C10
Built-Rite Airport	NPF	NPF	NPF
Commercial Garage, No. 15	65	70	80
Built-Rite Airport	NPF	NPF	NPF
Commercial Garage, No. 15	65	70	80

Built-Rite Army Battery Set.

Built-Rite Airport. Photo from Barbara and Jonathan A. Newman.

	C6	C8	C10
Garage and Super Service Station, No. 28	65	75	85
House, boxed set w/19" house and garage, twenty-seven pieces of furniture, sedan, baby buggy, shrubbery, etc., No. 415, c.1943, 13" x 20"	75	90	100
Miniature buildings, church, school, RR station, firehouse, drugstore, No. 56	30	55	60
Private Garage, brick, No. 7.............	30	40	50
Service Station, No. 17	65	70	80
Weapons Carrier, No. 83	NPF	NPF	NPF

C.A.W. NOVELTY COMPANY

It is remarkable, indeed, that collectors had not found this fine company until 1990. Charles A. Wood not only ran a substantial operation, but he made some of the finest replica toys in the slush-mold industry. Ironically, C.A.W. was in existence longer than most in the slush-mold industry. Founded about 1925, his company was active until lead casting came to a halt due to World War II.

Wood's output showed artistry, ingenuity and meticulous craftsmanship. All his toys were smooth, crisp, had detailed moldings and extra touches such as open windshields and two or three colors on each toy. The early production had metal disk wheels with black-painted tires or metal spoked wheels. When you find open, V-shaped, divided windshield, drivers inside cabs and tri-motored aircraft with the outboard engines mounted on the landing gear struts, you wonder how it was done for the five-cent price. According to Wood, it sometimes took him three or four years to make a mold. The molds are also works of art—machinist's art

Wood was born about 1891. He had lived and worked in Topeka, Kansas and in nearby Clifton, before moving to Clay Center. He was known for his civic pride and good works. After he helped establish the local airport, he built and operated his own aircraft maintenance hanger. A master machinist, he made all his toy molds, production tools and toy parts—even plastic wheels.

Over the years, there had been rumors of a "small molder in Clay Center." A few years ago, a small monoplane with initials "CAW" marked under its tailplane was found. Eventually, a collection in Mint condition owned by a relative of Wood's, as well as a few pieces and some paper memorabilia. Although a complete list has yet to be compiled, some of those "orphans" have been identified. Wood made airplanes, autos, novelties and trucks. Some of these have been well known to collectors, although unidentified. Clearly, this company and its toys deserve to be more fully known.

Abbreviations

The following abbreviations are for the details and variations useful in identification.

HG	horizontal grille pattern	SM	sidemounted spare
HL	horizontal hood louvers	SP	string-pull knob in handcrank area
HO	hood cap, Motometer or ornament	T	external trunk
L	lacquer finish	UV	unnumbered version
LI	landau irons on convertibles	VG	vertical grille pattern
MDW	metal disc wheels	VL	vertical hood louvers
MDSW	metal disc solid spokes	WS, W/S	windshield
MDWBT	wheels with black painted tires	WV	windshield visor
MSW	metal open spoke wheels	WHRT	wooden hubs, rubber tires
MWW	metal simulated wire wheels	WRDW	white hard rubber disc wheels
OW	open windows	WRW	white soft rubber wheels (balloon tires)
RM	rearmount spare tire/wheel		

The C&H Mfg. Co. was formed in 1940 by Rod Hemphill, the last C.A.W. employee, and Howard Clevenger. According to Mrs. Hemphill, they only used original C.A.W. models. Apparently, this effort at revival managed to reproduce some toys before C&H went under. These are heavier than C.A.W.'s and have black rubber wheels. Their claim to fame is in publication of the accompanying partial flyer that allowed us to solve the paternity of these handsome orphans. However, judging from the catalog numbers and our incomplete list below, there must be several orphans out there. Can any of you collectors help?

The seldom found C.A.W. trademark, consists of unique, lead-blind hubs fitted over a wire axle. They are sometimes found with ordinary nail axles piercing the hubs.

Contributor: Fred Maxwell, 4722 N. 33 St., Arlington, VA 22207. **Perry R. Eichor,** 703 North Almond Drive, Simpsonville, SC, 29681.

	C6	C8	C10
Air Drive Coach, No. 25; blimp-like bus w/fin and rear propeller drive; twelve OW, WRW w/unique fitted hubs which cap hidden axles; there ia also a version w/o propellor; 3-7/8" long (CWV005) .	30	45	60
DeSoto Sedan, No. 32, Airflow, divided WS, BOW, HL, VG, HO, WRW; 3-7/8" long (CWV009)	40	50	60
Dump Truck, no number, Ford (?), hinged dump body, divided open WS, two OW, HG, MDW; 3-1/8" long (CWV013)	20	30	40
Fuel Tanker, no number, Ford (?) truck, cab w/driver inside, no WS, HG, three tanks, hose compartment, MSW; 3-3/4" long (CWV004)	40	60	80

	C6	C8	C10
Marvel Racer, No. 31, Streamlined FWD Indy type, driver, torpedo tail w/very small fin, V-grille pattern, eight exhaust ports, aluminum wheels; 3-5/8" long (CWV008)	35	45	65
Marvel Racer, No. 31, Streamlined FWD Indy type, driver, torpedo tail w/very small fin, V-grille pattern, eight exhaust ports, aluminum wheels; also found in a modern bubble-pack, w/lucent hard plastic wheels, "Woodchuck Industries Metal Toys, Clay Center, Ks."; this name may have been a new idea or part of a rare market test; 3-5/8" long (CWV008A)	40	60	80

C.A.W. Novelty Air Drive Coach, rear propeller drive. Photo from Fred Maxwell.

C.A.W. Novelty DeSoto Sedan, airflow, divided windshield. Photo from Gary Franson.

C.A.W. Novelty Dump Truck, hinged dump body.

C.A.W. Novelty Dump Truck, hinged dump body.

C.A.W. Novelty Marvel Racer, Indy type, driver, eight exhaust ports. Photo from Gary Franson.

C.A.W. Novelty New Design Racer, 3-3/8", two oval open windows show driver, rounded tail. Photo from Gary Franson.

C.A.W. Novelty Overland bus, tour bus, no head-lamps, twelve windows. Photo from Gary Franson.

C.A.W. Novelty Sport Roadster, plain grille. Photo from Gary Franson.

	C6	C8	C10
New Design Racer, No. 38, streamlined coupe, rounded tail, driver visible through two oval OW, HO loop (stringpull?), WRW w/hubs; 3-3/8" long (CWV010) ...	30	40	50
Overland Bus, no number; Fageol (?) Yellow Line (?) tour bus, HG, no headlamps, twelve windows, shallow observer deck, MDW, left SM; 3-3/4" long (CWV003)	20	40	50
Sport Roadster, no number; Open Buick, driver w/gilt or silver cap, no WS, HG, VL, no headlamps, RM, MDW; 3-1/2" long (CWV001)	30	45	60
Sport Roadster, no number; later model Buick, no WS, plain grille, VL, RM, right SM, MDW; there is also a version with MSW; 3-1/2" long (CWV002)	30	40	50

	C6	C8	C10
Streamline Coupe, No. 30; airflow, V-pattern grille, HO, four OW, small rear fin, small winged design on rear-wheel skirts, MDW also WRW; bottom pan goes over rear axle, not under; 3" long (CWV006)	25	50	75
Tank Truck, no number; Ford (?), three fuel tanks, hinged dump body, divided open WS, two OW, HG, MDW; unusual two-piece body connected by rear axle; 3-3/16" long (CWV014)	25	35	45
Tank Truck, no number; Gasoline semi-trailer, two tanks; cab w/divided WS and open windows shows it is part of a set (CWV015)	30	40	60

TOYS THAT SELL THEMSELVES

Modern Metal Toys that Sell the Year Around, Realistic in Every
Detail. Finished in Bright Colors with the Best of Lacquers

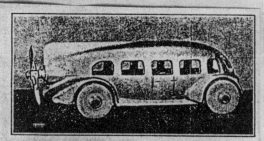

No. 25 AIR DRIVE COACH
Length 3⅞ in. Height 1⅜ in. Weight per
gro. 33 lbs. Retails for 10c.

Price per doz. ....

No. 32. DE SOTO SEDAN
Length 3⅞ in. Height 1⅜ in. Weight per
gro. 32 lbs. Retails for 10c.

Price per doz. ....

No. 30 STREAMLINE COUPE
Length 3 in. Height 1 in. Weight per gro.
19 lbs. Retails at 5c.

Price per doz. ....

No. 33 WONDER SPECIAL
Length 3⅜ in. Height 1 in. Weight per gro
19 lbs. Retails for 5c.

Price per doz. ....

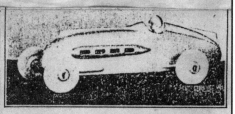

No. 31. MARVEL RACER
Length 3⅝ in. Height 1 3-16 in. Weight
per gro. 20 lbs. Retails at 5c.

Price per doz. ....

No. 38 NEW DESIGN RACER
Length 3⅜ in. Height 1¼ in. Weight per
gro. 20 lbs. Retails for 5c.

**No. 39
TRANSPARENT WINDSHIELD RACER**
Length 3 in. Height 1 in. Weight per gro.
15 lbs. Retails for 5c.

Each number packed one dozen
to box.

Colors: On all Airplanes 6 silver,
4 red, 2 green, to dozen. On all
Autos 6 red, 2 blue, 2 green, 2
silver to dozen.

Rubber Wheels on All Autos
Plastic Wheels on Airplanes Except No. 29

TERMS: 2% Ten Days, Net 30
Days. Prices are f. o. b. St. Louis,
Mo.

C & H Mfg. Co.

1610 So. Florissant Rd.
ST. LOUIS, MO.

No. 40 THREE PIECE AUTO SET
Three toys on card. Length 6⅜ in. Height 1 in. Weight per gro. 40 lbs. Retails for 10c
per card.

Price per doz. ....

C.A.W. Novelty vehicles, part of a catalog sheet issued by the St. Louis-based C&H Mfg. Co., around 1940
after the firm obtained C.A.W.'s molds.

	C6	C8	C10

Three Piece Auto Set, No. 40; includes: (a) Midget coupe racer, no number, HG, HL, divided open WS, two OW, two colored body, MDW, headlamps and cowl ventilators, 2-1/16" long; (b) Midget racer, no number, gilt driver, VL, HG, MDW (easily confused w/Barclay No. 53); 2-1/8" long; (c) Austin Bantam, no number, two-door sedanette, five OW, HL, plain grille, RM, MDW (easily confused w/other makers' Bantams); 2" long; value per each (CWV012) 20 30 40

	C6	C8	C10

Transparent Windshield Racer, No. 39; Indy FWD two man racer, v-shaped VG, dual exhausts, boattail, unique hubtires as in No. 25 (also WRW); not complete if divided plastic windshield is missing; 3" long (CWV011) 45 60 75

Wonder Special, No. 33, airflow coupe, three wheeled companion to No. 30 Streamline Coupe; VG, four OW, WRW, front wheel skirts; pan goes over front axle; 3-3/8" long (CWV007) 25 50 75

C.A.W. Novelty Streamline Coupe, small rear fin, 3". Photo from Perry Eichor.

C.A.W. Novelty Austin Bantam, part of the three-piece auto set.

C.A.W. Novelty Tank Truck, semi-trailer, two tanks. Photo from Ferd Zegel.

C.A.W. Novelty Transparent Windshield Racer, Indy-type, two-man ricer, dual exhausts.

C.A.W. Novelty Tank Truck, three fule tanks, 3-3/16". Photo from Gary Franson.

C.A.W. Novelty Wonder Special, 3-3/8", three wheels, front wheel skirts. Photo from Gary Franson.

CARETTE, GEORGES

Born in France, Carette went to Nuremberg to start his toy factory in 1886. He has since become a legend in the hobby. Next to Märklin, Carette is the most desirable of German toy car makers. Known for its fine detail and quality of materials, Carette stayed in business until 1917. At the onset of World War I, he fled to France, and his company was taken over by Karl Bub. The Carette limousines were made in three general lengths, nine-inch (twenty-two centimeters), 12-1/2-inch (thirty-two centimeters), and 15-1/2-inch (forty centimeters). The larger size is the most desirable and usually sells for five figures.

Contributor: Bob Smith, The Village Smith, 62 West Ave., Fairport, NY 14450-2102.

	C6	C8	C10		C6	C8	C10
Landaulet Limousine	2500	4000	6500	Limousine Driver, luggage rack, high headlamps, 15" long	2500	4000	6000
Limousine, clockwork motor, 16" long	2000	3500	5000	Limousine Driver, passenger, clockwork motor, 12-1/2" long	2000	3500	5000
Limousine, doors open, roof rack, c.1911, 12-1/4" long	1600	2700	4100	Open Car, Carette/Bub, clockwork motor, w/tin-plate or cloth dressed driver, red and black, hand brake, forward and reverse gear, c.1911, 6-1/2" long	900	1500	2000
Limousine, w/chauffeur, c.1910, 12-1/2" long	1200	2200	3100				

Carette Limousine, circa 1911, 9".

Carette Limousine, driver, luggage rack, high headlamps, 15". Photo from Bill Bertoia Auctions.

Carette Limousine, 1910, chauffeur, 12-1/2". Photo from Bill Bertoia Auctions.

Carette Limousine, chauffeur, passenger, clockwork motor, 12-1/2". Photo from Bill Bertoia Auctions.

Carette Open Tourer, four seat, two bisque figures, 12-1/2". Photo from Bill Bertoia Auctions.

Carette/Bub Open Car, red and black, 6-7/10".

	C6	C8	C10
Open Car, w/driver, 9" long..............	600	875	1200
Open Phaeton, w/driver, c.1906, 12" long...	2000	3500	5300

	C6	C8	C10
Open Tourer, wind-up, four-seat, w/two bisque figures, 12-1/2" long	6000	12,000	17,000
Phaeton, four-seat, w/two figures, 9" long...	1200	2200	3400
Rear Entrance Tonneau, clockwork motor, w/four figures, 8-1/2" long.	1500	2500	4000

CHAMPION

The Champion Hardware Co., though in business from 1883-1954, produced toys only from 1930-1936, as a Depression stopgap. As might be expected from a hardware firm, its toys were cast iron. During its toy years the Geneva, Ohio, outfit was headed by C.I. Chamberlin.

	C6	C8	C10
Airflow, 4-3/4" long	NPF	NPF	NPF
Coupe, Plymouth type, rumble seat opens, 7-1/2" long, auctioned in 1999...			760
Coupe, Reo type, 7-1/2" long..........	450	600	900
Delivery Truck, No. 536, 1930s, 8" long	NPF	NPF	NPF
Gas and Motor Oil Truck, cast iron, 8" long...	275	450	625

	C6	C8	C10
Mack Dump, 7" long.........................	150	225	325
Mack Express Truck, 7-1/2" long	100	150	225
Mack Stake Truck, 4-1/2" long, c.1930..	75	125	175
Mack Stake Truck, 7-1/2" long.........	300	525	750

Champion Delivery Truck, 1930s, 8". Photo from Rod Carnahan.

Champion Mack Dump Truck, 1930s, 7". Photo from Harry Wolf. Detroit Antique Museum.

Champion Mack Wrecker, 9".

Champion Motorcycle, solo policeman, rubber tires, 7-1/4".

From left: Champion Motorcycle, solo policeman, nickel wheels, 5"; Motorcycle, solo policeman, rubber tires. Photo from Kent M. Comstock.

Champion Panel Delivery, 7-3/4". Photo from Bill Bertoia Auctions.

	C6	C8	C10
Mack Wrecker, 9" long	350	550	800
Motorcycle, solo policeman, rubber tires, 5" long (CM001)	75	100	175
Motorcycle, solo policeman, nickel wheels, 5" long (CM002)	125	225	400
Motorcycle, solo policeman, rubber tires, 7-1/4" long (CM003)	150	250	425
Motorcycle, solo policeman, nickel wheels, 7-1/4" long (CM004)	175	300	475
Motorcycle, w/sidecar, policeman, rubber tires, 3" long (CM005)	50	80	120
Motorcycle, w/sidecar, policeman and passenger, rubber tires, 5" long (CM006)	125	200	325
Motorcycle, w/sidecar, policeman and passenger, rubber tires, 6" long (CM007)	200	325	475

	C6	C8	C10
Panel delivery, 7-3/4" long	700	1200	1900
Race Car, two riders, 5-1/2" long	160	250	375
Race Car, cast iron, detachable driver, 6" long.............................	150	250	370
Race Car, 1935, 7-1/2" long.............	300	450	650
Race Car, 9" long...........................	150	225	325
Radiator Car, four-casting, nickeled, approx. 4" long...........................	175	250	375
Sedan, 5-1/4" long	100	150	225
Stake Truck, 8" long........................	275	425	600
Wrecker, 4" long.............................	100	150	225
Wrecker, 9" long.............................	225	350	500
Wrecker, C-Cab, 8-1/4" long	900	1500	2250
Wrecker, cast iron, 7-1/2" long........	225	375	550

CHEIN

Chein (Pronounced "chain") was founded in 1903 by Julius Chein. The New Jersey company specialized in lithographed metal toys, the majority of them mechanical. In 1918, it was located at 310 Passaic Ave., in Harrison, New Jersey, with 250 employees. In 1934, it had 147 employees. In a 1946-47 directory, it listed 148 male and 132 female employees. Chein made toys until 1979, and is still in business today in Burlington, New Jersey.

Chein Hercules "C" Cab Mack Trucks

Chein introduced the Hercules series vehicles in 1925, the first model being the Dump Truck. It was made entirely of lightweight stamped-steel (heavy-gauge tin). Chein made at least fourteen different Hercules models, the smallest being seventeen inches long and stretching to thirty inches (with the C-Cab Bull Dog Mack mobile clam truck, including boom). These toys generally retailed between one dollar and $1.25. They were manufactured until the middle 1930s.

Contributor: Bob Smith. The Village Smith, 62 West Ave., Fairport, NY 14450-2102

	C6	C8	C10
Airflow, wind-up, w/garage	300	450	600
Army Truck, tin, cannon on back, early, 8-1/2" long	75	125	225
Army Truck, Mack, canvas top, 8" long	105	158	210
Army Truck, tin, open bed, early, 8-1/2" long	90	135	235
Chein Garage	NPF	NPF	NPF
Dan-Dee Dump Truck, wind-up	200	300	500
Greyhound Bus, wind-up, 9" long	120	200	400

	C6	C8	C10
Greyhound Lines Push Toy, 9" long	90	175	300
Junior Oil Tank Truck, 1920s, 8-1/2" long	125	250	475
Junior Truck, 1920s	125	225	400
Limosine, tin wind-up, 1930s, 7" long	225	375	550
Mack Army Truck, open bed, 8-1/2" long	200	300	450
Mack Ice Truck, 8-1/2" long	225	325	550
Mack Moving and Storage Van	400	650	750
Peanuts Bus, marked "Happiness Is An Annual Outing"	NPF	NPF	NPF

Left to Right: Chein Army truck, 8-1/2"; Chein Moving and Storage Van; Chein Ice Truck, 8-1/2" long. Photo from Bob Smith.

Chein Greyhound Lines Push Toy, 9". Photo from Bob Smith.

Chein Army Truck, open bed, 8-1/2".

Chein Peanuts Bus.

Chein Racer No. 52, tin windup, 6-1/2". Photo from Bob Smith.

Chein Rapid Delivery No. 10, tin windup. Photo from Bob Smith.

Back to front: Chein Woodie Sedan, tin windup; Chein Garage. Photo from Dave Leopard.

	C6	C8	C10
Playland Whip, four bump 'em cars, wind-up, No. 340	400	600	800
Racer, No. 3, wind-up, 1920s, 6-1/2" long	150	250	350
Racer, tin wind-up, marked "52," 6-1/2" long	90	150	275
Rapid Delivery Truck, tin wind-up, No. 10	275	425	600
Roadster, tin lithographed, c.1925, 8-1/2" long	315	472	630
Sedan, tin wind-up, six window, 8-1/2" long	250	475	675

Chein Hercules Crane, 23" 1920s. Photo from Bob Smith.

Chein Hercules Fire Pumper, 1920s, 18". Photo from Bob Smith.

	C6	C8	C10
Taxi, wind-up, 1920s, 7" long	185	325	450
Touring Car, tin lithographed, 7" long	250	375	500
Woodie Sedan, tin wind-up, 5-1/4" long	48	72	95
Woodie Sedan, tin windup	NPF	NPF	NPF
Woodie Station Wagon, wind-up	100	150	200

Hercules

	C6	C8	C10
Crane, c.1925, 23" long	225	300	550
Dump Truck, No. 250, open cab, c.1925, 18" long	400	550	850
Fire Pumper, No. 650, c.1926, 18" long	650	1150	1600
Mack Army Truck, brown w/canvas cover, 19-3/4" long	450	750	1500
Mack Coal Truck, black cab, chassis, green bed, tin coal chute, chute door opens, 20" long	550	900	1600

	C6	C8	C10
Mack Crane Truck, No. 1100, 18" long	750	1250	1800
Mack Dump Truck, black cab, chassis, red dump body, tailgate opens, 20" long	350	650	975

	C6	C8	C10
Mack Ice Truck, black cab, green cargo box, step plate at rear of bed, 19-1/2" long	550	900	1600
Mack Log Truck, all black, 18-1/2" long...................................	750	1300	2000
Mack Mobile Clam Truck, green, red and black, 30" long inlcuding boom...	1750	1300	1900
Mack Motor Express Truck, black cab, orange stake bed, 19-1/2" long...................................	550	900	1450
Mack Oil Tank Truck, black and orange, 19" long	600	1100	1700
Mack Ready-Mixed Concrete Truck, deluxe model, orange and black lithographed, rotating drum, 17" long...	750	1300	2000
Mack Wrecking Truck, black cab, chassis, tow boom, red bed, 23-1/2" long (including tow boom)	550	800	1300

Chein Hercules Mack Army Truck, canvas cover, 19-3/4".

Chein Hercules Mack Coal Truck, 20", black cab, green bed.

Chein Hercules Mack Dump Truck, black cab, red dump body, tailgate opens, 20".

Chein Hercules Mack Crane Truck, 18". Photo from Bob Smith.

Chein Hercules Mack Dump Truck with original box, 20". Photo from Bob Smith.

Chein Hercules Mack Ice Truck, 19-1/2" black cab, green cargo box.

Chein Hercules Mack Motor Express Truck, 19-1/2", black cab, orange stake bed.

Chein Hercules Mack Log Truck, black, 18-1/2".

Chein Hercules Mack Motor Express Truck, with original box. Photo from Bob Smith.

Chein Hercules Mack Mobile Clam Truck, 30", green, red, black.

Chein Hercules Mack Oil Tank Truck, 19", black and orange. Photo from Phillips, New York.

Chein Hercules Mack Ready-Mixed Concrete Truck, orange and black, rotating drum, 17".

Chein Hercules Mack Wrecking Truck, 23-/12", black cab, red bed.

Chein Hercules Roadster, 18", red and black, rumble seat, luggage rack.

Chein Hercules Motor Express Semi-Truck, driver printed on glass, 1930s, 15-1/2". Photo from Bob Smith.

Left to Right: Chein Hercules Roadster, black and red, 18"; Hercules Roadster, yellow with black fenders. Photo from Bob Smith.

Chein Hercules No. 8 Racer, red with yellow trim.

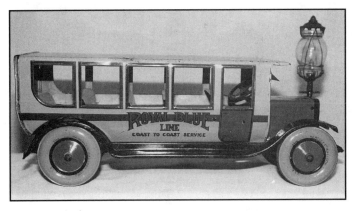

Chein Hercules Royal Blue Line Pullman Bus, gray, red, black, 18".

	C6	C8	C10
Motor Express Semi-Truck, driver printed on glass, No. 112, c.1934, 15-1/2" long	450	700	900
Packard Dump Truck	250	450	650
Racer, w/driver, spare tire (mounted on rear), red w/yellow trim, No. 8, 20" long	700	1500	2200

	C6	C8	C10
Roadster, red and black, rumble seat, luggage rack, 18" long	475	800	1200
Roadster, color variation of above, in green or yellow w/black fenders	550	900	1350
Royal Blue Line Pullman Bus, gray, red, black, 18" long	750	1500	2200
Wrecking Truck, open cab, 18" long	500	750	1350

CLARK, DAVID P. & CO.

D.P. Clark was the first manufacturer to use the heavy cast-iron flywheel on friction-drive Hill-Climber toys, patented by Israel and Edith Boyer. The cars and trucks were made of heavy sheet metal, wood and cast iron. Clark also made trains, animals and other novelty toys with the friction mechanism. William Schieble, who was a partner in the company, bought Clark's half of the business in 1909. Schieble then changed the firm's name to the Schieble Toy and Novelty Co. Schieble filed for bankruptcy in 1931.

Back on his own, Clark went on to begin a new business. Naming his company the Dayton Friction Toy Works, Clark felt free to use the patents from the now Schieble Toy Co. Lawsuits followed, with Schieble being the winner. Clark sold the Dayton Toy Works to Nelson Talbot in 1924. He passed away soon after. The company survived for eleven more years.

Contributor: Bob Smith, The Village Smith, 62 West Ave., Fairport, NY 14450-2102.

	C6	C8	C10		C6	C8	C10
Automobile, w/driver, No. 10, c.1908, 8-1/4" long......................	325	500	700	Fire Hook and Ladder, c.1908, driver, 19" long...........................	450	650	850
Automobile, No. 2, 10-1/4" long	307	550	775	Horseless Carriage, first toy w/flywheel drive; wood, tin and cast iron construction; blue and red, came lady passenger and driver, c.1898, 11-1/2" long..........	500	650	875
Electric Runabout, flywheel drive; two cast iron lady riders, wood, sheet metal and cast iron construction; red, black and gold, c.1902, 7-1/2" long.....................	550	800	1300				

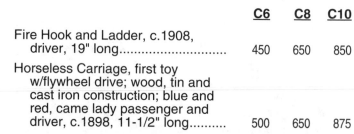

The Clark Horseless Carriage was the first toy with flywheel drive.

This vehicle appears to be a variation of the Clark No. 2 Automobile. Photo from B.R. Blaydes.

Clark No. 2 Automobile, 10-1/4". Photo from Joe and Sharon Freed.

Clark Electric Runabout, red, black, gold, early 1900s.

Hill-Climbing Friction Toys

No. 250. Chemical Engine.
10¾ inches long.
4 " wide.
7½ " high.

Equipped with ladder and chemical reservoir.

Packed 2 dozen in case.

Price, Doz., List..$11.50

No. 96. Automobile.
12¾ inches long.
4¾ " wide.
7½ " high.

Miniature representation of latest style Automobile. Runs forward, backward or in a circle.

Packed 2 dozen in case.

Price, Doz., List..$16.50

No. 100. Battleship.
19 inches long.
4 " wide.
8¾ " high.

Made of Sheet Steel, and painted gray. Boat rocks while in motion to reproduce actual sailing.

Has 4 Guns and 2 Turrets.
Packed 2 dozen in case.

Price, Doz., List..$16.50

No. 4. Hook and Ladder.
19½ inches long.
3¼ " wide.
6¾ " high.

Equipped with 3 ladders, and may be used for scaling purposes. Automatic gong that rings while machine is in operation.

Packed 2 dozen in case.

Price, Doz., List..$16.50

No. 1. Locomotive.
21 inches long.
5½ " wide.
7⅛ " high.

Representation of large American Locomotive. Capable of pulling ten cars.
Automatic Bell.

Packed 2 dozen in case.

Price, Doz., List..$16.50

No. 2. Automobile.
10¼ inches long.
3¾ " wide.
7 " high.

Contains four Passengers.
Up-to-date equipment.

Packed 2 dozen in case.

Price, Doz., List..$16.50

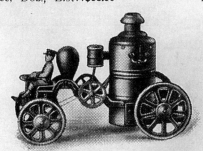

No. 3. Fire Engine.
11½ inches long.
4 " wide.
8 " high.

Made of Sheet Steel. Automatic Gong that rings while engine is in motion.

Packed 2 dozen in case.

Price, Doz., List..$16.50

No. 310. Automobile.
17 inches long.
7 " wide.
11 " high.

Miniature reproduction of finest automobiles on the market. Carries six passengers.

Packed one-half dozen in case.

Price, Doz., List..$72.00

A page from a 1908 toy catalog depicts eight Clark toys. Note the original prices compared to their values today.

The Clark Horseless Carriage Push Toy could be the first Clark toy. The wood, tin and cast-iron toy was patented in 1897.

Clark Police Patrol, 9-1/2", early 1900s.

Clark Open Touring Car, 8", circa 1903.

Clark Runabout, 7-1/4", red, circa 1903.

Clark Runabout, red, circa 1902, 7-3/4".

	C6	C8	C10
Horseless Carriage Push Toy, spring suspension, no flywheel mechanism; wood, tin and cast iron construction; green, red and yellow; possibly the first Clark toy. Patented November 2, 1897; 11" long	450	600	800
Open Touring Car, flywheel drive, tin head lamps, red, c.1903, 8" long	275	375	600
Police Patrol, flywheel drive, five riders, red and gold, c.1900, 9-1/2" long	600	850	1300
Runabout, flywheel drive, wood, sheet metal and cast iron construction; red, c.1903, 7-1/4" long	300	450	600

Hill-Climbing Friction Toys

No. 10. "Automobile."
8¼ inches long.
3¾ " wide.
7¼ " high.
Imitation of our modern Runabouts.
Packed 2 dozen in case.
Price, Doz., List...$8.30

No. 15. "Pullman Car."
13 inches long.
3⅝ " wide.
6 " high.
Substantially made and nicely painted.
Carries 6 passengers.
Packed 2 dozen in case.
Price, Doz., List...$8.30

No. 25. "Automobile."
9 inches long.
4¼ " wide.
6 " high.
A strong, durable toy.
Carries 3 passengers.
Attractively painted.
Packed 2 dozen in case.
Price, Doz., List...$8.30

No. 35. "Cruiser."
13 inches long.
3 " wide.
7 " high.
Constructed of sheet steel.
Equipped with 4 lifeboats.
Packed 2 dozen in case.
Price, Doz., List...$8.30

No. 40 "Scorcher."
11 inches long.
4 " wide.
5½ " high.
A perfect model of up-to-date racers.
Speedy machine.
Packed 2 dozen in case.
Price, Doz., List...$8.30

No. 20. Police Patrol.
10¾ inches long.
4 " wide.
7½ " high.
Made of steel. Equipped with 2 hand-cuffed prisoners, officer and chauffeur.
Packed 2 dozen in crate.
Price, Doz., List...$8.30

No. 220. "Patrol."
10¾ inches long.
4 " wide.
7½ " high.
Very good design.
Two prisoners, 1 driver and 1 officer.
Packed 2 dozen in case.
Price, Doz., List...$11.50

No. 210. Combination.
13 inches long.
4 " wide.
7 " high.
May be used as Ambulance, Moving Van or Delivery.
Nicely painted.
Packed 2 dozen in case.
Price, Doz., List...$11.50

Another page from a 1908 catalog showing Clark toys.

Clark Steam Pumper, gold and red, 11", circa 1908.

Clark Steam Pumper, early 1900s, 10-1/4".

	C6	C8	C10
Runabout, flywheel drive, wood head lamps, red, c.1902, 7-3/4" long	300	450	600
Steam Pumper, flywheel drive; wood, sheet metal and cast iron construction; red, silver and gold, c.1903, 10-1/4" long	650	850	1300

	C6	C8	C10
Steam Pumper, flywheel drive, gold and red, c.1908, 11" long	300	450	700

COMET-AUTHENTICAST

Comet-Authenticast, owned by the Slonim family, began toy making (as Comet) around 1940 in Queens, New York. Though it began with only toy soldiers, it switched to making ID models for the government, soon after World War II began. Following the war, it sold them as toys.

Comet-Authenticast went out of business in the early 1960s. Its vehicles sell in the $8-$10 range, and probably more for something rare, like the Lee Tank. In recent times, Quality Castings of Alexandria, Virginia, has been reissuing these toys, using the original molds in a generally $4-$6 range.

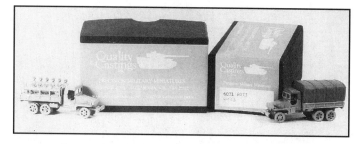

Using the original molds, Quality Castings has been reissuing vehicles like these Army trucks. Left to Right: No. 6033 and No. 6031. Prices are generally in the $4-$6 range. Photo from Ed Poole.

Back row from left: Quality Castings reproduces original German pieces like those shown here. Back row, left to right: 4017 Wespe; 4018, 7.5 PAK; 4023 Opel Blitz; and 4026 88 Flak on boogie wheels. Middle row, left to right: 4027 2 CM FLAF on and off trailer; 4031 3.7 PAK; 4035 7.5 INF gun; 4036 Kubelwagen; and 4037 BMW cycle with MB variant; 4041 Pz38t. Bottom row, left to right: 4042 Wirblewing FLAK; 4044 Hetzer; 4045 Marder III; 4046 250/l Halftrak; 4049 Hummell; RFE Lost Silver DAK (added for scale 22mm tall). Photo from Ed Poole.

Back row, left to right: 5175 LVTAA Amphibian Tank; 5176 LVT Amphibian; 5176 LTV Utility Tank (Quality Casting); 5178 Medium Tank 105 mm (Quality Casting). Front row. left to right: 5180 Walker Bulldog; 5179 General Patton; 5181 6x6 Truck; 5182 Command Car; 5183 Troop Carrier. Note: Comet-Authenticast marching GIs are 20mm tall. Photo from Ed Poole.

1:108-scale ID models of World War II Japanese tanks by Comet-Athenticast. Back row, left to right: 5051 Amphibian Tankette; 5052 Tankette; 5053 Medium Tank. Front row, left to right: 5054 Medium Tank; 5055 Tankette; 5056 Light Tank, 5057 Heavy Medium Tank. Note: Authenticast Gis are 21 mm tall. Photo from Ed Poole.

Two Comet-Authenticast 1:108-scale models (left to right: 5009 Cromwell, 5010 Churchill) and their original boxes. Comet address was given as New York, New York. Authenticast address was given as Richmond Hill, New York. Both have design copyright dates of 1943. Photo from Ed Poole.

Quality Casting 1:108-scale German tanks. Back row, left to right: 4051 5cm PAK; 4052 222 Armored Car; 4054 Brumbar; 4055 234/1 Armored Car; 4058 Tiger II (Porsche Turret). Front row, left to right: 4061 7/2 Halftrack with 3.7 FLAK; 4062 2 cm Quad FLAF and trailer; 4063 3.7 FLAK on trailer; 4064 88 PAK; 4065 105 Howitzer; 4066 Ferdinand; 4067 Elefant; 4068 250/7 Mortar Halftrack. The Authenticast 20 mm Gi is shown for comparison. Quality Cast makes many troops closer to the correst scale. Photo from Ed Poole.

Comet-Authenticast 1:108-scale ID World War II German vehicles. Back row, left to right: 5100 PzKwIII; 5101 PzKwI; 5102 Panzerjager; 5103 PzKw IV G; 5104 PzKw IV F. Middle row, left to right: 5105 PzKw II; 5106 PzKw III; 5107 Tiger; 5108 Eight-wheeled Armored Car. Front row, left to right:5109 Pz35T; 5110 Panther; 5111 Sturmgeschutz; 5112 Half-Track. The Authenticast German soldiers are up to 21mm tall. Photo from Ed Poole.

Comet-Authenticast 1:108-scale U.S. ID Models of the Cold War Era. Back row, left to right: 5184 Trailer; 5185. Weapons Carrier; 5186 M-67 Tank; 5187 M48 Tank; 5188 M103 Heavy Tank. Front Row: 5189 Atomic Cannon. (Quality Casting). Figures are 15mm tall. Photo from Ed Poole.

Cold War U.S. 1:108 ID Models. Back row, left to right: 5192 M3 Medium Tank; 5190 T98 S.P. 105mm Gun; 5191 S.P. 155mm Howizer; 5192 M3 Tank; 5193 Hawk Missile-Transporter (Quality Casting); Launcher and Mobile Radar with crew. Front row, left to right: 5194 Honest John Launcher and crew; 5195 Nike-Ajax Launcher and crew (Quality Cast); 5196 M42 Duster Twin 40mm AA (Quality Cast); 5197 Ontos S.P. Rocket Launcher. Standing figures are 15mm tall. Photo from Ed Poole.

Comet-Authenticast 1:108-scale U.S. ID Models. Back row, left to right: 5156 General Pershing; 5166 General Chaffee, 5167 Slugger II; 5168 Slugger; 5169 76mm Sherman. Front Row, left to right: 5170 Airborne Tank; 5171 Armored Car (Staghound); 5172 Armored Car (Twin 50); 5173 DUKW; 5174 M32 Tank Recovery. Soldiers were sculpted by Holger Eriksson; the tallest measures 20mm. Photo from Ed Poole.

Comet-Authenticast 1:108-scale metal World War II Russian ID Models. Back row, left to right: 5200 KV-1 Heavy Tank; 5201 KV-2 Heavy Tank; 5202 Josef Stalin; 5203 T34 Medium Tank. Middle row: Russian soldiers designed by Holger Erikson sold by Comet in sets R1 thru 8, the latter two containing tanks; figure are 20mm tall. Frontrow, left to right: 5204 T70 light tank; 5205 ST2 Armored Carrier; 5206 T34/85 medium tank; 5207 Josef Stalin III. Photo from Ed Poole.

Comet-Athenticast 1:108-scale U.S. World War II ID models identification models Back Row, left to right: 5150 75mm Gun on Half Track; 5151 Heavy Tank M6; 5152 Sherman Tank; 5153 Greyhound Armored Car; 5154 Half-Track. Middle row, left to right: 5155 Hellcat; 5156 Priest; 5157 General Scott; 5158 General Stuart; 5159 Wolverine. Front row, let to right: 5160 Jeep; 5161 Weasel; 5162 Scout Car; 5163 Quack; 5164 King Kong. Authenticat GI with Mine Detector is 20mm tall. Photo from Ed Poole.

CONVERSE

Beginning in 1878, Converse helped make Winchendon, Massachusetts, "Toy Town U.S.A." It made wooden, tin and steel toys and was felled in 1934 by the Depression. It was originally owned by Morton E. Converse.

	C6	C8	C10
Auto, pressed steel, painted, clockwork, w/fringe on top, three-seat, 1905, rubber tires	600	900	1200
Fire Engine Ladder Truck, wood headlamps, c.1915, 18" long	1800	3000	4250

	C6	C8	C10
Fire Engine Ladder Truck, bell, wooden headlight, 1915, 10" long	1250	1875	2500
Parcel Post, 1920s, 15" long	1500	2500	3700
Pick-Up Truck, very early, open cab	500	750	1000

	C6	C8	C10
Pierce-Arrow Touring Car, open, steers	1200	2200	3000
Roadster, wind-up, open cab, 1908, 15-1/2" long..............................	1200	2200	3000
Touring Auto, pressed steel, canvas roof, 1910....................................	1300	2200	3000
Touring Auto, open, four-seater	1200	2200	3000
Transitional Taxi, clockwork, 10-1/2" long	525	770	1050

Cor-Cor Supplee Ice Cream Truck. Photo from Tim Oei.

COR-COR

According to Margaret E. Holland (as reported by Ross Hermann in the July 27, 1992 *Antique News*), the granddaughter of Cor-Cor founder Louis A. Corcoran, this Washington, Indiana firm began on 21st Street in 1925, then expanded to East 3rd and Vantress. After a fire, Cor-Cor built its final plant on Front Street. At this latter location the company changed its name to Corcoran Metal Products. At its height, the firm employed up to 590 people. Corcoran retired in 1941 because of failing health, and died in 1945. His toys are marked "Cor-Cor" on the wheels.

	C6	C8	C10			C6	C8	C10
Airflow, wind-up, electric lights, 18" long	1000	1600	2200		Fire Truck, 24" long.........................	200	300	400
Army Truck..	NPF	NPF	NPF		Graham Paige Sedan, electric, 20" long...	600	1000	1600
Bus, electric lights	500	750	1000		Ice Truck	NPF	NPF	NPF
Bus, 23" long....................................	325	488	650		Semi Truck..	NPF	NPF	NPF
Chrysler Airflow	600	800	1200		Supplee Ice Cream Truck	NPF	NPF	NPF
DeSoto Airflow	650	850	1250		Van, painted metal, c.1928, 23" long	250	380	525
Dump Truck, dumps back or side to side, 23" long	225	338	450					

CORGI

Corgi is the registered trademark of Playcraft Toys. Its vehicles first appeared in 1956. Since Corgis are generally sold Mint in Box (C10), those are the prices shown here.

	C6	C8	C10			C6	C8	C10
Batcycle..	n/a	n/a	NPF		Major Aerial Rescue Truck..............	n/a	n/a	NPF
Chipperfield's Circus Crane Truck ...	n/a	n/a	NPF		No. 0010 Tank and Transporter.......	n/a	n/a	150
Daktari Set, two versions—cast wheels or Whizz Wheels..............	n/a	n/a	NPF		No. 0026 Beach Buggy & Sailboat...	n/a	n/a	80
					No. 0034 David Brown 1412 Tractor & Trailer	n/a	n/a	80
Husky Crime Busters Gift Set, includes Batmobile, Batboat, James Bond Aston Martin, Man From U.N.C.L.E. car	n/a	n/a	NPF		No. 0058 Beast Carrier	n/a	n/a	60
					No. 0061 Four Furrow Plow	n/a	n/a	35
James Bond Toyota 2000 GT	n/a	n/a	NPF		No. 0062 Farm Tipper Trailer...........	n/a	n/a	20

	C6	C8	C10
No. 0064 Jeep FC150 Conveyor......	n/a	n/a	100
No. 0069 Massye Ferguson Tractor.	n/a	n/a	120
No. 0073 Massey Ferguson Tractor w/saw................................	n/a	n/a	110
No. 0074 Ford Tractor w/haybine scoop................................	n/a	n/a	100
No. 0109 Penny Burn workman's trailer................................	n/a	n/a	35
No. 0150 007 Aston Martin	n/a	n/a	275
No. 0150 Vanwall...........................	n/a	n/a	55
No. 0152 BRM Formula 1	n/a	n/a	80
No. 0152 Ferrari 312 B2 Formula 1 .	n/a	n/a	40
No. 0153 Bluebird	n/a	n/a	120
No. 0154 Ferrari F-1......................	n/a	n/a	40
No. 0154 Lotus.............................	n/a	n/a	45
No. 0155 Shado Racer....................	n/a	n/a	45
No. 0156 Cooper Maserati	n/a	n/a	40
No. 0156 Embassy Shadow Racer ..	n/a	n/a	50
No. 0158 Elf Tyrrell Ford F-1...........	n/a	n/a	45
No. 0158 Lotus Climax F1...............	n/a	n/a	50
No. 0159 Patrick Eagle Indy Car......	n/a	n/a	45
No. 0160 Hesketh 308 Formula 1 Car................................	n/a	n/a	30
No. 0161 Santa Pod Commuter Dragster................................	n/a	n/a	45
No. 0162 Quatermaster Dragster.....	n/a	n/a	38
No. 0163 Capri, Glow Worm Dragster................................	n/a	n/a	75
No. 0164 Wild Honey Dragster	n/a	n/a	55
No. 0166 Ford Mustang Organ Grinder Drag Funny	n/a	n/a	38
No. 0167 U.S. Racing Buggy	n/a	n/a	42
No. 0169 Arnold Sundquist's Jet Car	n/a	n/a	55

	C6	C8	C10
No. 0200 Mini 1000.........................	n/a	n/a	45
No. 0201 Austin Cambridge.............	n/a	n/a	165
No. 0202 Morris Cowley...................	n/a	n/a	132
No. 0204 Morris Mini-Minor.............	n/a	n/a	75
No. 0206 Hillman Husky	n/a	n/a	120
No. 0208 Jaguar Saloon	n/a	n/a	132
No. 0210 Citroën D.S. 19................	n/a	n/a	100
No. 0211 Studebaker Golden Hawk	n/a	n/a	110
No. 0214 Ford Thunderbird Open Sports	n/a	n/a	120
No. 0217 Fiat 1800	n/a	n/a	75
No. 0218 Aston Martin DB4	n/a	n/a	60
No. 0219 Plymouth Wagon.............	n/a	n/a	120
No. 0220 Chevrolet Impala	n/a	n/a	67
No. 0221 Chevy Yellow Cab	n/a	n/a	100
No. 0222 Renault FloRide...............	n/a	n/a	82
No. 0223 Chevrolet Police Car	n/a	n/a	125
No. 0224 Bentley Continental	n/a	n/a	125
No. 0225 Austin Seven Mini............	n/a	n/a	100
No. 0226 Morris Mini-minor.............	n/a	n/a	75
No. 0228 Volvo P1800	n/a	n/a	90
No. 0229 Chevy Corvair...................	n/a	n/a	85
No. 0230 Mercedes 220..................	n/a	n/a	95
No. 0232 Fiat 2100	n/a	n/a	110
No. 0233 Heinkel Car......................	n/a	n/a	85
No. 0234 Ford Consul Classic	n/a	n/a	80
No. 0235 Olds Super 88	n/a	n/a	100
No. 0236 Motor School Car	n/a	n/a	100
No. 0237 Oldsmobile Sheriff Car	n/a	n/a	100
No. 0238 Jaguar Mark X	n/a	n/a	90
No. 0239 VW Kharmann Ghia	n/a	n/a	90
No. 0241 Ghia L6.4.........................	n/a	n/a	68
No. 0245 Buick Riviera	n/a	n/a	68
No. 0246 Chrysler Imperial	n/a	n/a	98
No. 0247 Mercedes 600 Pullman.....	n/a	n/a	75
No. 0248 Chevrolet Impala	n/a	n/a	85

Corgi Jaguar Saloon.

Corgi Ghia L6.4. Photo from Mark Arruda.

Corgi Penguinmobile. Photo from Mark Arruda.

Corgi Spider-Man Jeep. Photo from Mark Arruda.

Corgi The Saint's Volvo. Photo from Mark Arruda.

Corgi Chitty Chitty Bang Bang. Photo from Mark Arruda.

	C6	C8	C10
No. 0249 Mini Cooper Deluxe Wicker Work	n/a	n/a	120
No. 0252 Rover 2000	n/a	n/a	80
No. 0253 Mercedes 220 Coupe	n/a	n/a	85
No. 0256 VW Safari	n/a	n/a	225
No. 0258 The Saint's Volvo	n/a	n/a	135
No. 0259 LeDande Coupe	n/a	n/a	105
No. 0259 Penguinmobile	n/a	n/a	65
No. 0260 Metropolis Buick	n/a	n/a	60
No. 0260 Renault 16	n/a	n/a	50
No. 0261 James Bond Aston Martin	n/a	n/a	280
No. 0261 Spider-Man Jeep	n/a	n/a	195
No. 0262 Lincoln Continental	n/a	n/a	110
No. 0263 Captain America Jetmobile	n/a	n/a	95
No. 0263 Rambler Marlin	n/a	n/a	65
No. 0264 Olds Toronado	n/a	n/a	85
No. 0265 Supermobile	n/a	n/a	95
No. 0266 Chitty Chitty Bang Bang	n/a	n/a	380
No. 0267 Batmobile	n/a	n/a	325

One of several variations of the Corgi Batmobile from 1966. Photo from Mark Arruda.

	C6	C8	C10
No. 0268 Green Hornet Black Beauty	n/a	n/a	450
No. 0269 James Bond Lotus Esprit	n/a	n/a	110
No. 0270 James Bond Silver/Aston Martin	n/a	n/a	180
No. 0271 Aston Martin (first)	n/a	n/a	150

Corgi James Bond Lotus Esprit. Photo from Mark Arruda.

Corgi James Bond Silver Aston Martin.

Corgi James Bond Citroën 2CV. Photo from Mark Arruda.

Corgi Monkeemobile.

Corgi Hillman Hunter. Photo from Mark Arruda.

	C6	C8	C10
No. 0272 James Bond Citroën 2CV.	n/a	n/a	90
No. 0273 Rolls Royce Silver Shadow	n/a	n/a	90
No. 0274 Bentley Series T	n/a	n/a	90
No. 0275 Olds Toronado	n/a	n/a	75
No. 0275 Rover 200 TC	n/a	n/a	68
No. 0277 Monkeemobile	n/a	n/a	410
No. 0280 Rolls Royce Silver Shadow	n/a	n/a	40
No. 0281 Austin Metro Royal Wedding	n/a	n/a	25
No. 0281 Rover 2000TC	n/a	n/a	60
No. 0282 Mini Cooper	n/a	n/a	50
No. 0283 DAF City Car	n/a	n/a	50
No. 0284 Citroën sm	n/a	n/a	50

	C6	C8	C10
No. 0285 Jaguar XJ12C	n/a	n/a	50
No. 0285 Mercedes Benz 240D	n/a	n/a	30
No. 0287 Citroën Dyane	n/a	n/a	35
No. 0290 Kojak's Buick	n/a	n/a	70
No. 0291 AMC Pacer X	n/a	n/a	25
No. 0292 Starsky & Hutch Ford Torino	n/a	n/a	115
No. 0293 Renault 5TS	n/a	n/a	15
No. 0300 Chevrolet Stingray	n/a	n/a	100
No. 0301 ISO Grifo 7 litre	n/a	n/a	52
No. 0302 Hillman Hunter	n/a	n/a	105

Corgi The Saint's Jaguar.

Corgi Chevrolet Astro 1. Photo from Mark Arruda.

Corgi Vegas Ford Thunderbird. Photo from Mark Arruda.

	C6	C8	C10
No. 0302 VW Polo	n/a	n/a	15
No. 0303 Porsche 925 Rallye	n/a	n/a	30
No. 0304 Mercedes Benz 300SL Hardtop Roadster	n/a	n/a	100
No. 0306 Morris Marina	n/a	n/a	60
No. 0310 Corvette Sting Ray	n/a	n/a	80
No. 0311 Ford Capri 3 litre	n/a	n/a	50
No. 0312 Jaguar E. Competition	n/a	n/a	105
No. 0312 Marcos Mantis	n/a	n/a	55
No. 0313 Ford Cortina w/Graham Hill figure	n/a	n/a	70
No. 0314 Ferrari Berlinetta 250LM	n/a	n/a	55
No. 0315 Simca 1000 Competition	n/a	n/a	80
No. 0316 N.S.U. Sport Prinz	n/a	n/a	72
No. 0318 Lotus Elan	n/a	n/a	105
No. 0319 GT Miura-Lamborghini	n/a	n/a	60
No. 0320 The Saint's Jaguar	n/a	n/a	95
No. 0321 Porsche 924	n/a	n/a	30
No. 0322 Rover 2000 Monte Carlo	n/a	n/a	150
No. 0323 Citroen DS19 Monte Carlo	n/a	n/a	140
No. 0324 Ferrari Daytona	n/a	n/a	35
No. 0325 Ford Mustang Fastback	n/a	n/a	85
No. 0327 MGB	n/a	n/a	125
No. 0329 Mustang Mach	n/a	n/a	40
No. 0330 Porsche	n/a	n/a	55
No. 0331 Ford Capri GT	n/a	n/a	52

	C6	C8	C10
No. 0332 Lancia Fulvia Sport Zagato	n/a	n/a	65
No. 0334 Mini-Cooper Magnifique	n/a	n/a	48
No. 0335 Jaguar E2x2	n/a	n/a	140
No. 0336 007 Toyota 2000	n/a	n/a	465
No. 0337 Corvette Sting Ray	n/a	n/a	85
No. 0338 Chevy SS 350 Camaro	n/a	n/a	90
No. 0339 Monte Carlo Mini	n/a	n/a	200
No. 0341 Mini Marcos GT	n/a	n/a	60
No. 0342 Lamborghini	n/a	n/a	125
No. 0342 The Professionals Ford Capri	n/a	n/a	100
No. 0343 Firebird	n/a	n/a	62
No. 0344 Ferrari 206 DinoSport	n/a	n/a	62
No. 0345 MGB-GT Competition	n/a	n/a	90
No. 0347 Chevy Astro	n/a	n/a	65
No. 0348 Vegas Thunderbird	n/a	n/a	72
No. 0352 RAF Staff Car	n/a	n/a	105
No. 0358 Old H.Q. Staff Car, Military	n/a	n/a	150

	C6	C8	C10
No. 0359 Army Field Kitchen	n/a	n/a	175
No. 0370 Ford Mustang	n/a	n/a	16
No. 0372 Lancia Fulvia Sport...........	n/a	n/a	35
No. 0373 Peugeot 505	n/a	n/a	16
No. 0373 VW 1200 Police Car	n/a	n/a	60
No. 0377 Marco 3 litre....................	n/a	n/a	58
No. 0378 Ferrari 308 GTS...............	n/a	n/a	15
No. 0380 Alfa Rameo Pinin Farina...	n/a	n/a	38
No. 0381 GP Beach Buggy	n/a	n/a	36
No. 0382 Porsche 911S	n/a	n/a	54
No. 0383 VW 1200.........................	n/a	n/a	47
No. 0385 Mercedes 190E	n/a	n/a	10
No. 0385 Porsche 917	n/a	n/a	27
No. 0386 Bertone Runabout	n/a	n/a	40
No. 0389 Reliant Bond Bug.............	n/a	n/a	48
No. 0392 Bertone Shake Buddy.......	n/a	n/a	30
No. 0393 Mercedes Benz 350SL	n/a	n/a	48
No. 0395 Datsun 240Z....................	n/a	n/a	50
No. 0397 Can-Am Porsche 917	n/a	n/a	30
No. 0400 VW 1300 Motor School.....	n/a	n/a	70
No. 0402 Frod Crotina Police Car	n/a	n/a	50
No. 0403 Ski Dumper......................	n/a	n/a	40
No. 0405 Chevrolet Ambulance	n/a	n/a	45
No. 0405 Ford Transit Milk..............	n/a	n/a	20
No. 0406 Land Rover	n/a	n/a	80
No. 0411 Lucozade Van..................	n/a	n/a	150

	C6	C8	C10
No. 0412 Mercedes-Benz 240D Police...............................	n/a	n/a	36
No. 0413 Mazda Maintenance Truck	n/a	n/a	40
No. 0414 Coast Guard Jaguar XJ....	n/a	n/a	45
No. 0416 R.A.C. Rescue Land Rover	n/a	n/a	72
No. 0418 Austin Taxi......................	n/a	n/a	42
No. 0419 Ford Zephyr Patrol Car.....	n/a	n/a	90
No. 0420 Ford Airborn Caravan.......	n/a	n/a	90
No. 0421 Bedford Evening Sandard	n/a	n/a	200
No. 0422 Corgi Toy Van	n/a	n/a	350
No. 0422 Riot Police Armored Car...	n/a	n/a	40
No. 0424 Security Van	n/a	n/a	40
No. 0425 Booking Office	n/a	n/a	420
No. 0426 Citroën Safari	n/a	n/a	90
No. 0428 Mr. Softee Truck	n/a	n/a	120
No. 0430 T-Bird 1958 Bermuda Taxi	n/a	n/a	115
No. 0433 VW Delivery Van	n/a	n/a	80
No. 0434 Charlie's Angels Van	n/a	n/a	65
No. 0435 Superman Van	n/a	n/a	60
No. 0436 Spider-Man Van	n/a	n/a	45
No. 0437 Cadillac Ambulance..........	n/a	n/a	128
No. 0438 Land Rover......................	n/a	n/a	78
No. 0443 Plymouth Station Wagon, U.S. Mail	n/a	n/a	110
No. 0445 Plymouth Sports Station Wagon	n/a	n/a	100

Corgi Army Field Kitchen.

Corgi Cadillac Ambulance. Photo from Mark Arruda.

Corgi Plymouth Sports Station Wagon.

Corgi Man From U.N.C.L.E. THRUSH-Buster, dark
metallic blue.

Corgi Popeye Paddle Wagon; James Bond The Spy
Who Loved Me Helicopter.

	C6	C8	C10
No. 0447 Walls Ice Cream Van........	n/a	n/a	185
No. 0448 Police Set	n/a	n/a	175
No. 0450 Mini Van...........................	n/a	n/a	80
No. 0457 ERF Platform Lorry..........	n/a	n/a	75
No. 0458 ERF Earth Dumper..........	n/a	n/a	75
No. 0459 Raygo Rascal	n/a	n/a	30
No. 0460 Neville Cement Tipper......	n/a	n/a	115
No. 0463 Commer Ambulance.........	n/a	n/a	88
No. 0464 Commer Police Van..........	n/a	n/a	128
No. 0468 Routemaster Bus, Outspan	n/a	n/a	50
No. 0470 Forward Control Jeep.......	n/a	n/a	45
No. 0471 London Transport Silver Jubilee bus..................................	n/a	n/a	38
No. 0471 Smith's Mobile Canteen Joe's Diner	n/a	n/a	165
No. 0472 Vote for Corgi Land Rover	n/a	n/a	130
No. 0474 Walls Ice Cream (w/chimes)	n/a	n/a	225
No. 0475 Safari	n/a	n/a	125
No. 0477 Breakdown Truck..............	n/a	n/a	80
No. 0478 Hydraulic Tower Wagon ...	n/a	n/a	90
No. 0479 Commer Mobile Camera Van	n/a	n/a	145
No. 0482 Range Rover Ambulance .	n/a	n/a	45
No. 0487 Chipperfield Circus Range Rover	n/a	n/a	140
No. 0490 VW Breakdown Van	n/a	n/a	100
No. 0491 Ford Estate Car	n/a	n/a	85
No. 0494 Bedford Tipper Truck........	n/a	n/a	75
No. 0497 Ford Escort Radio Rentals	n/a	n/a	16
No. 0497 Man From U.N.C.L.E........	n/a	n/a	380
No. 0500 Police Car	n/a	n/a	35

Corgi Hardy Boys Rolls-Royce. Photo from Mark
Arruda.

	C6	C8	C10
No. 0503 Giraffe Truck.....................	n/a	n/a	195
No. 0506 Police Panda IMP.............	n/a	n/a	65
No. 0509 Porsche Targa Police Car	n/a	n/a	60
No. 0511 Performing Poodles Truck	n/a	n/a	525
No. 0524 Route Master Bus- Stevenson's	n/a	n/a	20
No. 0529 Route Master Bus- Graham Ward Calendar	n/a	n/a	20
No. 0530 Route Master Bus- Yorkshire Post	n/a	n/a	20
No. 0702 Breakdown Truck	n/a	n/a	20
No. 0802 Popeye Paddle Wagon.....	n/a	n/a	485
No. 0805 Hardy Boys Rolls Royce...	n/a	n/a	250

From left to right: Corgi Mobile Gas Tanker; Decca Radar van; Army Truck. Photo from The Collectors Toy & Model Shop.

	C6	C8	C10
No. 0809 Dick Dastardly Car	n/a	n/a	100
No. 0811 J.B. Moon Buggy	n/a	n/a	495
No. 0908 AMX Recovery Tank	n/a	n/a	75
No. 0909 Tractor Gun & Trailer	n/a	n/a	110
No. 1100 Low Loader	n/a	n/a	180
No. 1100 Mack Transcontinental	n/a	n/a	95
No. 1101 Warner & Swasey Hydraulic Crane	n/a	n/a	70
No. 1102 Crane Fruehauf Bottom Dumper	n/a	n/a	75
No. 1103 Chubb Pathfinder Crash Truck	n/a	n/a	80
No. 1104 Bedford Horse Transporter	n/a	n/a	75
No. 1105 Car Transporter	n/a	n/a	250
No. 1106 Decca Radar Van	n/a	n/a	125
No. 1106 Mack Container Truck ACL	n/a	n/a	95
No. 1107 Euclid Bulldozer	n/a	n/a	275
No. 1109 Ford Semi-Trailer	n/a	n/a	90
No. 1110 Mobile Gas Tanker	n/a	n/a	225
No. 1111 MF Combine Harvester	n/a	n/a	190
No. 1116 Shelvoke Trash Truck	n/a	n/a	45
No. 1123 Circus Cage Wagon	n/a	n/a	165
No. 1126 Ecurie Ecosse Transporter	n/a	n/a	225
No. 1127 Simon Snorkel Fire Engine	n/a	n/a	100
No. 1128 Priestman Cub Shovel	n/a	n/a	60
No. 1130 Chipperfield Horse Transporter	n/a	n/a	325

	C6	C8	C10
No. 1137 Ford Semi-Trailer Truck	n/a	n/a	240
No. 1138 Ford Car Transporter	n/a	n/a	145
No. 1139 Chipperfield Circus Managerie Truck	n/a	n/a	595
No. 1142 Ford Holmes Wrecker	n/a	n/a	130
No. 1143 American LaFrance Fire Engine	n/a	n/a	125
No. 1144 Berliet Wrecker Truck	n/a	n/a	80
No. 1145 Mercedes Unimog-Goose Dumper	n/a	n/a	50
No. 1146 Tri-Deck Car Transporter	n/a	n/a	185
No. 1147 Seammell Tractor & Trailer, Ferrymasters	n/a	n/a	120
No. 1150 Unimog Snow Plow	n/a	n/a	50
No. 1151 Mack Exxon Tank Truck	n/a	n/a	63
No. 1152 Mack Tanker, Esso	n/a	n/a	75
No. 1154 Mack Crane Truck	n/a	n/a	150
No. 1156 Volvo Concrete Mixer	n/a	n/a	60
No. 1159 Ford Car Transporter	n/a	n/a	75

Corgi Chipperfield Horse Transporter.

	C6	C8	C10		C6	C8	C10
No. 1160 Gulf Petrol Truck	n/a	n/a	90	No. 9001 1927 Bentley	n/a	n/a	65
No. 1163 Human Cannonball Truck.	n/a	n/a	85	No. 9011 1916 Model T Ford	n/a	n/a	40
No. 1170 Ford Car Transporter	n/a	n/a	50	No. 9013 1915 Ford	n/a	n/a	70
No. 1192 Ford Van Lucas	n/a	n/a	15	No. 9031 1910 Renault	n/a	n/a	65
No. 1953 Surtees T.S. 9b Racer	n/a	n/a	45	No. 9041 1912 Rolls Royce	n/a	n/a	63
No. 6547 Ford Tractor-Conveyor on Trailer	n/a	n/a	150	No. Karier Bantam	n/a	n/a	165
				Noddy's Car	n/a	n/a	NPF

COURTLAND

Walter Rudolph Reach, founder of Courtland toys, was born in Jersey City, New Jersey, in 1905. Educated in local schools, Reach eventually worked his way to Camden, New Jersey, where, in 1937, he opened a successful sign painting business. Beyond the usual commercial trade, he performed extensive contract work for the Campbell's Soup Company. In fact, he painted some of the early Campbell's advertising signs now eagerly sought by advertising collectors. Within a few years, Reach, sensing a rising wave of patriotism within the country, began a second business—The Camden Flag and Banner Company, again taking advantage of his artistic skills. The early war years saw a decline in his work for Campbell, but the flag and banner business flourished.

In the summer of 1943, Reach's friend, Harold Salter, a salesman working for a well-known Philadelphia toy distributor, A. Ponnock & Sons, approached Reach for suggestions on how he might dispose of a railroad boxcar full of "prepared" cardboard. Reach acquired the cardboard at a bargain price, with the thought he'd find some way to capitalize on this potential windfall. He decided on cardboard toys. He quickly fashioned two toys—a two-wheel rabbit cart and a horse cart. Sales success soon followed as a war-weary public, hungry for low-cost toys, snapped up the entire stock. Both sold well.

With the capital from the cardboard toys, Reach founded the Courtland Manufacturing Company, incorporating on May 29, 1944. His friends and business associates formed the company's management team. The first true Courtland toy was produced in 1944—a twelve-inch tractor and trailer truck, made entirely of wood and marked "Courtland" on the sides of the trailer. It achieved wide-spread sales success when it was introduced to the trade. His wooden Courtland success was short-lived, as his connections with Campbell soon provided him with a ready supply of "rejected" tin from their canning process. (Additionally, over the next several years, Reach purchased "reject" tin-plate from J&L Steel of Bethlehem, Pennsylvania.) A Courtland line of tin toys quickly followed; by the fall of 1945, several toy trucks and playsets fashioned from tin were introduced.

With Reach designing the toys, and his father Erwin as the plant's manager, Courtland was off and running. During 1945, toy production at the Haddon Avenue factory focused on forty-two dedicated employees. Courtland would eventually employ more than 350 persons, father and son, mother and daughter teams were quite common. By late 1945, Courtland began installing mechanical motors in a select number of toys, boosting sales even higher. Courtland prospered with gross sales in 1946 exceeding $600,000. In 1946, Courtland toys could be found in forty-three states and thirteen foreign countries. As evidence of the swift and dynamic growth of the company, the top three domestic orders for tin toys in 1946 came from Sears, Roebuck & Co. of Chicago, for $21,827,26; Loft Candy Company, Long Island, New York, for $14,704.50; and Butler Brothers of Chicago, for $11,711.74.

Reach and his management staff instituted a "child toy testing" program at the plant, whereby a small room in the building was set aside for local children to evaluate the play value of new toy designs by playing with the toys. He observed the children at play to see which toys kept their interest and which toys were played with the least, or not selected for play at all. Reach, over the years, pointed with pride to his "child testing" program, believing that this type of testing was greatly responsible for his overall success.

The 1947 toy sales were five times greater than the same period the preceding year, and factory production was taxed to its production capacity of 20,000 toys a day. During that same year, Courtland's Export Division came into being under the direction of John H. Jackson. The Export Division, located in Basking Ridge, New Jersey, was tasked with the responsibility of coordinating all sales to foreign countries and to administer a newly negotiated contract with General Metal Toys LTD, of Canada. Courtland had, in fact, just completed and shipped the first such order of Walt Reach Courtland Toys with the General Metal Toys, Ltd. markings.

Over the next few years, Courtland introduced several toy innovations, including the streamline design of its trucks and cars and, most notably, the famous "Guaranteed For Life" mechanical motor. This motor, completely enclosed and designed for easy removal from the toy, was offered in both key-wind and friction action, and came with a colorful printed warranty with each toy sold. Hailed by the trade as a decisive marketing tool, the "Motor Guaranteed For Life" warranty provided buyers with the unique opportunity to exchange defective motors for new motors.

Gross sales of more than $1.2 million was reported for the first time in 1948. In 1949, sales rose to a staggering $1.9 million. Also, during 1949, Courtland Manufacturing moved to a newly renovated plant at 6th & Jefferson Street in Camden. During the planning phase for the renovated plant, Reach hired a manufacturing consultant to design the production assembly line so that an entire toy—from start to finish, including piece assembly (hand work), packaging, boxing, sealing and labeling—could be completed with no toy ever leaving the flow of the production line.

Reach, having borrowed heavily to secure and outfit his new production facility, was hit a severe financial blow. On June 24, 1950, the United States, under a United Nations mandate, entered the Korean Conflict. Essential war materials, which included tin, were diverted to the war effort, effectively denying him the backbone of his toy production. The availability of tin for toy making was reduced to a trickle, with the only source once again being "reject" tinplate. Recalling the early years of the company, this scenario was nothing new to him. What was new this time was that he found himself competing with other toy and novelty manufacturers across America for the meager supply of available tin.

A second, and more devastating blow to Courtland was the discovery, in the fall of 1950, of the introduction of counterfeit toys. These cheap, look-alike knock-offs, with inferior mechanical motors, were flooding the toy market under the Courtland name. The perpetrator, in addition to producing counterfeit Courtland toys, was also printing bogus "Motor Guaranteed For Life" warranty certificates. This caused a two-fold problem. Not only was Courtland faced with the loss of the sale of the toy, but they were also forced to exchange Courtland motors for defective motors, and there were many. To refuse this exchange, at least initially, would have, in all probability, destroyed the highly regarded guarantee. His initial thoughts were that the toys came from an Asian country, such as China or Japan. Subsequent investigating revealed the possibility the toys were coming from Canada, or at least entering the United States from Canada. (The mystery of where the toys originated and by whom, has never seen solved).

With the combination of the effects of the war, the decline in sales due to counterfeit toys and the need to pay the mortgage on the new plant, Reach suddenly found himself with a cash-flow problem. Searching desperately for funds, he turned to the Geo. Borgfeldt Company, a large, national toy distributor, to secure the necessary financial assistance. Besides the debt-service, one of the concessions he made to Borgfeldt was that the sole distribution of all Courtland toys went to Borgfeldt. Sales continued to sag, and Reach, desperate to hold the company together, approached persons, now known to be less than honorable, for help. Help they did…they helped themselves to his company by taking over the directorship and management positions, firing the original directors and draining the company of its money by paying themselves high salaries and huge bonuses. Employee rosters were quickly reduced to a minimum.

Within two years, and without Reach, the fledgling toy empire with so much potential, evaporated. Reach, however, was a fighter. Moving to Philadelphia with his family and dreams in 1953, he opened the Courtland Toy Company, attempting to remanufacture several of the original toys and a few new designs under that name; thus, the toys with the Courtland Toy Company, Philadelphia markings. By 1953, though, time has passed for tin-plate as a material for mass toy production. Plastics were in. Even though Reach had used some plastics in his original streamline Courtland designs produced in the 1949-1951 period, he could not retool for plastic-injection molding, without considerable expense. Finally, Courtland Toys were truly committed to history and the drive to rival Louis Marx as America's toy king was no more.

Special thanks to Marie Reach, Walt Reach's widow, for the above information. Mrs. Reach, a most gracious lady, opened her home and her memories of Walt and his Courtland toys to us. She, herself employed at the Courtland plant in Camden, provided numerous documents, photographs, artifacts and anecdotes for our future book on the history of Courtland toys.

Source: *Collector's Guide to American Transportaion Toys* by Joe and Sharon Freed.

Contributor: John Taylor, P.O. Box 63, Nolensville, TN 37135-0063.

	C6	C8	C10		C6	C8	C10
Friction-Powered				Courtland Mechanical Gulf Gasoline Tractor-Trailer, No. 3875, 13" long, 3" wide, 3-1/4" high	150	225	350
Courtland Dump Truck w/dual rear wheels, 10-1/2" long, 3" wide, 3-3/8" high	250	350	475	Courtland Mechanical Military Gun Car, lithographed gunshield	100	175	250
Courtland FBI Riot Squad Car, No. 7600, 7-1/4" long, 3-1/4" wide, 2-3/4" high	100	150	200	Courtland Mechanical Military Gun Car, painted gun shield, 7-1/2" long, 3-1/4" wide, 2-1/2" high	100	175	225
Courtland Mechanical Fire Chief Car w/siren, No. 7500, 7-1/4" long, 3-1/4"wide, 3-1/4" high	150	200	250	Courtland Mechanical State Police Car with siren, No. 7500, 7-1/4" long, 3-1/4" wide, 2-3/4" high	150	200	250
Courtland Mechanical Gasoline Tractor-Trailer, similar to No. 2000; gasoline Truck w/Trailer, marked "Gasoline-Motor Oils", Philadelphia, PA, 13" long, 3" wide, 3-1/4" high	100	150	200	Courtland Pop-Up Ladder Fire Truck, No. 5450, 13" long, 3" wide, 3-1/4" high	250	350	450

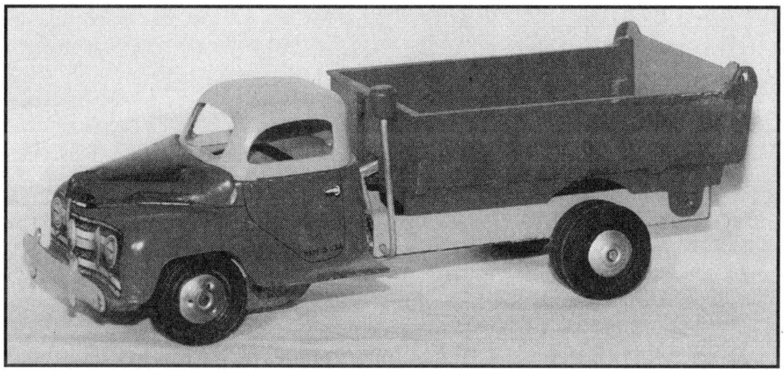

Courtland Dump Truck, dual rear wheels, 10-1/2".

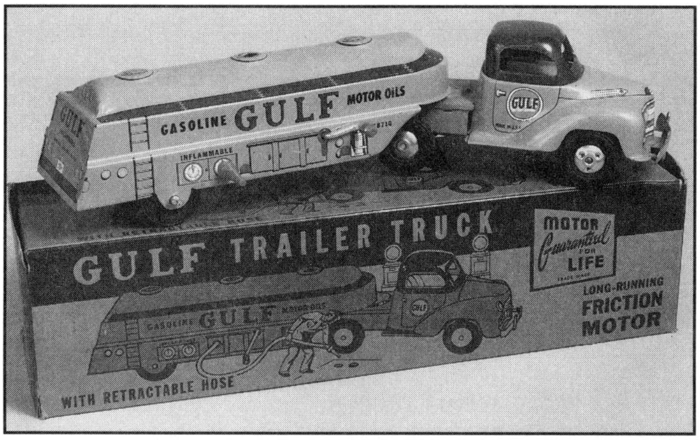

Courtland Mechanical Gulf Gasoline Tractor-Trailer, 13".

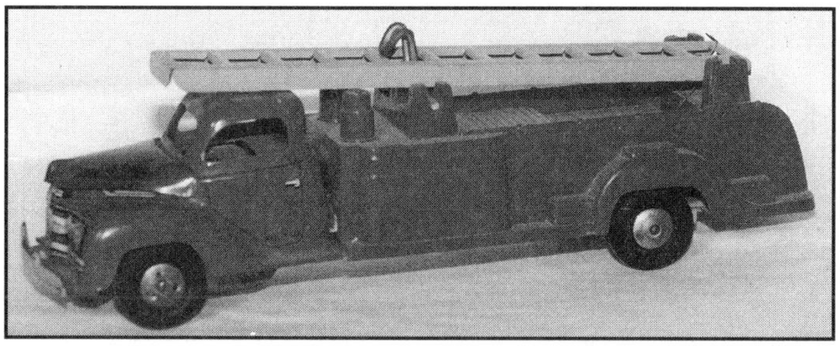

Courtland Pop-Up Ladder Fire Truck, red, yellow ladder.

	C6	C8	C10
Courtland Space Rocket Patrol Car, No. 4060, 1952, 7-1/4" long, 3-1/4" wide, 2-3/4" high	150	200	250
Courtland Woody Sedan, No. 4000, blue and tan, 7-1/4" long, 3-1/4" wide, 2-3/4" high. Note: This is one of only four Courtland styled toys stamped "A Walt Reach Toy by Courtland Toy Co. Phila., PA. Made in U.S.A." The only known Courtland-styled toys marked w/the Courtland Toy Company, Philadelphia stamping is this No. 4000 sedan, a non-powered "Fire Chief" car, a private garage similar to No. 9075 and a mechanical parking meter bank	65	75	100

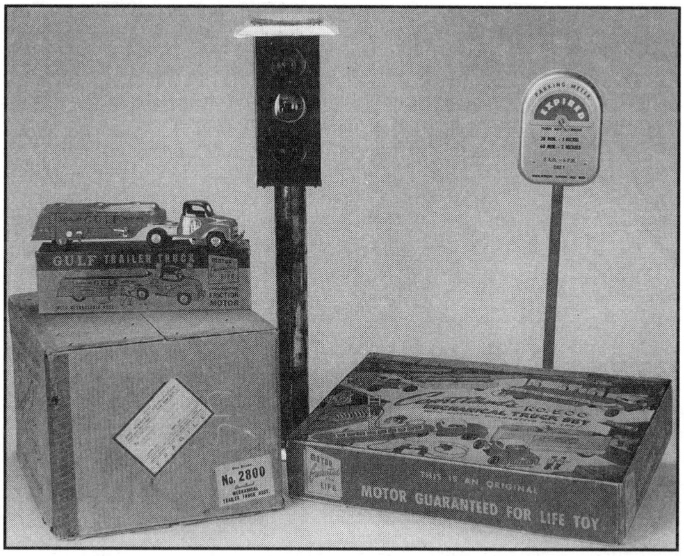

Left to Right: Courtland Gulf Gasoline Tractor-Trailer; unopened wholesale case; battery-operated Traffic Signal; Mechanical Truck Set, box with four trucks; Mechanical Parking Meter and bank, 24-1/2". Photo from Joe and Sharon Freed.

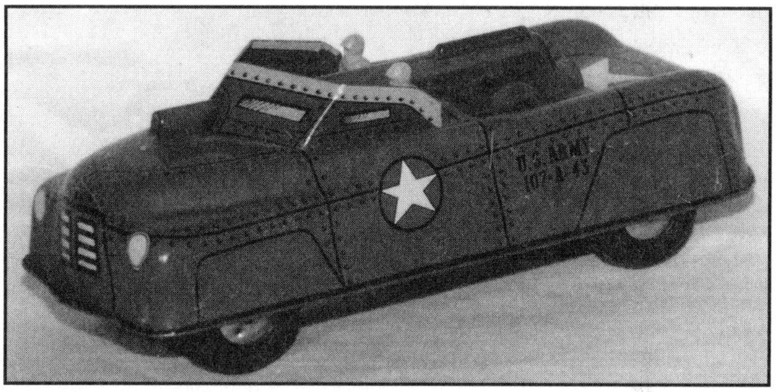

Courtland Mechanical Military Gun Car, painted gun shield, 7-1/2".

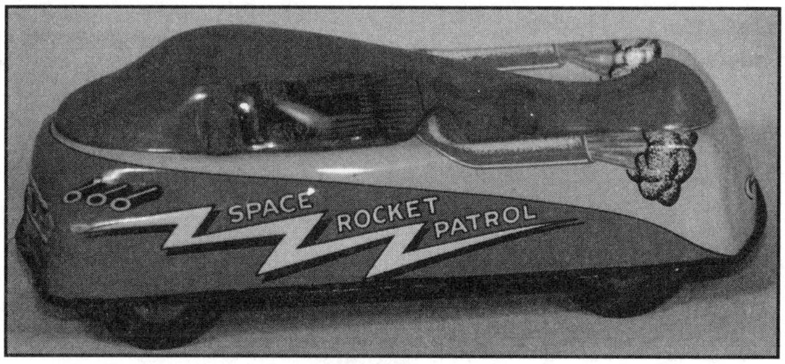

Courtland Space Rocket Patrol Car, red and yellow. Photo from Joe and Sharon Freed.

	C6	C8	C10
Courtland Woody Sedan, No. 4000, red and tan, 7-1/4" long, 3-1/4" wide, 2-3/4" height	65	75	100
Loft Candies Mechanical Tractor-Trailer	NPF	NPF	NPF

Courtland Woody Sedan, red and tan.

	C6	C8	C10
Non-Powered			
Courtland Big 4 Truck Parade, No. 1070, 1946, The four 900, 9-1/2" long, 3-1/4" wide, 3" high	NPF	NPF	NPF
Courtland Fire Patrol No. 2 Truck, No. 900, 1946, 9" long, 3" wide, 2-3/4" high..................	100	175	275

Courtland Mechanical Tractor-Trailer, Loft Candies.

Courtland Log Truck Tractor-Trailer (non-powered), 13".

Courtland Side Dump Tractor-Trailer, 13".

	C6	C8	C10
Courtland Log Truck Tractor-Trailer, No. 620, 1946, 13" long, 3" wide, 3-1/4" high	150	225	350
Courtland Logging Camp Train Set, No. 1050, 1946, 26-3/4" long, 3" wide, 3-1/4" high	NPF	NPF	NPF
Courtland Side Dump Tractor-Trailer, No. 1200, 13" long, 3" wide, 3-1/4" high	125	175	250
Courtland Tractor-Trailer, same tractor as No. 2000 except marked, "Loft-Fresh Candies"......	350	550	850
Courtland Trailer Truck Parade, No. 1060, 1946, 13" long, 3" wide, 3-1/4" wide..............	NPF	NPF	NPF
Easter Greetings Rabbit Truck, No. 800, 9" long.................................	325	525	750
Ice Cream Truck, No. 900, 1946......	125	200	300
Moving and Storage Truck, No. 900, 1946, 9" long, 3" wide, H 2-3/4" high	150	225	350
Open Van Tractor-Trailer, No. 600, 1946, 13" long, 3" wide, 3-1/4" high..............	100	150	200
Side Dump Tractor-Trailer, No. 700, 1946, 13" long, 3" wide, 3-1/4" high..............	100	150	200

Courtland Tractor-Trailer, "Loft Fresh Candy".

Courtland Easter Greetings Rabbit Truck, 9". Photo from Joe and Sharon Freed.

Courtland all-wood high-side trailer, open, 13".

Courtland Mechanical Parking Meter and Bank. Photo from Joe and Sharon Freed.

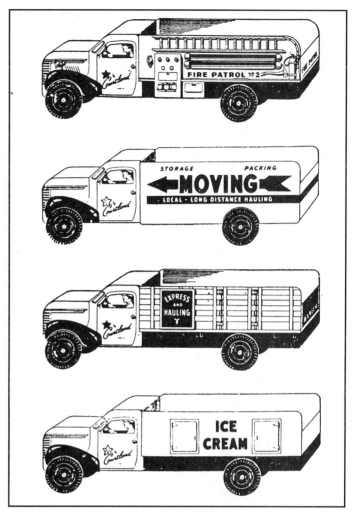

An assortment of four Courtland trucks. Photo from Richard MacNary.

	C6	C8	C10
Side Dump Tractor-Trailer, No 610, 1946, 13" long, 13" wide, 3-1/4" high	100	150	200
Trailer, all-wood open w/high-sides, 12" long	500	750	1000
Truck Assortment, No. 900, four trucks w/box	NPF	NPF	NPF

Tin Wind-up

	C6	C8	C10
Assortment, No. 3800, consists of six No. 3100 Dump Trucks; wholesale Assortment Only	NPF	NPF	NPF
Assortment, No. 2800, consists of two No. 2000 Gasoline Trucks, two No. 2050 Milk Trucks, two No. 2200 Log Trucks, two No. 2350 Open Van Trucks, two No. 2600 Freight Hauler Trucks and two No. 2700 Side Tipper Trucks; wholesale assortment only, in Mint condition	n/a	n/a	3000

	C6	C8	C10
Assortment, No. 5800, consists of three No. 2300 Aluminum Open Van Trucks, three No. 2150 Emergency Rescue Squad Trucks, three No. 2375 Sand and Gravel Trucks and three No. 2400 Towing Service Trucks; Wholesale Assortment Only	NPF	NPF	NPF
Bank, No. 7500, base 6" x 6", 24-1/2" high. Note: This is one of only four Courtland toys stamped "A Walt Reach Toy by Courtland Toy Co., Phila. PA. Made in U.S.A." The only known Courtland styled toys marked w/the Courtland Toy Company, Philadelphia stamping is this mechanical parking meter bank, a No. 4000 sedan, a non-power "Fire Chief" car, and a private garage similar to No. 9075	150	225	300
Checker Cab Car, No. 4000, green and yellow, 7-1/4" long, 3-1/4" wide, 2-3/4" high	175	200	325

	C6	C8	C10
Checker Cab Car, No. 4000, green and white, 7-1/4" long, 3-1/4" wide, 2-3/4" high	200	225	350
City Meat Market Delivery Sedan, No. 4000, 7-1/4" long, 3-1/4" wide, 2-3/4" high	75	150	175
Country Produce Pickup, No. 4500, 7-1/4" long, 3-1/4" wide, 2-3/4" high	75	125	175
Courtland Mechanical Side Tipper Tractor-Trailer, No. 3900, "Black Diamond Coal Company- 340," 13" long, 3" high, 3-1/4" wide	150	250	325
Express Service Pickup, No. 4500 7-1/4" long, 3-1/4" wide, 2-3/4" high	75	125	175
Fire Chief Car, No. 4000, red and white, 7-1/4" long, 3-1/4" wide, 2-3/4" high..............................	75	100	125
Fire Chief Car, No. 4000, red, 7-1/4" long, 3-1/4" wide, 2-3/4" high.......	100	125	150
Fire Department with automatic garage door, No. 9050, 7-3/4" x 10-1/8" x 6-3/4"; found to have a non-powered fire chief car w/the Courtland Toy Co., Phila. PA, markings, it is quite possible that some of the 9050 garages were also manufactured in Philadelphia .	45	55	75

	C6	C8	C10
Mechanical Automatic Ladder Fire Truck, No. 1400, 1947, 9" long, 3" wide, 2-3/4" high	175	250	350
Mechanical Big Four Truck Parade, No. 1070, 1947, 9" long, 3" wide, 2-3/4" high	NPF	NPF	NPF
Mechanical Black Diamond Coal Truck, No. 5100, 10-1/2" long, 3" wide, 3-3/8" high	150	225	300

Courtland Mechanical Black Diamond Coal Truck, 10-1/2". Photo from Joe and Sharon Freed.

Courtland Fire Chief Car, red and white, 7-1/4".

Courtland Checker Cab Car, green and yellow, 7-1/4".

Courtland City Meat Market Delivery Sedan, without motor, 7-1/4".

Courtland Fire Department with automatic garage door, non-powered fire chief car.

Courtland Mechanical Caterpillar Tractor with rubber treads, 6". Photo from Joe and Sharon Freed.

Courtland Chrome Trimmed Tow Truck, Walt's Garage, 8".

Courtland Excavating Mechanical Combination Steam Shovel carried by low-boy tractor-trailer, 15-1/2". Photo from Joe and Sharon Freed.

	C6	C8	C10
Mechanical Caterpillar Tractor w/rubber treads, No. 6100, 6" long, 3" wide, 4-1/2" high	250	350	450
Mechanical Chromed Trimmed Tow Truck, No. 8500, tow boom is solid color, 8" long, 3-1/4" wide, 3-1/2" high...................................	175	300	350
Mechanical Chromed Trimmed Tow Truck, No. 8500, tow boom shows detail, 8" long, 3-1/4" wide, 3-1/2" high...................................	75	175	225
Mechanical Combination Steam Shovel, No. 5300, carried by low-boy tractor-trailer, 15-1/2" long, 3-7/8" wide, 10-1/2" high..............	350	550	775
Mechanical Dump Truck, No. 3100, 7" long, 3" wide, 3-1/4" high.........	65	100	135
Mechanical Dump Truck, No. 1600, 7" long, 3" wide, 2-3/4" high.........	65	100	135

Top to bottom: Courtland Mechanical Dump Truck, 7" green, yellow, red; Mechanical Dump Truck, red, 7".

	C6	C8	C10
Mechanical Emergency Rescue Squad Tractor-Trailer, No. 2150, 13" long, 3" wide, 3-1/4" high.......	150	200	250
Mechanical ESSO Gasoline Tractor-Trailer, No. 2000, 13" long, 3" wide, 3-1/4" high	250	350	450
Mechanical Express and Hauling Truck, No. 1300, 1947, 9" long, 3" wide, 2-3/4" high	125	200	275

Courtland Mechanical Dump Truck, 7".

Courtland Mechanical Emergency Rescue Squad Tractor-Trailer, 13".

Courtland Mechanical Farm Tractor, 7-1/2".

Courtland Mecanical Fire Chief Car, with siren, 7-1/4". Photo from Joe and Sharon Freed.

	C6	C8	C10
Mechanical Farm Tractor w/o scraper, No. 6050, rear tires are large rubber and front are small rubber tires, 7-1/2" long, 4-3/4" wide, 4-1/2" high	75	100	150
Mechanical Farm Tractor w/o scraper, No. 6075, rear tires are large tin lithographed while the front are small rubber tires, 7-1/2" long, 4-3/4" wide, 4-1/2" high	250	350	450
Mechanical Farm Tractor w/scraper, No. 6000, rear tires are large rubber and front are small rubber tires, 8-3/4" long, 4-3/4" wide, 4-1/2" high..................................	100	150	200
Mechanical Fire Chief Car w/siren, No. 7000, 7-1/4" long, 3-1/4" wide, 2-3/4" high	125	175	225

	C6	C8	C10
Mechanical Fire Patrol No. 2 Truck, No. 1300, 1947, 9" long, 3" wide, 2-3/4" high	125	200	275
Mechanical Freight Haulers Tractor-Trailer, No. 2600, 13" long, 3" high, 3-1/4" wide	150	250	325
Mechanical Gasoline Tractor-Trailer, No. 2000, 13" long, 3" wide, 3-1/4" high	150	250	325
Mechanical Heavy Duty Sand and Gravel Tractor-Trailer, No. 2375, 13" long, 3" wide, 3-1/4" high.......	175	225	275
Mechanical Hook and Ladder Tractor-Trailer, No. 2100, 13" long, 3" wide, 3-1/4" high	100	150	175
Mechanical Ice Cream Scooter, No. 6500, 6-1/2" long, 3" wide, 4-1/2" high...	200	300	400

	C6	C8	C10		C6	C8	C10

Mechanical Ice Cream Truck, No. 1300, 9" long, 3" wide, 2-3/4" high — 150 200 250

Mechanical Logging Tractor-Trailer, No. 2200, 13" long, 3" wide, 3-1/4" high.................. 150 200 250

Mechanical Milk Tractor-Trailer, No. 2050, "American Dairies", 13" long, 3" wide, 3-1/4" high. Note: 1951 catalog shows Milk Trailer markings that read the same as above except "Approved" is used in the place of the words "Vitamin D." This variation is not known to have been produced. 150 250 325

Mechanical Moving and Storage Truck, w/No. 130 lithographed on the sides of the truck bed 175 250 375

Mechanical Moving and Storage Truck, No. 1300, 1947, 9" long, 3" wide, 2-3/4" high 175 250 375

Mechanical No. 51 Steam Shovel, No. 5200, 15-1/2" long, 3-3/4" wide, 9-1/2" high 135 185 235

Mechanical Open Van Tractor-Trailer, No. 2350, 13" long, 3" wide, 3-1/4" high 75 125 175

Courtland Mechanical Hook and Ladder Tractor-Trailer, 13".

Courtland Mechanical Ice Cream Truck, 9". Photo from Bob Smith.

Courtland Mechanical Gasoline Tractor-Trailer, 13".

Courtland Mechanical Heavy Duty Sand and Gravel Tractor-Trailer, 13".

Left to right: Courtland Fire Patrol No. 2 Truck, 9"; Moving and Storage Truck, 9".

Courtland Mechanical Logging Tractor-Trailer, 13".

Courtland Mechanical Milk Tractor-Trailer, American Dairies, 13".

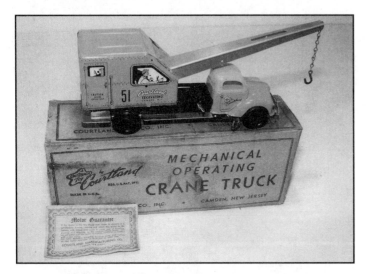

Courtland Mechanical Operation Crane Truck, 13". Photo from Bob Smith.

Courtland Mechanical Open Van Tractor-Trailer, 13".

Courtland Mechanical Side Tipper Tractor Trailer, 13".

Courtland Mechanical Road Roller Truck, 9".

	C6	C8	C10
Mechanical Open Van Tractor-Trailer, No. 2300, 13" long, 3" wide, 3-1/4" high	75	125	175
Mechanical Operation, No. 5000, No. 51 Crane Truck, 13" long, 3-5/8" wide, 5" high	225	325	400
Mechanical Road Roller Truck, No. 3000 9" long, 3" wide, 3-1/4" high	250	350	450

	C6	C8	C10
Mechanical Road Roller Truck, No. 1500, 9" long, 3" wide, 3-1/4" high	250	350	450
Mechanical Side Tipper Tractor-Trailer, No. 2700, 13" long, 3" high, 3-1/4" wide	200	300	375

Courtland Modern Bakery Delivery Sedan, 7-1/4".

Courtland No. 500 Mechanical Truck Set, box, four trucks. Photo from Joe and Sharon Freed.

	C6	C8	C10
Mechanical Stake Bed Truck, No. 3200, 7" long, 3" wide, 3-1/4" high	125	150	175
Mechanical State Police Car w/siren, No. 7500, 7-1/4" long, 3-1/4" wide, 2-3/4" high	150	200	250
Mechanical Trailer Tow Truck, No. 2400, 13" long, 3" wide, 3-1/4" high	225	300	375
Mechanical Trailer-Truck, No. 1200, 1947, 13" long, 3" wide, 3-1/4" high	200	250	375

	C6	C8	C10
Mechanical Truck Set, No. 500, w/box, four trucks, assorted, Nos. 2000, 2100, 2200, 2300	150	300	600
Modern Bakery Delivery Sedan, No. 4000, 7-1/4" long, 3-1/4" wide, 2-3/4" high	75	150	175
Modern Decorators Pickup, No. 4500, 7-1/4" long, 3-1/4" wide, 2-3/4" high	75	125	175
Private Garage w/automatic door, No. 9075, 7-3/4" x 10-1/8" x 6-3/4". Since the non-powered car which accompanies this garage is found w/Courtland Toy Co., Phila. PA markings, it is quite possible that some of the 9075 garages were also manufactured	50	75	100
Traffic Signal, No. 7800, battery-powered	275	400	550
Trucking Terminal Set, No. 600, two trucks, w/box	450	750	1100

CRAFTOYS

Craftoys, a small Omaha, Nebraska, firm, had a brief career casting slush-mold vehicles before World War II when the need for lead brought the potmetal era to a long halt. Craftoys acquired some of the molds when Ralstoy was reorganizing in 1940.

Contributor: Fred Maxwell, 4722 N. 33 St., Arlington, VA 22207. **Perry R. Eichor,** 703 North Almond Drive, Simpsonville, SC, 29681.

	C6	C8	C10
Cement Mixer, No. 78, two open windows, marked "Made in USA," 3-3/4" long	20	40	60

	C6	C8	C10
Fire Truck, No. 101, Hose Truck or Insurance Patrol, four open windows, 4-1/2" long	40	60	80

No. 102--Gasoline Transport
S. P. 25¢
Size 6¾ inches
Packed ½ Doz. to Ctn.
Doz. Wgt. 4 lbs.
Color--Cab, Blue; Truck, Red

No. 105--Station Wagon
S. P. 10¢
Size 3⅜ inches
Packed 1 Doz. to Ctn.
Doz. Wgt. 2¼ lbs.
Color--Red

No. 100--Racer with
removable Hood
S. P. 10¢
Size 4¼ inches
Packed 1 Doz. to Ctn.
Doz. Wgt. 2 lbs.
Color--Hood, Red;
Body, Aluminum

No. 104--Oil Truck
S. P. 10¢
Size 3¾ inches
Packed 1 Doz. to Ctn.
Doz. Wgt. 2¼ lbs.
Color--Red

Craftoys Inc.

Factory
2230 South 16th Street
Omaha 9, Nebraska

Executive Office
417 Omaha Loan Building
Omaha 2, Nebraska

No. 92--Sedan
S. P. 10¢
Size 4 inches
Packed 1 Doz. to Ctn.
Doz. Wgt. 2 lbs.
Color--Red

No. 101--Fire Truck
S. P. 10¢
Size 4½ inches
Packed 1 Doz. to Ctn.
Doz. Wgt. 2¼ lbs.
Color--Red

No. 17--Tractor
S. P. 10¢
Size 2½ inches
Packed 1 Doz. to Ctn.
Doz. Wgt. 2¼ lbs.
Color--Red

No. 103--Speed Car
S. P. 10¢
Size 4¼ inches
Packed 1 Doz. to Ctn.
Doz. Wgt. 2¼ lbs.
Color--Red

No. 78--Cement Mixer
S. P. 10¢
Size 3¾ inches
Packed 1 Doz. to Ctn.
Doz. Wgt. 2 1/3 lbs.
Color--Blue

No. 81--Racer
S. P. 10¢
Size 4½ inches
Packed 1 Doz. to Ctn.
Doz. Wgt. 2 lbs.
Color--Aluminum

No. 3600--Freight Train (5 Pcs.)
S. P. 49¢
Size 16½ inches
Packed 1 Doz. to Ctn.
Doz. Wgt. 8 lbs.

Colors--Locomotive, Aluminum
Coal Car, Black
Stock Car, Blue
Tank Car, Green
Caboose, Red

TERMS: 2% ten days, net 30 days, F.O.B. Omaha, Nebraska

An original Craftoys flyer.

Collectors Note

- No. 92 sedan has the same number as a Best Toy coupe, but they are not the same car.
- No. 100 racer is not the same as the Best Toy No. 100 sedan.
- Second-hand Kansas Toy molds were used for No.78 mixer, No. 81 racer, No. 102 gasoline semi-tanker, No. 101 fire truck, No. 103 speed car, No. 104 oil truck and No. 105 station wagon, possibly come from Ralstoy.
- The ancestry of Kansas toy is evident in No. 17 tractor and the freight-train set. The designs of the RR coal car, stockcar and tank car were changed
- These catalog numbers may or may not be found on the toys. Black rubber wheels are seen to be characteristic of this line, but they are not exclusive with Craftoy.

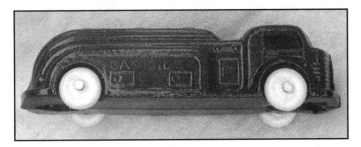

Craftoy Oil Truck, No. 104, tanker, two open windows, 3-3/4". Photo from Fred Maxwell.

Top to bottom: Craftoy Racer, No. 100, Indy type, driver, removable tin hood, rounded nose, 4-1/4"; Racer, slanted nose, tin hood, 3-3/4". Photo from Perry Eichor.

Craftoy Speed Car, No. 103, streamlined, closed racer, 4-1/4". Photo from Perry Eichor.

Craftoy Tanker, No. 103, semi-trailer, two open windows, 6-3/4". Photo from Ferd Zegel.

	C6	C8	C10
Oil Truck, No. 104, 1938 International (?), COE, two open windows, marked "Gas," "Oil" tanker, 3-3/4"	45	70	80
Racer, no number, Indy type, driver, removable tin hood, slanted nose, available as a reproduction, 3-3/ 4" long..............................	30	40	60
Racer, No. 100, Indy type, driver, removable tin hood, rounded nose available as a reproduction, 4-1/ 4" long.................................	35	50	70
Racer, No. 81, Miller FWD Indy racer, marked "Made in USA", 4-1/2"	20	40	60
Sedan, No. 92, streamlined two-door sedan, four open windows, screen pattern grille, 4" long	20	40	60

	C6	C8	C10
Speed Car, No. 103, streamlined closed racer, body trimmed in fantasy streamlines, available as a reproduction, 4-1/4" long, ...	45	70	85
Station Wagon, No. 105, streamlined, four open windows, 3-3/4" long	NPF	NPF	NPF
Tanker, No. 102, 1938, International K-Line (?), semi-trailer, two open windows, "Gasoline," See Ralstoy, 6-3/4" long	40	60	80
Tractor, No. 17, w/driver, rear wheels larger, visible engine; marked "Fordson" and "Made in USA"; 2-1/2" long........................	15	30	45

DAYTON FRICTION TOY WORKS

See David P. Clark history.

	C6	C8	C10
Armored Car, flywheel drive, sheet metal construction, red and gold, c.1909, 11" long	250	450	600
Bus, 1920s	350	525	700
Coal and Ice Truck, tin friction, c.1920	250	450	600
Coupe, pressed steel, 1928, 12" long	175	250	450
Coupe, c.1920, 12-1/2" long	400	550	800
Coupe, tin friction, 17" long	500	650	900
Dayton Friction, pressed steel, rubber tires, 1920s, 14-1/2" long..	250	400	550
Delivery Van, friction	250	400	550
Dump Truck.....................................	375	550	750
Fire Ladder Truck, friction, 22" long .	250	350	550

	C6	C8	C10
Fire Ladder Truck, 18" long..............	200	350	550
Fire Pumper Truck, flywheel drive, sheet metal construction, white/gold, c.1909, 14-3/4" long ..	450	600	800
Friction Car, 1914	NPF	NPF	NPF
Roadster, 14" long	200	300	400
Seven-Passenger Touring Car, flywheel drive, sheet metal contstruction, red and gold, patent date April 2, 1909, 13-1/4" long...	150	225	300
Stake Truck.....................................	300	450	600
Touring Car, unpowered, 13-1/2" long...	300	450	600

Dayton Fire Pumper Truck, white and gold, circa 1909, 14-3/4".

Dayton Armored Car, circa 1909, 11". Photo from Bob Smith.

Dayton Coupe, tin, friction, 17".

Dayton Seven-Passenger Touring Car, circa 1909, 13-1/4".

DENT HARDWARE COMPANY

Dent, of Fullerton, Pennsylvania, was in business from 1895-1973. Henry H. Dent, with four partners, was the owner. Dent is known for particularly fine castings in its vehicles. It was also one of the first manufacturers to try (with little success) aluminum toys (in the 1920s). Toys seem to have been phased out during the Depression. Dent toys are difficult to identify due to the fact that few, if any, of its toys are marked.

	C6	C8	C10
American Oil Co. Truck, cast iron, approx. 10-1/2" long....................	800	1250	1750
American Oil Truck, 15" long	1200	2000	300
Breyer's Ice Cream Truck, removable doors, 1932, 8-1/2" long	700	1150	1700

	C6	C8	C10
Bus, cast iron, 6-1/4" long	350	500	750
Bus, 10-1/2" long.............................	500	850	900
Bus Line, 9" long	450	600	1250
Coast to Coast Bus, 7-1/2" long.......	125	175	275
Coast to Coast Bus, 10" long	300	450	650
Coast to Coast Bus, c.1925, 15" long..	700	1000	1600
Contractors Mack Dump Truck, open cab, 10-1/2" long.................	1000	2000	3000
Convertible......................................	400	700	1000
Coupe, 5" long	125	175	250
Dump Truck, C-cab, 15-1/4"	800	1250	2000

Dent "American Oil Co.," cast-iron, 10-1/2".

Dent "American Oil" Truck, 15". Photo from Bill Bertoia Auctions.

Dent "Breyer's Ice Cream," removable doors, 1932, 8-1/2". Photo from Bill Bertoia Auctions.

Left to Right: Pattern for Dent "Coast to Coast" Bus, circa 1925, 15"; "Public Service" Bus, circa 1926, 13-1/2"; brass pattern for "Public Service" Bus. Photo from Bill Bertoia Auctions.

DENT TOYS

FIRE ENGINE

Number 290 finished in bright red with bronze trimmings. Equipped with solid rubber balloon wheels, red hubs.

IRON TOYS

No. 290R   Length 8½″   Height 4¾″
Packed Per Box 1 Doz. Per Case 3 Wt. Per Case 77 lbs.

Retailing at $ .50 each

FIRE CHIEF

Finished in bright red bronze trimmings, equipped with solid rubber balloon wheels, red hubs.

IRON TOY

No. 693R   Length 5½″   Height 2¾″
Packed Per Box 6   Doz. Per Case 6   Wt. Per Case 66 lbs.

Retailing at $.25 each

MOTOR FIRE TRUCK

A brand new snappy model, painted in bright red, equipped with solid rubber balloon wheels, red hubs.

IRON TOY

No. 692R   Length 6″   Height 2¾″
Packed Per Box 6   Doz. Per Case 6   Wt. Per Case 64 lbs.

Retailing at $ .25 each

FIRE ENGINE

Painted in bright red, with solid rubber balloon type wheels, red hubs.

IRON TOYS

No. 680R   Length 6½″   Height 3⅝″
Packed Per Box 6 Doz. Per Case 6 Wt. Per Case 74 lbs.

Retailing at $ .25 each

Another page from a 1932 Dent catalog shows a pair of Fire Engines, a Fire Chief car and a Motor Fire Truck.

DENT TOYS

LADDER TRUCK

Finished in bright red with gilt trimmings, with two 6" iron ladders on blue racks. Equipped with solid balloon type rubber wheels, red hubs.

IRON TOYS

No. 299R   Length 9¼"   Height 4¼"

Packed Per Box 1 Doz.Per Case 3 Wt.Per Case 81 lbs.

Retailing at $ .50 each

HOOK AND LADDER

Finished in bright red with ladders attached, with solid rubber balloon type rubber wheels, red hubs.

IRON TOYS

No. 679R   Length 7"   Height 3¼"

Packed Per Box 6 Doz.Per Case 6 Wt.Per Case 78 lbs.

Retailing at $ .25 each

HOOK AND LADDER

No. 291, finished in bright red with bronze trimmings, equipped with two 10" wooden ladders painted yellow. Equipped with solid rubber balloon wheels, red hubs.

IRON TOYS

No. 291R   Length 12½"   Height 4⅜"

Packed Per Box 1 Doz.Per Case 3 Wt.Per Case 90 lbs.

Retailing at $ .50 each

STEAM ROLLER

No. 717, a correct reproduction of steam road roller with moving piston rods.

No. 718 smaller size of same model except no movable piston rod. Finished in bright colors.

No. 717   Length 7"   Height 4"
Packed Per Box 1 Doz.Per Case 3 Wt.Per Case 42 lbs.

Retailing at $ .50 each

No. 718   Length 5"   Height 3"
Packed Per Box 1 Doz.Per Case 6 Wt.Per Case 38 lbs.

Retailing at $ .25 each

A Dent catalog from 1932 depicts a Ladder Truck, a pair of Hook and Ladder Trucks and a Steam Roller.

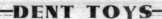

MACK CONTRACTOR'S TRUCK

No. 688 equipped with three buckets, mechanically operated, finished in bright red, gilt trimmings; black enameled top. Solid rubber balloon wheels, red hubs.

No. 707 equipped with two dumping buckets. Packed assorted red and green bodies. Solid rubber wheels, red hubs.

IRON TOYS

No.	Length	Height	Packed Per Box	Doz. Per Case	Wt. Per Case	Retailing at
688R	10¾″	4¼″	1	1	26 lbs.	$1.00 each
707R	7½″	3″	1	3	75 lbs.	$ .50 each

REO SPEED WAGON

A very up-to-date model, in bright finish, assorted colors in a box, solid rubber balloon wheels, red hubs.

IRON TOYS

Number 631R   Length 6¼″   Height 2¾″
Packed Per Box 6   Doz. Per Case 6   Wt. Per Case 88 lbs.
Retailing at $ .25 each

MACK EXPRESS VAN

Finished in bright red color. Equipped with solid balloon type rubber wheels, red hubs.

IRON TOYS

No. 685R   Length 6¼″   Height 2⅞″
Packed Per Box 6   Doz. Per Case 6   Wt. Per Case 92 lbs.
Retailing at $ .25 each

DUMP TRUCK

Painted in bright red with bronze trimmings, dump body, and drivers cab. Equipped with balloon type rubber wheels, red hubs.

IRON TOYS

No.	Length	Height	Packed Per Box	Doz. Per Case	Wt. Per Case	Retailing at
637R	8¼″	3¼″	1	3	68 lbs.	$ .50 each

Mack trucks from Dent. The 1932 catalog shows a Dump Truck; Express Van; Contractors Truck; and REO Speed Wagon.

Dent "New York-Chicago" Bus, 10-1/4". Photo from Bill Bertoia Auctions.

Dent "Police Patrol," 8-3/4".

Dent "Pioneer" Fire Ladder Truck, driver, 13-1/4". Photo from Bill Bertoia Auctions.

Dent "Public Service" Bus, 1920s, 13-1/2". Photo from Bill Bertoia Auctions.

	C6	C8	C10
Express J&B Stakebed Truck, driver, 1915, 14-1/2"	500	800	1250
Fire Ladder Truck, w/driver, 8-1/2" long	400	625	925
Fire Pumper, normal-sized driver, hose, 11" long	450	800	1250
Fire Pumper, tiny driver, early, 11" long	600	1100	1750
Fire Truck, cast iron, 7" long	125	200	325
Fire Truck, w/ladder and men, cast iron, 18" long	800	1250	1900
Fordson Tractor	200	350	525
Freemen's Dairy Truck, sliding doors, milkman, 6"	650	1150	1750
Hose Reeler, w/men, cast iron, large	450	700	1100
Ice Truck, 6" long	150	225	350
Ice Truck, 10" long	400	625	1000
Interburban bus, cast iron, 9" long	225	350	550
Interburban bus, cast iron, 10-1/2" long	400	700	1100
La Salle, 4-1/4" long	425	700	975
La Salle Panel Truck	425	700	975

	C6	C8	C10
Ladder Truck, two drivers, 10" long .	225	350	550
Ladder Truck, 12" long	275	425	625
Mack Cement Truck, extremely rare, 11-1/4" long	10,000	20,000	45,000
Mack Dump Truck, iron wheels, c.1925, 4-1/2" long	50	75	125
Mack Express State Truck	1500	2500	4400
Mack Express Van	2000	4500	9900
Mack Tank Truck	1500	2500	3960
Model T Sedan, two door, iron wheels, c.1925	125	175	275
New York-Chicago Bus, 10-1/4" long	350	550	800
Patrol, 6-1/2" long	125	175	275
Phantom, driver	160	250	350
Pioneer Fire Ladder Truck, driver, 13-1/4" long	1200	2000	3250
Police Patrol, 8-3/4" long	700	1125	1650
Public Service Bus, c.1926, 13-1/2" long	1750	3000	4750
Road Roller, 4-1/2"	70	100	160
Road Sweeper	1200	2000	3700

	C6	C8	C10
Runabout, driver, tiller, 6" long........	200	350	475
Sedan, 1920s, 4-1/2" long................	80	140	220
Sedan, spare tire, has stop and go light, full bumpers on front, 7-1/2" long	800	1250	1800
Sedan, 1920s, 7-1/2" long................	400	600	850
Stake Truck, driver, four tin milk cans, 15-1/2" long	2000	3600	5500
Steam Roller, cast iron, 6" long........	40	70	90
Touring Car, passengers, driver, 9-1/4" long.................................	500	800	1200
Touring Car, driver and passenger, 12" long......................................	450	700	1100
Truck, marked "Junior Supply Co. New York Philadelphia," c.1923, 16" long..	2000	2500	5250
Valley View Dairy, 8" long	500	900	1500
Yellow Cab, approx. 7-3/4" long........	800	1250	1800

Dent Road Sweeper. Photo from Bill Bertoia Auctions.

Dent Junior Supply Co. "New York-Philadelphia," 1920s, 16".

Dent Road Roller, 4-1/2". Photo from Bill Bertoia Auctions.

Another look at the Dent Junior Supply Co. "New York-Philadelphia" truck.

Left to Right: Dent Touring Car, driver, passengers, 9-1/4"; Touring Car, driver and passenger, 12". Photo from Bill Bertoia Auctions.

DINKY

When Dinky Toys were first issued in 1933, they were intended to add a touch of realism to the Hornby train models. The first offering to the public was a set of six small accessories referred to as Model Miniatures and were commonly known as the 22 Series.

The year 1937 saw the introduction of what developed into the finest range of mass-market die-cast military toys ever produced until the birth of Solido. And 1938 saw further consolidation of the vehicle range, which by then contained almost three varieties. During World War II, the Dinky operations were interrupted by the war effort. One of the few new or adapted models during this period was a replica of a petrol tanker painted gray with the word "pool" in white on its sides. The unfortunate part of this period was that many of the toy dies were lost during the equipment shuffling to make room for the wartime production. Christmas 1945 saw production get underway again, and some fifty different toy models went out to the retailers for sale to the public. The hopes for a quick return to the prewar status quo were, however, not to be fulfilled, as metal alloys were put to priority use for much-needed domestic products, and to feed the giant export projects on which the British economy now depended for its survival.

However, by 1952 the postwar boom was gathering momentum as railway accessories and model planes were re-introduced. New products flowed from the design studios to the production lines until finally, in 1954, the production of the first new group of army vehicles arrived on the scene. Also, one of the most significant events of that year for future collectors was the renumbering of all models. The suffix system was no longer manageable, and a lock-number system was allocated to types of vehicles. The larger-scale "Super Dinky Toys" in blue striped boxes with a white background were also introduced in the mid-1950s. It was 1958 before Dinky replied to the challenge of domestic competition from Corgi, which entered the market in 1956, by fitting special features to their models. Pausing for a breath from the introduction of gimmicks to keep abreast of their competition, in 1961, the company produced twenty or so new models and changed over from plain to tread tires on all their vehicles (although military models had them since the mid 1950s).

In June 1969, the company again made a significant change in this vehicle products to attempt to stay with the competition—the introduction of speed wheels, which were eventually to become standard on everything. Six years earlier, after the takeover by Lines Bros., the name of the firm was changed to "Meccano-Triang Ltd." A bad omen, for, in 1971, after a general recession in the toy trade, the company's bank loans were recalled and the whole of the Lines Group went into liquidation. The Meccano assets were transferred to a new company, Maoford, Ltd., which was subsequently named "Meccano (1971) Ltd." New toys were desperately needed. In 1972, the company went into the kit business for the first time.

But by now, the hand of doom was resting on production and even the introduction of space toys would not delay the inevitable, as the Binns Road factory was effectively closed on November 30, 1979. The closure did not save the parent company, which was also having difficulty in the American market. Although Dinky Toy continued to be produced elsewhere for several years, the eventual low labor cost and success of mass-plastic extrusion manufacturing from the Asian export market was the real culprit behind the demise of one of the English-speaking world's finest toy manufacturers, who, in its heyday, produced about three thousand varieties of transportation toys during a marvelous history of almost fifty years in England, France and India.

Dinky B.E.V. Truck, No. 14A/400, 1954-1960.

	C6	C8	C10
No. 014A/400 B.E.V. Truck, 1954-60	30	45	70
No. 014C Coventry Fork Lift	35	75	100
No. 022A Maserati Sport 2000	55	110	150
No. 022F Tank, gray or orange, 1933	75	150	200
No. 022S Search Light Lorry, 1935/41, six to a box	150	250	350
No. 023 J H.W.M. Racer	55	110	150

Condition

The following is a guide for those with items in less than Mint in Box (C10), Near Mint with Box (C8) and Excellent with Box (C6) condition.

- **Near Mint, without box.** Some rust, no scratches, all decals in place, deduct thirty percent from C10 value.
- **Very Good with box.** Some rust, scratched, all decals, no paint missing, deduct forty-five percent from the C10 value.
- **Very Good without box.** Some rust, scratches, no missing parts or paint, deduct fifty-five percent from the C10 value.
- **Good without box.** Rust, paint chipped, decals partially missing, no missing parts, deduct sixty percent from the C10
- **Fair without box.** Rusted wheels axle and base, scratches, chipped, missing paint, decals gone, missing tires or chains, but not broken, paint still good for the purpose of reconditioning; deduct fifty to sixty percent from the C10 value.

Items with broken or missing components or with pieces having less than forty percent of the original paint gone have no real value to the collector, unless reconditioned, and then they should only bring fifty percent of the C6 value. In addition, it should also be noted that boxes can bring $3 to $50, depending on age and condition

Note: Early military Dinky, except for boxed sets were sold in yellow boxes with black lettering, six or twelve pieces to the box. It should also be noted that prewar items differed from reissue as follows—prewar, smooth hub caps; post-war, rimmed hub caps.

	C6	C8	C10
No. 023G Cooper Bristol Racing Car	55	110	150
No. 023H Ferrari Racer	35	75	100
No. 024A New Yorker Convertible	65	130	175
No. 024B Peugeot	55	110	150
No. 024C Citroën DS19	65	132	180
No. 024H Mercedes 190SL	50	100	130

	C6	C8	C10
No. 024L 2CV Vespa	75	150	200
No. 024M Willy's Jeep, 1946/49, French	100	200	300
No. 024V Simca 9 Arnode	55	110	150
No. 024X Ford Vedette	65	130	165
No. 024Y Studebaker	45	95	125
No. 025 Ford Zodiac Police Car	40	55	85
No. 025M Bedford Tipper	40	80	100
No. 025V Bedford Refuse Truck	45	85	110
No. 027 Motorcart	55	110	150
No. 027F 1948 Plymouth Station Wagon	75	150	200
No. 030A Chrysler Airflow	85	150	250

Dinky Search Light Lorry, No. 22S, 1935-1941.

Dinky Chrysler Airflow, No. 30A.

Rolls Royce, No. 30B, 1946-50.

Top row, left to right: French Dinky AMX 13 Char Tank, No. 80C, 1958-1967; AMEX Self Propelled Gun, No. 813, 1965. Bottom: Panhard EBR Tank in box, No. 80A, 1957-1963.

Top to bottom: French Dinky Berliet Army Truck, No. 80D/818 1958-1967; 155mm Fieldgun, No. 80E/819, 1973-1977.

	C6	C8	C10
No. 030B Rolls Royce, 1946-50.......	45	95	125
No. 030E Breakdown Lorry..............	NPF	NPF	NPF
No. 033 AN Simca Bailly..................	55	110	150
No. 033 Simca Glass Truck	65	132	185
No. 034B Royal Mail	40	55	90
No. 036A Log Lorry	75	150	205
No. 036F British Salmson	45	90	120
No. 036F Taxi..................................	45	90	120
No. 037C Dispatch Rider RCS, 1938/41	25	40	70
No. 039A Unic Auto Transporter......	100	200	310
No. 039E Chrysler Royal..................	150	300	675
No. 042A Police Box	40	55	90
No. 044AA Motorcycle Patrol & Sidecar........................	40	50	80
No. 060Y Fuel Tender......................	100	200	400

	C6	C8	C10
No. 061 Ford Perfect.......................	40	50	80
No. 062 Singer Roadster	40	50	80
No. 064 Austin Lorry	40	55	90
No. 066 Bedford Flat Truck.............	45	85	110
No. 071 Dublo Volks Van.................	45	90	120
No. 073 Dublo Range Rover and Horse Trailer............................	45	95	125
No. 080A Panhard EBR Tank, 1957/63, French	45	55	95
No. 080B Willys Hotchkiss Jeep, 1957/60, French	45	55	95
No. 080BP Willys Hotchkiss Jeep, 1958/63, French	40	80	100
No. 080C AMX13 Char Tank, 1958/67, French	40	80	100
No. 080D Berliet 6x6 Truck, 1958/67, French	45	95	125
No. 080E 155mm. Fieldgun, 1958/67, French	40	80	105
No. 080F Renault Ambulance, 1959/67, French	40	50	80
No. 101 Sunbeam Alpine Sports Car	90	125	225
No. 103 Austin-Healey 100 Sports Car..	85	150	250
No. 103 Spectrum Patrol.................	80	125	220
No. 104 Spectrum Pursuit Vehicle ...	100	200	300
No. 105 Triumph TR2	95	125	225

	C6	C8	C10
No. 106 Austin Atlantic Convertible..	40	80	100
No. 106 The Prisoner Mini Moke......	45	85	105
No. 106 Thunderbird 2	45	95	125
No. 107 Sunbeam Alpine	45	95	125
No. 108 Sam's Car..........................	65	130	165
No. 110 Aston Martin	60	120	160
No. 111 Triumph TR2 Competition ..	80	125	225
No. 112 Purdy's TR7	40	55	85
No. 113 MGB	40	80	100
No. 120 Jaguar XKE	40	85	135
No. 122 Volvo 265..........................	10	15	25
No. 123 Princess 2200 HL Saloon ...	15	20	40
No. 124 Rolls Royce Phantom V......	40	50	82
No. 127 Rolls Royce Phantom V......	15	30	45
No. 128 Mercedes Benz 600...........	25	35	55
No. 129 VW Bug	45	55	95
No. 130 Ford Consul Corsair	40	55	90
No. 131 Cadillac Tourer	40	80	100
No. 131 Jaguar Type E 2 + 2	40	80	100
No. 131 Jaguar Type G...................	40	80	100
No. 132 Ford 40-RV	30	45	70
No. 132 Packard Convertible	65	130	190

	C6	C8	C10
No. 134 Triumph Vitesse	30	42	65
No. 138 Hillman Imp	30	42	65
No. 139A 1949 Ford Sedan	30	40	60
No. 140 Morris 1100	30	45	75
No. 1406 Sinpar 4x4 Military Police, 1977, French	30	45	75
No. 141 Vauxhall Victor	40	80	100
No. 142 Jaguar Mark X	40	55	85
No. 143 Ford Capri	45	90	120
No. 144 VW 1500...........................	40	55	90
No. 146 Daimler 2-1/2 litre V8.........	45	55	95
No. 148 Ford Fairlane	45	85	110
No. 149 Citroen Dyane	15	30	45
No. 150 Rolls Royce Silver Wraith...	45	55	95
No. 150 Royal Tank Corp. Personnel Set, 150 a, b, c, d; 1937/41, six pieces	45	90	120
No. 150A Royal Tank Corp Officer, 1937/41.................................	10	15	20
No. 150B Royal Tank Corp Private, seated, 1937/41..........................	15	20	25
No. 150C Royal Tank Corp NCO, 1937/41.................................	10	20	30
No. 150D Royal Tank Corp Driver, seated, 1937/41..........................	10	15	20
No. 151 Royal Tank Corp. Medium Set, 151 a, b, c, d; 1937/41, four pieces	100	200	300
No. 151 Triumph 1800 Saloon	40	55	90

Top to bottom: French Dinky 155mm Field gun, No. 80E, 1958-1967; Berliet Gazelle Truck, No. 824, 1963.

Dinky Transport Wagon, No. 151B, 1937-1941.

Dinky Medium Tank, with markings, No. 151A.

Dinky Light Tank, No. 152A, 1950s, reissued.

Dinky Medium Tank, without markings, No. 151A, 1930s-1940s.

Dinky Reconnaissance Car reissue, No. 152B, 1950s.

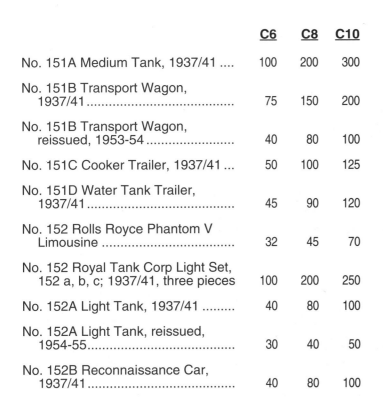

Dinky Austin Staff Car, No. 152C, 1937-1941.

	C6	C8	C10
No. 151A Medium Tank, 1937/41	100	200	300
No. 151B Transport Wagon, 1937/41	75	150	200
No. 151B Transport Wagon, reissued, 1953-54	40	80	100
No. 151C Cooker Trailer, 1937/41 ...	50	100	125
No. 151D Water Tank Trailer, 1937/41	45	90	120
No. 152 Rolls Royce Phantom V Limousine	32	45	70
No. 152 Royal Tank Corp Light Set, 152 a, b, c; 1937/41, three pieces	100	200	250
No. 152A Light Tank, 1937/41	40	80	100
No. 152A Light Tank, reissued, 1954-55	30	40	50
No. 152B Reconnaissance Car, 1937/41	40	80	100

	C6	C8	C10
No. 152B Reconnaissance Car, reissued, 1954-55	40	50	75
No. 152C Austin Staff Car, 1937/41.	75	100	125
No. 153A U.S. Jeep White Star, 1954/55	40	80	100

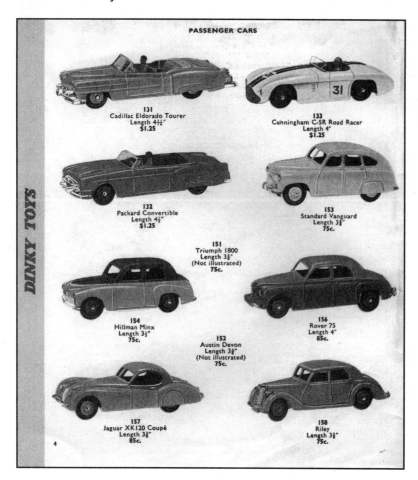

A selection of Dinky passenger cars from a Dinky Toys catalog.

Page 5 of a Dinky Toys catalog shows more Dinky passenger cars.

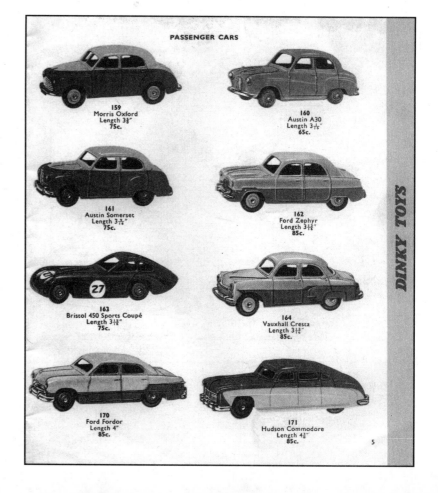

	C6	C8	C10
No. 155 Ford	40	50	80
No. 156 Mechanized Army Set, includes 151 a, b, c, d; 152, a, b, c; 161 a, b; 162, a, b, c, 1937/41, twelve pieces	200	1000	1500
No. 156 Rover 75	55	110	150
No. 156 Saab 96	55	90	135
No. 157 BMW 2000 Tilux	25	35	50
No. 157 Jaguar XK120	65	130	165
No. 158 Rolls Royce Silver Shadow	40	50	80
No. 160 Mercedes Benz 250 SE	30	45	70
No. 160 Royal Artillery Personnel Set, 160 a, b, c, d; 1939/40, six pieces	45	90	120
No. 160A Royal Artillery NCO, 1939/41	10	15	20
No. 160B Royal Artillery Gunner, seated, 1939/41	10	15	20
No. 160C Royal Artillery Gunlayer, 1939/41	15	20	25
No. 160D Royal Artillery Gunlayer, standing, 1939/41	10	15	20

	C6	C8	C10
No. 160X Ranco Seated Gunners (3), 1939/41	30	40	60
No. 161 Mobile Anti-Aircraft Set, 1939/41, Unit 161 a, b, c	600	800	1000
No. 161 Mustang Fastback	30	40	60
No. 161A AA Gun Trailer, reissued, 1954/55	40	50	70
No. 161A Transport Lorry with Search Light, 1939/41	250	300	500
No. 161B AA Gun Trailer, 1939/41	55	110	140
No. 162 Ford Zephyr Saloon	55	110	150
No. 162 Triumph 1130	40	55	90
No. 162A Lt. Dragon Motorized Tractor, reissued, 1954/55	35	50	75
No. 162A Lt. Dragon Motorized Tractor, 1939/41	40	80	100
No. 162B Ammunition Trailer, 1954/55	10	15	20

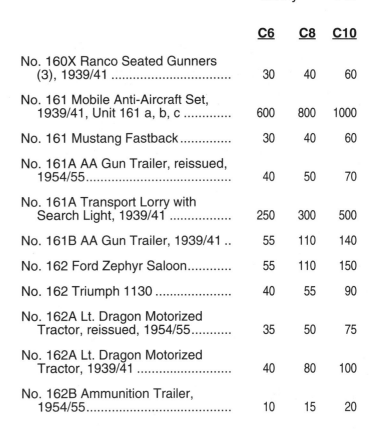

Left to Right: Dinky Transport Lorry with Search Light, No. 161A, 1939-1941; Cooker, No. 151C, Water Tanker, No. 151D.

Left to Right: Dinky No. 157 Jaguar KX120 Coupe; No. 344 Estate Car.

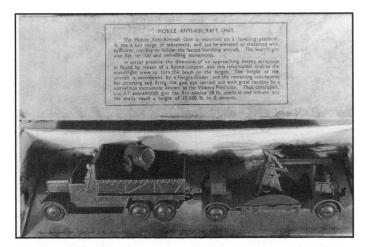

Dinky Mobile Anti-Aircraft Unit set, No. 161, 1939-1941.

Dinky Anti-Aircraft Gun on Trailer, No. 161B, 1950s, reissued.

Dinky Lt. Dragon Set, Nos. 162A, 162B, 162C, 1939-1941.

Left to Right: No. 174 Dinky Hudson Hornet Sedan; No. 172 Studebaker.

Dinky Hudson Hornet Sedan with its original box, No. 174.

Dinky Monteverdi 375L, No. 190.

	C6	C8	C10
No. 162B Ammunition Trailer, 1939/41	25	35	50
No. 162C 18 PD. Gun, reissued, 1954/55	10	15	20
No. 162C 18 PD. Gun, 1939/41	25	35	50
No. 163 Bristol 450 Sports Coupe	45	95	125
No. 163 Volkswagen 1600 TL Fastback	30	45	75
No. 164 Ford Zodiac	30	45	70
No. 164 Vauxhall Crest Saloon	55	110	150
No. 165 Ford Capri	45	55	95
No. 166 Sunbeam Rapier	55	115	155
No. 167 Aceca	55	90	130
No. 168 Ford Escort	15	25	50
No. 168 Singer Gazelle	55	110	145
No. 169 Ford Corsair 200E	30	42	65
No. 169 Studebaker Golden Hawk	55	110	145
No. 170 Lincoln Continental	45	55	95
No. 171 Hudson Sedan	55	110	150
No. 172 Studebaker	65	130	175
No. 173 Nash Rambler	45	90	120
No. 173 Pontiac Parisenne	30	42	65
No. 174 Ford Mercury Cougar	30	45	70
No. 174 Hudson Hornet	55	115	155
No. 175 Hillman Minx	65	130	190
No. 176 Austin A105 Saloon, first Dinky w/windows	65	130	170
No. 176 N SU R 80	30	45	75
No. 177 Opel Dapitan	45	95	125
No. 178 Mini Clubman	15	20	40
No. 178 Plymouth Plaza	55	90	130

	C6	C8	C10
No. 179 Studebaker President	55	110	150
No. 180 Packard Clipper Sedan	50	90	130
No. 180 Rover 3H	15	20	40
No. 181 Volkswagen	50	100	135
No. 182 Porsche 356A Coupe, deep pink	55	115	150
No. 184 Volvo	45	95	125
No. 185 Alfa Romeo Coupe	45	95	125
No. 186 Mercedes Benz	40	50	80
No. 187 DeTomaso Mangusta	25	35	50

	C6	C8	C10
No. 187 VW Karmann Ghia.............	45	95	125
No. 188 Jensen FF...........................	30	45	75
No. 189 Lamborghini Marzal...........	25	35	55
No. 189 Triumph Herald..................	40	80	105
No. 190 Caravan.............................	40	80	105
No. 190 Monteverdi 375L................	30	45	75
No. 191 Dodge Royal Sedan	55	110	145
No. 192 DeSoto Fireflite Sedan	45	90	140
No. 192 Range Rover	15	30	45
No. 193 Rambler Wagon.................	45	95	125
No. 195 Fire Chief's Car.................	15	20	35
No. 196 Holden Special	40	55	85
No. 197 Morris Mini Traveler...........	55	110	145
No. 198 Rolls Royce Phantom V......	40	80	105
No. 199 Austin Countryman.............	45	85	110
No. 200 Matra 630	15	20	40
No. 201 Plymouth Rally '76.............	15	20	40
No. 202 Fiat Abarth 2000................	15	20	35
No. 208 VW Porsche 914................	30	40	60
No. 210 Alfa Romeo 33 LeMans......	30	45	70
No. 212 Ford Cortina Rally..............	40	55	85
No. 213 Ford Capri Rally.................	25	35	50
No. 217 Alfa Scarabo	15	20	40
No. 220 Ferrari P5...........................	30	40	60
No. 221 Corvette Stingray................	30	40	60
No. 222 Hesketh 308E.....................	15	30	45
No. 223 McLaren M8A CanAm	15	20	33
No. 225 Lotus FI Racing Car...........	25	35	50
No. 226 Ferrari 312	15	30	45
No. 227 Beach Buggy	15	20	32
No. 228 Talbot-Lago Race Car	55	90	133
No. 231 Mercedes-Benz	45	95	125
No. 232 Alfa Romeo Race Car........	45	95	125
No. 233 Cooper Bristol Race Car.....	40	85	135
No. 236 Connaught Racer	40	85	135
No. 237 Mercedes Racer	55	115	155

	C6	C8	C10
No. 238 Jaguar Racer	60	120	160
No. 239 Vanwall Racer	45	95	125
No. 240 Cooper Racer	30	40	60
No. 240 Plymouth Belvedere	60	120	160
No. 242 BRM Racer........................	25	35	55
No. 242 Ferrari Racer	25	35	50
No. 245 Sports Car Gift Set	85	165	295
No. 250 Police Mini Cooper S..........	30	45	75
No. 251 Pontiac Police Car.............	30	45	75
No. 252 Pontiac RCMP Police Car ..	40	80	100
No. 254 Austin Taxi..........................	45	85	110
No. 254 Police Range Rover	15	30	45
No. 255 Zodiac Police Car	45	55	95
No. 257 Canadian Fire Chief's Car ..	55	115	150
No. 258 DeSoto Police Car.............	65	130	165
No. 259 Fire Engine	45	90	120
No. 260 Royal Mail Van	65	130	170
No. 261 Telephone Service Truck ...	65	130	165
No. 263 Airport Fire Rescue Tender	40	50	80
No. 264 Ford Fairlaine Police Car....	50	95	125
No. 265 Plymouth Taxi.....................	55	115	150
No. 266 ERF Fire Tender................	40	50	80
No. 267 Bedford Dump	30	45	75
No. 268 Range Rover Ambulance ...	15	20	30
No. 268 Renault Dauphine Mini Car	55	115	150
No. 269 Jaguar Police Car..............	65	130	175

Dinky Range Rover Ambulance, No. 268.

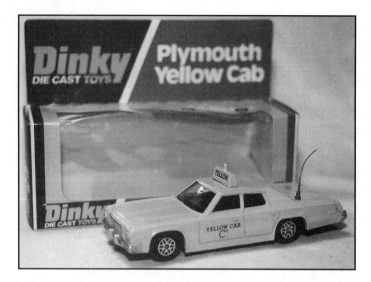

Plymouth Taxi, No. 278, 1970s.

Dinky B.O.A.C. Coach, No. 283.

Dent Road Roller, 4-1/2". Photo from Bill Bertoia Auctions.

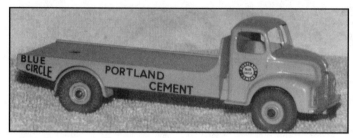

Dinky Leland Comet Cement Truck, No. 419/533, 1950s.

	C6	C8	C10
No. 270 Ford Panda Police Car	25	35	55
No. 271 Bedford Royal Van	15	20	40
No. 271 Ford Fire Appliance	15	20	40
No. 272 Police Accident Unit............	15	30	45
No. 275 Brinks Truck........................	25	40	60
No. 276 Ford Ambulance	15	20	40
No. 277 Superior Ambulance	40	55	85
No. 278 Plymouth Yellow Cab	25	35	50
No. 279 Diesel Road Roller..............	30	42	65
No. 279 Plymouth Taxi.....................	12	20	28
No. 280 Observation Coach.............	55	115	150
No. 281 Pathe News Camera Car....	65	132	180
No. 282 Land Rover Fire Appliance .	45	85	110
No. 283 B.O.A.C. Coach	15	20	40
No. 284 London Taxi........................	15	30	45
No. 285 Merryweather Fire Engine ..	45	55	95

	C6	C8	C10
No. 286 Ford Transit Fire Truck.......	30	45	70
No. 287 Police Accident Unit	30	40	60
No. 289 London Bus	15	20	40
No. 290 Double Decker Bus	55	115	155
No. 291 Atlantean Bus.....................	15	20	40
No. 292 Ribble Regent Bus	30	45	70
No. 295 Atlas Bus	40	80	100
No. 297 Cadillac Ambulance............	40	80	100
No. 300 Massey Harris Tractor	45	95	125
No. 301 Field-Marshall Tractor	40	55	85
No. 308 Leyland Tractor	30	40	60
No. 319 Tipping Trailer	15	20	35
No. 320 Harvest Trailer....................	15	20	40
No. 321 Manure Spreader	32	45	70
No. 322 Disc Harrow........................	15	30	45
No. 340 Land Rover and Trailer.......	65	130	175
No. 341 Land Rover.........................	15	20	35
No. 341 Land Rover Trailer, Army (sold w/No. 669 Super Dinky set), 1954, British..............................	15	20	40
No. 342 Motocart	30	45	75

	C6	C8	C10
No. 343 Dodge Farm Truck..............	65	130	195
No. 344 Estate Car..........................	30	40	60
No. 352 Ed Straker's Car	40	55	90
No. 419/933 Leland Comet Cement Truck, 1956-59..........................	85	150	250
No. 482 Bedford Van, 1956-58	60	115	200
No. 503/903 Foden Flat Truck	140	210	450
No. 514 Guy Van, Slumberland	135	300	575

	C6	C8	C10
No. 561 Blaw Knowx Bulldozer........	30	45	70
No. 601 Austin paramoke, 1966/77, British..	45	55	95
No. 602 Armoured Command Car, 1980, British.................................	30	45	75
No. 603 Army Personnel Privates, 1955/71, British...........................	25	35	50
No. 604 Landrover Bomb Disposal, 1977, British.................................	15	20	35
No. 609 U.S. 105mm Howitzer, 1977, British.................................	10	15	22
No. 612 Commando Jeep, 1980, British..	17	22	38
No. 616 AEC. Arctic Transporter, 1977, British.................................	40	80	100
No. 617 Volkswagen Anti-tank gun, 1977, British.................................	30	45	75

Dinky Bedford Van, No. 482, 1950s.

Dinky Foden Flat Truck.

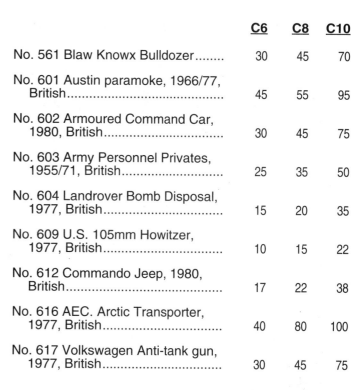

Dinky Blaw Knox Bulldozer, No. 561.

Dinky Guy Van Slumberland, No. 514.

Left to Right: Dinky Austin Paramoke, No. 601, 1966-1977; Scout Car, No. 673, 1953-1962.

Dinky Volkswagen and Anti-Tank Gun Set, No. 617, 1977.

Dinky Berliet Missile Launch, No. 620, 1973.

Top to bottom: Dinky Foden ten-ton Truck, No. 622, 1954-1964; Medium Artillery Tractor, No. 689, 1957-1965.

Top row, left to right: Dinky Army Covered Wagon, No. 623, 1954-1963; 5.5 Medium Gun, No. 692, 1955-1962. Bottom, left to right: 7.2 Howitzer, No. 693, 1958-1967; Three-Ton Army Wagon, No. 621, 1954-1963.

	C6	C8	C10
No. 618 AEC. Arctic Trans./Helicopter, 1980, British ...	55	115	150
No. 619 Bren Gun Set, 1980, British	40	50	80
No. 620 Berliet Missile Launch, 1977, British	40	55	90
No. 621 3 Ton Army Wagon, 1954/63 M/B, British	40	55	85
No. 622 10 Ton Army Truck, 1954/64, British	40	55	85
No. 622 Bren Gun Carrier, 1977, British	30	40	60
No. 623 Army Covered Wagon, 1954/63, British	40	55	90
No. 624 Daimler Ambulance #30H, 1944/54, British	40	55	85

	C6	C8	C10
No. 625 6 Pdr. Anti-tank Gun, 1977, British	15	30	45
No. 625 Austin Covered Lorry/30s, 1948/54, British	30	45	75
No. 626 Military Ambulance, 1956/65, British	40	55	85

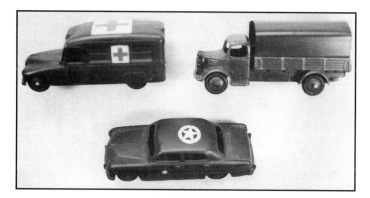

Top row, left to right: Dinky Daimler Ambulance, No. 624, 1944-1954; Austin Covered Lorry, No. 625, 1948-1954. Bottom: Ford Fordor U.S. Army, No. 675, 1944-1954.

Dinky Bedford Army Truck, No. 640, 1944-1954.

Top to bottom: Dinky One-Ton Cargo Truck, No. 641, 1954-1962; Armoured Command Vehicle, No. 677, 1952-1961.

Top to bottom: Dinky R.A.F. Pressure Fueller, No. 642, 1957-1960; Recovery Tractor, No. 661, 1957-1965.

Left to Right: Dinky Tank Transporter, No. 660, 1956-1964; Centurion Tank, No. 651, 1954-1970.

Dinky Honest John Launcher, No. 665, 1964-1976.

	C6	C8	C10
No. 640 Bedford Army Truck 25w, 1944/54, British...........................	30	45	75
No. 641 1 Ton Cargo Truck, 1954/62, British...........................	40	55	85
No. 642 R.A.F. Pressure Fueller, 1957/60, British...........................	65	132	185
No. 643 Army Water Tanker, 1958/64, British...........................	45	55	95
No. 651 Centurion Tank, 1954/70, British...........................	45	55	95
No. 654 155mm. Mobile Gun, 1980, British...........................	30	45	75
No. 654 155mm. Mobile Gun, 1980, British...........................	30	45	75

	C6	C8	C10
No. 656 Static 88mm. Gun, 1980, British...........................	40	55	90
No. 660 Tank Transporter, 1956/64, British...........................	65	132	180
No. 661 Recovery Tractor, 1957/65, British...........................	50	100	135
No. 665 Honest John Launcher, 1964/76, British...........................	65	130	175
No. 666 Missile Erector/Platform, 1959/64, British...........................	85	165	285
No. 667 Armoured Patrol Car, 1977, British...........................	15	20	35
No. 667 Missile Service Platform, 1960/64, British...........................	80	160	275
No. 668 Foden Army Truck, 1980, British...........................	25	35	55
No. 669 U.S. Army Jeep No. 405 sd/tr, 1944/54, British..................	25	35	50
No. 670 Armoured Car, 1954/70, British...........................	30	40	60

Dinky Missile Erector Platform, No. 666, 1959-1964.

Dinky Missile Service Platform, No. 667, 1960s.

Top row: Foden Army Truck, No. 668, 1980. Bottom row, left to right: Landrover Bomb Disposal Unit, no. 604, 1977; Convoy Truck, No. 687, 1980.

Dinky U.S. Army Jeep (No. 669) with trailer (No. 341), 1954.

Top to, left to right: Austin Champ "UN white," No. 674, 1954-1970; Austin Champ Jeep, No. 674, khaki, 1954-1970. Middle: Austin Champ box. Bottom row, left to right: Army Water Tanker, No. 643 1958-1964; Military Ambulance, No. 626, 1956-1965.

Top row, left to right: Armoured Personnel Car, No. 676, 1955-1962; Armoured Car, No. 670, 1954-1970. Bottom, left to right: Artillery Tractor, No. 688; Gun Trailer, No. 687; Field Gun, No. 686.

	C6	C8	C10
No. 673 Scout Car, 1953/62, British.	30	40	60
No. 674 Austin Champ Jeep, 1954/70, British	30	40	60
No. 674 Austin Champ UN white, 1954/70, British	100	200	300
No. 675 Ford Fordor U.S. Army No. 139, 1944/54, British	40	80	100
No. 676 Armoured Personnel Car, 1955/62, British	25	35	55
No. 677 Armoured Commando Vehicle, 1952/61, British	40	80	100
No. 680 Ferret Armoured Car, 1977, British	15	20	40

	C6	C8	C10
No. 681 D.U.K.W., 1977, British	10	15	25
No. 682 Stalwart Load Carrier, 1977, British	15	20	35
No. 683 Chieftain Tank, 1980, British	30	45	70
No. 686 Field Artillery Tractor, 1957/70, British	40	80	100
No. 687 Convoy Truck, 1980, British	12	20	27
No. 687 Trailer and 25 Pdr., 1957/70, British	10	20	30
No. 688 Gun Set, 1957/70, British	40	50	80
No. 689 Medium Artillery Tractor, 1957/65, British	40	80	105
No. 690 Scorpion Tank, 1979, British	40	50	80
No. 691 Striker Anti-tank Vech, 1979, British	30	42	65
No. 692 5.5 Medium Gun, 1955/62, British	30	45	75
No. 692 Leopard Tank, 1980, British	100	200	455
No. 693 7.2 Howitzer, 1958/67, British	15	20	40
No. 694 Hanomog Tank Destroyer, 1980, British	40	80	100
No. 696 Leopard Anti-Aircraft T, 1979, British	45	90	120
No. 699 Leopard Recovery Tank, 1977, British	30	45	75
No. 800 Renault SINAPAR Radio Tk, French	15	30	45
No. 802 (819) 155mm. Fieldgun, 1973/77, French	15	20	40
No. 807 Renault Ambulance Tous, 1973, French	32	45	70
No. 808/2 GMC Wrecker Sahara, 1972/73, French	65	130	170
No. 808/3 GMC Wrecker Khaki, 1974, French	55	115	150
No. 810 Dodge Command Car, 1973, French	65	132	185
No. 813 AMX Self Propelled Gun, 1965, French	65	130	195
No. 814 Panhard AML Amoured Car, 1962/67, French	45	85	110
No. 815 Panhard EBR Tank, 1962/67, French	40	55	85

	C6	C8	C10
No. 816 Berliet Gazelle Rkt. Launch, 1969, French..............................	55	110	140
No. 816/2 Hotchkiss Willys Jeep, w/tow hook, 1958/59, French.......	85	150	250
No. 821 UNIMOG Covered Truck, 1960, French...............................	45	55	95
No. 822 M3 Half Track, 1960, French..............................	45	85	115
No. 823 Field Kitchen, 1962/67, French..............................	40	55	85
No. 823 GMC Tanker, 1969, French	100	200	320

	C6	C8	C10
No. 824 Berliet Gazelle Truck, 1963, French	55	115	150
No. 825 D.U.K.W. Amphibian, 1964, French	65	130	165
No. 826 Berliet Wrecker, 1963, French	80	125	225
No. 827 Panhard FL10 Tank, 1963, French	45	85	110

Top row, left to right: French Dinky Panhard AML Armoured Car, No. 814, 1962-1967; Willys Hotckiss Jeep, No. 80B 1957-1960; Bottom: Willys Hotchkiss Jeep, No. 80BP, 1958-1963.

Top to bottom: French Dinky GMC Wrecker Sahara, No. 808/2, 1970s; GMC Wrecker Khaki, No. 803/3, 1974.

Top to bottom: French Dinky Panhard EBR Tank, No. 815, 1960s; Berliet Tank Transporter, No. 890, 1960.

Top row, left to right: French Dinky Dodge Command Car, No. 810, 1973; Jeep with Anti-Tank Missiles in box, No. 828, 1964. Bottom row, left to right: Jeep with recoil rifle in box, No. 829, 1964; Renault Sinpar, No. 815 1977.

Left to Right: French Dinky UNIMOG Covered Truck, No. 821, 1960; Field Kitchen, No. 823, 1960s.

French Dinky M3 Half Track, No. 822, 1960.

French Dinky AMX Bridge Layer, No. 883, 1964.

French Dinky Berliet Wrecker, No. 826, 1963.

French Dinky Brockway Bridgelayer, No. 884.

French Dinky Panhard FL10 Tank, No. 827, 1963.

Dinky Commer Fire Engine, No. 955.

	C6	C8	C10
No. 828 Jeep/anti-tank Missiles, 1964, French..............................	45	95	125
No. 829 Jeep with recoil rifle, 1964, French..	40	80	100
No. 883 AMX Bridge Layer, 1964, French..	65	132	180
No. 884 Brockway Bridging Truck, 1963, French..............................	85	165	295

	C6	C8	C10
No. 890 Berliet Tank Transporter, 1960, French	90	155	265
No. 955 Commer Fire Engine, 1955-69...	40	85	135

Dinky Road Grader, yellow and red No. 963.

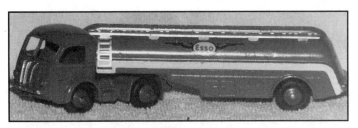

Dinky Panhard Esso Tanker, No. F32C, 1950s.

Dinky Euclid Dump Truck, No. 965.

Dinky Unic Bucket Truck, No. F38A/895.

	C6	C8	C10
No. 963 Road Grader, 1973-75........	30	45	70
No. 965 Euclid Dump Truck	45	85	115
No. F32C Panhard Esso Tanker, 1954-59..	85	150	250
No. F38A/895 Unic Bucket Truck, 1957-65..	75	120	225
Prisoner Mini-Moke	115	200	340

Dinky Prisoner Mini-Moke.

DOEPKE "MODEL TOYS"

Charles Wm. Doepke Mfg. Co., Inc., also known as Doepke, was located in Rossmoyne, Ohio. Each of their toys was an authorized replica of the actual vehicle, right down to the decals. The exception was the manufacturer's own "Model Toys" design. Doepke "Model Toys" advertised their toys as outlasting all others—three to one.

Doepke "Model Toys" were doomed to extinction by lower-priced, lightweight imitators of lesser quality, some of which were started in the 1920s. No company ever matched the heavy-duty construction and realistic operating qualities of the one and only "Model Toys."

Of the Doepke "Model Toys" that were mass produced, several had variations in their basic construction from time to time. Usually these changes were an elimination of the more intricate operating procedures and had little or no effect on the toy's overall appearance.

Doepke accepted orders to make models of actual vehicles for various companies, but the toys with the most allure, playability, feasible mass production design, and greatest entertainment value were mass produced. The others, those that would not withstand rough handling by young hands or were too expensive, were only manufactured in low numbers, sometimes only one. This is no doubt the explanation for the number gaps between the marketed items.

At the end of World War II, Doepke hit the market with five models, the first in a line of heavy-duty metal operating replicas employing metal tread or authentic miniature tires. The tires were either Goodyear or Firestone, with authentic tread and name and tire sizes. The first five numbers in the toy series were 2000, 2001, 2002, 2006, 2007. Following is a list of the Doepke vehicles.

No. 2000: Wooldridge H.D. Earth hauler, bright yellow, four large tires, twenty-five inches long, ten pounds. Two long doors, the length of the bottom of the dirt-hauling area, could be released to deposit a load..

No. 2001: The Barber-Greene high-capacity bucket loader, thirteen inches high, ten pounds, dark green, all steel and rolling on steel tread, was designed as a toy to lead earth haulers; hand crank.

No. 2002: Jaeger Concrete Mixer, bright yellow, fifteen inches long, eight pounds on four wheels, steerable via draw. Though perhaps the best-detailed, it did not sell well.

No. 2006: The Adams Diesel Roadgrader, dark orange, twenty-six inches long, fourteen pounds, all six wheels, three axles, and blade adjustable to all angles, exactly like the real thing, steerable via steering wheel.

No. 2007: The Unit Mobile Crane, dark orange, 11-1/2" long, 19-1/2" boom, eight pounds, eight ounces, with adjustable side jacks, steered via drawbar. It boasted a block and tackle and a removable operating clam shell as a standard accessory.

No. 2009: The Euclid Earth-Hauler Truck with uncoupling four-wheel tractor to use to tow other toys. It was twenty-seven inches long, eleven pounds, Euclid green or light roadgrader orange, and the trailer dumped in the same way as the Wooldridge.

No. 2010: The American LaFrance Pumper Fire Truck, eighteen inches long, seven pounds, was bright red with chrome trim, ladder, bell, fire extinguisher, hoses and nozzle, and had a reservoir that held water for hand-operated pressure pump.

No. 2011: The Heiliner Earth Scraper, twenty-nine inches long, thirteen pounds, bright dark red, loaded and dumped and operated on four wheels as the Wooldridge did.

No. 2012: The Caterpillar D6 Tractor and Bulldozer, caterpillar yellow, fifteen inches long, seven pounds, with real bulldozer treads for sharp realistic turning and adjustable bulldozer blade, plus heavy draw bar. Diesel motor was cast metal.

No. 2013 eliminated and replaced No. 2001: A Barber-Green mobile high-capacity bucket loader, twenty-two inches long, twelve inches high, and ten pounds, it had buckets on chains and rubber conveyor belt, and was adjustable and steered by steering wheel.

No. 2014: The American LaFrance Aerial Ladder Truck, twenty-three inches long, forty-two inches long extended ladder height, eleven pounds, bright red and chrome, with bell, red light, adjustable side jacks, was a single unit truck steered by steering wheel.

	C6	C8	C10
Farm Tractor-N-Wagon, No ??, wooden	68	102	135
No. 2000 Wooldridge H.D. Earth Hauler, 25" long	125	188	250
No. 2001 Barber-Greene High Capacity Bucket Loader, 13" high	242	365	485
No. 2002 Jaeger Concrete Mixer, 15" long	210	315	420
No. 2006 Adams Diesel Road Grader, 26" long	112	168	225

Doepke Wooldridge Earth Hauler, 25". Photo from Calvin L. Chausee.

Doepke Barber-Greene high capacity bucket loader, 13". Photo from Calvin L. Chausee.

Doepke Jaeger Concrete Mixer, 15". Photo from Calvin L. Chausee.

Doepke Adams Diesel Road Grader, 26". Photo from Calvin L. Chausee.

Doepke Unit Mobile Crane, 11-1/2".

A Doepke American La France Aerial Ladder Truck , as shown in a Doepke catalog.

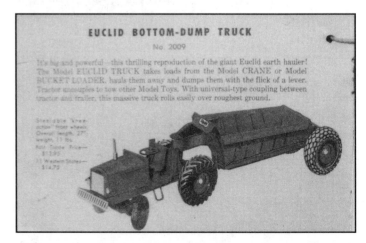

Doepke Euclid Earth Hauler Truck, 27" , as shown in a Doepke catalog.

Doepke American La France pumper fire truck, 18".

HEILINER-SCRAPER
No. 2011

It's *full speed ahead* on construction, with the big Model HEILINER on the job! This giant, triple-duty earth mover scoops up earth and loads itself - hauls and dumps loads for the Model ROAD GRADER to level or for the Model CRANE to pick up. It tows other Model Toys or can be towed. Dumping operations are mechanically controlled.

Universal-type coupling between tractor and trailer. Overall length, 29"; weight, 15 lbs.
Fair Trade Price—$13.95
11 Western States—$16.75

Doepke Heiliner Earth Scraper, 29" , as shown in a Doepke catalog.

Doepke American La France Aerial Ladder Fire Truck, 23". Photo from Calvin L. Chausee.

	C6	C8	C10
No. 2007 Unit Mobile Crane, 11-1/2" long	150	225	300
No. 2008 American La France Aerial Ladder Truck	190	285	380
No. 2009 Euclid Earth Hauler Truck, 27" long	142	215	285

Doepke Caterpillar D6 tractor and bulldozer, 15". Photo from Calvin L. Chausee.

Doepke Barber-Green mobile high-capacity bucket loader, 22" on tracks.

	C6	C8	C10
No. 2010 American-La France Pumper Fire Truck, 18" long	160	240	320
No. 2011 Heiliner Earth Scraper, 29" long	155	233	310
No. 2012 Caterpillar D6 Tractor and Bulldozer, 15" long	288	432	575
No. 2013 Barber-Greene Mobile High-capacity Bucket Loader, treads, wheels, 22" long	225	238	450
No. 2014 American-La France Aerial Ladder Fire Truck, 23" long	275	413	550
No. 2015 Clark Airport Tractor and Baggage Trailers	225	338	450

LOOK, DAD, ...IT WORKS JUST LIKE THE REAL ONES!

Fair Trade Price—$13.95
11 Western States—14.75

Right, son.

This new Model Bottom-Dump Truck looks and works just like the giant earth-hauling Euclids you see on big construction jobs. Like other Model Toys this authorized reproduction is all-steel, equipped with famous-make heavy rubber tires. It's sturdy enough to ride on! Detachable tractor can be used to tow other toys. Great fun—in sandbox or year-round playroom!

NOTE TO ST. NICK: Junior's eyes will outshine the Christmas Star when he finds a Model Toy under the tree!

COMMENDED PARENTS' MAGAZINE

Model TOYS ...outlast others 3 to 1

AT STORES WHEREVER FINE TOYS ARE SOLD
THE CHAS. WM. DOEPKE MFG. CO., Inc., ROSSMOYNE 7, OHIO

A Doepke "Model 'Toys" Advertisement.

Doepke Jaguar, 1955.

Doepke Searchlight Truck, 1955.

	C6	C8	C10
No. 2017 MG, 1954, 15" long..........	200	300	400
No. 2018 Jaguar, 1955....................	343	515	685
No. 2023 Searchlight Truck, 1955....	750	1300	1700

DYNA-MODEL PRODUCTS COMPANY

Dyna-Model Products Co., 93 S. St., Oyster Bay, Long Island, New York, may have pioneered the scale-models industry that now dominates today's markets with their "Dyna-Mo" brand of HO-scale toys. These high quality pot-metal toys can be identified by Dyna-Nodel's method of assembling body parts: clamping axles between small posts and the standardized appearance of the undersides of the whole line.

Probably produced in the 1930s, the toys were made by a coarse die-casting process. The earlier vintage cars were made into two to five parts, exclusive of wheels and axles— body, frame, steering wheel, top and windshield. These parts were then either pinned, clamped or glued together. Some were packaged as kits, with instructions printed on the box: "Pinch ends of axel [sic] after installing wheels" The toys were factory painted in as many as four colors per toy.

Contributors: Fred Maxwell 4722 N. 33 St., Arlington, VA 22207. **Perry R. Eichor,** 703 North Almond Drive, Simpsonville, SC, 29681.

	C6	C8	C10
Convertible, Buick, two-door sedan, top down, one-piece body, solid cast windshield, disk wheels, marked "R-68 HO Buick convertible 55c," late 1930s, 2-3/8" long (D013)	6	9	12
Convertible, Cadillac sedan, two door, late 1930s, 2-3/8" long (D016)	9	6	12
Delivery Van, Pontiac, open windshield and door windows, late 1930s, 2-3/8" long (D21)	4	6	8
Dump Truck, open windows, hinged body w/realistic load of coal, dual real wheels, three pieces, two colors, 2-3/4" long (D024)	6	9	12
Limousine, Cadillac, open windshield and windows incl. rear, late 1930s, 2-1/2" long (D020)	9	6	12
Pickup Truck, GMC (?), open windows, spoked wheels, two pieces, three colors, late 1930s, 2-1/2" long (D022)	4	6	8
Pickup Truck, GMC (?), one-piece, open windows, one color, 1930s, 2" long (D025)	4	6	8
Pickup Truck, Mack (?) marked "US Army" w/Air Corps star decals, late, two piece body, two colors, 1930s, 2" long (D026)	4	6	8
Roadster, Buick (?), open right-hand steering, three colors, 1-7/8" long, four pieces (D004)	4	6	8
Roadster, Packard convertible, top down, rumble seat, one-piece body w/glued windshield, spoked wheels, three colors, 1920s, 2" long (D008)	6	9	12

	C6	C8	C10
Roadster, Packard convertible, top up, rumble seat, one-piece body w/glued windshield, spoked wheels, three colors, 1920s, 2" long (D009)	6	9	12
Roadster, Model A Ford (?), top down, open rumble seat, disk wheels, one piece body, unpainted, 2" long (D011)	2	3	4
Sedan, Buick, open windshield and windows, two colors, 1930s, 2" long (D012)	4	64	8
Sedan, Buick, two door airflow, open windshield and windows, 2-3/8" long (D014)	6	6	12
Sedan, Cadillacsedan, two door, open windshield and windows, late 1930s, 2-3/8" (D017)	9	6	12
Sedan, Pontiac airflow, four door, open windshield and windows incl. rear, 2-3/8" long (D019)	9	6	12
Speedster, Mercer, right- hand steering, four colors, 2" long, three pieces (D003)	4	6	8

	C6	C8	C10
Surrey, horseless carriage, tiller steering, three colors, marked " R-26 HO Surrey, 35c," three piece body kit, 1-3/4" long (D001)	4	6	8
Taxi, Buick sedan, late 1930s, open windshield and windows, two colors, 2-3/8" long (D015)	9	6	12
Taxi, Cadillac sedan, open windshield and windows including rear, two colors, late 1930s, 2-3/8" long (D018)	9	6	12
Touring Car, Stanley Steamer, open tonneau, right-hand steering, four colors, 2" long, four pieces (D002)	4	6	8
Touring Car, realistic folded attachable top w/hinge pins, left-hand steering, two colors, 1 7/8" long, five pieces (D005)	4	6	8
Touring Car, 1914 Model T Ford, one-piece body, top up, three colors, marked "R-61 HO Model T Ford 1914 touring with top 60c," 1-5/8" long (D006)	4	6	8

Top to bottom, left to right: Dyna-Model Dyna Sedan (D14); Dyna Limousine (D20); Dyna Sedan, Buick, 1930s (D12); Dyna Sedan, Cadillac (D18), late 1930s. Middle row, left to right: Dyna Taxi, Buick, late 1930s (D15); Dyan Taxi, Cadillac, late 1930s (D18); Dyna Pickup Truck, 2-1/2," late 1930s (D21); Dyna Pickup Truck, 2-1/2," late 1930s (D22); Dyna Wrecker, 2-3/4", late 1930s (D23); Dyna Dump Truck, 2-3/4" (D24).

Top Row, left to right: Dyna-Model Surrey, horseless carriage (D1); Ford T Roadster, 1-7/8"; Dyna Touring Car, 1914 Ford (D7); Dyna Speedster, antique Mercer (D3); Touring Car, Stanley Steamer. **Middle Row, left to right:** Touring Car (D5); Model T Ford (D6); Roadster (D9); Touring Packard (D10); Roadster (D8); **Bottom row, left to right:** Roadster, top down, open rumble seat (D11); Cadillac sedan, late 1930s; Buick convertible (D23); Cadillac convertible (D16).

	C6	C8	C10		C6	C8	C10
Touring Car, 1914 Ford, cast in one-piece body, top down; glued windshield, three colors, 1-3/4" long (D007)	4	6	8	Truck, Mack (?), tarpaulin covered, two piece body, 2" long (D027) ...	4	6	8
Touring Car, Packard, top down, rumble seat, one-piece body w/glued windshield, spoked wheels, three colors, 1920s, 2" long (D010)	6	9	12	Wrecker, GMC (?), open windows, three pieces, four colors, late 1930s, 2-3/4" long (0D23)	6	9	12

ELASTOLIN

O&M Hausser (brothers Otto and Max) was founded in 1904 in Ludwigsberg near the German city of Stuttgart in Southern Germany. Hausser, Lineol's larger and fiercest competitor, made a somewhat larger variety of military toys and in the same popular 7-1/2 centimeter scale, but its pieces are generally considered to be a bit less sturdy and well-made (with a few exceptions). Thus, they do not command quite the same prices as do Lineol. Elastolin was Hausser's trade name. (In this section, prices run as part of the picture captions.) **Contributor:** Jack Matthews, 13 Bufflehead Dr., Kiawah Island, SC 29455, e-mail: meriam@concentric.net. Matthews was born in 1932 and grew up in a small New England town. Currently a Municipal Judge for two resort areas where he lives with his wife, Meriam. A seasoned collector, he has several thousand composition toy soldiers and German tin-plate military toys. He has won over fifty awards at regional and national shows. The author of Toys Go to War, Matthews has written for several publications, including Richard O'Brien's *Collecting Toy Soldiers*.

Elastolin Prime Mover, No. 730, U.S. crew, postwar, Value as shown $1,500. Jack Mathews Collection.

Elastolin Prime Mover, No. 731, "Chrysler" front, U.S. crew, postwar, value as shown $2,200. Jack Mathews Collection.

Elastolin Prime Mover, No. 730N, camouflaged, value as shown $2,500. Jack Mathews Collection.

Elastolin Kubelwagen No. 733/2 (Staff Car), war production, value as shown $900. Jack Mathews Collection.

Elastolin Six-wheel Prime Mover, No. 730/10, $3,000. Jack Mathews Collection.

Elastolin Command Car, No. 733/12, with luggage, very rare, value as shown, $4,000. Jack Matthews Collection.

Elastolin Large Prime Mover, No. 731, value as shown $16,000. Jack Mathews Collection.

Elastolin Communications Car, No. 733/10, very rare, value as shown $4,000. Jack Mathews collection.

Elastolin Zugsmachine, No. 734, rare, value as shown $3,600. Jack Mathews Collection.

Elastolin Searchlight Car, No. 734, with Luftwaffe crew, value as shown $2,400.

Elastolin Searchlight Truck, No. 743, with British crew, value as shown $1,200. Jack Mathews Collection.

Elastolin Panzer Spahwagen, No. 744, rare, value as shown $14,000. Jack Mathews Collection.

Elastolin Ambulance, No. 738, camouflaged with rubber tires, value as shown $3,000. Jack Mathews Collection.

Elastolin Flakwagen, No. 739N, camouflaged, with British crew, Value as shown $2,750. Jack Mathews Collection.

Elastolin Flakwagen, No. 739N, value as shown $2,200. Jack Mathews Collection.

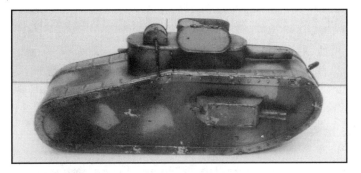

Elastolin Flakwagen, No. 739N, value as shown $2,200. Jack Mathews Collection.

Elastolin Anti-Aircraft Truck, No. 0/740, early, rare, value as shown $2,400. Jack Mathews Collection.

Elastolin Anti-Aircraft Truck, No. 1/740, early, rare, $2,750. Jack Mathews Collection.

Elastolin Kubelauto No. 1/733, with metal wheels, Kreigsproduction, rare, value as shown $700. Jack Mathews

Elastolin Zugwagen, No. 1/734, early, rare, value as shown $3,000. Jack Mathews Collection.

Elastolin Panzer Spahwagen, No. 1744, early, rare, value as shown $3,000. Jack Mathews Collection.

Elastolin Communications Truck, No. 745, light gray, rare, value as shown, $5,000. Jack Mathews Collection.

Elastolin Communications Truck, No. 745, camouflaged, rare, value as shown $5,000. Jack Mathews Collection.

Elastolin Heavy Truck towing Kitchen Wagon, No. 794, with crew, very rare, value as shown $4,250. Jack Mathews Collection.

Elastolin Searchlight Truck, camouflaged, with Luftwaffe crew, early, value as shown, $3,000. Jack Mathews Collection.

Elastolin Kubelauto, No. 1/733, value as shown $650. Jack Mathews Collection.

ERIE

According to James Apthrope, Erie toys were made by Parker White Metal Company, which apparently began in Erie, Pennsylvania, but moved to Fairview in the early 1960s. However, according to company officials, the firm made toys only prior to World War II. It printed no catalogs.

Contributor: Dave Leopard, 2507 Feather Run Trail, West Columbia, SC 29169-4915.

	C6	C8	C10		C6	C8	C10
Cabover Truck, no tail gate, c.1937, 3-1/4" long (EV015)	20	25	35	Coupe, futuristic, no chassis, c.1939, 4-1/4" long (EV019)	30	40	50
Champoin Coal Truck, c.1935, 5" long	40	55	95	Ford Ice Truck, "Pure Ice Co.," 1935, 5" long (EV013)	50	65	85
				Ford Pickup, painted (EV009)	40	55	70
				Ford Pickup Truck, low sides, plated, 1935, 5" long (EV010)	45	60	80
				Ford Pickup Truck, high sides, large rear window, 1935, 5" long (EV011)	40	55	70
				Ford Pickup Truck, high sides, small rear window, 1935, 5" long (EV012)	40	55	70
				Ford Tow Truck, "Servel Body," 1935, 5" long (EV014)	50	65	80
				Lincoln Zephyr Sedan, painted, 1936, 5-1/2" long (EV001)	40	50	70

Erie Champoin Coal Truck, 1935. Photo from John Talyor.

	C6	C8	C10
Lincoln Zephyr Sedan, plated, 1936, 5-1/2" long (EV002)	45	55	75
Lincoln Zephyr Sedan, painted, 1936, 3-1/2" long (EV003)	25	30	40
Lincoln Zephyr Sedan, 1936, 3-1/2" long, plated (EV004)	35	40	55
Packard Roadster, painted, 1936, 6" long (EV005)	45	65	95
Packard Roadster, plated, 1936, 6" long (EV006)	50	70	100

	C6	C8	C10
Packard Roadster, painted, 1936, 3-1/2" long (EV007)	25	30	40
Packard Roadster, plated, 1936, 3-1/2" long (EV008)	35	40	55
Sedan, futuristic, fin on trunk, no chassis, c.1939, 4-1/4" long (EV018)	30	40	50
Sedan, sharknose, no chassis, c.1939, 4-1/4" long (EV020)	30	40	50
Tow Truck, no chassis, c.1939, 4-1/4" long (EV017)	30	40	50

ERTL

Ertl was begun by Fred Ertl Sr., in 1945, working out of his Dubuque, Iowa, home. As business expanded, the firm moved to Dyersville, Iowa. Ertl learned about using sand molds in his native Germany; very early in the company's history, he began working directly from the original blueprints to make his toy tractors, trucks and other wheeled toys. Ertl's specialty is farm toys, with rights obtained from such manufacturers as International Harvester and John Deere. Today, Ertl is the largest manufacturer of toy-farm equipment in the world; in addition, it makes a number of other toys, such as cars, trucks and airplanes.

Ertl was purchased by Racing Champions in 1998 and now go by the name Racing Champions-Ertl.

	C6	C8	C10
Allis-Chalmers B-112 Tractor	70	110	165
Conoco Tanker................................	75	120	175
Fleetstar Dump Truck, red, ten wheel	125	185	250
Fleetstar Hi-Side Dump Truck, red and white	125	185	250
Fleetstar Tilt Bed, green...................	125	185	250
Ford 8000 Tractor, early...................	25	40	60
GE Truck, white..............................	15	22	30

	C6	C8	C10
Gleaner C-280 w/corn picker	25	45	60
Grain Hopper, early.........................	22	34	48
IHC Farmal 806, square fender	100	175	230
International Fleetstar Gravity Feed Truck..	150	250	350
International Scout, maroon or blue.	85	135	195
John Deere 500 Bulldozer, w/blade .	40	70	100
John Deere 6600 Combine	60	100	140
Loadstar Box Van, lavender and white	200	375	575

Ertl Fleetstar Dump Truck, red.

Ertl Fleetstar Hi-Side Dump Truck, white and red.

Ertl Fleetstar Tilt Bed, green.

Ertl grain Hopper, 14-1/2". Photo from Harvey K. Rainess.

Ertl International Scout, maroon (top up) and blue (top down).

Ertl International Harvester Fleetstar Gravity Feed Truck.

Ertl Loadstar Concrete Truck, red and white.

Ertl Loadstar Box Van, lavender and white.

Ertl Loadstar Tilt Bed.

Ertl Loadstar Tow Truck, white and red.

Ertl Van Lines Pup Trailer, white.

	C6	C8	C10
Loadstar Concrete Truck, red and white	200	350	500
Loadstar Dump Truck	140	250	325
Loadstar Grain/Cattle Stake Truck	140	250	325
Loadstar Tilt Bed, green and gray	125	175	300
Loadstar Tow Truck, white and red	150	275	425
Mary Kay Cosmetics Trailer Truck	65	115	150
Mobile Tanker	40	60	88
Picker	25	40	60
Texaco Tanker, No. 2	150	250	350
Van Lines Pup Trailer, white	100	150	225
White Cab-Over Dump Truck, white and red	165	265	400

Ertl Cab-Over Dump Truck, white and red.

F&F CEREAL PREMIUMS

The toy vehicles that were included in Post cereals during the 1950s-1960s were made by the F&F Mold and Die Works of Dayton, Ohio, a company that specialized in manufacturing plastic premiums for the food industry. The Fiedler and Fiedler company was in business from 1945 until 1987, and its entire product-line consisted of plastic premiums.

The small plastic vehicles, about three inches long, were included in Post Grape-Nut Flakes, Corn Flakes, Rice Krispies, etc. over a period of about fifteen years, beginning in 1954. Most of the cereal premiums were cars, but they also made speedboats, which were marked "Century"; several versions of a tractor-trailer truck, which were marked "Ford" on the cab and "Fruehauf" on the trailer; and two versions of a Greyhound bus.

All of the F&F vehicles from 1954 to 1967 are clearly marked with their trademark. Two earlier Fords, a 1950 and a 1951 sedan, have magnets glued underneath the roof, are the same scale and are very similar to other F&F vehicles. Collectors disagree as to whether these early Fords are in fact F&Fs. Likewise, a series of 1969 Mercurys, identical to earlier F&F vehicles in scale, style, and materials, are marked "JVZ Co." Whether these Fords and Mercurys are properly identified as F&F or not, they are very similar and fit nicely with known F&F vehicles.

Contributor: Dave Leopard, 2507 Feather Run Trail, West Columbia, SC 29169-4915.

	C6	C8	C10		C6	C8	C10
1950 Ford Sedan, four-door	15	20	40	1954 Ford Crestline Sedan, four-door	10	15	20
1951 Ford Sedan, four-door	15	20	40	1954 Ford Crestline Sunliner	10	15	20
1954 Ford Crestline Hardtop	10	15	20	1954 Ford Customline Ranchwagon	10	15	20

	C6	C8	C10
1954 Ford Customline Sedan, two-door	10	15	20
1954 Mercury Monterray Convertible	10	15	20
1954 Mercury Monterray Sedan, four-door	10	15	20
1954 Mercury Monterray Sedan, two-door	10	15	20
1954 Mercury XM-800 Show Car	10	15	20
1955 Ford Country Sedan (wagon)	10	15	20
1955 Ford Customline Sedan, two-door	10	15	20
1955 Ford Fairlane Crown Victoria	10	15	20
1955 Ford Fairlane Sunliner	10	15	20
1955 Ford Thunderbird Convertible	10	15	20
1957 Ford Ambulance	10	15	20
1957 Ford Convertible	10	15	20
1957 Ford Firechief Car	10	15	20
1957 Ford Hardtop Sedan, four-door	10	15	20
1957 Ford Highway Patrol	10	15	20
1959 Ford Thunderbird Convertible	10	15	20
1959 Ford Thunderbird Hardtop	10	15	20
1960 Plymouth Convertible	10	15	20

	C6	C8	C10
1960 Plymouth Hardtop Coupe	10	15	20
1960 Plymouth Station Wagon	10	15	20
1961 Ford Thunderbird Convertible	10	15	20
1961 Ford Thunderbird Hardtop	10	15	20
1961 Ford Thunderbird Roadster, single seat	10	15	20
1966 Ford Mustang Convertible	10	15	20
1966 Ford Mustang Fastback	10	15	20
1966 Ford Mustang Hardtop	10	15	20
1967 Mercury Cougar Hardtop	10	15	20
1969 Mercury Cougar Hardtop	10	15	20
1969 Mercury Cyclone Fastback	10	15	20
1969 Mercury Hardtop, two-Door	10	15	20
1969 Mercury Sedan, four-door	10	15	20
Ford Tractor/Trailer, flatbed	10	15	20
Ford Tractor/Trailer, lowboy	10	15	20
Ford Tractor/Trailer, moving van	10	15	20
Ford Tractor/Trailer, enclosed	10	15	20
Ford Tractor/Trailer Oil Tanker	10	15	20
Greyhound Bus	10	15	20
Greyhound Scenicruiser Double-Decker Bus	10	15	20

FISHER-PRICE

Fisher-Price was founded by Herman Fisher and Irving Price on October 1, 1930 in East Aurora, New York. It made (and makes) quality wood toys for small children, colorfully lithographed.

	C6	C8	C10
Donald Duck Choo-Choo, No. 450, 1940	350	600	1200
Elsie's Dairy Truck, No. 745	400	575	700

	C6	C8	C10
Husky Dump Truck, No. 145	50	75	100
Jalopy, No. 724	11	16	22
Looky Fire Truck, No. 7	85	125	170
Mickey Mouse Choo-Choo, No. 432, 1938	450	850	1800
Mickey Mouse Safety Patrol, No. 733	262	393	525
Nifty Station Wagon, No. 234	225	325	450
Peter Bunny Cart, No. 472	225	275	375
Popeye the Sailor, No. 703, 1936	600	1200	2400
Racing Rowboat, No. 730, 1952	105	225	475
Sports Car, No. 674	62	93	125
Tow Truck, No. 718	25	38	50
Tow Truck, No. 615	30	45	60
Tractor, No. 629	25	38	50

Fisher-Price issued two different Donald Duck Choo-Choo.

Fisher-Price Elsie's Dairy Cart. Photo from John Murray. Photo by Ross MacKearnin.

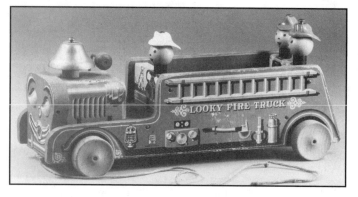

Fisher-Price Looky Fire Truck. Photo from John Murray. Photo by Ross MacKearnin.

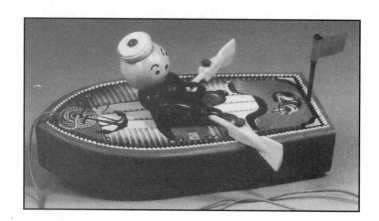

Fisher-Price Racing Rowboat, 1952.

Fisher-Price Mickey Mouse Choo-Choo, 1938.

Fisher-Price Bunny Truck. Photo from John Murray. Photo by Ross MacKearnin.

Fisher-Price Popeye the Sailor, 1936. Photo from John Murray. Photo by Ross MacKearnin.

FREIDAG

According to a well-illustrated article by Fred MacAdam in the March 1993 *Antique Toy World*, William Freidag formed Freidag Mfg. Co. and Foundry in Freeport, Illinois, in 1920. He pronounced his last name "Friday." Freidag's cast-iron toys are obscure but significant and can easily be confused with those by another maker. Thus, collectors might find it helpful to obtain a copy of the MacAdam article when they're uncertain about any cast-iron toy from 1920-1932.

	C6	C8	C10		C6	C8	C10
Auto, w/chauffeur, 1920s	375	562	750	Racer, w/driver and passenger, 6-1/2" long	400	600	800
Bus, 6-3/4" long	225	338	450	Roadster, 1922, 9-1/4" long	500	750	1000
Coupe, 1924, 5-3/4" long	290	435	580	Taxi, 1920s, 7" long	450	675	900
Double-Decker Bus, 9-1/4" long	850	1400	2100	Taxi, w/black driver	600	1000	1400
Panel Delivery Truck, 7-1/2" long	1200	2200	3200	Truck, flatbed, 10" long	500	750	1000
Pickup Truck, 7-1/2" long	500	750	1000	Yellow Cab, 5" long	550	850	1250

Freidag Double-decker Bus, 9-1/4" long. Photo from Bill Bertoia Auctions.

Freidag Roadster, 1922, 9-1/4". Photo from Bill Bertoia Auctions.

Left to right: Freidag Pickup Truck, 7-1/2"; Panel Delivery Truck, 7-1/2". Photo from Bill Bertoia Auctions.

GAMA

	C6	C8	C10
Aerial Ladder w/pump	138	210	275
Cadillac	350	550	850
Crane w/Clam Bucket	125	188	250
Tractor and Trailer, 17" long	95	140	190

Gama postwar tank, large (GT5), value as shown $350. Jack Mathews Collection.

Gama prewar tank, with chain treads (G1), value as shown $500. Jack Mathews Collection.

Gama prewar tank, large (GT2), value as shown $500. Jack Mathews Collection.

Gama postwar tank, large (GT6), value as shown $350. Jack Mathews Collection.

Gama postwar tank, large (GT7), value as shown $350. Jack Mathews Collection.

Gama postwar tank, large (GT8), value as shown $300. Jack Mathews Collection.

Gama prewar tank, medium size (GT9), value as shown $200. Jack Mathews Collection.

Gama prewar tank, medium size (GT10), value as shown $150. Jack Mathews Collection.

Gama prewar tank, small (GT11), value as shown $200. Jack Mathews Collection.

Two Gama small prewar tanks, left to right: (GT12) value as shown $100, (GT13), value as shown $125. Jack Mathews Collection.

Left to right: Two Gama small prewar tanks (left to right: GT14 and GT15), value as shown $125, each. Jack Mathews Collection.

Left to right: Two Gama small (5"-6") prewar tanks (left to right: GT16 and GT17), value as shown $125, each. Jack Mathews Collection.

Gama prewar tank, small, with box (GT18), value as shown $175. Jack Mathews Collection.

Gama Montage tank, small, with original box (GT19), value of tank Mint without box $200. Photo from Joe and Sharon Freed.

Gama tractor, early, value as shown $250. Jack Mathews Collection.

GIRARD

Girard Model Works was founded by C.G. Wood in 1906, in Girard, Pennsylvania. His son Frank was soon made a partner. In 1918, they began making mechanical toys for an unidentified New York firm. In 1920, they sold them under their name "Wood's Mechanical Toys." The business eventually passed into other hands and had 1,000 employees in 1931. During the Depression, Girard laid off its salesman, Louis Marx, who stalled Girard customers as he tried to get a plant of his own in business. Since Marx was better known to buyers than the people at Girard, he emerged triumphant, and in 1934, Marx took over the firm. Girard remained in business till 1980.

	C6	C8	C10
Army Truck, cloth top, c.1940	150	225	300
Auto Transport, carries two trucks, circa early 1930s	275	413	550
Bus, w/driver, wind-up, 12-1/2" long	188	282	375
Coupe, 6" long	30	45	60
Coupe, battery-operated, headlights, 14" long	350	525	700
Fire Chief Car, 15" long	260	300	400
Fire Chief Siren Coupe, wind-up, 14" long	275	450	600
Fire Truck, 1920s, 12" long	50	75	100

	C6	C8	C10
Gasoline Tanker, c.1939	85	135	225
Ladder Truck, 1930s, 7" long	175	263	350
Pierce-Arrow Coupe, green, orange and cream, wind-up, c.1932, 14" long	250	350	500
Pump Truck, battery-operated, headlights, 10" long	100	150	200
Race Car, pull rod, 1920s	138	205	275
Race Car, wind-up, No. 2, 8" long	300	450	600

Girard Fire Chief Siren Coupe, 14" wind-up.

Girard Pierce-Arrow Coupe, 14" 1930s, windup, green, orange and cream.

Girard Stake Truck, 10", electric headlights. Photo from Charles L. Jackson.

Girard Touring Bus, painted tin, circa 1920, 12". Photo from Mapes Auctioneers and Appraisers.

Girard Wrecker Truck, 1930s, mechanical boom, 10".

	C6	C8	C10
Roadster, electrified, 14-1/2" long....	212	318	425
Side Dump, 11-1/2" long..................	150	225	300
Stake Truck, electric headlights, 10" long.............	150	225	300
Tank Truck, wood wheels, 11-1/2" long..............	92	138	185
Touring Bus, painted tin, c.1920, 12" long.............	150	225	300
Truck, w/three trailers, 1928	130	195	260
Truck, w/trailer, 1930s, 17" long.......	100	150	200
Truck and Trailer, marked "Toyland Dairy".............	375	565	700
Wrecker Truck, mechanical boom, 1930s, 10" long, scarce	275	450	600

GOODEE

Goodee die-cast vehicles were made by the Excel Products Company of East Brunswick, New Jersey. All of the prototypes for Goodee vehicles appear to be from the years 1953-1955. It would seem that Goodee vehicles were produced in two sizes—three and six inches. Some of the larger models had wind-up motors, which would increase their value.

Contributor: Dave Leopard, 2507 Feather Run Trail, West Columbia, SC 29169-4915.

Both large and small versions of the Goodee 1953 GMC Pickup Truck. Photo from Dave Leopard.

	C6	C8	C10
Small Size			
1953 Cadillac Convertible	10	12	15
1953 Ford Police Cruiser	10	12	15
1953 Lincoln Capri Hardtop	10	12	15
1953 Studebaker Coupe	12	15	20
1954 DeSoto Station Wagon............	10	12	15
1955 Ford Fuel Truck	10	12	15
American LaFrance Pumper	10	12	15
Land Speed Racer, bubble fenders .	10	12	15

	C6	C8	C10
Land Speed Racer	10	12	15
Military Jeep	10	12	15
Moving Van	10	12	15
Step Van	10	12	15

Large Size

	C6	C8	C10
1953 Ford Police Cruiser	15	20	25

	C6	C8	C10
1953 GMC Pickup Truck	10	12	15
1953 GMC Pickup Truck	15	20	25
1954 DeSoto Station Wagon	15	20	25
1955 Ford Fuel Truck	15	20	25
American LaFrance Pumper	15	20	25
Military Jeep	15	20	25

GUNTHERMANN

Gunthermann's toy business flourished well into the 1900s despite the fact that S.G. Gunthermann passed away in 1890. His widow married the company manager, Adolf Weigel, and Weigel's initials were added to the "SG" logo until his death in 1919. The initials were removed and the logo was changed back to the original SG. The company was sold to Seimens in 1965 and is still in business today.

Contributor: Bob Smith, The Village Smith, 62 West Ave., Fairport, NY 14450-2102.

	C6	C8	C10
Auto Candy Container, driver in open, closed cab	550	900	1400
Blue Bird Racer, tin lithographed, clockwork motor, 20" long	1000	1700	2350
Car, two-seat, open, driver w/top hat, c.1899, 7" long	850	1600	2500
Clown Car, clockwork motor, 6" long	900	1700	2300
Double-Decker Bus, electric headlights, early 1930s, 12" long.	475	638	950
Fire Ladder Truck, four firemen, overhead ladder, 16" long	1800	3000	4400
Fire Pumper, handpainted tin, clockwork motor, two firemen, c.1898, 8-1/4" long	1500	2700	3900
Fire Pumper, three firemen (composition), 8-1/4" long	1600	2800	4000
Fire Pumper, wind-up, early 7-3/4"	800	1300	2000
Georgian Window Limousine, driver, clockwork motor, c.1908	1100	1700	2500
Gordon Bennett coupe, 5-3/4" long	1200	2200	3000
Hansom-type Auto	750	1300	1750

	C6	C8	C10
Horseless Carriage, clockwork motor, driver, 7" long	1100	1700	2500
Kaye Don's Sunbeam Silver Bullet Racer, 22" long	800	1400	2000
Limousine, green/black, clockwork motor, fur opening doors, painted driver, c.1920, 12" long	1150	1800	2600

Gunterman Kaye Don's Sunbeam Silver Bullet Racer, 22". Photo from Bill Bertoia Auctions.

Gunterman Limousine, 1920, green and black, four opening doors, painted driver, 12". Photo from Bob Smith.

Gunterman Blue Bird Racer, tin lithographed, 20". Photo from Bill Bertoia Auctions.

Guntherman Vis-a-Vis, driver, wind-up, 10-1/4". Photo from Bill Bertoia Auctions.

Another look ath the 10-1/4" Guntherman Vis-a-Vis. Photo from Bill Bertoia.

Guntherman two-way Limousine/Touring Car, brown and yellow, removable top, 1920s. Photo from Bob Smith.

	C6	C8	C10
Limousine/Touring Car, two-way, brown and yellow, clockwork motor, adjustable steering and headlamps, a removable top converts car to touring model. 10-1/4" long	850	1450	2100
Motorcycle and Rider, 7" long	1500	2800	3700
Motorcycle and Rider, 8-1/4" long	1000	1700	2400
Open Phaeton, driver, wind-up, 7" long	650	1100	1600
Paris-Berlin Race Car	1100	1700	2500
Taxi, convertible back, driver, clockwork motor, c.1912, 10-1/2" long	1100	2100	2900
Vis-à-Vis, driver, wind-up, 10-1/4" long	1250	2500	3100
Vis-à-Vis, driver, wind-up, 5" long	800	1400	2000

HESS PROMOTIONAL TOYS

One can trace the roots of the Amerada Hess Corp. (formally Hess Oil & Chemical) back many years before a promotional toy was even considered. Hess entered retail gasoline marketing around 1958 with a minority purchase of the Meadville Corp. Meadville operated clean, oversized service stations under the brands of Save Way and Safeway in some large Northeast cities. The Hess branch was introduced in 1959; by 1962 the company operated about twenty-eight stations under its own brand name. By 1965, several other fuel companies were bought, and some of their stations were renamed as "Hess."

It wasn't until 1964 that the first toy tanker truck was sold at Hess stations. Almost every year since then (around Thanksgiving Day) a high quality plastic toy vehicle bearing the Hess name has been offered. These highly detailed toys are said to be exact replicas of actual vehicles in the Hess fleet; although from 1987 to present, the toys design was changed to reflect non-fleet vehicles. The toys are produced in limited quantities and over the past few years, customers have been restricted to two toys, because of great demand. Each vehicle is packaged in a colorful box and batteries are included in the purchase price. It's important to note that to maintain the value, keep all the packaging that comes with the toy (box, inserts, battery card, etc.).

The 1964 toy truck commonly referred to as the "B Mack" was manufactured by Marx in Hong Kong and sold at the stations for $1.39. The cab of the truck was green with yellow fenders and red chassis. The tank trailer featured a green and white body with the Hess name applied to both sides of the tank and cab. The truck had operating head and tail lights, powered by a battery located under the tank. It came with a small red funnel that enabled the tank to be filled with liquid and a drain hose to empty it. This unique toy truck can be hard to find in original condition today.

Not commonly known by collectors, this same truck design was offered under the private labeling of several other fuel companies: Billups Pretroleum, Aetna (which was the North Carolina-based Taylor Oil Co., operating under the Travelers Brand), Wilco (also on the Delhi-Taylor supply system), Service of North Carolina and Gant. Each of these marketers sold the B Mack toy truck in 1964. By 1965, the Billups brand name had been eliminated in the Eastern part of the United States and their stations were sold to Hess. Hess continued the toy promotion the following year (1965) with the reissue of the B Mack.

A few highlights in the Hess Promotional Toys History:
- The year 1966 brought the only non-land vehicle to date in the Hess toy collection—the Hess Voyager.
- In 1967, Hess offered a newly-designed semi-tanker truck often referred to as the "red velvet bottom." This term describes the box, not the truck.
- The Merger of Hess Oil and Chemical with Amerada Petroleum Corp., took place in 1969, producing the present day name of Amerada Hess. To commemorate this occasion, the 1968-1969 toy truck, re-labeled with the new name, was given to Hess employees.
- The first pumper truck was offered in 1970 for $1.69.
- Amerada Hess opted not to offer a toy promotion at their stations in 1973.
- The first semi-box truck with opening side and rear doors made its appearance in 1975.
- Amerada Hess, in maintaining high standards of service, provided training to its service-station personnel on location by means of a modified GMC motor home. In 1980, a toy replica of the Hess Training Van was chosen as the holiday promotion.
- A reissue of the 1933 Chevy appeared in 1983, with a new feature—a savings bank.
- In 1987, an entirely new color scheme was introduced—white and green.

	C6	C8	C10		C6	C8	C10
1964 B Model Mack Tanker Truck, made in Hong Kong	n/a	n/a	1900	1968 Tank Truck, split window, without red velvet box, made in Hong Kong	n/a	n/a	675
1965 B Model Mack Tanker Truck, made in Hong Kong	n/a	n/a	1900	1969 Tank Truck, split window without red velvet box, made in Hong Kong	n/a	n/a	675
1966 Hess Voyager Tanker Ship, Made in U.S.A.	n/a	n/a	2300	1969 Tank Truck, split window, Amerada Hess, Hong Kong, never sold to the general public	n/a	n/a	2500
1966, B Mack Tanker Truck, silver, "W" tooled into grill	n/a	n/a	2500				
1967 Tank Truck, split window, w/faux red velvet base on box, Made in U.S.A.	n/a	n/a	2400				

Hess Promotional B Model Mack Tanker Truck, 1964.
Photo from Thomas G. Nefos.

Hess Promotional Hess Voyager Tanker Ship, 1966.
Photo from John and Suzanne Adivari.

Hess Promotional split-window Tank Truck with red velvet on box, 1967. Photo from John and Suzanne Adivari.

Hess Promotional Red Pumper Fire Truck, 1970. Photo from Thomas G. Nefos.

Hess Promotional Tank Truck, similar to 1967 except no red velvet box, 1968-69. Photo from John and Suzanne Adivari.

Hess Promotional Red Pumper Fire Truck, "Seasons Greetings," 1971. Photo from John and Suzanne Adivari.

Hess Promotional box-type Tractor Trailer with three oil drums, 1975, no labels on drums. Photo from John and Suzanne Adivari.

	C6	C8	C10
1970 Pumper Fire Truck, red, made in Hong Kong, by Marx	n/a	n/a	695
1971 Pumper Fire Truck, red, made in Hong Kong, by Marx, marked "Season's Greetings"	n/a	n/a	3000
1972 Tanker Truck, split window	n/a	n/a	395
1974 Tanker Truck, split window	n/a	n/a	350
1975 Tractor Trailer, box-type w/three oil drums, no labels on drums, one-piece cab, made in both Hong Kong and the United States	n/a	n/a	395
1976 Tractor Trailer, two-piece cab, three oil drums, marked "Hess," made in Hong Kong	n/a	n/a	395
1977 Tanker Tractor Trailer, made in Hong Kong, rear label is 1-1/2" x 1"	n/a	n/a	175

	C6	C8	C10
1978 Tanker Tractor Trailer, made in Hong Kong	n/a	n/a	185
1980 GMC Training Van, made in Hong Kong	n/a	n/a	395

Hess Promotional box-type Tractor Trailer, three "Hess" drums, 1976. Photo from Thomas G. Nefos.

Hess Promotional 1933 Chevy Tanker Delivery Truck, 1982. Photo from John and Suzanne Adivari.

Hess Promotional Tanker Tractor Trailer. Photo from John and Suzanne Adivari.

Hess Promotional Tanker Tractor Trailer, similar to the 1977 truck except it was issued as a bank, 1984. Photo from John and Suzanne Adivari.

Hess Promotional GMC Training Van, 1980. Photo from John and Suzanne Adivari.

Hess Promotional Red Aerial Ladder Fire Truck, 1986. Photo from John and Suzanne Adivari.

	C6	C8	C10
1982, 1933 Chevy Tanker Delivery Truck, marked "first Hess truck," made in Hong Kong	n/a	n/a	95
1983, 1933 Chevy Tanker Delivery Truck, marked "first Hess truck," made in Hong Kong	n/a	n/a	495
1984 Tanker Tractor Trailer, bank	n/a	n/a	495
1985, 1933 Chevy Tanker Delivery Truck, bank	n/a	n/a	125
1986 Aerial Ladder Fire Truck, bank, red, made in Hong Kong	n/a	n/a	100
1987 Tractor/Trailer, box-type, w/three drums labeled Hess, made in Hong Kong and China	n/a	n/a	75
1988 Race Car Transporter, w/friction-powered car, made in Hong Kong	n/a	n/a	470
1989 Aerial Ladder FireTruck, white, dual siren sounds, bank made in China	n/a	n/a	65
1990 Semi-tanker Truck, white, w/back-up/air horn sounds, made in China	n/a	n/a	45

	C6	C8	C10
1991 Race Car Transporter, w/friction-powered car, made in China	n/a	n/a	35
1992 Eighteen Wheeler Box Truck, track w/race car, made in China	n/a	n/a	40

Hess Promotional Aerial Ladder Fire Truck, 1989.

Hess Promotional box-type Tractor Trailer, three "Hess" oil drums, 1987. Photo from Thomas G. Nefos.

Hess Promotional Semi-Tanker Truck, air horn sounds, 1990. Photo from John and Suzanne Adivari.

Hess Promotional Race Car Transporter, 1988. Photo from John and Suzanne Adivari.

Hess Promotional Eighteen-wheeler Box Truck with race car, 1992. Photo from John and Suzanne Adivari.

Hess Promotional Patrol Car, white and green, 1993. Photo from John and Suzanne Adivari.

Hess Promotional Hess Premium Diesel truck, same as 1990 tanker except not sold to general public; given as gift to bulk diesel fuel dealers, 1993. Photo from John and Suzanne Adivari.

	C6	C8	C10
1993 Patrol Car, white and green w/sirens and lights, larger scale than previously-issued toys	n/a	n/a	28
1993 Semi-tanker Truck, white w/back-up/air horn sounds, not sold to general public, given as gift to bulk diesel fuel dealers	n/a	n/a	1000
1994 Rescue Truck, white and green w/red ladder, larger scale than previously-issued toys	n/a	n/a	25
1995 Flat-bed Semi, white and green w/helicopter cargo, both w/working lights	n/a	n/a	35

Hess Promotional Toy Truck and Helicopter, white and green, 1995.

HESS TOY COMPANY

Founded in 1825 by Matthieu Hess, this is one of the oldest toy makers in Germany. Matthieu passed away in 1886, leaving the business to his son, Johann Leonard, beginning the "J.L.H." trademark. Most Hess-mobile cars used a unique friction mechanism which had a power-lock on top of the cowl and a hand crank in the front. When cranking the handle, a momentum would build up. You would then lift the power-lock, releasing the driveshaft to turn the rear wheels.

Contributor: Bob Smith, The Village Smith, 62 West Ave., Fairport, NY 14450-2102.

	C6	C8	C10
Hessmobile Open Phaeton, driver, 8-1/2" long, c.1918	800	1300	1900
Hessmobile Racer, w/driver, hand crank, 8" long	400	700	950
Limousine, friction drive, green/black, c.1920, 7-1/2" long ..	575	675	900
Limousine, clockwork, green/red, 9" long	600	800	1100
Limousine, friction drive, blue/black, c.1920, 9" long	700	950	1300

	C6	C8	C10
Open Two-Seat Car, 10-1/2" long	750	1400	2000
Open Two-Seat Car, tin lithographed, approx. 8" long	750	1250	1800
Racer, tin lithographed, two seat, open, clockwork motor, 8-3/4" long	750	1250	1800
Racer, w/driver, 5"	500	800	1200
Speedster, w/driver, crank friction drive, 8" long	350	600	800

HOT WHEELS

It all started in 1968 when Mattel issued the original sixteen metallic colored toy cars. Today, most toy discount stores will have at least a four-foot section of space devoted Hot Wheels. Listed are issues from 1968 to 1979 (the red-line era). These are the most sought after by toy collectors, especially if they are still in their original blister package (C10). Most are found, however, in used condition (C6).

Contributors: Ron Smith, 33005 Arlesford, Solon, OH, 44139, 440-248-7066, fax 440-519-0906. **Reid Covey,** Box 2D Highmarket Rd., Constableville, NY, 13325, e-mail: sullivan@northnet.org. Covey lives in New York his wife Melissa, and works for B.O.C.E.S. as a computer technician. An avid collector, Covey boasts of a collection that includes more than 2,500 Hot Wheels, 200 Matchbox cars and a vast collection of Jeff Gordon items. His wife's collection of #97 Chad Little items complements Covey's items and her 300-plus salt-and-pepper shakers.

	C6	C8	C10
Alive '55, No. 6968, blue, 1974	n/a	90	350
Alive '55, No. 6968, green, 1974	n/a	50	110
Alive '55, No. 6968, assorted, 1973 .	n/a	75	500
Ambulance, No. 6451, assorted, 1970..........	n/a	30	50
American Hauler, No. 9118, blue, 1976..........	n/a	20	50
American Tipper, No. 9089, red, 1976..........	n/a	20	50
American Victory, No. 7662, light blue, 1975	n/a	20	60
AMX/2, No. 6460, assorted, 1971	n/a	30	100
Aw Shoot, No. 9243, olive, 1976......	n/a	15	25
Backwoods Bomb, No. 7670, light blue, 1975	n/a	40	125
Baja Bruiser, No. 8258, orange, 1974..........	n/a	30	75
Baja Bruiser, No. 8258, yellow, magenta in tampo, 1974	n/a	200	900
Baja Bruiser, No. 8258, light green, 1976..........	n/a	300	1000

	C6	C8	C10
Baja Bruiser, No. 8258, yellow, blue in tampo, 1974	n/a	200	900
Beatnik Bandit, No. 6217, assorted, 1968..........	n/a	15	45
Boss Hoss, No. 6406, pink, 1971.....	n/a	50	125
Boss Hoss, No. 6499, chrome, Club Kit, 1970	n/a	50	160
Brabham-Repco F1, No. 6264, assorted, 1969..........	n/a	10	25
Bugeye, No. 6178, assorted, 1971 ..	n/a	30	75
Buzz Off, No. 6976, blue, 1974........	n/a	30	90
Buzz Off, No. 6976, assorted, 1973 .	n/a	75	400
Bye Focal, No. 6187, assorted, 1971	n/a	90	375
Carabo, No. 7617, light green, 1974	n/a	25	70
Carabo, No. 6420, assorted, 1970 ...	n/a	20	60
Carabo, No. 7617, yellow, 1974.......	n/a	400	1200
Cement Mixer, No. 6452, assorted, 1970..........	n/a	20	45
Chapparal 2G, No. 6256, assorted, 1969..........	n/a	15	35
Chevy Monza 2+2, No. 7671, orange, 1975	n/a	40	110
Chevy Monza 2+2, No. 9202, light green, 1975	n/a	200	600
Chief's Special Cruiser, No. 7665, red, 1975	n/a	30	75
Classic '31 Ford Woody, No. 6251, assorted, 1969..........	n/a	20	70
Classic '32 Ford Vicky, No. 6250, assorted, 1969..........	n/a	20	50
Classic '36 Ford Coupe, No. 6253, blue, 1969..........	n/a	10	25
Classic '36 Ford Coupe, No. 6253, assorted, 1969..........	n/a	15	50
Classic '57 T-Bird, No. 6252, assorted, 1969..........	n/a	25	70

Hot Wheels Ambulance.

Hot Wheels Boss Hoss.

Hot Wheels Chaparral 2G.

Hot Wheels Carabo.

Hot Wheels Classic '32 Ford Vicky.

Hot Wheels Classic 36 Ford Coupe.

Hot Wheels Classic '36 Ford Coupe.

Hot Wheels Classic Nomad.

Hot Wheels Custom Mustang.

Hot Wheels Custom Charger.

Hot Wheels Custom Fleetside.

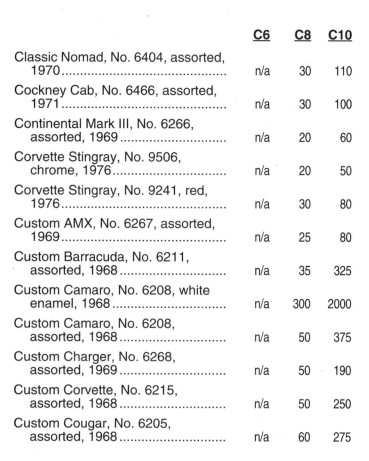

Hot Wheels Demon, 1970.

	C6	C8	C10
Classic Nomad, No. 6404, assorted, 1970	n/a	30	110
Cockney Cab, No. 6466, assorted, 1971	n/a	30	100
Continental Mark III, No. 6266, assorted, 1969	n/a	20	60
Corvette Stingray, No. 9506, chrome, 1976	n/a	20	50
Corvette Stingray, No. 9241, red, 1976	n/a	30	80
Custom AMX, No. 6267, assorted, 1969	n/a	25	80
Custom Barracuda, No. 6211, assorted, 1968	n/a	35	325
Custom Camaro, No. 6208, white enamel, 1968	n/a	300	2000
Custom Camaro, No. 6208, assorted, 1968	n/a	50	375
Custom Charger, No. 6268, assorted, 1969	n/a	50	190
Custom Corvette, No. 6215, assorted, 1968	n/a	50	250
Custom Cougar, No. 6205, assorted, 1968	n/a	60	275

	C6	C8	C10
Custom El Dorado, No. 6218, assorted, 1968	n/a	25	100
Custom Firebird, No. 6212, assorted, 1968	n/a	45	220
Custom Fleetside, No. 6213, assorted, 1968	n/a	60	250
Custom Mustang, No. 6206, assorted w/open hood scoops or ribbed windows, 1968	n/a	400	1200
Custom Mustang, No. 6206, assorted, 1968	n/a	75	425
Custom Police Cruiser, No. 6269, assorted, 1969	n/a	55	200
Custom T-Bird, No. 6207, assorted, 1968	n/a	50	165
Custom VW Bug, No. 6220, assorted, 1968	n/a	10	40
Demon, No. 6401, assorted, 1970	n/a	15	35
Deora, No. 6210, assorted, 1968	n/a	60	375
Double Header, No. 5880, assorted, 1973	n/a	120	450
Double Vision, No. 6975, assorted, 1973	n/a	110	400
Dune Daddy, No. 6967, assorted, 1973	n/a	110	400

Hot Wheels Deora.

Hot Wheels Double Header.

	C6	C8	C10
Dune Daddy, No. 6967, orange, 1975	n/a	175	450
Dune Daddy, No. 6967, light green, 1975	n/a	25	75
El Rey Special, No. 8273, light green, 1974	n/a	95	300
El Rey Special, No. 8273, green, 1974	n/a	40	75
El Rey Special, No. 8273, dark blue, 1974	n/a	225	450
El Rey Special, No. 8273, light blue, 1974	n/a	200	650
Emergency Squad, No. 7650, red, 1975	n/a	15	50
Evil Weevil, No. 6471, assorted, 1971	n/a	40	85
Ferrari 312P, No. 6973, red, 1974	n/a	40	80
Ferrari 312P, No. 6417, assorted, 1970	n/a	20	30
Ferrari 312P, No. 6973, assorted, 1973	n/a	300	1100
Ferrari 512-S, No. 6021, assorted, 1972	n/a	75	250
Fire Chief Cruiser, No. 6469, red, 1970	n/a	10	25
Fire Engine, No. 6454, red, 1970	n/a	25	60
Ford J-Car, No. 6214, assorted, 1968	n/a	10	60
Ford MK IV, No. 6257, assorted, 1969	n/a	10	35
Formula 5000, No. 9119, white, 1976	n/a	20	45

	C6	C8	C10
Formula 5000, No. 9511, chrome, 1976	n/a	30	65
Fuel Tanker, No. 6018, assorted, 1971	n/a	60	175
Funny Money, No. 6005, gray, 1972	n/a	60	325
Funny Money, No. 7621, magenta, 1974	n/a	30	80
Grass Hopper, No. 7621, light green, 1974	n/a	30	90
Grass Hopper, No. 6461, assorted, 1971	n/a	25	55
Grass Hopper, No. 7622, light green, no engine, 1975	n/a	90	350
Gremlin Grinder, No. 7652, green, 1975	n/a	25	60
Gun Bucket, No. 9090, olive, 1976	n/a	25	60
Gun Slinger, No. 7664, olive, 1975	n/a	25	50
Gun Slinger, No. 7664, olive, blackwall, 1976	n/a	15	30
Hairy Hauler, No. 6458, assorted, 1971	n/a	20	50
Heavy Chevy, No. 6189, chrome, Club Kit, 1970	n/a	50	175
Heavy Chevy, No. 7619, yellow, 1974	n/a	75	175
Heavy Chevy, No. 7619, light green, 1974	n/a	200	750
Heavy Chevy, No. 6408, assorted, 1970	n/a	25	55
Hiway Robber, No. 6979, assorted, 1973	n/a	75	250
Hood, No. 6175, assorted, 1971	n/a	15	90
Hot Heap, No. 6219, assorted, 1968	n/a	10	35
Ice T, No. 6184, yellow, 1971	n/a	40	200
Ice T, No. 6980, assorted, 1973	n/a	200	650
Ice T, No. 6980, yellow w/hood tampo, 1974	n/a	200	525
Ice T, No. 6980, light green, 1974	n/a	30	75

	C6	C8	C10
Indy Eagle, No. 6263, assorted, 1969	n/a	10	25
Indy Eagle, No. 6263, gold, 1969	n/a	50	200
Inferno, No. 9186, yellow, 1976	n/a	30	60
Jack Rabbit Special, No. 6421, white, 1970	n/a	10	55
Jack-in-the-Box Promotion, No. 6421, white, Jack rabbit w/decals, 1970	n/a	225	n/a
Jet Threat, No. 6179, assorted, 1971	n/a	45	160
Jet Threat II, No. 8235, magenta, 1976	n/a	35	80
Khaki Kooler, No. 9183, olive, 1976.	n/a	15	30
King Kuda, No. 6411, chrome, Club Kit, 1970	n/a	30	120
King Kuda, No. 6411, assorted, 1970	n/a	25	100
Large Charge, No. 8272, green, 1975	n/a	25	60
Light My Firebird, No. 6412, assorted, 1970	n/a	20	55

	C6	C8	C10
Lola GT 70, No. 6254, assorted, 1969	n/a	10	30
Lotus Turbine, No. 6262, assorted, 1969	n/a	10	30
Lowdown, No. 9185, light blue, 1976	n/a	30	75
Mantis, No. 6423, assorted, 1970	n/a	15	40
Masterati Mistral, No. 6277, assorted, 1969	n/a	50	125
Maxi Taxi, No. 9184, yellow, 1976	n/a	25	60
McClaren M6A, No. 6255, assorted, 1969	n/a	10	40
Mercedes 280SL, No. 6962, assorted, 1973	n/a	100	450
Mercedes 280SL, No. 6275, assorted, 1969	n/a	10	40
Mercedes C-111, No. 6978, assorted, 1973	n/a	300	1200

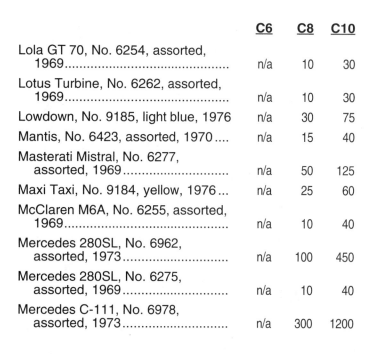

Hot Wheels King Kuda.

Hot Wheels Hiway Robber.

Hot Wheels Jack Rabbit Special.

Hot Wheels Mantis.

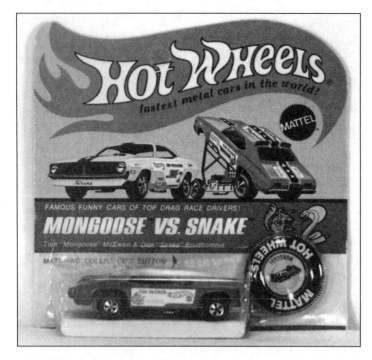

Hot Wheels Mongoose Funny Car.

Left to right: Hot Wheels Mongoose and Snake Funny Cars.

Hot Wheels Mongoose Dragster.

Hot Wheels Mongooseand SnakeDragsters.

Hot Wheels Noodle Head.

	C6	C8	C10
Mercedes C-111, No. 6978, red, 1974	n/a	40	90
Mercedes C-111, No. 6169, assorted, 1972	n/a	80	250
Mighty Maverick, No. 7653, blue, 1975	n/a	30	65
Mighty Maverick, No. 9209, light green, 1975	n/a	200	400
Mighty Maverick, No. 6414, assorted, 1970	n/a	35	85
Mod-Quad, No. 6456, assorted, 1970	n/a	15	40
Mongoose, No. 6970, red/blue, 1973	n/a	400	1400
Mongoose Funny Car, No. 6410, red, 1970	n/a	50	160
Mongoose II, No. 5954, metallic blue, 1971	n/a	75	350
Mongoose Rail Dragster, No. 5952, blue, two pack, 1971	n/a	75	600

	C6	C8	C10
Monte Carlo Stocker, No. 7660, yellow, 1975	n/a	45	90
Motocross I, No. 7668, red, 1975	n/a	50	160
Moving Van, No. 6455, assorted, 1970	n/a	50	125
Mustang Stocker, No. 9203, yellow w/red in tampo, 1975	n/a	300	900
Mustang Stocker, No. 7664, yellow w/magenta tampo, 1975	n/a	90	300
Mustang Stocker, No. 7664, white, 1975	n/a	400	1200
Mustang Stocker, No. 9203, chrome, 1976	n/a	40	90
Mutt Mobile, No. 5185, assorted, 1971	n/a	75	175
Neet Streeter, No. 9510, chrome, 1976	n/a	20	40
Neet Streeter, No. 9244, blue, 1976	n/a	20	60
Nitty Gritty Kitty, No. 6405, assorted, 1970	n/a	25	65
Noodle Head, No. 6000, assorted, 1971	n/a	40	150

	C6	C8	C10
Odd Job, No. 6981, assorted, 1973 .	n/a	100	600
Olds 442, No. 6467, assorted, 1971	n/a	275	625
Open Fire, No. 5881, 1972..............	n/a	100	400
Paddy Wagon, No. 6402, blue, 1970	n/a	15	30
Paddy Wagon, No. 6966, blue, 1973	n/a	30	120
Paramedic, No. 7661, white, 1975 ...	n/a	25	55
Paramedic, No. 7661, yellow, 1976 .	n/a	25	45
Peepin' Bomb, No. 6419, assorted, 1970..	n/a	10	25
Pit Crew Car, No. 6183, white, 1971	n/a	50	450
Poison Pinto, No. 9240, light green, 1976..	n/a	25	60

	C6	C8	C10
Poison Pinto, No. 9508, chrome, 1976.......................................	n/a	20	40
Police Cruiser, No. 6963, white, 1973.......................................	n/a	250	600
Police Cruiser, No. 6963, white, 1974.......................................	n/a	35	90
Porsche 911, No. 6972, orange, 1975.......................................	n/a	25	60
Porsche 911, No. 7648, yellow, 1975.......................................	n/a	40	75
Porsche 917, No. 6416, assorted, 1970.......................................	n/a	15	40
Porsche 917, No. 6972, assorted, 1973.......................................	n/a	300	950
Porsche 917, No. 6972, orange, 1974.......................................	n/a	40	75
Porsche 917, No. 6972, red, 1974 ...	n/a	175	500
Power Pad, No. 6459, assorted, 1970.......................................	n/a	25	65
Prowler, No. 6965, assorted, 1973 ..	n/a	200	1000
Prowler, No. 6965, orange, 1974	n/a	35	75
Prowler, No. 6965, light green, 1974	n/a	500	1000
Python, No. 6216, assorted, 1968 ...	n/a	10	55
Racer Rig, No. 6194, red/white, 1971.......................................	n/a	100	375
Ramblin' Wrecker, No. 7659, white, 1975.......................................	n/a	20	45

Hot Wheels Olds 442.

Hot Wheels Olds 442.

Hot Wheels Paddy Wagon.

Hot Wheels Pit Crew Car.

Hot Wheels Racer Rig.

Hot Wheels Sand Crab.

Hot Wheels S'Cool Bus.

Hot Wheels Seasider.

Hot Wheels Sky Show Fleetside.

	C6	C8	C10
Ranger Rig, No. 7666, green, 1975 .	n/a	20	65
Rash I, No. 7616, blue, 1974	n/a	300	800
Rash I, No. 7616, green, 1974	n/a	35	65
Rear Engine Mongoose, No. 5699, red, 1972.....................................	n/a	200	600
Rear Engine Snake, No. 5856, yellow, 1972..............................	n/a	200	600
Red Baron, No. 6400, red, 1970	n/a	15	40
Red Baron, No. 6964, red, 1973	n/a	30	200
Road King Truck, No. 7615, yellow set only, 1974	n/a	400	1000
Rock Buster, No. 9088, yellow, 1976	n/a	20	35
Rock Buster, No. 9507, chrome, 1976..	n/a	15	30
Rocket Bye Baby, No. 6186, assorted, 1971	n/a	60	200
Rodger Dodger, No. 8259, blue, 1974...	n/a	200	550
Rodger Dodger, No. 8259, magenta, 1974...	n/a	40	90
Rolls-Royce Silver Shadow, No. 6276, assorted, 1969	n/a	25	45
Sand Crab, No. 6403, assorted, 1970..	n/a	10	40
Sand Drifter, No. 7651, green, 1975	n/a	150	375
Sand Drifter, No. 7651, yellow, 1975	n/a	20	50
Sand Witch, No. 6974, assorted, 1973..	n/a	100	400
S'Cool Bus, No. 6468, yellow, 1971 .	n/a	175	750
Scooper, No. 6193, assorted, 1971 .	n/a	100	325

	C6	C8	C10
Seasider, No. 6413, assorted, 1970	n/a	50	120
Shelby Turbine, No. 6265, assorted, 1969..	n/a	10	25
Short Order, No. 6176, assorted, 1971..	n/a	35	100
Show-Off, No. 6982, assorted, 1973	n/a	140	400
Sidekick, No. 6022, assorted, 1972 .	n/a	80	200
Silhouette, No. 6209, assorted, 1968	n/a	20	90
Sir Sidney Roadster, No. 8261, light green, 1974	n/a	325	650
Sir Sidney Roadster, No. 8261, orange/brown, 1974....................	n/a	375	700
Sir Sidney Roadster, No. 8261, yellow, 1974................................	n/a	25	65
Six Shooter, No. 6003, assorted, 1971..	n/a	75	225
Sky Show Fleetside (Aero Launcher), No. 6436, assorted, 1970..	n/a	400	850

	C6	C8	C10
Snake, No. 6969, white/yellow, 1973	n/a	600	1500
Snake Dragster, No. 5951, white, two-pack, 1971	n/a	75	rare
Snake Funny Car, No. 6409, assorted, 1970	n/a	60	300
Snake II, No. 5953, white, 1971	n/a	60	275
Snorkel, No. 6020, assorted, 1971	n/a	60	150
Special Delivery, No. 6006, blue, 1971	n/a	45	150
Splittin' Image, No. 6261, assorted, 1969	n/a	10	35
Steam Roller, No. 8260, white w/seven stars, 1974	n/a	100	300
Steam Roller, No. 8260, white, 1974	n/a	25	70
Street Eater, No. 7669, black, 1975	n/a	30	50
Street Rodder, No. 9242, black, 1976	n/a	40	85
Street Snorter, No. 6971, assorted, 1973	n/a	110	400
Strip Teaser, No. 6188, assorted, 1971	n/a	65	200
Sugar Caddy, No. 6418, assorted, 1971	n/a	20	70
Super Van, No. 9205, chrome, 1976	n/a	20	40
Super Van, No. 7649, plum, 1975	n/a	90	250
Super Van, No. 7649, Toys-R-Us, 1975	n/a	100	350
Super Van, No. 7649, blue, 1975	n/a	650	rare
Superfine Turbine, No. 6004, assorted, 1973	n/a	300	1100
Sweet "16", No. 6007, assorted, 1973	n/a	90	375
Swingin' Wing, No. 6422, assorted, 1970	n/a	15	40

	C6	C8	C10
T-4-2, No. 6177, assorted, 1971	n/a	35	165
Team Trailer, No. 6019, white/red, 1971	n/a	95	225
TNT-Bird, No. 6407, assorted, 1970	n/a	25	70
Top Eliminator, No. 7630, blue, 1974	n/a	50	165
Torero, No. 6260, assorted, 1969	n/a	10	60
Torino Stocker, No. 7647, red, 1975	n/a	35	70
Tough Customer, No. 7655, olive, 1975	n/a	15	55
Tow Truck, No. 6450, assorted, 1970	n/a	30	80
Tri-Baby, No. 6424, assorted, 1970	n/a	15	40
Turbofire, No. 6259, assorted, 1969	n/a	10	45
Twinmill, No. 6258, assorted, 1969	n/a	10	35
Twinmill II, No. 9509, chrome, 1976	n/a	20	45
Twinmill II, No. 8240, orange, 1976	n/a	10	35
Vega Bomb, No. 7658, green, 1975	n/a	250	800
Vega Bomb, No. 7658, orange, 1975	n/a	40	85
Volkswagen, No. 7620, orange w/bug on roof, 1974	n/a	30	60
Volkswagen, No. 7620, orange w/stripes on roof, 1974	n/a	100	400

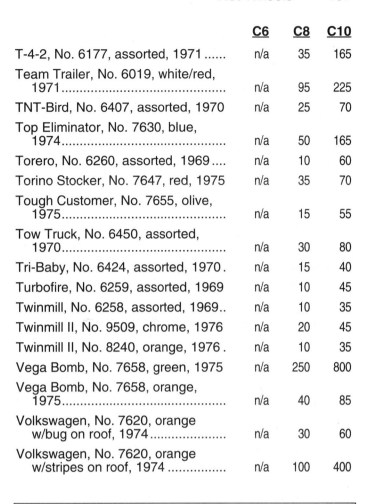

Hot Wheels Tow Truck.

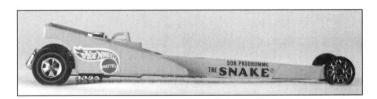

Hot Wheels Snake Dragster.

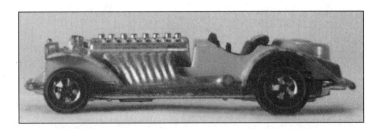

Hot Wheels Sweet 16.

Hot Wheels VW Beach Bomb.

	C6	C8	C10
Volkswagen Beach Bomb, No. 6274, surf boards in rear window, 1969	n/a	n/a	6000
Volkswagen Beach Bomb, No. 6274, surf boards on side raised panels, 1969	n/a	50	175
Warpath, No. 7654, white, 1975	n/a	50	110

	C6	C8	C10
Waste Wagon, No. 6192, assorted, 1971	n/a	90	325
What-4, No. 6001, assorted, 1971	n/a	50	150
Whip Creamer, No. 6457, assorted, 1970	n/a	15	40
Winnipeg, No. 7618, yellow, 1974	n/a	90	300
Xploder, No. 6977, assorted, 1973	n/a	100	500

HUBLEY

The Hubley Manufacturing Company was founded in 1892 by John Hubley. It made iron toys from the start at is plant in Lancaster, Pennsylvania. In the beginning, all toys were cast iron, and some early toys included coal ranges, circus wagons and mechanical banks. Hubley's cast-iron toys were popular almost from the start, and have long been collector's items because they were well-made and attractive. By 1940, however, the cast-iron toy, due to the increased cost of freight and foreign competition, was slowly becoming a thing of the past. At this time, when Hubley was the largest producer of cast-iron toys and cap pistols in the world, it began to introduce die-cast zinc alloy toys. During the World War II, Hubley was ninety-eight-percent engaged in war production.

After the war, Hubley manufactured die-cast toys and plastic toys exclusively. In 1952, Hubley manufactured 9,763,610 toys and 11,184,878 cap pistols, about ten times the amount of toys and pistols it produced in 1930, but with a line of toys eighty-percent smaller than in 1930. It is the combination of the relative scarcity (and multiplicity) of the older toys, plus the preference by collectors for cast-iron over die-cast zinc alloy and plastic toys that makes the prewar toys the most attractive to collectors. Hubley was acquired by Gabriel Industries in late 1965, and puts out holster sets, cap pistols, vehicles, hobby kits and a number of other toys.

Contributor: Motorcycles—Kent M. Comstock, 532 Pleasant St., Ashland Ohio 44805, 419-289-3308, 800-443-TOYS. Comstock is a life-long motorcycle enthusiast, and it was his interest in antique motorcycles that fueled his interest in toys. While at an Antique Motorcycle Club meet in Ohio, he saw small cast-iron motorcycles being traded—he was hooked. His advice to new collectors—buy what you like.

	C6	C8	C10
Ahrens Fox Hose Reel, 11-1/4" long	2000	4500	8000
Air Compress Truck, 7" long	37	56	75
Airflow type, marked "Hubley, U.S.A." c.1937, approx. 3-1/2" long	20	30	40
Allis Chalmers Model WC Tractor, w/driver, 7" long	100	160	225
American LaFrance Ladder and Hose Truck, 15" long	100	175	275
Army Ambulance, No. 476, late	60	90	120
Army Motor Truck, No. 807, w/driver, 15" long	1100	1800	2400
Auto, 6-1/2" long	80	120	160
Auto, die-cast, black plastic wheels, 1950s	12	18	25
Auto, No. 358, c.1928, 7-1/2" long	150	225	300
Auto, Chevy (?), 1922, 9" long	400	650	1000
Auto Carrier, w/three cars and one pickup truck, c.1939, 10" long			

	C6	C8	C10
Auto Carrier, w/two Packards, 1950s	80	120	160
Auto Express, cast iron, 9" long	900	1450	2000
Auto Transport, plastic, marked "Hubley Transport," 13" long	125	188	250
Auto Transport, all-metal, w/four different-color plastic Cadillacs, 18" long without ramp	175	263	350

Left to Right: Hubley Ladder Truck, 13"; Ahrens Fox Hose Reel, 11-1/4". Photo from Bill Bertoia Auctions.

Hubley Auto Carrier, 1950s, with two Packards.

Hubley Auto Transport, all-metal truck with four different color plastic Cadillacs, 18" without ramp. Photo from Harvey Rainess.

Hubley Avery Tractor, 4-3/4". Photo from Ron Carnahan.

Hubley Bell Telephone, postwar truck, 24". Photo from Thomas G. Nefos.

Hubley Bell Telephone, 5-1/4".

Hubley Borden's Milk Cream truck. Left to right: 6" long; 3-5/8" long. Photo from Bill Bertoia Auctions.

	C6	C8	C10
Avery tractor, marked "No. 2," very early, 4-3/4" long	120	180	240
Bell Telephone, post-WWII, 24" long	60	90	120
Bell Telephone Truck, 3-3/4" long	150	235	310
Bell Telephone Truck, w/tools, 8-1/4" long	400	600	800
Bell Telephone Truck, accessories, 1950s	85	128	170
Bell Telephone Truck, marked "Bell Telephone", w/tools, 12" long	179	263	350
Bell Telephone Truck, w/derrick and windlass, auger, trailer w/10" pole, three digging tools, and two loose ladders, 1931, 9-1/4" long	550	950	1300
Bell Telephone Truck, 5-1/4" long	200	320	450

	C6	C8	C10
Bell Telephone Truck, 3" long	200	300	400
Bell Telephone Truck, w/two ladders, tools, 7" long	600	1000	1400
Borden's Milk Truck, 3-5/8" long	250	375	500
Borden's Milk Truck, marked "Borden's Milk Cream," deluxe versions, rubber tires, clicker, 7-1/2" long	1250	1875	2500
Borden's Milk Truck, marked "Borden's Milk Cream," standard versions, 6" long	1000	1500	2000
Bulldozer, 12" long	150	225	300

Hubley Bell Telephone trucks. Top row, left to right: 3" long ; 3-3/4" long ; 5-1/4" long; 7" long. Bottom row, left to right: 8-1/4" long; 9-1/4" long. Photo from Bill Bertoia Auctions.

	C6	C8	C10
Bulldozer, 9" long	92	93	125
Bulldozer, die-cast, front scoop, rubber treads, c.1950, 10-1/4" long	78	118	155
Bus, cast iron, marked "Coast to Coast," 1927, 13" long	450	675	900
Bus, futuristic type, c.1935, 3-1/2" long	60	90	120
Bus, futuristic, No. 617, 7 3/4" long	150	225	300

	C6	C8	C10
Bus, c.1938, rubber wheels, 5-1/2" long	50	75	100
Bus, 1930s, 8" long	60	90	120
Bus, die-cast, 9" long	20	30	40
Cab, black and white, 1920s	1200	2000	3000
Cadillac, die-cast, 1941, 7" long	40	60	80
Car and Trailer, No. 2278 car and No. 2279 house trailer, c.1939	150	225	300
Caterpillar Tractor, 9" long	62	93	125
Caterpillar Tractor, driver in cab, 3-1/4" long	100	150	200
Cattle Truck, plastic, 12" long	30	45	60
Cement Mixer, marked "Jaeger"	475	712	950
Cement Mixer, Wonder, 1930s, 3-1/2" long	125	188	250
Cement Mixer, 18" long	400	600	800
Cement Mixer Truck, 8" long	2000	3800	6500
Champion Stake Truck, white rubber tires, 1930s, 8-1/2" long	140	210	280

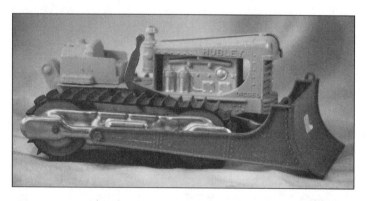

Hubley Bulldozer, 12". Photo from Calvin L. Chaussee.

Hubley Coast to Coast Bus, cast-iron, 1927, 13". Photo from Bill Bertoia Auctions.

Hubley Bus, futuristic type, 3-1/2", 1930s. Photo from Mapes Auctioneers and Appraisers.

Hubley Caterpillar Tractor, 3-1/4".

Hubley Cement Mixer Truck, 8". Photo from Bill Bertoia Auctions.

Hubley Cattle Truck, plastic, 12".

Hubley made several versions of the Chrysler Airflow, the most valuable of which is an eight-inch car with white rubber tires on wood hubs.

Hubley Coal Truck, 1920s, 9-1/2". Photo from Christie's East.

Hubley Chrysler Airflow, 4-1/2".

	C6	C8	C10
Chemical Truck, w/ladders, 13" long	200	300	400
Chevrolet 1932 Coupe Kit, w/box.....	12	18	25
Chevrolet 1932 Paheton Kit, 1960s, w/box	27	41	55
Chevrolet 1932 Roadster Kit, 1960s, w/box	20	30	40
Chrysler Airflow, racing car, c.1938 .	100	150	200
Chrysler Airflow, electrified, white rubber tires on wood hubs, 8" long............................	600	900	1200

	C6	C8	C10
Chrysler Airflow, take-apart body, 4-1/2" long	125	188	250
Chrysler Airflow, take-apart body, 6-3/4" long	312	468	625
Coal Truck, marked "Coal," c.1922, 9-1/2" long	438	657	875
Coal Truck, cast iron, w/driver, 16-3/4" long	1200	1800	2500

	C6	C8	C10
Compressor Truck, Ingersoll Rand, 8-1/4" long....................	2500	4500	7000
Convertible, die-cast and iron, 7" long..............................	100	150	200
Convertible, hard top, 1950s...........	50	75	100
Corvette, No. 509, 13-1/2" long........	162	243	325
Coupe, 1920s, 4-1/2" long	100	150	200
Coupe, c.1939, 6-1/2" long	110	165	220
Coupe, 1933 Ford	90	135	180
Coupe, 1930s, 3-1/2" long............	40	60	80
Coupe Roadster, rumble seat, rubber tires, 11" long..................	125	187	250
Crane, wooden wheels, 1940s.........	67	100	135
De Soto Air flow, 4" long	100	150	200
Delivery Van, 1932, 4-1/2" long	700	1300	1800
Delvery Truck, marked "Merchants Delivery," 1920s, 6" long.............	400	600	800
Diesel Low Boy, w/grader	115	172	230
Diesel Road Roller, 10" long	50	75	100

	C6	C8	C10
Duesenberg Town Car, built-it, model, w/box, 9" long	26	39	52
Dump Truck, 1930s, 3-1/2" long	40	60	80
Dump Truck, plastic and metal, 8" long................................	25	38	50
Dump Truck, No. 902, late	55	83	110

Hubley Crane, 1940s, wooden wheels. Photo from Harvey Rainess.

Hubley Compressor Truck, Ingersoll Rand, 8-1/4". Photo from Bill Bertoia Auctions.

Hubley Delivery Van, 4-1/2", 1932.

Hubley Corvette, 13-1/2".

Hubley Merchants Delivery, 1920s, 6". Photo from Bill Bertoia Auctions.

Hubley Fire Ladder Truck, early, 7-1/2". Photo from Rod Carnahan.

Hubley Flatbed Truck, all metal, No. 506. Photo from Harvey Rainess.

Hubley Tractor, Ford Powermaster, No. 961.

	C6	C8	C10
Dump Truck, Mack, six tires, 1930s, 10-3/4" long	1000	1800	2800
Dump Truck, 1952	112	168	225
Dump Truck, 5-1/2" long	50	75	100
Dump Truck, c.1938, 7-1/2" long	1000	1600	2400
Fire Engine, die-cast, white rubber tires w/wooden rims, c.1941	40	60	80
Fire Engine, No. 526, c.1936, 10-1/2" long	175	263	350
Fire Engine Pumper, 1930s, 5" long	65	98	130
Fire Engine Pumper, early, No. 504	350	525	700
Fire Engine Pumper, w/searchlight, 7" long	55	83	110
Fire Engine Pumper, terraplane front, 1930s, 6-1/4" long	185	275	370
Fire Engine Pumper, 1930s, No. 2254	170	255	340
Fire Engine Pumper, cast iron, black rubber tires, driver, boiler-trailer, c.1920, 12-1/2" long	350	525	700
Fire Engine Pumper, two firemen, early, No. 554, 14" long	1700	3200	6820
Fire Engine Pumper, postwar?, 7" long	55	82	110
Fire Engine Pumper, w/two firemen, 8-1/2" long	275	362	550
Fire Engine Pumper, Ahrens-Fox, 10" long	250	375	500

	C6	C8	C10
Fire Engine Pumper, Ahrens-Fox, 7" long	400	600	800
Fire Ladder Truck, driver, early 1930s, 14" long	500	800	1200
Fire Ladder Truck, 19-1/2" long	850	1400	1900
Fire Ladder Truck, early, 8-1/2" long	250	375	500
Fire Ladder Truck, early, 7-1/2" long	130	195	260
Fire Truck, 5" long	100	150	200
Fire Truck, w/searchlight, white rubber tires w/wooden rims	55	82	110
Fish Hatchery Truck, w/net, fish, 1950s	65	98	130
Flatbed Truck, all metal, No. 506	118	177	235
Ford Coupe, 1936	40	50	80
Ford Model A Coupe Kit, 1960s, w/box	25	38	50
Ford Model A Phaeton Kit, 1960s, w/box	25	38	50
Ford Model A Pickup Kit, 1960s, w/box	25	38	50
Ford Model A Roaster Kit, 1960s, w/box	32	48	65
Ford Model A Station Wagon Kit, 1960s, w/box	25	38	50
Ford Model A Town Car Kit, 1960s, w/box	25	38	50
Ford Model A Victoria Kit, 1960s, w/box	25	38	50
Ford Powermaster Tractor, No. 961	NPF	NPF	NPF
Ford Tractor and Disk	85	128	170
Fordson Front-End Loader, cast iron, early 1930s, 9" long	1000	1800	2700
Fuel Truck, cast iron, 5-1/2" long	100	150	200
Grader	56	84	112
Graham, 4" long	85	125	170
Hook and Ladder, No. 473	82	123	165

Hubley Huber Road Rollers. Left to right: 5-3/8" long; 4-1/2" long; 3-1/2" long. Photo from Bill Bertoia Auctions.

	C6	C8	C10
Hook and Ladder, No. 463	28	42	56
Hook and Ladder, No. 468	130	195	260
Hook and Ladder Truck, cast iron, 19-1/2" long..............................	200	300	400
Huber Road Roller, 5-3/8" long	125	188	250
Huber Road Roller, wind-up, 1932, 7-1/2" long..............................	3500	6500	9500
Huber Road Roller, 4-1/2" long	110	165	220
Huber Road Roller, 8" long	455	682	960
Huber Road Roller, 13" long	2500	3850	5000
Huber Road Roller, 14" long	1600	2500	3800
Huber Road Roller, 15" long	3000	4500	6000
Huber Road Roller, 3-1/2" long	75	112	150
Indianapolis 500 Racer Kit, metal, 9" long	150	225	300
Jaguar, die-cast, 7-1/2" long	62	93	125
Jeep, metal, 6-3/4" long	15	22	30
Jeep and Speedboat, late	25	38	50
Kiddie Toy, plastic, black rubber tires, marked "3," 6-5/8" long	150	200	250

	C6	C8	C10
Kiddie Toy, aluminum, "457," 7" long	50	75	100
Kiddie Toy Auto Transport, w/Cadillacs	80	120	160
Kiddie Toy Buick Convertible, No. 465, 7" long.................................	65	98	130
Kiddie Toy Convertible, 1930s	100	150	200
Kiddie Toy Dump Truck, No. 510	125	188	250
Kiddie Toy Dump Truck, No. 475, plastic cab w/metal dump, 8" long	50	75	150

Hubley Jaguar, 7-1/2".

Hubley Huber Road Roller, 8". Photo from Mapes Auctioneers and Appraisers.

Hubley Kiddietoy Dump Truck, 8".

Banner Stake Truck, wood wheels, 1940s, 8". Photo from John Taylor.

Hubley Kiddie Toy Stake Truck. Photo from Bob and Alice Wagner.

Hubley Kiddie Toy Motor Express, 6-1/2", tailgate opens, plastic. Photo from Harvey Rainess.

Hubley Kiddie Toy Taxi.

	C6	C8	C10
Kiddie Toy Dump Truck, No. 476	70	105	140
Kiddie Toy Fire Ladder Truck, No. 520, 19" long..............................	250	375	500
Kiddie Toy Fire Truck, plastic, w/rubber wheels..........................	17	26	35
Kiddie Toy Hook and Ladder, No. 454, 7" long..............................	65	98	130
Kiddie Toy Ladder Truck, 1950s, 6" long.....................................	67	100	135
Kiddie Toy Log Truck, No. 356, 12" long.....................................	72	105	145
Kiddie Toy MGTD Roadster, No. 432, 6" long..............................	110	165	220
Kiddie Toy Motor Express, plastic, tailgate opens, 6-1/2" long	30	45	60
Kiddie Toy Pickup Truck, 1930s.......	100	150	200
Kiddie Toy Pumper, 1950s, 6" long..	67	10	135
Kiddie Toy Racer, die-cast rubber tires, No. 457, 6-1/2" long	46	69	92

	C6	C8	C10
Kiddie Toy Road Roller, plastic, No. 315, 6" long................................	50	75	100
Kiddie Toy Sedan, two-door, 1930s.	100	150	200
Kiddie Toy Sedan, four-door, 1930s	115	172	230
Kiddie Toy Stake Truck, Ford 1946, No. 461	45	90	170
Kiddie Toy Stake Truck, marked "Patrol," c.1937	27	41	55
Kiddie Toy Taxi, No. 5, marked "Taxi"	7	12	25
Kiddie Toy Tow Truck, 1950s "No. 2" on roof, No. 452, 6-3/8" long ...	37	56	75
Kiddie Toy Tractor, No. 472	42	63	85
Kiddie Toy Tractor, die-cast, 1960s, 5-1/2" long	12	18	25
Kiddie Toy Wrecker, 8" long.............	67	105	135
Ladder Truck, terraplane front, 1930s, 6" long............................	70	105	140

	C6	C8	C10
Ladder Truck, w/eagles, early, 16" long..............................	700	1150	1600
Ladder Truck, c.1940, 13-1/2".........	375	562	750
Ladder Truck, 1929, 13" long...........	500	750	1000
Ladder Truck, 1930s, 10" long........	110	165	225
Ladder Truck, 7" long.....................	175	263	350
Ladder Truck, circa late 1930s, 5" long..............................	45	67	90
Ladder Truck, w/three ladders, w/two aces, 7-1/4" long.................	225	338	450
LaSalle, die-cast, 1940s..................	90	135	180
Life Saver Truck, small hole in rear, can't hold Life Savers..................	NPF	NPF	NPF
Life Saver Truck, hole in rear is large enough to hold pack of Life Savers, 4-1/4" long	700	1150	1600
Limousine, six-door, 1920s, 7" long .	165	250	330
Lincoln Zephyr, 7-1/4" long	233	350	465
Lincoln Zephyr, 6" long	120	180	240
Lincoln Zephyr, die-cast, 5-1/4" long	25	38	50
Lincoln Zephyr and House Trailer, cast iron, 14" long overall.............	400	600	800
Log Truck, w/five chained logs, black rubber tires, die-cast, approx. 19" long.........................	138	205	275
Log Truck, plastic, No. 356, 12" long	75	112	150
Log Truck, No. 469.........................	45	100	200
Log Truck, 16" long	70	105	140
Log Truck, 13" long	100	150	200

	C6	C8	C10
Low Boy Hauler, w/road grader, 21" Long.............................	115	172	230
Low Boy Truck, trailer, tractor	200	300	400
Mack Dump Truck, 8-1/2" long........	600	950	1400
Mack Dump Truck, w/driver, 11-1/2" long.............................	900	1400	2200
Mack Gasoline Truck, c.1925, 13-1/4" long	550	900	1300
Mack Gasoline Truck, 8-3/4" long	700	1100	1500
Mack Gasoline Truck, 10 3/4" long ..	800	1350	1800
Mack Truck Steam Shovel-Digger, nickel wheels and scoop, c.1920, 7" long.........................	450	675	920
MG, 9" long	60	90	120
MG, 5-3/4" long	48	72	95
Mighty Metal Power Shovel	100	150	200
Milk Truck, cast iron, white rubber tires, "Milk Cream," 1930s, 3-1/2" long.........................	262	393	525
Model T Coupe, 4" long	100	150	200
Monarch Tractor, 5-1/2" long	600	900	1200
Motor Express Tractor and Trailer, black rubber tires, 500 series, approx. 19" long.........................	130	195	260

Hubley Mack Gasoline Truck, 8-3/4". Photo from Bill Bertoia Auctions.

Hubley Life Saver Truck, 1930s, holds pack of Life Savers, 4-1/4". Photo from Bill Bertoia Auctions.

Hubley Lincoln Zephyrs. Left to right: 6" long; 5-1/4 long. Photo from Bill Bertoia Auctions.

Hubley Mack Gasoline Truck, 10-3/4". Photo from Bill Bertoia Auctions.

Hubleys, as shown in Woolworth's 1954 Christmas catalog/comic book.

Hubley Milk Cream Truck, 1930s, cast-iron, white rubber tires, 3-1/2". Photo from Mapes Auctioneers and Appraisers.

Hubley Mr. Magoo Car, battery-operated, 1961.

Hubley Nite Coach, 3-1/2" metal wheels, 1930s, went on Nu-Car carrier.

Hubley Nucar Transport, w/four cars, 17". Photo from Christie's East.

Hubley made several versions of the Packard in the 1920s-1930s.

	C6	C8	C10
Motor Express Truck and Trailer, No. 2287, 8" long	175	263	350
Motor Express Truck and Trailer, No. 352, plastic, 12" long	75	112	150
Motor Express Truck and Trailer, plastic, 12" long..........................	70	105	140
Motorized Steam Pumper, 4" long ...	50	75	100
Mr. Magoo Car, battery-operated, includes cloth roof top, five actions, 1961, 9" long	145	215	290
Nite Coach, metal wheels, went on "Nu-Car" carrier, 1930s, 3-1/2" long	30	45	60
Nucar Transport, five cars, 17" long w/trailer	500	900	1250

	C6	C8	C10
Oliver Orchard Tractor, 5-1/2" long ..	88	132	175
Packard, "Phaeton" Kit, w/box, 1930	25	38	50
Packard, fifteen parts, straight eight, 1929, 11" long.............................	6000	12,000	16,000
Packard Dietrick Convertible Model Kit, w/box	25	38	50
Packard Roadster Kit, w/box............	25	38	50
Packard Sedan, 1939-1940s, 5-1/2" long..	25	40	75
Panama Digger, hard to find, approx. 3-1/2" long	300	450	600
Panama Digger, 9-1/2" long............	800	1200	1650
Panama Digger, Mack, 13" long	1100	1650	2200

	C6	C8	C10
Patrol Car, w/driver and three firemen, 8-1/4"long......................	312	468	625
Patrol Car, w/driver and policeman, 15 1/2" long.................................	700	1200	1600
Pickup, Dump, die-cast, Ford, No. 470, 1958, 9-1/2" long..................	20	30	40
Pickup, cast iron, 3-1/2"long	22	33	45
Pipe Truck, No. 803, 9-1/2" long	35	52	70
Power Shovel, 14" long....................	60	90	120
Racer, aluminum and cast iron, No. 22, 1940, 7-3/8" long....................	105	158	210
Racer, "22," aliminum and cast iron, 7-3/8" long..................................	100	150	200

	C6	C8	C10
Racer, cast iron, exhaust stacks, white rubber tires, wooden hubs, tail fins, marked "1791" on driver and "2233" on cast iron, 6" long ..	150	200	250
Racer, No. 5, early wheels, 9-3/8" long...	1100	1800	2600
Racer, cast iron, flat slanted grille, tail fin 4-1/4" long	50	100	150
Racer, No. 5, hood raises to show engine, painted and nickeled iron and aluminum, 9-1/2"long............	1300	2000	3000
Racer, No. 5, die-cast, large wheels	75	11	2150

Hubley Packard, fifteen parts, 1929, 11". Photo from Bill Bertoia Auctions.

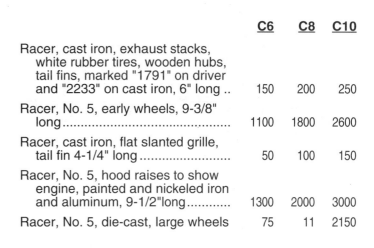

Hubley Panama Digger, Mack, 13". Photo from Joe and Sharon Freed.

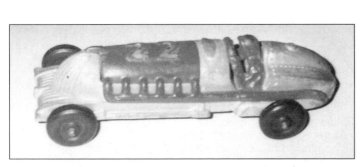

Hubley Racer, No. 22, 7-3/8", aluminum and cast-iron, circa 1940. Photo from Rod Carnahan.

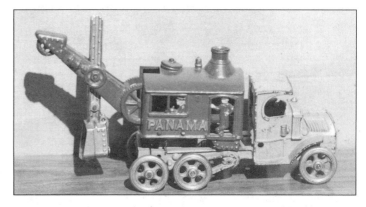

Hubley Racer, No. 5, nickeled iron and aluminum, hood opens, 9-1/2". Photo from Christie's East.

Hubley Racers. Left to right: 9-1/2" long; with exhaust stacks, 11" long; with early wheels, 9-3/8" long; streamlined, 7-1/4" long. Photo from Bill Bertoia Auctions.

Hubley Racer, 5". Photo from Bill Kaufman.

Hubley Racer, 7-1/2", 1930s.

Hubley Railway Express Truck, 5" rubber tires.

	C6	C8	C10
Racer, No. 7, early 1930s, 5-1/4" long	188	282	375
Racer, No. 8, streamlined, 7-1/4" long	225	338	450
Racer, No. 629, 1936, 6-3/4" long	300	475	650
Racer, No. 677, 8-1/2" long	700	1200	1600
Racer, marked "1790," approx. 5" long	160	240	320
Racer, No. 2241, 1930s, 7-1/2" long	45	68	90
Racer, No. 2330, aluminum	500	800	1200
Racer, "1," cast iron, white rubber wheels	150	200	250
Racer, cast iron, exhaust stacks, tail fins, white rubber tires w/wooden hubs, driver part of casting, marked "2229" on car, 5-3/8" long	75	100	125
Racer, cast iron, white rubber tires w/wooden hubs, electric light, marked "2125B on casting" and 1878B18" on driver, 6-1/2" long	350	450	550
Racer, "12," cast iron, white rubber tires, red grille, 5-1/2" long	100	125	150
Racer, animated exhaust stacks, driver, 11" long	1200	2000	3000
Racer, die-cast, black rubber tires, 4" long	25	38	50
Racer, aluminum, white rubber tires, tail fin, 3-3/4" long	50	75	100
Racer, driver, tail fin, 1930s, 6" long	210	325	450

	C6	C8	C10
Racer, "6," nickel-plated cast iron, white rubber tires w/wooden hubs, one piece driver, exhaust and grille, marked "2137," 4-3/4" long	200	250	300
Racer, driver, 1930s, 6-1/2" long	200	300	400
Racer, plastic, 6-1/2" long	44	66	88
Racer, driver, 1930s, 7" long	215	322	430
Racer, w/two passengers, 1930s, 5-1/2" long	125	188	250
Racer, animated exhaust stacks, driver, 8 " long	550	875	1250
Racer, Closed Cabin, 1930s, 8" long	250	375	500
Racer, driver, rubber tires, 8" long	125	188	250
Racer, 1930s, tail fin, exhaust stacks, driver, 8-1/2" long	650	1000	1500
Racer, die-cast, 12" long	65	93	130
Racer, "7," cast iron, white rubber tires w/wooden hubs, large scalloped tail, one-piece casting, marked "2309," 5-3/4"	150	200	250
Racer, marked "No. 1," 8" long	250	375	500
Racer, "7," cast iron, marked "1791" on driver, 5-1/4" long	150	200	250
Racer, "5," cast iron, white rubber tires w/wooden hubs, tail fin, marked "1791," 5-1/16" long	200	250	300
Racer, driver, electric headlights, 7" long	NPF	NPF	NPF
Railway Express Truck, rubber tires, 5" long	200	300	400
Renault Dauphine, plastic	45	68	90
Road Grader, 1950s, 15" long	40	60	80
Road Grader, 12" long	70	105	140
Road Grader, die-cast, 10" long	27	41	55

"HUBLEY"

9 STYLES

Rubber Tires!

Average 3¾ In.

9 Styles—Roadster, coupe, sedan, phaeton, wrecker, etc., streamline models, beautiful 2-color enamel finishes, nickeled radiator and lamps, some styles with black enameled trunks.

61-1920—1 doz in box..........Doz **.80**

Order numbers below for individual items

61-1925—Sedan......................	1 doz in box
61-1926—Phaeton....................	
61-1927—Coupe.....................	Doz
61-1928—Truck.....................	**.80**
61-1929—Roadster..................	

Hubley automobiles, as shown in an ad from the September 1934 Butler Bros. catalog.

	C6	C8	C10
Road Roller, w/driver, late 1920s, 8" long	300	450	600
Road Roller, plastic, wood wheels	25	38	50
Road Roller, Hercules, 4-5/8" long	80	120	160
Road Scraper, No. 481	37	52	75
Roaster, driver, early 1920s, 7-1/4" long	900	1600	2200
School Bus, die-cast, 1960s, 9" long	35	52	70
Sedan, cast iron, 1920, 7" long	100	150	200
Sedan, looks like Ford, rubber wheels, two-door, 3-1/2", c.1938	60	90	120
Sedan, sidemount tire, 1930s, 5" long	165	198	230
Sedan, cast iron, 1928, 7" long	150	225	300
Sedan, early, 4-1/8" long	67	100	135
Sedan, die-cast, 7" long	62	93	125
Sedan, cast iron, four-door, 1930s, 6" long	110	165	220
Service Car, 4-1/4" long	60	90	120
Service Car, cast iron, including wheels, 1930s, 5" long	200	300	400
Shovel Truck, No. 726, c.1930, 10" long	NPF	NPF	NPF
Shovel Truck, c.1938, 8-1/2" long	550	900	1250
Speedster, No. 6, early, 7" long	225	350	435
Sport Car, No. 485	70	105	140
Stake Bed Truck, 7" long	225	338	450
Stake Bed Truck, 5" long	95	142	190
Stake Bed Truck, cast iron, 3-1/2" long	50	75	100
Stake Dump, die-cast	30	45	60

	C6	C8	C10
Stake Truck, white cab, blue bed	NPF	NPF	NPF
Stake Truck, cast iron, marked "10 ton," 7" long	300	425	600
Stake Truck, w/trailer, No. 927, 21" long, two pieces	40	60	80
Stake truck, white cab w/blue bed, 12" long	NPF	NPF	NPF
Stake Truck, late 1930s	160	240	325
Stake Truck, No. 460	44	66	88
Stake Truck, No. 614, 1930s	75	112	150
Stake Truck, marked "10 ton," 8-1/4" long	350	525	700

Hubley Stake Bed Truck, 7". Photo from Mapes Auctioneers and Appraisers.

Hubley Stake Truck, white cab, blue bed.

Hubley Sport Car

Hubley 10 Ton Stake Truck, 7".

Hubley 10 Ton Stake Truck, 8-1/4". Photo from Bill Bertoia Auctions.

Hubley Stake Truck, No. 452, postwar.

Hubley Elgin Street Sweeper, 8", cast-iron, 1931.

	C6	C8	C10
Stake-type Truck, No. 452, black rubber tires, post WWII	40	60	80
Station Wagon, No. 476, 1940s-50s, 8-1/2" long	35	52	70
Steam Roller, 5" long	150	225	300
Steam Shovel, marked "General," 15" long	450	700	1000
Steam Shovel, marked "General," 10-1/2" long	440	660	880
Steam Shovel, marked "General," 9" long	400	625	850
Steam Shovel, marked "General," 8-1/4" long	300	450	600
Steam Shovel, marked "General," 7" long	375	562	750
Steam Shovel, marked "General," 6" long	175	263	350
Steam Shovel, No. 325, 4-1/2" long	115	173	230
Stock Truck, plastic, 12" long	112	168	225
Street Sweeper, cast iron, marked "The Elgin," 1931, 8" long	3500	5000	7500
Studebaker Car Carrier, 10" long	200	300	400
Studebaker Roadster, frame and body separate	300	450	600
Studebaker Stake Truck	20	30	40
Studebaker Touring Car, cast iron	325	518	650

	C6	C8	C10
Studebaker Town Car, cast iron, 5" long	250	375	500
Take-Apart Coupe, 6" long	225	338	450
Take-Apart Roadster, 1930	120	180	240
Take-Apart Sedan, early 1930s, 6" long	150	230	325
Take-Apart Stake Truck, 4-3/4" long	200	300	400
Take-Apart Station Wagon, 1920s	250	400	550
Take-Apart Two Truck, early	238	355	475
Tank Truck	100	150	200
Tanker, plastic, marked "Hubley Tanker," 12-1/2" long	NPF	NPF	NPF
Taxi, die-cast, black rubber tires	20	30	40
Telephone Truck, plastic	25	38	50
Thunderbird	120	180	240
Touring Auto, 1920s, 7" long	165	248	330
Touring Auto, cast iron, chauffeur and rider, 1915, 9-1/2" long	750	1125	1500
Touring Auto, 1921, 11-1/2" long	NPF	NPF	NPF
Tow Truck, cast iron, 8-3/4" long	140	210	280
Tow Truck, Ford, die-cast, 9" long	62	93	125
Tractor, No. 472	40	60	80
Tractor, Ford No. 961, w/plow, 15" long	100	150	200
Tractor, Ford 4000, 10-1/2" long	40	60	80
Tractor, Ford 6000	80	120	160
Tractor, 960 H	68	102	1035
Tractor, scale model, 7" long	88	132	175
Tractor, steam boiler in front, early 1920s, 4-3/4" long	125	187	250
Tractor, 1930s, 5" long	250	450	600

- Hubley

	C6	C8	C10
Tractor, die-cast, w/scoop, 13" long.	58	87	115
Tractor, No. 490	50	75	100
Tractor Loader, No. 501, 1950s, 11" long	78	118	155
Tractor Shovel, driver, 9-1/2" long ...	750	1300	1750
Tractor Trailer, 1950s	75	112	150
Tractor Trailer and Road Scraper, No. 506, die-cast, 19" long	150	225	300
Trailer Truck, c.1936-38	100	150	200
Transitional Fire Patrol, cast iron, driver, firemen, 1920, 12" long	1000	1500	2000
Truck, w/eight wooden barrels, marked "5 Ton Truck," c.1920, 17" long	750	1200	1700
VW, metal w/sunroof, marked "Beetle Bug," 1969	50	75	100
Water Tower, early, two drivers, 14" long	850	1400	2000
Woody Station Wagon, takeapart, 5" long	NPF	NPF	NPF
Wrecker, white wheels on large hubs, c.1940, 6" long	100	150	200
Wrecker, Service Car, chrome wheels	45	68	90
Wrecker, 3-1/2" long	42	63	85

	C6	C8	C10
Wrecker, 4-3/4" long	75	112	150
Wrecker, Ford, No. 474, 10" long	82	123	165
Wrecker, rubber wheels, 1930, 4-1/2" long	110	165	220
Wrecking Truck, cast iron, rubber tires, 1930, 7-1/2" long	150	225	300
Yellow Cab, spare tire, 1920s, 8-1/4" long	600	950	1400
Yellow Cab, rear luggage racks folds down, 8" long	300	450	600
Yellow Cab, 1920s, 7-3/4" long	550	850	1200

Motorcycles

	C6	C8	C10
Motorcycle, rubber or nickel wheels, marked "Cop," 4" long (HM01)	50	75	100
Motorcycle, tandem, marked "PDH" rubber or nickel wheels, 4-1/8" long (HM04)	100	150	250

Hubley Yellow Cab, 1920s, 7-3/4". Photo from Sotheby's, New York.

Hubley Woody Station Wagon, takeapart, 5". Photo from Bill Bertoia Auctions.

Hubley Wrecker, No. 20, 6", circa 1940. Photo from Mapes Auctioneers and Appraisers.

Hubley Motorcycle solo, Cop, rubber or nickel wheels, 4". Photo from Mapes Auctioneers and Appraisers.

Hubley Motorcycle, removable rider, 4-1/4". Photo from Kent M. Comstock.

Hubley Motorcycle, plastic Kiddie Toy, 5".

Hubley Motorcycle, Harley-Davidson with sidecar, two policemen, rubber or nickel wheels, 5-1/4". Photo from Kent M. Comstock.

Hubley Motorcycle with civilian driver, rubber or nickel wheels, 6-1/4". Photo from Kent M. Comstock.

	C6	C8	C10
Motorcycle, w/detachable cop, battery-operated headlight, red, 8-1/2" long (HM18)	600	750	1000
Motorcycle, Harley Davidson, sidecar, civilian driver, woman passenger, 9" long (HM33)	800	1400	2200
Motorcycle, removable rider, 4-1/4" long (HM34)	50	75	125
Motorcycle, w/cast-in policeman, black rubber tires, 4-1/2" long (HM34A)	50	75	100
Motorcycle, Harley Davidson w/sidecar, two policemen, rubber or nickel wheels, 5-1/4" long (HM35)	250	350	500
Motorcycle, Popeye Patrol, 8-3/8" long (HM38)	2000	3500	5500

	C6	C8	C10
Motorcycle, Kiddie Toy, plastic, 5" long (HM40)	15	22	30
Motorcycle Civilian Driver, rubber or nickel wheels, 6-1/4" long (HM13)	250	400	600
Motorcycle Hillclimber, rubber or nickel wheels, marked "HD-45," 6-1/2" long (HM11)	400	600	800
Motorcycle Package Truck, "Harley Davidson Parcel Post," w/detachable blue rider 9-1/2" long (HM25)	1300	2000	2900
Motorcycle Package Truck, "Indian Air Mail," w/detachable blue rider, 9-1/2" long (HM26)	1100	2000	2700
Motorcycle Policeman, nickel wheels, marked "Harley Davidson," 5-1/2" long (HM09)	275	363	550

• Hubley

Hubley Motorcycle Hillclimber, rubber or nickel wheels, 6-1/2".

Hubley Motorcycle policeman, Harley-Davidson, nickel wheels, 5-1/2".

Hubley Motorcycle Package Truck, Harley-Davidson Parcel Post, 9-1/2".

Hubley Motorcycle policeman, Harley-Davidson, swivel head, rubber or nickel wheels, 7-1/4". Photo from Mapes Auctioneers and Appraisers.

Hubley Motorcycle Package Truck, Indian, Air Mail, 9-1/2". Photo from Bill Bertoia Auctions.

Hubley Motorcycle policeman, 1950s, die-cast with plastic driver, 8-1/2".

	C6	C8	C10
Motorcycle Policeman, marked "Harley Jr.," nickel wheels, 5-1/2" long (HM09A)	150	300	450
Motorcycle Policeman, swivel head, rubber or nickel wheels, marked "Harley Davidson," 7-1/4" long (HM10)	500	750	1200
Motorcycle Policeman, die-cast w/plastic driver, "PD," 1950s, 8-1/2" long (HM15)	400	500	750
Motorcycle Policeman, battery-operated headlight, 6" long (HM17)	300	450	600
Motorcycle racer, marked "Speed," 4-1/4" long (HM03)	165	248	330
Motorcycle Racer, nickel wheels, 5-3/4" long (HM12)	375	550	800
Motorcycle Trike, rubber or nickel wheels, marked "Crash Car," 4-3/4" long (HM05)	50	75	125
Motorcycle Trike, traffic car nickel wheels, 3-5/8" long (HM06)	75	125	200
Motorcycle Trike, nickel wheels, blue, marked "Flowers," 3-3/8" long (HM07)	500	800	1200

	C6	C8	C10
Motorcycle Trike, rubber or nickel wheels, blue, marked "Flowers," 4-1/2" long (HM08)	500	800	1200
Motorcycle Trike, marked "Flowers," 5-1/4" long (HM08A)	900	1500	3100
Motorcycle Trike, "Traffic Car" Indian, rubber tires, 9" long (HM16)	700	1000	1600
Motorcycle Trike, "Indian Crash Car," removable rider, axes and hose red 11-1/2" long (HM27)	1500	2000	3000
Motorcycle Trike, "Indian Traffic Car," removable rider, red and blue, 12" long (HM28)	1500	2000	3000

Hubley Motorcycle Trike, "Flowers," rubber (left) or nickel (right) wheels, blue, 4-1/2". Photo from Kent M. Comstock.

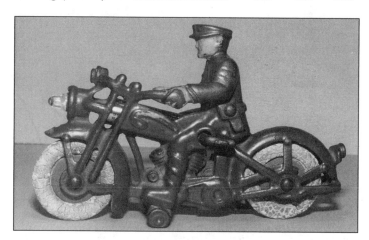

Hubley Motorcycle policeman, battery-operated headlight, 6".

Hubley Motorcycle trike Indian Traffic Car, removable rider, 12", red and blue. Photo from Bill Bertoia Auctions.

Hubley Motorcycle Racer, nickel wheels, 5-3/4".

Hubley Motorcycle Trike Indian Crash Car, 11-1/2". Photo from Bill Bertoia Auctions.

	C6	C8	C10
Motorcycle Trike, cast iron, "Say It with Flowers," 10-1/2" long (HM31)	8000	13,000	18,000
Motorcycle Trike, "Indian Crash Car," 9-3/8" long (HM36)	1400	2200	4500
Motorcycle Trike, Popeye Spinach Cycle, separate rider, 5-3/8" long (HM37)	650	1100	1750
Motorcycle Trike, "Crash Car," 6-1/2" long (HM39)	225	338	450

	C6	C8	C10
Motorcycle w/removable civilian rider, "Harley Davidson," olive green, blue, or orange, 9" long (HM22)	1250	2000	3000
Motorcycle w/removable cop, "Harley Davidson," olive green, blue, or orange, 9" long (HM23) .	700	1500	1880

Hubley Motorcycle Trike Crash Car, 6-1/2". Photo from Bill Bertoia Auctions.

Hubley Motorcycle Trike, "Say It With Flowers," cast-iron, 10-1/2". Photo from Bill Bertoia Auctions.

Hubley Motorcycle Trike Indian Crash Car, 9-3/8". Photo from Bill Bertoia Auctions.

Hubley Motorcycle with removable civilian driver, Harley-Davidson, 9". Photo from Kent M. Comstock.

Left to Right: Hubley Motorcycle trike Popeye Spinach Cycle, 5-3/8"; Hubley Popeye Patrol, 8-3/8". Photo from Bill Bertoia Auctions.

Hubley Motorcycle with removable cop, Harley-Davidson, 9", olive green, blue or orange. Photo from Bill Bertoia Auctions.

Hubley Motorcycle with removable cop, 9-1/4", red, green or yellow. Photo from Kent M. Comstock.

Hubley Motorcycle with sidecar, Harley-Davidson, two removable cops, 9" olive green.

Hubley Motorcycle with sidecar, Cop rider and passenger (passenger missing), 4".

Hubley Motorcycle with sidecar, Indian, two cops, 9" red. Photo from Kent M. Comstock.

Hubley Motorcycle with sidecar, two removable cops, battery-operated headlight, 8-1/2" red.

	C6	C8	C10
Motorcycle w/removable cop, "Indian," nickel four-cylinder motor, red, green, or yellow, 9-1/4" long (HM24)	800	1300	1800
Motorcycle w/sidecar, Cop rider and passenger, 4" long (HM02)	110	165	220
Motorcycle w/sidecar, civilian driver and passenger, 6-1/2" long (HM14) ....,....................	300	500	750
Motorcycle w/sidecar, two removable cops, battery-operated headlight, red, 8-1/2" long (HM19)	800	1900	2650
Motorcycle w/sidecar, "Harley Davidson," two removable cops, olive green, 9" long (HM20)	600	1000	1400

	C6	C8	C10
Motorcycle w/sidecar, "Indian," two removable cops, red, 9" long (HM21)	600	900	1200
Motorcycle w/sidecar, "Indian Armored Car," two removable cops, red, 8-1/2" long (HM29)	1200	2000	2750

Hubley Motorcycle with sidecar, Indian Armored Car, two removable cops, 8-1/2" red. Photo from Bill Bertoia Auctions.

IDEAL

	C6	C8	C10		C6	C8	C10
American LaFrance Aerial Ladder Truck............	95	143	190	Car Trailer, c.1945, plastic, 3" long ..	20	30	40
American LaFrance Fix-It Tow Truck, w/1952 Pontiac car and tools	150	225	300	Carousel Truck............	50	75	100
				Cattle Truck, 13" long............	25	38	50
Army Ambulance, 5" long............	20	30	40	Coal Truck, 1949, 5-1/2" long	21	31	42
Army Jeep, "Mighty Mo," siren, plastic, 1953, 13" long............	25	38	50	Corvette	75	112	150
Army Van, 4" long	20	30	40	Dairy Farm Van............	27	41	54
Atomic Rocket Launching Truck, 12" long............	32	48	65	Danger Patrol Truck, 1950s	90	135	180
Auto Laundry............	55	83	110	Dragnet Talking Police Car	60	90	120
Barracuda Coupe, 1964, plastic, 4" long............	15	23	30				
Bulldozer, plastic............	50	75	100				
Cadillac, four-door, 1948, plastic, 4" long............	25	38	50				

Ideal Dragnet Talking Police Car.

Left to right: Ideal Army Ambulance, 5"; Van, 6". Photo from Bob and Alice Wagner.

Ideal Cattle Truck, 13". Photo from Terry Sells.

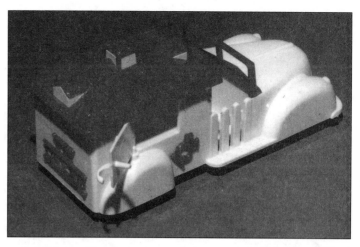

Ideal Ice Cream Truck, 5-1/2", 1948-1954. Photo from Bob and Alice Wagner.

Ideal Dump Truck, 5-3/4". Photo from dave Leopard.

Ideal FBI Car, No. 3072, talks. Photo from Tim Oei.

Ideal Jeep, with original box, 1940s. Photo from Terry Sells.

	C6	C8	C10
Dump Truck, 5-3/4" long	21	32	42
Emergency Van, 6" long	10	35	45
FBI Car, No. 3072, talks	NPF	NPF	NPF
Fire Pumper	34	51	68
Fix-It Cadillac, 12" long	75	112	150
Fix-It Fire Chief Fire Truck	72	108	145
Fix-It Sport Convertible, 13" long	65	98	130
Fix-It Tow Truck	90	135	180
Fix-It Tow Truck and Car w/Dented Fender, metal and plastic, 20-1/2" long	NPF	NPF	NPF
Fix-It Truck, w/tools, plastic, 8-1/2" long	62	93	125
Ford Truck	40	60	80
Ford Wagon	40	60	80
Gambles Semi Truck, plastic, 12" long	36	54	72
Hy-Speed Car Wash w/car, 1950s	32	48	65
Ice Cream Truck, 1948-54, 5-1/2" long	30	60	100

	C6	C8	C10
Ideal Car Trailer, plastic, four cars, 27" long	40	60	80
Jeep, c.1945	20	30	40
Jet Racer	50	75	100
Ladder Truck	65	98	130
Mercedes Sedan, 9" long	35	52	70

Left to right: Ideal Pickup Truck, streamlined with canopy and gas tank filler, 4-1/2"; Pickup Truck, streamlined, 4-1/2". Photo from Bob and Alice Wagner.

Ideal Robert the Robot, battery-operated. Photo from Don Hultzman.

Ideal Rocket Cycle, 6-1/2". Photo from Terry Sells.

Ideal Rolls-Royce, 8", plastic. Photo from Ron Fink.

Ideal Sanitation Truck, 5-1/2" plastic. Photo from Terry Sells.

	C6	C8	C10
Motorific, 1951 GMC Wrecker	20	30	40
Nellybelle Jeep	14	21	28
Oldsmobile, 1954, 19" long	150	225	300
Panel Truck, No. 3085, 1951-52	27	41	54
Panel Truck, No. 1-1729	20	30	40
Patton Tank, 6" long	12	18	25
Pickup Truck, American, 1948, 4" plastic	20	30	40
Pickup Truck, streamlined, w/canopy and gas tank filler, 1950s, 4-1/2" long	4	10	20

	C6	C8	C10
Pickup Truck, Ford, 1940, 4" plastic	14	21	27
Pickup Truck, streamlined, 1950s, No. 1-788, 4-1/2" long	7	11	14
Police Car	6	9	12
Race Car, 8" wind-up	60	90	120
Race Car, 10" wind-up	50	75	100
Robert the Robot, battery-operated	150	225	300
Rocket Car, w/wind-up launcher, 11" long	NPF	NPF	NPF
Rocket Cycle, 6-1/2" long	100	150	200
Rocket Launcher Truck, 12" long	55	83	110
Rolls Royce, 8" long, plastic	12	18	25
Rolls Royce, 12" long	11	16	22
Sanitation Truck, plastic, 5-1/2" long	20	35	50

Ideal Scooter, 4" plastic. Photo from Terry Sells.

Ideal Shell Truck, 12-1/2". Photo from Terry Sells.

Ideal Steam Shovel, plastic, 7-1/2". Photo from Dave Leopard.

Ideal Sedan, 9-1/4". Photo from Terry Sells.

Ideal Turbo-Jet Car, No. 4867. Photo from Tim Oei.

	C6	C8	C10
Scooter, plastic, 4" long	NPF	NPF	NPF
Sedan, 5" long.................................	14	21	28
Sedan, plastic, 9-1/4" long	20	35	50
Sedan w/Teardrop Trailer, 8-1/8" long..	26	39	52
Semi Truck, 12" long.......................	26	39	52
Service Truck, 8" long.....................	22	33	45
Service Van, 5" long........................	20	30	40
Shell Truck, 12-1/2" long.................	25	38	50
Signal Corps Truck, 5" long	20	30	40
Speed King Dream Racer, plastic, 13" long............................	50	75	100

	C6	C8	C10
Speedy Pete pulltoy racer, early 1950s..	60	90	120
Steam Shovel, 7-1/2" long	22	33	45
Steering Farm Tractor......................	7	11	15
Steve Canyon Glider Bomb Truck, 17" long...	60	90	120
Television Repair Truck	40	60	80
Tow Truck, plastic and metal, 17" long..	100	150	200
Tractor, 1948, plastic, 4" long	20	30	40
Trailer, No. 1-409	7	11	15

Back row, left to right: Ideal Van, sliding front door, 4-1/2"; Dairy Farm Van. Front row: Van, 6". Photo from Bob and Alice Wagner.

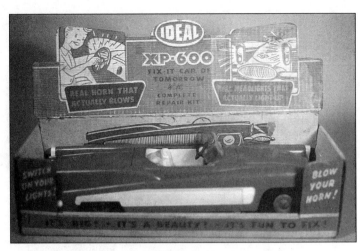

Ideal XP-600 Fix-It Car of Tomorrow, 16". Photo from Terry Sells.

	C6	C8	C10
Turbo-Jet Car, No. 4867	60	90	120
Van, sliding front door, 4-1/2" long...	10	25	60
Van, 6" long....................................	10	35	45

	C6	C8	C10
Work Truck.....................................	35	52	70
XP-600 Fix-It Car of Tomorrow, 16" long...	85	128	170

IRWIN TOY CORPORATION

Irwin was founded in 1922 by Irwin Cohn. Located at first in New York City, it began as a maker of celluloid baby rattles and pinwheels, soon becoming the largest manufacturer of pinwheels in the United States. In the late 1940s, it produced the first polyethylene toy—a seven-inch car. Irwin, which eventually moved to Leominster and Fitchburg in Massachusetts (with an additional plant in Nashua, New Hampshire), sold out to Miner Industries in 1973.

	C6	C8	C10
Army Bus...................................	27	41	55
Army Cadillac Staff Car, plastic windshield	15	22	30
Army Dump Truck, plastic................	12	18	25
Barney Rubble Car..........................	12	18	25

Irwin Chevrolet Pickup Truck, 1952. Photo from Dave Leopard.

	C6	C8	C10
Big Mike Tow Truck, battery-operated	55	82	110
Buick Convertible, 1948, 5" long......	10	15	20
Chevrolet Panel Delivery, 6" long	10	15	20
Chevrolet Pickup Truck, 1952, 5-1/3" long	10	15	20
Dream Car Convertible, metal, 16" long..	200	300	400
Dump Truck, 1950s, 8-1/2" long	15	22	30
Ford Sunliner, plastic friction, 9" long	50	15	100
GI Joe Motorcycle and Sidecar........	100	150	200
Horse Van, 16" long.......................	25	38	50
Human Cannonball Truck, w/net and two figures, 1960s, 19" long	41	62	83
Ice Cream Truck, plastic	55	82	110
Jaguar Roadster, 6" long	35	52	70
Log Truck	20	30	40

Irwin Pickup Truck, 6", metal. Photo from Ron Fink.

Irwin Pontiac Hardtop Coupe, 6", friction. Photo from Dave Leopard.

Irwin Police Car, 12", plastic friction. Photo from Ron Fink.

Irwin State Police Car, 6-1/2", plastic friction. Photo from Ron Fink.

	C6	C8	C10
Packard Sedan, friction, 1952, 9" long	25	30	35
Pickup Truck, metal, 6" long	24	36	48
Plumbing and Heating Truck, w/tools, etc., 1960s	62	93	125
Police Car, plastic, 12" long	25	38	50
Pontiac Hardtop Coupe, friction, 1952, 6" long	15	20	25

	C6	C8	C10
Racer	17	26	35
Skipper convertible, 1962	150	225	300
State Police Car, plastic friction, 6-1/2" long	15	22	30
Steeraway Wonder Car	95	143	190
Taxi Cab, trunk opens, 12" long	125	188	250
Telephone Repair Truck	100	150	200
Tow Truck, 8"	27	41	55

IVES

	C6	C8	C10
Fire Patrol, cast-iron, 20-1/2" long	500	700	900
Hook and Ladder Wagon, cast-iron, 26-1/2" long	600	800	1000
Horse Drawn Ladder Truck, cast-iron, 21" long	900	1200	1500
Horseless Carriage Runabout, 6-1/2" long, 6" high to the top of jockey cap on driver	2500	3750	5000
Steamer, cast iron, two drivers, 19-1/2" long	500	750	1000

Ives Fire Patrol, 20-1/2" cast-iron.

Ives Hook & Ladder Wagon, 26-1/2" cast-iron.

Ives Horse Drawn Ladder Truck, 21" cast-iron.

JANE FRANCIS TOYS

Jane Francis Toys operated in Wilkinsburg, Pennsylvania, from 1942-1946 and in Somerset, Pennsylvania, from 1947-1949. Starting as a stuffed-toy maker, the company introduced a line of die-cast cars in 1945. The last Jane Francis toys were manufactured in 1949.

	C6	C8	C10
Gulf Service Station	400	575	750
Gulf Service Station, complete	235	475	950
Gulf Truck, tin cover, No. 447, 5" long (JF05)	30	45	75
Pickup Truck, 6-1/2" long (JF01)	30	40	50
Pickup Truck, No. 347, 5" long (JF02)	20	25	30

	C6	C8	C10
Pickup Truck, 5" long, No. 447 (JF03)	20	25	30
Sedan, fastback, futuristic, 6-1/2" long (JF06)	25	30	40
Sedan, fastback, futuristic, w/wind-up motor, 6-1/2" long (JF07)	30	40	50
Tow Truck, No. 447, 5" long (JF04)	30	40	65

Jane Francis Gulf Service Station, 1940s. Photo from Barbara Francis Vanyo.

Jane Francis Pickup Truck, 5". Photo from Dave Leopard.

Jane Francis Gulf Truck, 5", tin cover. Photo from Dave Leopard.

Jane Francis Tow Truck, 5". Photo from Dave Leopard.

JAPANESE BATTERY-OPERATED VEHICLES

"Made in Japan" are the words toy collectors look for in their pursuit of high-quality mechanical tin toys. Before World War II, these words were synonymous with cheap, poor-quality, drab-looking toys made from recycled materials and ideas. Most of the toys were people-animal oriented, with less emphasis on vehicle, nautical or aircraft-type toys. They were powered either by a spring or a flywheel and didn't last too long or do too much, as far as play-value goes. These cheap toys kept Japan a third-rate toy-manufacturing nation until after World War II, when Japan's surrender resulted in economic chaos for this industrial nation.

In its quest for economic recovery and to compete in a toy market already dominated by Germany and America, the Japanese knew they had to come up with a new, different and exciting type of toy that would make them more desirable than their competitors. The Japanese toy designers concentrated their technology on a different type of toy operation. Not satisfied with the limited edition and short duration of spring-driven or flywheel-propelled toys, the toy engineers developed a small electric motor, powered by flashlight batteries. This mini-motor took up less room than other mechanisms, had a longer-running duration and enabled the toy to perform more functions. This development opened up an entirely new dimension in toy design and introduced the concept of the battery-operated toy.

The Toy designers integrated this new concept into hundreds of automaton-like toys, capable of as many as eight different types of actions, all in one cycle. These unique toys were an instant hit with the foreign market, especially in the United States. These clever, unusual and high-quality toys made Japan the dominant toy producer and exporter for the next twenty-thirty years.

Again, Japan flooded the market with these ingenious, well-made toys while quality control remained a high priority. These merits were not only apparent in their figural toys, but also in their vehicle line. Here, the Japanese toy makers concentrated on very fine detail and quality, especially in their scale-model passenger cars, with the ultimate goal of making them look like the real thing. They succeeded. Their workmanship carried over into their other vehicle lines, such as motorcycles, emergency and construction vehicles, as well as their novelty (silly) and comic character cars, trucks and space toys.

No other nation was able to equal or surpass the impetus and determination of the Japanese toy makers, until Japan relinquished its domination by realigning its economy in the electronic-automotive field.

Now that they are approaching middle age, it is no wonder that these fine toys remain in great demand today and are often very pricey!

Condition Of A Toy And Its Relation To Price

The value of a battery-operated toy depends not only on its desirability, rarity and complexity, but very much on its condition. A toy in Mint condition is generally worth twice as much as a toy in Good condition. A toy in Very Good condition will be equally priced between Good and Mint.

C10, Mint: It means just that—the condition in which the toy was originally issued regardless of age. It will also be in perfect mechanical condition, complete with all accessory parts, when applicable, and will look brand new. The cloth or fur (plush) covering on some battery toys may reveal some discoloration or yellowing due to age, but this should not affect its value as a Mint toy, as long as it is clean. All toys in this category must be in perfect working condition. The original box in Mint condition will significantly enhance the value of any Mint toy.

C8, Excellent: Indicates the condition of a battery toy that has seen some use and is starting to show its age. It will still be in perfect working order and have all its accessory parts, where applicable. It will have some age-soiling, but will have no rust or corrosion. Overall, it will have an appearance of freshness and still be highly desirable to the fussy collector.

C6, Good: Applies to a battery toy that has seen considerable use, wear and tear, some age soiling, but still in perfect working condition with no missing parts or accessories. The "wet" toys may show some slight surface rust that can be easily removed. A toy in Good condition is still a welcome addition to any toy collection, but will be targeted for upgrading by a piece in better condition.

Any battery toy below the condition of Good will reflect a drastic reduction in value. Toys in good shape, but missing accessory parts, will not lose as much value as those that are severely rusted, corroded, painted over, have parts broken off and are totally inoperable. These toys in Poor condition are usually collected for their scrap value by the toy repairer, and seldom are they worth more than $10.

The key to grading is to use common sense and avoid wishful thinking. Since grading the condition of a toy may be difficult at times, consulting with an expert in the field, if possible, could clear up any lingering doubts. (See back section of this guide for references of toy collectors.)

Source: *Collecting Battery Toys* by Don Hultzman

	C6	C8	C10
007 Aston Martin, 1966, Gilbert Co., 11-1/2" long, eight actions (includes ejectable passenger)	250	375	500
007 Secret Agent's Car (Impala), 1960s, Spesco Co., (Joy Toy), 15" long, five actions	200	300	400
American Circus Television Truck, 1950s, Exelo Co., 9-1/4" long, six actions, RAE (includes detachable metal antenna)	600	900	1200
Anti-Aircraft Jeep, 1950s, T-N Co. 11" long, six actions (includes detachable tin radar antenna)	150	225	300
Anti-Aircraft Jeep, 1950s, "K" Co., 9-1/2" long, five actions	100	150	200
Antique Gooney Car, 1960s, Alps Co., 9" long, four actions	70	105	140
Armored Attack Set, 1960s, Marx Co., jeep 6-1/4" long and tank 5-1/4" long, plus fifteen 2" plastic figures	200	300	400
Army Radio Jeep—J1490, 1950s Linemar Co., 7-1/4" long, four actions	90	135	180

	C6	C8	C10
Automatic Toll Gate, 1955, Sears, 16"x17" base, six actions (includes 8" tin Valiant)	150	225	300
Auto-top Ferrari Convertible, 1960s, Bandai Co., three actions, 11" long..............................	450	675	900
Batmobile, 1972 National Periodical Publications, ASC Co., 12" long, three actions	200	300	400
Big Ring Circus Truck, 1950s, M-T Co., 13" long, three actions	150	225	300
Big Shot Cadillac, 1950s, T-N Co., 10" long, four actions, rare...........	200	300	400
Big Wheel Coca-Cola Truck, 1970s, Taiyo Co., three actions...............	80	120	160
Big Wheel Family Camper, 1970s, 10" long, three actions	80	120	160
Big Wheel Ice Cream Truck, 1970s 10" long, three actions	70	105	140
Bulldozer, 1950s, M-T Co., 11" long, six actions	90	135	180
Bulldozer, 1950s, T-N Co., 7-1/2" long, five actions........................	80	120	160

Guidelines For The Care And Repair Of Your Battery-Operated Toy

Your prized battery toy needs special care. When it stops working, you now have a frustrating disaster on your hands. To avoid this, the following suggestions should be of some help.

Battery toys, like other mechanical toys, should be operated periodically to keep them loosened up. Using a lightweight spray lubrication now and then will help considerably, if the mechanism is accessible. Do not over-lubricate, as the excess may stain any cloth or fur covering on some battery toys.

A good quality car wax or polish will keep the lithographed and bare metal parts looking like new—especially on the "wet" toys. Always test an obscure lithographed area to make sure the polish doesn't soften or dissolve the paint. Care should be exercised when polishing metal parts adjoining any cloth or plush covering, as the substance may stain the coverings. Light surface rust usually disappears with a careful polishing. Nothing can be done for deep rust or corrosion without ruining the value of the toy. Repainting will only further reduce the value and is not recommended.

Should your battery toy fail to operate, the following steps might be helpful.

1. Make sure it is not gunked-up, and that no moving parts are binding.

2. Make sure the battery contacts are not dirty or corroded—if so, clean them with crocus cloth. Always use fresh batteries.

3. Lightly tap the toy with your finger or lightly nudge one of the moving parts while the switch is on.

If none of these steps work, your toy needs major surgery. This means the toy must be completely torn down, repaired and reassembled. Most battery toys are repairable as long as they have not been destructively tampered with and no parts are missing or corroded beyond repair. This job is best left to an expert in toy repair and should never be attempted by one who doesn't know what he is doing. Expert repairs will not affect the value of a battery toy, so long as the repair is undetectable and the toys look and function exactly as it did before the repair. Such repairs are acceptable in toy collecting circles. Expert repairs are also expensive but well worth the investment, if it means the difference between a Mint and Good toy, since an inoperable toy is practically worthless, regardless of condition.

Japanese battery-operated Anti-Aircraft Jeep, T-N, 1950s, 11". Photo from Don Hultzman.

Japanese battery-operated Antique Gooney Car, Alps, 1960s, 9". Photo from Don Hultzman.

Japanese battery-operated Batmobile, ASC, 1972, 12". Photo from Don Hultzman.

Japanese battery-operated Big Wheel Coca-Cola Truck, Taiyo, 1970s. Photo from Don Hultzman.

Japanese battery-operated Caterpillar Tank M-1, 1950s, M-T, 11". Photo from Don Hultzman.

	C6	C8	C10
B-Z Porter Baggage Truck, 1950s, M-T Co., 7-1/2" long, 6-1/2" high, minor toy, includes three pcs. of luggage (tin)	150	205	300
Cadillac Car, 1949, Ashai Toy Co., 10" long, three actions	150	225	300
Caterpillar Tank M-1, 1950s, M-T Co., five actions, 8-1/2" long, 11" long w/barrel extended	150	220	300
Chaparral 2F Car, 1960s, Alps Co., 11" long, five actions	90	135	180
Chemical Fire Engine, 1950s, HTC Co., 10" long, four actions	110	165	220

	C6	C8	C10
Circus Fire Engine, 1960s, M-T Co., 11" long, four actions	140	210	280
Climbing Donald Duck On His Friction Fire Engine, 1950s Linemar Co., four actions, 12" long	400	600	800
Clown Circus Car, 1960s, M-T Co., 8-1/2" long, 9" high, five actions	130	195	260
Coin Taxi, 1960s, Daiya Co., 6-1/2" long, minor toy	50	75	100
Comic Hungry Bug, VW auto, 1970s, Tora (S-T) Co., 7-3/4" long, five actions	40	60	80
Comic Musical Car, 1960s, T-N Co., four actions, 6" long, 8-1/2" tall	70	105	140
Comic Road Roller, 1960s, Bandai Co., four actions, 9" long	70	105	140
Corvair Bertone, 1970s, Bandai Co., four actions, 12" long	50	75	100
Corvette Sting Ray Sport Coupe, 1968, Eldon Co., 13-1/2" long, minor toy	100	150	200
Cragstan Beep Beep Greyhound Bus, 1950s, Cragston Co., 20" long, three actions	120	330	240
Cragstan Firebird III, 1956, Alps Co., 11-3/4" long, three actions	300	450	600
Crane Tractor, 1950s, SKK Co., 7-1/2" long, 11-1/2" high extended	70	105	140
Crazy Car, 1950s, Marusan Co., five actions, 9" long	70	105	140
Desert Patrol Jeep, 1960s, M-T Co., 11" long, four actions, includes turret gunner	100	150	200
Dick Tracy Police Car, 1949, TN Co., 9" long, four actions	100	150	200
Disney Fire Engine, 1950s, Linemar Co., 11" long, four actions	440	660	880
Disneyland Fire Engine, 1950s, Linemar Co., 18" long, five actions	300	450	600

	C6	C8	C10
Dreamboat Hot-Rod--See Hot Rod, "Dump Truck No. 7343," 1960s, T-N Co., 10-1/4" long, seven actions	150	225	300
Electric School Bus, 1950s, M-T Co., 9-1/2" long, minor toy	80	120	160
Electro Special Racer, 1950s, Yonezawa Co., 10" long, three actions	100	150	200
Electro Toy Racer, 1950s, Yonezawa Co., three actions, 10" long	1000	1500	2000
Electronic Fire House, 1940s, Banner Co., 7" square, minor toy (includes plastic fire engine)	80	120	160
Expert Motor Cyclist, 1950s, MT Co., 12" long, five actions	450	675	900
F.D. Fire Engine, 1960s, Y-M Co., 10" long, 12" high when ladder is extended, four actions	100	150	200
Farm Truck, 1950s, T-N Co., five actions, 9" long	100	150	200
Farm Truck, 1960s, Alps Co., 11" long, three actions	120	180	240
Ferris Wheel Truck, 1950s, T-N Co., 11" long, four actions	400	600	900
Fire Chief Mystery Action Car, 1960s, T-N Co., 9-3/4" long, four actions	120	180	240

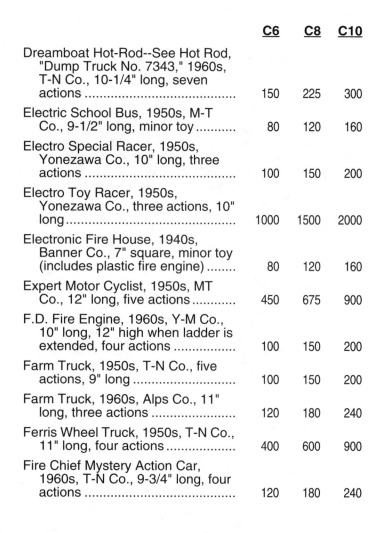

Japanese battery-operated Crazy Car, Marusan, 1950s, 9". Photo from Don Hultzman.

Japanese battery-operated Farm Truck, T-N, 1950s, 9". Photo from Don Hultzman.

Japanese battery-operated Fire Command Car, T-N Co., 1950s. Photo from Don Hultzman.

Japanese battery-operated Fork Lift Truck, 1960s, M-T Co., 10-1/4". Photo from Don Hultzman.

Japanese battery-operated Go-Kart, M-T Co., 1960s, 6-1/2". Photo from Don Hultzman.

Japanese battery-operated Greyhound Bus. Photo from Don Hultzman.

	C6	C8	C10
Fire Chief No. 8 Car, 1960s, Y Co., 11-1/4" long, three actions	90	135	180
Fire Command Car, 1950s, T-N Co., five actions	170	255	340
Fire Engine, 1950s, Marusan Co., four actions, 9" long	150	225	300
Fire Engine, 1950s, T-N Co., (Electro Toy), three actions, 9" long-ladder extends 13"	150	225	300
Fire Engine, 1950s, Y Co., 12" long, ladder extends 16", six actions	100	150	200
Fire Engine, 1950s, S-H Co., three actions, 8" long	100	150	200
Firebird Racer, 1950s, Tomiyama Co., four actions, 14-1/4" long	300	450	600
Ford Model T, 1950s, Nihonkogei Co., 10-1/4" long, four actions (includes detachable tin roof)	60	90	120
Ford Mustang 2x2, 1960s, Wenmac-AMF Co., four actions, 16" long ...	70	105	140

	C6	C8	C10
Fork Lift Truck, 1960s, M-T Co., 10-1/4" high, minor toy	100	150	200
Go Kart, 1960s, M-T Co., 6-1/2" long, minor toy (includes control wire w/steering key)	100	150	200
Go Kart, 1950s, Rosko Co., 10" long, three actions, includes detachable head	100	150	200
Go-Stop Benz Racer, 1950s, Marusan Co., three actions, 11" long	150	220	300
Grand-Pa Car, 1950s, Y Co., 9" long, four actions	60	90	120
Greyhound Bus, 1950s, KKK. Co., minor toy, 7-1/4" long..................	100	150	200

Japanese battery-operated Highway Patrol Police Special, Y Co., 1960s, 11-1/2".

Japanese battery-operated John's Farm Truck, T-N, 1950s, 9". Photo from Don Hultzman.

Japanese battery-operated John's Farm Truck, T-N, 1950s, 9". Photo from Don Hultzman.

	C6	C8	C10
Greyhound bus with Headlights, 1950s, Linemar Co., 10-1/4" long, three actions	120	180	240
Greyhound Bus-Scenicruiser, 1950s, I.Y. Metal Toy Co., 16" long, three actions	100	150	200
Handy-Hank Mystery Tractor, 1950s, T-N Co., 9" long, four actions	90	135	180
Happy Clown Car, 1960s, Y Co., 6-1/2" long, three actions	80	120	160
Happy Tractor, 1960s, Daiya Co., 8" long, four actions	40	60	80
Highway Drive, 1950s, T-N Co., 15-1/2" long, three actions (includes tin magnetic car)	60	90	120
Highway Patrol Jeep, 1950s, Daiya Co., 10" long, four actions	70	105	140
Highway Patrol Police Special, 1960s, Y Co., five actions, 11-1/2" long	100	150	200
Highway Skill Driving, 1960s, K Co., 13" long, three actions	70	105	140

	C6	C8	C10
Hot Rod Car, 1950s, T-N Co., 10" long, minor toy	200	300	400
Hot Rod Custom 'T' Ford, 1960s, Alps Co., four actions, 10-1/2" long	100	150	200
Hot Rod Limousine, 1960s, Alps Co., four actions, 10-1/2" long	200	300	400
Ice Cream Truck, 1960s, Bandai Co., 10-1/2" long, five actions	150	225	300
James Bond-007 Car-M101, 1960s, Daiya Co., 11" long, seven actions, includes ejectable driver, See M101 Aston Martin	NPF	NPF	NPF
James Bond's Aston-Martin, See 007 Aston Martin	NPF	NPF	NPF
Jeep No. 10560, 1950s, Cragstan, 5-1/2" long, a minor action toy	70	105	140
Jeep-USA, 1950s, TKK Co., 12-1/2" long, a minor toy	60	90	120
John's Farm Truck, 1950s, T-N Co., 9" long, seven actions	140	210	280
K-55 Electric Tractor, M-T Co., three actions, 7" long	70	105	140
King Size Fire Engine, 1960s, Bandai Co., three actions, 12-1/2" long	150	225	300

	C6	C8	C10
Kissing Couple, 1950s, Ichida Co., 10-3/4" long, five actions..............	150	225	300
Ladder Fire Engine, 1950s, Linemar Co., five actions, 13" long	170	255	340
Love-Beetle-Volks, 1960s, K.O. Co., 10" long, three actions	60	90	120
M-101 Aston Martin Secret Ejector Car, 1960s, Daiya Co., 11" long, six actions (includes ejectable passenger).....................	200	300	400
Magic Action Bulldozer, 1950s, T-N Co., 9-1/2" long, three actions	100	150	200
Marvelous Car, T-Bird, 1956, T-N Co., three actions, 11" long..........	250	375	500
Marvelous Fire Engine, 1960s, "Y" Co., 11" long, four actions............	100	150	200
Melody Camping Car, 1970s, "Y" Co., 10" long, three actions..........	100	150	200
Merry-Go-Round Truck, 1950s, M.T. Co., 11" long, four actions............	400	600	800

	C6	C8	C10
Mickey Mouse and Donald Duck Fire Engine, 1960s, M-T Co., 16" long, three actions	200	300	400
Mickey Mouse Sand Buggy, 1960s M-T Co., 11" long, four actions	150	225	300
Military Air Defense Truck, 1950s, Linemar Co., four actions, 15-1/4" long..	100	150	200
Military Command Car, 1950s T-N Co., five actions, 11" long	150	225	300
Million Bus, 1950s, KKK Co., three actions, 12" long, rare..................	1250	1875	2500
Mobile Satellite Tracking Station, 1960s, Y Co., six actions, 9" long, (includes detachable antenna) rare	400	600	800
Monkee-Mobile, 1967, ASC Co., (Aoshin Co.) Minor Toy, 12" long.	250	375	500

Japanese battery-operated Kissing Couple, Ichida, 1950s, 10-3/4". Photo from Don Hultzman.

Japanese battery-operated Marvelous Fire Engine, Y Co., 1960s, 11". Photo from Don Hultzman.

Japanese battery-operated M-101 Aston Martin Secret Ejector Car, Daiya, 1960s, 11". Photo from Don Hultzman.

Japanese battery-operated Military Command Car, T-N Co., 1950s, 11". Photo from Don Hultzman.

Japanese battery-operated Mobile Satellite Tracking Station, Y Co., 1960s, 9". Photo from Don Hultzman.

Japanese battery-operated Monkee-Mobile, ASC Co., 1967, 12". Photo from Don Hultzman.

Japanese battery-operated Musical Ice Cream Truck, Bandai, 1960s, 10-1/2". Photo from Don Hultzman.

Japanese battery-operated Mystery Police Car, T-N, 1960s, 9-3/4". Photo from Don Hultzman.

	C6	C8	C10
Motorcycle Cop, 1950s, Daiya Co., 10-1/2" long, 8-1/4" high, five actions	200	300	400
Musical Cadillac Car, 1950s, Irco Co., 9" long, minor toy	300	450	600
Musical Comic Jumping Jeep, 1970s, M-T Co., 12" long, six actions	90	135	180

	C6	C8	C10
Musical Ice Cream Truck, 1960s, Bandai Co., 10-1/2" long, five actions	100	150	200
Mystery Fire Chief Car No. 81, 1950s, Sanshin Co., 9-1/4" long, three actions	120	180	240
Mystery Police Car, 1960s, T-N Co., 9-3/4" long, 6" wide, 4" high, three actions	100	150	200
Newbuggy Crazy Car, 1970s, M-T Co., 10" long, minor toy	50	75	100
News Service Car, 1960s, TPS Co., 10" long, four actions	150	225	300

	C6	C8	C10
Nutty Mads Car (Drincar), 1960s, Marx Co., 9-1/4" long, three actions	200	300	400
Ol' MacDonald's Farm Truck, 1960s, Frankonia, four actions (includes plastic pig, cow and chicken)	110	165	220
Old Fashioned Car, 1950s, S-H Co., 10" long, four actions	50	75	100
Old Fashioned Fire Engine, 1950s, M-T Co., four actions, 12-1/2" high	110	165	220
Old Ford Touring Car, 1950s, Z Co., 10" long, four actions	50	75	100

	C6	C8	C10
Old Time Automobile, 1950s, "Y" Co., 8-3/4" long, three actions (includes detachable tin lithographed driver and steering wheel)	100	150	200
Old Timer, Car, 1950s, Cragstan Co., 9" long-three actions	100	150	200
Oldtimer Automoball, 1950s, M-T Co., 10" long, three actions, includes celluloid ball	90	135	180
Oldtimer Sunday Driver, 1960s, Daiya Co., 9" long, four actions	70	105	140
P.D. No. 5--Police Patrol Car (Buick), 1960s, Askakusa Toy Co., 11-1/2" long, three actions	90	135	180
Passenger Bus, 1950s, "Y" Co., 16" long, four actions	300	450	600
Patrol Auto-Tricycle, 1960s, T-N Co., 19" long, 7-1/2" high, four actions	160	240	320
Pick-Up Truck, T-N Co., 10" long, four actions	90	135	180
Piston Action Bulldozer, 1960s, Linemar Co., 7-1/2" long, two cycles	100	150	200

Japanese battery-operated Ol' MacDonald's Farm Truck, 1960s. Photo from Mapes Auctioneers and Appraisers.

Japanese battery-operated Old Timer Car, Cragstan, 1950s, 9". Photo from Mapes Auctioneers and Appraisers.

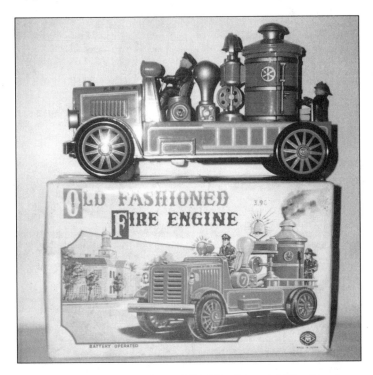

Japanese battery-operated Old Fashioned Fire Engine, M-T, 1950s, 12-1/2". Photo from Don Hultzman.

Japanese battery-operated Police Auto Cycle, Bandai, 1960s. Photo from Don Hultzman.

	C6	C8	C10
Police Auto Cycle, 1960s, (motorcycle and plastic driver), Bandai Co., five actions, remote control	150	225	300
Police Motorcycle, 1950s, M-T Co., 11-3/4" long, seven actions..........	160	240	320
Police No. 5 Police Car, 1950s, T-N Co., four actions, 9-1/2" long	100	150	200
Police Patrol Jeep, 1960s, T-N Co., four actions, lights, bump and go, noise, smoke, 9-1/4" long	100	150	200
Pom Pom Tank, 1950s, S&E Co., 12" long, five actions....................	100	150	200
Popcorn Vendor Truck, 1960s, T-N Co., 9" long, three actions...........	130	195	260
Porsche With Visible Engine, 1964, Bandai Co., 10" long, three actions	90	135	180

	C6	C8	C10
Power Shovel, 1950s, Alps Co., 15" long, extended, six actions	150	225	300
Racecar No. 25, 1950s, Alps Co., three actions, 9" long, rare..........	800	1200	1600
Radar Jeep, 1950s, T-N Co., 11" long, four actions	100	150	200
RCA-NBC Mobile Color TV Truck, 1950s, Yonezawa Co., 9" long, four actions	350	525	700
Reversible Diesel Electric Tractor, 1950s, Marx Co., minor toy	90	135	180
Road Construction Roller, 1950s, Daiya Co., 8-1/2" long, four actions	90	135	180
Road Grader, 1960s, T-N Co., 12" long, three actions	80	120	160
Road Roller, 1950s, M-T Co., 9" long, four actions	110	165	220
Robotank TR-2, 1960s, T-N Co., four actions, 5" high	200	300	400
Romance Car M-841, 1950s, "M" Co., 8" long, three actions	110	165	220

Japanese battery-operated Police Motorcycle, M-T, 1950s, 11-3/4". Photo from Don Hultzman.

Japanese battery-operated Power Shovel, Alps Co., 1950s, 15". Photo from Don Hultzman.

Japanese battery-operated Police Car, T-N, 1950s, 9-1/2". Photo from Don Hultzman.

Japanese Road Roller, M-T, 1950s, 9". Photo from Don Hultzman.

	C6	C8	C10
Santa Claus on Hand Car	100	150	200
Santa Claus on Scooter, 1960s, M-T Co., 10" high, four actions............	100	150	200
School Bus, 1950s, Cragstan, 20-1/2" long, minor toy.................	60	90	120
Searchlight Jeep, 1950s, T-N Co., 16" long overall, (7-1/2" Jeep and 8-1/2" artillery) four actions..........	100	150	200
Secret Service Action Car (Green Hornet motif), 1960s, ASC Co., 11" long, four actions, rare..........	300	450	600
Shaking Classic Car, 1960s, T-N Co., 7" long, four actions..............	60	90	120
Shaking Old-Timer Car, No. 2511-1, 1960s, T-N Co., 9" long, four actions, includes plastic driver	60	90	120
Sheriff Car, 1950s, T-N Co., four actions, 10" long	90	135	180
Sight Seeing Bus, 1950s, Yonezawza Co., minor toy, 9" long	150	225	300
Sight Seeing Bus, 1960s, Bandai Co., 14-1/2" long, four actions	150	225	300
Siren Fire Car, 1950s, M-T Co., 9" long, four actions	130	195	260
Siren Patrol Car, 1960s, M-T Co., four actions, 12-1/2" long	80	120	160

	C6	C8	C10
Siren Patrol Motorcycle, 1960s, M-T Co., three actions, 12" long	200	300	400
Smokey the Bear Jeep, 1950s, M-T Co., 10" long, four actions	300	450	600
Smoking Bulldozer, 1960s, WKC Co., 9" long, four actions	100	150	200
Smoking Volkswagen, 1960s, Aoshin Co., 10-1/2" long, four actions	60	90	120
Smoky Bill on Old Fashioned Car, 1960s, T-N Co., 9" long, four actions	110	165	220
Smoky Joe-Fancy Mobile, 1960s, T-N Co., four actions, smokes, lights, bump and go, noise, 9" long..	90	135	180
Sports Car Race Set, 1960s, TPS Co., Minor Toy, 8"x14" base, includes four plastic race cars	100	150	200
Steam Roller, 1950s, "Y" Co., 8" long, four actions (includes tin trailer)	110	165	220
Steam Roller (Road Roller), 1950s, T-N Co., (Rosko), 12" long w/trailer, four actions	150	225	300
Steerable Tank, 1950s, Linemar Co., 9" long, five actions	60	90	120
Strange Explorer, 1960s, DSK Co., 7-1/2" long, four actions..............	70	105	140
Sunbeam Jeep No. 1, 1940s, 10" long, unmarked, three actions	100	150	200

Japanese battery-operated Santa Claus on Scooter, M-T, 1960s, 10". Photo from Don Hultzman.

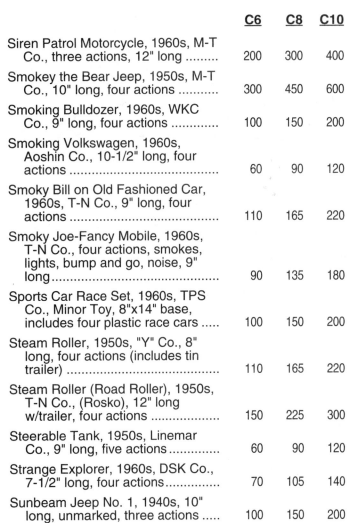

Japanese battery-operated Strange Explorer, DSK, 1960s, 7-1/2".

Japanese battery-operated Sunday Driver, M-T, 1950s, 10". Photo from Don Hultzman.

Japanese battery-operated Turn-O-Matic Gun Jeep, T-N, 1960s, 10". Photo from Don Hultzman.

	C6	C8	C10
Sunbeam Side Car (Motorcycle), 1950s, Marusan Co., 9-1/2" long, three actions	800	1200	1600
Sunday Driver, 1950s, M-T Co., 10" long, four actions (includes detachable driver)	70	105	140
Superman Truck, 1950s, Linemar Co., 10-1/4" long, three actions, rare	800	1200	1600
Surrey Jeep, 1960s, T-N Co., 11" long, three actions	90	135	180
Swinger, The (Mustang Mach I), 1960s, T.P.S. Co., 10-1/2" long, three actions	50	75	100
Talking Police Car-Mystery Action, 1960s, Y Co., 14" long, three actions	70	105	140
Tank, Daisymatic No. 80	100	150	200
Tank, Daisymatic No. 64	100	150	200
Tank M-103, 1950s, M-T Co., 7" long, three actions	90	135	180
Tank M-107-US Army, 1950s, Y Co., 6" long, four actions, includes four missiles	110	165	220
Tank M-35, 1950s, HTC Co., 8" long, three actions	110	165	220
Tank M-4 Combat Tank, 1960s, Taiyo Co., 11-1/2" long, 13" w/gun barrel extended, five actions	80	120	160
Tank M-41, 1970s, J Co., 8-1/4" long, four actions	110	165	220
Tank M-48-T, 1960s, T-N Co., 8-1/4" long, four actions	100	150	200
Tank M-56, 1940s, M-T Co., 7-1/2" long, wheel drive	100	150	200

	C6	C8	C10
Tank M-71, 1950s, M-T Co., 5-3/4" long, five actions	100	150	200
Tank M-81, 1960s, M-T Co., 8-1/2" long, seven actions	100	150	200
Tank M-X, 1950s, T-N Co., 8-1/2" long, five actions	70	105	140
Tank Robot, 1960s, S-H Co., five actions, 10" tall	250	375	500
Tank T-5, 1950s, T-N Co., 8-1/2" long, three actions, includes detachable radar antenna	120	160	240
Tank X-3 (Explorer Defense), 1950s, Cragstan Co., 7-3/4" long, five actions, includes six cartridge shells	130	195	260
Tank X-75, 1950s, M-T Co., 9" long, three actions, includes tin gun and darts	110	165	220
Taxi (yellow cab), 1950s, Linemar Co., 7-1/2" long, five actions	70	105	140
Taxi Cab, 1960s, "Y" Co., four actions, 9" long	80	120	160
Taxi Cab, 1950s, "Y" Co., 8-1/2" long, five actions	70	105	140
Teddy-Go-Kart, 1960s, Alps Co., 10-1/2" long, four actions	90	135	180
Tiny Jeep, 1950s, WACO Co., 4-1/4" long, minor action	30	45	60
Tiny Tank, 1950s WACO Co., 4-1/4" long, minor action	30	45	60
Tom and Jerry Highway Patrol, 1960s, M-T Co., 8" long, three actions	120	180	240
Tom and Jerry Jumping Jeep, 1960s, M-T Co., 9" long, three actions	150	225	300
Tractor, 1950s, Showa Co., 7-1/2" long, four actions, includes lithographed tin figure (driver)	110	165	220
Tractor, 1960s, Y Co., 6" long, three actions	100	150	200

	C6	C8	C10
Tractor On Platform, 1950s, T-N Co., tractor 9" long, trailer 7" long, minor toy	100	150	200
Turn-O-Matic Gun Jeep, 1960s, T-N Co., 10" long, five actions	100	150	200
Twin Racing Cars, 1950s, Alps Co., three actions, 7" long; 10" long w/coupling rod)	200	300	400
Visible Ford Mustang, 1960s, Bandai Co., 10" long, four actions	90	135	180
Volkswagen Convertible, 1950s, T-N Co., three actions, 9-3/4" long	250	375	500
Volkswagen No. 7653, 1960s, Bandai Co., 10" long, three actions	80	120	160
Volkswagen With Visible Engine, 1960s, K.O. Co., 7" long, three actions	110	165	220
Volkswagen With Visible Engine No. 4049, 1960s, Bandai Co., 8" long, three actions	110	165	220
Volkswagen-Eletrik, 1950s, Mignon Co., 8-1/2" long, three actions	100	150	200

Japanese battery-operated Twin Racing Cars, Alps, 1950s. Photo from Don Hultzman.

JAPANESE (ETC.) TIN CARS

Tin toy cars have been manufactured since the first horseless carriages roamed the streets of the United States and Europe. They ranged in size and price from the tiny one-inch penny toy to the twenty-eight-inch Eldorado, which sold for $10. Although there are German, Spanish and French toy cars listed here, our concentration will be the 1950s—the Golden Era of Japanese tin toy cars. These examples enjoy much popularity today, and prices have been raised by the limitlessness of some people's insanity. Keep one thing foremost in your mind when trying to sell a toy at the mint price—the person who paid that price already has one. (All photos by Ron Smith except where noted.)

Contributor: Ron Smith, 33005 Arlesford, Solon, OH, 44139, 440-248-7066, fax 440-519-0906. Smith has always loved toy cars and planes, he can still show you his first Dinky Toy his aunt bought him at Fred Harvey's Toy Store in Cleveland's Terminal Tower Building. Smith has collected die-cast cars, trucks and planes, cast-iron toys and plastic promotional cars, but for the past fifteen years he has specialized in tin-plate cars and planes. Smith lives in Ohio with his wife Joan and their two cats, T-2 and Bogart.

	C6	C8	C10		C6	C8	C10
1930s DeSoto, friction, Masudaya, 8" long (J081)	300	400	800	1950 Cadillac, battery, Marusan, 11" long (J019)	500	800	1500
1946 Ford, wind-up, Italy, 10" long (J092B)	100	200	400	1950 Champion Racer No. 15, friction, German, 18" long (J289)	500	750	1400
1949 Ford Sedan, wind-up, Guntherman, 11" long (J093)	150	300	400	1950 Champion Racer No. 42, friction, German, 18" long (J288)	500	750	1400
1950 BMW 600 Isetta, friction, Bandai, 9" long (J016)	200	400	600	1950 Chrysler, friction, Guntherman, 11" long (J070)	100	300	600
1950 BMW Isetta (three wheels), friction, Bandai, 6-1/2" long (J017)	75	125	200	1950 Daihatsu Midget, friction, Kokyu Shokai, 5" long (J269)	75	100	200
1950 Cadillac, friction, Marusan, 11" long (J018)	300	500	1000	1950 Ford Good Humor Ice Cream Truck, friction, KTS, Japan, 10-3/4" long (J095)	150	500	750

Japanese Tin 1946 Ford, Italian, wind-up, 10". Photo from Ron Smith.

Japanese Tin 1949 Ford Sedan, Guntherman, wind-up, 11". Photo from Ron Smith.

Japanese Tin 1950 Champion Racer No. 42, German, friction, 18". Photo from Ron Smith.

Japanese Tin 1950 Cadillac, Marusan, friction, 11". Photo from Ron Smith.

Japanese Tin 1950 Champion Racer No. 15, German, friction, 18". Photo from Ron Smith.

Japanese Tin 1950s Agajanian Racer No. 98, Y, friction, 18". Photo from Ron Smith.

	C6	C8	C10
1950 International Grain Hauler, friction, SSS, 23" long (J153)	275	300	800
1950s Agajanian Racer No. 98, friction, Y Co., 18" long (J286)	500	1000	3000
1950s Buick Futuristic Le Sabre, friction, Yonezawa, 7-1/2" long (J276)	100	200	400
1950s Champion's Racer No. 98, friction, Y Co., 18" long (J287)	500	800	1600
1950s Daihatsu Auto Tricycle, friction, Nomura, 11" long (J275)	100	150	300

	C6	C8	C10
1950s Daihatsu Midget, friction, Yonezawa, 7" long (J270)	75	100	200
1950s DeSoto Hardtop, friction, Japan, 7" (J081A)	50	75	150
1950s Divco Dugans Bakery Truck, friction, unknown, Japan, 7-1/2" long (J080)	300	400	600
1950s Dream Car Buick Phantom, friction, Tipp & Co., 12" long (J278)	300	400	800
1950s International Cement Mixer, friction, SSS, 19" long (J152)	275	300	800

Japanese Tin 1950s Buick Futuristic Le Sabre, Yonezawa, friction, 7-1/2". Photo from Ron Smith.

Japanese Tin 1950s Lancia, friction, Bandai, 8". Photo from Ron Smith.

Japanese Tin 1950s Champion's Racer No. 98, Y, friction, 18". Photo from Ron Smith.

Japanese Tin 1950s Mazda Auto Tricycle, Bandai, friction, 8". Photo from Ron Smith.

Japanese Tin 1950s DeSoto, Hardtop, friction, 7". Photo from Ron Smith.

	C6	C8	C10
1950s Lancia Coupe and Convertible, friction, Bandai, 8" long (J161B)	50	90	150
1950s Lotus Elite, friction, Bandai, 8-1/2" long (J170)	25	35	45
1950s Mazda Auto Tricycle, friction, Bandai, 8" long (J274)	75	100	200
1950s Mazda Auto Tricycle K 360, friction, Bandai, 6" long (J268)	75	100	200
1950s Mercedes-Benz 300 SL, battery, T.N., 11" long (J183)	125	150	200
1950s Mercedes-Benz 300 SL, battery, KS, 7" long (J184)	45	65	85

Japanese Tin 1950s Mercedes Benz 300 SL, T.N., battery, 11". Photo from Ron Smith.

	C6	C8	C10
1950s Mercedes-Benz 300 SL, battery, Dist. Cragstan, 9" long (J185)	65	95	125
1950s Mercedes-Benz 300 SL Coupe and Convertible, friction, Bandai, 8" long (J186)	65	95	150
1950s Mercedes-Benz Racer, friction, Line Mar, 9-1/2" long (J173)	95	150	185

	C6	C8	C10
1950s Mercedes-Benz Racer W196, battery, Marusan, 10" long (J174)	150	200	250
1950s Mercedes Limousine, friction, Tipp & Co., 14" long (J172)	500	800	1000
1950s Mitsubishi Auto Tricycle, friction, Bandai, 11" long (J272) ..	100	150	300
1950s Mitsubishi Auto Tricycle Leo, friction, Bandai, 5" long (J271)	75	100	200
1950s Nash, battery, MSK, 8" long (J206)	40	70	90
1950s Opel Sedan, friction/battery, Yonezawa, 11-1/2" long (J217) ...	70	90	125
1950s Orient Auto Tricycle, friction, Yonezawa, 9" long (J273)	75	100	200
1950s Pontiac Convertible, friction, KS, 14" long (J218B)	150	300	450
1950s Pontiac Coupe, friction, KS, 14" long (J218C)	150	300	450
1950s Pontiac Dream Car, friction, Mitsubishi, 10" long (J282)	100	300	600
1950s Porsche Speedster, battery, Distler, 10-1/2" long (J235)	350	400	600
1950s Record Racer NSU, friction, Bandai, 18" long (J285)	100	150	250
1950s Volkswagen, wind-up, German, 6" long (J262A)	75	150	300

	C6	C8	C10
1950s Volkswagen Bus, battery, Tipp & Co., 9" long (J257)	300	400	600
1950s Volkswagen Convertible, friction, T.N., 9-1/2" long (J258) ..	100	150	250
1950s Volvo, wind-up, Sweden, 11" long (J265A)	600	700	1800
1950s Zuendapp Janus, friction, Bandai, 8" long (J267)	125	150	300
1951 Ford Sedan, wind-up, Guntherman, 11" long (J094)	150	300	400
1952 Cadillac, friction, Alps, 11-1/2" long (J020)	200	400	800
1952 Cadillac, battery, T.N., 13" long (J021)	100	250	450
1952 MG TF, friction, unknown, 8-1/2" long (J198)	50	75	95
1952 Oldsmobile, friction, Y Co., 11" long (J207A)	150	350	500
1953 Buick, friction, Marusan, 7" long (J003)	75	125	250
1953 Chevrolet Corvette, friction, Bandai, 7" long (J037)	75	100	200
1953 Packard Convertible/Sedan, friction, Alps, 16" long (J222)	500	900	1800
1954 Buick Station Wagon, battery, unknown, 8" long (J004)	75	150	200

Japanese Tin 1950s Pontiac Convertible, KS, friction, 14". Photo from Ron Smith.

Japanese Tin 1950s Porsche Speedster, battery, Distler, 10-1/2". Photo from Ron Smith.

Japanese Tin 1950s Pontiac Coupe, KS, friction, 14". Photo from Ron Smith.

Japanese Tin 1950s Volkswagen Convertible, T.N., friction, 9-1/2". Photo from Ron Smith.

Japanese Tin 1950s Volvo, wind-up, 11". Photo from Ron Smith.

Japanese Tin 1952 Cadillac, Alps, friction, 11-1/2". Photo from Ron Smith.

	C6	C8	C10
1954 Cadillac, friction, Gama, 12" long (J022)	200	300	500
1954 Cadillac, battery, Joustra, 12" long (J023)	200	300	500
1954 Chevrolet, friction, Marusan, 11" long (J049)	300	600	800
1954 Ford Hardtop and Police and Fire Chief and Yellow Cab, friction, Marusan, 11" long (J095A)	125	175	350
1954 Lincoln, friction, unknown, 12" long (J162)	175	275	400

	C6	C8	C10
1954 Mercury Hardtop, battery, Rock Valley Toys, 9-1/2" long (J192)	100	125	200
1954 MG TD, friction, SSS, 6-1/2" long (J199)	35	65	85
1954 Pontiac Hardtop/Convertible, friction, Minister-India, 11" long, new issue, made from old Asahi molds (J218A)	n/a	n/a	15
1954 Pontiac Star Chief, friction, Asahi, 11" long (J218)	250	350	500
1954 Studebaker, friction, Yoshiya, 9" long (J243)	150	200	400
1955 Buick Roadmaster, friction, Yoshiya, 11" long (J005)	200	300	400

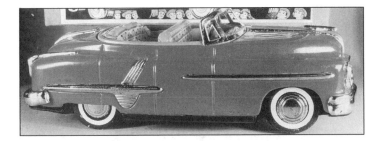

Japanese Tin 1952 Oldsmobile, Y, friction, 11". Photo from Ron Smith.

Japanese Tin 1953 Chevrolet Corvette, Bandai, friction, 7". Photo from Ron Smith.

Japanese Tin 1952 Cadillac, T.N., battery, 13". Photo from Ron Smith.

Japanese Tin 1953 Packard Convertible/Sedan, Alps, friction, 16". Photo from Ron Smith.

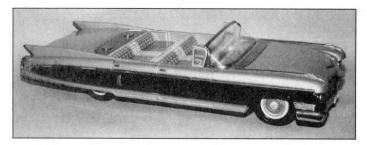

**Japanese Tin 1954 Cadillac, battery, Joustra, 12".
Photo from Ron Smith.**

**Japanese Tin 1954 Studebaker, Yoshiya, friction, 9".
Photo from Ron Smith.**

**Japanese Tin 1954 Chevrolet, Marusan, friction, 11".
Photo from Ron Smith.**

Japanese Tin 1955 Buick Roadmaster, Yoshiya, friction, 11". Photo from Ron Smith.

**Japanese Tin 1954 Ford Hardtop, Marusan, friction,
11". Photo from Ron Smith.**

**Japanese Tin 1955 Chevrolet, battery, Marusan, 10-
3/4". Photo from Ron Smith.**

**Japanese Tin 1954 Pontiac Hardtop/Convertible, Min-
ister-Indai, friction, 11". Photo from Ron Smith.**

**Japanese Tin 1955 Chrysler, friction, Yonezawa, 8".
Photo from Ron Smith.**

	C6	C8	C10
1955 Chevrolet, battery, Marusan, 10-3/4" long (J050)	500	900	1500
1955 Chrysler, friction, Yonezawa, 8" long (J071)	100	200	300
1955 Ford Ambulance, friction, Bandai, 12" long (J098)	150	250	300
1955 Ford Convertible, friction, Bandai, 12" long (J100)	300	500	700
1955 Ford Panel Truck, friction, reads "Flowers," Bandai, 12" long (J099)	200	400	600
1955 Ford Panel Truck, friction, reads "Standard Coffee," Bandai, 12" long (J99A)	600	800	1500

	C6	C8	C10
1955 Ford Pickup, friction, Bandai, 12" long (J096)	100	200	250
1955 Ford Station Wagon, friction, Bandai, 12" long (J097)	150	200	250
1955 Ford Thunderbird Convertible, friction, Bandai, 7" long (J126A) .	50	100	150
1955 Lincoln Sedan, friction, Yonezawa, 12" long (J163)	250	325	600
1955 MG, friction, SSS, 6" long (J200B)	50	70	100
1955 MG TF, friction, Bandai, 8" long (J200)	95	125	150
1956 Chevrolet Convertible, friction, Bandai, 9-1/2" long (J053)	80	100	150

Japanese Tin 1955 Ford Ambulance, Bandai, friction, 12". Photo from Ron Smith.

Japanese Tin 1955 Ford Pick Up, friction, Bandai, 12". Photo from Ron Smith.

Japanese Tin 1955 Ford Convertible, Bandai, friction, 12". Photo from Ron Smith.

Japanese Tin 1955 Ford Station Wagon, Bandai, friction, 12". Photo from Ron Smith.

Japanese Tin 1955 Ford Panel Truck "Flowers," Bandai, friction, 12". Photo from Ron Smith.

Japanese Tin 1955 Lincoln Sedan, Yonezawa, friction, 12". Photo from Ron Smith.

Japanese Tin 1955 MG, friction, SSS, 6". Photo from Ron Smith.

Japanese Tin 1956 Ford Convertible, Haji, friction, 11-1/2". Photo from Ron Smith.

Japanese Tin 1956 Ford Sedan, Marusan, friction, 13". Photo from Ron Smith.

Japanese Tin 1956 Ford Thunderbird, T.N., friction, 11". Photo from Ron Smith.

Japanese Tin 1956 Ford Thunderbird, T.N., battery, 11". Photo from Ron Smith.

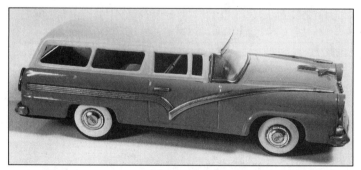

Japanese Tin 1956 Ford Wagon, Nomura, friction, 10-1/2". Photo from Ron Smith.

	C6	C8	C10
1956 Chevrolet Pickup, friction, Bandai, 9-1/2" long (J052)	60	90	120
1956 Chevrolet Station Wagon, friction, Bandai, 9-1/2" long (J051)	60	90	120
1956 Ford, friction, Bandai, 7" long..	60	125	175
1956 Ford Convertible, friction, Haji, 11-1/2" long (J102)	400	600	1000+
1956 Ford Hardtop, friction, Yonezawa, 12" long (J101)	300	500	800
1956 Ford Sedan, friction, Marusan, 13" long (J103)	500	800	2000+

	C6	C8	C10
1956 Ford Thunderbird, friction, T.N., 11" long (J127)	200	300	400
1956 Ford Thunderbird, battery, T.N., 11" long (J129)	200	300	400
1956 Ford Thunderbird Hardtop Clear Top, friction, T.N., 11" long (J128)	200	300	400
1956 Ford Wagon, friction, Nomura, 10-1/2" long (J104)	75	100	200
1956 GM's Gas Turbine Powered Firebird II, friction, Ashahi, 8-1/2" long (J281)	100	200	500

	C6	C8	C10
1956 Lincoln, friction, Ichiko, 16-1/2" long (J165)	150	250	375
1956 Lincoln Continental Mark II, friction, Linemar, 12" long (J164)	400	800	1200+
1956 Mercury Hardtop, friction, Alps, 9-1/2" long (J193)	600	800	1500
1956 Nash Ambassador, friction, Sankei Gangu, 8" long (J207)	100	125	150
1956 Oldsmobile Sedan, friction, Ichiko/Kanto, 10-1/2" long (J208)	400	800	1200
1956 Oldsmobile Super 88 Sedan, friction, Masudaya, 16" long (J209)	300	400	600
1956 Plymouth Hardtop, friction, unknown, 8-1/2" long (J224)	100	200	400
1956 Plymouth Hardtop, battery, Alps, 12" long (J225)	300	400	800
1956 Pontiac Hardtop, friction, TN, 8" long (J218D)	150	300	500
1957 Chrysler New Yorker, friction, Alps, 14" long (J072)	600	900	2000
1957 Ferrari 250 G. Convertible, friction, A.T.C., 9-1/2" long (J147)	200	300	600
1957 Ford Hardtop, friction, T.N., 12" long (J106)	100	200	300

Japanese Tin 1956 Lincoln, friction, Ichiko, 16-1/2". Photo from Ron Smith.

Japanese Tin 1956 Lincoln Continental Mark II, Linemar, friction, 12". Photo from Ron Smith.

Japanese Tin 1956 Mercury Hardtop, Alps, friction, 9-1/2". Photo from Ron Smith.

Japanese Tin 1956 Oldsmobile Sedan, Ichiko/Kanto, friction, 10-1/2". Photo from Ron Smith.

Japanese Tin 1956 Oldsmobile Super 88 Sedan, Masudaya, friction, 16". Photo from Ron Smith.

Japanese Tin 1956 Plymouth Hardtop, friction, 8-1/2". Photo from Ron Smith.

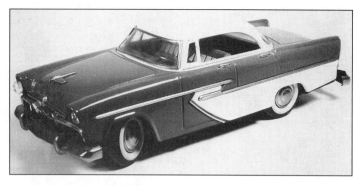

Japanese Tin 1956 Plymouth Hardtop, Alps, battery, 12". Photo from Ron Smith.

Japanese Tin 1956 Pontiac Hardtop, TN, friction, 8". Photo from Ron Smith.

Japanese Tin 1957 Chrysler New Yorker, Alps, friction, 14". Photo from Ron Smith.

Japanese Tin 1957 Ford Hardtop, T.N., friction, 12". Photo from Ron Smith.

Japanese Tin 1957 Ford Sedan/Con./Wagon/Pickup, Joustra, friction, 12". Photo from Ron Smith.

Japanese Tin 1957 Packard Hawk Convertible, Schuco, battery, 10-3/4". Photo from Ron Smith.

Japanese Tin 1957 Plymouth Fury Hardtop, Y, friction, 11-1/2". Photo from Ron Smith.

	C6	C8	C10
1957 Ford Sedan/Con./Wagon/Pickup, friction, Joustra, 12" long (J107) .	200	250	300
1957 Ford Sedan/Convertible/Wagon/Pickup, friction, Bandai, 12" long (J108)	200	250	300
1957 Ford Station Wagon, friction, Nomura, 7-1/2" long (J109)	60	80	100
1957 Mercedes Benz 300 SL, friction, Marusan, 8-1/2" long (J187)	150	250	325
1957 MGA, friction, A.T.C., 10" long (J201)	175	300	600
1957 Packard Hawk Convertible, battery, Schuco, 10-3/4" long (J223)	300	400	800

	C6	C8	C10
1957 Plymouth Fury Hardtop, friction, Y Co., 11-1/2" long (J226)	300	400	800
1958 Buck Century, friction, Bandai, 8" long (J007)	60	80	100
1958 Buick Century, friction, Yonezawa, 12" long (J006)	400	800	1600
1958 Chevrolet Convertible, friction, Bandai, 8" long (J056)	60	90	125
1958 Chevrolet Corvette, friction, Yonezawa, 9-1/2" long (J038)	200	300	500
1958 Chevrolet Pickup Truck, friction, Bandai, 8" long (J055)	50	65	90

	C6	C8	C10
1958 Chevrolet Red Cross Ambulance, friction, Bandai, 8" long (J054)	20	30	50
1958 Chevrolet Sedan, friction, Bandai, 8" long (J058)	75	100	150
1958 Chevrolet Station Wagon, friction, Bandai, 8" long (J057)	50	60	85
1958 Chrysler, battery, unknown, 13" long (J073)	200	300	600
1958 Dodge Sedan, friction, T.N., 11" long (J082)	300	400	600
1958 Edsel, friction, Yonezawa, 10-1/2" long (J092)	300	400	600
1958 Edsel Ambulance, friction, Haji, 11" long (J088)	200	250	300
1958 Edsel Convertible/Sedan, friction, Haji, 10-1/2" long (J086)	300	400	800

Japanese Tin 1958 Buick Century, Bandai, friction, 8". Photo from Ron Smith.

Japanese Tin 1958 Chevrolet Station Wagon, Bandai, friction, 8". Photo from Ron Smith.

Japanese Tin 1958 Buick Century, Yonezawa, friction, 12". Photo from Ron Smith.

Japanese Tin 1958 Chrysler, battery, 13". Photo from Ron Smith.

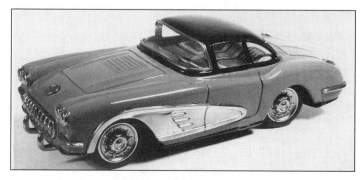

Japanese Tin 1958 Chevrolet Corvette, Yonezawa, friction, 9-1/2". Photo from Ron Smith.

Japanese Tin 1958 Dodge Sedan, T.N., friction, 11". Photo from Ron Smith.

Japanese Tin 1958 Edsel Convertible/Sedan, Haji, friction, 10-1/2". Photo from Ron Smith.

Japanese Tin 1958 Edsel Wagon, Haji, friction, 10-1/2". Photo from Ron Smith.

Japanese Tin 1958 Edsel Hardtop, friction, Toy Nomura, 8-1/2". Photo from Ron Smith.

Japanese Tin 1958 Ford Hardtop, battery, 12". Photo from Ron Smith.

Japanese Tin 1958 Edsel Station Wagon, T.N., friction, 11". Photo from Ron Smith.

Japanese Tin 1958 Mercury Hardtop, Yonezawa, friction, 11-1/2". Photo from Ron Smith.

	C6	C8	C10
1958 Edsel Hardtop, friction, Asahi, 10-3/4" long (J090)	300	400	800
1958 Edsel Hardtop, friction, Toy Nomura, 8-1/2" long (J091)	100	150	250
1958 Edsel Station Wagon, friction, T.N., 11" long (J089)	150	200	300
1958 Edsel Wagon, friction, Haji, 10-1/2" long (J087)	200	300	400
1958 Ferrari, battery, Bandai, 11" long (J148)	90	150	300
1958 Ford Country Squire Station Wagon, friction, Bandai, 8" long (J112)	40	60	100

	C6	C8	C10
1958 Ford Fairlane Hardtop/Convertible, friction, Bandai, 8" long (J113)	40	60	125
1958 Ford Fairlane Hardtop/Convertible, friction, Sankei Gangu, 9" long (J114)	90	115	125
1958 Ford Hardtop, battery, Japan, 12" long (J114A)	150	200	400
1958 Ford Retractable Top, friction, K. Japan, 10" long (J110)	70	90	150
1958 Ford Retractable Top, battery, T.N., 11" long (J111)	100	125	175
1958 Mercury Hardtop, friction, Yonezawa, 11-1/2" long (J195)	250	325	600

Japanese Tin 1958 Oldsmobile Sedan, friction, A.T.C., 12". Photo from Ron Smith.

Japanese Tin 1959 Buick, Ichiko, battery-operated/friction, 12". Photo from Ron Smith.

Japanese Tin 1958 Plymouth Fury, Bandai, friction, 8". Photo from Ron Smith.

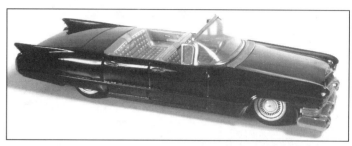

Japanese Tin 1959 Cadillac Convertible, Bandai, friction, 12". Photo from Ron Smith.

Japanese Tin 1959 Buick, T.N., friction, 11". Photo from Ron Smith.

Japanese Tin 1959 Cadillac Sedan, Bandai, friction, 12". Photo from Ron Smith.

	C6	C8	C10
1958 Mercury Station Wagon, friction, Bandai, 8" long (J194)	60	80	100
1958 Oldsmobile Sedan, friction, A.T.C., 12" long (J210)	200	300	600
1958 Oldsmobile Sedan, friction, Y Co., 16" long (J212)	300	400	700
1958 Oldsmobile Super 88 Sedan, friction, A.T.C., 13" long (J211) ...	250	325	425
1958 Plymouth Fury Convertible, Sedan, Wagon, friction, Bandai, 8" long (J227)	75	90	150
1959 Austin-Healey 100 Six Convertible, friction, Bandai, 8" long (J002B)	60	80	160
1959 Austin-Healey 100 Six Coupe, friction, Bandai, 8" long (J002A) .	60	80	160
1959 Buick, friction, T.N., 11" long (J008)	80	125	250

	C6	C8	C10
1959 Buick, B/O-friction, Ichiko, 12" long (J009)	100	250	300
1959 Cadillac Convertible, friction, Bandai, 12" long (J025)	75	100	150
1959 Cadillac Sedan, friction, Bandai, 12" long (J024)	75	100	150
1959 Chevrolet Sedan/Convertible/Wagon, friction, SY, 11-1/2" long (J059) ..	200	300	600
1959 Chrysler Imperial Convertible, friction, Bandai, 8" long (J074)	75	90	150
1959 Chrysler Imperial Sedan, friction, Bandai, 8" long (J075)	75	90	150
1959 Dodge Pickup, friction, unknown, 18-1/2" long (J084)	350	500	900

	C6	C8	C10
1959 Dodge Truck, friction, unknown, 24" long (J083)	350	500	1000
1959 Ford Fairlane Skyliner, friction, Sankei Gangu, 9" long (J115)	90	115	125
1959 Ford Retractable, friction, T.N., 11" long (J117)	100	150	200
1959 Ford Station Wagon, friction, T.N., 12" long (J116)	100	150	200
1959 Ford Thunderbird, friction, Bandai, 8" long (J130)	50	60	80

	C6	C8	C10
1959 Ford Thunderbird Convertible, friction, Bandai, 8" long (J131)	50	60	80
1959 Lincoln Continental Mark III Convertible, friction, Bandai, 12" long (J166)	75	100	150
1959 Lincoln Continental Mark III Sedan, friction, Bandai, 12" long (J167)	75	100	150
1959 Oldsmobile Sedan, friction, Ichiko, 12-1/2" long (J213)	75	125	175
1959 Plymouth Convertible, friction, A.T.C., 10-1/2" long (J229)	250	400	600
1959 Plymouth Hardtop, friction, A.T.C., 10-1/2" long (J228)	200	400	600
1960 Buick, friction, Ichiko, 17-1/2" long (J010)	150	250	600
1960 Cadillac, friction, Yonezawa, 18" long (J027)	150	200	350

Japanese Tin 1959 Chevrolet Sedan/Convertible/Wagon, SY, friction, 11-1/2". Photo from Ron Smith.

Japanese Tin 1959 Chrysler Imperial Convertible, Bandai, friction, 8". Photo from Ron Smith.

Japanese Tin 1959 Dodge Pick Up, friction, 18-1/2". Photo from Ron Smith.

Japanese Tin 1959 Ford Retractable, T.N., friction, 11". Photo from Ron Smith.

Japanese Tin 1959 Ford Station Wagon, T.N., friction, 12". Photo from Ron Smith.

Japanese Tin 1959 Lincoln Continental Mark III Convertible, Bandai, friction, 12". Photo from Ron Smith.

Japanese Tin 1959 Lincoln Continental Mark III Sedan, Bandai, friction, 12". Photo from Ron Smith.

Japanese Tin 1960 Chevrolet, Marusan, friction, 11-1/2". Photo from Ron Smith.

Japanese Tin 1959 Oldsmobile Sedan, Ichiko, friction, 12-1/2". Photo from Ron Smith.

Japanese Tin 1960 Chevrolet Hardtop, friction, 9". Photo from Ron Smith.

Japanese Tin 1959 Plymouth Hardtop, A.T.C., friction, 10-1/2". Photo from Ron Smith.

	C6	C8	C10
1960 Chevrolet, friction, Marusan, 11-1/2" long (J060)	200	300	600
1960 Chevrolet Hardtop, friction, Japan, 9" long (J060A)	100	150	200
1960 Chrysler Valiant, friction, Bandai, 8" long (J076)	20	40	50
1960 Citroen DS 19 Convertible, friction, Bandai, 12" long (J067)	100	150	300
1960 Citroen DS 19 Sedan, friction, Bandai, 12" long (J068)	100	150	300
1960 Citroen DS19 Sedan, Convertible, Wagon, friction, Bandai, 8" long (J66A)	75	125	200
1960 Citroen ID 19 Station Wagon, friction, Bandai, 12" long (J069)	100	150	300
1960 DKW 1000 Convertible, friction, Bandai, 8" long (J078)	90	200	300

Japanese Tin 1960 Citroen DS 19 Sedan, Bandai, friction, 12". Photo from Ron Smith.

	C6	C8	C10
1960 Ferrari Super America Coupe, friction, Bandai, 12" long (J149)	100	200	300
1960 Ford, friction, Haji, 11" long (J119)	100	200	400
1960 Ford Gyron, battery, Ichida, 11" long (J280)	75	150	300

	C6	C8	C10
1960 Ford Panel Delivery, reads "Standard Coffee," friction, 10" long (J119A)	800	1500	2500
1960 Jaguar XK150 Hardtop Convertible, friction, Bandai, 9-1/2" long (J154)	75	125	200
1960 Lincoln Hardtop/Convertible, friction, Yonezawa, 11" long (J168)	100	150	300
1960 Mercedes-Benz 230 SL, battery, Yanoman, 14-1/2" long (J180)	125	155	185
1960 Mercedes-Benz 250 S, friction, Daiya, 14" long (J182)	110	155	175

	C6	C8	C10
1960 Porsche 911, battery, Bandai, 10" long (J234)	65	95	125
1960 Renault, friction, Bandai, 7-1/2" long (J241)	50	75	100
1960 Rolls-Royce Silver Coupe Convertible, friction, Bandai, 12" long (J236)	100	150	200
1960 VW Karmann-Ghia Coupe/Convertible, friction, Bandai, 7" long (J252)	100	150	250
1960s Aston-Martin DB5 (James Bond), friction, Gilbert, 11-1/2" long (J001)	75	150	400
1960s Aston-Martin DB6, friction, Asahi Toy Co., 11" long (J002)	100	300	500
1960s BMW1500, friction, Ichiko, 8" long (J002C)	90	150	250

Japanese Tin 1960 Ford, Haji, friction, 11". Photo from Ron Smith.

Japanese Tin 1960 Lincoln Hardtop/Convertible, Yonezawa, friction, 11". Photo from Ron Smith.

Japanese Tin 1960 Renault, Bandai, friction, 7-1/2". Photo from Ron Smith.

Japanese Tin 1960 Rolls Royce Silver Coupe Convertible, Bandai, friction, 12". Photo from Ron Smith.

Japanese Tin 1960 VW Karmann-Ghia, Bandai, friction, 7". Photo from Ron Smith.

Japanese Tin 1960s Aston-Martin DB5 (James Bond), Gilbert, friction, 11-1/2". Photo from Ron Smith.

Japanese Tin 1960s Aston-Martin DB6, Asahi , friction, 11". Photo from Ron Smith.

Japanese Tin 1960s Ferrari Berlinetta, Bandai, friction, 9-1/2". Photo from Ron Smith.

Japanese Tin 1960s BMW 1500, Ichiko, friction, 8". Photo from Ron Smith.

Japanese Tin 1960s Ferrari Berlinetta 250 Le Mans, Asahi. Photo from Ron Smith.

Japanese Tin 1960s Chevrolet Corvair, Bandai, friction, 8". Photo from Ron Smith.

	C6	C8	C10
1960s Cadillac, friction, Bandai, 17" long (J026)	125	175	375
1960s Chevrolet Corvair, friction, Bandai, 8" long (J043)	30	50	75
1960s Coke Truck, battery, Japan, 12" long (J17B)	125	225	400
1960s Datsun Bluebird 1200, friction, Bandai, 8" long (J079)	90	125	250
1960s Dream Car Firebird III, friction, Alps, 11" long (J279)	100	200	300

	C6	C8	C10
1960s Ferrari Berlinetta, friction, Bandai, 9-1/2" long (J092A)	50	75	125
1960s Ferrari Berlinetta 250 Le Mans, Asahi	NPF	NPF	NPF
1960s Ferrari Super America Convertible, friction, Bandai, 12" long (J150)	100	200	300
1960s Fiat 600 Sedan, friction, Bandai, 8" long (J151)	50	65	95
1960s Ford Falcon, friction, Bandai, 8" long (J118)	20	30	50
1960s Ford GT, battery, Bandai, 10" long (J146)	65	85	125
1960s Ford Taunus 17M Convertible, friction, Bandai, 8" long (J145)	30	40	60
1960s Jaguar 3.4 Convertible, friction, Bandai, 8" long (J160)	50	60	120
1960s Jaguar 3.4 Sedan, friction, Bandai, 8" long (J159)	50	60	120
1960s Jaguar XK140, friction, Bandai, 9-1/2" long (J157)	40	60	90

	C6	C8	C10
1960s Jaguar XKE, battery, Bandai, 10" long (J158)	90	125	200
1960s Jaguar XKE Convertible, friction, T.T., 10-1/2" long (J155)	95	125	150
1960s Jaguar XKE Coupe, friction, Lendolet Auto, 10-1/2" long (J156)	50	75	100
1960s Land Rover 88 Station Wagon, friction, Bandai, 8" long (J171)	30	40	60
1960s Lotus Ford Racer, battery, Junior, 16" long (J170A)	200	400	600
1960s Mercdes-Benz 219 Sedan, friction, Bandai, 8" long (J176)	50	80	150
1960s Mercedes, friction, Ichiko, 12-1/2" long (J175)	115	155	200
1960s Mercedes-Benz 219 Convertible, friction, Bandai, 8" long (J177)	50	80	150

	C6	C8	C10
1960s Mercedes-Benz 230 SL, battery, Modern Toys, 15" long (J178)	175	210	250
1960s Mercedes-Benz 230 SL, battery, Alps, 10" long (J179)	65	75	95
1960s Mercedes-Benz 250 SE, battery, Ichiko, 13" long (J181) ...	110	140	185
1960s Mercedes-Benz 600, friction, unknown, 10" long (J188)	95	125	175
1960s Mercedes-Benz Taxi, battery, Bandai, 10" long (J189)	75	100	125

Japanese Tin 1960s Lotus Ford Racer, Junior, battery, 16". Photo from Strine.

Japanese Tin 1960s Ford Taunus 17M Convertible/Hardtop, Bandai, friction, 8". Photo from Ron Smith.

Japanese Tin 1960s Mercedes Benz 219 Sedan, Bandai, friction, 8". Photo from Ron Smith.

Jaguar XKE Convertible, friction, T.T., 10-1/2". Photo from Ron Smith.

Japanese Tin 1960s Mercedes Benz 219 Convertible, Bandai, friction, 8". Photo from Ron Smith.

Japanese Tin 1960s Messerchmitt Three-wheel Sedan, Bandai, friction, 8". Photo from Ron Smith.

Japanese Tin 1960s Porsche, T.T., friction, 9-1/2". Photo from Ron Smith.

Japanese Tin 1960s No. 3 Ferrari, Bandai, friction, 8". Photo from Ron Smith.

Japanese Tin 1960s Porsche, Geshia German, 9". Photo from Ron Smith.

	C6	C8	C10
1960s Messerschmitt Four-wheel Convertible, friction, Bandai, 8" long (J204)	200	500	600
1960s Messerschmitt Three-wheel Sedan/Convertible, friction, Bandai, 8" long (J205)	200	250	350
1960s MG Magnette Mark III Convertible, friction, Bandai, 8" long (J203)	95	125	150
1960s MG Magnette Mark III Sedan, friction, Bandai, 8" long (J202)	95	125	150
1960s No. 3 Ferrari, friction, Bandai, 8" long (J147B)	85	150	190
1960s Porsche, friction, T.T., 9-1/2" long (J233B)	75	125	200
1960s Porsche, wind-up, JNF (Ger.), 9" long (J233C)	200	400	600
1960s Porsche, W/W, Geshia (Ger.), 9" long (J233D)	200	400	600
1960s Porsche 911, friction, T.T., 9-1/2" long (J234B)	75	125	200

	C6	C8	C10
1960s Rambler Rebel Station Wagon, friction, Bandai, 12" long (J240)	50	85	125
1960s Rolls, friction, HTC, 6" long (J235B)	75	100	150
1960s Rolls-Royce (w/Electric Lights), battery, Bandai, 12" long (J238)	100	200	400
1960s Rolls-Royce Sedan, friction, TN, 10" long (J235C)	300	500	800
1960s Rolls-Royce Silver Coupe Sedan, friction, Bandai, 12" long (J237)	100	150	200
1960s Saab 93 B, friction, Bandai, 7" long (J244)	40	60	80
1960s Studebaker Avanti, friction, Bandai, 8" long (J242)	125	175	250

**Japanese Tin 1960s Porsche 911, T.T., friction, 9-1/2".
Photo from Ron Smith.**

**Japanese Tin 1960s Rolls, HTC, friction, 6". Photo
from Ron Smith.**

**Japanese Tin 1960s Rambler Rebel Station Wagon,
Bandai, friction, 12". Photo from Ron Smith.**

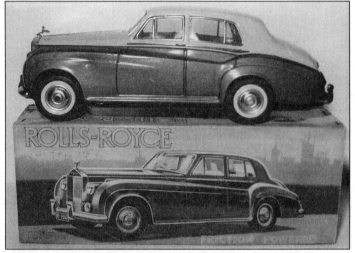

**Japanese Tin 1960s Rolls Royce Sedan, TN, friction,
10". Photo from Ron Smith.**

**Japanese Tin 1960s Rolls Royce Silver Coupe Sedan,
Bandai, friction, 12". Photo from Ron Smith.**

	C6	C8	C10
1960s Triumph TR-3 Coupe, friction, Bandai, 8" long (J247)	50	75	150
1960s Vespa, friction, Bandai, 9" long (J251)	50	75	125
1960s Volkswagen, friction, Bandai, 8" long (J262)	25	40	80
1960s Volkswagen, battery, Bandai, 10-1/2" long (J263)	25	50	75
1960s Volkswagen, battery, Bandai, 11" long (J264)	25	50	75
1960s Volkswagen Bus, friction, A.T.C., 12" long (J253)	125	175	350
1960s Volkswagen Bus, friction, Bandai, 8" long (J255)	50	60	75
1960s Volkswagen Bus, battery/friction, Bandai, 9-1/2" long (J256)	75	125	175

	C6	C8	C10
1960s Subaru 360, friction, Bandai, 7" long (J245)	75	100	125
1960s Toyopet Crown, friction, Bandai, 9" long (J248)	100	200	300
1960s Toyota, friction, Ichiko, 16" long (J249)	150	275	325
1960s Triumph TR-3 Convertible, friction, Bandai, 8" long (J246)	50	75	150

Japanese Tin 1960s Studebaker Avanti, Bandai, friction, 8". Photo from Ron Smith.

Japanese Tin 1960s Volkwagen, Bandai, battery, 11". Photo from Ron Smith.

Japanese Tin 1960s Volkswagen Convertible, Bandai, battery, 11". Photo from Ron Smith.

Japanese Tin 1960s Volkswagen with/without sun roof, Bandai, friction, 15". Photo from Ron Smith.

Japanese Tin 1960s Volvo, K.S., friction, 7". Photo from Ron Smith.

Japanese Tin 1961 Cadillac Fleetwood, SSS, friction, 17-1/2". Photo from Ron Smith.

Japanese Tin 1961 Chevrolet Impala Convertible, Bandai, friction, 11". Photo from Ron Smith.

Japanese Tin 1961 Chevrolet Impala Sedan, Bandai, friction, 11". Photo from Ron Smith.

	C6	C8	C10
1960s Volkswagen Convertible, battery, Bandai, 7-1/2" long (J259)	50	70	90
1960s Volkswagen Convertible, battery, Bandai, 11 long (J260) ...	110	145	185
1960s Volkswagen Convertible, battery, Taiyo, 10-1/2" long (J261)	25	40	70
1960s Volkswagen Pickup Truck, friction, Bandai, 8" long (J254)	50	60	75
1960s Volkswagen with/without Sun Roof, friction, Bandai, 15" long (J265)	60	90	175
1960s Volvo 444 and 445, friction, KS, 7" long (J265B)	100	200	350
1960s Volvo P-1800 Coupe, friction, Ichiko, 9" long (J265C)	200	300	600
1960s Volvo P-1800 Coupe, friction, SSS, 11" long (J265E)	600	1200	1800
1960s Volvo P-1800 Wagon, friction, Ichiko, 9" long (J265D)	200	300	600
1960s Willys Jeep FC - 150 Pickup, friction, T.N. Toy Nomura, 11" long (J266)	50	75	95
1961 Buick, friction, T.N., 11" long (J011)	50	100	200
1961 Buick Emergency Car, friction, T.N., 14" long (J012)	50	75	100
1961 Cadillac 60, friction, unknown, 9" long (J028)	70	80	100
1961 Cadillac Fleetwood, friction, SSS, 17-1/2" long (J029)	150	300	600
1961 Chevrolet Impala Convertible, friction, Bandai, 11" long (J063) ..	100	150	300
1961 Chevrolet Impala Sedan, friction, Bandai, 11" long (J062) ..	100	150	250
1961 Ford Country Sedan, friction, Bandai, 10-1/2" long (J120)	125	150	250
1961 Ford Thunderbird Retractable, battery, Yonezawa, 11" long (J132)	90	120	175

	C6	C8	C10
1961 Oldsmobile Convertible/Wagon, friction, Yonezawa, 12" long (J214)	75	125	200
1961 Plymouth Sedan, friction, Ichiko, 12" long (J230)	125	300	500
1961 Plymouth Station Wagon, friction, Ichiko, 12" long (J231) ...	125	150	300
1961 Plymouth T.V. Car, battery, Ichiko, 12" long (J232)	125	200	400
1962 Cadillac, friction, Yonezawa, 22" long (J030)	100	250	400
1962 Chevrolet, friction, unknown, 11" long (J065)	150	300	600
1962 Chevrolet Corvette, friction, Bandai, 8" long (J039)	30	50	75
1962 Chevrolet Secret Agent, battery, unknown, 14" long (J064)	75	110	170

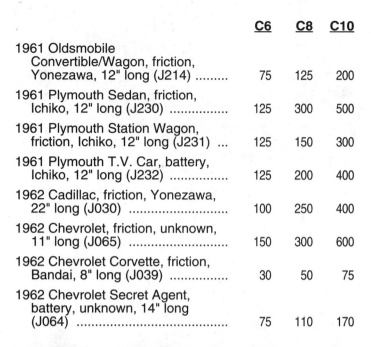

Japanese Tin 1961 Oldsmobile Convertible/Wagon, Yonezawa, friction, 12". Photo from Ron Smith.

Japanese Tin 1961 Plymouth Sedan, Ichiko, friction, 12". Photo from Ron Smith.

Japanese Tin 1961 Ford Country Sedan, Bandai, friction, 10-1/2". Photo from Ron Smith.

Japanese Tin 1961 Plymouth Station Wagon, Ichiko, friction, 12". Photo from Ron Smith.

Japanese Tin 1961 Plymouth T.V. Car, Ichiko, battery, 12". Photo from Ron Smith.

Japanese Tin 1962 Chevrolet, friction, 11". Photo from Ron Smith.

Japanese Tin 1962 Chevrolet Secret Agent, battery, 14". Photo from Ron Smith.

Japanese Tin 1962 Chrysler Imperial, Asahi, friction, 16". Photo from Ron Smith.

Japanese Tin 1962 Ford Country Sedan, Asahi, friction, 12". Photo from Ron Smith.

Japanese Tin 1963 Buick Wildcat, Ichiko, friction, 15". Photo from Ron Smith.

Japanese Tin 1963 Cadillac, Bandai, friction, 17". Photo from Ron Smith.

	C6	C8	C10
1962 Chrysler Imperial, friction, Asahi Toy Co., 16" long (J077) ...	600	1200	10,000+
1962 Ford Country Sedan, friction, Asahi, 12" long (J121)	200	300	600
1962 Ford Thunderbird Retractable, battery, Yonezawa, 11" long (J133)	90	120	175
1962 Mercedes-Benz, battery, SSS, 12" long (J190)	200	250	350
1963 Buick Wildcat, friction, Ichiko, 15" long (J013)	125	250	500

	C6	C8	C10
1963 Cadillac, friction, Bandai, 17" long (J031)	125	200	350
1963 Chevrolet Corvair, friction, Ichiko, 9" long (J044)	50	65	95
1963 Chevrolet Impala, friction, Bandai?, 18" long (J066)	150	300	600
1963 Corvair Bertone, battery, Bandai, 12" long (J277)	75	200	400

	C6	C8	C10
1963 Ford Thunderbird Retractable, battery, Yonezawa, 11" long (J134)	90	120	175
1964 Chevrolet Corvette, battery, Ichida, 12" long (J041)	150	225	350
1964 Ford Convertible, friction, Rico, 17" long (J124)	300	500	800
1964 Ford Hardtop, friction, Ichiko, 13" long (J122)	200	400	600
1964 Ford Hardtop, friction, Rico, 17" long (J123)	300	500	800
1964 Ford Thunderbird, friction, Ichiko, 16" long (J137)	100	200	400
1964 Ford Thunderbird Convertible, friction, Asahi, 12-1/2" long (J135)	150	200	400

	C6	C8	C10
1964 Ford Thunderbird Hardtop, friction, Asahi, 12" long (J136)	150	200	400
1964 Lincoln, friction, unknown, 10-1/2" long (J169)	90	175	275
1964 Plymouth Fury Hardtop, friction, Kusama, 10" long (J233)	60	80	100
1965 Cadillac, friction, Ashahi Toy Co., 17" long (J032)	200	400	600
1965 Cadillac, friction, Ichiko, 22" long (J033)	200	400	600
1965 Chevrolet Corvette, friction, Bandai, 8" long (J040)	40	60	80
1965 Ford Galaxie Hardtop, friction, MT, 11" long (J125)	125	150	250
1965 Ford Mustang (FBI), friction, Bandai, 11" long (J141)	75	100	300

Japanese Tin 1963 Chevrolet Impala, Bandai, friction, 18". Photo from Ron Smith.

Japanese Tin 1963 Ford Thunderbird Retractable, Yonezawa, battery, 11". Photo from Ron Smith.

Japanese Tin 1964 Chevrolet Corvette, Ichida, battery, 12". Photo from Ron Smith.

Japanese Tin 1964 Ford Hardtop, Ichiko, friction, 13". Photo from Ron Smith.

Japanese Tin 1964 Ford Thunderbird Hardtop, Asahi, friction, 12". Photo from Ron Smith.

Japanese Tin 1964 Lincoln, friction, 10-1/2". Photo from Ron Smith.

Japanese Tin 1965 Ford Mustang Fastback, Bandai, friction, 11". Photo from Ron Smith.

Japanese Tin 1965 Ford Mustang Hardtop/Convertible, Bandai, friction/battery, 11". Photo from Ron Smith.

Japanese Tin 1965 Ford Thunderbird Hardtop, Bandai, friction, 10-3/4". Photo from Ron Smith.

Japanese Tin 1966 Ford Mustang F.B., T.N., friction, 17". Photo from Ron Smith.

Japanese Tin 1966 Oldsmobile Toronado, Bandai, battery, 11". Photo from Ron Smith.

Japanese Tin 1967 Cadillac, friction, K.O., 10-1/2". Photo from Ron Smith.

	C6	C8	C10
1965 Ford Mustang Convertible, battery, Yonezawa, 13-1/2" long (J142)	90	125	250
1965 Ford Mustang Fastback, friction, Bandai, 11" long (J139)	45	65	90
1965 Ford Mustang Hardtop/Convertible, friction/battery, Bandai, 11" long (J140)	75	125	150
1965 Ford Thunderbird Hardtop, friction, Bandai, 10-3/4" long (J138)	60	85	125
1965 Jaguar XKE120, friction, Alps, 6-1/2" long (J161)	90	150	350

	C6	C8	C10
1966 Buick Le Sabre, friction, Ashai Toy Co., 19" long (J014)	100	200	400
1966 Ford Mustang Fastback, friction, T.N., 17" long (J143)	100	175	250
1966 Oldsmobile Toronado, battery, Bandai, 11" long (J215)	65	110	150
1967 Cadillac, friction, K.O., 10-1/2" long (J034)	100	150	300
1967 Cadillac, friction, unknown, 10-3/4" long (J035)	75	100	125
1967 Cadillac El Dorado, friction, Ichiko, 28" long (J036)	200	300	500
1967 Chevrolet Camaro, friction, Taiyo, 9-1/2" long (J045)	10	20	30
1967 Chevrolet Camaro, friction, T.N., 14" long (J046)	150	250	400
1967 Chevrolet Camaro, friction, Modern Toys, 11" long (J047)	25	50	75

	C6	C8	C10
1967 Ford Mustang, battery, Bandai, 13" long (J144)	45	65	100
1967 Mercury Cougar Hardtop, battery, Taiyo, 10" long (J196)	25	45	65
1967 Mercury Cougar Hardtop, friction, Asakusa Toys, 15" long (J197)	175	225	300
1967 Pontiac Firebird, friction, Akasura, 15-1/2" long (J219)	90	250	500
1967 Pontiac Firebird, friction, Bandai, 10" long (J220)	30	55	75
1967 Pontiac Firebird (w/wipers), battery, Bandai, 9-1/2" long (J221)	40	55	75

	C6	C8	C10
1967 Toyota 2000 GT, friction, A.T.C., 15" long (J250)	150	275	325
1968 Buick Sportswagon, friction, Asakusa, 15" long (J015)	100	150	200
1968 Chevrolet Corvette, battery, Taiyo, 9-1/2" long (J042)	35	50	75
1968 Dodge Yellow Cab and Checker cab, friction, T.N., 12" long (J085)	90	125	200
1968 Ford Torino, friction, S.T., 16" long (J126)	200	250	400
1968 Oldsmobile Toronado, friction, Ichiko, 17-1/2" long (J216)	300	400	500
1969 Dodge Hardtop, X, Buddy L, 13" long (J085A)	50	70	90
1970 Mercedes-Benz, friction, Ichiko, 24" long (J191)	125	150	200

Japanese Tin 1967 Chevrolet Camaro, T.N., friction, 14". Photo from Ron Smith.

Japanese Tin 1967 Pontiac Firebird, Bandai, friction, 10". Photo from Ron Smith.

Japanese Tin 1967 Mercury Cougar Hardtop, Asakusa Toys, friction, 15". Photo from Ron Smith.

Japanese Tin 1968 Chevrolet Corvette, Taiyo, battery, 9-1/2". Photo from Ron Smith.

Japanese Tin 1967 Pontiac Firebird, Akasura, friction, 15-1/2". Photo from Ron Smith.

Japanese Tin 1968 Ford Torino, friction, S.T., 16". Photo from Ron Smith.

Japanese Tin 1968 Oldsmobile Toronado, Ichiko, friction, 17-1/2". Photo from Ron Smith.

Japanese Tin Dream Car, Y, friction, 17". Photo from Ron Smith.

Japanese Tin 1971 Chevrolet Camaro Rusher, Taiyo, battery, 9-1/2". Photo from Ron Smith.

Japanese Tin Electrospecial No. 21, Y, battery, 10". Photo from Ron Smith.

Japanese Tin Atom Car, Yonezawa, friction, 17". Photo from Ron Smith.

Japanese Tin Midget Special No. 6, Y, friction, 7". Photo from Ron Smith.

	C6	C8	C10
1971 Chevrolet Camaro Rusher, battery, Taiyo, 9-1/2" long (J048)	10	20	35
Atom Car, friction, Yonezawa, 17" long (J284)	200	400	1000
Atom Jet Car, friction, Y Co., 30" long (J283)	500	1000	2000
Dream Car, friction, Y Co., 17" long (J278A)	600	800	1500
Electrospecial No. 21, battery, Y Co., 10" long (J290)	300	500	1000

	C6	C8	C10
Ford Fairlane Sedan, friction, Ichiko, 10" long (J105)	100	200	300
Ford Panel Truck, friction, reads "Standard Coffee," Bandai, 12" long (J108A)	1000	2000	3000+
Midget Special No. 6, friction, Y Co., 7" long (J291)	200	400	600

JOHNNY LIGHTNING / TOPPER

	C6	C8	C10
'32 Roadster, 1969	20	25	125
A.J. Foyt Indy Special, black wall tires, 1970	20	40	250
Al Unser Indy Special, black wall tires, 1970	50	100	500
Baja, 1970	n/a	20	45
Big Rig, came w/add on extras called Customs; prices reflect fully accessorized cars, 1971	35	65	275
Bubble, Jet Powered, 1970	25	45	150
Bug Bomb, black wall tires, 1970	25	40	225
Condor, black wall tires, 1970	75	150	1000
Custom Camaro, prototype, only six known to exist, 1968-69	n/a	n/a	5000
Custom Charger, prototype, only six known to exist, 1968-69	n/a	n/a	5000
Custom Continental, prototype, only six known to exist, 1968-69	n/a	n/a	6000
Custom Dragster, without canopy, 1969	10	35	125
Custom Dragster, mirror finish, 1969	n/a	100	150
Custom Dragster, w/plastic canopy, 1969	35	60	150
Custom El Camino, w/opening doors, 1969	50	100	475
Custom El Camino, mirror finish, 1969	n/a	100	200
Custom El Camino, w/sealed doors, 1969	70	100	55
Custom Eldorado, w/opening doors, 1969	75	125	350
Custom Ferrari, w/opening doors, mirror finish, 1969	n/a	150	300
Custom Ferrari, w/opening doors, 1969	45	150	n/a
Custom Ferrari, w/sealed doors, 1969	15	35	125
Custom GTO, mirror finish, 1969	100	200	1000
Custom GTO, w/sealed doors, 1969	75	125	1000
Custom GTO, w/opening doors, 1969	45	100	2000
Custom Mako Shark, w/opening doors, mirror finish, 1969	n/a	100	200
Custom Mako Shark, w/sealed doors, 1969	15	40	225
Custom Mako Shark, w/opening doors, 1969	n/a	50	125
Custom Mustang, prototype, only six known to exist, 1968-69	n/a	n/a	5000
Custom Spoiler, black wall tires, 1970	20	35	125
Custom T-Bird, w/opening doors, 1969	40	75	450
Custom T-Bird, mirror finish, 1969	100	200	5000
Custom T-Bird, w/sealed doors, 1969	65	80	600
Custom Toronado, mirror finish, 1969	n/a	300	450
Custom Toronado, w/sealed doors, 1969	n/a	200	300
Custom Toronado, w/opening doors, 1969	175	225	1000
Custom Turbine, w/unpainted interior, 1969	15	25	100
Custom Turbine, red, black, white painted interior, 1969	25	25	175
Custom Turbine, mirror finish, 1969.	100	150	425
Custom XKE, w/opening doors, 1969	n/a	45	150
Custom XKE, w/opening doors, mirror finish, 1969	n/a	150	300
Custom XKE, w/sealed doors, 1969	15	35	100
Double Trouble, black wall tires, 1970	40	75	5000
Flame Out, black wall tires, 1970	30	60	200
Flying Needle, Jet Powered, 1970	25	45	225
Frantic Ferrari	n/a	15	35
Glasser, Jet Powered, 1970	20	40	150
Hairy Hauler, came w/add on extras called Customs; prices reflect fully accessorized cars, 1971	35	65	275
Jumpin' Jag, black wall tires, 1970	15	35	175
Leapin' Limo, black wall tires, 1970 .	25	50	400
Mad Maverick, black wall tires, 1970	40	75	450
Monster, Jet Powered, 1970	20	40	150
Movin' Van, black wall tires, 1970	20	35	90
Nucleon, black wall tires, 1970	15	35	225
Parnelli Jones Indy Special, black wall tires, 1970	20	40	250
Pipe Dream, came w/add on extras called Customs; prices reflect fully accessorized cars, 1971	35	65	275
Sand Stormer, black wall tires, 1970	10	20	90

	C6	C8	C10
Sand Stormer, black roof, black wall tires, 1970	25	50	200
Screamer, Jet Powered, 1970	25	45	200
Sling Shot, black wall tires, 1970	25	50	250
Smuggler, black wall tires, 1970	20	35	150
Stiletto, black wall tires, 1970	40	60	300
T.N.T.	n/a	15	30
TNT, black wall tires, 1970	20	40	175
Triple Threat, black wall tires, 1970	20	40	200

	C6	C8	C10
Twin Blaster, came w/add on extras called Customs; prices reflect fully accessorized cars, 1971	35	65	275
Vicious Vette, black wall tires, 1970.	10	35	225
Vulture w/wing, black wall tires, 1970	45	75	500
Wasp, black wall tires, 1970	45	80	400
Wedge, Jet Powered, 1970	25	45	200
Whistler, black wall tires, 1970	45	75	300
Wild Winner, came w/add on extras called Customs; prices reflect fully accessorized cars, 1971	35	60	250

KANSAS TOY & NOVELTY COMPANY

Arthur Haynes, an auto mechanic, began molding toys in his Clifton, Kansas, shed for local stores in 1923. With clever hands and an artist's eye, he charmed his friends and local townspeople with his bright-colored toys. He made his patterns from advertising pictures, from local vehicles and probably from other makes of toys, such as Tootsietoy. He made his own production tools. His range was diverse, for he made miniatures of aircraft, autos, trains, farm equipment, zeppelin and a few animals, novelties and charms.

Haynes believed that he invented the hollow-casting of metal toys, so he must have started with solid toys. One day, he dropped his full mold, spilling its hot metal. To his delight he had a perfect, hollow toy vehicle, with promise of savings of metal and shipping costs.

This was a town enterprise from the beginning. Jess Foster, news editor, helped with alloy mixtures; Mr. Hadsell, Union Pacific agent, suggested they send samples to Woolworth's in New York. Clayton D. Young, a traveling salesman, saw the toys, joined the company and built a profitable business with the chain stores, including Kress, Kresge and Sears-Roebuck; he later became a partner. At its peak of international sales in the late 1920s, the firm employed as many as sixty-five in two shifts during the Christmas-order season.

They were young people who had grown up together, this familiarity lead to an informal and relaxed workplace. This informality was reflected in the local name for the plant, "The Hoopie Factory." Two or three of their early toys, No. 26 and No. 33, were stripdowns—hoopies, probably raced locally. Whether "Whoopee", tractor toy No. 48, was a local spelling of this or whether it celebrated a fat, cheering order, is not known

Teamwork was a must, for a molder, according to Ernest Istas, could produce 2,000 toys a day. Helen Istas was the secretary; Bill Haynes was another molder, showing the family nature of the work force, with its clippers (trimmers), painters, clampers (axles) and boxers. Butch Morgison, one of our sources, was each of these during his long career with the company. It was discovered that Clayton Stevenson (see Lincoln White Metal Works and Midwest Toy), a basement toymaker and then employee a foundry, furnished some molds and patterns. He must have created those realistic designs from three-piece molds with their intricate front-ends (see No. 8, No. 58, No. 60, No. 80, No. 88, No. 91). These features must have slowed production and added to costs, but made for collector value and rarity.

During its good years, Kansas Toy & Novelty created more designs and produced more toys than any producer of white-metal toys except Barclay. Young withdrew his share and retired around 1930. With the loss of these assets and the onset of the Depression, the company went downhill. George Hoeffer reorganized the company and moved the factory down the road, but this effort lasted only a few months. An era was coming to an end. This later history is scanty, but there is evidence that Haynes kept trying until toy No. 100 in 1935.

High-numbered toys are rare. Changes of wheel types suggest that Haynes was having problems. Perhaps he had always overreached, for looking back at the diversity of his toys and novelties, it is remarkable from a few mechanics in a small Midwest town.

Contributor: Fred Maxwell, 4722 N. 33 St., Arlington, VA 22207. **Perry R. Eichor,** 703 North Almond Drive, Simpsonville, SC, 29681.

Kansas Toy Molds

Because KT&N founded a molding dynasty, with its molds still in use today after passing through several companies, extra details and comments have been included to eliminate collector and dealer confusion. Many Kansas Toy & Novelty toys were not numbered, some of them were twins of the numbered versions; and not all numbered toys were Kansas Toy & Novelty.

- Some toys were made in two or three versions/variations.
- Some toys were made in two or three sizes (5 cents, 10 cents and 15)
- Most wheels were metal (disk or simulated spoked or wire. Tractor/farm wheels were large disk or open spoke with wide rims; a unique track laying version with rubber tracks used metal or wood wheels.) Rubber tires on wood hubs (popularized by Tootsietoy Grahams in 1932) were tried on No. 75 and later; followed by soft rubber (balloon) wheels and hard-rubber white discs with painted black tires.
- Many had string-pull loops or knobs on the lower grille.
- All colors were used, including gold, silver and pink.
- A few were found with bi-colored bodies (may have been salesman samples). Many early toys were finished in Egyptian lacquer, so this the bright metal gleamed through. A mint example with this unique finish has a modern, glittery look.
- "Made in USA" embossing is a clue to Best Toy and later, for this copyright addition came from laws of the mid-1930s. Black rubber tires were used later by Ralstoy and others.
- For Kansas Toy & Novelty airplanes, cannon and novelties, see "Aircraft" and "Miscellaneous" sections in *Collecting Toys*. For additional pictures and different views see "Best Toy & Novelty" in this book.
- The "dynasty" mentioned above included Best Toy, Ralstoy, Craftoy and Eccles Bros., in that order. The Ralstoy of today, with its line of die-cast trucks, is the same company on a different track.
- The following sequential listing has been carefully researched, but additions are still trickling in. The first toy is controversial. One source said it was a solid casting; probably true, but did it ever reach the market? Some said it was the large Indy racer; others said it was the midget racer without a driver.

Note: There are so few original Kansas Toy & Novelty toys with higher numbers in today's market, compared to later reproductions, that it is not known which went into production. They are shown earlier in this book as Best Toys to save duplication.

	C6	C8	C10
Army Tank, No. "74"; marked "US Army," WWI-type, high turret, large front, small rear wheels; olive drab color; 2-1/4" long (KTV056)	20	30	40
Box Car, No. "38"; marked "KT & N RR," Union Pacific shield (possibly an early promotional), four MDW, 3-1/4" long (KTV029)	15	25	35

	C6	C8	C10
Caboose, No. "40"; marked "KT & N RR," stack, brakeman's cab, MDW, 2-3/4" long (KTV031)	15	25	35
Coupe, no number; crude, slant roof, no head lamps, shallow rear body, no fenders, lacquer; posibly first "hoopie" or stripdown made; 3-1/8" long (KTV004)	32	48	65
Coupe, No. "8"; Cadillac Convertible (?), three-piece mold casting different from the three No. 8 versions, basic body suggests same pattern-maker, if not Kansas Toy & Novelty, then it is Midwest Toy; rectangular VG, HO, no headlamps, VL, MWW, SM, WV, two OW, body trim, kickplates, door handles, LI, T, MDWBT, rare, 3-1/4" long (KTV006)	40	60	80
Coupe, No. "8"; Convertible, LI, VL, HG, WV, SP, RM, MWW, no HO, no headlamps, enamel finish. 3-1/8" long; there is also UV w/"Chrysler," headlamps and HO, or w/MDSW (KTV007)	20	30	40

Kansas Toy Army Tank, No.74, high turret, large front, 2-1/4". Photo from Perry Eichor.

Abbreviations

The following abbreviations are for the details and variations useful in identification.

HG	horizontal grille pattern	SM	sidemounted spare
HL	horizontal hood louvers	SP	string-pull knob in handcrank area
HO	hood cap, Motometer or ornament	T	external trunk
L	lacquer finish	UV	unnumbered version
LI	landau irons on convertibles	VG	vertical grille pattern
MDW	metal disc wheels	VL	vertical hood louvers
MDSW	metal disc solid spokes	WS, W/S	windshield
MDWBT	wheels with black painted tires	WV	windshield visor
MSW	metal open spoke wheels	WHRT	wooden hubs, rubber tires
MWW	metal simulated wire wheels	WRDW	white hard rubber disc wheels
OW	open windows	WRW	white soft rubber wheels (balloon tires)
RM	rearmount spare tire/wheel		

	C6	C8	C10
Coupe, No. "8"; trunk Convertible, T, HO, VG, SM, MDW; 3-1/8" long; Note: No. 8 is the lowest numbered vehicle found. Its realistic, high quality signals the ending of a novice toymaker's experimental phase (KTV008)	20	30	40
Coupe, No. "35"; convertible, LI, VL, HG, HO, RM, MWW; 2-1/4" long; also an UV (KTV026)	20	30	40
Coupe, No. "66"; stream-lined three-wheeler, six OW, MWW; 3-1/2" long (KTV051)	60	80	100

	C6	C8	C10
Dirt scraper, No. "65"; 1-7/8" blade, adjustable, on same frame as number 62; 3-5/8" long; Note: This is part of a unique towed farm set w/several hinged or moving parts, each a different color and large 1-1/4" spoked tractor wheels (KTV050)	40	60	80
Dirt Tumble, No. "64"; adjustable dumping scoop, 1-1/2" wide on same frame as No. 62, six pieces, four colors; 4" long; Note: This is part of a unique towed farm set w/several hinged or moving parts, each a different color and large 1-1/4" spoked tractor wheels (KTV049)	50	75	100

Top row, left to right: Kansas Toy Coupe, no number; Sedan, no number. Middle row: a pair of 3-1/8" Coupes (No. 8). Bottom row, left to right: a pair of 2-1/4" Coupes (No. 35); Sedanette, No. 58, 2-1/4". Photo from Fred maxwell.

Left to right: Kansas Toy Coupe, No. 8, 3-1/8"; Coupe, No. 8, 3-1/4". Photo from Fred Maxwell.

Top row, left to right: Kansas Toy Coupe, No. 8, 3-1/8"; Roadster, No. 15, 3-1/8". Bottom row, left to right: Sedan, No. 60, 3-1/2"; Coupe, No. 80, 3-1/2". Photo from Perry Eichor.

Back row: Kansas Toy Dump Truck, No. 42, driver, no cab, 3-1/2". Front row: two Ralstoy versions of the Kansas Toy truck. Photo from Perry Eichor.

Left to right: Kansas Toy Dump Truck, No. 42, 3-1/2" and a later version of the Dump Truck. Photo from Fred Maxwell.

Kansas Toy Coupe, No. 35, 2-1/4". Photo from Bob Ackerly.

Left to right: Kansas Toy Farm Tractor, No. 17, 2-7/8"; Disc Harrow, No. 62, 4"; Planter, No. 61, 4".

Kansas Toy Coupe, No. 66, three-wheeler, 3-1/2". Photo from Ferd Zegel.

Top to bottom: Kansas Toy Large Coupe, no number, 5"; Coupe, No. 35, 2-1/4". Photo from Ferd Zegel.

A pair of Kansas Toy Deere Model D tractors, 4-/78".

Kansas Toy Large Indy Racer, no number, driver, boat-tail, 6".

	C6	C8	C10
Disk Harrow, No. "62"; eight disks on same 1-5/8" wide frame as No. 61; thirteen pieces, including disks and wheels, four colors, 4" long. Note: This is part of a unique towed farm set w/several hinged or moving parts, each a different color and large 1-1/4" spoked tractor wheels. Has been seen w/tin snap-on seats. (KTV047)	40	60	80
Dump Truck, No. "42"; Ford (?), driver, no cab, diamond emblem on hinged dump body, VL, HG, SP, MWW; 3-1/2" long (KTV033)	30	45	60
Farm Tractor, No. "17"; "Fordson", driver, HG, crank, no tow hook, large 1-1/4" and 3/4" MDW w/four holes in disks; also found w/same size six spoke wheels; 2-7/8" long; see No. 57 (KTV017)	25	35	45
Farm Tractor, no number; "Fordson" on radiator and crankcase, VG and towhook, w/small plain MDW, three-piece molded grille; 2-5/8" long (KTV018)	25	35	45
Farm Tractor, No. "48"; "Caterpillar," "Whoopee," driver, VL, HG, HO, SP, tow loop, w/larger-3/4" track-laying wheels, metal or wood, for rubber track (KTV036A)	25	40	55
Farm Tractor, No. "57"; Fordson, driver, SP, MDW rear, MSW front; 1-3/4" long; smaller version of No. 17 there is also an UV (KTV042)	25	35	45
Fire Engine, No. "70"; Seagrave (?) pumper, driver, VL, HG, MDW; 2-1/4" long (KTV053)	25	45	60
Indy Racer, No. "10"; driver, boattail, exhaust right, VL, HG, HO, SP, M.S.W. or MWW; 3-1/8" long; There is also UV (KTV014)	20	30	40

	C6	C8	C10
Large Coupe, no number; crude, high-bodied "Ford," HO, HG, no headlamps, SP, VL, five windows, door handles, wheel type unknown because only a reproduction has been found, 3-1/4" long (KTV000)	20	30	40
Large coupe, no number; Chrysler Convertible, MWW and and golf doors; 5" long; larger version of No. 8 (KTV009)	20	30	40
Large Farm Tractor, no number; Deere Model D, two color, steering shaft, fly wheel, belt drive wheel, rear fenders, large 2" and 1" twelve-spoke wheels; 4-7/8" long (KTV019)	35	50	75
Large Indy Racer, no number; driver, boattail, HO, MDW, lacquer, 6" long (KTV003)	40	60	80
Locomotive-tender, No. "36"; marked "KT & N RR," six MSW, four MDW, 0-6-4; 4-3/8" long (KTV027)	20	30	40
Midget Racer, no number; no driver, torpedo tail, HO, SP, VL, HG; 5/8" MDW w/simulated lug nuts; lacquer finish (KTV001)	20	30	40
Midget Racer, no number; no driver, torpedo tail, HO, SP, VL., HG, 3" long w/driver, plain MDW, lacquer; easily confused w/another maker's copy; see No. 31 and No. 67 (KTV002)	70	105	140
Midget racer, No. "31"; driver, torpedo tail, VL, HG, HO, MWW, lacquer; 2-1/8" long; there is also UV; see No. 67 (KTV024)	14	21	28
Midget Racer, No. "67"; Driver, torpedo-tail, VL, HG, HO, MDW; 1-1/2"; smaller version of No. 31; there is also an UV (KTV052)	25	45	55
Overland Bus, No. "9"; "Fageol," solid windows; 3-1/2" long (KTV012)	25	35	45

	C6	C8	C10
Overland Bus, no number; "Fageol", nine male passengers, driver and "baggage" cast on windows; HG, RM, MDW 3-1/2" long; There is also an UV w/various family passengers on windows (KTV013)	35	50	70
Pickup Truck, No. "51"; Ford w/cab; VL, HG, tow loop, MDW, lacquer; 2-3/4" long; there is also an UV (KTV038)	20	30	40
Planter, No. "61"; marked "KTN No. 61," V-blade plough w/seed hopper, four-piece including wheels, three colors; 4" long; Note: This is part of a unique towed farm set w/several hinged or moving parts, each a different color and large 1-1/4" spoked tractor wheels. Has been seen w/tin snap-on seats. (KTV046) ...	40	60	80
Plough, No."63"; single blade on same shaft as number 61, 4" long; Note: This is part of a unique towed farm set w/several hinged or moving parts, each a different color and large 1-1/4" spoked tractor wheels (KTV048)	40	60	80

	C6	C8	C10
Pullmar Car, No. "37"; marked "KT & N RR," four MDW; 3-1/2" long (KTV028)	15	25	35
Racer, No. "26"; "Bearcat" stripdown, long hood, motometer, three intakes, driver, open frame, left four cylinder exhaust, 4" long; see No. 33 (KTV022)	75	100	125
Racer, No. "33"; "Bearcat" stripdown, 3" long; smaller version of No. 26 (KTV025)	85	125	150
Racer, No. "46"; 1929 Golden Arrow record car, driver, large tail fin, MWW; 2-7/8" long (KTV035)	25	35	45
Racer, no number; miniature solid-cast version of No. 10, moving wheels, charm loop on nose; 1" long (KTV057)	15	25	35
Roadster, No. "14"; open "Chrysler," solid W.S., plain grille, HO, VL, SP, RM, MDSW; 3-1/8" long (KTV015)	20	30	45

From left: Racer, No. 26, 4"; Racer, No. 33, 3". Photo from Perry Eichor.

Top row, left to right: Kansas Toy Midget Racer, no number, no driver, 3"; Midget Racer, no number, with driver, 3". Bottom row, left to right: Indy Racer, No. 10, driver, 3-1/8"; Midget Racer, No. 24, driver, 2-1/28"; Midget Racer, No. 67, driver, 1-1/2". Photo from Fred Maxwell.

Kansas Toy Racer, No. 46, Golden Arrow Record Car. Photo from Fred Maxwell.

Overland Bus, No. 9, 3-1/2". Photo from Fred maxwell.

This is a catalog photo of the Kansas Toy No. 92 Toy Racer. Photo from M.C.P. Catalog.

Kansas Toy Roadster, no number, open rumble seat. Photo from Bob Straub.

Kansas Toy Roadster, No. 54, rumble seat, plain hood and grille, no headlamps, 2-3/8". Photo from Fred Maxwell.

Kansas Toy Sedanette, No. 58, Austin Bantam, unique fighting cock on door panels, 2-1/4". Photo from Ferd Zegel.

From left: Kansas Toy Coupe, three-piece mold grille, No. 58, 3-1/4"; Sedanette, No. 8, 2-1/4".

	C6	C8	C10
Roadster, no number; solid WS, plain grille, HO, VL, SP, RM, MDSW, HG, two golf club doors; 3-1/8" long (KTV015A)	25	40	60
Roadster, no number; solid WS, plain grille, HO, VL, SP, RM, MDSW, HG, w/open rumble seat; might not be Kansas Toy & Novelty (KTV016)	NPF	NPF	NPF
Roadster, No. "54"; Buick, driver w/cap, rumble seat, T, plain hood and grille, no headlamps, SM, MWW; 2-3/8" long; there is also an UV; see No. 77 (KTV039)	30	50	70
Roadster, "54", Buick, driver w/cap, rumble seat, no trunk, plain hood and grille, no headlamps, SM, MWW; 2-1/4" long; there is also an UV; see No. 77 (KTV040)	60	75	100
Sedan, no number; crude limousine or stretch taxi, six windows, louvered rear quarters, HO, VL, HG, T, SP, large MDW, lacquer; 3-3/8" long (KTV005)	15	25	35
Sedan, no number; "Chevrolet," six windows, LI, WV, VL, SP, RM, MWW; 2-7/8" long (KTV010)	20	30	40
Sedan, no number; "Chevrolet," six windows, LI, WV, VL, SP, RM, MWW, HG, HO, MSW; 3-1/4" long (KTV011)	20	30	40

	C6	C8	C10
Sedan, No. "60", 1930 Reo Royale (?) or Chrysler two-door. brougham, plain hood, vee-VG, square rear deck, MDW, MDWSM; 3-1/2" long; there is also an UV w/MWW and MWWSM, three-piece molded grille (KTV045)	30	45	60
Sedanette, No. "58"; Austin Bantam, unique fighting cock on door panels, four OW, H.L., VG, RM, MWW, three-piece molded grille; 2-1/4" long (KTV043)	25	35	45
Separator-Thresher, No. "27"; tow hook, auto-type MSW (not tractor rims), lacquer or enamel; 3" long; there is also UV; see No. 72 (KTV023)	25	40	50
Separator-Thresher, No. "72"; tow hook for No. 71 (KTV055)	NPF	NPF	NPF
Steam Road Roller, No. "43"; driver, SP, boiler, wooden rollers; 3-1/4" long (KTV034)	30	45	60

	C6	C8	C10
Steam Tractor, No. "25"; "Case," crew of two, tow loop, large front, small rear M.S.W. and flywheel; 3" long; see number 71; also an UV w/no name (KTV021)	25	40	60
Steam Tractor, No. "71"; crew of two, tow-loop; 2-1/2" long; small version of No. 25 (KTV054)	30	40	60
Stock Car, No. "41"; marked "KT & N RR," MDW (KTV032)	15	25	35
Tank Car, No. "39"; marked "KT & N RR," ladder, filler, MDW; 3-1/8" long (KTV030)	15	25	35

	C6	C8	C10
Tour Bus, No. "49"; 1928 Pickwick COE "Nite Coach," HG, SP, MDW duals; 2-3/8" long; there is also an UV; see No. 59 (KTV037)	20	30	40
Tour Bus, No. "59"; 1928 Pickwick COE double-deck night-coach, screen grille; 3-3/8" long; larger version of No. 49; also an UV w/dual wheels (KTV044)	75	100125	150
Truck, No. "20"; Ford (?), solid W.S., two OW, three tanks, VL, HG, rear faucet, M.W.W; there are versions w/ and w/o driver. 3-1/8"; there is also an UV version (KTV020)	40	60	80
Truck-Semi, No. "55"; Ford, stake trailer, VL, HG, MDW; 4" long (KTV041)	NPF	NPF	NPF

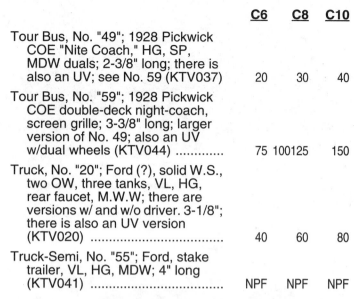

Kansas Toy Tour Bus, No. 59, 1928 Pickwick double-deck night-coach, 3-3/8". Photo from Fred Maxwell.

From left: Kansas Toy Tour Bus, No. 49; Fire Engine, No. 70.

Top row, left to right: Kansas Toy Separator-Thresher, No. 27, 3"; Steam Tractor, No. 21, Case, 3". Bottom row: Steam Tractor, No. 71, crew of two, 2-1/2". Photo from Fred Maxwell.

Left to right: Kansas Toy Dump Truck, No. 42; Truck-Semi, No. 55, stake trailer, 4". Photo from Ferd Zegel.

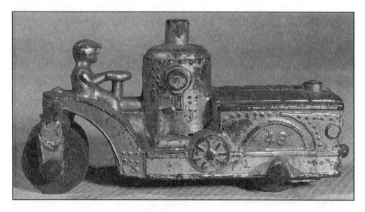

Kansas Toy Steam Road Roller, No. 43, driver, boiler, wooden rollers, 3-1/4". Photo from R.F. Sapita.

Kansas Toy Truck, No. 20, three tanks, 3-1/8". Photo from Fred Maxwell.

Kansas Toy Warehouse Tractor, No. 48, Caterpillar, driver, 3". Photo from Fred Maxwell.

Back row, left to right: Kansas Toy Sedan, No. 79, two-door, 4-1/4"; Racer, No. 76., Auburn Speedster, 4-1/4". Middle row, left to right: Coupe, No. 80, 3-1/2"; Sedan, No. 60, 1930s REO or Chrysler, 3-1/2". Bottom row: Sedanette, No. 58, three-piece molded grille, 2-1/4". Photo from Perry Eichor.

Kansas Toy Racer, No. 81, 1933 issue, 4-3/8". Photo from Bob Ackerly.

A pair of Kansas Toy Pierce-Arrow Silver Arrow Sedans (No. 82), 4". Photo from Ferd Zegel.

	C6	C8	C10
Warehouse Tractor, No. "48"; "Caterpillar," "Whoopee," driver, VL, HG, HO, SP, tow loop, MWW; 3" long; there is also an UV (KTV036)	25	38	50

Kansas Toy Transitional Vehicles

	C6	C8	C10
Army Tank, No. "74"; marked "US Army," two gun turret, olive dab color; 2-1/4" long; a different tank than No. 74 listed earlier (KTV061)	NPF	NPF	NPF
Concrete Mixer, No. "78", truck w/water tank and mixing barrel, VG, HL, WHRT; Found both w/ and w/o a bottom pan; sometimes called a fuel tanker; 3-3/4" long (KTV065)	NPF	NPF	NPF
Coupe, No. "75"; Graham-like (Tootsietoy), VG, SM, T, WHRT, 1933 issue, 4-1/4" long (KTV062)	NPF	NPF	NPF
Coupe, No. "80"; convertible, top up, LI, two OW, VG, T, MWW w/MWW, SM, three-piece molded grille; 3-1/2" long (KTV067)	30	45	60
Coupe, No. "80"; convertible, top up, LI, two OW, VG, T, HRDW w/MDW, SM (a different sidemounts castings); 3-1/2" long (KTV068)	NPF	NPF	NPF

	C6	C8	C10
Indy Racer, No. "83"; FWD, driver, VG, H.L., right exhaust, WHRT, 4-5/8" long (KTV071)	NPF	NPF	NPF
Racer, No. "76"; Auburn speedster, low driver, headrest fairing, SP, HG, slanted louvers, large oval fin, kickplates, HWRW or WHRT; 4-1/4" long (KTV063)	25	38	50
Racer, No. "81"; 4-3/8". Miller FWD, driver, eight cylinder right exhaust, HG, WHRT, 1933 issue (KTV069)	NPF	NPF	NPF
Roadster, No. "77"; open sport Duesenberg, W.S down, driver, VG, slanted louvers, SM, T, WHR; 4" long (KTV064)	25	38	50
Sedan, No. "79," two-door, Graham-like, four OW, VG, HL, RM, WHRT w/five removable tires; found both w/ and w/o bottom pan; 4-1/4" long (KTV066)	20	30	40

	C6	C8	C10
Sedan, No. "82"; Pierce-Arrow Silver Arrow fastback, six OW, HRDW, three-piece molded grille; 4" long (KTV070)	NPF	NPF	NPF
Sedan, No. "84", DeSoto (?) Airflow, four OW, HO, HG, HL, HRDW, 1934 issue; 3-5/8" long (KTV072)	NPF	NPF	NPF

Kansas Toy Sedan, No. 84, 3-5/8", possibly a DeSoto Airflow, 1934 issue. Photo from Bob Ackerly.

KARL BUB

Bub had one of the longest reigns in the toy business. He took over the Carette Toy Co., in 1917, after Georges Carette fled to France at the onset of World War I. He also took over the Bing Toy Works in 1932. Bub used much of the technology practiced by Carette. His toys were of the better-quality toys to come out of Germany in the early 1900s. Bub produced many of the fine toys sold by F.A.O. Schwarz Co., of New York.

Contributor: Bob Smith, The Village Smith, 62 West Ave., Fairport, NY 14450-2102.

	C6	C8	C10
Coupe, rumble seat, clockwork motor	NPF	NPF	NPF
Limousine, red and black, clockwork motor, opening doors, hand brake, c.1915, 14" long	1200	2000	2700
Limousine, clockwork, 14" long	2000	4000	7500
Limousine, green and black, doors open, front crack clockwork motor, 9-3/4" long	700	1150	1600
Limousine, wind-up, driver, 11" long	700	1400	2000
Limousine, wind-up, 8" long	400	600	800
Mercedes Limousine, green and black, doors open, windshield folds, head lamps, tool box's clockwork motor, head lamps, steering, c.1928, 13-1/2" long	1050	1750	2400

Karl Bub Limousine, 9-3/4".

Karl Bub Limousine, red and black, circa 1915, 14".

Karl Bub Limousine, clockwork, 1920s, 14". Photo from Sotheby's, New york.

Karl Bub Mercedes Limousine, circa 1928, 13-1/2".

Karl Bub Roadster, driver, circa 1908, 9". Photo from Bill Bertoia Auctions.

	C6	C8	C10
Roadster, driver, c.1908, 9" long......	800	1500	2300
Sedan, wind-up, high headlamps, 1919, 14" long..............................	800	1600	2500
Toures, wind-up, two seat, 9-1/2" long..	900	1700	2400

Karl Bub Sedan, 1919, high headlamps, wind-up, 14". Photo from Bill Bertoia Auctions.

KELMET
Also known as Trumodel and Big Boy

Kelmet was founded in Chicago in 1925 by several wholesale toy representatives. It was their wish to compete with the large toy-steel vehicles of the period. Some work was through A.C. Gilbert. White trucks were a Kelmet staple. The toys were big (about two feet) and heavy (about ten pounds).

	C6	C8	C10
Aerial Ladder Truck, 30" long...........	800	1250	1700
Army Truck, 1929, 25" long..............	800	1250	2000
Chemical Truck	900	1400	2000

Kelmet Aerial Ladder Truck, 30". Photo from Bill Bertoia Auctions.

Kelmet Army Truck, 1929, 25". Photo from Joe and Sharon Freed.

Kelmet White Dump Truck, No. 501, 25". Photo from Joe and Sharon Freed.

	C6	C8	C10
Coal Pocket Loader	1200	2000	3000
Crane Truck	2500	4000	6000
Sand Loader	1000	1700	2400
Scissor Dump Truck, 25" long	600	950	1400
Steam Shovel, Big Boy	325	488	650
Tank Truck, 27" long	1500	2700	4700
Trumodel Derrick, w/power hoist and tip bucket	1000	1700	2400
White Dump Truck, No. 501, 25" long	1200	2000	2700
White Fire Truck, w/ladder	1200	2000	3000

KENTON

Kenton Lock Manufacturing Co., was incorporated in May 1890, in Kenton, Ohio. In November of 1894, it became the Kenton Hardware Manufacturing Co. Around this period, it began producing toys. In 1903, it brought out its first toy vehicle line, calling them the "Red Devils," since most cars in those days were painted red. The firm was a guild. In 1930, L.S. Bixler, of Jones & Bixler, was its president. Cast-iron was its material.

	C6	C8	C10
Ambulance, cast iron, 7" long	700	1200	1800
Army Motor Truck 807, cast iron, 14" long	600	950	1450
Auto, clockwork, tiller, driver w/top hat, very early, approx. 4" long	250	400	650

	C6	C8	C10
Auto, cast iron, 6" long	900	1600	2400
Auto Dray Truck, black driver, passenger, 9" long	9000	1700	2600
Auto Express 548, w/driver, 9-1/4" long	1500	2500	3800
Auto Hansom, 7-3/4" long	475	550	800
Boat-tail Cut-Down Speedster, 1910, 7" long	120	180	260
Buckeye Ditcher, 9" long	500	750	1200
Buckeye Ditcher, 11-3/4" long	1400	2500	4250
Bus, double-decker, 13-1/2" long	1500	2600	4500
Bus, twin coach, 8-1/2" long	950	1500	2350
Bus, 12-3/4" long	600	900	1500
Bus, 1920s, 10-3/4" long	375	525	750
Bus, cast iron, 8" long	325	500	700

Kenton Ambulance, 7". Photo from Sotheby's.

Kenton Army Motor Truck, 14". Photo from Sotheby's.

Kenton Auto Hansom, 7-3/4". Photo from Bill Bertoia Auctions.

Kenton Buckeye Ditcher, 9". Photo from Sotheby's.

Kenton Bus, 12-3/4". Photo from Bill Bertoia Auctions.

Kenton Bus, double-decker, 13-1/2". Photo from Sotheby's.

Kenton Bus, double-decker, 8-1/8". Photo from Sotheby's.

Kenton Seeing New York 899 Bus, 10-1/2". Photo from Bill Bertoia Auctions.

Kenton Bus, double-decker, 12". Photo from Bill Bertoia Auctions.

	C6	C8	C10
Bus, double-decker, c.1902s, 8-1/8" long	1000	1600	2500
Bus, double-decker, 12" long	500	800	1300
Bus, w/Mama Katzenjammer, Uncle Heine, Alphonse, Gloony Gus, Happy Hoaligan, marked "Seeing New York 899," 10-1/2" long	2000	3900	6350
Bus, double-decker, 1920, 7-1/4" long	1000	1500	2200
Bus, double-decker, 1920s, 6" long	375	575	900
Bus, double-decker, 9-1/2" long	500	750	1100

	C6	C8	C10
Cattle Truck, cast iron, c.1938, 8" long	150	225	325
Cement Mixer Truck, 1932, 8-1/2" long	1400	2500	4000
Circus Truck, 10" long	1300	2000	2700
City Service Truck, C-cab, 10-1/4" long	1500	2800	3700
Coal Dump Truck, w/driver, c.1932, 10-1/2" long	800	1350	2000
Coal Dump Truck, 8-1/2" long	140	210	280
Coast-to-Coast Bus	350	525	700

	C6	C8	C10
Contractors Dump Truck, 3-bucket, 9-3/4" long..........................	500	800	1150
Contractors Dump Wagon, cast iron, 8-1/2" long..........................	500	750	1000
Coupe, 5" long	230	345	460
Coupe, 6-1/2" long	450	638	850
Coupe, 8" long	700	1100	1600
Coupe, separate driver, 10" long, 1926	1500	4500	9000
Dump Truck, 6" long	337	505	675
Dump Truck, hinged self-locking gate, 8-1/2" long..........................	500	800	1100

	C6	C8	C10
Emergency Truck, black rubber tires, takes batteries for headlights and spotlight, 1930s ...	180	270	360
Fire Apparatus Truck	400	600	800
Fire Pump Truck, early w/driver, approx. 10" long..........................	185	278	350
Fire Pumper, 1911, 11-1/2" long	NPF	NPF	NPF
Fire Pumper, 1920s, 14-1/2" long	800	1200	1600
Fire Pumper, early, 5-3/4" long	120	180	240

Kenton Coal Dump Truck, with driver, 1930s, 10-1/2". Photo from Bill Bertoia Auctions.

Kenton Bus, double-decker, 1920s, 6". Photo from Bill Bertoia Auctions.

Kenton Contractors Dump Truck, 3-bucket, 9-3/4". Photo from Sotheby's.

Kenton Bus, double-decker, 9-1/2". Photo from Sotheby's.

Kenton Coal Dump Truck, with driver, 1930s, 10-1/2". Photo from Bill Bertoia Auctions.

Kenton Fire Pumper Truck, early, with driver, approximately 10". Photo from Rod Carnahan.

Kenton Fire Pumper, circa 1920, 18". Photo from Mapes Auctioneers and Appraisers.

Kenton Franklin, air-cooled, 8-1/2". Photo from Sotheby's.

Kenton Ice Truck, driver, 7-7/8". Photo from Bill Bertoia Auctions.

Kenton Ice Truck, tractor trailer, 1930s, 10-1/2". Photo from Bill Bertoia Auctions.

Kenton Jaeger Cement Mixer Truck, 8". Photo from Hake's.

	C6	C8	C10
Fire Pumper, w/gong, c.1920, 18" long	350	525	700
Fire Truck, w/pumper, 15" long	1200	2000	2800
Franklin, air-cooled, 8-1/2" long	1300	1950	2600
Hose Reel Fire Truck, 8-3/4" long	325	488	650
Hose Truck, open cab, green, driver, rider, hose, ladders, 1920s, approx. 6-3/4" long	350	525	700
Hudson, postwar electric lights	50	75	100
Ice Truck, tongs and glass ice, 7-1/2" long	1000	2000	3000
Ice Truck, w/driver, 7-7/8" long	425	638	850
Ice Truck, tractor trailer 1930s, 10-1/2" long	1000	1700	2400
Jaeger Cement Mixer, 8" long	1000	1500	2000
Jaeger Cement Mixer, iron wheels, 6-1/2" long	262	393	525
Jaeger Cement Mixer, 7" long	550	825	1250
Jaeger Cement Mixer, 7-3/8" long	650	950	1500

	C6	C8	C10
Jeager Cement Mixer Truck, cast iron, 9" long	1000	2000	3000
Ladder Truck, cast iron, approx. 7-1/2" long	300	450	600
Ladder Truck, driver, early 1930s, 9" long	90	135	180
Ladder Truck, 11-1/2" long	280	420	560
Ladder Truck, pressed steel ladders, 16" long	500	850	1100
Ladder Truck, 17-1/4" long	750	1200	1700
Ladder Truck, 20" long	1100	1800	2500
Ladder Truck, 22" long	1500	2400	3500
Limousine, driver, c.1915, 7-3/4" long	500	700	1000

	C6	C8	C10
Merchant Delivery Truck	450	675	900
Oil Gas Truck, 10-1/2" long	800	1400	2100
Overland Circus, w/hippo, 7-1/4" long	700	1150	1600
Overland Circus, w/lion, 9" long	800	1300	1800
Overland Circus Cage Truck, w/driver, 7-1/2" long	900	1500	2000
Overland Circus Calliope Truck, rare, 10" long	NPF	NPF	NPF
Patrol Wagon, w/driver and three fireman, 1920s-1930s, 9" long	650	1100	1600
Phaeton touring Car, 12" long	350	562	700
Pickwick Nite Coach, cast iron, 14" long	1900	2750	3800
Pickwick Nite Coach, 11" long	NPF	NPF	NPF
Pickwick Nite Coach, 9-1/2" long	1400	2500	3700
Pickwick Nite Coach, 7-1/2" long	600	1100	1500
Pickwick Nite Coach, 6" long	500	850	1200

	C6	C8	C10
Pontiac, 4-1/2" long	262	393	525
Pontiac and Trailer, 10" long	350	525	725
Racer, 7-1/2" long	142	213	285
Racer, cast iron, early, 9" long	600	1000	1400
Red Devil Auto, w/driver, 1906, 6" long	225	338	450
Red Sedan, 1929, 8" long	NPF	NPF	NPF
Road Grader, 5-1/2" long	125	188	250
Road Grader, 1950, 7-1/4" long	135	205	275
Road Grader, cast iron, rubber tires, nickel-plated moveable blade, 7-1/2" long	155	230	310

Kenton Jaeger Cement Mixer, 6-1/2" iron wheels. Photo from Sotheby's.

Kenton Jaeger Cement Mixer, rubber wheels. Photo from Sotheby's.

Kenton Limousine, driver, circa 1915, 7-3/4". Photo from Sotheby's.

Kenton Overland Circus Cage Truck with hippo, 7-1/4". Photo from Bill Bertoia Auctions.

Kenton Patrol Wagon, driver, three firemen, 9".

Kenton Runabout Auto, driver, circa 1908, 6-1/2". Photo from Christie's East.

Kenton Pickwick Nite Coach, 11". Photo from Phillips.

Kenton Road Roller, Galion Master, 7". Photo from Bill Bertoia Auctions.

Kenton Speed Stake Truck, circa 1927, 5-1/2". Photo from Bill Bertoia Auctions.

Left to Right: Kenton Pickwick Nite Coaches, 7-1/2" and 9-1/2". Photo from Bill Bertoia Auctions.

Left to Right: Kenton Sedan, 1923, separate driver, 10"; Coupe, 1926, separate driver, 10"; Sedan, 1926, separate driver, 10-1/4". Photo from Bill Bertoia Auctions.

Kenton Speed Stake Truck, 9-1/8". Photo from Bill Bertoia Auctions.

Kenton Touring Car, open, driver and passenger, 1923, 9". Photo from Bill Bertoia Auctions.

	C6	C8	C10
Road Roller, "Galion Master," 5-1/2" long	115	172	230
Road Roller, "Galion Master," 7" long	150	225	300
Roadster, w/driver, c.1908, 6" long	300	450	600
Runabout Auto, 1900, 5" long	170	225	340
Runabout Auto, cast iron, driver, c.1908, 6-1/2" long	700	1050	1400
Sand and Gravel Truck, 1940s	165	248	330
Sedan, separate driver, 1923, 10" long	1500	3000	6000
Sedan, separate driver, 1926, 10-1/4" long	4500	9500	15.000
Sedan, rubber tires, take apart body, late 1930s, 7" long	1400	2100	2800
Sedan, 4" long	110	165	225
Sedan, separate drive, 1923, 10" long	1500	3000	6000
Sedan, 8-1/2" long	2000	3000	5000

	C6	C8	C10
Speed Stake Truck, c.1927, 5-1/2" long	50	75	100
Speed Stake Truck, 9-1/8" long	450	850	1250
Sprinkler Truck, early, 8" long	300	450	600
Stake Truck, 6" long	337	405	675
Steam Roller, marked "Galion Master," 6-1/2" long	225	338	450
Steam Shovel, Marion, 7-1/4" long	600	900	1200
Tank, cast iron, 2-1/2" long	80	120	160
Touring Car, w/driver, 6" long	225	338	450
Touring Car, open, driver and passenger, detachable steering wheel, 1924, 7-3/4" long	NPF	NPF	NPF
Touring Car, open, driver and passenger, 1923, 9" long	650	975	1300
Tow Auto, 1920s, 9-1/2" long	1600	2400	3200
Yellow Cab, 1950s, 6-3/8" long	300	450	600

KEYSTONE

Keystone of Boston had an odd assortment of products—movie projectors, steel trucks, wooden boats and pressed-wood forts and garages. Founded in 1922 or 1923 by Chester Rimmer and Arthur Jackson, it was first located in a small shop in Malden, Massachusetts under the name Jacrim, using parts of partners' last names. Rimmer retired in 1958 and sold out to various companies. Address in Boston was 288 A Street.

	C6	C8	C10
Aerial Ladder, No. 79, 30-1/2" long	600	1000	1400
Ambulance, military, No. 73, 27" long	775	1400	1950
American Railway Express, No. 43, 26" long	1000	1700	2500
Bus, plastic, 7-1/4" long	NPF	NPF	NPF
Chemical Pump Engine, No. 57, 27-1/2" long	700	1200	1600

	C6	C8	C10
Coast to Coast Bus, wind-up, No. 84, 31" long	1100	1900	2700
Dugan Brothers Truck, "ridem," 27" long	1200	2200	3200
Dump Truck, No. 41, 26-1/2" long	450	750	1100
Dump Truck, "Keystone" embossed on door, electric lights, 1937, 23" long	300	500	700
Dump Truck, cab over, 25" long	230	345	460

Keystone American Railway Express, 26". Photo from Joe and Sharon Freed.

Keystone Dugan Brothers Ridem Truck, 27". Photo from Joe and Sharon Freed.

Keystone Dump Truck, 26-1/2". Photo from PB Eighty Four.

Keystone Dump Truck, 26-1/2". Photo from PB Eighty Four.

Keystone Fire Truck, No. 49, 27-1/2". Photo from Joe and Sharon Freed.

Keystone made several Koaster Trucks, the version with skids, a hoist cable and windlass is considerably more valuable than the truck without those features. Photo from Joe and Sharon Freed.

	C6	C8	C10
Express Truck, wind-up, 20" long	105	158	210
Fire Truck, No. 49, 27-1/2" long	275	412	550
Fire Truck, No. 52, 27-1/2" long	600	1100	1500
Hydraulic Dump Truck, No. 62, 26" long	325	488	650
Koaster Truck, without skids and windlass, No. 55	450	675	900

	C6	C8	C10
Koaster Truck, w/skids, hoist cable, windlass, No. 54, 26" long when skids retracted	800	1350	1825
Ladder Truck, 24" long.....................	250	385	525
Mack Fire Truck, Ride 'Em, cab over engine...	235	355	470
Milk Truck, 27" long.........................	1400	2300	3300
Moving Van, No. 58, 26" long	750	1300	1850
Plastic Bus, 7-1/4" long	NPF	NPF	NPF
Plastic Sedan, hood lifts, gas tank fills and drains, c.1950, 4-1/2" long..	27	41	55

	C6	C8	C10
Police Patrol, No. 51, 27-1/2" long ...	700	1200	1700
Police Van, 1920s	NPF	NPF	NPF
Pure Milk Divco, motor drive, No. D-402	150	225	300
Ride 'Em, "Water Tower w/Real Pump," 1945, 29" long	200	300	400
Ride 'Em Dump Truck, c.1945, 29" long	200	300	400
Riding Steam roller, No. 60, 26" long	232	348	465
Service Center w/vehicles................	70	105	140

	C6	C8	C10
Sprinkler Truck, No. 53, tank 12" long...	800	1300	2000
Steam Roller, red and black, air pressure whistle, brass bell, 20" long...	400	600	800
Steam Shovel, No. 47, 34-1/2" long when arm is extended	250	375	500

Keystone Moving Van, 26". Photo from Mapes Auctioneers and Appraisers.

Keystone Plastic Bus, 7-1/4". Photo from Joe and Sharon Freed.

Keystone Plastic Sedans, circa 1950, 4-1/2". Photo from Terry Sells.

Keystone Police Van, 1920s.

Keystone Ride 'em Water Tower with Real Pump, 1945, 29". Photo from Joe and Sharon Freed.

Keystone Ride 'em Dump Truck, circa 1945, 29". Photo from Joe and Sharon Freed.

"KEYSTONE" HEAVY DUTY STEEL TOYS
TRUCKS WILL SUPPORT 200 POUNDS

Heavy gauge steel....bright color baked enamel finishes....disc wheels....fully equipped....the finest and most up-to-date line of heavy duty steel toys made. Here we present the best sellers from last year with many new numbers....a line scientifically built to meet every demand. All 4-wheel models have steering front wheels.

Trucks will support 200 pounds

1F2271—(Mfrs 265) Airplane, 25 in. long, 24 in. wing spread, red and drab, 8 in. revolving propeller, imit. 8 cylinder motor, ratchet produces loud noise, rubber tires, windows. Each in carton (k.d., with 2 bolts for easy assembling), 6 lbs. Each $1.95

1F2274—(Mfrs 263) Mail plane, 25x24, green & red body, nickel plated revolving propeller, ratchet attachment produces loud noise, swinging door on aviator's cabin, heavy rubber tires, leather bound mail bags, pull rope. 1 in carton, 6½ lbs. .... Each $2.25

With Extension Arm

1F2494—(Mfrs 47) Steam shovel, 26 x 12 x 6½, black with red trim, 16½ in. extension arm, 14 in. derrick, shovel raised and extended by turning crank, lowered by pressing lever, opened by pulling string. 1 in carton, 11 lbs. .... Each $2.80

1F2272—(Mfrs 30) Dump truck, 26x12, black body, drop end with chute door, nickeled headlights and radiator cap, lifting lever for raising body, red wheels, balloon type rubber tires. 1 in carton, 13 lbs. Each $3.25

1F2266—(Mfrs 44) Truck loader, 18 x 17 x 4½, green with red and black trim, 10 buckets. 1 in box, 13 lbs. Each $3.30

Lifts 200 lbs.

1F2260—(Mfrs 41) Dump truck, 26x9½x8¼, black with red trim, balloon type rubber tires, drop end with chute door, signal arm, crank and worm gear raises body. 1 in carton, 15 lbs. .... Each $3.70

1F2269—(Mfrs 48) U. S. Army truck, 26x11¼x7¾, khaki, balloon type rubber tires, drop tail piece, heavy canvas top. 1 in carton, 13 lbs. Each $3.95

1F2273—(Mfrs 60) Steam roller, 30x12½, red & black, extra heavy roller, steering rear wheel controls front roller, air pressure whistle, brass bell, will sustain wt. of 150 lbs. 1 in carton, 14 lbs. Each $4.50

1F2261—(Mfrs 51) Police patrol, 27½x11½x7½, black with red trim, balloon type rubber tires, 2 full length seats inside, brass railing, signal arm. 1 in carton, 18 lbs. .... Each $4.25

1F2259—(Mfrs 43) American Railway Express, 26x10½x7½, green with black and red trim, balloon type rubber tires, signal arm, doors with lock and key, 4 miniature mail pouches. 1 in carton ...... Each $4.15

1F2262—(Mfrs 45) U. S. Mail truck, 26x10½x7½, green with black and red trim, balloon type rubber tires, signal arm, doors with lock and key, 4 miniature mail pouches. 1 in carton, 17 lbs. Each $4.50

1F2276—(Mfrs 78) Wrecker, 27x22¾ (when crane is raised), red trimmed in black, solid rubber tires, nickel crank gears and folding crank, brass rails, lifts 100 lbs. 1 in carton, 16 lbs. .... Each $4.70

1F2277—(Mfrs 73) Ambulance, 27½x11½, khaki, solid rubber tires, khaki canvas curtains, snap fasteners, brass rails, signal arm, white flag with green cross. 1 in carton, 17 lbs. .... Each $5.10

1F2265—(Mfrs 40) Fire truck, 28x8¼x11, red body, brass railings and bell, hose reel, imitation hose and nozzle, two 18 in. extension ladders, attachment for raising ladders, balloon type rubber tires. 1 in carton, 17 lbs. Each $5.20

1F2278—(Mfrs 64) Locomotive, 27½ x 11½, red and black, brass bell, steam dome and railing, rubber tires. 1 in carton, 16½ lbs. .... Each $5.60

FIRE DEPARTMENT TOYS

Ladder extends to 51 in.

Water Pumper Fire Engine—37½ In. Long

1F2539—(Mfrs 57) 37½ x 10¾ x 8½, red body, 7 x 4¼ brass water tank, pressure pump operated by front crank, brass railings, extension ladders (extend to 5 ft.), rubber hose, with brass nozzle, brass bell, hose reel, balloon type rubber tires. Shoots water from 25 to 35 ft. 1 in carton, 19 lbs. .... Each $7.05

Aerial Ladder Truck—30½ In. Long

1F2279—(Mfrs 79) 30½ x 10¾ x 8½, red body, nickel plated ladders (extend to 51 in.), chain drive extension, 2 extra 15 in. red ladders, brass bell, aluminum covered running board, solid rubber tires. 1 in carton, 21 lbs. .... Each $7.35

Water Pump and Tower—29 In. Long

1F2544—(Mfrs 56) 29x10¾x8½ (30 in. long when tower is raised), brass water tank, pressure pump operated by front crank, nickeled mechanism for raising tower, 10¾ in. ladders, brass railing, aluminum running board, brass bell, Klaxon horn, balloon type rubber tires. Shoots water 25 to 35 ft. 1 in carton, 21½ lbs. Each $8.40

"SON-NY" HEAVY DUTY STEEL TRUCK

1F2526—26 in. long, enameled, orange with black trim, orange disc wheels and imitation balloon tires, steering front wheels, drop end, lever for raising body. 1 in carton .... Each $2.10

82

BUTLER BROTHERS ST. LOUIS

Keystone vehicles, as shown in a 1928 Butler Bros. catalog.

One of several versions of Keystone's Steam Shovel—the 26" version shown here is more valuable than the 34-1/2". Photo from Calvin L. Chaussee.

Keystone U.S. Army Truck, 26". Photo from Calvin L. Chaussee.

Keystone Tank, wooden, metal firing mechanism, 6". Photo from Ed Poole.

Keystone World's Greatest Circus Truck, 1930s, 26". Photo from Calvin L. Chaussee.

	C6	C8	C10
Steam Shovel, No. 46, 26" long when arm is extended..................	425	638	450
Steam Shovel, Ride 'Em	200	300	400
Tank, wooden w/metal firing mechanism, 6" long	NPF	NPF	NPF
Truck Loader, No. 44, 17-3/4" high ..	500	800	1100
U.S. Army Truck, No. 48, 26" long ...	432	648	865

	C6	C8	C10
U.S. Mail Truck, No. 45, 26" long.....	750	1300	1850
Water Pump Tower, No. 56, 29" long..............................	700	1250	1650
Water Tower, No. 59.......................	1300	2100	3000
World's Greatest Circus Truck, 26" long, 1930s	1500	2700	4000
Wrecking Car, No. 78, 27" long........	775	1400	1950

KILGORE

Kilgore, of Westerville, Ohio, appears to have begun toy making in the 1920s. Its toys were cast iron and low priced, with cap pistols its most popular line. But it also did well with a number of attractive trucks, fire engines and cars, as well as scattered aircraft and ships. Some subsidiary manufacturing was done in Lancaster, Pennsylvania and Canada. In 1937, Kilgore began making plastic cars, trucks, planes and buses, and later added plastic cap pistols, placing it among the first companies to produce plastic toys. Kilgore remained in business until 1978.

	C6	C8	C10
Arctic Ice Cream Truck, 8" long	600	1000	1400
Arctic Ice Cream Truck, 9" long	500	750	1000
Arctic Ice Cream Truck, w/three interchangeable bodies, 6-3/8" long..........	550	1000	1400
Auto, LF 1300A, w/driver.................	180	270	360
Aviation Semi Tanker Ford, 1931, 12-1/4" long.........................	2000	4000	5200

	C6	C8	C10
Bus, double decker, c.1930, 6" long	450	675	900
Bus, plastic, advertised in 1937, 4" long..............	20	25	30
Convertible with Rumble Seat, w/driver, early 1930s, 7" long	160	240	320
Coupe, cast iron, 1930s, 5" long......	70	105	140
Coupe, cast iron, 4" long.................	60	90	120
Coupe, streamlined, plastic, advertised in 1939, 4" long	22	33	45
Dump Truck, cast iron, c.1934, 8-1/2" long.....................	800	1500	2180
Dump Truck, cast iron, c.1934, 5-3/4" long.....................	160	240	320

One of several versions of Kilgore's Arctic Ice Cream Truck—this is the 9" version.

Kilgore Arctic Ice Cream Truck, 6-3/8" with three inerchangeable bodies. Photo from Bill Bertoia Auctions.

Kilgore Bus, double decker, circa 1930, 6". Photo from Christie's East.

Kilgore Aviation Semi Tanker Ford, 12-1/4". Photo from Bill Bertoia Auctions.

Kilgore Coupe, streamlined, plastic, 4". Photo from Dave Leopard.

Kilgore Dump Truck, circa 1934, 5-3/4". Photo from James S. Maxwell and Viginia Caputo.

Kilgore Livestock truck, 8". Photo from Rod Carnahan.

Kilgore Express Truck, plastic, 4". Photo from Dave Leopard.

Kilgore Stake Truck, take-apart, 5". Photo from Bill Bertoia Auctions.

Kilgore Fire Chief Sedan, plastic, 4". Photo from Dave Leopard.

	C6	C8	C10
Dump Truck, 1930s, 7" long	180	270	360
Express Truck, plastic, advertised in 1937, 4" long	22	33	45
Fire Chief Sedan, plastic, advertised in 1937, 4" long	22	33	45
Fire Ladder Truck, 7-1/2" long	200	300	400
Fire Pumper, cast iron, 5" long	88	132	175
Fire Pumper, cast iron, 4" long	80	120	160
Ford Deluxe Sedan, 1934, 7" long	NPF	NPF	NPF
Ford Wrecker, 1931, 10-3/4" long	1200	2100	3100
Livestock Truck, 8" long	600	900	1200
Livestock Truck, 1930s, 7" long	700	1050	1400
Livestock Truck, 6-1/4" long	165	248	330

	C6	C8	C10
Low Boy Machinery Hauler, 1931, 12-1/4" long	900	1500	2300
Model T Coupe, 5" long	200	300	400
Open Town Car, plastic, 4" long	15	20	25
Packard Luxury Sedan, take-apart body, 8-1/4" long	800	1200	1600
Pierce-Arrow Roadster, take-apart body, 6-1/8" long	250	375	500
Police Car, plastic, 1937, 4" long	22	33	45
Pontiac, cast iron, 1930, 10" long (See Stutz)	NPF	NPF	NPF
Race Car, Rocket, 1930s, 4-1/4" long	112	168	225
Race Car, Rocket, 1930s, 6-1/2" long	225	338	450
Roadster, driver, rumble seat, 8" long	375	563	750
Roadster, 4" long	68	102	135
Roadster, driver, rumble seat, 6" long	230	345	460
Sedan, 3-1/4" long	70	105	140
Sedan, 5" long	175	263	350
Stake Truck, take-apart, 5" long	112	168	225
Stake Truck, 3-1/2" long	62	93	125
Stutz Roadster, thirteen parts	1100	1500	2500

Kilgore Stutz Roadster, thirteen parts.

Kilgore Toy Town Delivery Truck, 6-1/8". Photo from Bill Bertoia Auctions.

Kilgore Tank, 2-1/2". Photo from Ed Poole.

Kilgore Motorcycle with delivery box, nickel wheels, 5-7/8". Photo from Kent M. Comstock.

Kilgore Taxi, plastic, 4". Photo from Dave Leopard.

Left to Right: Kilgore Motorcycle Trike Special Delivery, white rubber tires, 4-1/4"; Kilgore Motorcycle with sidecar, nickel wheels. Photo from Kent M. Comstock.

	C6	C8	C10
Tank, cast iron, 2-1/2" long	30	45	60
Taxi, plastic, advertised in 1937, 4" long	22	33	45
Toy Town Delivery Truck, 6-1/8" long	200	300	400
Tractor, w/scoop.............................	100	150	200

Motorcycles

	C6	C8	C10
Motorcycle, w/sidecar nickel wheels, 4-1/4" long (KM003)	125	200	300
Motorcycle, w/sidecar nickel wheels, 5" long (KM004)	175	250	400

	C6	C8	C10
Motorcycle, solo, rubber tires, 5-3/4" long (KM005)	150	225	350
Motorcycle, solo, removable rider, rubber tires, 6-1/2" long (KM006)	400	600	1000
Motorcycle, w/delivery box, nickel wheels, 5-7/8" long (KM007)	250	500	750
Motorcycle solo, police, white rubber tires, 4" long (KM001)	75	100	150
Motorcycle Trike, Special Delivery, white rubber tires, 4-1/4" long (KM002)	150	225	350

KINGSBURY

Kingsbury had its origins in 1886 in Keene, New Hampshire. Its owner was Harry T. Kingsbury, who bought the Wilkins Toy Co., apparently not phasing out that firm's name until 1919. Steel and spring motors characterize Kingsbury's toys, with cars, fire engines, farm equipment and racing cars its primary output. Kingsbury is still in business, but gave up toy production in 1942.

	C6	C8	C10
Aerial Ladder Truck, wind-up, 1920s, 33" long	1200	2000	3000
Aerial Ladder Truck, wind-up, 1920s, 9" long	250	375	550
Aerial Ladder Truck, pressed steel, wind-up, ladder rises automatically to height of 38" when the truck runs into any obstruction, fireman on ladder climbs up and down by turning crank at base of ladder, early version new in 1905; c.1941, 24" long	250	375	625
Airflow, pressed steel, rubber tires, c.1934, 14" long	275	375	600
Airflow, clockwork, 14" long	275	375	600

	C6	C8	C10
Army Truck, c.1941	125	175	250
Auto, steel, wind-up, very early, 9-3/4" long	325	525	750
Auto Delivery Truck, No. 749, c.1908	700	1200	1800
Bluebird Racer	750	1200	2000
Brougham Sedan, pressed steel, wind-up, 13" long	550	900	1500
Cannon Truck, clockwork, very early, 11" long	150	250	350
Cannon Truck, wind-up, c.1939, 15" long	150	250	350
Caterpillar, wind-up, 8-1/2" long	150	250	350
Cattle Truck, 1930s, 19" long	100	185	275
Chemical Fire Truck, clockwork motor, c.1929, 14" long	950	1750	2750
Chemical Ladder Truck, 35" long	1100	2000	3000
Combination Chemical Truck, 26" long	1250	2250	3500
Contractors Tractor	150	225	300
Coupe, No. 74200	550	900	1300
Coupe, No. 244	800	1300	2000
Coupe, wind-up, 11" long	800	1400	1900
Coupe, wind-up, has music box, electric lights, 14" long	500	825	1250
Coupe, No. 344, 13-1/2" long	500	900	1100
Coupe, rumble seat, electric light, c.1930, 12-1/2" long	325	488	650
Coupe, electric lights, No. 444, 13-1/2" long	500	800	1200

One version of Kingsbury's Airflow.

Kingsbury Auto Delivery Truck, No. 749, circa 1908. Photo from Phillips.

Kingsbury Cannon Truck, circa 1939, 15" wind-up. Photo from Orville C. Britor.

Kingsbury Coupe, circa 1930, rumble seat, electric lights, 12-1/2". Photo from Christie's East.

Kingsbury Fire Chief Coupe, wind-up, 12-1/4".

Kingsbury Fire Pumper, 1930s, 20". Photo from Calvin L. Chaussee.

Kingsbury Fire Pumper, cast-iron.

Kingsbury Golden Arrow Racer, pressed steel, wind-up, 20". Photo from Kevin Sharp. Detroit Antique Toy Museum.

	C6	C8	C10
Delivery Stake Truck, w/driver, 1923, 9" long	225	325	450
DeSoto, pressed steel wind-up, c.1938, 14-1/2" long	275	375	600
Divco Borden's Van	350	525	750
Divco Grocery Van	300	450	650
Divco U.S. Air Mail Truck	300	450	675
Dray Stake Truck, early 1930s	150	225	325
Dump Truck, clockwork, early 1930s, 16" long	350	525	750
Dump Truck, tin, driver, 10" long	200	300	450
Dump Truck, 11-1/2" long	450	700	1100
Express Truck, late	200	275	375
Fire Chief Coupe, 1930s, 14" long	325	550	850
Fire Chief Coupe, wind-up, 12-1/4"	750	1250	2000
Fire Pumper, 1930s, 20" long	300	450	650
Fire Pumper, 9-1/2" long	200	300	400
Fire Pumper, 1920s, 23" long	1000	1700	2700
Fire Pumper, very early, clockwork, iron and steel, 11" long	300	450	675
Fire Truck, mechanical ladder, cast-iron driver, 1915, 9-1/2" long	235	355	470
Fire Truck, 18" long	220	330	440
Ford Sedan and House Trailer, pressed steel, 1937, 23" long	350	535	700

	C6	C8	C10
Golden Arrow Racer, pressed steel, wind-up, 20" long	465	700	930
Greyhound Bus, wind-up, 18" long	500	750	1000
Huckster Truck, 9-1/2" long	800	1200	2090

	C6	C8	C10
Ladder Truck, steel, driver, 22" long	150	250	350
Ladder Truck, pressed steel, wind-up, No. 225, 1930s, 15" long	275	375	475
Ladder Truck, 33" long....................	1000	2300	3600
Ladder Truck, early, 19" long	1700	3000	4700
Ladder Truck, 10-1/2" long..............	100	150	200
Ladder Wagon Fire Truck, tin, rubber tires, 23-1/2" long	100	175	275
Lincoln Zephyr and Travel Trailer, c.1936, 22-1/2" long....................	325	500	700
Little Jim Delivery Truck, 13" long....	300	450	550
Little Jim Tow Truck, 11" long	300	450	650
Little Jim Tractor.............................	250	375	500

	C6	C8	C10
Little Jim Truck	700	1100	1600
Mail Truck, w/driver, early, 7" long ...	500	800	1100
Panama Dump Truck, clockwork, 1923, 14" long.............................	750	1000	1400
Phaeton Auto, rubber slip tires, 1900, 9-1/2" long	750	1125	1500
Pure Milk Truck	132	198	265
Rack Truck, pressed steel, wind-up, 16" long.............................	350	525	700
Roadster, 11" long	350	525	700
Roadster, electric headlights, spring motor, luggage rack, No. 242, 13" long...	400	600	800
Roadster, No. 433, same as No. 242	NPF	NPF	NPF
Sand Loader, 12" long	125	188	250
Sedan, No. 300	1300	2000	2900
Semi-Truck, cab over.......................	155	250	325
Stake Truck, clockwork, c.1926, 25" long..	300	450	600
Studebaker Cannon Truck	150	225	400
Sunbeam Racer, sheetmetal, red w/rubber tires on steel wheels, clockwork motor, 19" long............	500	750	1050
Tractor, mechanical, w/driver, 8" long..	160	240	320
Tractor and Cart, tin, w/iron driver, white rubber wheels, 1930s	150	250	450
Transit Truck, 1930s, 19" long	150	250	400

Kingsbury Greyhound Bus, wind-up, 18".

Kingsbury Ladder Truck, 1930s, windup, 15". Photo from John Taylor.

Kingsbury Lincoln Zephyr and Travel Trailer, 22-1/2", circa 1936.

Kingsbury Sand Loader, 12". Photo from Calvin L. Chaussee.

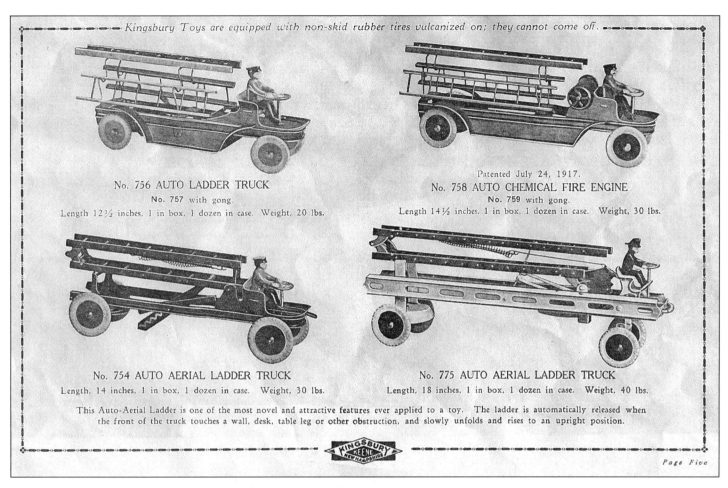

Kingsbury Toys are equipped with non-skid rubber tires vulcanized on; they cannot come off.

No. 756 AUTO LADDER TRUCK
No. 757 with gong.
Length 12½ inches, 1 in box, 1 dozen in case. Weight, 20 lbs.

Patented July 24, 1917.
No. 758 AUTO CHEMICAL FIRE ENGINE
No. 759 with gong.
Length 14½ inches, 1 in box, 1 dozen in case. Weight, 30 lbs.

No. 754 AUTO AERIAL LADDER TRUCK
Length, 14 inches, 1 in box, 1 dozen in case. Weight, 30 lbs.

No. 775 AUTO AERIAL LADDER TRUCK
Length, 18 inches, 1 in box, 1 dozen in case. Weight, 40 lbs.

This Auto-Aerial Ladder is one of the most novel and attractive features ever applied to a toy. The ladder is automatically released when the front of the truck touches a wall, desk, table leg or other obstruction, and slowly unfolds and rises to an upright position.

Page Five

An illustration from an early 1920s Kingsbury catalog.

Kingsbury Truck with Crane, 1930s. Photo from Calvin L. Chaussee.

Kingsbury Wrecker, late 1920s, windup, 14". Photo from John Taylor.

	C6	C8	C10
Truck with C Cab, tin, 10" long.........	175	262	350
Truck with Crane, 1930s, 20" long ...	175	300	500
Windup Car, curved dash, driver, 9" long	225	337	450

	C6	C8	C10
Wrecker, pressed steel, wind-up, 13" long..	250	375	500
Wrecker, pressed steel, wind-up, 1927, 14" long.............................	550	750	950
Yellow Cab, 1934.............................	350	525	700

LANSING SLIK-TOYS

Lansing Slik-Toys were made in Lansing, Iowa, and sometimes bear the name "Kipp," in addition to the "Lansing" and "Slik-Toy" trademarks. Most Slik-Toys are made of aluminum in a single casting. but some were made of hard plastic. it seems that all Slik-Toys have a four-digit number beginning with "9." If a toy bears such a number, even if it has no other markings, it is almost surely a Slik-Toy.

Contributor: Dave Leopard, 2507 Feather Run Trail, West Columbia, SC 29169-4915.

	C6	C8	C10
Bulldozer	65	98	130
Combine	150	225	300
Corn Picker, goes w/Oliver 77 Tractor	225	338	450
Fire Truck, No. 9606, 6" long	20	30	40
Fire Truck, plastic, No. 9706, 4" long	20	25	30
Fire Truck, No. 9700, 3-1/2" long	25	35	45
Grader, 9-1/2" long	50	75	100
Grader, 17" long	88	132	175
Metro Van, No. 9618, 5" long	25	30	40
Oliver 77 Tractor, approx, 7-3/4" long	142	217	285
Open Stake Truck, No. 9602, 7" long	25	35	50
Pickup Truck, No. 9601, 7" long	25	35	50
Pickup Truck, No. 9605, 6" long	20	30	40
Pickup Truck, plastic, No. 9703, 4" long	20	25	30
Roaster, No. 9701, 3-1/2" long	25	35	45
Sand and Gravel Dump, 12" long	70	105	140
Sedan, fastback, taxi version, No. 9600, 7" long	30	45	60

	C6	C8	C10
Sedan, Buick, plastic, c.1949, No. 9702	15	20	30
Sedan, fastback, No. 9600, 7" long	25	35	50
Sedan, four-door, No. 9604, 6" long	20	30	40
Stake Truck, No. 9616, 6" long	25	30	40
Stakebody Truck, No. 9500, 11" long	45	60	75
Station Wagon, plastic, No. 9704, 4" long	20	25	30
Tank Truck, No. 9603, 7" long	25	35	40
Tank Truck, No. 9607, 6" long	20	30	40
Tank Truck, plastic, No. 9705, 4" long	20	25	30
Tractor/Trailer Rig, grain trailer, No. 9611, 8" long	30	40	55
Tractor/Trailer Rig, (log trailer) 18" long, No. 9612	25	40	55
Tractor/Trailer Rig, milk tanker, No. 9610, 8" long	30	40	55
TractorTtrailer Rig, (flatbed trailer), 8" long, No. 9613	25	35	45
Wrecker, 4" plastic, No. 9707	20	25	30
Wrecker, 5" long, No. 9617	20	25	35

Left to Right: Lansing Slik-Toys Pickup Truck, 4"; Tank Truck, 4", plastic; Sedan 1949 Buick, plastic. Photo from Dave Leopard.

A Lansing-Slik Toys ad as seen in the July 1946 issue of *Toys & Novelties*.

LEHMANN, ERNST PAUL

Ernst Paul Lehmann began manufacturing toys in 1881, using the EPL trademark. Its founder passed away in 1934, but the company continued in business under the management of his cousin, Johannes Richter. At the end of World War II, Richter moved to West Germany. He opened a new factory in Nuremberg in 1951. The Lehmann Company is still in business making toys.

Lehmann Toys have become a common word among early tin-toy collectors. These wonderful mechanical machines are more sought-after than any other wind-up toy, though they usually command a high price. The company used many different color variations from year to year on some of its toys, giving the collector a wide variety to choose from. While some Lehmanns are very rare, it is not too difficult to build a collection of them. Most Lehmanns carry a model number for easy reference. A box adds twenty to forty percent to the value.

Contributor: Bob Smith, The Village Smith, 62 West Ave., Fairport, NY 14450-2102.

	C6	C8	C10
Aha Delivery Van, tin wind-up, 1920s, 5-1/2" long	500	850	1200
Auto Post, tin wind-up, 5" long	650	1100	1500
Autobus, tin wind-up	800	1400	2000
Autohutte Garage, No. 771, 6" long	200	300	400
Baker and Chimney Sweep, tin wind-up, c.1900-1935, 5-1/4" long	2000	3800	6000
Berolina Car, tin wind-up	1500	2500	3500
Deutsche Reichspost, wind-up, postal truck w/driver, 1927	800	1400	2200
Echo Motorcycle, tin wind-up, No. 725, 1907, 9" long	1000	1700	2800
EHE & Co. Truck, tin wind-up, open bed	320	550	800
Galop Racer, No. 1, tin wind-up w/garage	800	1200	1600
Gnom No. 808 Autohutt Garage, w/two no. 807 Sedans, tin lithographed, c.1935	500	750	1200

	C6	C8	C10
Gnom Series No. 807 Sedan, various colors, tin lithographed, c.1935, 4-1/2" long	200	350	500
Gnom Series No. 808 Racing Car, various colors colors, tin lithographed, c.1935, 4-1/2" long	250	400	650
Gnom Series No. 813 Opel Dump Truck, red/green, tin lithographed, c.1935, 4-1/2" long	200	350	550
Gnom Series No. 835 BV-Aral Tanker, blue/gray, tin lithographed, c.1938, 4-1/2" long	250	400	600
IHI Meat Van, lithographed tin, clockwork, cloth sides, 6-5/8" long	1200	1800	2200
Ito Sedan, tin wind-up, 1920s, 6-1/2" long	500	850	1200
Lana Auto, tin wind-up	1200	2000	2800
Lehmann Am Pol, 5-3/4"	NPF	NPF	NPF
Lehmann's Autobus 590, tin wind-up, red	800	1400	2000
Lehmann's Autobus 590, tin wind-up, brown	1000	1800	2500

**Lehmann Aha Delivery Van, 1920s tin wind-up, 5-1/2".
Photo from Bill Bertoia Auctions.**

Lehmann Autobus tin wind-up. Photo from Bill Bertoia Auctions.

Lehmann Baker and Chimney Sweep, tin wind-up, 5-1/4". Photo from Kent M. Comstock.

Lehmann Galop Racer, tin wind-up with garage. Photo from Bill Bertoia Auctions.

Lehmann Echo Motorcycle, 1907, 9". Photo from Kent M. Comstock.

Lehmann Gnom Autohutte with two tin-lithographed sedans. Photo from Bob Smith.

Lehmann EHE & Co., open bed, tin wind-up.

Top row, left to right: Gnom Series BV-Aral Tanker, 4-1/2"; Gnom Series Opel Dump Truck, 4-1/2". Bottom row, left to right: Gnom Series Racing Car, 4-1/2"; Gnom Series Sedan. Photo from Bob Smith.

Lehmann Ito Sedan, 1920s, 6-1/2". Photo from Christie's East.

Lehmann Am Pol, 5-3/4". Photo from Bill Bertoia Auctions.

Lehmann Lu Lu Delivery Truck tin wind-up, 7-1/4". Photo from Bill Bertoia Auctions.

	C6	C8	C10
Li La Car, tin wind-up, early, 5-1/2" long	1000	1700	2500
Lo Lo Car, tin wind-up, w/driver, early	500	750	1100
Lu Lu Delivery Truck, tin wind-up, 7-1/4" long	1500	2700	4000

Lehman Uhu Amphibious Car. Photo from Sotheby's.

Lehmann Mensa Delivery Van, circa 1912, 5-1/4". Photo from Bob Smith.

	C6	C8	C10
Mensa Delivery Van, No. 688, red/blue, clockwork motor, three wheel, steering, c.1912, 5-1/4" long	1200	1900	3000
Mixtum Comic Car, 4" long	1200	2200	3200
Motor Car Kutsche, tin wind-up, 1897, 5-1/2" long	400	550	800
Motor Coach, tin wind-up, 1920s, 5-1/2" long	325	475	600
Naughty Boy, tin wind-up	650	1200	1500
New Century Cycle, tin wind-up, 1907, 5" long	400	650	1000

Nr. 688 Mensa

Dreirad mit Motorgeräusch. Vorderrad beliebig einstellbar. Laderaum mit Tür zum Öffnen und Füllen.

No. 688 Mensa

Three wheel car, table toy, making noise like a petrol engine. The front wheel can be adjusted at will. Has door to open at back for loading.

N⁰ 688 Mensa

Triciclo imitando el ruido del motor. La rueda delantera ajustable a voluntad. Carrocería con tapa para llenar la caja.

Nr. 345 Onkel

Der Reiseonkel fährt durch die Welt, mit dem Hute grüßend, während der Neger den Schirm dreht. Fahrtrichtung: geradeaus, links- und rechtsherum.

No. 345 Onkel

Uncle touring the world, raising his hat, while the nigger turns the parasol. Running direction; straight ahead, to the left, to the right.

345 El Trotamundos

Un turista que da la vuelta al mundo, saludando con el sombrero, mientras que el paje hace girar la sombrilla. Circula hacia adelante, a la izquierda y a la derecha.

The Mensa Delivery Van and the Onkel, as they appeared in a reprint of an 1881 Lehmann catalog.

Nr. 733 Nunu

Chinese, natürlich gehend, zieht eine Teekiste. Während des Aufziehens und beim Anheben wird Werk selbsttätig gesperrt.

No. 733 Nunu

Chinese, natural walking movement, pulls a tea chest. The clockwork is automatically braked while being wound up.

N⁰ 733 Nunu

un chino que anda con movimiento natural y arrastra una caja de te. El movimiento se enclava solo al dar cuerda o levantar la figura.

Nr. 560 Tap-Tap

Gärtner mit Karre und Spaten, macht sehr natürliche Bein- und Kopfbewegungen.

No. 560 Tap-Tap

Gardener with cart and spade. Makes very realistic leg and head movements.

N⁰ 560 Tap-Tap

Un jardinero con carretilla y pala que mueve las piernas y la cabeza de modo muy natural.

Reprint of an 1881 Lehmann catalog.

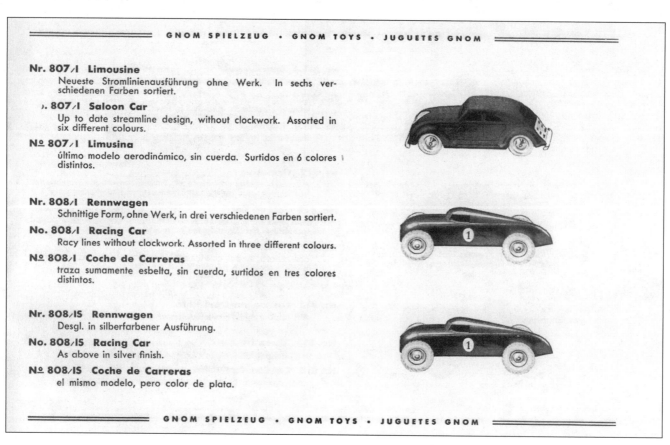

GNOM SPIELZEUG • GNOM TOYS • JUGUETES GNOM

Nr. 807/I Limousine
Neueste Stromlinienausführung ohne Werk. In sechs verschiedenen Farben sortiert.

). 807/I Saloon Car
Up to date streamline design, without clockwork. Assorted in six different colours.

Nº 807/I Limusina
último modelo aerodinámico, sin cuerda. Surtidos en 6 colores distintos.

Nr. 808/I Rennwagen
Schnittige Form, ohne Werk, in drei verschiedenen Farben sortiert.

No. 808/I Racing Car
Racy lines without clockwork. Assorted in three different colours.

Nº 808/I Coche de Carreras
traza sumamente esbelta, sin cuerda, surtidos en tres colores distintos.

Nr. 808/IS Rennwagen
Desgl. in silberfarbener Ausführung.

No. 808/IS Racing Car
As above in silver finish.

Nº 808/IS Coche de Carreras
el mismo modelo, pero color de plata.

GNOM SPIELZEUG • GNOM TOYS • JUGUETES GNOM

Another reprint of an 1881 Lehmann catalog.

Lehmann Mixtum Comic Car, 4". Photo from Bill Bertoia Auctions.

Lehmann Motor Coach, 1920s, 5-1/2". Photo from Sotheby's.

Lehmann Terra tin wind-up. Photo from Bill Bertoia Auctions.

Lehman Uhu Amphibious Car. Photo from Sotheby's.

Lehmann Tut Tut, man in car with horn, 6-3/4". Photo from Christie's East.

	C6	C8	C10
Oho, tin wind-up, c.1903	325	575	850
Onkel, tin wind-up	375	575	900
Panne Touring Car, tin wind-up, 6-1/2" long	550	850	1200
Peter Clown Car	1000	1600	2200

	C6	C8	C10
Royal Mail Van, lithographed tin, clockwork, w/driver, 6-3/4" long	1200	1800	2200
Sedan, tin wind-up, 5-1/2" long	275	400	550
Terra, tin wind-up	650	1100	1650
Tut-Tut, tin wind-up, man in car w/horn, 6-3/4" long	650	1100	1700
Uhu Amphibious Car, tin wind-up	800	1850	2400
Velleda, lithographed tin, clockwork, open sedan w/chauffer	900	1500	2000

LINCOLN TOYS

Contributor: John Taylor, P.O. Box 63, Nolensville, TN 37135-0063.

	C6	C8	C10
Allied Van Lines Truck, 23" long	175	275	375
Auto Transport, 24" long	150	225	375
Cement Truck, 13" long	95	143	190
Coca Cola Truck, 16" long	330	550	800
Crane Truck	175	263	350
Department of Highways Dump Truck, 19" long	125	175	225
Dump Truck, 7" long	75	125	175
Dunlop Wrecker, 13" long	100	175	250

	C6	C8	C10
Dunlop Wreckers, 10" long	100	175	275
Express Truck, 17" long	200	325	475
Heinz Pickle Truck	300	450	600
Hi Dump Truck, 20" long	100	175	200
Highway Express, 17" long	200	325	475
Ice Truck, 1949	225	338	450
Ladder Truck, steel, 1950s, available in both 15" and 17" version	125	200	275

Lincoln Toys Sand Truck Dump, 14".

	C6	C8	C10
Lincoln Transport, early 1950s, 24" long	175	275	350
Lincoln Van Lines	230	345	460
Phil Wood Dump Truck, 12" long	75	125	175
Phil Wood Dump Truck, 17" long	125	175	225
Phil Wood dump Truck, 7" long	65	98	130
Sand Dump Truck, 14" long	100	175	200
Shovel, 16" long	125	175	275
Telephone Service Truck	150	250	300
Tow Truck, w/two spares, 17" long	175	300	400
Tow Truck, round fenders, 13" long	75	150	225

LINCOLN WHITE METAL WORKS

This Lincoln, Nebraska, firm is now recognized as the maker of many high-quality prewar slush mold "orphan toys." This long obscurity is all the more surprising because Clayton E. Stevenson, founder, was a many-talented personage in the Dime Store Toy industry—an artist, skilled craftsman and salesman with worldwide contacts. He had made toys at home since the early 1920s (see Mid-West Metal Novelty Co.); as a salesman for Western Diecasting Co., he furnished some molds to Kansas Toy and may have furnished some to Tip Top Toy and others. His specialty were toys made from a the three-piece mold. The third piece was used to case those uniquely realistic front-ends (grille, headlamps, fenders). These molds, and the more-complex molds for those beautiful tri-motored aircraft (Lincoln's Fokker and C.A.W.'s Fords), were surprising in this competitive industry, because it slowed production and added to costs. For us collectors it created rarity.

Stevenson had a remarkably long toy making career, about fifteen years, through the Great Depression. What we know came from a story in the Nov. 20, 1931, *Nebraska State Journal*, an article in the January 1984 *Antique Toy World*, and from biographical information, photos and toys saved by his daughter, Marian Horn. Stevenson, an auto mechanic, she was born in 1896 and raised in Axtell, Kansas. He, and his wife, Ester, moved to Lincoln in 1931, and started marketing toys in his name at 1250 Dakota Street. For a new business, he had a rapid rise. In his first season he made 800,000 toys in three months. He was manager, purchaser, worker and salesman. As his business grew (30,000 toys a day and twenty-seven to thirty laborers at one time), he moved to a larger facility at 2204 Y Street. In 1935, he was listed at 3433 J Street. The toys were sold to Woolworth, Kress, Kresge and Schwartz Paper Co., stores, as well as all over the country, especially California and New York, and even abroad.

The factory was sold in 1940, after nine years of production, due to shortages of lead and rubber and the rising costs of labor—all due to expansion of war production. (We were not told who bought what, although a few clues point to nearby Ralstoy. Although 1940 is the date given by a family member, the business was not listed in Lincoln directories after 1937.)

A variety of toys were made—tiny airplanes, midget racers, larger speed cars, brilliant sedans, small coupes, tri-motor plane models and miniature sawmills. They range in size from three inches to seven inches long. Stevenson, who made the molds, used pictures of planes and cars shown in magazines. For his midget racer, he used a picture of a Miller special. His sedan was a replica of the front-drive Cord. His coupe was a Nash model. His tri-motor plane was taken from a photo of a Ford product. Early toys used metal wheels and tin propellers and had neat patterned bottom pans. Later toys had rubber wheels. This list below is incomplete. Collectors with more information are welcome to send the info either of the contributors listed below, or directly to the editor at the address listed on the title page of this book.

Contributors: Fred Maxwell, 4722 N. 33 St., Arlington, VA 22207. **Perry R. Eichor,** 703 North Almond Drive, Simpsonville, SC, 29681

Abbreviations

The following abbreviations are for the details and variations useful in identification.

HG	horizontal grille pattern		SM	sidemounted spare
HL	horizontal hood louvers		SP	string-pull knob in handcrank area
HO	hood cap, Motometer or ornament		T	external trunk
L	lacquer finish		UV	unnumbered version
LI	landau irons on convertibles		VG	vertical grille pattern
MDW	metal disc wheels		VL	vertical hood louvers
MDSW	metal disc solid spokes		WS, W/S	windshield
MDWBT	wheels with black painted tires		WV	windshield visor
MSW	metal open spoke wheels		WHRT	wooden hubs, rubber tires
MWW	metal simulated wire wheels		WRDW	white hard rubber disc wheels
OW	open windows		WRW	white soft rubber wheels (balloon tires)
RM	rearmount spare tire/wheel			

	C6	C8	C10
Brougham, Graham (?), vertical V-grille, SM, fiour OW, T, made from three-piece mold, 3-1/2" long (LWV021)	40	60	80
Bus, Overland, HO, HG, VL, ten OW, 3-1/2" long (LWV027)	25	40	65
Coupe, streamline, Pontiac, HO, VG, HL, two OW, H trim on front fenders, embossed folded "trunk rack", patterned pan, 3-3/8" long (LWV014)	35	55	75
Coupe, Graham (?), slanted vee-grille, divided WS, two OW, SM, T, from three-piece mold, 3-3/8" long (LWV015)	30	40	50
Coupe, Oldsmobile, streamlined, slanted vee-grille, HO, HL, divided W.S., two OW, RM, patterned pan, 4" long (LWV016)	30	40	50
Coupe, streamlined Lincoln (?), slanted vee-grille, divided WS, two OW, patterned pan, 3-1/2" long (LWV017)	35	50	70
Coupe, Graham (?), VG, SM, two OW, LI, T, made from three-piece mold, 3-1/2" long (LWV018)	30	40	50

	C6	C8	C10
Coupe, slanted hood, rear-mount hub for rubber tire, slanted grill (see Tootsie Graham); 4-1/2" long (LWV019)	40	60	80
Coupe, vertical hood, wrap-around (?), rear window, T (LWV020)	40	60	80

Top to bottom: Lincoln White Metal Coupe, streamlined Pontiac, 3-3/8"; Coupe, three-piece mold, 3-1/2"; Brougham, vertical vee-grille, three-piece mold, 3-1/2". Photo from Fred Maxwell.

Lincoln White Metal Overland Bus, 3-1/2". Photo from Bob Ackerly.

Left to Right: Lincoln White Metal Sedan, Pierce-Arrow Silver Arrow; Coupe, possibly a Graham, 3-3/8"; Sedan, Chrysler Airflow, 3-3/4". Photo from Perry Eichor.

Lincoln White Metal Coupe, slanted hood, 4-1/2". Photo from Ferd Zegel.

Lincoln White Metal Fire Engine, steam pumper, two-man crew, 3-1/4". Photo from Fred Maxwell.

Left to right: Lincoln White Metal Indy Racer, 5-1/8"; Indy Racer, large, driver, torpedo tail. Photo from Perry Eichor.

Lincoln White Metal Fire Engine with fireman on rear step, Graham-like grille, 3-3/4". Photo from Perry Eichor.

	C6	C8	C10
Fire Engine, steam pumper, two man crew, hose real compartment, HO, HG, 3-1/4" long (LWV012)	25	50	75
Fire Engine Pumper, w/fireman on rear step, Graham-like grille, fenders faired bumper to bumper, patterned pan, marked "Made in USA," "Patrol No. 79," 3-3/4" long (LWV009)	75	100	125
Indy Racer, Miller FWD Special, driver, rounded grille, horizontal cooling fins alongside hood, torpedo tail, 5-1/8" long (LWV001)	60	80	100

	C6	C8	C10
Indy Racer, small, two-man, FWD, rounded hood, four cylinder, exhaust left side (LWV025)	40	60	80
Indy Racer, large driver, slanted V-grille, horizontal cooling fins, torpedo tail (LWV028)	50	75	100
Indy Racer, large, driver, unusual grille design (LWV029)	50	75	100
Indy Racer, large (LWV030)	NPF	NPF	NPF
Limousine, Graham (?) VG, MDW SM, four OW, LI, T, made from three-piece mold, 3-1/4" long (LWV023)	40	60	80

	C6	C8	C10
Limousine, Nash (?), VG, VL, MWW SM, four OW, T, made from three-piece mold, 2-1/2" long (LWV024)	40	60	80
Racer, Indy Miller type, smaller version of Indy Racer Miller FWD Special, 4" long (LWV033)	30	45	60
Racer, Indy Miller type, similar to above, 4-1/4" long (LWV034)	NPF	NPF	NPF
Railcar, Streamline, marked "UNION PACIFIC" and shield symbol, two OW in cab, eighteen OW in passenger section, hidden rubber wheels, patterned pan, marked "Made In USA," 4-1/2" long (LWV011)	80	110	140

	C6	C8	C10
Sedan, Pierce-Arrow Silver Arrow, vertical vee-grille, head-lamps and front fenders faired, six OW, divided WS, plain pan, 3-1/2" long (LWV005)	40	60	80
Sedan, Chrysler airflow, two-door, HO, divided open WS, HL, plain pan, 3-3/4" long (LWV006)	35	45	60
Sedan, Pontiac, two-door, HO, grid pattern grille, HL, four OW, trunk, 3-7/8" long (LWV007)	30	40	50
Sedan, Lincoln Auto Co. (?) (LWV031)	NPF	NPF	NPF
Sedan, Ford V-8 (LWV032)	NPF	NPF	NPF
Sedan, DeSoto (?), two-door, HO, HL, four OW, very streamlined airflow rear (LWV035)	40	60	80

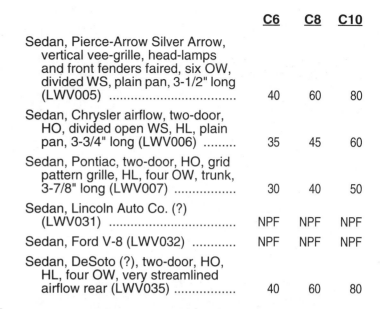

Railcar, hidden rubber wheels, 4-1/2". Photo from Perry Eichor.

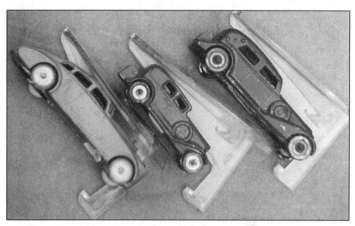

Left to right: Lincoln White Metal Sedan, Pierce-Arrow Silver Arrow, 3-1/2"; Coupe, slanted vee-grille; Coupe, Oldsmobile, streamlined vee-grille, 4". Photo from Fred Maxwell.

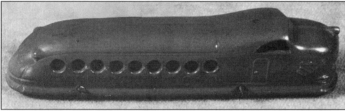

Left to right: Lincoln White Metal Sedan, Pierce-Arrow Silver Arrow, 3-1/2"; Lincoln White Metal Sedan, Chrysler Airflow, 3-3/4". Photo from Perry Eichor.

Top to Bottom: Lincoln White Metal Limousine, possibley a Nash, 2-1/2"; Limousine, possibly a Graham, 3-1/4"; Lincoln White Metal Coupe, possibly a Graham, 3-3/8". Photo from Fred Maxwell.

Lincoln White Metal Sedan, possibly Lincoln Auto Co. Photo from Fred Maxwell.

Left to right: Lincoln White Metal Fire Engine; Sedan, Ford V-8; Fire Engine variation. Photo from Fred Maxwell.

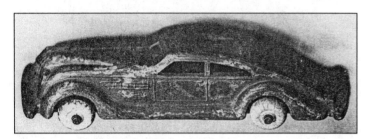

Lincoln White Metal Sedan, possibly a two-door DeSoto. Photo from Bob Ackerly.

Lincoln White Metal Speed Car, Bluebird record car, triangular fin with wing design, 6". Photo from Chic Gast.

Top to bottom: Lincoln White Metal Speed Car, Bluebird record car, driver, V-8 engine with intake ports, 6"; Lincoln White Metal Speed Car, Bluebird, smaller version of above, 4". Photo from Perry Eichor.

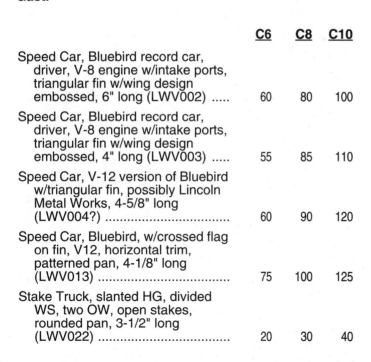

Lincoln White Metal Speed Car, Bluebird, 4". Photo from John Taylor.

	C6	C8	C10
Speed Car, Bluebird record car, driver, V-8 engine w/intake ports, triangular fin w/wing design embossed, 6" long (LWV002)	60	80	100
Speed Car, Bluebird record car, driver, V-8 engine w/intake ports, triangular fin w/wing design embossed, 4" long (LWV003)	55	85	110
Speed Car, V-12 version of Bluebird w/triangular fin, possibly Lincoln Metal Works, 4-5/8" long (LWV004?)	60	90	120
Speed Car, Bluebird, w/crossed flag on fin, V12, horizontal trim, patterned pan, 4-1/8" long (LWV013)	75	100	125
Stake Truck, slanted HG, divided WS, two OW, open stakes, rounded pan, 3-1/2" long (LWV022)	20	30	40

	C6	C8	C10
Tanker Truck, COE, two OW, six tranks, eight compartments, patterned pan, marked "Made in USA", 3-3/4" long (LWV010)	60	80	100
Tractor, small Fordson (LWV026) ...	15	25	40
Wrecker, high style w/chopped top, Graham-like grille, two OW, fenders faired bumper to bumper, solid crane w/grid pattern and hook, patterned pan, marked "Made in USA," 3-1/2" long (LWV008)	40	60	80

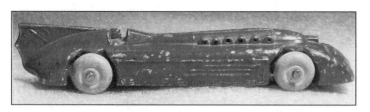

Lincoln White Metal Speed Car, Bluebird, V12, 4-1/8". Photo from Perry Eichor.

Lincoln White Metal Tanker Truck, six tanks, eight compartments, 3-3/4". Photo from Fred Maxwell.

Lincoln White Metal Stake Truck, open stakes, 3-1/2". Photo from Bob Ackerly.

Lincoln White Metal Wrecker, high style with chopped top, Graham-like grille. Photo from Perry Eichor.

LINEOL

Germany's Lineol was founded by Oscar Weiderholz in 1906, in the Berlin suburb of Brandenburg. Its military tinplate line was considered superior to all others (although in sales, Elastolin dominated the field). Authentic in detail, most were painted in camouflage colors. With a few exceptions, all Lineol military tinplates toys were made in scale for its 7-1/2 centimeters (2-15/16 inches) composition toy soldiers.

Contributor: Jack Matthews, 13 Bufflehead Dr., Kiawah Island, SC 29455, e-mail: meriam@concentric.net.

Lineol Ambulance, No. 1041, value as shown $4,000. Jack Mathews Collection.

Lineol Armored Car, No. 1215, rare, value as shown $3,500. Jack Mathews Collection.

Lineol Bridge Truck, No. 1218, value as shown $6,500. Jack Mathews Collection.

Lineol Command Staff Car, No. 1211 (camouflage), value as shown $1,500. Jack Mathews Collection.

Lineol Command Staff Car, No. 1211 (solid olive drab), value as shown $1,300. Jack Mathews Collection.

Lineol Communications Car, No. 1205/5, very rare, value as shown $6,000. Jack Mathews Collection.

Lineol Panzer Tank, No. 1280, value as shown $2,000. Jack Mathews Collection.

Lineol Six-wheeled Prime Mover, No. 1225/6, gray, lade vehicle made, value as shown $3,000. Jack Mathews Collection.

Lineol Six-wheeled Prime Mover with camouflage top, No. 1225/6, camouflage top, last vehicle made, $3,000. Jack Mathews Collection.

Lineol Searchlight Truck, No. 1010, value as shown $4,500. Jack Mathews Collection.

Lineol Troop Lorry, No. 1011, early, value as shown $3,500. Jack Mathews Collection.

Lineol Staff Car, No. 1206/5, with luggage rack, value as shown $6,000. Jack Mathews Collection.

Lineol early tank, value as shown $450. Jack Mathews Collection.

LLEDO

Lledo was founded in 1983 by Jack Odell, a former executive at Lesney Products & Co. Odell's goal was to produce quality die-cast at an affordable price. Lledo, Odell spelled backwards, is the only major die-cast manufacturer to produce models in the United Kingdom (Enfield, Essex). In 1996, the company was purchased by HCG Group Limited (the Hobbies Collectables and Gifts Group).

The first six models, part of the Day Gone line, were launched in April 1983and consisted of five horse-drawn vehicles. Also issued was a 1920 Model "T" Ford Van which could very well be the most popular toy vehicle ever produced. The scale of the early models was erratic, especially for buses and trucks. Most models were motor vehicles from the 1920s-1940s era with a few exceptions. In 1996, the Vanguard line was launched. Based on vehicles from the 1950s and 1960s, they are generally 1:45-scale for cars and 1:64-scale for trucks.

From the beginning, Lledo exploited the collectibles market and over the years many millions of models have been produced. Its product proved very popular in the promotional market and steps were taken to distinguish general release lines from promotional lines.

A systematic numbering system was developed. Day Gone models are marked with a "DG" followed by a casting number. Promotional models, marked with at "LP" followed by a casting number, each have a different face plate and weren't intended for general release. The Vanguard series are identified by "VA" followed by the casting number, while the promotional models done from this line are marked with a "PM". There are about eighty-eight different DG/LP castings and twenty-six PM castings. The Marathon series is made up of six different truck or bus castings done in a larger scale.

The casting number in each series is followed by a three-digit livery number while the annual catalogs published by RDP Publications, the main source of information for Lledo models, applies a final letter to define variants—which can be extremely important in identifying the more expensive models. Specific lines were included a gray series of 144 sets of seventeen of the DG castings issued in 1986 for promotional use in the United States; a United States-dedicated series (the so-called 500 series) which consisted of eight DG castings without logos; eight castings were released under the name Edocar in the Netherlands in 1986; and the "Fantastic Set of Wheels" series, distributed by Hartoy, Inc., was developed in 1985 for the U.S. market in 1985.

Logos on the models available to the general public are tampo printed while the logos on the promotional models were label printed for small runs and tampo printed for larger runs.

While the models are popular in Great Britain, there has been considerable expansion of their distribution in the United States, and an American collector's club has been formed.

Lledo models have virtually no value if they are not Mint in box (C10). Many of the models can be secured for relatively low prices ($10-$15) but it seems unlikely there will be any significant increase in price for the average model. A complete set of the castings (amounting to more than 150) can be secured for a relatively modest investment, although individual liveries cost considerably more. Promotional releases tend to bring higher prices because of the scarcity as compared to general release liveries. However, the collector should be aware that limited edition models with certificates of authenticity are rapidly increasing in value.

Some typical prices would be as follows:
- DG1-000C Horse-drawn tram Westminster, $15; however, variant DG1-000E is valued at $160.
- DG6 1920 Ford Model T—Most prices for general release models are in the $10 to $40 range, while the LP series tends to fall in the $20 to $100 range.
- DGG-033C Barclay Bank livery, $1,600

With nearly 140 castings and possibly some 7,000 in total different liveries, detailed pricing becomes more impossible but the above figures will give some guide to a collector.

More information on Lledo can be found in the *Days Gone Collector and Lledo Information Service Contact*. They can be contacted at RDP Publications, P.O. Box 1946, Halesowen, West Midlands B63 3T6, England

Contributor: Iain C. Baillie, Town Mill, 191 high Street, Old Amersham, Bucks HP7 0EQ, England. Baillie is a Scots-born naturalized American living in London with his wife, Joan, while their only son resides in California. Baillie is an intellectual property lawyer and a Senior European partner of an American law firm. Originally drawn to model vehicles because of the advertising, Baillie specializes in Lledo but also collects Matchbox and Corgi. In addition to vehicles, Baillie collects military figures, models of ducks and ship models.

An assortment of Lledo vehicles. Photo from Iain C. Baillie.

A.C. Williams Coast to Coast Cartage Co. Stake Trailer Truck, 10-1/8". Photo from Bill Bertoia Auctions.

A.C. Williams Racer, two passengers, 7-1/8". Photo from Tim Oei.

Woodhaven Animate Climbing Tractor, tin windup. Photo from John Monteleone.

Left to right: A.C. Williams Machinery Hauler, three Lowboy Trailers, Roadscraper, Roadroller, Tractor, overall length 28-5/8". Photo from Bill Bertoia Auctions.

Left: Arcade Model AA Coupe, 1928, rumble seat, 6-3/4". Photo from Bill Bertoia Auctions.

Below, Left to right: Arcade Stake Trailer Truck, 1931, 11-5/16"; International Dump Truck, 1931. Photo from Bill Bertoia Auctions.

Above, Left to right: Arcade White Moving Van "USCO" variant sold for $16,000 at a 1994 auction; this variant brought $11,000 at the same auction. Photo from Bill Bertoia Auctions.

Right: Arcade International Dump Truck, 1937, 9-1/2". Photo from Bill Bertoia Auctions.

Arcade Panel Delivery Truck, 1925, 8-1/8". Photo from Bill Bertoia Auctions.

Below, Left to right: Arcade Fire Engine, 1941, 13-1/2"; Hubley Ahrens Fox Hose Reel. Photo from Bill Bertoia Auctions.

Arcade Ford Express Truck, 1929, 8-1/4". Photo from Bill Bertoia Auctions.

Arcade White Dump Truck, 1929, 11-1/2", auctioned in 1994 for $13,200. Photo from Bill Bertoia Auctions.

Left to right: C.A.W. Transparent Windshield Racer, 3"; Austin Bantam; Kansas Toy Sedanette, three-piece grille. Photo from Chic Gast.

Above, Top to bottom: Cor-Cor Graham Paige Sedan, electric, 20"; Sturditoy Oil Company Tanker, 27"; Buddy "L" Ice Truck. Photo from Christie's East.

Left: Auburn Fire Engine, 1940s.

Dinky Unic Auto Transporter. Photo from Christie's South Kensington.

Left to right: Hubley General Steam Shovel, 9"; Arcade Mack Hoist Truck, 1932, 8"; Hubley General Steam Shovel, 8-1/4". Photo from Bill Bertoia Auctions.

Hubley Packard, fifteen parts, 1920s. Photo from Clint Seeley Collection.

Motorcycles were a forte of Hubley's. Values range from the hundreds to the thousands.

Corgi James Bond Silver Aston-Martin.

Hot Wheels Tri Baby.

Hot Wheels Sand Crab.

Hot Wheels McLaren.

Hot Wheels Beatnik Bandit.

Hot Wheels Torero.

Hot Wheels Strip Teaser.

Hot Wheels Deora.

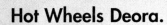

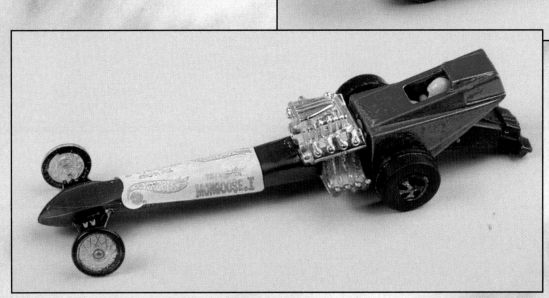

Hot Wheels
Mongoose Dragster.

Above: Keystone Moving Van.

Right: Keystone Truck Loader, 17-3/4".
Photo from Joe Freed.

Left: Kenton's double-decker Buses from the 1920s are extremely valuable. The "least" expensive, a 12" version.

Below: Manoil Rocket, futuristic bus-like vehicle.

Left: Wooden Tank, World War II, value as shown $80. Photo from Jack Mathews Collection.

Below: Wooden Tank, US W57, circa World War II, value as shown $35. Photo from Jack Mathews Collection.

Below: Composition Jeep, possibly by Krak-A-Jap, value as shown $40. Photo from Jack Mathews Collection.

Above: Cardboard Tank, circa World War II, possibly by the D.A. Pachter Co., value as shown $30. Photo from Jack Mathews Collection.

Left: World War II-era cardboard vehicles, value as shown $15 each. Photo from Jack Mathews Collection.

Marx Milton Berle Crazy Car, tin windup, 1950s.

Below: Marx Mortimer Snerd's Tricky Auto, 1939, tin windup.

Marx Linemar NAR Television Truck, 1950s, battery-operated.

Marx Queen of the Campus tin windup with college boy passengers.

Marx Charlie McCarthy in his Benzine Buggy, tin windup.

Below: Marx made several G-Man Pursuit Cars in the 1930s.

Below: How could one realistically play Marx Motorcycle policeman without a trip to the Marx Gas Island? Photo from Richard MacNary.

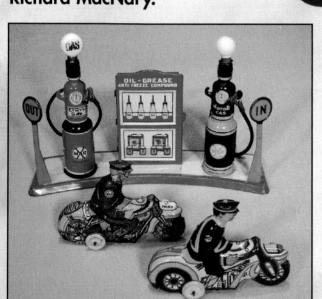

Above: Marx Amos & Andy Fresh-Air Taxi, 1930s, tin windup, 8".

Marx Hi-Way Express Truck, $400. Photo from Calvin L. Chaussee.

Strauss Big Show Circus, 1920s, tin windup, 9".
Photo from Bob Smith.

Below, Top to bottom: Strauss Green Racer,
1920s, 8-1/2"; Red Flash Racer, 9-1/2"; Racer,
No. 21, tin windup, 1920s. Photo from Bob
Smith.

Top to bottom: Tru-Scale/Ertl International Fleetstar Cab, Anderson
Payload, 1970s; Tru-Scale International Semi-Tractor Hydraulic Dump
Truck, orange and yellow, 1960s.

Left to right: Sun Rubber White Bus,
streamlined; Coupe, 1936. Photo
from Bob and Alice Wagner.

Turner Yellow Taxicab, 1920s, 9-3/4". Photo from John Taylor.

Turner Stake Truck, closed cab, 22". Photo from John Taylor.

Turner Ladder Truck, 1940s. Photo from John Taylor.

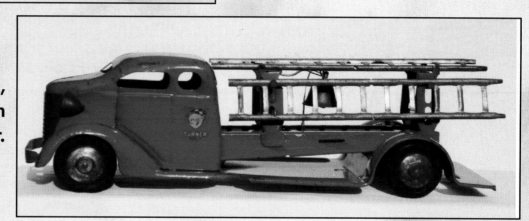

Turner Dump Truck, 1940s, 21". Photo from John Taylor.

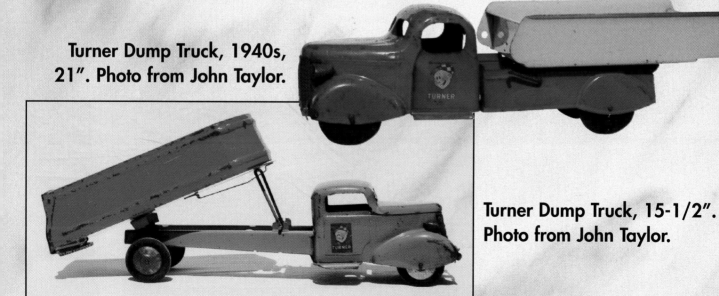

Turner Dump Truck, 15-1/2". Photo from John Taylor.

Finnegan the Porter, tin windup.
Photo from Richard MacNary.

Above: Vindex P&H power shovel, handle revolves rig. Photo from Bill Bertoia Auctions.

Left to right: Vindex Hay Loader, 9"; John Deere Thresher, 15". Photo from Bill Bertoia Auctions.

Wolverine Express Bus, 14".

Wolverine Trailer House. Photo from Calvin Chaussee.

LONDONTOY

Londontoy die-cast vehicles were produced in London, Ontario, from 1945-1950. They were also molded in the United States by the Leslie Henry Company, by special arrangement with Londontoy. The American versions are characterized by the absence of the "Made in Canada" marking, and the larger American versions sometimes had a three-dimensional baseplate, which simulated the vehicle drivetrain. The larger versions were sometimes equipped with a heavy flywheel friction-motor or a wind-up mechanism. Oil tankers and beverage trucks sometimes bore advertising for actual brandnames. Either motors or advertising would add to the values below.

Contributor: Dave Leopard, 2507 Feather Run Trail, West Columbia, SC 29169-4915.

Four-inch Size	C6	C8	C10	Six-inch Size	C6	C8	C10
1941 Chevrolet Master Deluxe Coupe	15	20	25	1941 Chevrolet Master Deluxe Coupe	25	30	40
1941 Ford Open Cab Fire Truck	15	20	25	1941 Ford Pickup Truck	25	30	40
1941 Ford Pickup Truck	15	20	25	Beverage Truck	25	30	40
Beverage Truck	15	20	25	Candian Greyhound Bus	NPF	NPF	NPF
City Bus	20	25	30	City Bus	25	30	40
Oil Tanker	15	20	25				

Left to Right: Londontoy Pickup Trucks, 1941, 4"; Londontoy Ford Pickup, 1941, 6". Photo from Dave Leopard.

Left to Right: Londontoy Chevrolet Master Deluxe Coupes, 1941, 4"; Chevrolet Master Deluxe Coupe, 1941, 6". Photo from Dave Leopard.

Left to Right: Londontoy 1941 Ford Open Cab Firetruck, 4"; Firetruck, 6". Photo from Dave Leopard.

Left to Right: Londontoy Oil tanker, 4"; Londontoy Oil Tanker, 6". Photo from Dave Leopard.

	C6	C8	C10
Fire Truck	25	30	40
Oil Tanker	25	30	40
Panel Delivery	NPF	NPF	NPF
Six-window Sedan	NPF	NPF	NPF
Thunderbolt Racer	NPF	NPF	NPF
Tractor and Van Trailer	60	80	100

Larger Than Six Inches

	C6	C8	C10
Car Transporter	NPF	NPF	NPF
Dump Truck	NPF	NPF	NPF
Lumber Truck	NPF	NPF	NPF
Moving Van, tin body	NPF	NPF	NPF
Stake Body Truck	NPF	NPF	NPF

MANOIL

Manoil was owned by two brothers, Jack and Maurice Manoil. Its sole sculptor was Walter Baetz, the man responsible for Manoil's seven early vehicles, which were Manoil's first toys, debuting in 1934. The firm, originally located in Manhattan, then Brooklyn, and finally in Waverly, New York, closed down about 1955.

	C6	C8	C10
No. 070 Soup Kitchen, large number	9	13	18
No. 071 Shell Carrier With Soldier On Shell Box, has loop	11	16	23
No. 071A Armored Car w/Siren, siren cast separately	25	38	50
No. 071A Armored Car w/Siren, siren cast w/vehicle	32	48	65
No. 071A Shell Carrier w/Soldier On Shell Box, no loop	10	15	20
No. 072 Water Wagon, larger number	10	15	20
No. 072A Water Wagon, small number	10	15	20
No. 072B Water Wagon, No. number	10	15	20
No. 073 Tractor, loop front	10	15	20

	C6	C8	C10
No. 073A Tractor, plain front	11	16	23
No. 074 Armored Car w/Anti-Tank Gun	22	33	45
No. 075 Armored Car w/Anti-Aircraft Gun	27	41	55
No. 095 Tank	8	12	17
No. 096 Large Shell on Truck	9	13	18
No. 097 Pontoon on Wheels	22	33	45
No. 098 Torpedo on Wheels	10	15	20
No. 103 Gasoline Truck	10	15	20
No. 104 Chemical Truck	11	16	22
No. 105 Five Barrel Gun on Wheels	12	18	25
No. 700 Sedan, futuristic	40	60	80
No. 701 Sedan, futuristic	45	68	90

Top row, left to right: Manoil Sedan, futuristic, No. 705; Roadster, No. 708; Roadster, vertical radiator, No 708. Bottom row, left to right: Sedan, No. 707; Oil Tanker, 710; Fire Engine, 4", No. 709. Photo from Marjorie and Peter Ruben.

Manoil Aerial Ladder with original box. Photo from *Old Toy Soldier* magazine.

Manoil Aerial Ladder, No. 711. Figures were not included with engine. Photo from *Old Toy Soldier* magazine.

Manoil Pumper, No. 712, with original box. Figures were not included with the engine. Photo from *Old Toy Soldier* magazine.

	C6	C8	C10
No. 702 Coupe, futuristic..................	45	68	90
No. 703 Wrecker, futuristic..............	80	120	160
No. 704 Roadster, futuristic, Pat. No. 95701	45	68	90
No. 705 Sedan, futuristic, Pat. No. 95792..................................	45	68	90
No. 706 Rocket, futuristic bus-like vehicle, Pat. No. 95793................	60	90	120
No. 70A Soup Kitchen, small number..........................	9	13	18

Plastic Vehicles

	C6	C8	C10
No. P-10 Towing Truck	12	18	25
No. P-11 Towing Truck	12	18	25
No. P-12 Tractor..............................	12	18	25
No. P-13 Dump Cart.........................	12	18	25
No. P-7 Roadster	12	18	25
No. P-8 Sedan................................	12	18	25
No. P-9 Pick-Up	12	18	25

Postwar Vehicles

	C6	C8	C10
Four Speedsters Boxed Set, includes roadster and sedan	250	375	500
No. 707 Sedan	22	33	44
No. 708 Roadster, horizontal radiator	27	41	55
No. 708A Roaster, vertical radiator ..	50	75	100
No. 709 Fire Engine, 4" long	18	28	38
No. 710 Oil Tanker...........................	13	19	26
No. 711 Aerial Ladder	200	300	400
No. 712 Pumper..............................	200	300	400
No. 713 Bus	12	18	24
No. 714 Towing Truck......................	10	15	20
No. 715 Commercial Truck	10	15	20
No. 716 Sedan	10	15	20
No. 717 Hard Top Convertible	12	18	24
No. 718 Convertible	10	15	20
No. 719 Sport Car	10	15	20
No. 720 Rance Wagon.....................	10	15	20

MÄRKLIN VEHICLES

Well-known today for currently manufactured toy trains, the German Märklin Company enjoyed a fine reputation for quality toys long before 1933-1934, when a series of constructional motor vehicles was introduced. Märklin had been making multipurpose construction sets similar in concept to Erector in the United States and Meccano in England, but now it was building specialized sets that would appeal to the young automotive engineer.

A clever merchandising scheme was developed. You could buy a boxed set of parts to build a complete chassis, but a motor would have to be purchased separately. The body of your choice was still another kit to buy, and up to six types were available by the late 1930s. If you wished to have other types of vehicles, alternative body kits were available. Complete sets with body, motor and chassis were also sold, and some sets included more than one body. Märklins were costly, and, in the 1930s, many could afford to buy only one piece at a time. The quality of finish is superb, and some pieces are decorated with hand striping.

The group of constructional vehicles could be referred to as The 1100 series. However, there was no 1102. The 1100 Series was revived after the war, but 1104P, 1106T, 1108G, 1110B, 1133R and 99R were not made again. Märklin phased out the remaining constructional vehicles in the mid-1950s. Why is no value guide possible for Märklin toys. Very few are changing hands in the 1990s, and not enough data exists to develop a reliable and useful listing of values.

Since 1990, Marklin has issued seven limited-edition constructional vehicles that look as though they could be members of the original 1100 series, but there are many detail differences. The Tanker, Racing Car and Lorry are very similar to the originals, but the three vans and the Fire Engine are probably based upon 1930s prototypes that had never reached production. Perhaps one of these could have been the missing link, Number 1102! All of the "new" Märklins have electric headlights, and they were completely assembled at the factory. It remains to be seen whether there will be additions to the series.

Prewar Numberings.

* – Means not reissued postwar.

1101C Chassis

1103St Streamline Coupe body; early version is two-tone blue; later version is all green with brown roof.

*1104 Pullman Limousine body; early version is beige and green; later version is ivory with gray roof.

1105L Lorry (Pick-up) body; red/green.

*1106T Tanker Body; red/blue.

1107R Racing (Sports Car) body, red/white.

*1108G Armored Car body, camouflaged (more than one pattern).

1109M Clockwork motor.

*1110B Electric Lighting Set

*99R Driver (lightweight composition material)

*1133R Mercedes Racing Car. red, complete with chassis and motor; smaller scale

1133AL Mercedes Racing Car. aluminum. Complete with chassis and motor. smaller scale.

	C6	C8	C10
Construction Sets			
1101C Chassis	NPF	NPF	NPF
1103St Streamline Coupe Body, Early is 2-tone blue, later is all green w/brown roof	NPF	NPF	NPF
1104 Pullman Limousine Body, early is beige and green, later is ivory w/gray roof	NPF	NPF	NPF
1105L Lorry (Pick-up) Body, red/green	NPF	NPF	NPF

	C6	C8	C10
1106T Tanker Body, red/blue	NPF	NPF	NPF
1107R Racing (Sports Car) body, red/white	NPF	NPF	NPF
1108G Armored Car Body, camouflaged (more than one pattern)	NPF	NPF	NPF
1109M Clockwork motor	NPF	NPF	NPF
1110B Electric Lighting Set	NPF	NPF	NPF
1133AL Mercedes Racing Car, aluminum, complete w/chassis and motor, smaller scale	NPF	NPF	NPF

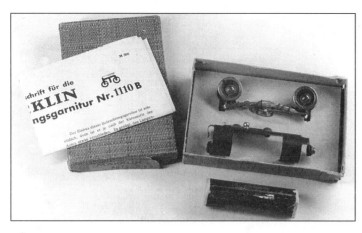

Märklin Lighting Set with instructions and original battery. Photo from Gates Willard. Photo by E.W. Willard.

Märklin No. 1106T Tanker with orginal box; two tinplate cars were included. Photo from Gates Willard. Photo by E.W. Willard.

Märklin No. 1103St Streamlined Coupe. Photo from Gates Willard. Photo by E.W. Willard.

Märklin No. 1104 Pullman Limousine. Photo from Gates Willard. Photo by E.W. Willard.

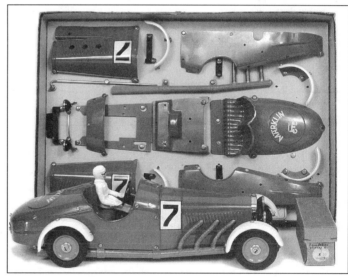

Märklin No. 1107R racing car with original composition 99R driver; behind it is the unassembled car in its box. Photo from Gates Willard. Photo by E.W. Willard.

Märklin No. 1105L Lorry. Photo from Gates Willard. Photo by E.W. Willard.

Märklin No. 1108G Armored Car, camouflage-type paint. Photo from Gates Willard. Photo by E.W. Willard.

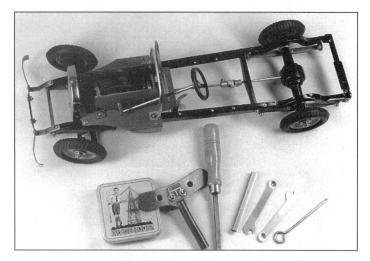

Märklin Assembled Chassis with parts box, cast-iron key and tools; No. 1109M clockwork motor is installed. Photo from Gates Willard. Photo by E.W. Willard.

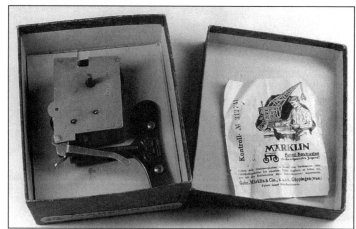

Märklin boxed No. 1110B Lighting Set with instructions and original battery. Photo from Gates Willard. Photo by E.W. Willard.

	C6	C8	C10
1133R Mercedes Racing Car, red, complete w/chassis and motor, smaller scale	NPF	NPF	NPF
99R Driver, made of lightweight composition material	NPF	NPF	NPF

Die-Cast

	C6	C8	C10
308 El Racer, 12" long	250	375	500
Armored Car, camouflaged, 14-1/2" long	1000	1700	2400
Kubelwagen, 3-1/2" long	325	490	650
Mercedes Racing Car, wind-up, 12" long	425	638	850
Road Working Machine, 3-5/8" long	100	150	200
Troop Carrier, ten wheels, 5" long ...	450	675	900
Troop Carrier, 4-1/2" long	325	490	650
Water Truck, early, faucet works, 15" long	1300	2500	3600

Märklin Kubelwagen, die-cast, 3-1/2". Photo from Terry Sells.

Märklin • Mercedes Racing Car, composition driver, cast-iron key, wind-up, 12". Photo from Gates Willard. Photo by E.W. Willard.

Märklin Road Working Machine, 3-5/8". Photo from Virginia Caputo.

Märklin Troop Carrier, die-cast metal, ten wheels, 5". Photo from Terry Sells.

Märklin Water Truck, faucet works, 15". Photo from Bill Bertoia Auctions.

Märklin Troop Carrier, die-cast metal, 4-1/2". Photo from Terry Sells.

Limited editions, Left to right: Märklin Reichspost Van, 1994; Racing Car, 1995. Photo from Gates Willard. Photo by E.W. Willard.

Left to right: Märklin Standard Tanker, 1993; Geld Transporter, 1993. Photo from Gates Willard. Photo by E.W. Willard.

Limited Editions

	C6	C8	C10
Fire Engine, red, No. 1990, 1990	NPF	NPF	NPF
Geld Transporter (Armored Truck), blue/black, No. 1993, 1993	NPF	NPF	NPF

	C6	C8	C10
Lorry, red/green, No. 1992, 1992	NPF	NPF	NPF
Racing Car, red/white, No. 1995, 1995	NPF	NPF	NPF
Reichspost (Postal Van), dark red/black, No. 1994, 1994	NPF	NPF	NPF
Reichspost (Postal Van), yellow/black, No. 1990, 1990	NPF	NPF	NPF
Standard Tanker, red/blue, No. 1993, 1993	NPF	NPF	NPF

MARX

By the 1950s, Louis Marx was the largest manufacturer of toys in the world; six large factories in the United States and ownership of interest in factories in seven other countries. Marx, born in Brooklyn in 1896, was working for the so-called toy king Ferdinand Strauss when he was in his teens. By 20, his energy and enterprise had made in a director of that company. A falling out with Strauss persuaded him to go into business for himself. In 1921, he and his brother began making their own toys, including some adaptations of items by the now-defunct Strauss. Marx's watchword seems to have been quality at the lowest possible price, and he was such a favorite with toy buyers that he had virtually no need for salesmen or advertising.

Marx made virtually every type of toy, with the exception of dolls. In April 1972, he sold his company to the Quaker Oats Company, which, in 1976, sold it to Europe's largest toy manufacturer, Dunbee-Combex-Marx. The company went into bankruptcy in 1980. Marx died in 1982, at the age of 85. In 1982, American Plastics bought much of the Marx assets; in 1990, it began producing toys from the original molds. Marx eventually ended up in the hands Jay Horowitz, the current president. Horowitz produces Marx action figures based on the original molds and has licensed Jim and Debby Flynn to produce new tin-lithographed trains. For more information on Marx trains, see *O'Brien's Collecting Toy Trains*.

Contributors: Michael W. Curran, Heritage America Company, P.O. Box 545, Hampton, IL 61256, 309-496-9426. John Taylor, P.O. Box 63, Nolensville, TN 37135-0063.

	C6	C8	C10
1st Batt. F.D. Chief's Car, tin wind-up, w/siren, battery-operated headlights, 16" long	215	322	430
A&P Truck, 28" long	75	125	200
Acme Markets Trailer Truck, late	150	275	325
Aerial Ladder Truck, late	135	202	270
Aerial Water Tower Truck, wind-up, 15" long	275	363	550

	C6	C8	C10
Aero Oil Company Truck, friction, c.1930, 5-1/2" long	225	375	500
Air Force Truck, canvas top, 20" long	105	158	210
Air Force Truck, "Air Defense Group" ride 'em toy, No. 3290, 32" long	125	188	250
Airflow, 4" long	40	50	100
Airport Transport, 6-1/2" long	30	40	65
Allied Van Lines, tin friction, Linemar, 1950s	100	150	200
Allstate Super Trailer	325	490	650
Ambulance, tin wind-up, marked "M.D. War Dept.," 1930s	300	450	800
Ambulance, No. 8500, 1930s, approx. 14" long	150	275	475

Marx A&P Truck.

Marx Acme Markets Trailer Truck. Photo from John Taylor.

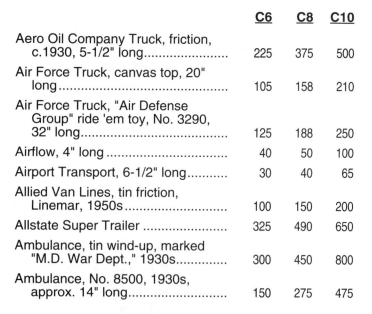

Marx Aero Oil Company Truck, friction, 5-1/2". Photo from Bob Smith.

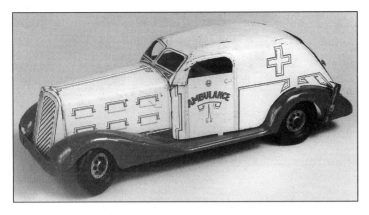

Marx Ambulance, with siren, 1930s, tin wind-up, 14-1/2". Photo from Mapes Auctioneers and Appraisers.

Marx Armored Bank, 6". Photo from Richard MacNary.

Marx Amos & Andy Fresh-Air Taxi, 1930s, 8". Photo from Bob Smith.

Marx Army Command Car, friction, tin and plastic, siren, 19-1/2". Photo from Terry Sells.

	C6	C8	C10
Ambulance, No. 8600, 1930s, approx. 14" long	240	360	550
Ambulance w/Siren, tin wind-up, 1930s, 14-1/2" long	250	375	550
American LaFrance Hose Truck, late, 21" long	175	263	350
American Railroad Express Agency, Inc., open cab, early 1930s, 7" long	150	250	450
American Railway Express Agency Van, wind-up, closed driver's window, 9" long	300	450	625
American Railway Express Agency Van, wind-up, Bulldog Mack	250	400	575
American Tractor, tin wind-up, w/implements, 1920s, 10" long	132	198	265
American Truck Co. Moving Truck, friction, No. 65	65	98	130
Amos & Andy Fresh-Air Taxi, tin wind-up, 1930s, 8" long	500	850	1400
Anti-Aircraft, friction, plastic and tin, Unit No. 1 Fire Control Truck	90	135	180

	C6	C8	C10
Anti-Aircraft Unit Civilian Defense Truck, No. 12, friction, plastic, 12" long	110	165	220
Armored Bank Truck, c.1940, 6" long	75	112	150
Armored Trucking Co., tin wind-up	150	275	400
Army Command Car, friction, tin and plastic, siren and flashing signal light, 19-1/2" long	NPF	NPF	NPF
Army Corps of Engineers, canvas top, 20" long	125	188	250
Army Jeep w/Searchlight Trailer, steel	100	150	250
Army Scout Stake Truck, c.1940	60	90	120
Army Staff Car, tin wind-up, w/flasher and siren, 1940s, No. W-601158, 11" long	200	300	425
Army Staff Car, plastic friction, 9" long	9	14	18

	C6	C8	C10
Army Staff Car, tin wind-up, 1930s ..	150	225	325
Army Tractor, wind-up, 1930s	135	203	270
Army Troop Carrier, plastic, w/searchlight	62	93	125
Army Truck, tin wind-up, cloth cover, 1930s, 10" long	350	525	700
Army Truck, tin lithographed, c.early 1930s, 8" long	108	162	215
Army Truck, plastic cab..................	85	128	170
Army Truck, w/canopy, mark "U.S. Army 5th Div.," late 1950s	80	120	160
Army Truck, w/covered trailer and cannon trailer, c.1940	200	300	400
Army Truck, w/cannon, 1950s..........	65	98	130
Army Truck, c.1952, marked "USA 4153147," 13-3/4" long	100	150	200
Arrow Special Delivery Truck, 1940s, 13" long	125	175	225
Arrow Racer, tin wind-up, No. 2, 1930s, 4" long	70	110	155
Arrow Special Delivery Truck, wind-up, 1940s, 13" long	150	225	275
Arrow Special Delivery Truck, 1940s, 13" long	125	175	225
Auto Hauler, w/four plastic cars	135	102	270

	C6	C8	C10
Auto Hauler, w/two Airflows, 1930s .	150	210	300
Auto Hauler, friction, w/three 1965 Mustangs, 18" long	175	263	350
Auto Hauler, wind-up, two cars, c.1950, 10" long.....................	125	200	275
Auto Transport, friction powered, with three racers	NPF	NPF	NPF
Auto Transport, wind-up, Mack C-Cab, w/three cars, 1920s, 12" long...	250	375	575
Auto Transport, w/three cars, 1950s, 21" long....................................	225	338	450
Auto Transport, includes two Corvettes, two T-Birds, everything tin, c.1958, 31" long ...	275	363	550
Auto Transport, w/two tin lithographed cars, 1950s, 34" long..	150	225	300
Auto Transport, four steel cars, c.1939	275	400	500
Auto Transwalk, truck w/three cars, No. T-50447B, 1930s	185	278	350
Auto-Laundry Car Wash	125	188	250
Automatic Fire House Fire Chief Car, tin wind-up, 1950s, 7-1/2"-long car, w/19"-long Volunteer Fire Dept. Garage	110	165	250
Automatic Garage, comes w/one friction car	35	52	70

Marx Army Truck, cloth cover. Photo from Phillips.

Marx Arrow Special Delivery, 1940s, 13". Photo from John Taylor.

Marx Auto Transport, friction powered, with three racers. Photo from Continental Hobby House.

Marx made several versions of the Auto Transport. The 31" version from 1958 with two Corvettes and two Thunderbirds is the most valuable. Photo from Calvin L. Chaussee.

Marx Automatic Fire House, 1950s, Fire Chief Car, Volunteer Fire Dept. Garage. Photo from Don Hultzman.

Marx Brake Kar with screeching noise. Photo from Continental Hobby House.

	C6	C8	C10
Automatic Reversing Road Roller, tin wind-up, 1925, 9" long	200	300	400
Baby Wrecker Truck, battery-operated	50	75	100
Bakery Truck, reads "Rolls Pies & Cakes," 11" long	125	188	250
Beat It the Komikal Kop, tin wind-up, 1930s	250	375	500
Big Boss Car Carrier, 42" long	80	120	160
Big Bruiser Tow Truck, 1960s	50	75	100
Big Job Dump Truck, plastic, 28" long	50	75	100
Big Lizzie Car, tin wind-up, early 1930s, 7-1/4" long	130	225	300
Big Load Van Company Truck, wind-up, Bulldog Mack, 1930s, 13" long	235	352	470
Big Parade, tin wind-up, moving vehicles, soldiers, etc., 24" long	500	900	1200
Big Shot Cannon Truck, plastic, fires cap-loaded missiles, 22" long	52	76	105

Marx Dippy Dumper, Brutus celluloid figure, 1930s, 9". Photo from Don Hultzman.

Marx Bud Bowman's Milk Express Truck. Photo from John Taylor.

	C6	C8	C10
Big Silver Mack Dump Truck, tin wind-up	250	375	500
Blondie's Jalopy, tin wind-up, 16" long	1500	2300	3100
Blue Bird Gas Station	150	225	300
Bluestreak Racer, No. 3, tin, wind-up, 1930s, 4" long	55	83	110
Bottom Dump, late	40	60	80
Bouncing Benny Pull Car, 1939, 7" long	150	225	300
Brake Kar, w/screeching noise	105	157	210
Brutus Dippy Dumper	450	675	900
Bud Bowman's Milk Express Truck	175	250	350
Bulldozer Climbing Tractor, tin wind-up, caterpillar type, 1950s, 10-1/2" long	175	275	400
Bumper Auto, tin wind-up, streamlined, large bumpers, c.1939	120	180	240
Bus, c.1940, 4-1/2" long	90	135	180
Busy Bridge, tin wind-up	325	488	650
Busy Parking Station, wind-up, 1930s, 17" long, w/2" tin race car	150	225	300
Cadillac, Untouchables type, 5-1/4" long	35	52	70
Cadillac Coupe, wind-up, 1931, 12" long	432	648	865

	C6	C8	C10
Cadillac Roadster, tin wind-up, trunk w/tools on luggage carrier, 1930s, 13" long,	250	400	550
Car Carrier, wind-up, carries Airflow	58	85	115
Car Wash and Garage, tin lithographed	125	188	250
Cargo Truck, postwar, 16" long	80	120	160
Carousel Truck, marked "1967," 8" long	50	75	100

	C6	C8	C10
Carpenter Stakebed Truck, w/dolly, approx. 14" long	100	150	200
Caterpillar Climbing Tractor, tin wind-up, 10" long	10	140	190
Charlie McCarthy and Mortimer Snerd Private Car, tin wind-up	1100	1800	2600
Charlie McCarthy in his Benzine Buggy, tin wind-up	400	550	750
Chief-Fire Dept. No. 1, friction drive, c.1948	90	135	180
Circus Truck, plastic, 10" long	110	165	220
Cities Service Towing Service, 20-1/2" long	150	225	375
City Freight Trailer Truck, 1950s, 19" long, rare	175	250	325

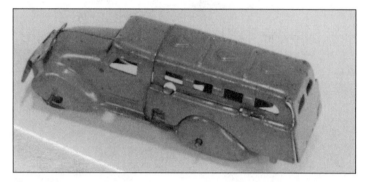

Marx Bus, circa 1940, 4-1/2". Photo from Richard Mac-Nary.

Marx Cadillac, Untouchables-type, 5-1/4". Photo from Gary Linden.

Marx Carousel Truck, 1967, 8". Photo from Scott Smiles.

Marx Charlie McCarthy in his Benzine Buggy tin wind-up. Photo from Bob Smith.

Marx City Sanitation Dept. Help Keep Your City Clean, 12-3/4". Photo from Calvin L. Chaussee.

Marx Cloverdale Farms Milk Truck, 11-1/2". Photo from John Taylor.

Marx Coca-Cola Truck, 1950s, shelf sidecases. Photo from Don Hultzman.

Marx Coast to Coast Delivery Truck, 1930s, 6". Photo from Richard MacNary.

Marx Coca-Cola Truck, plastic, 10-1/2". Photo from Terry Sells.

	C6	C8	C10
City Hospital Ambulance, tin wind-up, 10" long	475	713	950
City Sanitation Dept. Help Keep Your City Clean, c.1940, 12-3/4" long	150	250	350
Climbing Tractor, tin wind-up, sparkling, 1960s, 8-1/2" long	90	135	180
Climbing, Fighting Tank, tin wind-up	175	263	350
Climbing, Fighting Tank, tin and plastic, 5-1/2" long	22	33	45
Cloverdale Farms Milk Truck, 11-1/2" long	100	150	200
Coal Dump Truck, No. 964, 21" long	140	210	280
Coal Truck, electric motor and lights, early	200	300	500
Coal Truck, No. 964J	122	188	245
Coast to Coast Delivery Truck, 1930s, 6" long	75	100	150
Coast to Coast Transfer Semi Truck, 1950s, 24" long	100	150	200
Coca-Cola Truck, shelf sidecases, 1950s	200	300	450

	C6	C8	C10
Coca-Cola Truck, Sprite decal, stamped steel, late 1940s to early 1950s, 20" long	160	250	450
Coca-Cola Truck, 17" long	200	275	425
Coca-Cola Truck, Linemar, friction, tin, 3" long	50	75	100
Coca-Cola Truck, plastic, 10-1/2" long	175	263	350
Coke Coal City Coal Co. Truck, tin wind-up	255	383	510
Comicar the Snappy Flivver	275	363	550
Construction Tractor Hauler, reverses, w/driver, 14" long	175	263	350
Contractors and Builders Dump Truck, 1939, 11" long	100	150	200
Convertible Roadster, nickel-plated tin, 1930s, 11" long	200	300	400
Coo Coo Car, 1920s, 7-1/2" long	175	415	550
Corvette Coupe, plastic, friction, 8" long	42	63	85
Coupe, steel wind-up, electric headlights, 14" long	390	585	780

	C6	C8	C10
Crane Truck, approx. 20" long	188	292	375
Crazy Dora Nodder-Head, tin wind-up	100	150	200
Crescent Ice Truck, 11" long...........	75	150	195
Cunningham Drug Stores Truck, plastic, 1950s, scarce	30	45	75
Curtiss Candy Truck, plastic	10	20	30
Dairy Truck and Trailer, w/bottles, 1930s	125	263	350
Dan Dipsey Car, plastic nodder, wind-up, 1950s, 5-1/2" long	138	205	275
Daredevil Motor Drome, wind-up car, 1930s, 5-1/2" high, 9" diameter..	100	150	200
Day and Nite Service Service Center	75	112	150
DC Semi Tractor Trailer, late	100	150	200

	C6	C8	C10
De Luxe Tractor, six wheels, four w/treads, tin wind-up, c.1932.......	250	375	500
Delivery Truck, w/friction motor, 1950s..	175	250	325
Delivery Van.....................................	75	112	150
Delivery Van, plastic	60	90	120
Deluxe Auto Transport, w/o cars, approx. 22" long..........................	60	125	175
Deluxe Auto Transport, w/two plastic cars, approx. 22" long..................	95	175	250
Deluxe Coupe, wind-up, electric lights, 15" long	450	650	950
Deluxe Delivery Super Series Truck, wind-up, 1940s, 13" long	150	225	275
Deluxe Delivery Truck, 13" long.......	100	175	225

Marx Curtiss Candy Truck, plastic. Photo from Gary Linden.

Marx Coo Coo Car, 1920s, 7-1/2". Photo from Don Hultzman.

Marx Deluxe Coupe, electric headlights, 15". Photo from Bob Smith.

Marx Cunningham Drug Stores Truck, plastic, 1950s. Photo from John Taylor.

Marx Deluxe Delivery Truck, 13". Photo from John Taylor.

Marx Deluxe Trailer Truck, plastic cab, metal trailer, 1950s. Photo from John Taylor.

Marx Doughboy Tank, World War II pot helmet, circa 1950. Photo from Harvey K. Rainess.

Marx Disney Parade Roadster. Photo from Don Hultzman.

One of Marx's numerous Dump Trucks. Photo from Perry Eichor.

	C6	C8	C10
Deluxe Delivery Truck, tin, 1950s 11" long	75	125	175
Deluxe Mechanical Coupe, 1930s, 8" long	155	235	310
Deluxe Trailer Truck, plastic cab, metal trailer, 1950s	35	60	85
Dept. of Police Car, friction, 1930s, 8" long	125	228	450
Dick Tracy Police Station, w/7" long automatic siren car, 1950s	225	400	600
Dick Tracy Riot Car, friction motor, c.1946, 7-1/2" long	140	210	280
Dick Tracy Squad Car, friction, No. 1, 6-3/4" long	125	175	275
Dick Tracy Squad Car, friction, No. 1, 11" long	200	300	400
Dipsy Doodle Bug Dodgem Car, Dan or Dora, tin wind-up, 6" high.	67	105	135
Disney Parade Roadster, w/four characters	240	360	480

	C6	C8	C10
Donald Duck Dipsy Car, tin wind-up w/plastic Mickey or Donald, 1950s, 5-1/4" long	260	390	550
Donald Duck on Tractor, friction, plastic, 1950s, 3-1/2" long	100	150	200
Dora Dipsy Car, plastic nodder, wind-up, 1950s, 5-1/2" long	188	282	375
Dottie the Driver, wind-up, 1950s, 6-1/2" long	80	120	160
Doughboy Tank, WWII pot helmet, c.1950	130	195	260
Doughboy Tank, tin wind-up, no extending side turrets	150	225	300
Doughboy Tank, tin wind-up, soldier w/gun pops out, two extending side turrets, w/top turret, 1930, 9-1/4" long	160	240	320
Driver Training Car, tin wind-up, 1950s, 6" long	105	160	250
Drive-UR-Self Car, tin wind-up, 1950s, 11" long	225	338	450
Dump Truck, No. 695B, 17" long	75	112	150

	C6	C8	C10
Dump Truck, c.1940, 4-1/2" long	50	95	140
Dump Truck, c.1941, 7-1/2" long	60	90	120
Dump Truck, late, 9-1/2" long	50	75	100
Dump Truck, 14" long	37	56	75
Dump Truck, No. 1018, 1950s, 18" long	192	290	385
Dump Truck, No. 2083, late, 20" long	50	75	100
Dump Truck, two-color, No. T751, 1930s	82	124	165
Dump Truck, No. 1084	30	45	60
Dump Truck, 1955 Chevy	62	93	125
Dump Truck, hard plastic	42	63	85
Dump Truck, w/treads, 1920s	137	205	375
Dump Truck, tin wind-up, 13" long ...	200	300	400
Dump Truck, wind-up, 6" long	85	160	220
Dump Truck, c.1940, 4" long............	50	95	140
Dump Truck, steel wind-up, c.1940, 4-1/2" long....................................	75	130	175

	C6	C8	C10
Dump Truck, 6" long	60	135	195
E-12 Tank, sponsons swing down ...	88	132	175
Earth Hauler, c.1964	110	165	220
Easter Dump Truck, 1930s, 6" long, scarce	150	225	300
Easter Stake Truck, w/coal chute, c.1940, 7" long.........................	162	243	325
Easter Stake Truck, 1938, 10-1/2" long..	190	275	380
East-West Fast Freight Trailer Truck .	100	150	225
Electric Combat Tank, battery-operated	80	120	160
Electric Lighted Car, Silver finish, Pontiac, 10" long......................	60	90	120
Electric Motor Driven Coupe, electric lights, c.1933, 15" long	350	550	850

Marx Easter Dump Truck, late 1930s, 6". Photo from John Taylor.

Marx Dump Truck, circa 1940, 4-1/2". Photo from Bob Smith.

Marx Easter Stake Truck, 1940, 7". Photo from John Taylor.

Marx E-12 Tank, sponsons swing down for flint replacements; very similar to the Sparkling Climbing Fighting Tank. Photo from Bill Holt.

Marx East-West Fast Freight Trailer Truck. Photo from John Taylor.

Marx Electric Combat Tank, battery-operated. Photo from Continental Hobby House.

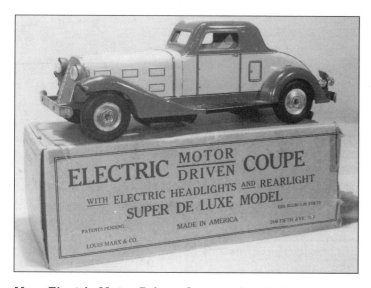

Marx Electric Motor Driven Coupe, electric lights, circa 1933, 15". Photo from Bob Smith.

	C6	C8	C10
Electric Speedway Cars, track, transformer	300	450	600
Electrically Lighted Truck and Trailer Set, No. T-5715, 1930s, 15" long.	150	220	300
Elmer's Racing Fuel trailer Truck, tin, 1950s	112	168	225
Falcon, w/plastic bubble top, black rubber tires..................................	125	188	250
Fanny Farmer Candy Truck, plastic .	50	75	125
Farm Tractor, battery-operated	40	60	80

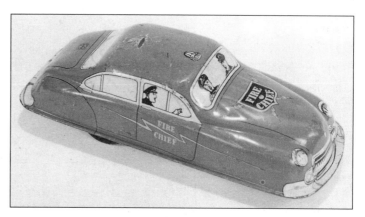

Marx Fire Chief Car, right-hand drive (made in England), 7-1/2". Photo from Richard MacNary.

	C6	C8	C10
Fighting Tank, wind-up, plastic top, No. 462, 6" long	37	56	75
Fire Chief Car, 1920s....................	175	263	350
Fire Chief Car, right-hand drive (made in England), 7-1/2" long	100	150	200
Fire Chief Car, friction	68	102	135
Fire Chief Car, 1948 Hudson, 12" long	162	245	350
Fire Department Car	100	150	200
Fire Dept. Chief Car, tin wind-up, 1950s, 11" long...........................	40	60	80
Fire Engine Pumper, friction, late 1920s...	275	363	550
Fire Ladder Truck, 14" long............	60	90	120
Fire Ladder Truck, c.1940, 6" long...	50	75	100
Fire Truck, friction, 25" long	225	338	450
Fire Truck, plastic, w/siren, 1950s ...	70	105	140
Firestone Truck, 14-1/2" long...........	312	468	625
First National Stores Tractor Trailer, late 1950s-early 1960s, 25" long .	150	275	325
Fix-All Convertible and Wrecker Set	125	188	250
Fix-All Farm Tractor, 1953	112	168	225
Fix-All Hard-top Convertible, w/tools, equipment......................	88	132	175
Fix-All Mercury Station Wagon	115	172	230
Fix-All Motorcycle, plastic, 12" long .	NPF	NPF	NPF
Fix-It Motorcycle, plastic, 12" long ...	88	132	175
Fix-It Tow Truck, w/accessories.......	100	150	200
Ford Convertible, 1951, 11" long	55	83	110
Funny Flivver, tin wind-up, 8" long, c.1925...	160	240	360
Gang Buster Car, No. 7200, 1930s, approx. 14" long........................	550	825	1100
Garage, tin, marked "Volunteer Fire Department" and "Chief FD," w/1950s car	130	195	260

	C6	C8	C10
Gas Island, 1930s	100	200	300
Gasoline Trailer Truck, wind-up	188	282	375
General Alarm Fire House	350	525	700
Giant King Racer, tin wind-up, marked "711," 1930s	110	165	220
Giant Reversing Tractor Truck, tin wind-up, w/tools, marked "Hauling," 14" long,	100	150	200
Glendale Coat Company Dumper	125	175	275
Glendale Wrecker	100	150	225
G-Man Pursuit Car, tin wind-up, 1930s	300	450	600

	C6	C8	C10
G-Man Pursuit Car, No. 7000, 1930s, 15" long	375	562	750
Gold Star Transfer Company Trailer Truck	150	200	275
Gravel Mixer, 1940s, 9-1/2" long	150	225	325
Gravel Mixer, secure, 1940s, 9-1/2" long	150	225	325
Gravel Truck, 13" long	88	132	175
Gravel Truck, 9" long	55	83	100
Grocery Truck, 1950s, 14-1/2" long	62	93	125
Guided Missile Truck, No. 4488	220	330	440
Gulf Service Station	300	450	600
Gyro Rocket Car	85	128	170
Handyman Repair Truck, 16-1/2" long	100	175	225
Happitime Service Station	238	357	475
Hauler and Closed Van Trailer, plastic	62	93	125
Hauler and Open Van Trailer, plastic	90	135	180
Hauling tractor, wind-up, six-wheel, 14" long	150	220	300
Heavy Duty Express Truck, cloth cover	95	142	190
Heavy Duty Hydraulic Dump	72	108	145
Heavy Duty Power Shovel	112	168	225

Marx Funny Flivver, 1920s, 8". Photo from Bill Bertoia Auctions.

Marx Giant King Racer, 1930s. Photo from 1929 Butler Bros. Catalog.

Marx Gold Star Transfer Company Trailer Truck. Photo from John Taylor.

Marx G-Man Pursuit Car, 1930s.

Marx Gravel Mixer, 1940s, 9-1/2". Photo from John Taylor.

Marx Highboy Climbing Tractor, sparkles, 1950s, 10".
Photo from Don Hultzman.

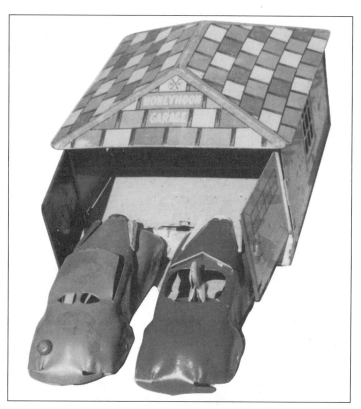

Marx Honeymoon Garage with the two original cars.
Photo from James Apthorpe.

Marx Home Dairy Truck, 10-1/2", bottles missing.
Photo from John Taylor.

Marx Hook and Ladder Fire Truck. Photo from Continental Hobby House.

	C6	C8	C10
Highboy Climbing Tractor, tin wind-up, 10-1/2" long	75	112	150
Highboy Tractor, tin wind-up, sparkles, 10" long	100	150	200
High-Lift Loader, c.1964	112	168	225
Highway Patrol Car (TV series), plastic and metal, friction, 9" long	88	132	175
Hi-Mac Dump Truck and Driver	125	188	250
Hi-Way Express Truck	125	200	300
Hi-Way Express Van Lines Truck	100	150	200

	C6	C8	C10
Home Dairy Semi Truck, metal, w/bottles, 10-1/2" long	100	150	200
Home Dairy Truck, plastic cab, w/bottles, 1950s, 11-1/2" long	50	75	125
Honeymoon Garage, tin lithographed, 1930s	50	100	175
Hook and Ladder Fire Truck	NPF	NPF	NPF
Hot Rod, open cab, driver, plastic, 7-1/2" long	45	68	90
Hot Rod, marked "777 Super"	160	240	320
Hot Rod Coupe, plastic, 5" long	42	63	85
Howard Johnson's Truck, plastic, 10" long	50	75	125

	C6	C8	C10
Hydraulic Dump	75	100	150
Ice Truck, c.1941	75	150	200
Ice Truck, w/tongs and ice	262	393	525
Intercity Delivery, 18" long	100	175	225
International Agent Car, tin wind-up.	30	55	125
International Agent Car, lithographed tin, friction, 1950s	60	100	195

	C6	C8	C10
International Task Force Truck, w/soldiers	55	82	110
Invasion Force Truck	45	68	90
Jalopy Pickup Truck, tin wind-up, 7" long	80	120	160
Jeep, 11" long	100	150	200
Jeep and Trailer	108	162	225
Jet Speed Racer, battery-operated, with box	NPF	NPF	NPF
Joy-Rider, tin wind-up, college boy driver, 1929, 8" long	250	375	500
Jumpin' Jeep, tin wind-up, WWII-era, 6" long			
Kellogg's Express Stake Truck	80	120	160
King Racer, tin wind-up, 1930s, 8-1/2" long	500	800	1100
Landau, 6" long	38	58	75
Lazy-Day Dairy Farm Pick-up Truck, w/trailer, 22" long	115	172	230
Lazy-Day Farms Stake Truck, late, 18" long	65	98	130
Liberty Bus Co., 1930s	150	225	300
Lifesavers Truck, plastic, 9-1/2" long	75	100	150
Light Duty Climbing Tractor, tin wind-up, 1930s	162	243	325

Marx Hydraulic Dump. Photo from Continental Hobby House.

Marx Ice Truck, 1941. Photo from Terry Sells.

Marx International Agent Car, tin wind-up.

Marx Jet Speed Racer, battery-operated, with box. Photo from Continental Hobby House.

Marx Joy-Rider, 1929, College Boy driver, 8". Photo from Bill Bertoia Auctions.

Marx Lifesavers Truck, plastic, 9-1/2". Photo from Terry Sells.

Marx Lonesome Pine Trailer and Convertible Sedan, 1930s, 19".

Marx Magnetic Crane Truck, 1940s, 8-1/2". Photo from Bob Smith.

	C6	C8	C10
Limping Lizzie Car, tin wind-up	200	300	400
Livestock Truck	75	112	150
Loader Dump, 17" long	100	150	200
Loblaws Trailer Truck, late	132	198	265
Lone Eagle Oil Company Tank Truck, Bulldog Mack, wind-up, 12" long....................................	700	1100	1600
Lonesome Pine Trailer and Convertible Sedan, 1930s, 19" long...	360	540	720
Lowboy, 1953, 34" long....................	112	168	225
M.D. War Dept. Ambulance, 1930s..	650	975	1300
Machinery Moving Truck, No. 1016 .	90	175	300
Mack Dump Truck, tin wind-up, City Coal Co., 1930s 13" long	350	525	700
Mack Tank Truck...............................	250	375	500
Magic Barn, w/tractor	95	143	190

	C6	C8	C10
Magic Garage and Car, wind-up, garage, 1950s, 10" long, car: 7" long	85	128	170
Magnetic Crane, 17" long.................	100	150	275
Magnetic Crane Truck, 1940s, 8-1/2" long	425	640	850
Main Street, tin wind-up, 1929	263	395	525
Maintenance Truck, two ladders at each side of truck, c.1929, 6" long	30	45	60
Mammoth Truck Train, truck w/five trailers, No. T-50-12345, 1930s...	175	262	350
Marbrook Farms Sparkling Tractor and Trailer Set, tin wind-up, , 21" long...	75	112	150
Marco Oil Tanker, c.1940.................	150	225	300
Marcrest Livestock Semi, 20" long...	75	125	175
Marshall's Delivery Van, late............	100	150	200
Marx-A-Power Giant Bulldozer, battery-operated	68	102	135

	C6	C8	C10
Mayflower Van, 13" long	115	173	230
Meadow Brook Dairy, stake truck w/trailer	225	338	450
Meat Delivery Truck, plastic, 9-3/4" long	90	135	180
Mechanical Coupe, tin wind-up, c.1933, 8" long	275	400	575
Mechanical Gasoline Truck, wind-up	325	488	650
Mechanical Roadster, tin wind-up, 1950s, 11" long	100	150	200
Mechanical Sparkling Tank, late	35	52	70
Mechanical Speedway Racer, tin wind-up	125	188	250
Mechanical Station Wagon, tin wind-up	125	188	250
Mechanical Taxi Cab, tin wind-up, 1950s, 11" long	80	120	160
Mechanical Tractor, plastic and tin wind-up, 6" long	62	93	125
Mechanical Tractor, tin wind-up, 6" long, 1930s	110	165	220
Mechanical Tractor with Earth Grader, tin wind-up, 21-1/2" long	105	158	210
Mechanical Trailer Truck, wind-up ...	300	450	600
Merchants Transfer Truck, tin wind-up, 1929, 10" long........................	275	450	700
Mickey Mouse Dipsy Car, tin car, plastic Mickey, 1950s, 5-1/4" long	200	300	450
Mickey Mouse Motorcycle, Linemar, tin friction, 1950s, 3-1/2" long	300	475	700
Midget Climbing Fighting Tank, tin wind-up, c.1935, approx. 5-1/2" long	75	112	150
Midget Climbing Fighting Tank, third version, 195	60	90	120
Midget Climbing Tractor, tin wind-up, c.1950, 5-1/2" long................	60	90	120

	C6	C8	C10
Midget Racer, premier wind-up, No. 7...	100	150	200
Midget Racer, plastic wind-up, 1950s, 6" long.............................	50	75	100
Midget Special Race Car, tin wind-up, driver in old headgear and goggles, No. 2, 1930s, 5" long.....	100	150	200
Midget Special Race Car, driver in old headgear and goggles, No. 7 racer, tin wind-up, 1930s, 5" long	100	150	200
Midtown Service Center....................	200	300	400
Mighty Marx Jeep.............................	10	15	20
Military Power-Mite Bulldozer	45	68	90
Military Power-Mite Dump Truck......	45	68	90
Military Truck, mark "U.S. Mobile Guided Missile Squadron"	180	270	360

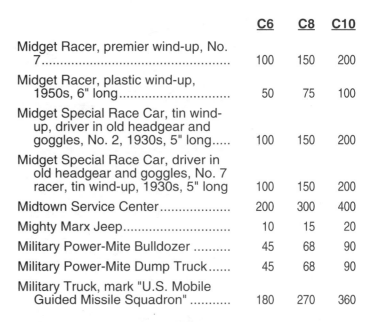

Marx Midget Climbing Fighting Tank, third version, 1951. Photo from Harvey K. Rainess.

Marx Mickey Mouse Dipsy Car, 1950s, 5-1/4". Photo from Don Hultzman.

Marx Midget Climbing Fighting Tank, 1930s, 5-1/2". Photo from K. Warren Mitchell.

Marx Midtown Service Center. Photo from Ron Fink.

Marx Midget Racer, No. 7, premier wind-up. Photo from Richard MacNary.

Marx Midget Special Racer, No. 2, driver in old headgear and goggles, 5". Photo from Richard MacNary.

	C6	C8	C10
Milk Truck, Studebaker-type	450	675	950
Milton Berle Car, tin wind-up, 1950s	200	325	475
Mobile Crane, c.1940	80	120	160
Model T Ford, plastic........................	40	60	80
Mortimer Snerd's Tricky Auto, tin wind-up, 1939	438	658	875
Moto-Fix Truck	80	120	160
Motor Market, 14" long....................	100	150	200
Motorcycle Policeman w/Sidecar, tin wind-up, marked "Police" and "3," license plate reads "102D," c.1940, approx. 8" long	200	325	450
Motorcycle Trooper, tin wind-up, 1935..	175	275	400

	C6	C8	C10
Moving Van, c.1940, 4-1/2" long	100	150	200
Mystery Car, tin wind-up, press down to operate	145	318	290
Mystery Police Cycle, 1930s, 4-1/2" long...	175	275	400
Mystery Taxi, press down to operate, 1930s...........................	100	150	275
Mystic Motorcycle, tin wind-up, 1930s..	75	112	150
Navy Jeep, No. 1078	65	97	130
Navy Jeep, w/searchlight trailer	100	150	200
Nevins Cut Rate Stores Stake Truck, 1940s...............................	75	125	225

	C6	C8	C10
New Flivver, tin wind-up, 1920s, 7" long	250	350	500
New Rocket Racer, 1930s, 16" long	200	300	450
Newberry's Box Van, 1950s, 12" long	125	200	275
Newberry's Semi Truck	125	200	300
North American Van Lines, wind-up, 14" long..........................	150	225	300

	C6	C8	C10
Nutty Mads Car (Drincar), battery-operated, three action, 1960s, 9-1/4" long	125	210	300
Old Jalopy, tin wind-up..................	128	192	255
Old Jalopy, tin wind-up, w/college boys, postwar	150	225	300
Old-Fashioned Antique Automobile, plastic	20	30	35

Marx Moving Van, circa 1940, 4-1/2". Photo from Richard MacNary.

Left to right: Marx Old Jalopy tin wind-up; Linemar Old Jalopy, smaller. Photo from Ed Hyers Antique Toys.

Marx New Flivver, 1920s, 7", tin wind-up. Photo from Bob Smith.

Marx Old-Fashioned Antique Automobile. Photo from Gary Linden.

Marx Newberry's Semi Truck. Photo from John Taylor.

Marx P.D. Motorcycle Cop, wind-up, siren, late 1930s, 8". Photo from Kent M. Comstock.

Mark Pepsi-Cola Truck, 10-1/2". Photo from Terry Sells.

Marx Pepsi-Cola Truck, plastic, 7". Photo from Terry Sells.

Marx Pet Shop Delivery, 1950s, 10".

Marx Pickup Truck, electric headlights, 11", with original box. Photo from Richard MacNary.

	C6	C8	C10
P.D Police Motorcycle w/Sidecar, tin wind-up, 1930s, 3-1/2" long	200	325	450
P.D. Motorcycle Cop, wind-up, siren, 8" long, late 1930	200	275	375
P.D. Motorcyclist, tin wind-up, approx. 4" long	150	225	325
Paddy Wagon, 5" long	150	225	300
Panel Truck, plastic, 8-1/4" long	NPF		
Panel Wagon	40	60	80
Parcel Post U.S. Mail, tin wind-up, early, 8-1/2" long	225	338	450
Pepsi-Cola Truck, 1945, 8" long	95	150	250
Pepsi-Cola Truck, 1950s, 11" long	50	125	200
Pepsi-Cola Truck, plastic, 1950s, 7" long	100	150	200
Pepsi-Cola Truck, plastic, 10-1/2" long	175	250	375
Pepsi-Cola Truck, plastic, 7" long	145	215	290
Pet Shop Delivery, 1950s, 10" long	55	82	110
Peter Rabbit Eccentric Car, tin wind-up	145	225	325
Pickup Truck, marked "Package Service," electric headlights, c.1941, 11" long	100	175	225
Pickup Truck, marked "Package Service," w/box and load, electric headlights, c.1941, 11" long	125	225	325

	C6	C8	C10
Pickup Truck, 1968, 6" long	12	18	25
Pinched, tin wind-up, c.1927	450	700	1000
Polar Ice Truck, steel, 14" long	75	150	225
Police Car, 1954, Chevy	NPF	NPF	NPF
Police Patrol motorcycle w/Sidecar, tin wind-up, 1935	150	225	300
Police Siren Motorcycle, tin wind-up, 1930s, 8" long	175	275	400
Police Squad Sidecar, wind-up, yellow, 8" long	200	325	450
Pontiac, friction, 1954, 10" long	30	45	60
Popeye Dippy Dumper Truck	450	675	900
Popeye Transit Co. Trailer Truck	550	825	1200
Power Caterpillar Climbing Tractor, tin wind-up	125	188	250
Power Grader, No. 1759, black or white wheels, 17-1/2" long	35	52	70
Power House Dump Truck, late, 25" long	50	75	100
Power Shovel, c.1964	90	135	180

	C6	C8	C10
Power Snap Caterpillar Climbing Tractor, tin wind-up, 1950s, 8" long	80	120	160
Powerhouse Dump Truck	250	375	500
Precinct Police Patrol Armored Truck, tin wind-up, circa early 1930s, 10-1/2" long	2000	3000	4000
Pure Milk Dairy Truck, w/glass bottles, pressed steel, tin wheels, c.1940	125	225	350
Racer, No. 3, tin wind-up, 1930s, 5" long	75	112	150
Racer, No. 3, plastic wind-up	162	243	325
Racer, tin wind-up, No. 4, 1930s, 5" long	75	112	150
Racer, tin wind-up, No. 5, 1930s, 5" long	75	112	150

	C6	C8	C10
Racer, tin wind-up, No. 7, 1930s, 5" long	75	112	150
Racer, No. 8, nickel-plated	100	150	200
Racer, tin wind-up, sedan-like, No. 4, 1942	88	132	175
Racer, No. 2, tin wind-up, 1930s, 5" long	75	112	150
Racer, tin wind-up, No. 2, 1930s 13" long	100	150	200
Racing Car, tin wind-up, w/two-man team, marked "12," c.1940	150	200	250
Racing Car, wind-up, marked "61," 1930s, 6" long	90	135	180
Racing Car, wind-up, lithographed, plastic driver, marked "27," c.1950	150	225	300
Racing Car, wind-up, lithographed, w/plastic driver, marked "12," 1950s	300	450	600
Racing Car, marked "21," early, 7" long	175	263	350

Marx Racer, No. 3, 1930s, 5". Photo from Richard MacNary.

Marx Racer, No. 7, tin wind-up, 5". Photo from Richard MacNary.

Marx Racer, 1930s, tin wind-up, 5". Photo from Richard MacNary.

Marx Racer, No. 8, nickel-plated. Photo from Perry Eichor.

Marx Racer, No. 4, 1942, sedan-like. Photo from Richard MacNary.

Marx RCA Panel Truck, 1950s, with original box, 8".
Photo from John Taylor.

Marx Rex Race Car, 1920s, tin wind-up. Photo from
Thomas G. Nefos.

	C6	C8	C10
Rapid Express Truck, wind-up, 9" long..................................	125	175	225
RCA Panel Truck, w/accessories, 1950s, 8" long............................	100	135	185
REA Express Truck, No. 1021	325	488	650
Reads Drugstore Stake Truck, plastic cab, 14-1/2" long..............	75	125	175
Reads Drugstore Stake Truck, c.1940, 14" long	162	243	325
Reversible Coupe, tin wind-up, marked "The Marvel Car," c.1938	275	415	550
Reversing Road Roller, tin wind-up..	125	188	250

Marx Road Grader, 17".

Marx Roy Rogers Horse Trailer. Photo from Harvey K.
Rainess.

	C6	C8	C10
Reversing Tank, tin wind-up, 1930s.	65	98	130
Rex Mars Planet Patrol, tin wind-up, 1950s, 9-1/2" long........................	212	318	425
Rex Race Car, tin wind-up, 1920s ...	162	244	325
Ridem Fire Truck, 30" long	162	243	325
Road Grader, heavy-duty, 17" long..	37	56	75
Road Roller, has driver, tin wind-up, c.1930, 8-1/2" long.......................	125	188	250
Roadside Rest, four pumps, car, garage, 1930	450	700	1000
Rocker Dump, No. 1752, 17-1/2" long..	110	165	220
Rocket Racer, tin wind-up, 1930s	350	425	625
Rookie Cop, w/siren, 1930s, 8-1/2" long, tin wind-up	232	348	465
Rookie Cop, wind-up, yellow, c.1950, 8" long.............................	188	282	375
Roy Rogers Horse Trailer, w/Jeep...	245	475	600
Roy Rogers Horse Trailer	225	450	550
Royal Bus Line, tin wind-up, 10" long..	100	150	200
Royal Coupe, 1920s, 9" long	375	563	750
Royal Oil Company Truck, Mack, 9" long..	400	600	800
Royal Van Co., tin wind-up, reads "We Haul Anywhere," 9" long	350	525	700
Sabre Car...	87	132	175
Safe Driving School - see Driver Training Car.................................			

	C6	C8	C10
Salerno Cookies and Crackers Truck	125	175	225
Salerno Cookies - Crackers Dodge Cab, 1950s, 11"	125	175	225
Sand & Gravel Truck, w/scoop, 16" long	70	105	140
Sand and Gravel Dump Truck, 21" long	115	172	230
Sand and Gravel Dump Truck, late 1940s, 11" long	75	125	175
Sand and Gravel DumpTruck, 10" long, 1940s	50	75	125
Sand and Gravel Truck, tin wind-up, "reads Builders Supply Co.," 1920	100	150	200
Sand Loader	60	90	120
Sand Mechanical Dump Truck, c.1939, 9" long	45	68	90
Scenic Bus, plastic, 10" long	40	60	80
School Bus, 12" long	35	52	70
Scoop Dump, postwar, 20" long	138	206	275
Searchlight Truck, c.1941, 9" long	150	225	325
Secret Agent Car	110	165	220

	C6	C8	C10
Sedan, c.1937, 4" long	50	95	140
Sedan, c.1940, 4-1/2" long	50	95	140
Service Station, 1929	262	393	525
Sheriff Sam and His Whoopee Car, tin wind-up, 1950s, 6" long	180	270	360
Shop-Rite Tractor/Trailer, late	50	75	125
Side Dump Truck, four-color, No. T-475, c.1940	60	90	120
Signal Corps Truck, plastic	50	75	95
Silver Streak Racer, plastic wind-up, 6" long	70	105	140
Sinclair Truck, steel	200	325	475
Single Track Speedway, wind-up car, eight track sections, 1938, 4" long	60	90	120
Siren Fire Chief, reads "F.D. 1st Batt.," c.1930, 15" long	375	550	750

Marx Searchlight Truck, 1941, 9". Photo from John Taylor.

Marx Royal Van Co. 9".

Marx Salerno Cookies-Crackers, Dodge cab, 1950s, 11". Photo from John Taylor.

Marx Siren Sparkling Fire Engine, 9" friction, 1930s. Photo from John Taylor.

Marx Sparkling Climbing Fighting Tank, cannon recoils, 10". Photo from Bill Holt.

Marx Speed Boy, 9-1/2" motorcycle. Photo from Kent M. Comstock.

Marx Sparkling Climbing Tractor, 8-1/2" tin wind-up. Photo from Continental Hobby House.

Marx Speed Cop, two 4" tin wind-up cars, track, 1930s.

	C6	C8	C10
Siren Police Car, 1930s	215	322	430
Siren Police Patrol, 1930s, 15" long.	375	550	750
Siren Sparkling Fire Engine, friction, 1930s, 9" long	125	225	350
Snappy Gus Car	500	750	1050
Sparkling Climbing Fighting Tank, tin wind-up, cannon recoils	138	206	275
Sparkling Climbing Tank, 1939	140	210	280
Sparkling Climbing Tractor, tin wind-up, 8-1/2" long	62	93	125
Sparkling Climbing Tractor, tin wind-up, 1940s	150	225	300
Sparkling Climbing Tractor and Trailer, tin wind-up, 16" long	55	82	110
Sparkling Doughboy Tank	175	263	350

	C6	C8	C10
Sparkling Heavy Duty Bulldog Tractor w/Road Scraper, tin wind-up, 11" long	125	188	250
Sparkling Hot Rod Racer, plastic wind-up, 1950s, 8" long	37	56	75
Sparkling Jet Futuristic Car, friction motor, 10" long	87	132	175
Sparkling Soldier Motorcycle, tin wind-up, c.1940	250	375	500
Sparkling Super Power Tank, tin wind-up, 9-1/2" long	110	165	220
Sparkling Tank, tin wind-up, 4" long.	55	82	110
Sparkling Tank, tin wind-up, prewar, 9" long	120	180	240
Sparkling Tractor, tin wind-up, tractor w/plow blade, 1939	140	210	280
Sparkling Turn Over Tank, tin wind-up	40	60	80
Speed Boy 4 Motorcycle, wind-up, 9-1/2" long	250	375	550

	C6	C8	C10
...ery Delivery Motorcycle, tin ...s, 9-3/4" long	262	393	525
...od Boy Delivery Motorcycle, tin wind-up, battery lights, 1930s, 9-3/4" long	250	425	625
Speed Cop, includes two tin wind-up cars and track, 1930s, cars: 4" long	175	275	795
Speedway Bus, plastic wind-up, 4" long	25	38	50
Speedway Coupe, plastic wind-up, 4" long	250	375	500
Speedway Jeep	25	38	50
Sports Coupe, 1930s, 15" long	200	300	400
Stake, wind-up, 4-1/2" long	75	130	175
Stake Truck, No. 1008	60	90	120
Stake Truck, c.1940, 14" long	50	95	140
Stake Truck, c.1940, 4-1/2" long......	50	95	140
Stake Truck, c.1941, 6" long	60	135	195
Stake Truck, c.1939, 20" long	100	150	200
Stake Truck, three-color, No. E-271, c.1940	100	150	200
Stake Truck, two-color, 1930s, 12" long	65	98	130
Streamline Convertible, friction	138	207	275

	C6	C8	C10
Streamline Speedway, tin figure-eight track, two wind-up cars, 1938, 31" long............................	140	210	280
Streamlined Coupe, tin wind-up	110	165	220
Streamlined Coupe, steel, hardtop, no windshield supports, c.1937, 6" long............................	180	270	360
Studebaker Dump, 1950s	110	165	220
Studebaker Shovel Truck................	125	188	250
Studebaker Stake Truck, 1950s.......	100	150	200
Stutz, 11" long............................	650	1050	1450
Stutz Electric Car, tin wind-up, w/driver, 1930, 36" long	225	338	450
Sunnyside Service Station, 1930s, complete	400	600	800
Sunshine Fruit Growers Semi, wind-up, 14" long	175	250	325
Super Hi-Way Service Wrecker	42	63	85
Super Hot Rod 777	150	225	300
Super Roadster, plastic..................	NPF	NPF	NPF
Super Service Center......................	175	263	350
Super Streamline Racer, tin wind-up, 1950s, 17" long....................	120	180	240
Superman Rollover Tank, 1940s, 4" long............................	400	600	800
Superman Tank, battery-operated, three actions, 1950s, Linemar Co., 10-1/4" long......................	500	750	1000
Superman Tank, Linemar, 4" long ...	500	800	1100
Take-Apart Jaguar, 1950s	115	172	230
Tank, plastic and metal wind-up, 392-U.S. Tank Division................	22	33	45
Tank, tin wind-up, No. 3, two machine guns or cannon on top of roof (no turret)........................	80	120	160

Marx Stake Truck, 4-1/2". Photo from Richard MacNary.

Marx Sunny Side Service Station, 1930s, complete. Photo from Don Hultzman.

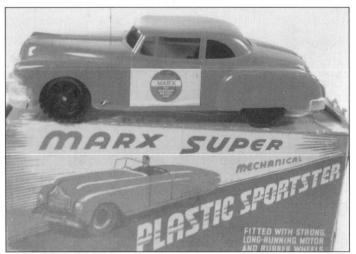

Marx Super Roadster, plastic. Photo from Continental Hobby House.

Marx Tip Over Motorcycle, 1930s, 8". Photo from Bob Smith.

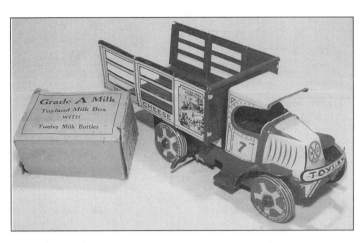

Marx Toyland Farm Products Truck, 1931, 10-1/2".
Photo from Bob Smith.

Marx Tri-City Express Truck. Photo from John Taylor.

Marx Toy Town Express Van Lines Deluxe Service Truck. Photo from Ron Chonjnacki.

	C6	C8	C10
Tank, late, machine gun on top of turret	55	82	110
Tank, wind-up, marked "U.S. Tank Co. No. 4," 1931, 5-1/4" long	60	90	120
Tank, wind-up, No. 4, marked "U.S. Army"	100	150	200
Tank, tin, sparkles, friction, 1940, 3-1/2" long	20	30	40
Tank 392-U.S. Tank Division, battery-operated, three actions, 1950s 9-1/2" long	60	90	120
Tank Truck, scarce, 6" long	85	160	220
Tank Truck, c.1940, scarce, 4-1/2" long	75	100	150
Taxi Hauler, two cabs, c.1940	150	225	300
Telephone Repair Unit, thirty pieces	275	415	550
Telephone Truck, plastic, 11" long	50	75	125
Thimble-Drome Racer No. 1, plastic wind-up, 6" long	35	52	70

	C6	C8	C10
Thrifty Stores State Truck, c.1940	160	240	320
Tip Over Motorcycle, tin wind-up, c.1933, 8" long	225	375	500
Tow Truck, c.1941, 11" long	100	175	250
Toy Town Express Van Lines Deluxe Service Truck	100	150	250
Toyland Dairy	135	202	270
Toyland Farm Products Truck, tin wind-up, w/twelve wooden bottles, 10-1/2" long, c.1931	500	675	1000
Track and Trailer Set, wind-up, 1930s, similar to climbing tractor set, but w/rounded and radiator front and copper finish metal. Tin plow attaches to front, silver metal trailer attaches to rear; has tin, copper finish and "balloon" tires	160	240	320
Track and Trailer Set, no balloon tires	125	188	250
Tractor, tin wind-up, early 1940s	50	75	100
Tractor, plastic	20	30	40
Tractor, tin wind-up, 1920s	60	90	120
Tractor and Trailer, tin wind-up, 16-1/2" long	95	138	190
Tractor Service, tractor, cardboard garage box, three pieces of farm equipment, 1940s	225	338	450
Tri-City Express Truck	150	225	300
Tricky Motorcycle, non-fail action w/wind-up, 1930s, 4-1/4" long	90	135	180

	C6	C8	C10
Tricky Taxi, tin wind-up, 1940s, 4-1/2" long	78	117	155
Tricky Taxi, friction, 4-1/2" long	60	90	120
Tricky Tommy Big Brain Tractor, battery-operated	62	93	125
Truck w/Trailer, c.1940, 19" overall	88	132	175
Trucking Terminal	90	135	180
Turn Over Tank, tin wind-up, No. 8	70	105	140
U.S. Air Force Radio Jeep, w/driver and rider	138	207	275
U.S. Air Force Searchlight Truck	88	132	175
U.S. Air Force Truck, cloth top	92	138	185
U.S. Army Seachlight Trailer	30	45	60
U.S. Army Troop Transport, plastic, 6" long	15	22	30

	C6	C8	C10
U.S. Army Truck, plastic, 6-1/2" long	12	18	25
U.S. Army Truck, cloth top, late	72	108	145
U.S. Army Truck, Mack, wind-up, cloth cover, 1920s, 10" long	90	135	180
U.S. Army Truck, late, canvas cover, plastic cab	60	90	120
U.S. Army Truck, w/horns, cloth top, 18-1/2" long	80	120	160
U.S. Army Truck, 4-1/2" long, c.1940	100	150	200
U.S. Mail Truck, 14" long	100	150	200
U.S. Mail Truck, tin wind-up, 9-1/2" long	250	350	475
U.S. Mail Truck, 12-1/2" long	45	68	90
U.S. Mail Truck, late, 24" long	200	300	400
U.S. Navy Jeep, w/seachlight, 23" long	138	205	275
U.S.A. Mobile Artillery Truck	55	80	115
Uncle Wiggily Crazy Car, tin wind-up	500	800	1100
United Van Lines Semi, wind-up, 14" long	175	250	325
Univeral Gas Service Station, 1940s, 6-1/2" high, base 12" long	138	208	275
Universal Bus Terminal, 12" long	95	142	190
Untouchables Rolls Royce, tin friction, 5-1/4" long	42	63	85

Marx made several Tricky Taxis.

Marx Turnover Tank. Photo from Max Heiss.

Marx U.S. Army Truck, plastic, 6-1/2". Photo from Ron Fink.

Marx U.S. Army Troop Transport, plastic, 6". Photo from Ron Fink.

Marx U.S. Army Truck, with horns, cloth top, 18-1/2". Photo from Joe and Sharon Freed.

Marx U.S. Army Truck, 4-1/2". Photo from Richard Mac-Nary.

Marx U.S. Mail Truck, 9-1/2". Photo from Phillips.

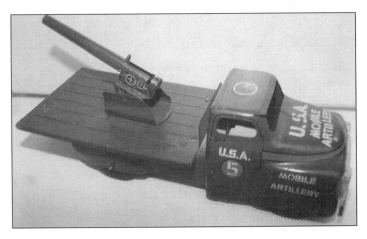

Marx U.S.A. Mobile Artillery Truck. Photo from Bill Holt.

Marx Utility Service Truck, with trailer, linemen, 1950s. Photo from John Taylor.

Marx Walgreen's Ice Cream Trailer Truck, 21". Photo from John Taylor.

Marx Whoopee Car, laughing cows on wheels, driver looks like cowboy. Photo from Bill Bertoia Auctions.

	C6	C8	C10
Untouchables Touring Car, tin friction	35	52	70
UPS Truck, plastic, 10" long	75	125	175
Utility Service Truck, w/trailer	175	325	475
Wacky Taxi, tin wind-up	75	112	150
Walgreen's Ice Cream Trailer Truck, 21" long, rare	175	350	425

	C6	C8	C10
Walt Disney Television Car, 1950s, 7-1/2" long	225	325	500
War Tank, tin wind-up, 5-1/4" long	68	102	135
Wars Service Station	138	205	275
Western Auto Truck, 25" long	60	90	120
Whoopee Car, tin wind-up, laughing cows on wheels, driver looks like cowboy, 1929	250	400	575
Whoopee Car, tin wind-up, marked "Yale-Princeton" pennants on wheels	225	338	450
Whoopee Car with Flappers, tin wind-up, 7-1/2" long	100	150	200
Willys Jeep, w/lights, horn	90	135	180
Willys Jeep, steel, hood opens, windshield folds down, c.1940, 12" long	60	90	120

Marx Whoopee Car, Yale-Princeton pennants, with original box. Photo from Bill Bertoia Auctions.

Marx Willys steel Jeep, hood opens, windshield folds down, 12". Photo from Richard Jensen.

Marx Woolworth's Trailer Truck, 1960s. Photo from John Taylor.

Left to right: Marx Wrecker, 4-1/2"; Sedan, 4-1/2". Photo from Richard MacNary.

Marx Linemar Air Defence Pom-Pom Gun, battery-operated, 14". Photo from Don Hultzman.

	C6	C8	C10
Willys Jeep and Trailer, 22" long......	100	150	200
Willys Jeepster, plastic wind-up	75	112	150
Willys Tow Jeep, c.1940	100	150	195
Woodie Sedan, tin lithographed wind-up, 6-3/4" long	48	72	95
Woodie Sedan, tin lithographed wind-up, 11" long	100	150	200
Woolworth's Trailer Truck, 1960s.....	200	375	450
Wreckage Service Truck, tin, battery lights	75	112	150
Wrecker, plastic..............................	20	30	40
Wrecker, Studebaker, 7" long	75	1335	195
Wrecker, No. T-16, 1930s	150	225	300
Wrecker, 10" long, 1920s.................	100	150	200
Wrecker, 6" long, c.1940..................	60	135	195
Wrecker, c.1940, 4-1/2" long............	50	95	140

	C6	C8	C10
Wrecker, c.1941, 4" long..................	50	95	140
Yellow Cab, tin wind-up, marked "LMN 52," 1940s, 6-1/2" long	162	245	325
Yellow Cab, first Marx plastic car, 4" long. Original has "MADE IN U.S.A." under roof. (1990s reissue has Marx emblem)	27	41	55

Linemar

	C6	C8	C10
Air Defense Pom-Pom Gun, battery-operated, five action, 14" long	120	180	240
Army Pickup Truck, tin friction, 6-1/2" long....................................	35	52	70
Army Searchlight Truck....................	100	150	200
Army Stake Truck, tin, friction, 7" long..	35	52	70
Donald Duck Convertible, tin friction, 1950s, 5" long.................	250	350	500

	C6	C8	C10
Donald Duck Crazy Car, wind-up, 1950s, 5-1/2" long......................	275	363	550
Donald Duck Dipsy Car, wind-up, 1950s, 6" long	350	525	750
Donald Duck Disney Flivver, 1950s, 5-1/2" long..........................	250	375	550
Donald Duck Dump Truck, 1950s, 5" long	250	375	550
Donald Duck Fire Chief Crazy Car, tin wind-up, rubber hat	750	1300	1700
Donald Duck In His Convertible, friction, 1950s, 6" long	225	350	525
Ferris Wheel Truck, battery-operated, four actions, 11" long ..	140	210	280

Marx Linemar Army Pickup Truck, tin friction, 6-1/2". Photo from Ron Fink.

Marx Linemar Army Stake Truck, tin, friction, 7". Photo from Ron Fink.

Marx Linemar Donald Duck Dipsy Car, 1950s, 5-1/4", tin wind-up. Photo from Don Hultzman.

	C6	C8	C10
Friction Car, 8-1/2" long	30	45	60
Mercedes Racer, 9" long..................	138	208	275
Military Police Car, battery-operated, six actions, 1950s, 8-1/2" long	90	135	180
NAR Television Truck, battery-operated, four actions, included six film strip inserts, 1950s, 12" long..	280	420	560
NBC Television Truck, battery-operated, five actions, 1950s, 9" long	240	360	480
Nutty Mad Car, friction, c.1965, 4" long...................................	70	105	150
Old Jalopy, tin wind-up, small, 1950s................................	48	72	95
Police Car, 1954 Chevy, 7-1/2" friction	60	90	120
Searchlight Truck, Studebaker.........	90	135	180
Stake Truck, friction, 15-1/2" long....	108	162	215
Steerlab Tank, battery-operated, five actions, 1950s, 9" long.........	50	75	100
Taxy Yellow Cab, battery-operated, five actions, 7-1/2" long	60	90	120
Television Truck, three actions, battery-operated, 1950s, 11" long	200	300	400

Lumar

	C6	C8	C10
Aerial Ladder Truck...........................	118	177	235
Allied Van Lines	50	100	175
Army Truck......................................	80	120	160
Army Truck and Electric Searchlight Trailer	100	150	200

Marx Linemar Nutty Mad Car, battery-operated, 1965, 4". Photo from Don Hultzman.

Marx Lumar Contractors Dump Truck, 17". Photo from Continental Hobby House.

Marx Lumar Inter-city Delivery Service, 1950s, 16-1/2". Photo from John Taylor.

Marx Lumar Emergency Searchlight Unit, 1950s, 19". Photo from John Taylor.

Marx Lumar Utility Truck, with tools. Photo from Continental Hobby House.

	C6	C8	C10
Auto Transport, 28" long	145	218	290
Carry All Low Boy	32	48	65
Contractors Crane	65	98	130
Contractor's Dump, No. 1084, 21" long	100	150	200
Contractors Dump Truck, No. 962, approx. 17" long	110	150	220
Contractors Steam Shovel	70	105	140
Dairy Truck	75	100	175
Dump, 22" long	85	128	170
Dump Truck	100	150	200
Emergency Searchlight Unit, tin lithographed, 19" long	175	300	425
Emergency Searchlight Unit Truck, 18" long	175	300	425
Hi-Lift Loader	90	135	275
Hook and Ladder, 33" long	212	318	425
Hydraulic Dump	75	112	150
Inter-city Delivery Service Truck, 16-1/2" long	100	175	225
Jeep and Trailer	112	168	228
Police Car, battery-operated, 1954 Chevy	68	102	135
Power Grader	52	78	105
Rocker Dump, 18" long	60	90	120

Marx Lumar Van Lines, straight body. Photo from Bob Smith.

	C6	C8	C10
Rocket Truck	77	108	155
Scoop-A-Dump	140	210	280
Searchlight Truck, 19" long	138	208	275
Shop-Rite Trailer Truck, 1970s, 24" long	27	41	55
Stake Truck, 14" long	60	90	120
Steam Shovel	75	112	150
Telephone Service Truck	120	180	240

	C6	C8	C10
U.S. Army Truck, cloth top, 18-1/2" long	75	112	150
Utility Truck, w/tools	200	300	400
Van Lines, straight body	175	275	400
Van Lines Trailer Truck, 17" long	175	235	350
Willys Jeep	75	112	150
Wrecker Service Truck, 1950s, 22" long, rare	150	200	300

Marx Lumar Wrecker Service, 1950s, 22". Photo from John Taylor.

MATCHBOX

Matchbox Toys grew out of a company begun in 1947 by two Navy friends, Leslie Smith and Rodney Smith (no relation). Manufacturing toys was not even planned at this point. On June 19, 1947, the two partners combined portions of their first names, and the name Lesney was born. In 1948, Lesney Products produced their first toy, a 4 1/2-inch Aveling Barford Road Roller. Encouraged by the brisk sales, three other toys were produced that year—a 4 1/2-inch Caterpillar Bulldozer, a 3 1/8-inch Caterpillar Tractor, and a 3 3/4-inch Cement Mixer. Value on these rare early Lesney toys today is near $1,000. It was decided to package the toys in a matchbox-type box, and thereafter the toys would be known as "Matchbox."

These small vehicles quickly became very popular, and all other toy lines were discontinued. These first small vehicles had metal wheels, but these were quickly changed to plastic. These type wheels are now known to collectors as "regular" wheels, no to be confused with the "Superfast" wheels that were introduced in 1969. It is not uncommon to find slight color and style variations for the same vehicle. These variations were often due to paint or part shortages, and these variations are now highly sought-after by collectors. The year 1956 saw the introduction of the "Models of Yesteryear" line. The king-size line was first developed and marketed in 1957 and was known as Major Packs. Matchbox toys were first marketed in the United States in 1958; by the early 1960s, they became a household standard. 1993 marked the 40th anniversary of Matchbox toys, and these small vehicles are rapidly gaining popularity and value among collectors. Listed are all of the basic models and some important variations.

Prices are for Mint in Box, since that is how most collectible Matchboxes are sold.

Contributor: Reid Covey, Box 2D Highmarket Rd., Constableville, NY, 13325, e-mail: sullivan@northnet.org.

	C6	C8	C10
No. 01 Aveling Barford Road Roller, 1964	n/a	n/a	28
No. 01 Diesel Road Roller, 1953	n/a	n/a	195
No. 01 Dodge Challenger, 1976	n/a	n/a	15
No. 01 Mercedes Benz Lorry, 1968	n/a	n/a	17
No. 01 Mod Rod, 1971	n/a	n/a	13
No. 02 Dumper, 1953	n/a	n/a	110
No. 02 Hot Rod Jeep, 1971	n/a	n/a	13
No. 02 Mercedes Trailer, 1968	n/a	n/a	14
No. 02 Muir-Hill Dumper, 1962	n/a	n/a	22
No. 03 Bedford Ton Tipper, 1961	n/a	n/a	82
No. 03 Cement Mixer, 1953	n/a	n/a	55
No. 03 Mercedes-Benz Ambulance, 1968	n/a	n/a	20
No. 03 Monteverdi Hai, 1973	n/a	n/a	12

	C6	C8	C10
No. 03 Porsche Turbo, 1978	n/a	n/a	15
No. 04 '57 Chevy, 1981	n/a	n/a	6
No. 04 Gruesome Twosome, 1971	n/a	n/a	7
No. 04 Pontiac Firebird, 1976	n/a	n/a	7
No. 04 Stake Truck, 1967	n/a	n/a	35
No. 04 Tractor, 1954	n/a	n/a	125
No. 04 Triumph Motorcycle and sidecar, 1959	n/a	n/a	100
No. 05 London Bus, 1954	n/a	n/a	40
No. 05 Lotus Europea Sports Car, 1969	n/a	n/a	17
No. 05 Seafire, 1976	n/a	n/a	6
No. 05 U.S. Mail Truck, 1981	n/a	n/a	12
No. 06 Euclid Ten-wheel Quarry, 1964	n/a	n/a	55
No. 06 Ford Pick-up, 1969	n/a	n/a	19

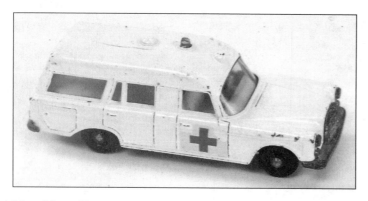

Matchbox Mercedes-Benz Ambulance, No. 3, 1968.

Matchbox Merryweather Marquis Fire Engine, No. 9, 1959. Photo from Gary Linden.

Matchbox Land Rover, No. 12, 1953. Photo from Gary Linden.

	C6	C8	C10
No. 06 Mercedes Tourer, 1974	n/a	n/a	11
No. 06 Quarry Truck, 1955..............	n/a	n/a	100
No. 07 Ford Anglia, 1961	n/a	n/a	27
No. 07 Ford Refuse Truck, 1967......	n/a	n/a	17
No. 07 Hairy Hustler, 1971...............	n/a	n/a	13
No. 07 VW Golf, 1976	n/a	n/a	5
No. 08 Caterpillar Tractor, 1955.......	n/a	n/a	150
No. 08 De Tomaso Pantera, 1975 ...	n/a	n/a	8
No. 08 Ford Mustang Fastback, 1966..	n/a	n/a	28
No. 08 Wildcat Dragster, 1971	n/a	n/a	17
No. 09 Boat & Trailer, 1967..............	n/a	n/a	17
No. 09 Dennis Fire Engine, 1955.....	n/a	n/a	110
No. 09 Ford Escort RS200, 1978.....	n/a	n/a	8
No. 09 Javelin, 1972	n/a	n/a	11
No. 09 Merryweather Marquis Fire Engine, 1959............................	n/a	n/a	39

	C6	C8	C10
No. 10 Mechanical Horse and Trailer, 1955	n/a	n/a	122
No. 10 Pipe Truck, 1967	n/a	n/a	17
No. 10 Piston Popper, 1973.............	n/a	n/a	18
No. 10 Plymouth 'Gran Fury' Police Car, 1980..................................	n/a	n/a	10
No. 10 Sugar Container Truck, 1961	n/a	n/a	93
No. 11 Car Transporter, 1977	n/a	n/a	10
No. 11 Flying Bug, 1972	n/a	n/a	16
No. 11 Jumbo Crane (Taylor), 1964	n/a	n/a	22
No. 11 Petrol Tanker (Esso decal), 1955..	n/a	n/a	103
No. 11 Scaffolding Truck (Mercedes), 1969	n/a	n/a	17
No. 12 Big Bull, 1975	n/a	n/a	8
No. 12 Citroen CX, 1981	n/a	n/a	8
No. 12 Land Rover, 1953.................	n/a	n/a	22
No. 12 Safari Land Rover, 1965	n/a	n/a	36
No. 12 Setra Coach, 1971	n/a	n/a	11
No. 13 Baja Buggy, 1971	n/a	n/a	14
No. 13 Bedford Wreck Truck, 1955..	n/a	n/a	85
No. 13 Dodge Wreck Truck (BP Label), 1961...............................	n/a	n/a	33
No. 13 Snorkel Fire Engine, 1977....	n/a	n/a	6
No. 13 Thames Wreck Truck (MB Garages), 1959..........................	n/a	n/a	103
No. 14 Bedford Lomas Ambulance, 1962..	n/a	n/a	22

	C6	C8	C10
No. 14 Daimler Ambulance, 1955	n/a	n/a	93
No. 14 Grifo Sports Car, 1968..........	n/a	n/a	17
No. 14 Mini Ha Ha, 1975..................	n/a	n/a	10
No. 15 Dennis Refuse Truck, 1963..	n/a	n/a	50
No. 15 Fork Lift Truck, 1972.............	n/a	n/a	11
No. 15 Prime Mover, 1955	n/a	n/a	55
No. 15 Volkswagen 1500 Saloon, 1968...	n/a	n/a	25
No. 16 Badger, 1974	n/a	n/a	11
No. 16 Case Tractor Bulldozer, 1969	n/a	n/a	33
No. 16 Low-Loading Trailer, eight wheels, 1955..............................	n/a	n/a	55
No. 16 Low-Loading Trailer, six wheels, 1955..............................	n/a	n/a	57

	C6	C8	C10
No. 16 Pontiac, 1981	n/a	n/a	3
No. 16 Scammel Mountaineer Dump with Plow, 1961	n/a	n/a	31
No. 17 18-Wheel Tipper Hoveringham, 1964	n/a	n/a	22
No. 17 Austin Taxi, 1960..................	n/a	n/a	99
No. 17 Bedford Removal Van, 1955	n/a	n/a	137
No. 17 Horse Box Ergomatic Cab, 1969...	n/a	n/a	17
No. 17 Londoner, 1973	n/a	n/a	13
No. 18 Caterpillar Bulldozer, 1955 ...	n/a	n/a	66
No. 18 Field Car, 1969	n/a	n/a	17
No. 18 Hondarora, 1975	n/a	n/a	10
No. 19 Aston-Martin F.I., 1961	n/a	n/a	93
No. 19 Cement Truck, 1976.............	n/a	n/a	10
No. 19 Lotus Racing Car, 1965........	n/a	n/a	17
No. 19 MG Midget Sports Car, 1955	n/a	n/a	104
No. 19 MGC Sports Car, 1959.........	n/a	n/a	33
No. 19 Road Dragster, 1971	n/a	n/a	11
No. 20 E.R.F. Lorry Truck, 1955	n/a	n/a	88
No. 20 Lamborghini Marzel, 1969....	n/a	n/a	11
No. 20 Police Patrol, 1975	n/a	n/a	8
No. 20 Taxi Cab (Chevrolet Impala), 1965...	n/a	n/a	25
No. 21 Commer Milk Truck, 1961	n/a	n/a	25
No. 21 Foden Concrete Truck, 1969	n/a	n/a	17
No. 21 Long Distance Coach London To Glasgow, 1955	n/a	n/a	104
No. 21 Rod Roller, 1973	n/a	n/a	10
No. 22 Blaze Buster, 1975	n/a	n/a	10

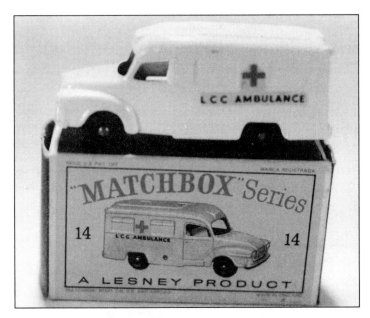

Matchbox Bedford Lomas Ambulance, No. 14, 1962. Photo from Gary Linden.

Matchbox Dennis Refuse Truck, No. 15, 1963.

Matchbox MG Midget Sports Car, No. 19, 1955. Photo from Gary Linden.

Matchbox B.P. Tanker, No. 25, 1960.

Matchbox Bedford Compressor Truck, No. 28, 1956. Photo from Gary Linden.

Matchbox Bedford Dunlop Van, No. 25, 1956. Photo from Gary Linden.

	C6	C8	C10
No. 22 Freeman Inter City Commuter, 1970	n/a	n/a	12
No. 22 Pontiac 'Grand Prix' Sports Coupe, 1964	n/a	n/a	30
No. 22 Vauxhall Cresta, 1955	n/a	n/a	66
No. 23 Atlas, 1975	n/a	n/a	8
No. 23 Caravan Trailer, 1956	n/a	n/a	17
No. 23 House Trailer Caravan, 1967	n/a	n/a	30
No. 23 Volkswagen Camper, 1970	n/a	n/a	17
No. 24 Diesel Shunter, 1979	n/a	n/a	8
No. 24 Excavator, 1956	n/a	n/a	30
No. 24 Rolls Royce Silver Shadow, 1967	n/a	n/a	17
No. 24 Team Matchbox, 1973	n/a	n/a	11

	C6	C8	C10
No. 25 B.P. Tanker, 1960	n/a	n/a	20
No. 25 Bedford 'Dunlop' Van, 1956	n/a	n/a	66
No. 25 Flat Car & Container, 1979	n/a	n/a	5
No. 25 Ford Cortina G.T., 1968	n/a	n/a	17
No. 25 Mod Tractor, 1972	n/a	n/a	12
No. 25 Volkswagen 1200 Sedan, 1958	n/a	n/a	110
No. 26 Big Banger, 1972	n/a	n/a	11
No. 26 G.M.C. Tipper Truck, 1968	n/a	n/a	20
No. 26 Ready Mix Concrete Truck, 1956	n/a	n/a	55
No. 26 Site Dumper, 1976	n/a	n/a	8
No. 27 Bedford Low Loader, 1956	n/a	n/a	93
No. 27 Cadillac Sedan, 1960	n/a	n/a	104
No. 27 Lamborghini Countach, 1974	n/a	n/a	10
No. 27 Mercedes Benz, 230SL, 1965	n/a	n/a	22
No. 28 Bedford Compressor Truck, 1956	n/a	n/a	66
No. 28 Lincoln Continental, 1980	n/a	n/a	6
No. 28 Mack Dump Truck, 1968	n/a	n/a	17
No. 28 Mark Ten Jaguar, 1964	n/a	n/a	25
No. 28 Stoat, 1974	n/a	n/a	11
No. 28 Thames Compressor Truck, 1959	n/a	n/a	93
No. 29 Austin A55 Cambridge, 1961	n/a	n/a	50
No. 29 Bedford Milk Delivery Van, 1956	n/a	n/a	55

	C6	C8	C10
No. 29 Fire Pumper Truck, 1965	n/a	n/a	30
No. 29 Racing Mini, 1971	n/a	n/a	17
No. 29 Shovel Nose Tractor, 1976	n/a	n/a	7
No. 30 Articulated Truck, 1981	n/a	n/a	6
No. 30 Beach Buggy, 1971	n/a	n/a	14
No. 30 Favin Crane, eight wheel, 1965	n/a	n/a	22
No. 30 Ford Prefect with Towbar, 1956	n/a	n/a	83
No. 30 German Crane Truck, 1961	n/a	n/a	54
No. 30 Swamp Rat, 1977	n/a	n/a	6
No. 31 Caravan, 1977	n/a	n/a	5
No. 31 Ford Customline Station Wagon, 1956	n/a	n/a	103
No. 31 Ford Fairlane Station Wagon, 1959	n/a	n/a	103
No. 31 Lincoln Continental, 1964	n/a	n/a	20
No. 31 Volks Dragon, 1971	n/a	n/a	17
No. 32 Excavator, 1981	n/a	n/a	15
No. 32 Jaguar, E Type	n/a	n/a	84
No. 32 Leyland Tanker, 1968	n/a	n/a	25
No. 33 Datsun 126X, 1973	n/a	n/a	11
No. 33 Ford Zephyr 6 MKIII, 1963	n/a	n/a	25
No. 33 Ford Zodiac MKII, 1956	n/a	n/a	93
No. 33 Lamborghini Muira P400, 1969	n/a	n/a	13
No. 33 Police Motorcyclist, 1977	n/a	n/a	12
No. 34 Chevy Pro Stocker, 1981	n/a	n/a	8
No. 34 Formula 1 Racing Car, 1971	n/a	n/a	13
No. 34 Vantastic, 1976	n/a	n/a	7
No. 34 Volkswagen Camper, 1961	n/a	n/a	36
No. 34 Volkswagen Microvan 'Matchbox' Express, 1956	n/a	n/a	75
No. 35 Fandango, 1975	n/a	n/a	17
No. 35 Marschall Horse Box, 1956	n/a	n/a	71
No. 35 Merryweather Marquis Fire Engine, 1970	n/a	n/a	20
No. 35 Sno-Trac Tractor, 1961	n/a	n/a	30
No. 36 Austin A50 with Towbar, 1956	n/a	n/a	61
No. 36 Formula 5000, 1975	n/a	n/a	7
No. 36 Hot Rod Draguar, 1971	n/a	n/a	17
No. 36 Lambretta & Sidecar, 1960	n/a	n/a	71
No. 36 Opel Diplomat, 1966	n/a	n/a	20
No. 36 Refuse Truck, 1981	n/a	n/a	14
No. 37 Cattle Truck (Dodge), 1967	n/a	n/a	20
No. 37 Coca-Cola Truck, 1956	n/a	n/a	275
No. 37 Skip Truck, 1976	n/a	n/a	8
No. 37 Soopa Coopa, 1973	n/a	n/a	11

Matchbox Volkswagen Camper, No. 34, 1961.

Matchbox Lambretta Motorcycle with sidecar, No. 36, 1960. Photo from Gary Linden.

Matchbox Jaguar, E Type, No. 32.

Matchbox Opel Diplomat, No. 36, 1966.

Matchbox Coca-Cola Truck, No. 37, 1956. Photo from Gary Linden.

Matchbox Darrier Refuse Collector, No. 38. Photo from Gary Linden.

	C6	C8	C10
No. 38 Armored Jeep, 1976	n/a	n/a	16
No. 38 Camper, 1981	n/a	n/a	11
No. 38 Darrier Refuse Collector	n/a	n/a	93
No. 38 Honda Motorcycle with Trailer, 1968	n/a	n/a	22
No. 38 Stingeroo, 1973	n/a	n/a	11
No. 38 Vauxhall Estate, 1963	n/a	n/a	38
No. 39 Clipper, 1973	n/a	n/a	13
No. 39 Ford Tractor, 1967	n/a	n/a	25
No. 39 Ford Zodiac Convertible, 1956	n/a	n/a	93
No. 39 Pontiac Convertible, 1962	n/a	n/a	62
No. 39 Rolls-Royce Silver Shadow MKII	n/a	n/a	15
No. 40 Bedford 7 Ton Tipper, 1956	n/a	n/a	103
No. 40 Guildsman, 1971	n/a	n/a	11
No. 40 Hay Trailer, 1967	n/a	n/a	20
No. 40 Horse Box, 1977	n/a	n/a	8
No. 40 Leyland 'Royal Tiger' Coach/Long Distance, 1961	n/a	n/a	30
No. 41 Ambulance, 1978	n/a	n/a	10
No. 41 'D' Type Jaguar Racing Car, 1956	n/a	n/a	110
No. 41 Ford G.T. 40 (Sports Racer), 1965	n/a	n/a	20
No. 41 Siva Spyder, 1972	n/a	n/a	11
No. 42 Bedford 'Evening News' Van, 1956	n/a	n/a	75
No. 42 Container Truck, 1977	n/a	n/a	15
No. 42 Iron Fairy Crane, 1969	n/a	n/a	54
No. 42 Studebaker Lark Wagonaire, 1965	n/a	n/a	19
No. 42 Tyre Fryer, 1972	n/a	n/a	16
No. 43 Aveling-Barford Shovel, 1962	n/a	n/a	42
No. 43 Dragon Wheels, 1972	n/a	n/a	11
No. 43 Hillman Minx, 1957	n/a	n/a	83
No. 43 Pony Trailer, 1968	n/a	n/a	10
No. 44 Boss Mustang, 1972	n/a	n/a	7
No. 44 Passenger Coach, 1978	n/a	n/a	14
No. 44 Refrigerator Truck, GMC, 1967	n/a	n/a	25
No. 44 Rolls-Royce Silver Cloud, 1957	n/a	n/a	66
No. 45 BMW, 1976	n/a	n/a	8
No. 45 Ford Corsair with Green Boat, 1959	n/a	n/a	22
No. 45 Ford Group Six, 1970	n/a	n/a	18
No. 45 Vauxhall Victor, 1957	n/a	n/a	39
No. 46 Ford Tractor, 1978	n/a	n/a	5

Matchbox Morris Minor 1000, 1957, No. 46. Photo from Gary Linden.

Matchbox Trojan Brooke Bond Van, No. 47, 1957. Photo from Gary Linden.

Matchbox Army Half Track MKIII, No. 49, 1958. Photo from Gary Linden.

	C6	C8	C10
No. 46 Mercedes-Benz 300Se, 1968	n/a	n/a	18
No. 46 Morris Minor 1000, 1957	n/a	n/a	93
No. 46 Pickfords Removal Van, 1960	n/a	n/a	71
No. 46 Stretcha Fetcha, 1972	n/a	n/a	11
No. 47 Beach Hopper, 1973	n/a	n/a	14
No. 47 DAF Tipper Container Truck, 1968	n/a	n/a	17
No. 47 Neilson Ice Cream Van, 1963	n/a	n/a	36
No. 47 Trojan 'Brooke Bond' Van, 1957	n/a	n/a	77
No. 48 Dodge Dumper Truck, 1967	n/a	n/a	26
No. 48 Pi-Eyed Piper, 1973	n/a	n/a	11
No. 48 Sambron Jack Lift, 1977	n/a	n/a	8
No. 48 Sports Boat & Trailer, 1957	n/a	n/a	28
No. 49 Army Half Track MKIII, 1958	n/a	n/a	54
No. 49 Chop Suey, 1973	n/a	n/a	20
No. 49 Crane Truck, 1976	n/a	n/a	12
No. 49 Mercedes Unimog Truck, 1967	n/a	n/a	22
No. 50 Articulated Truck, 1973	n/a	n/a	9
No. 50 Commer Pick-up Truck, 1958	n/a	n/a	83
No. 50 Ford Kennel Truck, 1969	n/a	n/a	13
No. 50 Harley Davidson Motorcycle, 1981	n/a	n/a	6
No. 50 John Deere-Lanz Tractor, 1963	n/a	n/a	30
No. 51 8 Wheel Tipper Truck, 1969	n/a	n/a	28

	C6	C8	C10
No. 51 Albion Truck 'Portland Cement', 1958	n/a	n/a	90
No. 51 Citroen SM, 1972	n/a	n/a	7
No. 51 Combine Harvester, 1979	n/a	n/a	6
No. 51 Tipping Farm Trailer, 1963	n/a	n/a	20
No. 52 BRM Racing Car, 1965	n/a	n/a	22
No. 52 Dodge Charger MKIII, 1970	n/a	n/a	11
No. 52 Maserati 4 CLT, 1958	n/a	n/a	103

	C6	C8	C10
No. 52 Police Launch, 1976	n/a	n/a	10
No. 53 Aston-Martin, DB2/4, 1959 ...	n/a	n/a	39
No. 53 C.J. 6 Jeep, 1977	n/a	n/a	8
No. 53 Ford Zodiac MKIV, 1968.......	n/a	n/a	17
No. 53 Mercedes-Benz 220SE, 1968...	n/a	n/a	42
No. 53 Tanzara, 1972	n/a	n/a	13
No. 54 Army Saracen Personnel Carrier, 1959..........................	n/a	n/a	55
No. 54 Cadillac Ambulance, 1965....	n/a	n/a	24
No. 54 Ford Capri, 1971..................	n/a	n/a	11
No. 54 Mobile Home, 1981	n/a	n/a	10
No. 54 Personnel Carrier, 1976	n/a	n/a	15
No. 55 D.U.K.W. (Army Amphibian), 1959...	n/a	n/a	71
No. 55 Ford Cortina, 1980...............	n/a	n/a	6

	C6	C8	C10
No. 55 Ford Police Car, 1963	n/a	n/a	35
No. 55 Hell Raiser, 1975.................	n/a	n/a	13
No. 55 Mercury Parkland Police Car, 1969...................................	n/a	n/a	13
No. 55 Mercury Police Car (Station Wagon), 1970	n/a	n/a	22
No. 56 BMC 1800 Pininfarina, 1970	n/a	n/a	11
No. 56 Fiat 1500, 1965	n/a	n/a	18
No. 56 Hi Trailer, 1975...................	n/a	n/a	11
No. 56 London Trolley Bus, 1959	n/a	n/a	93

Matchbox Ford Zodiac MKIV, No. 53, 1968.

Matchbox Ford Police Car, No. 55, 1963. Photo from Gary Linden.

Matchbox Army Saracen Personnel Carrier, No. 54, 1959. Photo from Gary Linden.

Matchbox Fiat 1500, No. 56, 1965. Photo from Gary Linden.

Matchbox DAF Girder Truck, No. 58, 1968.

Matchbox Scammel Army Wreck Truck, No. 64, 1959.
Photo from Gary Linden.

Matchbox Ford Singer Van, No. 59, 1959. Photo from
Gary Linden.

	C6	C8	C10
No. 56 Mercedes 450SEL, 1980	n/a	n/a	8
No. 57 Chevrolet Impala, 1966	n/a	n/a	90
No. 57 Eccles Caravan, 1970	n/a	n/a	33
No. 57 Wild Life Truck, 1973	n/a	n/a	14
No. 57 Wolseley 1500, 1959	n/a	n/a	66
No. 58 British European Airways Coach, 1959	n/a	n/a	93
No. 58 DAF Girder Truck, 1968	n/a	n/a	17
No. 58 Drott Excavator, 1963	n/a	n/a	66
No. 58 Faun Dumper, 1976	n/a	n/a	8
No. 58 Woosh-N-Push, 1972	n/a	n/a	13
No. 59 Fire Chief Car, 1966	n/a	n/a	16
No. 59 Ford Fairlane Fire Car, 1964	n/a	n/a	300
No. 59 Ford 'Singer' Van, 1959	n/a	n/a	110

	C6	C8	C10
No. 59 Planet Scout, 1975	n/a	n/a	11
No. 59 Porsche 928, 1981	n/a	n/a	8
No. 60 Holden Pick-up, 1977	n/a	n/a	8
No. 60 Lotus Super Seven, 1971	n/a	n/a	14
No. 60 Morris OmniTruck J2 Pick-up	n/a	n/a	72
No. 60 Truck with Site Officer, 1967	n/a	n/a	18
No. 61 Alvis Stalwart, 1967	n/a	n/a	42
No. 61 Blue Shark, 1971	n/a	n/a	7
No. 61 Military Scout Car (Ferret), 1959	n/a	n/a	72
No. 61 Wreck Truck, 1978	n/a	n/a	6
No. 62 Chevrolet Corvette, 1980	n/a	n/a	8
No. 62 General Army Lorry, 1959	n/a	n/a	83
No. 62 Mercury Cougar, 1969	n/a	n/a	18
No. 62 Rat Rod Dragster, 1971	n/a	n/a	13
No. 62 Renault 17TL, 1974	n/a	n/a	13
No. 62 TV Service Van, 1964	n/a	n/a	36
No. 63 Airport Fire Fighting Crash Tender, 1964	n/a	n/a	49
No. 63 Army Ambulance, 1959	n/a	n/a	35
No. 63 Dodge Crane Truck, 1968	n/a	n/a	18
No. 63 Freeway Gas Tanker, 1973	n/a	n/a	11
No. 64 Caterpillar Tractor, 1981	n/a	n/a	8
No. 64 Fire Chief Car, 1976	n/a	n/a	14
No. 64 Jaguar 3.4 Litre Salon, 1959	n/a	n/a	83
No. 64 MG 1100, 1966	n/a	n/a	18
No. 64 Scammell Army Wreck Truck, 1959	n/a	n/a	95

	C6	C8	C10
No. 64 Slingshot Dragster, 1971	n/a	n/a	18
No. 65 Airport Coach, 1977.............	n/a	n/a	20
No. 65 Claas Combine Harvester, 1968...................................	n/a	n/a	18
No. 65 Saab Sonnet, 1973...............	n/a	n/a	11
No. 66 Citroen DS19, 1959.............	n/a	n/a	83
No. 66 Ford Transit, 1977	n/a	n/a	15
No. 66 Greyhound Bus, 1967...........	n/a	n/a	18
No. 66 Harley Davidson Motorcycle & Sidecar, 1963	n/a	n/a	150
No. 66 Mazda RX500, 1972.............	n/a	n/a	11
No. 67 Datsun 260Z, 1978..............	n/a	n/a	8
No. 67 Hot Rocker, 1973.................	n/a	n/a	11
No. 67 'Saladin' Armored Car, 1959.	n/a	n/a	33
No. 67 Volkswagen 1600 T.L., 1968	n/a	n/a	18
No. 68 Army Austin MKII Radio Truck, 1959..........................	n/a	n/a	61
No. 68 Chevrolet Van, 1980.............	n/a	n/a	8
No. 68 Cosmobile, 1975..................	n/a	n/a	15
No. 68 Mercedes Coach, 1965	n/a	n/a	18
No. 68 Porsche 910, 1970	n/a	n/a	17
No. 69 Commer 30 Cwt. Van 'Nestles', 1959	n/a	n/a	140
No. 69 Hatra Tractor Shovel, 1965 ..	n/a	n/a	42
No. 69 Rolls-Royce Silver Shadow, 1970...................................	n/a	n/a	17
No. 69 Turbo Fury, 1973.................	n/a	n/a	11
No. 69 Wells Fargo Security, 1978 ..	n/a	n/a	8

	C6	C8	C10
No. 70 Atkinson Grit-Spreading Truck, 1965.....................	n/a	n/a	16
No. 70 Dodge Dragster, 1971	n/a	n/a	17
No. 70 Ferrari, 1981	n/a	n/a	8
No. 70 Ford Thames Estate Car, 1959.................................	n/a	n/a	50
No. 70 S.P. Gun, 1977	n/a	n/a	8
No. 71 Army Water Truck, 1959	n/a	n/a	96
No. 71 Cattle Truck, 1976	n/a	n/a	11
No. 71 Ford Heavy Wreck Truck, 1968.................................	n/a	n/a	44
No. 71 Jeep Pick-up Truck, 1964.....	n/a	n/a	67
No. 72 Bomag Road Roller, 1980	n/a	n/a	7
No. 72 Fordson Tractor (Power Major), 1959	n/a	n/a	71
No. 72 Standard Jeep, 1967	n/a	n/a	20
No. 73 Ferrari Racing Car, 1963......	n/a	n/a	36

Matchbox Commer 30 CWT Van, Nestle's, No. 69, 1959. Photo from Gary Linden.

Matchbox Army Austin MKII Radio Truck, No. 68, 1959. Photo from Gary Linden.

Matchbox Dodge Dragster, No. 70, 1971.

Matchbox RAF 10-Ton Pressure Refueler Tanker, No. 73, 1959. Photo from Gary Linden.

Matchbox 1911 Renault Two-seater, Y-2, 1963.

	C6	C8	C10
No. 73 Mercury Station Wagon (Commuter), 1969	n/a	n/a	18
No. 73 Model 'A' Ford, 1981	n/a	n/a	8
No. 73 RAF 10-Ton Pressure Refueler Tanker, 1959	n/a	n/a	93
No. 73 Weasel, 1974	n/a	n/a	12
No. 74 Cougar Villager, 1978	n/a	n/a	8
No. 74 Daimler Bus, 1966	n/a	n/a	24
No. 74 Mobile Refreshment Bar (Canteen), 1959	n/a	n/a	88
No. 74 Toe Joe, 1972	n/a	n/a	7
No. 75 Alfa Carabo, 1971	n/a	n/a	11
No. 75 Ferrari Berlinetta, 1965	n/a	n/a	18
No. 75 Ford Thunderbird, 1959	n/a	n/a	115
Y-01 1936 Jaguar SS 100, 1977	n/a	n/a	17
Y-02 1911 'B' Type London Bus, 1955	n/a	n/a	90
Y-02 1911 Renault 2-Seater, 1963	n/a	n/a	36
Y-02 Prince Henry Vauxhall, 1970	n/a	n/a	21
Y-03 1907 London 'E' Class Tramcar, 1955	n/a	n/a	125
Y-03 1910 Benz Limousine, 1965	n/a	n/a	50
Y-03 1934 Riley MPH, 1972	n/a	n/a	20
Y-04 1909 Opel Coupe, 1966	n/a	n/a	30
Y-04 1930 Duesenberg Model J, 1976	n/a	n/a	10
Y-04 Sentinel Steam Wagon, 1955	n/a	n/a	120
Y-05 1907 Peugeot, 1968	n/a	n/a	33
Y-05 1927 Talbot Van, 1978	n/a	n/a	10

	C6	C8	C10
Y-05 1929 LeMans Bentley, 1955	n/a	n/a	75
Y-05 1929 Supercharged 4-1/2 Litre Bentley, 1960	n/a	n/a	30
Y-06 1913 Cadillac, 1967	n/a	n/a	33
Y-06 1916 A.E.C. Y type Lorry Truck, 1955	n/a	n/a	72
Y-06 1926 Type 35 Bugatti, 1961	n/a	n/a	89
Y-06 Rolls-Royce Fire Engine, 1978	n/a	n/a	14
Y-07 1912 Rolls-Royce, 1967	n/a	n/a	48
Y-07 1913 Mercer Raceabout Sportcar, 1961	n/a	n/a	16
Y-07 1914 4-Ton Leyland, 1955	n/a	n/a	125
Y-08 1914 Stutz Roadster, 1968	n/a	n/a	36
Y-08 1914 Sunbeam Motorcycle with Sidecar, 1962	n/a	n/a	113
Y-08 1926 Morris Cowley Bullnose, 1955	n/a	n/a	66
Y-08 1945 MGTC Sports Car, 1978	n/a	n/a	11
Y-09 1912 Simplex, 1967	n/a	n/a	54
Y-09 1924 Fowler Big Lion Showman Engine, 1967	n/a	n/a	54
Y-10 1906 Rolls-Royce Silver Cloud, 1968	n/a	n/a	20
Y-10 1908 Grand Prix Mercedes Racing Car, 1957	n/a	n/a	30
Y-10 1928 Mercedes-Benz, 36/220, 1963	n/a	n/a	54
Y-11 1912 Packard Landaulet, 1963	n/a	n/a	42
Y-11 1920 Aveling & Porter Steam Roller, 1957	n/a	n/a	93

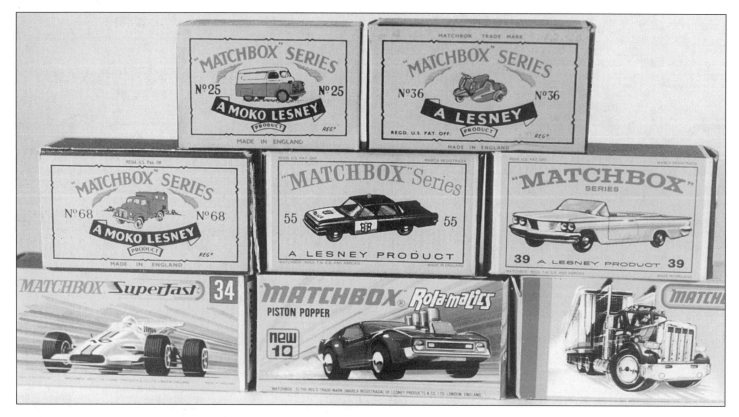

Different versions of Matchbox boxes. Photo from Gary Linden.

Matchbox Y-14 Stutz Bearcat, 1972. Photo from Gary Linden.

	C6	C8	C10
Y-11 1938 Lagonda Drophead Coupe, 1972	n/a	n/a	19
Y-12 1899 Horse-Bus (London), 1957	n/a	n/a	110
Y-12 1909 Thomas Flyabout, 1967	n/a	n/a	50

	C6	C8	C10
Y-12 1912 Model T Ford, 1979	n/a	n/a	15
Y-13 1911 Daimler, 1965	n/a	n/a	60
Y-13 1918 Crossley Truck, 1972	n/a	n/a	22
Y-14 1911 Maxwell Roadster, 1965	n/a	n/a	27
Y-14 1931 Stutz Bearcat, 1972	n/a	n/a	18
Y-15 1907 Rolls-Royce Silver Ghost, 1960	n/a	n/a	48
Y-15 1930 Packard Victoria, 1969	n/a	n/a	16
Y-16 1904 Spyker Veteran Automobile, 1961	n/a	n/a	48
Y-16 1928 Mercedes SS, 1971	n/a	n/a	19
Y-17 1938 Hispano Suiza, 1972	n/a	n/a	19
Y-18 1937 Cord 812, 1979	n/a	n/a	20
Y-19 1935 Auburn 851, 1980	n/a	n/a	21
Y-20 1938 Mercedes 540K, 1981	n/a	n/a	17
Y-21 1929 Woody Wagon, 1981	n/a	n/a	11
Y-22 Model A Van	n/a	n/a	15

MECCANO

The Meccano Company closed its doors at the Liverpool, England, factory on Nov. 30, 1979. It was a sad ending to a great company founded by Frank Hornby early in the twentieth century. His construction sets had become very popular by the time the first specialized Meccano car constructor sets appeared for Christmas in 1932. The largest of the three cars to be made, it was later dubbed the No. 2 Motor Car Constructor Outfit. In 1933, the smaller No. 1 outfit became available at a much lower price. At about the same time, an accessory electric lighting set was made available for the No. 2 car only. The two-seater sports car probably appeared in 1934. It is in scale with the No. 1 constructor and has the same wheels and was sold fully assembled. The two car constructor sets were marketed in the United States, but the two-seater sports car was imported in very small numbers, if at all. In any case, it is rare in the United States and scarce in England. Meccano cars went out of production in 1940. A wooden garage was made, but few were sold. A beautiful miniature Kaye Oil can, made of copper and brass, is a much-sought-after accessory.

The French Meccano Factory also manufactured both car construction sets, and these are identified by decals stating that they were made in France. Earlier models appear to be the same as their English counterparts, but the tires of the French No. 1 car can be marked Hutchinson, instead of Dunlop. Later French No. 1 cars continued to have removable tires on stamped steel wheels, while the English No. 1 cars changed to solid-rubber wheels with metal disks on the outside only. The last French No. 1 cars retained the original chassis and wheels, but all of the sheet metal and radiators were revised to create a more modern appearance.

Recognizing that a complete construction set in a large box could be a bit formidable for a novice collector. Meccano produced some lower-priced, factory-assembled cars in both sizes, and the box was big enough only for one assembled car, with no extra alternative pieces. Individually boxed assembled cars are identical to those sold in the larger sets. They were not very popular, and individually boxed cars are rare today.

Why is no value guide possible for Meccano toys? Very few are changing hands in the 1990s, and not enough data exists to develop a reliable and useful listing of values.

Identification

The following should help you identify approximately when an English Meccano car was made (note that over the years, parts can get substituted and moved around).

English No. 1 Meccano Car Constructor

Early (1933 to 1934)—Removable rubber tires on stamped steel wheels; yellow opaque headlight lenses, large oval decal (hood).

Later (1934 to 1940)—Solid-rubber wheels with metal disks; translucent gray headlight lenses, small round decal (hood).

Colors
   Fenders: yellow/Body: green
   Fenders: cream/Body: blue
   Fenders: red/Body: cream
   Fenders: red/Body: black
   Fenders: blue/Body: red

English No. 2 Meccano Car Constructor

Early (1932 to 1933): Soft alloy wheels; Dunlop tires; rubber spare tire; no holes in seat or dashboard; tall handbrake lever; opaque yellow headlight lenses; splitpin steering mechanism assembly; large oval decal (rear body sections); smaller box; colors—All had cream fenders; body was painted red, blue, or green. (Note from O'Brien: This set was auctioned in 1995 in excellent condition for $990.)

Later (1933 to 1940)—Hard die-cast wheels (subject to metal fatigue); Dunlop (more common) or Firestone tires; soft alloy cast metal tire cover; holes in seat and dashboard for figure and switch for lighting set; short handbrake lever; gray translucent headlight lenses; simplified steering assembly; round decal (rear body sections); larger box.

Colors
   Fenders: yellow/Body: green
   Fenders: cream/Body: blue
   Fenders: red/Body: cream
   Fenders: red/Body: black
   Fenders: blue/Body: red

Two-Seater Sports Car

Early—Opaque yellow headlight lenses; colors—same as No. 1 and No. 2 constructor cars (two-tone) except yellow-green and red-black combination were not made; picture on box lid shows a red car with cream fenders; but the reverse of this combination was actually used; all had hand-painted black running boards.

Later—Translucent gray headlamp lenses; colors—the lasts cars were painted single colors-all blue with slightly darker blue wheel discs and all red with maroon wheel discs; hand painting of running boards black was phased out, cost savings passed on to the buyer, prices were slightly reduced; no picture label on box lid.

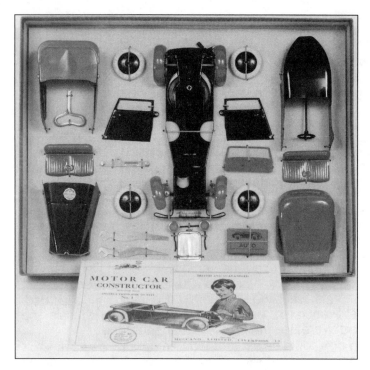

Later (1939-40) No. 1 Car Constructor in its original box. Photo from Gates Willard. Photo by E.W. Willard.

Left to right: Late French No. 1 Car; Late English No. 1 Car. Photo from Gates Willard. Photo by E.W. Willard.

Left to right: Early (1933) No. 1 Car; 1933-40 No. 1 Car. Photo from Gates Willard. Photo by E.W. Willard.

Left to right: Late Fench No. 1 Car; Late English No. 1 Car. Photo from Gates Willard. Photo by E.W. Willard.

Left to right: No. 1 Constructor Car; Two-Seater Sports Car (non-constructional). Photo from Gates Willard. Photo by E.W. Willard.

A factory-assembled No. 1 Constructional Car with original box. Photo from Gates Willard. Photo by E.W. Willard.

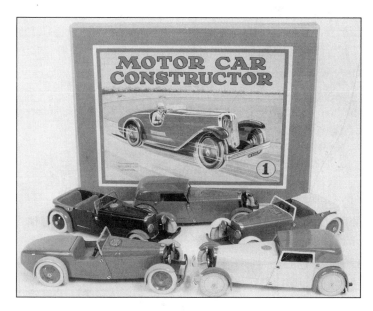

Five different ways to assemble the English No. 1 Car—an original box is also pictured. Photo from Gates Willard. Photo by E.W. Willard.

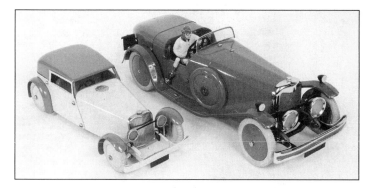

A size comparison of the No. 1 and No. 2 Constructor Cars. Photo from Gates Willard. Photo by E.W. Willard.

No. 2 Car assembled and placed on a store display stand with an original box in the background. Photo from Gates Willard. Photo by E.W. Willard.

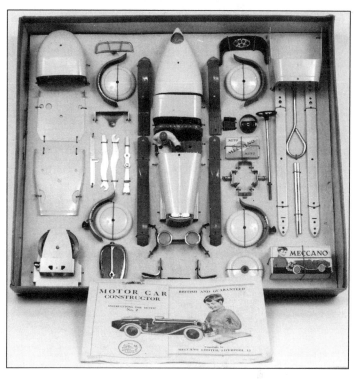

No. 2 Car Constructor shown as purchased at the store. Photo from Gates Willard. Photo by E.W. Willard.

Left to right: Early (1932) No. 2 Constructor Car; Late (1933-40) No. 2 Constructor Car. Photo from Gates Willard. Photo by E.W. Willard.

Left to right: Firestone and Dunlop (more common) tires for No. 2 Car. Photo from Gates Willard. Photo by E.W. Willard.

Left to right: Miniature K oil can compared to a real one; Electric Lighting Set with instructions; No. 2 Car to give concept of scale. Photo from Gates Willard. Photo by E.W. Willard.

Left to right: Meccano 1932 No. 2 Constructor Car; 1933-40 No. 2 Constructor Car. Photo from Gates Willard. Photo by E.W. Willard.

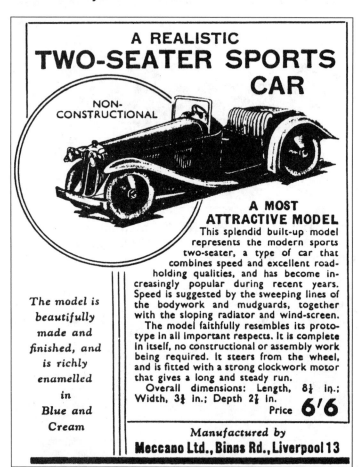

A December, 1936 ad in "Meccano Magazine" for the Meccano two-seater sports car. Photo from Gates Willard.

Meccano Two-Seater Sports Car (non-constructional). Photo from Gates Willard. Photo by E.W. Willard.

A late 1930s French Meccano Constructional Car with original box, alternative parts and instruction sheet. Photo from Gates Willard. Photo by E.W. Willard.

Left to right: Early two-seater Sports Car with box; later two-seater Sports Car with box (picture box was discontinued). Photo from Gates Willard. Photo by E.W. Willard.

METAL CAST

Metal Cast Products, formed by the reorganization (circa 1925) of the toy soldier and novelty company S. Sachs, made hand-operated slush-casting molds for small businesses and hobbyists—what some have called the home-casting industry. Since identical molds were sold to many, actual makers cannot be identified unless the maker engraved their names on their products. One who did was Fred Green Toys, whose name is found prominently on its toys. Metal Cast offered full-support services to its customers, including marketing, printing, publishing and parts. A variety of wheels may be found on its vehicles, including Tootsietoy-like metal disk wheels, metal spoke wheels, wood wheels with rubber tires, and white or black rubber wheels. There aren't many of these home-cast vehicles on the market today, not many were made, perhaps it was the lack of identity; demand today seems weak. However, collectors of the unusual should find many collectibles; most of those I have seen were well designed and professionally finished.

Contributor: Fred Maxwell, 4722 N. 33 St., Arlington, VA 22207. Perry R. Eichor, 703 North Almond Drive, Simpsonville, SC, 29681.

	C6	C8	C10
Cadillac Sedan, No. 40, two-door, 5-1/4" long	20	30	40
Cadillac Sedan, No. 40, second version, two-door, 5-3/4" long	20	30	40
Coupe, No. 63, convertible, two open windows, sidemounts, trunk	NPF	NPF	NPF
Dump Truck, No. 43, COE unique chassis w/activating mechanism, 5-1/4" long	20	30	40
Dump Truck, No. 42	20	30	40
Fire Engine, No. 61, hook and ladder truck, crew of two, 4-1/2" long	25	50	60

	C6	C8	C10
Fire Engine, No. 65, steam pumper w/water cannon, driver, 4" long	NPF	NPF	NPF
Fire Engine, no number, similar to No. 65 w/o water cannon, 3-7/8" long	6	10	14
Greyhound Bus, no number	NPF	NPF	NPF
Limousine, no number	NPF	NPF	NPF
Open Rack Truck, No. 01-04, COE cab, stake semi-trailer, 6" long	15	25	35
Packard Convertible, No. 45, 6" long	20	30	40
Packard Convertible, No. 41, 2-door, top down, 5-1/4" long	20	30	40
Packard Convertible, No. 41, second version, 5-3/4" Long	20	30	40
Racer, No. 92, large Indy-type w/bulging radiator, no driver, torpedo tail	40	60	80
Racer, No. 62, Bluebird type, blunt-nosed, V-8, record car, driver, 4-1/2" long	40	60	80
Sedan, No. 44, postwar, 6" long	20	30	40

Metal Cast Cadillac Sedan, No. 40, second version, 5-3/4". Photo from Metal Cast catalog.

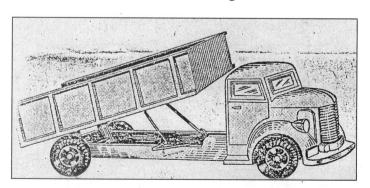

Metal Cast Dump Truck, No. 42. Photo from Metal Cast catalog.

Metal Cast Fire Engine, hook and ladder truck, No. 61, 4-1/2". Photo from Metal Cast catalog.

Metal Cast Streamline Sedan, six open windows, No. 60, 4", $20. Photo from Metal Cast catalog.

Top row, left to right: Metal Cast Greyhound Bus; Racer, Bluebird type, Nol. 62, 4-1/2". Middle row, left to right: Limousine, No. 40; Sport Coupe, No. 60. Bottom row: Truck, No. 20, stake-body, 1920s. Photo from Perry Eichor.

Metal Cast Packard Convertible, second version, No. 41, 5-3/4". Photo from Metal Cast catalog.

Top to bottom: Van Truck, No. 01-02, 6", $40; Tank Truck, No. 01-03; Cadillac Sedan, No. 04, 5-3/4". Photo from Perry Eichor.

Metal Cast Racer, No. 92, Indy type with bulging radiator, no driver, torpedo tail. Photo from Bob Ackerly.

Metal Cast War Tank, No. 39. Photo from Metal Cast catalog.

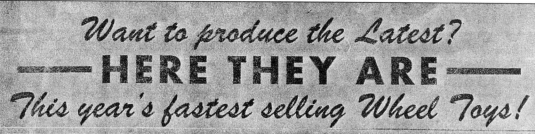

Want to produce the Latest?
—HERE THEY ARE—
This year's fastest selling Wheel Toys!

The First Scale Models of Trailer-Trucks on the market. The newest in Sedans and Convertibles. Accurate in every detail. Fascinating Toys and attractive for Model Railway layouts, etc.

A LEADING LINE WITH ALL TOY AND NOVELTY DEALERS — DEPARTMENT AND CHAIN STORES.

No. 44 SEDAN
6 Inches Long
Bronze castingform
for hollow casting $75.00

No. 01-02 VAN TRUCK
6 Inches Long

Bronze form No. 01
for hollow casting
CAB OVER ENGINE
TRACTOR $50.00
Bronze form No. 02 for hollow casting
VAN TRAILER UNIT $50.00

No. 45 CONVERTIBLE
6 Inches Long
Bronze castingform
for hollow casting $95.00
(Includes mould for casting windshield which is easily assembled to casting.)

No. 01-04 OPEN RACK TRUCK
6 Inches Long

Bronze form No. 01
for hollow casting CAB
OVER ENGINE
TRACTOR ... $50.00

Bronze form No. 04
for hollow casting
RACK BODY
TRAILER UNIT $50.00

No. 01-03 TANK TRUCK
6 Inches Long
Bronze form No. 01
for hollow casting
CAB OVER ENGINE
TRACTOR $50.00
Bronze form No. 03 for hollow casting
TANK TRAILER UNIT $50.00

NOTE:—As the same Cab-Over-Engine Tractor is used for all Trailer Sets, only one No. 01 form is needed for manufacturing all three.
Trailer Trucks sell separately or in Sets
(See attached price list.)

Castings come from moulds with axle holes and rubber wheels are easily assembled by simply slipping over standard nails. A new exclusive method eliminates need of spreading or crimping axles.
Wheels supplied manufacturers at $____ per thousand.

METAL CAST PRODUCTS CO.
1696 BOSTON ROAD
NEW YORK 60, N. Y.

Copyrighted 1949

A page from a 1949 Metal Cast catalog.

	C6	C8	C10		C6	C8	C10
Sport Coupe, No. 60, vee grille, Graham (?), from three-piece mold; very similar to Kansas Toy's No. 75	20	30	40	Truck, No. 64, Dodge (?), stake-body, 1920s, two open windows, 4-1/4" long	NPF	NPF	NPF
Streamline Sedan, No. 60, DeSoto (?) Airflow, six open windows, smooth grille, rubber tires, 4" long	20	30	40	Van Truck, No. 01-02, COE, cab, semi-trailer moving van; trailer also found in a Fred Green version, 6" long	20	30	40
Tank Truck, No. 01-03, same COE cab, semi-fuel tanker, marked "FRED GREEN TOYS," "Made in U.S.A.," 6" long	20	30	40	War Tank, No. 39, early heavy Sherman Tank, 4" long	35	50	65
				War Tank, No. 55, early WWI type w/side turrets	20	30	40

METAL MASTERS

Contributor: Dave Leopard, 2507 Feather Run Trail, West Columbia, SC 29169-4915.

	C6	C8	C10		C6	C8	C10
Bus, c.1938, 7-1/4" long (MM002)	25	38	50	Station Wagon, c.1940, 8-1/2" long (MM007)	40	50	65
Fire Truck, variation of pickup, c.1938, 7" long (MM004)	35	55	75	Station Wagon, wind-up motor, c.1940, 8-1/2" long (MM008)	45	55	75
Fire Truck, removable ladders, c.1940, 10" long (MM012)	50	65	85	Station Wagon, ambulance version, c.1940, 8-1/2" long (MM009)	45	55	75
Fire Truck, wind-up motors, w/ladders, c.1940, 10" long (MM013)	60	90	120	Tow Truck, variation of pickup, c.1938, 7" long (MM005)	35	55	50
Jeep, c.1947, 5-1/2" long (MM006)	20	30	55	Tow Truck, marked "ABC Towing Service," c.1940, 10" long (MM010)	50	75	100
Pickup Truck, c.1938, 7" long (MM003)	25	38	50	Tow Truck, wind-up motor, c.1940, 10" long (MM011)	55	80	110
Roadster, c.1938, 7" long (MM001)	25	38	50	Tractor, w/driver, 5" long (MM014)	55	82	110

METALCRAFT

Metalcraft, of St. Louis, Missouri, began producing its pressed-steel trucks in 1931. About a million were sold, most as advertising toys. In 1937, defeated by the Depression, Metalcraft closed. According to a collector-researcher, Al Korte was the designer of all of the firm's trucks and worked there from 1931 to 1936.

Contributor: John Taylor, P.O. Box 63, Nolensville, TN 37135-0063.

	C6	C8	C10		C6	C8	C10
BFG Wrecker	300	450	600	Coca-Cola Truck, ten bottles, long nose, stamped metal, late 1930s, 12" long	450	675	900
Bunte Candies Truck, 12" long	250	350	450	Coca-Cola Truck, w/bottles in racks, c.1928	438	655	875
Buster Brown Shoes Truck	300	450	600	CW Coffee Delivery Van, 11" long	250	400	525
Clover Farm Stores Truck	450	675	900	CW Coffee Dump Truck, 10-3/4" long	225	400	525
Coca-Cola Truck, pressed steel, rubber tires, w/ten bottles in rack, late 1920s-early 1930s, reads "Every Bottle Sterilized," 11" long	400	600	900	CW Coffee Wrecker	350	525	700
Coca-Cola Truck, w/ten bottles, 1930s, 10-1/2" long	350	525	700	Deckers Iowana Truck	500	700	1000

Metalcraft Clover Farm Stores. Photo from Bob Smith.

Metalcraft Coca-Cola Truck, late 1920s to early 1930s, ten bottles in rack, 11". Photo from Detroit Antique Museum. Photo by Harry Wolf.

Left to right: Metalcraft Coca-Cola Truck, 11"; Heinz Truck with original box. Photo from Bill Bertoia Auctions.

Metalcraft Machinery Hauling. Photo from Calvin L Chaussee.

Metalcraft CW Coffee Dump Truck, 10-3/4".

Metalcraft Decker's Iowana, sweet heart grille. Photo from Bob Smith.

Metalcraft Heinz Truck, 12". Photo from Calvin L. Chaussee.

Metalcraft Meadow Gold Butter Truck, battery lights, 13". Photo from Bob Smith.

Metalcraft Sand-Gravel Dump. Photo from Bob Smith.

Metalcraft Plee-zing Quality Products Delivery Van, 11". Metalcraft tried to beat the Depression by tying its toys to participating advertisers. Its pressed-steel toys were inexpensive, but by 1937 the company was defunct. Photo from Mapes Auctioneers and Appraisers.

Metalcraft Pure Oil Co. tanker, electric lights, sweetheart grille, 14-3/4". Photo from Bob Smith.

Metalcraft Shell Motor Oil, with eight oil drums. Photo from Bob Smith.

	C6	C8	C10
Delivery Truck Van, steel, 11" long ..	200	300	450
Dump Truck, electric headlights, 24" long	200	300	450
Esso Stake Truck, w/barrels, 12" long	300	700	1100
Goodrich Silvertown Tires Wrecker, w/three spare tires	225	350	425
Hardy's Salt Truck.............................	225	375	450
Heinz Truck, marked "Baked Beans, Bottled Vinegar" and "Rice Flakes," c.1932, 12" long	250	350	425
Ice Truck	245	368	490
Kroger Food Express Truck, 11" long	300	450	600
Krug Bakery Truck	450	675	935
Leslie Vacuum Packed Coffee Truck	425	638	850
Machinery Hauling Truck	500	700	900
Meadow Gold Butter Truck, battery-operated lights, 3" long	425	550	750
Plee-zing Quality Products Delivery Van, c.1928, 11" long..................	250	375	500

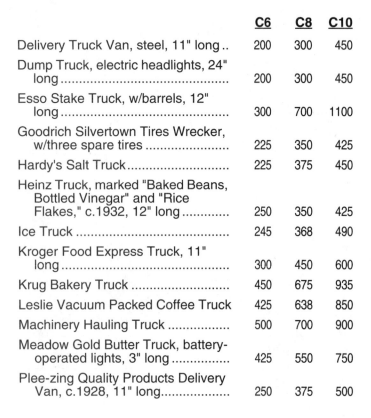

Metalcraft Steam Shovel. Photo from Calvin L Chaussee.

	C6	C8	C10		C6	C8	C10
Pure Oil Co. tanker, electric lights, 14-3/4"	500	700	1000	Towing & Repairs Truck	250	425	500
Sand-Gravel Dump Truck	175	275	375	Toy Town Grocery Truck	275	425	550
Shell Motor Oil Truck, includes eight oil drums	325	600	900	Waldorf Lager Truck	400	600	900
				Weatherbird Shoes Truck	245	375	490
St. Louis Truck, c.1930, 11" long	175	325	400	Werks Tag Soap Truck	300	450	600
Steam Shovel	115	150	200	Weston's English Biscuits Truck	250	375	500
Sunshine Biscuits Truck	250	385	500	White King Express Truck, 12" long	258	385	515

METTOY

	C6	C8	C10		C6	C8	C10
Bus, streamlined, wind-up, 7-1/4" long	95	140	190	Motorcycle, c.1940	425	638	850
Citroen Sedan, 11" long	188	282	375	Racer, No. "7," 5" long	750	1400	1800
Clown on Motorcycle, 7-1/4" long	550	800	1210	Rolls Royce, 14" long	500	800	1200
Coupe	400	600	800	Sedan, 14" long, c.1930	300	450	600
Motorcycle, No. 49, tin wind-up, 8" long	262	393	525	Steam Roller, clockwork	100	150	200
				Tractor, tin wind-up, 8" long	55	83	110

MIDGETOY

During postwar slack times at A&E Tool & Gage Co. of Rockford, Illinois, a die-cast toy company was born that would eventually rank second only to Tootsietoy in the industry.

A&E, named for owners Alvin and Earl Herdklotz, had making precision gages since 1943. Reluctant to let workers go when business slowed after the war, the Herdklotz brothers turned to toy making. The company had already made tooling work for regional toy companies, including Nylint.

Their first toy was the Chevy truck of 1946. Interchangeable bodies snapped onto the chassis, to make a stake, oil or dump truck.

That toy, and many which followed, reflected an appealing and distinctive sense of design at work, essentially a 1930s deco sensibility that was especially apparent in the King-Size and Jumbo series of vehicles.

Two futuristic designs appeared next—the Spaceship and the Rear Engine Auto. The spaceship was modeled after a comic strip Buck Rogers spaceship but never marketed as such, for licensing reasons. The Rear-Engine Auto, with its swept-back, two-door body and swept-up tail lights, was an original design.

After this flirtation with the future, Midgetoy settled on the course it would take the next three decades, producing solidly built toys based on existing vehicle models.

Leaving toys in production for many years was standard practice for the company. The popular train sets, for instance, were issued continuously from their introduction in the late 1950s until the company closed its doors in the early 1980s. They remain common in collecting circles today, even in Mint in Package (C10) form.

In 1981, the Herdklotz brothers sold the company to a group of investors. The new owners unfortunately let the business languish, introducing no new toy designs. The new Midgetoy company also packaged toys produced by other companies. After one investor suffered a fatal heart attack, the Herdklotz brothers bought back the company in 1985 to shut it down.

The Herdklotz brothers retained ownership of the company's old inventory during the change of ownership. They started releasing these essentially factory-fresh toys in the 1990s, with the result that collectors have a plentiful supply of later, plastic-wheeled versions of Midgetoy's line in excellent condition. These later versions of the toys frequently had masking and decals, unlike earlier versions. Some collectors show preference for these over older examples.

The axle arrangement used in the toys was patented by Midgetoy in 1957. The hidden wheels gave the toys their distinctive look until the 1970s, when the company introduced a line of small, exposed-axle vehicle toys akin to Tootsietoy's Jam-Pac vehicles. The move was made necessary by the rising cost of zinc. Midgetoy did continue producing some larger vehicles until the end, however.

In the listings below, dates in parentheses refer to the year of first release of the model. Early versions of the smaller vehicles possessed black rubber tires, here designated **brt**, as opposed to the later black plastic tires, or **bpt**. The later versions are usually worth sixty to seventy percent of the earlier versions. Larger toy vehicles apparently had black rubber tires from beginning to end, although the early tires have a fatter and rounder appearance, and the later ones have a central ridge. Masking and decals, however, are sure signs of later production.

The given dates refer to the year of the model's introduction.

Contributor: Mark Rich, P.O. Box 971, Stevens Point, WI 54481-0971.

	C6	C8	C10
Pee-Wee Series, Two-inch mini vehicle			
American La France Fire Truck, 1969	1	2	3
Chevy-style Dragster, 1969	1	2	3
Corvette Convertible Dragster, 1969	1	2	3
Drag Racer, 1969	1	2	3
Ford Dragster, 1969	1	2	3
Ford GT, 1969	1	2	3
Jeep, 1969	n/a	1	2
MG Roadster, 1969	1	2	3
Open Cockpit Racer, 1969	n/a	1	2
Porsche Convertible Dragster, 1969	1	2	3
New Junior Series, 2-1/2" to 3" vehicles			
Cadillac Ambulance, 1971	5	8	12
Corvette '68 L88 Stingray, 1971	2	3	4
Ford Mark IV, 1971	2	4	5
Ford Mustang	1	2	3
Ford Pickup Truck, 1971	2	4	5
Ford Torino, 1971	1	2	3
Ford Torino Fire Chief Car, 1971	2	4	6
Ford Torino Police Car, 1971	2	4	6
Ford wrecker, 1971	3	5	7
Jaguar XKE, 1971	3	5	8
Junior Series, 2-1/2" to 3-1/2" vehicles			
American La France Pumper, open cab, late 1950s	6	9	13
American La France Pumper, closed cab, early 1950s	6	10	15
Army Amphibious Vehicle, brt, 1949	8	14	22
Army Howitzer, bpt	2	5	7
Army Howitzer, brt, 1949	4	7	10
Army Jeep, brt, 1950	4	7	10
Cadillac Convertible, brt, 1949	6	11	17

	C6	C8	C10
Chevy Dump Truck, 1946	10	17	25
Chevy Oil Truck, 1946	10	17	25
Chevy Stake Truck, 1946	10	17	25
Corvette Convertible, brt, late '50s	5	8	12
Ford Hot Rod, 2-1/2 inches, brt	5	8	12
Ford V-8 Hot Rod, brt, 1948, 3" long	8	14	22
Ford V-8 Hot Rod, bpt	5	8	12
Ford Wrecker, brt, late 1950s	5	8	12
MG Sports Roadster, brt, 1958	6	9	13
Open Cockpit Curtis Craft Racer, 1950	8	14	22
Rear-Engine Auto, rear window outlined, bpt	7	12	18

Midgetoy Stake Truck. Photo from Mark Rich.

Midgetoy Scenicruiser Bus. Photo from Thomas G. Nefos.

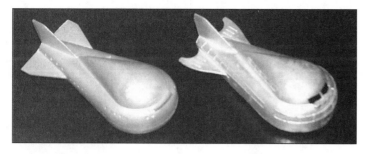

Left to right: Midgetoy Spaceship without open windows; Midgetoy Spaceship with open windows. Photo from Mark Rich.

Midgetoy American La France Fire Truck, 1957, 6". Photo from Thomas G. Nefos.

Midgetoy Oil Tank Truck, 1957, 6". Photo from Thomas G. Nefos.

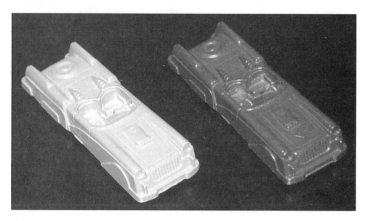

Two examples of Midgetoy convertibles. Photo from Mark Rich.

	C6	C8	C10
Rear-Engine Auto, no rear window, brt, 1948	12	25	35
Scenicruiser Bus, brt, 1955	6	10	15
Spaceship, no open window, two brt	25	40	50
Spaceship, open window, two brt	20	32	45
Spaceship, no open window, three brt	30	45	60
Spaceship, open window, two bpt	8	14	22
Sunbeam Racer, bpt	5	8	12
Sunbeam Racer, bpt, heavily decaled	7	12	18
Sunbeam Racer, brt, 1950	8	14	22
Volkswagen Beetle, bpt, 1960	6	10	15

King-Size Series, Four-inch vehicles

	C6	C8	C10
American La France Pumper, brt, early 1950s	8	14	22
Army Half-Track, late '50s, brt	7	13	20
Army Personnel Carrier, late '50s, brt	7	13	20
Army Tank, brt	7	13	20
Cadillac Four-door Sedan, late '50s, brt	7	13	20
Cadillac Four-door Sedan, military	7	12	18

	C6	C8	C10
Cadillac Two-door Coupe, early '50s, brt	9	15	24
Chrysler-style Convertible Roadster, brt	8	14	22
Ford Pickup Truck, early 1950s, brt	8	14	22
Oil Tanker Truck, military, brt	7	13	20
Oil Tanker Truck, late '50s, brt	9	15	24
Van, open side windows, late 1950s, brt	7	12	18
Van Ambulance, Red Cross, late '50s, brt	7	12	18
Van Ambulance, late 1950s, brt	6	10	15

Jumbo Series, Six-inch vehicles

	C6	C8	C10
American La France Pumper, brt	11	18	27
Cadillac Four-door Convertible, brt	10	17	25
Ford Oil Tanker, marked "Midgetoy Oil Co."	10	17	25
Ford Oil Tanker, 1957, brt	10	17	25
Mobile Artillery, 1957, brt	10	17	25
Scenicruiser Bus, marked "Midgetoy Bus Line"	10	17	25
Scenicruiser Bus, late 1950s, brt	12	20	30
Utility Truck, brt	10	17	25

Chevrolet Tractor-Trailer Series, Eight-inch vehicles

	C6	C8	C10
Auto Transporter with loading ramp, 1962	11	18	27
Hook and Ladder Aerial Fire Truck, 1963	12	20	30

Midgetoy Shipping Van, "Midgetoy Van Lines, Inc."
Photo from Mark Rich.

Midgetoy Truck Set, Chevrolet chassis with three inerchangeable bodies, 1946. Photo from Thomas G.
Nefos.

	C6	C8	C10
Oil Tanker, 1962..............................	11	18	27
Oil Tanker, marked "Midgetoy Oil Co."...	12	20	30
Shipping Van, 1962........................	11	17	27
Shipping Van, marked "North American Van Lines"..................	NPF	NPF	NPF
Shipping Van, marked "Midgetoy Van Lines, Inc."..........................	12	20	30
Shipping Van, marked "Allied Van Lines"...	NPF	NPF	NPF

Miscellaneous

	C6	C8	C10
Boat Trailer, various designs............	3	5	8
Camping Trailer...............................	6	10	15
Gas Pumps, plastic	n/a	1	2
Gas Pumps, metal...........................	6	10	15

Part of a Midgetoy salesman's sample box. Photo from
Thomas G. Nefos.

	C6	C8	C10
Race Car Trailer for Pee Wee Car, w/car..	3	5	8
Utility Trailer, military, 1-1/2" long	2	4	5
Utility Trailer, 1-1/2" long.................	2	4	5
Utility Trailer, 2" long......................	3	5	8

Sets

	C6	C8	C10
Dixie Chargers, three car set, 1981 .	5	8	12
Interchangeable Truck Set, on cardboard tray	n/a	n/a	55
Interchangeable Truck Set, Chevy cab w/stake, oil and dump options, 1946	12	25	35
Train, western, four-piece set	7	13	20
Train, Western, package marked "Train That Won the West," Mint in blister pack...............................	n/a	n/a	25
Train, passenger, marked "Amtrak," Mint on blister pack.....................	n/a	n/a	27
Train, passenger, Mint on blister pack	n/a	n/a	25
Train, passenger, five-piece set.......	7	13	20
Train, freight, Mint on blister pack....	n/a	n/a	25
Train, freight, five-piece set..............	7	13	20
Train, diesel, Mint on blister pack	n/a	n/a	25
Train, diesel, five-piece set	7	13	20

MID-WEST METAL NOVELTY MANUFACTURING COMPANY

In the late 1920s, the American auto industry, led by Ford, was not only booming but dominating global production, and vehicle toys were keeping up with their prototypes. There were three companies that developed a thriving slushmold toy business—C.A.W. Novelty Co., Mid-West Metal Novelty Co., and Kansas Toy and Novelty Co. These were in small Northern Kansas towns, Clay Center and Clifton, only a few miles apart. These toy makers had other things in common—they loved racers, they all used metal-disk wheels and black-painted tires, they tended to follow the lead of Tootsietoy, and the companies left almost no paper trail.

This lack of documentation accounts for the difficulty toy historians have had identifying some excellent models and toys. The above clues suggest that Mid-West was C.E. Stevenson's business title. Stevenson, an active businessman, was at the center of all this. In 1923, he started casting toys at home. In 1925, he joined Western Diecasting of Clay Center, probably as an outside salesman. Shortly after Kansas Toy started, he contracted to furnish molds to them. He may also have sold master patterns and those prepainted wheels to C.A.W. and Kansas Toy, for all these were probably made in the foundry of Western Diecasting. The sole surviving newsclip on Mid-West in a 1929 *Toys and Novelties* magazine shows a deluxe (five-window) coupe, a fairly exact copy of the Tootsietoy Buick, but with Kansas Toy black-painted tires.

But what else did Mid-West make? Over the years a group of vehicle toys with a similar look have been found—Tootsietoy copies or look-a-likes; Tootsietoy wheels, including those distinctive lug boltheads; metal-disk wheels with a suggested rim between wheel and tire; most important, several versions of Buick coupe seen in the 1929 *Toys and Novelties*. The most likely maker was Stevenson, before he moved on to a larger city in 1931 and started Lincoln (Nebraska) White Metal Works, with which he thrived for years, despite the Depression.

Contributors: Fred Maxwell, 4722 N. 33 St., Arlington, VA 22207. **Perry R. Eichor,** 703 North Almond Drive, Simpsonville, SC, 29681.

Abbreviations

The following abbreviations are for the details and variations useful in identification.

HG	horizontal grille pattern	SM	sidemounted spare
HL	horizontal hood louvers	SP	string-pull knob in handcrank area
HO	hood cap, Motometer or ornament	T	external trunk
L	lacquer finish	UV	unnumbered version
LI	landau irons on convertibles	VG	vertical grille pattern
MDW	metal disc wheels	VL	vertical hood louvers
MDSW	metal disc solid spokes	WS, W/S	windshield
MDWBT	wheels with black painted tires	WV	windshield visor
MSW	metal open spoke wheels	WHRT	wooden hubs, rubber tires
MWW	metal simulated wire wheels	WRDW	white hard rubber disc wheels
OW	open windows	WRW	white soft rubber wheels (balloon tires)
RM	rearmount spare tire/wheel		

	C6	C8	C10
Buick Coupe, no lamps, disk wheels, five grooved solid windows, HG, HO, VL, SM, three variations, four open windows; five smooth windows; MDW w/"lug bolts," 3" long (MW003) ...	25	40	55
Bus, overland/safety, no lamps, no doors, no spares, HG, HO, ten open windows, disk wheels (same bus later reissued by by Lincoln White Metal Works), 3-1/2" long (MW012)	40	50	60

	C6	C8	C10
Bus, Yellow Coach, school-bus body, no doors, thirteen solid grooved windows, HG, RM, painted disk wheels, 3-3/4" long (MW010)	30	40	50
Large Coupe, no lamps, large die-cast (?), five grooved solid windows, disk wheels w/lug bolts, HG, HO, VL, 3-1/2" long (MW001)	40	60	80

Two versions of the 3" Mid-West Buick Coupe. Photo from Fred Maxwell.

Top: Two versions of the Mid-West Midget Racer, 2-3/4"; Bottom row: Large Racer, 3-5/8". Photo from Fred Maxwell.

Top to bottom: Mid-West Large Roadster, 3-5/8"; Another version of the Large Roadster; Town Car, 3-5/8". Photo from Fred Maxwell.

Left to right: An unlisted Mid-West vehicle and the Mid-West Sedan, two-door Ford A, 2-3/4".

	C6	C8	C10
Large Racer, driver crouched and hunched over steering wheel, boattail, medium-sized disk wheels w/lug bolts, HG, HO, VL, 3-5/8" long (MW005)	40	60	80
Large Roadster, AC Mack, Buick or Packard, long hood, top up, HG, HO, VL, door handles and hinges, RM, rear bumper, 3-5/8" long; variation—two colors, three solid windows, painted disk wheels (MW007)	40	60	80
Large Truck, AC Mack, gas tank ahead of windshield, V6, screen louvers, full-sized solid stake body w/open rear (for pouring), 3-1/4" long; Unique slushmold design w/solid, curved pan (MW006)	40	60	80

	C6	C8	C10
Midget Racer, driver crouched and hunched over steering wheel, torpedo tail, small disk wheels w/lug bolts, HG, HO, VL, 2-3/4"; variation: narrower body and large wheels (the postwar Barclay?); M & L reproduction is more often found (MW004)	40	50	60
Sedan, Ford A, two-door, finely detailed screen grille, headlamps and fenders (made w/a three-piece mold, a Stevenson specialty); VL, WSV, four open windows, door handles and hinges, painted disk wheels, 2-3/4" long (MW013)	40	60	80
Sedan (?), Buick, finely detailed screen grille, headlamps and fenders, "B" cast on grille, HO, VL, side lamps, WSV, six open windows, door-hinges, RM, painted wheels, 3-1/16" long; a similar car has been attributed to Barclay Mfg. (MW014)	40	60	80

Left to right: Mid-West Touring Car, top up, no seats, 3-1/8"; Touring Car, driver and lady, top down, 3-1/8". Photo from Fred Maxwell.

NEW LINE OF CAST TOYS

Of particular interest to jobbers and quantity buyers will be the announcement of the three new attractively colored cast metal toys which are being offered by

the Mid-West Metal Novelty Manufacturing Co. of Clay Center, Kan.

This manufacturer of novelties and art castings has instituted a new finish process enabling them to use lacquers which do not chip. Also by the use of plenty of metal, strength is obtained and breakage avoided. Each one of their toys, including the coupe illustrated here, moves on its own wheels and the toys are packed securely and neatly three colors to each carton. A wide variety of these colors is offered from which choice may be made. Cartons contain either half gross or gross.

These toys retail at popular prices and are particularly interesting as 10 cents to $1 merchandise.

An advertisement for Mid-West Metal Novelty Manufacturing Co.

From left: Mid-West Yellow Taxicab, grooved solid windows, 2-3/4"; Large Coupe, disc wheels, 3-/2". Photo from Fred Maxwell.

Two versions of the Mid-West Yellow Taxicab. Photo from Fred Maxwell.

	C6	C8	C10
Touring Car, Ford T, driver and lady passenger w/muff, top down, no lamps, plain grille, HO, VL, door handles, disk wheels, 3-1/8" long (MW008)	50	75	100
Touring Car, top up, no seats, HG, HO, VL, RM, side lamps, door handles, disk wheels, 3-1/8" long (MW009)	30	40	50
Town Car, w/chauffeur, long hood, HG, HO, VL, LI, three colors, five solid windows, grooved, door handles and hinges, disk wheels, 3-5/8" long (MW011)	50	75	100

	C6	C8	C10
Yellow Taxicab, no lamps, door handles, seven "grooved" solid windows, MDW w/rims but no bolts, HG, HO, VL, 2-3/4" long; other versions have driver and passenger embossed on front windows, other windows open (MW002)	40	60	80

MILITARY VEHICLES

Identification Models and Miscellaneous items

1:24-scale metal Identification Models; World War II. Top row, left to right: Amphibian Tractor, 105mm S.P. (illegible) M7; Half-trak car; M2. Front row, left to right: Jeep (some of these movable wheel versions are also marked "Dale"); "4X4 Ton Truck- Jeep" (fixed wheel version); "Cletrac" (bulldozer). Note: Manoil 3-1/4" GI for scale. Photo from Ed Poole.

1:36-scale Metal Identification Models; World War II U.S. Top row, left to right: "Heavy Tank M-6"; "Med. Tank, M4-2" (Turret Revolves); "Med. Tank M-4"; "Med. Tank M-3". Front row, left to right: "Light Tank M-3"; "Light Tank M-3" (turrent revolves); "3" Gun Car. M-5"; "105 MM Howitzer Motor T32 My M7 Priest M-7". Note: Britians Ltd. GI included for scale. Photo from Ed Poole.

Movable Wheel Versions of 1:36-scale Metal Identification Models; World War II U.S. Top row, left to right: "Med. Tank M4"; "General Sherman" (turret rotates); "105 MM Howitzer Motor T32 M7 Priest M7". Front row, left to right: "Armored Car T-17 Dale model Co. Chicago"; "75 MM Gun Car M3 Dale - Model Co. Chicago"; "Stuart M5". Note: Company name and city imprinted on hubs of wheeled vehicles - other data on hulls. Britains Ltd. 54mm GI included for scale. Photo from Ed Poole.

1:36-scale Metal Identification Models; World War II U.S. Top row, left to right: "Half TRK Car M2"; "Half TRK pers. car - M3"; "75 MM Gun Car. M-3 Half Track Car M2" (decal not original but AAF Acceptance tag dated "Jul 3 1946" is); "Scout Car M-3 A-1". Front row, left to right: "Armoured Car T-17"; "Duck" (1/48th scale); "37MM Gun Car. M6". Note: Britains Ltd. GI included for scale. Photo from Ed Poole.

1:36-scale Metal Identification Model, World War II German. Top row, left to right: "Ger. Light med. tank L.T. 3.5"; "Praga" Ger. Tank 7 ton T.N.H.P. Ex. (Czech); "Ger. Light Med. Tank C.K.V.D.8.H." Front row, left to right: "German Light Amphibian Tank C.K.D.F.4.H.E."; "Ger. Light Arm. car Horch 1936 SD:K 223"; "Ger. Heavy 8 wheeled armor, car." Note: Jones 54mm soldier included for scale. Photo from Ed Poole.

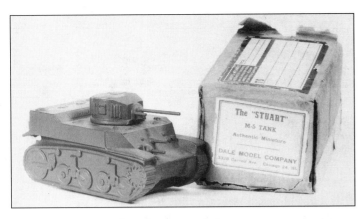

Dale 1:36-scale Identification model bought in an Army "PX" post World War II; mailing label already attached to box. Photo from Ed Poole.

Some contemporary Russian die-casts. Top row, left to right: 76mm Gun; T34-85 Tank; 100mm Gun in 1:43-scale by UEHA (?). Front row, left to right: T34 Tank; Two YA3-469 Cars in 1:43 scale by Schelano B CCCP. Dinky soldiers added for scale is 30mm tall. Photo from Ed Poole.

1:36-scale Metal Identification Models; WWII Japanese (Decals not original). Top row, left to right: "Japanese Medium Tank - Cometal"; "Japanese Cruiser Tank - Cometal"; "Japanese Heavy Medium Tank - Cometal." Front row, left to right: "Japanese Amphibian Tank"; "Japanese 1938 Tankette"; "Japanese L.M. Tank M2595 Comet"; "Japan. Tankette M2592 - 1932 Comet." Note: Britains Ltd. 54mm Soldier added for scale. Photo from Ed Poole.

1:108-scale Metal Identification Models; WWII British. Numbering is that of the manufacturer Comet/Authenticast but a Denzil Skinner model is substituted for No. 5012. Front row, left to right: No. 5000 Convenanter IV; No. 5001 Churchill MKV; No. 5002 Universal Carrier; No. 5003 Humber Armoured Car; No. 5004 Carden Loyd Carrier. Middle row, left to right: No. 5005 Valentine; No. 5006 Matilda; No. 5007 Crusader; No. 5009 Cromwell. Front row, left to right: No. 5008 Daimler Armoured Car, No. 5010 Churchill MKVII; No. 5011 Sherman VC 5012 Centurion. Note: Authenticast GI by Holger Eriksson is 23mm tall. Photo from Ed Poole.

1:36-scale Metal Identification models; World War II British. Top row, left to right: Churchill Tank, "Infantry Tank MKIV Comet NY"; armoured car, "Humber MKII Comet NY"; Convenanter Tank, "Cruiser MKV"; Bren Gun, "UK Cruiser MKVI Crusader Comet NY," "Universal Carrier." Front row, left to right: Bren Gun Carrier, "Universal Carrier"; Valentine Tank, "MKIII UK Cruiser Comet NY"; Matilda II Tank, "UK Infantry Tank MKIIA Comet NY"; armoured car, "MKI Daimler Comet NY"; "Carden Loyd Carrier." Note: Britains 54mm "Tommy" for scale. Photo from Ed Poole.

Miscellaneous small metal AFVs. Top row, left to right: Crescent (England) Russian Tank; British Cruiser Tank and Humber Armoured Car; Daimler Ambulance and tank by unknown makers. Front row, left to right: Series by Unknown Maker—Patton Tank, Sherman Tank, Armored car, Tank and Amphibian. U.S. Markings but imprinted "JAPAN". Note: Comet GI is 20 mm tall. Photo from Ed Poole.

Some Military Vehicles by Miscellaneous British manufacturers Top row, left to right: Lone Star Bren Gun Carrier towing Gun; Skybirds Artillery Tractor towing Howitzer; TriAng Mini-Toys Jeep, Lledo Days Gone Ambulance. Front Row, left to right: Charbens Armoured Car; Crescent Armoured Car towing Limber and Gun Corgi Major; International 6x6 Truck; Corgi Toys Hong Kong King Tiger Tank; Lone Star Jeep. Note: Skybird soldier shown for scale is 30mm tall. Photo from Ed Poole.

Die-cast Military Vehicles from Various Countries. Top row, left to right: "Henschel Bau J 1926 Made in W. Germany" (maker unknown); Mercedes Benz 1937 Cabriolet Feuhrerwagen by RIO (Italy); Fiat Antocarro Militaire 1914 by RIO; Military truck; Rader Truck by TEKNO (Denmark); Ambulance by TEKNO. Front row, left to right: Liasson Car by Brumm (Italy); "Dodge 6X6 Made in France" (marked FJ within a geared wheel); three tanks by Play Art (Hong Kong)—Tiger I, Panther and Sherman; Two jeeps—front by Play Art and behind by Fun Ho! (New Zealand); Zylmex "King Tiger" (Hong Kong). Note: Starlux soldiers shown are 30mm tall. Photo from Ed Poole.

Miscellaneous small die-cast military vehicles. Top row, left to right: Mattel "Hot Wheels Gun Bucket"; Corgi Junior (England) Daimler Scout Car; Lesney "Matchbox Rola-matics" No. 73 Weasel; Sherman Tank (made in Hong Kong, pencil sharpener). Front row, left to right: Efsi (Holland) T-Ford 1919 Ambulance; Budgie Toy (England) Tank Transporter; 25pdr Gun Howitzer (maker unknown). Note: Comet GI 20mm tall. Photo from Ed Poole.

Miscellaneous Small metal AFVs. Top row, left to right: HR Products WWI Rhomboidal tanks; Renault FT tank; Quality Castings Desert War 2018 Stuart "Honey"; 2019 MKVI light tank; 2020 Cruiser MK IV. Front row, left to right: Denzil Skinner (England)—British tank Series BZ Centurion, B25 Vickers MKVI and MKII Medium; British Armoured Car Series Bill Daimler; B23 Rolls Royce and Armoured Truck (number unknown). Note Comet GI is 20mm tall. Photo from Ed Poole.

Some contemporary Russian die-casts. Top row, left to right: 76mm Gun; T34-85 Tank; 100mm Gun in 1:43-scale by UEHA (?). Front row, left to right: T34 Tank; Two YA3-469 Cars in 1:43 scale by Schelano B CCCP. Dinky soldiers added for scale is 30mm tall. Photo from Ed Poole.

Arnold (Germany) Jeep with Five and Dime Corps troops and mascot; Jeep 17cm long. Photo from Ed Poole.

Three Battle of Britain 50th Anniversary Commemorative sets; vehicles each about 8cm in length. Photo from Ed Poole.

Prime Mover (after Barclay) and Howitzer (after Tootsietoy) from Junior Caster Model No. E45; homecast. Photo from Ron Eccles. Photo by Ed Poole.

MINIATURE VEHICLE CASTINGS

Though these appear to be toys from the 1930s, they were first produced in 1985. The models were carved and cast by owner Robert E. Wagner. Made of die-cast lead from silicone molds, they were sold for $21 each; at least 3,500 have been sold. Some are beginning to appear at toy shops and on dealer lists. The average length is about 4-1/2 inches, and the New Jersey firm's name is visible (sometimes dimly) on a piece of tin soldered to the bottom. The toys today seem to sell at slightly more than double their original price.

Following is a list of Miniature Vehicle Castings:
1937 Ford Two-door Sedan
1938 Ford Standard Sedan Delivery
1934 Olds Two-door Humpback
1936 Olds Four-door Humpback
1937 Hudson Terraplane Two-door
1938 Dodge Step Van
1937 Plymouth Five-window Coupe
1937 Dodge Two-door Humpback
1938 Plymouth Two-door Sedan
1941 Ford COE Truck (flatbed or dump)
1935 Hudson two-door Sedan
1937 Studebaker Three-window Coupe
1936 Plymouth Four-door Sedan
1936 Plymouth Four-door Taxi
1935 Pontiac Three-window Coupe
1940 Dodge Two-door Sedan
1939 Dodge Two-door Sedan
1941 Divco Milk Truck (Sunrise Dairy)

Left to right: 1937 Hudson Terraplane; 1935 Hudson. Photo from Bob and Alice Wagner.

Left to right: Miniature Vehicle Castings 1934 Olds; 1936 Olds. Photo from Bob and Alice Wagner.

Miniature Vehicle Castings 1938 Dodge Step Van. Photo from Bob and Alice Wagner.

Left to right: Miniature Vehicle Castings 1941 Ford C.O.E. Truck; 1937 Studebaker three-window Coupe; 1936 Plymouth Taxi. Photo from Bob and Alice Wagner.

From left: Miniature Vehicle Castings 1938 Plymouth two-door Sedan; 1937 Plymouth Coupe, five windows; 1937 Dodge two-door Humpback. Photo from Bob and Alice Wagner.

MINIC

Established by George Lines in the 1870s, the original Lines company of England made wooden rocking horses. Lines' brother, Joseph joined the firm and ultimately bought out his share. After World War I, three of Joseph Lines' sons formed a company called Lines Bros., Ltd. and its logo was a triangle, and its products came to be known as Tri-ang Toys. By the mid 1930s, the company was making prams, cycles, pedal cars, stamped steel trucks, wooden toys, doll houses, and many other kinds of playthings.

In 1935, the Tri-ang Minic Miniature Clockwork Vehicles were introduced. Only fourteen models were available that first year. Three to seven inches in length, they were robustly made of heavier gauge steel than that used by competing German manufacturers. They had brightly plated radiators and wheels. The trucks and some of the cars even had plated fenders. Painting was done by a dipping and baking process which caused runs, as well as thick and thin areas, but the finishes were durable. Subtle shades of red, blue, green, beige, orange and yellow, plus black and chrome were tastefully combined to make some unusually attractive color schemes. The road vehicles and white rubber tires and each Minic came boxed with a stamped steel key and a little color folding catalogue inside the box.

The first Minics must have successful, because in 1936 many new types were added and a few even had electric lights. A miniature Shell gasoline can appeared on the left running board of most cars and trucks. By early September 1939, England was at war and the Shell can had been deleted. The white tires were replaced with black, and the plated trunk rack on the ordinary cars was replaced by a decal number plate and a plain rear bumper. Since 1935, many new models were added and none discontinued. The factory claimed that more than seventy types were available. However, by 1940, some vehicles were painted in army camouflage, while others, such as the electric lighted types, were phased out. The non-military vehicles had some parts chemically blackened instead of plated. Steering wheels were later attached with miniature split pins instead of being pressed onto a brass column.

After the war ended, Minics were rushed back into production. The British economy required exports, and large quantities of Minics were sent to the United States, which was starved for metal toys. Minics seem to have been available in many areas of the country, whereas there had been very few outlets before the war. The first postwar Minics often had leftover prewar parts and boxes. Stronger colors were used (mostly bright red, dark blue, and shades of green) and the quality of finish was below the prewar standard. Tolling was wearing out and the stampings often lacked definition. In time, quite a few new types and variations were produced before the company ceased operations in the 1970s.

In addition to the vehicles, various garages, service stations, and even a fire station were made prewar and postwar. The numbering system used below was instituted about 1938 or 1939. In general, the lower the number, the cheaper the item. However, new toys announced 1939 or 1940 were tacked on to the end of the existing list (65M-79M). Some of this last group were never put into production before toy manufacturing ended during World War II.

Why is there no value guide for prewar Minic toys? Very few are changing hands in the 1990s and not enough data exists to develop a reliable and useful listing of values.

Mint in Box versions of postwar Minic vehicles average between $95 and $225.

01M Ford Saloon Sedan, 1936

01MCF Ford Saloon, camouflaged, fewer than 100 known, 1939-1940 (none produced postwar)

02M Ford Light Van, 1936

03M Ford Royal Mail Van, 1936

04M Sports Saloon, two-window sedan; headlights, radiator and bumper stamped from one piece, 1935; it is a possibility that a small number were made following WWII w/a new tooling for radiator and matte-black baseplate

05M Limousine, three-window sedan; headlights, radiator and bumper stamped from one piece, 1935; a small number were made following WWII w/a new tooling for radiator and matte-black baseplate

06M Cabriolet, coupe, headlights, radiator and bumper stamped from one piece, 1935; a small number were made following WWII w/a new tooling for radiator and matte-black baseplate

07M Town Coupe (Town Car), headlights, radiator and bumper stamped from one piece, 1935; a small number were made following WWII w/a new tooling for radiator and matte-black baseplate

08M Open Touring Car, headlights, radiator and bumper stamped from one piece, 1935; a small number were made following WWII w/a new tooling for radiator and matte-black baseplate

09M Streamline Saloon Airflow Sedan, 1935

10M Delivery Lorry (Pickup Truck), headlights, radiator and bumper stamped from one piece, 1935

11M Tractor, headlights riveted to bar held in place by radiator, 1935

11MCF Tractor, camouflaged, 1940 (none produced postwar); fewer than fifty known to exist

12M Learner's Car, 1936, 1, 5

13M Racing Car, headlights, radiator and bumper stamped from one piece, 1936, fewer than 100 known to exist

14M Streamline Sports, 1935

15M Petrol Tank Lorry Oil Tanker, 1936, fewer than 100 known to exist

15MCF Petrol Tank Lorry, headlights, radiator and bumper stamped in one piece, camouflaged, 1940 (none produced postwar); fewer than 100 known to exist

Left to right: Minic Fire Station; small 00 Service Station. Photo from Gates Willard. Photo by E.W. Willard.

Minic Service Station with pumps, oil bin and electric lamps advertising Shell and Pratts. Photo from Gates Willard. Photo by E.W. Willard.

Left to right: 2M Minic Ford Light Van, 1936; 3M Ford Royal Mail Van; 1M Ford Saloon (Sedan); 1MCF Ford Saloon, camouflaged. Photo from Gates Willard. Photo by E.W. Willard.

Left to right: 15M Minic Petrol Tank Lorry (Oil Tanker), 1936; 78M Pool Tanker, 1940; 31M Mechanical Horse and Fuel Oil Tanker, 1936; 79M Mechanical Horse and Pool Tanker, 1940. Photo from Gates Willard. Photo by E.W. Willard.

Left to right: 17M Minic Vauxhall Tourer, 1937; 18M Vauxhall Town Coupe; 19M Vauxhall Cabriolet; 19MCF Vauxhall Cabriolet, camouflaged, 1940. Photo from Gates Willard. Photo by E.W. Willard.

Left to right: 4M Minic Sports Saloon, 1935; 5M Limousine, 1935. Photo from Gates Willard. Photo by E.W. Willard.

Left to right: 7M Minic Town Coupe, 1935; 6M Cabriolet, 1935; 8M Open Touring Car, 1935. Photo from Gates Willard. Photo by E.W. Willard.

16M Caravan, non-electric, house trailer, 1937

17M Vauxhall Tourer, headlights riveted to bar held in place by radiator, 1937

18M Vauxhall Town Coupe, headlights riveted to bar held in place by radiator, 1937

19M Vauxhall Cabriolet, headlights riveted to bar held in place by radiator, 1937

19MCF Vauxhall Cabriolet, camouflaged, headlights riveted to bar held in place by radiator, 1940 (none produced postwar); fewer than 100 known to exist

20M Light Tank, painted either dark glossy green or gray, 1935 (none produced postwar)

20MCF Light Tank, camouflaged, 1940 (none produced postwar); fewer than fifty known to exist

21M Transport Van, headlights, radiator and bumper stamped in one piece, decals not used during first year produced, 1935

21MCF Transport Van, camouflaged, headlights, radiator and bumper stamped in one piece, 1940 (none made after WWII); fewer than 100 known to exist

22M Carter Paterson Van, headlights, radiator and bumper stamped in one piece, 1936

23M Tip Lorry Dump Truck, headlights, radiator and bumper stamped in one piece, 1936

24M Luton Transport Van Moving Van, headlights, radiator and bumper stamped in one piece, 1936

24MCF Luton Van, camouflaged, 1940 (none produced postwar)

25M Delivery Lorry w/cases, headlights, radiator and bumper stamped in one piece, 1936

26M Tractor and trailer with cases, 1936

27M, 28M - Numbers not used

29M Traffic Control Car (Police Car), headlights rivited to bar held inplace by radiator, 1938

Left to right: 18M Minic Vauxhall Town Coupe, plain bumper and number plate, 1937; 8M Open Touring Car, with luggage rack and Shell can, 1935. Photo from Gates Willard. Photo by E.W. Willard.

Left to right: 24MCF Minic Luton Van, camouflaged, 1940; 24M Luton Transport Van, 1936. Photo from Gates Willard. Photo by E.W. Willard.

Left to right: 21M Minic Transport Van, 1935; 22M Carter Paterson Van, 1936; 21M Transport Van, 1935; 21MCF Transport Van, camouflaged, 1940. Photo from Gates Willard. Photo by E.W. Willard.

Four Minic Tourers. Left to right: 35M Rolls; 36M Daimler; 37M Bentley, non-electric (electric versions were never made); 55ME electric-lighted Bentley Tourer. Note the battery box in back in place of the rear seat. Photo from Gates Willard. Photo by E.W. Willard.

Top to bottom: Minic Delivery Lorry with cases, 1936; Mechanical Horse and Trailer with cases; Delivery Lorry (Pickup Truck), 1935; Tip Lorry (Dump Truck), 1936. Photo from Gates Willard. Photo by E.W. Willard.

Left to right: 33M Minic Steam Roller; 11MCF Camouflaged Tractor; 26M Tractor and 11M Trailer with cases. Photo from Gates Willard. Photo by E.W. Willard.

Minic Mechanical Horse and Pantechnicon. Left to right: typical 1935-1936 version; rare Brockhouse promotional. Photo from Gates Willard. Photo by E.W. Willard.

Left to right: 37M Minic Bentley Tourer, non-electric, 1938; 55ME Bentley Tourer, electric. Photo from Gates Willard. Photo by E.W. Willard.

Two 38M Minic Caravan Sets. Left to right: 5M Limousine and 16M non-electric Caravan, 1937; 34M Tourer with Passengers, 1937, 34ME Caravan with electric light. Photo from Gates Willard. Photo by E.W. Willard.

The Minic Rolls Royce Sedanca with electric head-lamps as sold by Bloomingdale's department store in New York City for $1.98. Also shown are the key and catalog that were included with every Minic, plus instruction/information sheets. Photo from Gates Willard. Photo by E.W. Willard.

Minic electric-lighted Sunshine Saloons. Left to right: Rolls; Daimler; Bentley. Photo from Gates Willard. Photo by E.W. Willard.

Minic Sunshine Saloons. Left to right: 47M Rolls, non-electric; 45M Daimler, non-electric; 46M Bentley, non-electric. Photo from Gates Willard. Photo by E.W. Willard.

30M Mechanical Horse and Pantechnicon, headlights, radiator and bumper stamped in one piece, decals not used during first year of production, 1935; a special non-numbered issue Brockhouse promotional was made c.1937; reportedly fewer than 100 made

31M Mechanical Horse and Fuel Oil Tanker, headlights rivited to bar held inplace by radiator, 1936

32M Dust Cart (Garbage Truck), headlights rivited to bar held inplace by radiator, 1936

33M Steam Roller, 1935

34M Tourer with Passengers, headlights, radiator and bumper stamped in one piece, 1937 (none produced postwar); fewer than 100 known to exist

35M Rolls Tourer, Non-electric, headlights rivited to bar held inplace by radiator, no front bumper, 1937 (none produced postwar)

36M Daimler Tourer, Non-electric, headlights rivited to bar held inplace by radiator, 1937 (none produced postwar)

37M Bentley Tourer, Non-electric, headlights rivited to bar held inplace by radiator, 1938 (none produced postwar)

38M Caravan Set (Limousine and Non-electric caravan), 1937; fewer than fifty known to exist

39M Taxi, 1938, rare if found in colors other than dark blue

40M Mechanical Horse and Trailer with cases, headlights, radiator and bumper stamped in one piece, 1936; fewer than 100 known to exist

41ME Caravan with electric light, 1937 (none produced postwar); fewer than 100 known to exist

42M Rolls Sedanca, Non-electric, headlights rivited to bar held inplace by radiator, no front bumper, 1937; fewer than 100 known to exist

43M Daimler Sedanca, Non-electric, headlights rivited to bar held inplace by radiator, 1937; fewer than 100 known to exist

44M Traction Engine, 1938; fewer than 100 known to exist

45M Bentley Sunshine Saloon, (Sunroof Sedan), Non-electric, headlights rivited to bar held inplace by radiator, 1938; fewer than fifty known to exist

46M Daimler Sunshine Saloon, non-electric, headlights rivited to bar held inplace by radiator, 1938; fewer than fifty known to exist

47M Rolls Sunshine Saloon, Non-electric, headlights rivited to bar held inplace by radiator, 1938; fewer than fifty known to exist

XXIV

THE MECCANO MAGAZINE

MINIC Regd. Trade Mark

ALL TO SCALE CLOCKWORK TOYS

Almost every type of vehicle on the road represented; some with ELECTRIC LIGHTS. Strongly constructed and fitted with powerful, long-running mechanism, they will run anywhere, EVEN ON THE CARPET. Each model is beautifully finished in a variety of colours, and packed singly in an attractive box.

MINIC Ford £100 Saloon
LENGTH 3½ ins.   Price 6d.

MINIC Racing Car
LENGTH 5¼ ins.   Price 1/-

MINIC Luton Transport Van
LENGTH 5½ ins.   Price 1/6

MINIC Breakdown Lorry
with Mechanical Crane
LENGTH 5¼ ins.   Price 3/6

MINIC Mechanical Horse and
Fuel Oil Trailer
LENGTH 7 ins.   Price 2/-

MINIC Dust Cart
LENGTH 5½ ins.   Price 2/-

MINIC Steam Roller
LENGTH 5¼ ins.   Price 1/6

MINIC Light Tank
LENGTH 3½ ins.   Price 1/6

MINIC Streamline Saloon
LENGTH 5 ins.   Price 1/-

MINIC Petrol Tank Lorry
LENGTH 5½ ins.   Price 1/-

MINIC Searchlight Lorry
with Electric Searchlight and
Battery
LENGTH 5¼ ins.   Price 3/6

MINIC Single Deck Bus
LENGTH 7¼ ins.
Price 3/6. Red or green.

MINIC Lorry with cases
LENGTH 5½ ins.   Price 1/6

MINIC Tip Lorry
LENGTH 5½ ins.   Price 1/3

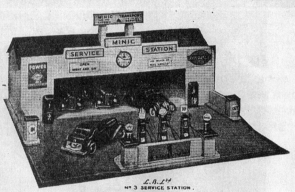

No 3 SERVICE STATION.

MINIC Service Station No. 3
Realistic design, imitation red tiled roof with sign, three large petrol pumps, one large oil cabinet, two electric lights and battery, dummy clock face and other signs. LENGTH 16 ins. 7/6
Other models 1/6, 3/11, 5/-, 15/-, 25/-

L.B.Lᵈ MINIC CONSTRUCTION SET N°1

MINIC Contruction Set No. 1
A complete set of parts for making six types of MINIC all to scale clockwork models. All parts, including powerful clockwork motor units, are made with precision tools and machines. Full instructions and tools are included in each set which is packed in a handsome oak finished cabinet 18 ins. x 9¾ ins. x 2½ ins.
PRICE 15/-

MINIC Caravan Trailer
LENGTH 4½ ins.
COMPLETE WITH ELECTRIC LIGHT AND BATTERY 3/6
CAR NOT INCLUDED, BUT CAN BE OBTAINED PRICE 1/-

There are thirty-four models to choose from; some with ELECTRIC LIGHTS.

TRI-ANG TOYS
OBTAINABLE AT ALL GOOD TOY SHOPS AND STORES

Ask your dealer to show you the complete range, also the **MINIC** Service Stations.

Made in England by

LINES BROS. LTD., Tri-ang Works, Morden Rd., London, S.W.19

The Minic line was becoming more sophistic when this ad appeared in *Meccano Magazine*. **Photo from Gates Willard.**

48M Breakdown Lorry (Wrecker Truck), headlights, radiator and bumper stamped in one piece, 1936

48MCF Breakdown Lorry, camouflaged, headlights, radiator and bumper stamped in one piece, 1940 (none produced postwar); fewer than fifty known to exist

49ME Searchlight Lorry, headlights, radiator and bumper stamped in one piece, 1936 (none produced postwar)

49MECF Searchlight Lorry, camouflaged, headlights, radiator and bumper stamped in one piece, 1940 (none produced postwar); fewer than fifty known to exist

50ME Rolls Sedanca, electric, no front bumper, electric headlights, 1936 (none produced postwar); fewer than fifty known to exist

51ME Daimler Sedanca, electric, electric headlights, 1937 (none produced postwar); fewer than fifty known to exist

52M Single Deck Bus, red, 1936

53M Single Deck Bus, green, 1936

54M Traction Engine and Trailer, 1939; fewer than fifty known to exist

55ME Bentley Tourer, electric (production probably delayed), electric headlights, 1938 (none produced postwar); fewer than fifty known to exist

Left to right: 50ME Minic Rolls Sedanca; 51ME Daimler Sedanca; 42M Rolls Sedance; 43M Daimler Sedanca. The two Minic Sedancas on the left have electric lights; the battery is inside the opening trunk. A turn screw operated the lamps. The two cars on the right are non-electric and there is no separate trunk lid. All postwar Rolls, Bentleys an. Photo from Gates Willard. Photo by E.W. Willard.

Left to right: 48M Minic Breakdown Lorry; 48CF Camouflaged Breakdown Lorry; 49ME Searchlight Lorry; 49MECF Camouflaged Searchlight Lorry. Also shown is an original Everready battery. Photo from Gates Willard. Photo by E.W. Willard.

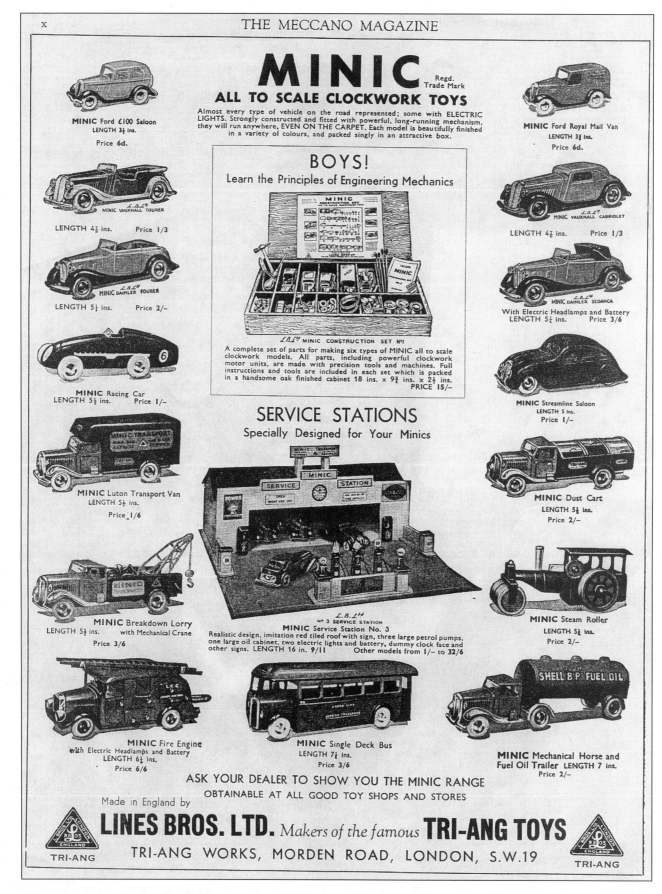

MINIC
Regd. Trade Mark

ALL TO SCALE CLOCKWORK TOYS

Almost every type of vehicle on the road represented; some with ELECTRIC LIGHTS. Strongly constructed and fitted with powerful, long-running mechanism, they will run anywhere, EVEN ON THE CARPET. Each model is beautifully finished in a variety of colours, and packed singly in an attractive box.

MINIC Ford £100 Saloon
LENGTH 3¼ ins.
Price 6d.

MINIC Vauxhall Tourer
LENGTH 4⅞ ins.   Price 1/3

MINIC Daimler Tourer
LENGTH 5¼ ins.   Price 2/–

MINIC Racing Car
LENGTH 5½ ins.   Price 1/–

MINIC Luton Transport Van
LENGTH 5¼ ins.
Price 1/6

MINIC Breakdown Lorry with Mechanical Crane
LENGTH 5½ ins.
Price 3/6

MINIC Ford Royal Mail Van
LENGTH 3¼ ins.
Price 6d.

MINIC Vauxhall Cabriolet
LENGTH 4⅞ ins.   Price 1/3

MINIC Daimler Sedanca
With Electric Headlamps and Battery
LENGTH 5¼ ins.   Price 3/6

MINIC Streamline Saloon
LENGTH 5 ins.
Price 1/–

MINIC Dust Cart
LENGTH 5¼ ins.
Price 2/–

MINIC Steam Roller
LENGTH 5¼ ins.
Price 2/–

BOYS!
Learn the Principles of Engineering Mechanics

L.B.Lᵗᵈ MINIC CONSTRUCTION SET Nº 1

A complete set of parts for making six types of MINIC all to scale clockwork models. All parts, including powerful clockwork motor units, are made with precision tools and machines. Full instructions and tools are included in each set which is packed in a handsome oak finished cabinet 18 ins. x 9¾ ins. x 2¼ ins.
PRICE 15/–

SERVICE STATIONS
Specially Designed for Your Minics

MINIC Nº 3 SERVICE STATION
MINIC Service Station No. 3
Realistic design, imitation red tiled roof with sign, three large petrol pumps, one large oil cabinet, two electric lights and battery, dummy clock face and other signs. LENGTH 16 in. 9/11   Other models from 1/– to 32/6

MINIC Fire Engine with Electric Headlamps and Battery
LENGTH 6¼ ins.
Price 6/6

MINIC Single Deck Bus
LENGTH 7½ ins.
Price 3/6

MINIC Mechanical Horse and Fuel Oil Trailer LENGTH 7 ins.
Price 2/–

ASK YOUR DEALER TO SHOW YOU THE MINIC RANGE
OBTAINABLE AT ALL GOOD TOY SHOPS AND STORES

Made in England by
LINES BROS. LTD. *Makers of the famous* TRI-ANG TOYS
TRI-ANG WORKS, MORDEN ROAD, LONDON, S.W.19

TRI-ANG

TRI-ANG

Minic toys, as pictured in the September 1937 issue of *Meccano Magazine*. Photo from Gates Willard.

56ME Rolls Sunshine Saloon, electric, electric headlights, 1938 (none produced postwar); fewer than fifty known to exist

57ME Bentley Sunshine Saloon electric, electric headlights, 1938 (none produced postwar); fewer than fifty known to exist

58ME Daimler Sunshine Saloon electric, electric headlights, 1938 (none produced postwar); fewer than fifty known to exist

59ME Caravan Set, tourer with passengers and caravan with electric light, 1937 (none produced postwar); fewer than fifty known to exist

60M Double Deck Bus, red, 1935

61M Double Deck Bus, green, 1935 (none produced postwar); fewer than fifty known to exist

62ME Fire Engine, electric headlights, 1936

63M No. 1 Presentation Set, 1937 (none produced postwar); fewer than fifty known to exist

64M No. 2 Presentation Set, 1937 (none produced postwar); fewer than fifty known to exist

65M Construction Set, 1936 (none produced postwar); fewer than fifty known to exist

66M Six Wheel Army Lorry, ten wheel, painted dark glossy green, headlights, radiator and bumper stamped in one piece, 1939 (none produced postwar); fewer than 100 known to exist

Left to right: 50ME Rolls Sedanca; 51ME Daimler Sedanca; 42M Rolls Sedanca; 43M Daimler Sedanca. Four Minic Sedancas, the Rolls and Daimler on the left have electric lights, but the Rolls and Daimler on the right are non-electric. Bentley Sedancas were never made. Photo from Gates Willard. Photo by E.W. Willard.

Left to right: 56ME Minic Rolls Sunshine Saloon, electric, 1938; 51ME Daimler Sedanca, electric, 1937; 55ME Bentley Tourer, electric, 1938; 47M Rolls Sunshine Saloon, non-electric, 1938; 43M Daimler Sedanca, non-electric, 1937; 37M Bentley Tourer, non-electric, 1938. Photo from Gates Willard. Photo by E.W. Willard.

Left to right: 61M Minic Double-Deck Bus; 53M Single-Deck Bus. These buses were produced in red, beige or two-tone green. All four were separately numbered in trade catalog. Photo from Gates Willard. Photo by E.W. Willard.

Left to right: 67M Minic Farm Lorry; 68M Timber Lorry; 72M Mechanical Horse and Lorry with barrels. Photo from Gates Willard. Photo by E.W. Willard.

Left to right: 62ME Minic Fire Engine, with electric headlamps and attachments (hoses are in an opening compartment), 1936; 39M Taxi, 1938; 29M Traffic Control Car (Police Car), 1938. Photo from Gates Willard. Photo by E.W. Willard.

Left to right: 71M Minic Mechanical Horse and Milk Trailer, 1939; 72M Mechanical Horse and Lorry with barrels, 1939. Photo from Gates Willard. Photo by E.W. Willard.

66MCF Six Wheel Army Lorry, camouflaged, headlights, radiator and bumper stamped in one piece, 1939-1940; fewer than 100 known to exist

67M Farm Lorry, headlights, radiator and bumper stamped in one piece, 1939-1940; fewer than fifty known to exist

68M Timber Lorry, headlights, radiator and bumper stamped in one piece, 1939; fewer than fifty known to exist

69M Canvas Tilt Lorry (Enclosed Army Truck), ten wheel, painted dark glossy green, headlights, radiator and bumper stamped in one piece, 1939-1940; fewer than fifty known to exist

69MCF Canvas Tilt Lorry, camouflaged, ten wheel, headlights, radiator and bumper stamped in one piece, 1940-1940

70M Coal Lorry not made, cataloged but never made, 1939

Left to right: 69M Minic Canvas Tilt Lorry; 69MCF Camouflaged Canvas Tilt Lorry; 66M Six-wheel Army Lorry; 66MCF Camouflaged Six-wheel Army Lorry. Photo from Gates Willard. Photo by E.W. Willard.

xii

THE MECCANO MAGAZINE

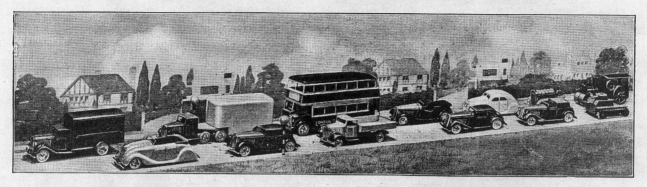

LOOKS LIKE A REAL ROAD DOESN'T IT?

Though it's difficult to believe, the traffic jam in this photograph is actually made up of MINIC scale model clockwork toys.

This unique clockwork series will contain almost every vehicle to be seen on the roads. Each model is true to scale so that the bus is exactly the right amount larger than the lorry and the limousine in the right proportion to the open tourer.

These MINIC vehicles are wonderfully built and have reliable long-running clockwork; they are most reasonably priced too, the smaller ones costing only 1/– each. They have a front wheel drive, so that they will run on carpet and can be used in any room.

Start collecting your road full now.

MINIC scale model LIMOUSINE
Strong construction, with powerful long-running clockwork motor. Colours: Dark Green, plated guards; Ivory, Red guards; New Blue, Ivory guards. Radiator and bumpers plated, also wheels, with rubber tyres. Length, 4¾ in.   Price 1/–

MINIC scale model STREAMLINE CLOSED.
Strong construction, with powerful long-running clockwork motor. Colours: Red, Ivory, New Blue. Plated bumpers, radiator, also wheels, with rubber tyres. Length, 5 in.   Price 1/–

MINIC scale model STREAMLINE OPEN.
Strong construction, with powerful long-running clockwork motor. Colours: Ivory, Red hood; Red, Ivory hood; or Light Green, Ivory hood. Plated radiator, bumpers, also wheels, with rubber tyres. Length, 5 in.   Price 1/–

MINIC scale model SPORTS SALOON.
Strong construction, with powerful long-running clockwork motor. Colours: Ivory, New Blue, Primrose, with plated mudguards, radiator, bumpers, also wheels, with rubber tyres. Length, 4¾ in.   Price 1/–

MINIC scale model TRACTOR.
Strong construction, with powerful long-running clockwork mechanism. Colours: Green with Red wheels, or Red with Green wheels. Length, 3 in.   Price 1/–

MINIC scale model TOWN COUPÉ.
Strong construction, with powerful long-running clockwork motor. Colours: New Blue, plated mudguards; Light Brown, Black mudguards; or Ivory, Red mudguards. Plated radiator, bumpers, also wheels, with rubber tyres. Length, 4¾ in.   Price 1/–

MINIC scale model CABRIOLET.
Strong construction, with powerful long-running clockwork motor. Colours: Ivory and Green with plated mudguards, or Red with Ivory mudguards. Radiator, bumpers, plated, also wheels, with rubber tyres. Length, 4¾ in.   Price 1/–

MINIC scale model OPEN SPORTS TOURER.
Strong construction, with powerful long-running clockwork motor. Colours: Green, plated mudguards, Ivory hood; Red, Ivory mudguards and hood; Ivory, Red mudguards and hood. Plated bumpers, radiator, also wheels, with rubber tyres. Length, 4¾ in.   Price 1/–

MINIC
Regd. Trade Mark

CLOCKWORK TOYS ALL TO SCALE
Obtainable from all good Toy Shops and Stores
Made by Lines Bros. Ltd., Tri-ang Works, Merton, S.W.19

This was the first Minic advertisement as shown in *Meccano Magazine*. Photo from Gates Willard.

71M Mechanical Horse and Milk Trailer, number on box is "70M," headlights, radiator and bumper stamped in one piece, 1939; fewer than fifty known to exist

72M Mechanical Horse and Lorry with Barrels, number on box is "71M," headlights, radiator and bumper stamped in one piece, 1939; fewer than fifty known to exist

73M Cable Lorry, prewar, not made, cataloged as prewar, but not made until postwar, 1939

74M Log Lorry, number on box is "75M," headlights, radiator and bumper stamped in one piece, 1939; fewer than fifty known to exist

75M Ambulance, prewar, not made, cataloged as prewar, but not made until postwar, 1939

76M Balloon Barrage Wagon and Trailer, production delayed until 1940 made in camouflage only; should have been numbered 76MCF; 1939-1940; fewer than fifty known to exist

77M Double Deck Trolley Bus, cataloged but never made, 1939

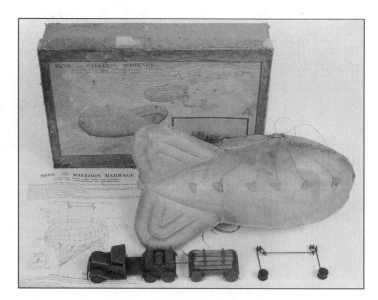

76M Minic Balloon Barrage Wagon and Trailer. Photo from Gates Willard. Photo by E.W. Willard.

78M Pool Tanker, headlights, radiator and bumper stamped in one piece, 1939-1940; fewer than fifty known to exist

79M Mechanical Horse and Pool Tanker, headlights, radiator and bumper stamped in one piece, 1939-1940; fewer than fifty known to exist

MINNITOYS BY OTACO LIMITED (ONTARIO, CANADA)

Contributor: John Taylor, P.O. Box 63, Nolensville, TN 37135-0063.

	C6	C8	C10		C6	C8	C10
Beaver Lumber Truck, 1950s, 29" long	200	350	500	Country Good Soups Trailer Truck, w/french side, 29" long	300	500	700

Minnitoys Good Soups Tractor Trailer, French inscription. Photo from John Taylor.

Minnitoys Ketchup Trailer Truck, 1950s, 29". Photo from John Taylor.

	C6	C8	C10
Country Good Soups Trailer Truck, 1950s, 29" long	200	400	600
Heinz Ketchup Trailer Truck, 1950s, 29" long	200	400	600
Heinz Pickles Trailer Truck, w/French side, 29" long	300	500	700
Heinz Pickles Trailer Truck, 1950s, 29" long	200	400	600
Ice Truck, 1950s, 29" long	200	300	400
Irving Gasoline Tanker Truck, 1950s, 16" long	400	800	1000
Minni Construction Dump Truck, 1950s, 16" long	150	225	300
Minni Construction Hydraulic Dump Truck, 1950s, 16" long	150	225	300
Minnitoy Wrecker, 1950s, 18" long	200	300	400
Shell Tanker Truck, 1950s, 29" long	300	500	800
Texaco Gasoline Tanker Truck, 1950s, 29" long	400	800	1000
White Rose Tanker Trailer, 1950s, 29" long	200	400	600

Minnitoys Heinz Pickles Trailer Truck, Canada, 1950s, 29". Photo from John Taylor.

MURRAY

	C6	C8	C10		C6	C8	C10
Buick Pedal Car, 1949	1500	2700	4600	Pace Car Pedal Car, 1959	500	800	1100
Camaro Pedal Car, 1968	88	132	175	Pontiac Station Wagon Pedal Car, 1948	950	1500	2200
Champion Pedal Car	500	850	1150	Racer Pedal Car, No. 8, 1960	215	322	430
Clipper Pedal Car	550	900	1200	Radio Sports Car, 1959	480	720	960
Comet Pedal Car, 1956	800	1400	2000	Speedway Pace Car, 1959	500	800	1100
Country Squire Station Wagon Pedal Car, 1955	325	488	650	Suburban Pedal Car, 1950	550	850	1200
Earth Mover Pedal Car, 1959	550	850	1200	Super Wildcat Pedal Car, 1961	350	525	700
Fire Chief Pedal Car	500	800	1100	Tee Bird Pedal Car, 1961	140	210	280
Fire Truck Pedal Car	200	300	400	Tractor Pedal Car, c.1950	400	600	800
Golden Wildcat Pedal Car, 1961	425	635	850				

NEFF-MOON

Neff-Moon, of Sandusky, Ohio, was owned by William Moon and Charles Neff. Production of its pressed steel toys began in 1923. The firm, which was located above a grocery, was apparently an early victim of the Depression.

	C6	C8	C10
10 Toys in 1 Set, No. 14....................	500	750	1040
Coupe...	NPF	NPF	NPF
Dump truck......................................	NPF	NPF	NPF
Emergency Truck............................	NPF	NPF	NPF
Groceries Van	175	262	350
Sedan...	NPF	NPF	NPF
Sedan, 12" long..............................	500	800	1100
Sedan Delivery Truck......................	350	525	700
Taxi, 12" long	350	525	700
Tow Truck, c.1925, 16" long	200	300	400
Truck, interchangable......................	NPF	NPF	NPF

Neff-Moon Emergency Truck. Photo from Don Hultzman.

Neff-Moon Coupe. Photo from Don Hultzman.

Neff-Moon Sedan, 12". Photo from Don Hultzman.

Neff-Moon Dump Truck. Photo from Don Hultzman.

Neff-Moon Convertible Auto Sets and Interchangeable Toys. Photo from Don Hultzman.

NYLINT

The Nylint Tool and Manufacturing Company was formed in 1937 by Bernard C. Klint and David Nyberg (thus its name) in Rockford, Illinois. Toy production began in the spring of 1946. Since 1951, the firm has concentrated on the production of heavy-duty scale reproductions, in steel, of earth-moving equipment and over-the-road trucks. Jeff L. Hubbard provided part of the following list.

	C6	C8	C10
Austin Western Crane	125	188	250
Brinks Truck	48	72	95
Chase & Sanborn, stake sides	100	140	200
Elevating Scraper, 1950s	NPF	NPF	NPF
Fire Truck, 1970, 20" long	27	41	55
Ford Cab-over Tow Truck, 17" long	95	143	190
Harley Davidson Tanker, 25" long	100	150	200
Hot Rod and Trailer	60	90	120
Jungle Wagon	100	150	200
Vacationer Bronco and Travel Trailer, 1960s, 20" overall	100	150	200
No. 0600 Amazing Car, wind-up, 1946-49, 13-3/4" long	100	150	200
No. 0800 Scootcycle, wind-up, 1948-50, 7-1/4" long	200	300	400

	C6	C8	C10
No. 1000 Deliverall, wind-up, 1948-51, 10" long	300	450	600
No. 1100 Elgin Street Sweeper, wind-up, 1950-52, 8-1/4" long	250	375	500
No. 1200 Pumpmobile, wind-up, 1950-52, 8-5/8" long	125	188	250
No. 1300 Tournarocker, open tractor w/driver, 1951-52, 18" long	62	93	125
No. 1300 Tournarocker 1953-57, no driver, closed cab, 1953-57, 18" long	105	158	210
No. 1400 Road Grader, small wheels, 1951, 19-1/4" long	65	98	130

Nylint Ranch Truck, Chase & Sanborn version, 14". Photo from Bob Smith.

Nylint Ford Cab-over Tow Truck, 17". Photo from Bob Smith.

Nylint Elevating Scraper.

Nylint Vacationer Bronco and Travel Trailer, 1960s, 20". Photo from John Taylor.

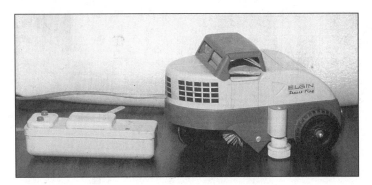

Nylint Elgin Street Sweeper, 1950s, battery-operated, closed cab. Photo from Frank McCormick.

Nylint Tournarocker, 1950s, open tractor, driver, 18". **Photo from Thomas G. Nefos.**

Nylint Payloader, No. 1600, 1950s. Photo from Continental Hobby House.

Nylint Traveloader, 1950s, 30". Photo from Thomas G. Nefos.

Nylint Speed Swing, No. 2000, 1955-58, 19". Photo from Thomas G. Nefos.

	C6	C8	C10
No. 1400 Road Grader, larger wheels, 1952-58	70	105	140
No. 1500 Tournahopper, 1951-56, 22-1/2" long	175	263	350
No. 1600 Payloader, red, 1951-54, 18" long	75	112	150
No. 1600 Payloader, tan, 1955	125	188	250
No. 1600 Payloader, light green, 1956-57	100	150	200
No. 1600 Payloader, yellow, 1958; earlier version were done in green, add twenty percent to yellow price	100	150	200

	C6	C8	C10
No. 1700 Tournahauler, 1953-56, 30-1/4" long	70	105	140
No. 1800 Traveloader, 1953-55, 30" long	113	170	225
No. 1900 Tournatractor, 1954-55, 14-3/4" long	150	225	300
No. 2000 Speed Swing, 1955-58, 19" long	100	150	200
No. 2100 Tournadozer, 1956-59, 20" long	110	165	220
No. 2200 Michigan Shovel, 1955-65, 31-1/2" long	78	117	155
No. 2300 Elgin Street Sweeper, battery-operated version, closed cab, 1956-57	120	180	240
No. 2400 Electronic Cannon, no radar antenna, 1956	100	150	200
No. 2400 Electronic Cannon, has radar antenna, 1956, 22-1/2" long	88	132	175
No. 2500 Telescoping Crane, 1957-60, 27" long	125	188	250

	C6	C8	C10
No. 2600 Missile Launcher, 1957-60, 31-1/2" long........................	125	188	250
No. 2700 Uranium Hauler, 1958-59. 22-1/2" long........................	125	188	250
No. 2800 Guided Missile Carrier, first version, nose cone of missile doesn't fire, 1958, 15-1/2" long	150	225	300
No. 2800 Guided Missile Carrier, later (made through 1960), cone of missile fires	75	112	150
No. 2900 Jack Hammer, 1958-60, 19-1/2" long, w/box	150	225	300
No. 3000 Grader-Loader, 1959-61, 23-3/4" long..............................	92	138	185
No. 3100 Payloader Tractor Shovel, 1959-61, 17-5/8" long	100	150	200
No. 3200 Power & Light Lineman Truck, 1959-61, 35-3/4" long	150	225	300
No. 3300 Power & Light Posthole Digger, 1959-61, 35-3/4" long......	150	225	300
No. 3400 Highway Emergency Unit, 1959-63, 18-5/8" long	72	108	145
No. 3500 Countdown Rocket Launcher, 1959-61, 21" long........	125	188	250
No. 3600 Ford Rapid Delivery, 18-1/4" long................................	163	245	325
No. 3700 Street Sprinkler Truck, 18" long	140	210	280

	C6	C8	C10
No. 3800 Ford Sales & Service, 13-5/8" long	140	210	280
No. 3900 Ford Platform Tilt Truck, 15-3/4" long	125	188	250
No. 4000 Ford Speedway Truck w/Racer, 24-3/4" long	122	185	250
No. 4100 Ford Pickup & U-Haul Box Trailer	110	165	220
No. 4125 Rhino Pickup	22	33	45
No. 4200 Bulldozer, 14" long	65	98	130
No. 4300 Ford U-Haul Rental Fleet, three pieces	175	263	350
No. 4400 Camper on Pickup, 13-1/2" long	70	105	140
No. 4500 Ranch Truck, 14" long	75	112	150
No. 4600 Construction Four-wheel Platform Dump, 15-3/4" long	88	132	175
No. 4700 Happy Acres Truck, w/horses, 14" long	65	98	130
No. 4800 U-Haul Trailer, 8" long	50	75	120
No. 4900 U-Haul Trailer, 9" long	50	75	100
No. 5000 Dump Truck w/Cement Mixer, 20-1/2" long........................	125	188	250

Nylint Michigan Shovel, No. 2200, 1955-65, 31-1/2".

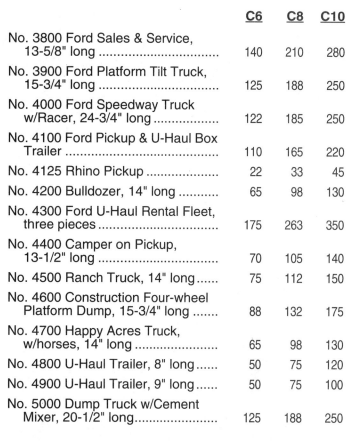

Nylint Guided Missile Carrier, No. 2800, 1958. Photo from Calvin L. Chausee.

Nylint Electronic Cannon, No. 2400, 1956. Photo from Calvin L. Chaussee.

Nylint Ford U-Haul Rental Fleet, No. 4300, three pieces. Photo from Thomas G. Nefos.

Nylint Pepsi Truck, No. 5500, 16-1/2". Photo from Bob Smith.

Nylint U-Haul Truck, Chevy, 1975. Photo from Thomas G. Nefos.

Nylint American Oil Emergency Truck, No. 6000, 11-1/4". Photo from Bob Smith.

	C6	C8	C10
No. 5100 Dump Truck, 13-1/2" long.	75	112	150
No. 5200 Pickup Truck (Econoline), 11-1/4" long	80	120	160
No. 5300 Custom Camper, 12-1/2" long	75	112	150
No. 5400 Custom Camper, w/boat, 23-1/2" long	120	180	240
No. 5500 Pepsi Truck, 16-1/2" long .	125	188	250
No. 5800 Ford Econoline Van, 12" long	72	105	145
No. 6000 American Oil Emergency Truck, 11-1/4" long	100	150	200

	C6	C8	C10
No. 6200 Kennel Truck, w/dogs, 11-1/2" long	88	132	175
No. 6300 Horse Van, 23-1/2" long ...	78	117	155
No. 6600 Mobile Home, semi type, 1964, 30" long	125	188	250
No. 6700 Ambulance, 12" long	100	150	200
No. 6800 Jalopy, 9-5/8" long	30	45	60
No. 6900 Airport Courtesy Van, "Holiday Inn," 12" long	275	332	550
No. 700 Lift Truck (fork lift), wind-up, 1947-49	75	112	150
No. 7100 Fun on Farm Econohne Truck, 11-1/4" long, twenty-nine pieces	87	130	175
No. 7300 Army Ambulance, 12" long	60	90	120
No. 7900 Road Grader, 15" long	62	93	125
No. 8000 Pony Farm Van, 11-1/4" long, seven piecs set	135	198	270
No. 8100 Suburban Fire Pumper, 12-1/2" long	100	150	200
No. 8200 Bronco, 12-1/2" long	75	112	150
No. 8300 Texaco Service Van, 12" long	150	225	300
No. 8400 U-Haul Cube Van, 1965, 22" long	87	130	175
No. 8410 Ford U-Haul Truck & Trailer, 1974, 22" long	75	112	150
No. 8411 U-Haul Truck, Chevy	75	112	150

OH BOY

KIDDIE METAL TOYS, PLAINFIELD, NEW JERSEY

President Louis Portolano was also a tool and die maker for Kiddies Metal Toys. Established in the early part of the twentieth century, Kiddie Metal Toys produced toy vehicles under the logo O Boy!. In the early 1920s, the company hired Louis Emmets, a skilled lithographer previously employed by J. Chein & Co. Emmets worked with George Borgfeldt to produce the type of toys the public wanted. Very successful early on, Kiddie Metal Toys' volume was close to $1,000,000 in the early 1920s.

In 1925, Kiddie Metal Toys began a line of large light pressed-steel vehicles. These trucks ranged in length from nineteen to twenty-seven inches. The gauge of metal used on the Oh Boy! trucks was the same gauge metal that Chein used on its Hercules Trucks. Other similarities in these trucks, include body style and wheel types. Some collectors believe that Louis Emmets brought this strong influence with him from J. Chein & Co. The Oh Boy! toys, however, were finished with enamel paint, while Chein used lithography on the Hercules vehicles. Another peculiarity of the Oh Boy toys was the installing of decals on only one side.

Kiddie Metal toys made a wide variety of toys such as tea sets, sand pails and roulette games. Kiddies Metal Toys, Inc. closed its door in 1931, after going through tough times from the Depression.

Contributor: Bob Smith, The Village Smith, 62 West Ave., Fairport, NY 14450-2102.

	C6	C8	C10		C6	C8	C10
No. 100 Dump Truck, black/red or all black, w/or without decals, c.1926, 19" long	400	600	875	No. 135 Fire Engine, red w/orange boiler and hand rails, c.1926, 19" long	600	850	1350
No. 100 Dump Truck, black/gray, w/or without decals, c.1926, 19" long	450	700	1000	No. 135 Fire Engine, red w/copper plated boiler and hand rails, c.1926, 19" long	700	1100	1650
No. 105 Bus, blue, c.1926, 19-1/2" long	700	1500	2000	No. 140 Fire Patrol Truck, red, c.1926, 23" long	450	850	1350
No. 110 Racer, red, c.1926, 19" long	800	1600	2400	No. 200 Auto Steam Shovel, four-wheel chassis w/vertical boiler, red/black, c.1927, 23" long	700	1300	2000
No. 115 Ice Truck, green, c.1926, 19-1/2" long	500	750	1000	No. 200 Auto Steam Shovel, red/black, mounted on open cab truck chassis, c.1927, 27" long	650	1250	1900
No. 120 Delivery Truck, pen cab, stake sides, black/red, c.1927, 19" long	400	800	1200	No. 205 American Express Truck, green, c.1927, 22" long	800	1600	2200
No. 120 Delivery Truck, closed cab, stake sides, black/red, c.1927, 19" long	500	900	1250	No. 209 Mail Truck, olive green, c.1927, 22" long	800	1600	2200
No. 125 Wrecker Truck, black/red, c.1926, 19" long	500	1050	1550	No. 210 Moving Van, black/red, c.1927, 22" long	800	1600	2200
No. 130 Hook & Ladder Truck, red, c.1926, 21" long	650	850	1250				

Oh Boy Dump Truck, same as No. 100 Dump Truck except black and red. Photo from Bob Smith.

Oh Boy Dump Truck, No. 100, 1920s, 19". Photo from Bob Smith.

Oh Boy toys, as shown on a page from a late 1920s Butler Bros. catalog. Manufacturer's numbers are in parentheses.

Oh Boy Racer, No. 110, red, 1920s, 19". Photo from Bob Smith.

Oh Boy Wrecker Truck, No. 125, black, red, 1920s, 19". Photo from Bob Smith.

Oh Boy Hook & Ladder Truck, No. 130, red, 1920s, 21". Photo from Bob Smith.

Oh Boy Fire Engine, No. 135, orange boiler, hand rails. Photo from Bob Smith.

Oh Boy American Express Truck, No. 205. Photo from Bob Smith.

Oh Boy Fire Patrol Truck, No. 140, red, 1920s, 23". Photo from Bob Smith.

Oh Boy American Express Truck, No. 205. Photo from Bob Smith.

OROBR

Orobr Toy Works was founded by three partners, Neil, Muller, and Blechschmidt. The company produced numerous lower-end toy vehicles, many of which were made for the American market. Even though a large amount of toy vehicles are found with the Orobr mark, there is not much information in print about the company. Orobr made some toys that do carry a fair value, and they make a nice accent to any collection.

Contributor: Bob Smith, The Village Smith, 62 West Ave., Fairport, NY 14450-2102.

	C6	C8	C10
Bus	500	800	1200
Double-Decker Bus, wind-up, c.1915, 6" long	300	500	600
Double-Decker Bus, wind-up, 9-1/2" long	400	700	1100
Express Wagon, wind-up, 1920s, 6" long	300	550	700
Limousine, open front cab, luggage rack on top, clockwork motor, c.1910, 5-1/2" long	350	600	800

	C6	C8	C10
No. 24 Orobr Mercedes Pullman Limousine, six window, lithographed in three-tone green/red/white, electric lights, clockwork motor, four opening doors, driver, c.1920, 9-1/2" long.	1100	1700	2400
No. 25 Touring Car, red/gray, clockwork motor, fold down rear seats, c.1918, 8-3/4" long	500	700	950

Orobr Six-Window Mercedes Pullman Limousine, green, red and white, electric lights, opening doors, driver, circa 1920, 9-1/2". Photo from Bob Smith.

Top row: Orobr Model T Ford Sedan, 6". Front row, left to right: Model T Ford Sedan, 7-3/4"; Model T Ford Touring Car, 7-3/4". Photo from Bob Smith.

	C6	C8	C10
No. 26 Model T Ford Sedan, black, 6" long, clockwork motor, 1920s; add $200 for different color..........	300	375	600
No. 27 Model T Ford Sedan, black, 7-3/4" long, clockwork motor, full interior, 1920s	550	750	1000
No. 28 Model T Ford Touring Car, black/gray, clockwork motor, 7-3/4" long..................................	550	750	1000

	C6	C8	C10
Steam Roller, tin wind-up, 6" long....	200	300	450
Taxi, tin, 6" long	350	500	750

PROMOTIONALS

Promotionals are scale models of the full-size cars (usually) offered by car salesmen to the children of protential buyers. Almost always produced in 1:25-scale plastic or pot metal, most potmetal promos were discontinued by the early 1950s. The most dominant manufacturers were—Aluminum Model Toys (AMT), Banthrico (BAN), JoHan Models (JH), Master Caster (MC), Model Products Corp. (MPC), National Products (NP), Product Miniatures (PM), and Scale Model Products (SMP).

This price guide deals mostly with those produced up to 1972. They are still being made today, but in reduced numbers. In recent years, as few as three or four different models were produced, whereas in the mid 1960s, as many as fifty different models were produced. The most popular full-size cars are usually the popular promo.

When using this guide, remember the sometimes even Mint in box items may not get you the C10 price. The plastic of the 1950s and early 1960s had a tendency to warp and each car had a specific place where warp occurred. In addition, the plating on the grille or bumpers might be flaking or dull. Something as small as a missing hood ornament or a cracked vent window post can reduce your C10 to a C6.

Contributor: Ron Smith, 33005 Arlesford, Solon, OH, 44139, 440-248-7066, fax 440-519-0906.

	C6	C8	C10		C6	C8	C10
Aero Willys Four-door Sedan, 1953, BIR..	80	160	325	Barracuda Two-door Hardtop, 1968, MPC..	40	75	140
Aerocar Convertible, 1953 GLA	40	80	150	Barracuda Two-door Hardtop, 1971, MPC..	80	160	325
AMX Two-door Hardtop, 1969, JH ...	20	30	60	Barracuda Two-door Hardtop, 1969, MPC..	30	45	100
AMX Two-door Hardtop, 1970, JH ...	20	30	60	Barracuda Two-door Hardtop, 1967, AMT..	15	35	75
Barracuda Two-door Fastback, 1965, AMT	15	45	95				
Barracuda Two-door Fastback, 1966, AMT	15	35	75	Barracuda Two-door Hardtop, 1970, MPC..	65	135	260

	C6	C8	C10
Buick Century Convertible, 1956, AMT	30	60	110
Buick Convertible, 1955, AMT	20	40	75
Buick Electra 225 Convertible, 1963, AMT	30	70	120
Buick Electra 225 Convertible, 1962, AMT	30	50	100
Buick Electra 225 Two-door Hardtop, 1963, AMT	2	50	100
Buick Electra 225 Two-door Hardtop, 1962, AMT	20	50	100
Buick Four-door Hardtop, 1956, BAN	30	50	95
Buick Four-door Sedan, 1954, AMT	20	40	85
Buick Four-door Sedan, 1955, AMT	20	40	65
Buick Four-door Sedan, 1947, NP	40	80	150
Buick Four-door Sedan, 1948, NP	30	65	130
Buick Four-door Sedan, 1952, BAN	30	60	110
Buick Invicta Convertible, 1959, AMT	20	40	85
Buick Invicta Convertible, 1961, AMT	30	60	110
Buick Invicta Convertible, 1960, AMT	30	60	110
Buick Invicta Two-door Hardtop, 1961, AMT	20	40	90
Buick Invicta Two-door Hardtop, 1959, AMT	20	40	75
Buick Invicta Two-door Hardtop, 1960, AMT	30	60	110
Buick Riviera Two-door Hardtop, 1964, AMT	20	50	95
Buick Riviera Two-door Hardtop, 1969, AMT	20	40	75
Buick Riviera Two-door Hardtop, 1967, AMT	20	30	60
Buick Riviera Two-door Hardtop, 1963, AMT	30	70	130
Buick Riviera Two-door Hardtop, 1966, AMT	20	30	70
Buick Riviera Two-door Hardtop, 1965, AMT	45	80	160
Buick Riviera Two-door Hardtop, 1968, AMT	30	50	105
Buick Roadmaster Convertible, 1958, AMT	20	60	100
Buick Roadmaster Convertible, 1957, AMT	30	60	110
Buick Roadmaster Four-door Hardtop, 1956, AMT	20	40	80
Buick Roadmaster Two-door Hardtop, 1958, AMT	20	40	90
Buick Roadmaster Two-door Hardtop, 1957, AMT	30	60	110
Buick Sedan, 1950, NP	30	55	110
Buick Sedan, 1953, BAN	30	50	110
Buick Skylark Convertible, 1954, AMT	40	80	140
Buick Skylark Two-door Hardtop, 1966, AMT	36	81	160
Buick Special Station Wagon, 1962, AMT	10	25	50
Buick Special Station Wagon, 1961, AMT	20	40	60
Buick Two-door Hardtop, 1955, BAN	20	40	75
Buick Two-door Hardtop, 1954, BAN	20	40	90
Buick Wildcat Convertible, 1965, AMT	54	108	215
Buick Wildcat Two-door Hardtop, 1965, AMT	54	117	235
Buick Wildcat Two-door Hardtop, 1966, AMT	20	40	80
Buick Wildcat Two-door Hardtop, 1964, AMT	60	110	225
Buick Wildcat Two-door Hardtop, 1969, AMT	10	30	60
Buick Wildcat Two-door Hardtop, 1970, AMT	10	20	40
Cadillac 60 S, Four-door Sedan, 1958, JH	10	30	60
Cadillac 62, Two-door Hardtop, 1956, AMT	20	40	80
Cadillac Convertible, 1963, JH	10	30	60
Cadillac Convertible, 1967, JH	20	30	60
Cadillac Convertible, 1966, JH	20	40	80
Cadillac Convertible, 1965, JH	20	40	80
Cadillac Convertible, 1968, JH	10	20	40
Cadillac Convertible, 1964, JH	20	40	80
Cadillac Eldorado Two-door Hardtop, 1967, JH	20	40	80
Cadillac Eldorado Two-door Hardtop, 1968, JH	10	20	40
Cadillac Eldorado Two-door Hardtop, 1972, JH	10	20	40
Cadillac Eldorado Two-door Hardtop, 1971, JH	10	30	60
Cadillac Eldorado Two-door Hardtop, 1956, BAN	30	65	130
Cadillac Eldorado Two-door Hardtop, 1969, JH	10	30	40
Cadillac Eldorado Two-door Hardtop, 1970, JH	20	30	60
Cadillac Fleetwood Four-door, 1959, JH	20	40	80

	C6	C8	C10
Cadillac Fleetwood Four-door Hardtop, 1961, JH......................	20	40	80
Cadillac Fleetwood Four-door Hardtop, 1960, JH......................	20	40	80
Cadillac Fleetwood Four-door Hardtop, 1962, JH......................	20	40	85
Cadillac Four-door Sedan, 1952, BAN	30	60	120
Cadillac Four-door Sedan, 1955, BAN	40	60	120
Cadillac Four-door Sedan, 1954, BAN	30	60	120
Cadillac Two-door Hardtop, 1969, JH	10	30	40
Cadillac Two-door Hardtop, 1970, JH	10	20	40
Cadillac Two-door Hardtop, 1968, JH	10	20	40
Cadillac Two-door Hardtop, 1966, JH	20	40	80
Cadillac Two-door Hardtop, 1964, JH	20	40	80
Cadillac Two-door Hardtop, 1963, JH	10	30	60
Cadillac Two-door Hardtop, 1955, AMT	20	50	95
Cadillac Two-door Hardtop, 1965, JH	20	40	80
Cadillac Two-door Hardtop, 1967, JH	20	30	60
Camaro Convertible, 1968, MPC	50	90	185
Camaro Convertible, 1969, AMT......	40	90	180
Camaro Convertible, 1967, AMT......	40	80	140
Camaro Convertible Pace Car, 1969, AMT	80	150	310
Camaro Convertible Pace Car, 1967, AMT	125	250	500
Camaro Two-door Hardtop, 1969, AMT	40	80	150
Camaro Two-door Hardtop, 1970, AMT	30	60	120
Camaro Two-door Hardtop, 1971, MPC	20	40	80
Camaro Two-door Hardtop, 1972, MPC	20	40	80
Camaro Two-door Hardtop, 1967, AMT	40	80	160
Chevelle Convertible, 1969, AMT	40	80	100
Chevelle Malibu SS Two-door Hardtop, 1965, AMT	20	40	80
Chevelle Malibu Station Wagon, 1965, AMT	30	50	95

	C6	C8	C10
Chevelle SS Convertible, 1970, AMT	30	60	120
Chevelle SS Two-door Hardtop, 1970, AMT......................	30	60	120
Chevelle SS Two-door Hardtop, 1972, MPC......................	20	40	80
Chevelle Station Wagon, 1964, AMT	20	40	80
Chevelle Two-door Hardtop, 1969, AMT......................	30	60	125
Chevelle Two-door Hardtop, 1964, AMT......................	30	50	120
Chevelle Two-door Hardtop, 1971, MPC......................	2	40	80
Chevrolet 11 Two-door Hardtop, 1965, AMT	25	50	100
Chevrolet 150 Four-door Sedan, 1954, PMC......................	40	80	180
Chevrolet 150 Four-door Sedan, 1953, PMC......................	30	60	120
Chevrolet 150 Two-door Sedan, 1953, PMC......................	30	70	130
Chevrolet 150 Two-door Sedan, 1954, PMC......................	40	80	160
Chevrolet 210 Four-door Sedan, 1954, PMC......................	30	60	120
Chevrolet 210 Four-door Sedan, 1953, PMC......................	30	70	120
Chevrolet 210 Two-door Sedan, 1953, PMC......................	30	60	120
Chevrolet 210 Two-door Sedan, 1954, PMC......................	40	80	160
Chevrolet Apache Pickup, 1961, AMT	40	80	150
Chevrolet Bel Air Convertible, 1954, PMC......................	50	100	200
Chevrolet Bel Air Four-door Sedan, 1953, PMC......................	30	60	120
Chevrolet Bel Air Four-door Sedan, 1954, PMC......................	40	60	125
Chevrolet Bel Air Two-door Hardtop, 1952, PMC......................	30	60	120
Chevrolet Bel Air Two-door Hardtop, 1951, PMC......................	30	60	130
Chevrolet Bel Air Two-door Hardtop, 1953, PMC......................	30	60	140
Chevrolet Bel Air Two-door Hardtop, 1950, BAN	30	60	120
Chevrolet Bel Air Two-door Hardtop, 1954, PMC......................	40	80	160
Chevrolet Bel Air Two-door Sedan, 1954, PMC......................	27	63	125
Chevrolet Bel Air Two-door Sedan, 1953, PMC......................	30	70	125

Promotionals, Chevrolet El Camino Pickup, 1960, AMT. Photo from Ron Smith.

	C6	C8	C10
Chevrolet Cameo Pickup, 1956, PMC	40	80	135
Chevrolet Convertible, 1959, SMP	30	60	125
Chevrolet Convertible, 1958, AMT	30	60	115
Chevrolet Convertible, 1949, BAN	40	80	160
Chevrolet Convertible, 1953, PMC	40	80	160
Chevrolet Convertible, 1952, PMC	60	110	240
Chevrolet Convertible, 1950, BAN	40	80	150
Chevrolet Convertible, 1951, PMC	60	120	240
Chevrolet Convertible, 1957, SMP	40	60	120
Chevrolet El Camino Pickup, 1960, AMT	20	60	120
Chevrolet El Camino Pickup, 1964, AMT	30	60	120
Chevrolet El Camino Pickup, 1965, AMT	36	63	125
Chevrolet Fleetline Four-door, 1949, BAN	40	80	150
Chevrolet Fleetline Four-door, 1951, PMC	40	80	160
Chevrolet Fleetline Four-door, 1950, BAN	30	60	120
Chevrolet Fleetline Two-door, 1948, NP	40	80	160
Chevrolet Fleetline Two-door, 1947, NP	40	80	160
Chevrolet Fleetline Two-door, 1951, PMC	40	80	150
Chevrolet Fleetline Two-door, 1949, BAN	40	80	150
Chevrolet Fleetline Two-door, 1952, PMC	30	60	150
Chevrolet Fleetline Two-door, 1950, BAN	40	70	140
Chevrolet Fleetside Pickup, 1967, AMT	30	60	115

	C6	C8	C10
Chevrolet Fleetside Pickup, 1965, AMT	40	80	160
Chevrolet Fleetside Pickup, 1968, MPC	30	55	115
Chevrolet Fleetside Pickup, 1969, AMT	30	60	120
Chevrolet Fleetside Pickup, 1972, MPC	30	50	100
Chevrolet Fleetside Pickup, 1966, AMT	50	140	180
Chevrolet Fleetside Pickup, 1971, MPC	30	60	110
Chevrolet Fleetside Pickup, 1970, AMT	30	60	120
Chevrolet Four-door Hardtop, 1958, PMC	20	40	60
Chevrolet Four-door Hardtop, 1957, PMC	30	60	120
Chevrolet Four-door Hardtop, 1956, PMC	30	60	120
Chevrolet Four-door Sedan, 1955, PMC	30	60	115
Chevrolet Four-door Sedan, 1956, PMC	30	60	120
Chevrolet Impala Convertible, 1970, AMT	20	40	80
Chevrolet Impala Convertible, 1969, AMT	20	40	80
Chevrolet Impala Convertible, 1968, MPC	40	80	160
Chevrolet Impala Convertible, 1967, AMT	40	60	115
Chevrolet Impala Convertible, 1966, AMT	30	60	120
Chevrolet Impala Convertible, 1964, AMT	40	70	140
Chevrolet Impala Convertible, 1971, MPC	20	40	80
Chevrolet Impala Convertible, 1961, AMT	50	100	200
Chevrolet Impala Convertible, 1960, SMP	30	60	110
Chevrolet Impala Convertible, 1963, AMT	80	160	300
Chevrolet Impala Convertible, 1962, AMT	50	100	200
Chevrolet Impala Four-door Hardtop, 1960, SMP	20	30	90
Chevrolet Impala Four-door Hardtop, 1961, AMT	60	120	200
Chevrolet Impala SS Budget Rent-A-Car, 1966, AMT	40	80	175
Chevrolet Impala SS Convertible, 1965, AMT	30	70	140

	C6	C8	C10
Chevrolet Impala SS Two-door Hardtop, 1966, AMT	30	60	120
Chevrolet Impala Two-door Hardtop, 1962, AMT	80	10	300
Chevrolet Impala Two-door Hardtop, 1969, AMT	20	40	80
Chevrolet Impala Two-door Hardtop, 1960, SMP	20	30	60
Chevrolet Impala Two-door Hardtop, 1963, AMT	60	110	220
Chevrolet Impala Two-door Hardtop, 1971, MPC	20	40	80
Chevrolet Impala Two-door Hardtop, 1965, AMT	30	60	115
Chevrolet Impala Two-door Hardtop, 1967, AMT	25	60	115
Chevrolet Impala Two-door Hardtop, 1968, MPC	30	60	120
Chevrolet Impala Two-door Hardtop, 1964, AMT	40	80	150
Chevrolet Impala Two-door Hardtop, 1970, AMT	20	40	70
Chevrolet Impala Two-door Hardtop, 1972, MPC	15	30	60
Chevrolet Monte Carlo Two-door Hardtop, 1971, AMT	25	50	100
Chevrolet Monte Carlo Two-door Hardtop, 1970, AMT	20	40	75
Chevrolet Monte Carlo Two-door Hardtop, 1972, MPC	20	40	85
Chevrolet Nomad Station Wagon, 1960, SMP	20	40	70
Chevrolet Nova Convertible, 1963, AMT	40	80	170
Chevrolet Nova Convertible, 1962, AMT	30	60	120
Chevrolet Nova Station Wagon, 1963, AMT	15	30	60
Chevrolet Nova Two-door Hardtop, 1962, AMT	40	80	160
Chevrolet Nova Two-door Hardtop, 1963, AMT	25	50	100
Chevrolet Pickup, 1963, AMT	60	120	250
Chevrolet Pickup, 1962, AMT	60	120	250
Chevrolet Pickup, 1960, SMP	50	40	185
Chevrolet Pickup, 1959, PMC..........	40	80	170
Chevrolet Pickup, 1958, AMT	20	40	80
Chevrolet Pickup, 1957, PMC..........	30	60	120
Chevrolet Station Wagon, 1958, PMC	20	50	75
Chevrolet Station Wagon, 1957, SMP	30	60	120

Promotionals, Chevrolet Impala Two-door hardtop, 1963, AMT. Photo from Ron Smith.

	C6	C8	C10
Chevrolet Station Wagon, 1956, PMC..	20	40	80
Chevrolet Station Wagon, 1959, SMP	20	40	80
Chevrolet Styline Four-door Sedan, 1951, PMC..............................	30	60	120
Chevrolet Styline Four-door Sedan, 1949, BAN	40	70	130
Chevrolet Styline Four-door Sedan, 1950, BAN	30	60	120
Chevrolet Styline Four-door Sedan, 1952, PMC..............................	30	60	120
Chevrolet Styline Two-door, 1949, BAN	30	60	120
Chevrolet Styline Two-door Sedan, 1950, BAN	30	60	120
Chevrolet Styline Two-door Sedan, 1952, PMC..............................	40	70	150
Chevrolet Styline Two-door Sedan, 1951, PMC..............................	30	60	130
Chevrolet Two-door Coupe, 1950, BAN	30	60	115
Chevrolet Two-door Coupe, 1949, BAN	60	120	240
Chevrolet Two-door Coupe, 1951, PMC..............................	30	60	130
Chevrolet Two-door Coupe, 1952, PMC..............................	40	80	150
Chevrolet Two-door Hardtop, 1956, BAN	40	70	140
Chevrolet Two-door Hardtop, 1955, BAN	40	80	145
Chevrolet Two-door Hardtop, 1956, PMC..............................	30	60	120
Chevrolet Two-door Hardtop, 1955, PMC..............................	30	60	120
Chevrolet Two-door Hardtop, 1958, AMT	27	54	110
Chevrolet Two-door Hardtop, 1957, SMP..............................	30	60	120

	C6	C8	C10
Chevrolet Two-door Hardtop, 1959, SMP	20	40	80
Chrysler 300 Convertible, 1967, JH	10	20	45
Chrysler 300 Convertible, 1968, JH	10	20	45
Chrysler 300 Convertible, 1966, JH	15	30	60
Chrysler 300 Convertible, 1965, JH	30	60	120
Chrysler 300 Convertible, 1963, JH	35	70	140
Chrysler 300 Convertible, 1962, JH	15	30	60
Chrysler 300 Convertible Pace, 1963, JH	60	130	270
Chrysler 300 Two-door Hardtop, 1966, JH	40	60	150
Chrysler 300 Two-door Hardtop, 1968, JH	10	20	45
Chrysler 300 Two-door Hardtop, 1967, JH	10	20	35
Chrysler 300 Two-door Hardtop, 1965, JH	40	80	170
Chrysler 300 Two-door Hardtop, 1962, JH	15	30	60
Chrysler 300 Two-door Hardtop, 1963, JH	30	6	120
Chrysler Convertible, 1964, JH	30	70	140
Chrysler Four-door Hardtop, 1957, JH	15	40	60
Chrysler Four-door Sedan, 1948, NP	20	40	90
Chrysler Four-door Sedan, 1950, BAN	30	60	120
Chrysler Four-door Sedan, 1954, BAN	30	60	95
Chrysler New Yorker Four-door, 1958, JH	15	35	65
Chrysler New Yorker Four-door Hardtop, 1959, JH	10	20	45
Chrysler New Yorker Two-door Hardtop, 1960, JH	10	20	45
Chrysler New Yorker Two-door Hardtop, 1961, JH	10	20	60
Chrysler Turbine Two-door Hardtop, 1964, JH	10	30	65
Chrysler Two-door Hardtop, 1964, JH	20	40	80
Chrysler Two-door Hardtop, 1953, BAN	3	50	100
Comet Convertible, 1963, AMT	10	30	60
Comet Cyclone GT Pace Car (red), 1966, AMT	50	90	180
Comet Cyclone GT Pace Car (white), 1966, AMT	50	90	180
Comet Four-door Sedan, 1960, AMT	10	20	30

	C6	C8	C10
Comet Two-door Hardtop, 1964, AMT	60	120	240
Comet Two-door Sedan, 1971, JH	10	20	30
Comet Two-door Sedan, 1961, AMT	10	20	30
Comet Two-door Sedan, 1962, AMT	10	25	50
Continental Convertible, 1961, AMT	20	40	80
Continental Four-door Convertible, 1963, AMT	20	30	60
Continental Four-door Convertible, 1965, AMT	10	20	40
Continental Four-door Convertible, 1964, AMT	20	40	85
Continental Four-door Convertible, 1962, AMT	30	60	120
Continental Four-door Sedan, 1968, AMT	10	20	40
Continental Four-door Sedan, 1967, AMT	20	40	85
Continental Four-door Sedan, 1966, AMT	20	40	80
Continental Four-door Sedan, 1965, AMT	30	60	90
Continental Four-door Sedan, 1963, AMT	20	40	60
Continental Four-door Sedan, 1961, AMT	20	40	80
Continental Four-door Sedan, 1964, AMT	40	80	170
Continental Four-door Sedan, 1962, AMT	30	60	120
Continental Mark II Two-door Hardtop, 1957, AMT	40	80	150
Continental Mark II Two-door Hardtop, 1956, AMT	40	80	150
Continental MK III Four-door Hardtop, 1958, AMT	10	30	60
Continental MK IV Convertible, 1959, AMT	20	40	60
Continental MK IV Two-door Hardtop, 1959, AMT	20	40	60

Promotionals, Lincoln Continental MK III Four-door hardtop, 1958, AMT. Photo from Ron Smith.

	C6	C8	C10
Continental MK V Convertible, 1960, AMT	10	30	50
Continental MK V Two-door Hardtop, 1960, AMT	10	20	50
Corvair 700 Four-door Sedan, 1961, AMT	20	40	80
Corvair Corsa Convertible, 1965, AMT	30	63	120
Corvair Corsa Convertible, 1966, AMT	20	30	60
Corvair Corsa Two-door Hardtop, 1965, AMT	40	80	150
Corvair Corsa Two-door Hardtop, 1966, AMT	30	60	130
Corvair Four-door Sedan, 1960, AMT	20	40	80
Corvair Monza Convertible, 1964, AMT	40	90	170
Corvair Monza Convertible, 1963, AMT	30	60	115
Corvair Monza Coupe, 1961, AMT	25	50	100
Corvair Monza Two-door Hardtop, 1967, AMT	30	60	120
Corvair Monza Two-door Hardtop, 1964, AMT	40	90	170
Corvair Monza Two-door Hardtop, 1963, AMT	30	65	120
Corvair Monza Two-door Hardtop, 1962, AMT	50	100	200
Corvette Convertible, 1961, SMP	150	275	560
Corvette Convertible, 1962, AMT	150	275	560
Corvette Convertible, 1960, AMT	90	180	390
Corvette Convertible, 1958, AMT	80	180	360
Corvette Convertible, 1954, PMC	90	200	410
Corvette Convertible, 1959, AMT	80	180	325
Corvette Convertible (orig.), 1954, BAN	20	50	95
Corvette Convertible w/Hardtop, 1961, AMT	60	120	240
Corvette Sting Ray Convertible, 1967, AMT	200	400	800
Corvette Sting Ray Convertible, 1969, AMT	90	180	360
Corvette Sting Ray Convertible, 1966, AMT	2	450	900
Corvette Sting Ray Convertible, 1965, AMT	120	250	500
Corvette Sting Ray Convertible, 1964, AMT	120	250	500
Corvette Sting Ray Convertible, 1970, AMT	80	160	320
Corvette Sting Ray Convertible, 1968, MPC	100	200	400

	C6	C8	C10
Corvette Sting Ray Convertible, 1963, AMT	70	140	300
Corvette Sting Ray Coupe, 1969, AMT	140	280	560
Corvette Sting Ray Coupe, 1971, MPC	90	180	360
Corvette Sting Ray Coupe, 1970, AMT	80	160	320
Corvette Sting Ray Coupe, 1968, MPC	120	140	380
Corvette Sting Ray Coupe, 1967, AMT	225	450	900
Corvette Sting Ray Coupe, 1966, AMT	200	400	800
Corvette Sting Ray Coupe, 1965, AMT	150	300	600
Corvette Sting Ray Coupe, 1963, AMT	150	300	600
Corvette Sting Ray Coupe, 1972, MPC	90	180	360
Corvette Sting Ray Coupe, 1964, AMT	120	250	500
Cougar Two-door Hardtop, 1968, AMT	10	20	60
DeSoto Adventurer Two-door Hardtop, 1960, JH	20	30	50
DeSoto Fireflight Four-door Hardtop, 1958, JH	20	30	60
DeSoto Fireflight Four-door Hardtop, 1959, JH	10	25	55
DeSoto Four-door, 1956, JH	20	40	60
DeSoto Four-door Sedan, 1955, JH	20	40	75
DeSoto Sedan, 1948, NP	20	40	80
DeSoto Sportsman Four-door Hardtop, 1957, JH	20	40	80
Diamond T Dump Truck, 1956, PMC	20	40	90
Diamond T Semi-Truck, 1956, PMC	20	40	90
Divco Milk Truck, 1951, AMT	70	120	250
Dodge Challenger Two-door Hardtop, 1970, MPC	60	120	230
Dodge Challenger Two-door Hardtop, 1972, MPC	30	60	120
Dodge Challenger Two-door Hardtop, 1971, MPC	50	100	200
Dodge Charger R/T Two-door Hardtop, 1970, MPC	50	100	210
Dodge Charger R/T Two-door Hardtop, 1969, MPC	60	100	200
Dodge Charger Two-door Hardtop, 1967, MPC	50	100	200
Dodge Charger Two-door Hardtop, 1972, MPC	30	60	120

	C6	C8	C10
Dodge Charger Two-door Hardtop, 1966, MPC	40	80	150
Dodge Charger Two-door Hardtop, 1968, MPC	65	130	260
Dodge Charger Two-door Hardtop, 1971, MPC	70	140	265
Dodge Coronet 500 Convertible, 1965, MPC	40	90	180
Dodge Coronet 500 Two-door Hardtop, 1965, MPC	50	100	200
Dodge Coronet Convertible, 1969, MPC	50	10	200
Dodge Coronet Two-door Hardtop, 1968, MPC	60	120	240
Dodge Coronet Two-door Hardtop, 1969, MPC	50	100	200
Dodge Custom 880 Convertible, 1965, MPC	40	80	160
Dodge Custom Royal Two-door Hardtop, 1958, JH	20	30	65
Dodge Custom Royal Two-door Hardtop, 1959, JH	10	25	50
Dodge Dart Convertible, 1962, JH	20	30	60
Dodge Dart Police Car, 1962, JH	60	120	240
Dodge Dart Two-door Hardtop, 1962, JH	10	30	60
Dodge Four-door Sedan, 1950, BAN	20	40	95
Dodge Four-door Sedan, 1948, NP	20	60	95
Dodge Four-door Sedan, 1951, BAN	20	40	90
Dodge Four-door Sedan, 1954, BAN	20	40	80
Dodge Four-door Sedan, 1953, BAN	20	50	95
Dodge Lancer Four-door Hardtop, 1956, AMT	30	60	110
Dodge Lancer Two-door Hardtop, 1955, BAN	20	30	70
Dodge Monaco 500 Two-door Hardtop, 1966, MPC	40	80	150
Dodge Monaco Two-door Hardtop, 1965, MPC	30	60	120
Dodge Phoenix Two-door Hardtop, 1960, JH	20	40	70
Dodge Phoenix Two-door Hardtop, 1961, JH	20	30	65
Dodge Pickup, 1950, NP	30	60	120
Dodge Polara 500 Convertible, 1966, MPC	40	80	160
Dodge Polara Convertible, 1963, JH	20	40	80
Dodge Polara Convertible, 1964, JH	30	40	90
Dodge Polara Two-door Hardtop, 1964, JH	30	40	85
Dodge Polara Two-door Hardtop, 1963, JH	30	40	85

Promotionals, Ford Edsel convertible, 1958, AMT. Photo from Ron Smith.

	C6	C8	C10
Dodge Police Car, 1961, JH	20	40	85
Dodge Stake Truck, 1950, NP	30	60	120
Edsel Convertible, 1958, AMT	50	100	190
Edsel Corsair Convertible, 1959, AMT	40	80	160
Edsel Corsair Two-door Hardtop, 1959, AMT	40	80	160
Edsel Ranger Convertible, 1960, AMT	40	80	160
Edsel Ranger Two-door Hardtop, 1960, AMT	40	80	160
Edsel Two-door Hardtop, 1958, AMT	40	60	90
Euclid Dump Truck, 1965, BAN	10	20	60
Euclid Dump Truck, 1958, BAN	20	30	60
Euclid Quarry Dump Truck, 1950, PM	20	40	80
F-85 442 Two-door Hardtop, 1968, JH	20	40	60
F-85 Convertible, 1964, JH	30	60	120
F-85 Cutlass Convertible, 1962, JH	20	40	60
F-85 Cutlass Two-door Sedan, 1962, JH	20	40	60
F-85 Station Wagon, 1961, JH	10	20	30
F-85 Two-door Hardtop, 1964, JH	30	60	120
Fairlane 500 Two-door Hardtop, 1964, AMT	20	40	80
Fairlane Cobra Two-door Hardtop, 1970, AMT	10	30	60
Fairlane Two-door Hardtop, 1963, AMT	20	40	65
Fairlane Two-door Hardtop, 1966, AMT	20	60	110
Fairlane Two-door Hardtop, 1965, AMT	20	30	60
Fairlane Two-door Sedan, 1962, AMT	20	40	60
Falcon Convertible, 1963, AMT	30	60	115
Falcon Convertible, 1965, AMT	20	40	80

	C6	C8	C10
Falcon Futura Two-door, 1966, AMT	20	40	80
Falcon Futura Two-door Sedan, 1962, AMT	10	20	30
Falcon Ranchero Pickup, 1961, SMP	10	30	60
Falcon Sprint Convertible, 1964, AMT	20	40	80
Falcon Sprint Two-door Hardtop, 1964, AMT	20	40	80
Falcon Two-door Hardtop, 1965, AMT	20	40	80
Falcon Two-door Hardtop, 1969, AMT	10	20	40
Falcon Two-door Sedan, 1961, AMT	10	20	30
Falcon Two-door Sedan, 1960, AMT	10	30	60
Firebird 400 Two-door Hardtop, 1972, MPC	20	30	70
Firebird 400 Two-door Hardtop, 1971, MPC	20	30	70
Firebird Convertible, 1968, MPC	60	110	225
Firebird Convertible, 1969, MPC	30	70	120
Firebird Convertible, 1967, MPC	50	100	180
Firebird Two-door Hardtop, 1969, MPC	27	63	115
Firebird Two-door Hardtop, 1967, MPC	50	10	180
Firebird Two-door Hardtop, 1970, MPC	20	40	80
Firebird Two-door Hardtop, 1968, MPC	40	80	160
Ford Convertible, 1954, AMT	20	50	100
Ford Custom 300 Two-door Sedan, 1957, AMT	70	140	300
Ford Custom Four-door Sedan, 1952, AMT	20	40	75
Ford F- 100 Pickup, 1961, AMT	40	60	130
Ford F-100 Pickup, 1962, AMT	30	60	110
Ford Fairlane Convertible, 1957, AMT	30	50	100
Ford Fairlane Convertible, 1958, AMT	30	60	110
Ford Fairlane Four-door Sedan, 1961, HUB	20	30	60
Ford Fairlane Four-door Sedan, 1960, HUB	20	30	60
Ford Fairlane Two-door Hardtop, 1958, AMT	20	30	75
Ford Fairlane Two-door Hardtop, 1957, AMT	20	40	80
Ford Four-door Sedan, 1948, AMT	30	60	120
Ford Four-door Sedan, 1950, BAN	30	60	120
Ford Four-door Sedan, 1950, AMT	20	40	80

	C6	C8	C10
Ford Four-door Sedan, 1951, AMT	20	40	85
Ford Four-door Sedan, 1953, BAN	20	35	75
Ford Four-door Sedan, 1953, AMT	20	35	75
Ford Four-door Sedan, 1954, AMT	20	40	80
Ford Four-door Sedan, 1956, AMT	30	50	100
Ford Galaxie 500 Convertible, 1966, AMT	20	30	60
Ford Galaxie 500 Two-door Hardtop, 1966, AMT	20	30	60
Ford Galaxie 500XL Convertible, 1964, AMT	20	40	85
Ford Galaxie 500XL Two-door Hardtop, 1964, AMT	20	40	85
Ford Galaxie Convertible, 1959, AMT	30	50	95
Ford Galaxie Convertible, 1965, AMT	20	30	60
Ford Galaxie Convertible, 1963, AMT	20	40	80
Ford Galaxie Convertible, 1962, AMT	30	50	100
Ford Galaxie Four-door Hardtop, 1960, AMT	20	40	80
Ford Galaxie Two-door Hardtop, 1968, AMT	20	30	60
Ford Galaxie Two-door Hardtop, 1959, AMT	30	50	95
Ford Galaxie Two-door Hardtop, 1967, AMT	20	30	60
Ford Galaxie Two-door Hardtop, 1965, AMT	20	30	60
Ford Galaxie Two-door Hardtop, 1963, AMT	20	40	80
Ford Galaxie Two-door Hardtop, 1962, AMT	15	30	65
Ford Galaxie Two-door Hardtop, 1961, AMT	20	40	80
Ford Grand Torino Two-door Hardtop, 1972, JH	10	20	40
Ford LTD Four-door Hardtop, 1970, AMT	20	30	60
Ford LTD Two-door Hardtop, 1969, AMT	20	30	60
Ford Pace Car Convertible, 1953, AMT	70	150	300
Ford Panel Truck, 1951, NP	20	40	90
Ford Pickup, 1960, AMT	30	60	120
Ford Pickup, 1953, BAN	40	80	160
Ford Pickup, 1950, NP	40	80	150
Ford Pickup, 1951, NP	20	50	100
Ford Ranchero Pickup, 1959, PMC	20	40	60
Ford Stake Truck, 1951, NP	20	40	80

Promotionals, Chrysler Imperial Two-door hardtop, 1958, AMT. Photo from Ron Smith.

Promotionals, International Pickup, 1956, Product Miniatures. Photo from Ron Smith.

	C6	C8	C10
Ford Starliner Hardtop, 1961, AMT ..	25	60	120
Ford Starliner Hardtop, 1960, AMT ..	20	50	100
Ford Station Wagon, 1962, HUB......	20	40	80
Ford Station Wagon, 1955, PMC	30	50	100
Ford Station Wagon, 1959, AMT......	20	40	80
Ford Station Wagon, 1956, PMC	30	50	100
Ford Station Wagon, 1957, PMC	20	40	80
Ford Station Wagon, 1961, HUB......	20	40	80
Ford Station Wagon, 1960, HUB......	20	40	80
Ford Station Wagon, 1958, PMC	20	40	100
Ford Sunliner Convertible, 1961, AMT	20	50	110
Ford Sunliner Convertible, 1955, AMT	40	80	150
Ford Sunliner Convertible, 1960, AMT	20	50	110
Ford Sunliner Convertible, 1956, AMT	20	40	85
Ford Torino Two-door Hardtop, 1969, AMT	30	60	115
Ford Two-door Sedan, 1950, MC.....	30	60	120
Ford Two-door Sedan, 1948, MC.....	30	60	120
Ford Victoria Four-door Sedan, 1955, BAN	30	60	120
Ford Victoria Four-door Sedan, 1956, AMT	20	40	85
Ford Victoria Two-door Hardtop, 1955, BAN	20	50	100
GMC Dump Truck, 1950, NP..........	30	60	100
GMC Pickup, 1950, NP..................	30	60	100
Henry J Two-door Sedan, 1951, AMT	40	80	150
Hornet Two-door Sedan, 1970, JH ..	10	20	40
Hudson Four-door Sedan, 1951, MC	40	80	160
Hudson Four-door Sedan, 1948, MC	50	100	200
Hudson Sedan, 1950, MC................	40	80	150
Imperial Convertible, 1964, AMT......	45	90	180

	C6	C8	C10
Imperial Convertible, 1966, AMT	60	110	230
Imperial Convertible, 1965, AMT	50	100	200
Imperial Convertible, 1958, AMT	20	45	90
Imperial Convertible, 1959, SMP	20	45	90
Imperial Convertible, 1960, SMP	10	30	60
Imperial Convertible, 1963, AMT	20	50	100
Imperial Convertible, 1961, AMT	40	60	120
Imperial Convertible, 1962, AMT	20	50	100
Imperial Crown Two-door Hardtop, 1964, AMT	45	90	180
Imperial Two-door Hardtop, 1967, AMT	40	80	140
Imperial Two-door Hardtop, 1965, AMT	20	40	80
Imperial Two-door Hardtop, 1968, JH	10	20	50
Imperial Two-door Hardtop, 1962, AMT	20	50	100
Imperial Two-door Hardtop, 1966, AMT	60	110	230
Imperial Two-door Hardtop, 1959, SMP	20	45	90
Imperial Two-door Hardtop, 1960, SMP	10	30	60
Imperial Two-door Hardtop, 1961, AMT	40	60	120
Imperial Two-door Hardtop, 1963, AMT	50	100	175
Imperial Two-door Hardtop, 1958, AMT	20	45	90
International Dump Truck, 1958, PMC	10	20	50
International Dump Truck, 1953, PMC	25	50	100
International Dump Truck, 1951, PMC	30	60	120
International Four-door Sedan, 1958, PMC	10	20	50

	C6	C8	C10
International Pickup, 1956, PMC......	20	40	85
International Pickup, 1951, PMC......	40	80	150
International Pickup, 1947, PMC......	50	100	190
International Pickup, 1950, PMC......	40	70	140
International Pickup, 1957, PMC......	20	45	90
International Scout Convertible, 1965, ESK......	20	30	60
International Semi (plain), 1953, PMC......	30	60	120
International Semi Mayflower, 1953, PMC......	20	40	90
International Semi-Truck, 1951, PMC......	30	60	110
International Stake Truck, 1953, PMC......	30	60	120
International Stake Truck, 1951, PMC......	30	60	120
International Telephone Truck, 1947, NP......	30	60	130
International Tilt Cab Semi, 1955, PMC......	25	50	100
Javelin Two-door Hardtop, 1968, JH	10	30	60
Javelin Two-door Hardtop, 1969, JH	10	30	60
Javelin Two-door Hardtop, 1970, JH	20	30	65
Javelin/AMX Two-door Hardtop, 1971, JH......	10	30	50
Javelin/AMX Two-door Hardtop, 1972, JH......	10	30	50
Jeep Station Wagon, 1950, AUT......	40	90	180
Kaiser Four-door Sedan, 1953, BAN	80	150	310
Lincoln Cosmopolitan Four-door Sedan, 1950	100	250	425
Lincoln Four-door Sedan, 1951, BAN	30	60	100
Lincoln Four-door Sedan, 1953, BAN	30	60	100
Lincoln Two-door Hardtop, 1954, BAN	30	60	100
Mack Tanker Truck, 1950, NP	30	60	120
Maverick Two-door Sedan, 1969, JH	10	15	25
Mercedes 300 SL Convertible, 1958, HUB	25	40	80
Mercedes 300 SL Coupe, 1958, HUB	25	40	80
Mercury Breezeway Two-door Hardtop, 1964, AMT	40	80	160
Mercury Four-door Sedan, 1951, BAN	30	60	120
Mercury Four-door Sedan, 1953, BAN	20	40	95
Mercury Monterey Convertible, 1961, AMT	20	35	70

	C6	C8	C10
Mercury Monterey Convertible, 1963, AMT	20	40	80
Mercury Monterey Convertible, 1962, AMT	30	60	120
Mercury Monterey Two-door Hardtop, 1963, AMT	20	40	80
Mercury Monterey Two-door Hardtop, 1962, AMT	30	60	120
Mercury Monterey Two-door Hardtop, 1961, AMT	10	20	40
Mercury Park Lane Convertible, 1964, AMT	20	40	80
Mercury Park Lane Convertible, 1959, AMT	20	35	70
Mercury Park Lane Convertible, 1960, AMT	20	35	70
Mercury Park Lane Two-door Hardtop, 1965, AMT	10	20	40
Mercury Park Lane Two-door Hardtop, 1964, AMT	20	35	70
Mercury Park Lane Two-door Hardtop, 1966, AMT	10	25	50
Mercury Park Lane Two-door Hardtop, 1959, AMT	20	40	75
Mercury Park Lane Two-door Hardtop, 1960, AMT	20	35	70
Mercury Two-door Hardtop, 1954, BAN	20	40	95
Mercury Two-door Hardtop, 1955, BAN	30	60	120
Meteor Custom Two-door Sedan, 1962, AMT	30	60	120
Meteor Two-door Hardtop, 1963, AMT	30	60	120
Metro Panel Truck (double), 1952, PMC	20	40	80
Metro Panel Truck (single), 1952, PMC	20	40	80
Metropolitan Convertible, 1958, HUB	60	120	240
Metropolitan Two-door Hardtop, 1958, HUB	60	120	240
Mustang 2 + 2 Two-door Hardtop, 1967, AMT	60	120	220
Mustang 2 + 2 Two-door Hardtop, 1966, AMT	40	80	175
Mustang Convertible, 1966, AMT	20	40	80
Mustang Convertible, 1965, AMT	30	50	100
Mustang Convertible Pace, 1964, AMT	50	100	200
Mustang Mach I Two-door Fastback, 1969, AMT	60	120	245
Mustang Mach I Two-door Fastback, 1971, AMT	40	80	150

	C6	C8	C10
Mustang Mach I Two-door Hardtop, 1972, AMT	30	60	120
Mustang Two-door Convertible, 1964, AMT	30	60	120
Mustang Two-door Fastback, 1965, AMT	30	50	100
Mustang Two-door Hardtop, 1965, AMT	20	40	90
Mustang Two-door Hardtop, 1964, AMT	25	50	90
Mustang Two-door Hardtop, 1966, AMT	30	60	115
Nash Four-door Sedan, 1954, PMC.	30	50	100
Nash Four-door Sedan, 1950, NP	20	40	60
Nash Four-door Sedan, 1953, PMC.	20	40	95
Nash Golden Airflight Four-door, 1952, PMC	3	50	100
Oldsmobile 442 Two-door Hardtop, 1970, JH	20	40	60
Oldsmobile 442 Two-door Hardtop, 1969, JH	20	40	80
Oldsmobile 442 Two-door Hardtop, 1971, JH	20	40	60
Oldsmobile 88 Convertible, 1965, AMT	30	60	110
Oldsmobile 88 Four-door Hardtop, 1961, JH	20	30	60
Oldsmobile 88 Four-door Hardtop, 1962, JH	20	40	80
Oldsmobile 88 Two-door Hardtop, 1965, AMT	20	50	100
Oldsmobile 98 Four-door Hardtop, 1957, JH	20	40	75
Oldsmobile 98 Four-door Hardtop, 1959, JH	20	40	75
Oldsmobile 98 Two-door Hardtop, 1960, JH	20	30	60
Oldsmobile Four-door Hardtop, 1956, JH	25	40	85
Oldsmobile Four-door Hardtop, 1958, JH	20	40	65
Oldsmobile Four-door Sedan, 1953, BAN	25	40	85
Oldsmobile Starfire Convertible, 1963, JH	10	30	50
Oldsmobile Starfire Convertible, 1962, JH	20	40	80
Oldsmobile Starfire Two-door Hardtop, 1963, JH	10	30	60
Oldsmobile Toronado Two-door Hardtop, 1966, JH	10	30	50
Oldsmobile Toronado Two-door Hardtop, 1969, JH	10	30	50

	C6	C8	C10
Oldsmobile Toronado Two-door Hardtop, 1970, JH	10	20	40
Oldsmobile Toronado Two-door Hardtop, 1971, JH	20	40	60
Oldsmobile Toronado Two-door Hardtop, 1972, JH	10	20	30
Oldsmobile Two-door Hardtop, 1955, BAN	25	40	85
Oldsmobile Two-door Hardtop, 1954, BAN	25	40	85
Opel GT 1900 Coupe, 1969, AMT	20	50	100
Opel Sedan, 1959, PMC	10	20	30
Packard Convertible, 1948, MC	30	60	120
Packard Four-door Sedan, 1953, BAN	35	60	120
Packard Four-door Sedan, 1954, BAN	35	60	120
Packard Henesey Ambulance, 1951, AMT	60	120	250
Pinto Runabout Two-door Sedan, 1972, AMT	10	15	25
Pinto Two-door Sedan, 1971, AMT	10	15	25
Plymouth Belvedere Four-door, 1956, JH	20	40	80
Plymouth Belvedere Two-door Hardtop, 1957, JH	20	40	80
Plymouth Belvedere Two-door Hardtop, 1958, JH	10	30	60
Plymouth Cuda Two-door Hardtop, 1972, MPC	50	90	175
Plymouth Drivers Ed.	80	120	180
Plymouth Duster, 1972, MPC	30	60	120
Plymouth Duster Two-door Hardtop, 1971, MPC	20	50	100
Plymouth Four-door Sedan, 1953, BAN	30	60	120
Plymouth Four-door Sedan, 1955, JH	20	40	80
Plymouth Four-door Sedan, 1953, PMC	20	40	80
Plymouth Four-door Sedan, 1954, PMC	30	40	80
Plymouth Four-door Sedan, 1950, AMT	20	40	85
Plymouth Four-door Taxi, 1953, PMC	20	40	85
Plymouth Fury Convertible, 1967, JH	20	30	60
Plymouth Fury Convertible, 1964, JH	20	40	80
Plymouth Fury Convertible, 1962, JH	30	50	100

	C6	C8	C10
Plymouth Fury Convertible, 1963, JH	20	40	85
Plymouth Fury III Convertible, 1968, JH	20	30	60
Plymouth Fury III Convertible, 1965, JH	30	70	130
Plymouth Fury III Convertible, 1966, JH	20	40	80
Plymouth Fury III Convertible Pace, 1965, JH	60	120	265
Plymouth Fury III Driver's Training, 1966, JH	35	70	125
Plymouth Fury III Driver's Training, 1965, JH	25	50	110
Plymouth Fury III Two-door Hardtop, 1968, JH	10	30	50
Plymouth Fury III Two-door Hardtop, 1965, JH	30	60	120
Plymouth Fury III Two-door Hardtop, 1966, JH	20	40	80
Plymouth Fury Police Car, 1962, JH	40	80	150
Plymouth Fury Taxi, 1962, JH	50	100	200
Plymouth Fury Taxi, 1960, JH	30	65	130
Plymouth Fury Taxi, 1959, JH	30	50	110
Plymouth Fury Two-door Hardtop, 1962, JH	30	50	100
Plymouth Fury Two-door Hardtop, 1967, JH	10	30	50
Plymouth Fury Two-door Hardtop, 1963, JH	20	40	85
Plymouth Fury Two-door Hardtop, 1960, JH	20	40	60
Plymouth Fury Two-door Hardtop, 1961, JH	20	40	90
Plymouth Fury Two-door Hardtop, 1959, JH	20	40	80
Plymouth Fury Two-door Hardtop, 1958, JH	30	60	115
Plymouth GTX Two-door Hardtop, 1970, JH	20	50	100
Plymouth GTX Two-door Hardtop, 1969, JH	20	40	80
Plymouth Police Car, 1961, JH	25	50	100
Plymouth Roadrunner Two-door Hardtop, 1971, MPC	30	65	130
Plymouth Roadrunner Two-door Hardtop, 1972, MPC	30	60	120
Plymouth Sedan, 1948, NP	30	60	120
Plymouth Sedan, 1955, BAN	20	40	80
Plymouth Station Wagon, 1954, PMC	30	70	140
Plymouth Station Wagon, 1960, JH	10	30	60

	C6	C8	C10
Plymouth Taxi, 1958, JH	40	60	120
Plymouth Taxi, 1961, JH	30	65	135
Plymouth Taxi, 1957, JH	40	65	130
Plymouth Two-door Hardtop, 1964, JH	30	60	120
Plymouth Two-door Sedan, 1956, BAN	20	40	80
Pontiac Bonneville Convertible, 1965, AMT	40	65	130
Pontiac Bonneville Convertible, 1967, MPC	30	60	115
Pontiac Bonneville Convertible, 1966, MPC	40	65	130
Pontiac Bonneville Convertible, 1963, AMT	40	80	130
Pontiac Bonneville Convertible, 1962, AMT	60	120	240
Pontiac Bonneville Convertible, 1964, AMT	40	80	140
Pontiac Bonneville Convertible, 1961, AMT	30	60	120
Pontiac Bonneville Convertible, 1969, MPC	20	40	80
Pontiac Bonneville Convertible, 1960, AMT	20	40	80
Pontiac Bonneville Convertible, 1958, AMT	30	60	120
Pontiac Bonneville Convertible, 1968, MPC	30	50	110
Pontiac Bonneville Convertible, 1959, AMT	20	40	80
Pontiac Bonneville Two-door Hardtop, 1966, MPC	40	75	150
Pontiac Bonneville Two-door Hardtop, 1968, MPC	20	40	75
Pontiac Bonneville Two-door Hardtop, 1967, MPC	30	60	115
Pontiac Bonneville Two-door Hardtop, 1965, AMT	40	90	140
Pontiac Bonneville Two-door Hardtop, 1964, AMT	30	60	120
Pontiac Bonneville Two-door Hardtop, 1963, AMT	30	50	90
Pontiac Bonneville Two-door Hardtop, 1962, AMT	40	80	160
Pontiac Bonneville Two-door Hardtop, 1961, AMT	30	60	120
Pontiac Bonneville Two-door Hardtop, 1959, AMT	20	40	80
Pontiac Bonneville Two-door Hardtop, 1958, AMT	20	40	80
Pontiac Bonneville Two-door Hardtop, 1960, AMT	20	40	80

	C6	C8	C10
Pontiac Bonneville Two-door Hardtop, 1969, MPC	20	40	80
Pontiac Bonneville Two-door Hardtop, 1970, MPC	10	25	50
Pontiac Four-door Hardtop, 1956, JH	20	40	60
Pontiac Four-door Sedan, 1952, AMT	20	40	60
Pontiac Four-door Sedan, 1947, NP	40	60	120
Pontiac Four-door Sedan, 1951, AMT	20	40	60
Pontiac Four-door Sedan, 1948, NP	40	60	120
Pontiac Four-door Sedan, 1955, JH.	20	40	60
Pontiac Grand Prix Two-door Hardtop, 1964, AMT	40	80	140
Pontiac Grand Prix Two-door Hardtop, 1965, AMT	40	80	150
Pontiac Grand Prix Two-door Hardtop, 1972, MPC	20	40	80
Pontiac Grand Prix Two-door Hardtop, 1971, MPC	20	40	80
Pontiac Grand Prix Two-door Hardtop, 1970, MPC	20	40	80
Pontiac Grand Prix Two-door Hardtop, 1969, MPC	20	40	80
Pontiac GTO Two-door Hardtop, 1971, MPC..................................	20	40	85
Pontiac GTO Two-door Hardtop, 1970, MPC..................................	30	25	100
Pontiac GTO Two-door Hardtop, 1972, MPC..................................	20	40	80
Pontiac Sedan, 1953, BAN	30	60	90
Pontiac Sedan, 1955, BAN	20	40	60
Pontiac Star Chief Convertible, 1957, AMT	40	80	160
Pontiac Star Chief Four-door Hardtop, 1957, AMT	30	60	120
Pontiac Two-door Sedan, 1954, AMT	20	40	60
Pontiac Two-door Sedan, 1955, JH .	20	40	60
Pontiac Two-door Sedan, 1953, AMT	20	40	60
Rambler Ambassador Convertible, 1967, JH	10	20	30
Rambler Ambassador Convertible, 1968, JH	10	20	30
Rambler Ambassador Two-door Hardtop, 1969, JH......................	10	20	30
Rambler Ambassador Two-door Hardtop, 1967, JH......................	10	20	30
Rambler Ambassador Two-door Hardtop, 1968, JH......................	10	20	30
Rambler Ambassador Two-door Hardtop, 1966, JH	10	20	30
Rambler American Convertible, 1964, JH	10	20	30
Rambler American Convertible, 1963, JH	10	30	40
Rambler American Convertible, 1962, JH	10	20	40
Rambler American Convertible, 1966, JH	10	20	40
Rambler American Two-door Hardtop, 1964, JH	10	20	50
Rambler American Two-door Hardtop, 1966, JH	10	20	40
Rambler American Two-door Sedan, 1962, JH......................	10	20	40
Rambler American Two-door Sedan, 1961, JH......................	10	30	40
Rambler C.C. Station Wagon, 1966, JH	10	20	30
Rambler Classic Convertible, 1965, JH	10	20	40
Rambler Classic Four-door Sedan, 1965, JH	10	20	40
Rambler Classic Four-door Sedan, 1964, JH	10	20	40
Rambler Classic Four-door Sedan, 1963, JH	10	30	50
Rambler Classic Four-door Sedan, 1962, JH	10	20	40
Rambler Classic Station Wagon, 1964, JH	10	20	40
Rambler Classic Station Wagon, 1962, JH	10	20	40
Rambler Classic Station Wagon, 1963, JH	10	30	50
Rambler Convertible, 1951, NP	30	60	120
Rambler Cross Country Station Wagon, 1961, JH...................	10	30	40
Rambler Dauphine Four-door, 1958, HUB	10	20	45
Rambler Marlin Two-door Fastback, 1965, JH	20	40	80
Rambler Marlin Two-door Fastback, 1966, JH	20	40	80
Rambler Sedan, 1953, BAN.............	20	50	100
Rambler Station Wagon, 1959, JH ..	10	30	40
Rambler Station Wagon, 1960, JH ..	10	30	40
Rambler Two-door Hardtop, 1954, BAN	30	60	120
Rambler Two-door Hardtop, 1952, BAN	30	60	120

	C6	C8	C10
Rambler Unit Construction Demo, 1961, JH	50	100	150
Rolls Royce Silver Ghost Four-door Sedan	30	60	120
Studebaker Golden Hawk Two-door, 1956, AMT	30	60	90
Studebaker Lark Convertible, 1962, JH	10	25	50
Studebaker Lark Two-door Hardtop, 1962, JH	10	25	50
Studebaker Lark Two-door Hardtop, 1961, JH	10	25	50
Studebaker Lark Two-door Hardtop, 1959, JH	10	25	50
Studebaker Lark Two-door Hardtop, 1960, JH	10	25	50
Studebaker Stake Truck, 1950, NP	90	180	350
Studebaker Starliner Coupe, 1953, AMT	20	40	80
Studebaker Starliner Coupe, 1954, AMT	20	40	80
Studebaker Starliner Coupe, 1953, BAN	20	40	80
Studebaker Two-door Sedan, 1947, NP	40	80	150
Studebaker Two-door Sedan, 1948, NP	30	60	120
Studebaker Two-door Sedan, 1950, AMT	30	60	110
Studebaker Two-door Sedan, 1951, AMT	30	60	110
Studebaker Two-door Sedan, 1952, AMT	20	40	80
Studebaker Two-door-Hardtop, 1955, AMT	20	40	80
Tempest Four-door Sedan, 1961, AMT	20	30	60
Tempest GTO Convertible, 1966, MPC	70	140	300
Tempest GTO Convertible, 1965, AMT	65	140	300
Tempest GTO Convertible, 1969, MPC	40	80	160
Tempest GTO Convertible, 1968, MPC	40	80	160
Tempest GTO Convertible, 1967, MPC	70	140	300
Tempest GTO Two-door Hardtop, 1969, MPC	40	80	100
Tempest GTO Two-door Hardtop, 1968, MPC	40	80	160
Tempest GTO Two-door Hardtop, 1967, MPC	70	140	300

	C6	C8	C10
Tempest GTO Two-door Hardtop, 1965, AMT	65	140	300
Tempest GTO Two-door Hardtop, 1964, AMT	65	120	250
Tempest GTO Two-door Hardtop, 1966, MPC	70	140	300
Tempest LeMans Convertible, 1962, AMT	20	30	60
Tempest LeMans Convertible, 1964, AMT	30	60	120
Tempest LeMans Convertible, 1963, AMT	30	60	120
Tempest LeMans Two-door Hardtop, 1964, AMT	30	60	120
Tempest LeMans Two-door Sedan, 1962, AMT	20	30	60
Tempest LeMans Two-door Sedan, 1963, AMT	30	60	120
Thunderbird Convertible, 1961, AMT	30	60	120
Thunderbird Convertible, 1955, AMT	50	75	150
Thunderbird Convertible, 1957, AMT	30	40	60
Thunderbird Convertible, 1966, AMT	20	40	75
Thunderbird Convertible, 1959, AMT	20	40	75
Thunderbird Convertible, 1965, AMT	20	40	75
Thunderbird Convertible, 1960, AMT	20	50	100
Thunderbird Convertible, 1956, AMT	40	60	80
Thunderbird Convertible, 1964, AMT	30	60	120
Thunderbird Convertible, 1962, AMT	50	110	195
Thunderbird Convertible, 1963, AMT	50	90	180
Thunderbird Two-door Hardtop, 1966, AMT	20	40	60
Thunderbird Two-door Hardtop, 1967, AMT	10	25	50
Thunderbird Two-door Hardtop, 1970, AMT	10	25	50
Thunderbird Two-door Hardtop, 1969, AMT	10	25	50
Thunderbird Two-door Hardtop, 1971, AMT	10	25	50
Thunderbird Two-door Hardtop, 1968, AMT	10	25	50
Thunderbird Two-door Hardtop, 1964, AMT	20	40	80
Thunderbird Two-door Hardtop, 1963, AMT	20	40	80
Thunderbird Two-door Hardtop, 1962, AMT	30	60	120
Thunderbird Two-door Hardtop, 1961, AMT	30	60	120
Thunderbird Two-door Hardtop, 1959, AMT	20	40	75

	C6	C8	C10
Thunderbird Two-door Hardtop, 1958, AMT	20	40	75
Thunderbird Two-door Hardtop, 1965, AMT	20	40	75
Thunderbird Two-door Hardtop, 1960, AMT	20	40	75
Torino Cobra Two-door Hardtop, 1971, AMT	10	20	60
Triumph TR-3A Convertible, 1958, HUB	20	40	90
Triumph TR-3A Hardtop, 1958, HUB	20	40	90
Valiant Four-door Sedan, 1961, AMT	10	20	40
Valiant Four-door Sedan, 1960, AMT	10	20	40
Valiant Hatchback Two-door, 1972, MPC	10	20	30
Valiant Signet 200 Two-door Hardtop, 1964, AMT	10	60	80
Valiant Signet 800 Two-door Hardtop, 1963, AMT	10	60	80
Valiant Signet 800 Two-door Hardtop, 1962, AMT	30	60	120

	C6	C8	C10
Valiant Two-door Hardtop, 1965, AMT	20	30	60
Valiant Two-door Hardtop, 1966, AMT	80	160	320
Valiant Two-door Hardtop, 1961, AMT	10	20	40
Vega Hatchback Two-door Hardtop, 1971, MPC	10	20	30
Volkswagen Karmann Ghia Convertible, 1959, PM	10	20	40
Volkswagen Sedan, 1959, PM	10	20	30
White C.O.E Truck, 1950, NP	50	100	200
Willys 3/4-ton Army Truck, 1969, BAN	20	40	80
Willys Jeep FC Pickup, 1961, AUT	30	50	100
Willys Jeep FC Stake Truck w/plow, 1961, AUT	30	50	100
Willys Jeep Jolly, 1961, AUT	20	50	100
Willys Jeep Stake Truck, 1961, AUT	30	50	100
Willys Jeepster, 1968, MPC	10	20	40

PYRO

Pyro is probably best known for its plastic model kits produced in the 1950s and 1960s, but it did produce a nice line of toy vehicles in the 1950s. The originals of these were military vehicles made around the time of the Korean War. Available in two sizes, they came in three different colors—khaki, olive drab, and gray (for Navy and Marine) plastic. Each model was heat-stamped with stars and other identifying marks. Lionel used the large Pyro military vehicles as loads for its Navy and Marine trains. The loads were all gray and had no figures glued in place. After the Korean War came the inevitable decline in sales of war toys, and the vehicles were issued in civilian roles (i.e., Horse Transport) and specialty roles (i.e., Coca-Cola Truck). Pyro also produced a wide range of toys and trinkets for Planters Peanuts.

Specialty advertising issued included at least one political truck—an "Elect Marvin Griffin for Governor-Get On The Griffin Bandwagon" truck. Griffin was governor of Georgia from 1954 to 1958. Military sets continued in production into the mid to late 1950s. A 1956 Pyro advertisement in *Toys & Novelties* magazine declared: "Military Toys Are Hot Again!" The ad pictured boxed military sets C-242, C-243, and C-244. Toys gradually faded behind Pyro's growing line of model kits. The company went out of business in 1969. It was located in Pyro Park, Union City, New Jersey. At its height, it had 400 employees.

Contributor: Terry Sells. Sells is a graphic artist who works with music and entertainment accounts. He draws cartoons for fun and collects all types of plastic and celluloid toys. Sells began collecting in 1972 when his wife gave him a toy car for his birthday.

	C6	C8	C10
Army Tank P-1020	30	45	60
Balloon Racer, 3-1/2" long	12	18	25
Bulldozer, front loader	35	70	100
Canteen Truck	30	45	60
City Bottling Truck, 4" long	11	16	22

	C6	C8	C10
City Builders Truck, 5-1/2" long	NPF	NPF	NPF
Coca-Cola Truck, 5-1/2" long	75	112	150
Design-A-Car Set, builds fourteen models, w/box	35	52	70
Express Truck, 1950s	15	22	30

Pyro City Builders Truck, 5-1/2". Photo from Terry Sells.

Pyro Design-A-Car set, builds fourteen models, with box. Photo from Terry Sells.

Pyro Coca-Cola Truck, 5-1/2". Photo from Terry Sells.

Pyro Ice & Coal Truck, 5-1/2". Photo from Terry Sells.

Pyro Mr. Peanut's Peanut Wagon, 5-1/2". Photo from Terry Sells.

	C6	C8	C10
F7U Cutlass, 6" long	15	22	30
Ford, No. C-295, 1932	5	8	10
Ice & Coal Truck, 5-1/2" long	NPF	NPF	NPF
Lumber Loader	20	35	50
Lunch Wagon Truck, 5-1/2" long	18	27	37
Mobile Anti-Aircraft Truck, P-1015	48	72	95
Mobile Radar Truck, P-957	48	72	95
Mobile Searchlight Truck, P-958	48	72	95
Mobile Sound Truck, P-956	48	72	95
Motorcycle	32	48	65
Mr Peanut's Peanut Wagon, 5-1/2" long	NPF	NPF	NPF
Planters Peanuts Semi w/Trailer, 5-1/2" long	NPF	NPF	NPF

	C6	C8	C10
Planters Peanuts Stake Truck, semi, 5-1/2" long	NPF	NPF	NPF
Race Car, 3-1/2" long	10	15	21
Race Car, 4" long	20	30	40
Ranch Horse Transport, 5-1/2" long	NPF	NPF	NPF
Range Patrol Truck, 5" long	15	22	30
Road Roller	12	18	25
Soap Box Supersonic Racer, 4-3/4" long	75	112	150
Soldier Transport, P-955	20	30	40
Steam Roller	12	18	25
Truck, marked "Elect Marvin Griffin Governor" or "Get On The Griffin Bandwagon," 5-1/2" long	NPF	NPF	NPF
Twin 40-mm Mobile Gun, P-1087	48	72	95
U.S Army Ambulance	12	18	24

Pyro toys, as advertised in a December 1951 Woolworth's catalog.

Pyro Planters Peanuts semi with trailer, 5-1/2". Photo from Terry Sells.

Pyro Elect Marvin Griffin Covernor, Get On The Griffin Bandwagon Truck, 5-1/2". Photo from Terry Sells.

Pyro Planters Peanuts Stake Truck, semi, 5-1/2". Photo from Terry Sells.

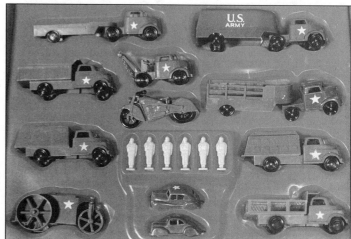

Contents of Pyro's twenty-one-piece U.S. Army Set. Photo from Terry Sells.

Pyro Ranch Horse Transport, 5-1/2". Photo from Terry Sells.

	C6	C8	C10
U.S Army Mobile Units Set	NPF	NPF	NPF
U.S Army Set, twenty-one pieces	17	26	35
U.S Army Stake Trailer Truck, 5-1/2" long...	10	15	20
U.S Army Truck...............................	9	13	19
U.S Navy Truck...............................	10	15	20
U.S.M.C. Truck	10	15	20

RALSTOY

Ralston Toy & Novelty Co. was founded in July 1939 to manufacture slush mold toys and novelties. It was formed by Dr. Felix Despecher, former mayor of Ralston, Nebraska, A.M. Erickson, and Henry C. Nestor to acquire the assets of Best Toy Co. of Manhattan, Kansas, and the surviving molds of Kansas Toys Co. of Clifton, Kansas. These assets included the temporary services of John M. Best, his molder Conrad Morsch, and about 140 molds from these pioneering slush mold toy-vehicle companies. The new enterprise was located in a building formerly occupied by the American Legion at 7632 Burlington St. This continued a low-cost toy line familiar to collectors since Kansas Toy was founded in 1923.

With the death of its founder, the young company was forced into reorganization. Lawyer Paul Massey, reorganized the company, but had to give up production of pot metal toy vehicles soon thereafter due to the need of lead for World War II. To survive, Massey turned to the production of wooden toys. One of Ralstoys well know wooden toys was a model of the an Army Jeep, of which about two million copies were sold through the dimestores, mainly Woolworth and Kresge. Other wooden toys included an Army tank, a Navy PT boat, and a (rumored) DUKW amphibious landing craft. These toys were completely made in Ralston, except for Jeep wheels, which were made in Omaha by blind workers (when war-time labor became short, handicapped workers were hired).

After the war the company turned to die-casting toys and novelties. As the business expanded it moved to 5707 S. 77th St., where it is today producing a well-known line of promotional trucks under Art Massey.

The history of those numbered molds is confusing. Although market values will depend on other factors than the actual makers, the following information should be of assistance to collectors. Ralstoy did label a few of its toys. They liked bottom pans, introduced by Best to increase rigidity of these fragile toys; this provided a surface to emboss "Ralstoy" and "Made in USA." Military olive-drab colors reflected the growing war consciousness. Wheels are not a good clue, even when the latest fad, black rubber wheels, were used.

Ralstoy probably reproduced many pieces from its acquired molds, but there is no practical way to know who made them when they are not labeled. (See Best Toy Co. and Kansas Toy Co. in this book.)
The toys described below are mostly new issues.

Contributors: Fred Maxwell, 4722 N. 33 St., Arlington, VA 22207. **Perry R. Eichor,** 703 North Almond Drive, Simpsonville, SC, 29681.

Abbreviations
The following abbreviations are for the details and variations useful in identification.

HG	horizontal grille pattern		SM	sidemounted spare
HL	horizontal hood louvers		SP	string-pull knob in handcrank area
HO	hood cap, Motometer or ornament		T	external trunk
L	lacquer finish		UV	unnumbered version
LI	landau irons on convertibles		VG	vertical grille pattern
MDW	metal disc wheels		VL	vertical hood louvers
MDSW	metal disc solid spokes		WS, W/S	windshield
MDWBT	wheels with black painted tires		WV	windshield visor
MSW	metal open spoke wheels		WHRT	wooden hubs, rubber tires
MWW	metal simulated wire wheels		WRDW	white hard rubber disc wheels
OW	open windows		WRW	white soft rubber wheels (balloon tires)
RM	rearmount spare tire/wheel			

	C6	C8	C10
Army Jeep Wooden, WWII issue, marked "Ralstoy 78 HR1," white star on hood, white grille and headlamps, no steering wheel, rearmount spare; crude, assembled w/nails; 5-1/8" long; also available in metal version, details not available; (RAV010)	20	30	40
Army tank, No. "74," marked "US Army," two gun turret; entirely different tank than Kansas Toy No. 74; 2-1/4" long (RAV003)	13	20	26
Army Tank, No. "107," reads "US Army," wood grooved-3/4" tracklaying wheels, two-gun turret, larger version of No. 74; 3-1/8" long; two other versions: also version w/black rubber wheels, and one unnumbered version (RAV007)	13	20	26

	C6	C8	C10
Army Tank, wooden, marked "USA W356" and "Rakstoy" on bottom, WWII issue (RAV011)	37	56	75
Dump Truck, No. "42," International (?) COE, two OW, hinged tin dump body, different casting than Kansas Toy Dump Truck No. 42; 3-3/8" long (RAV00I1)	NPF	NPF	NPF
Fire-rescue Truck, die-cast, streamlined, w/cast on roof, six open windows, tandem rear axles w/wheel skirts, possibly an early postwar issue, 6" long (RAV013)	NPF	NPF	NPF
Ford Tractor, 1948, w/trailer, 9" overall	30	45	60

**Ralstoy Army Tank, No. 107, two-gun turret, 3-1/8".
Photo from Fred Maxwell.**

Ralstoy Army Tank, wooden. Photo from Ed Poole.

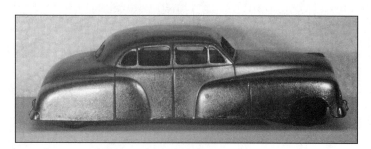

Ralstoy Large Sedan, No. 2R, black rubber wheels, 5-5/8". Photo from Fred Maxwell.

Back row: Ralstoy Tanker Truck, No. 102, 6-3/4". Middle row, two variations on No. 48 Tractor—one without the rubber tracks and one with. Photo from Perry Eichor.

	C6	C8	C10
Indy Racer, slanted grille, removable tin hood, torpedo tail. 3-3/4" long; earlier attributed to Craftoy, it is now known to be a different casting since it is also found w/large white rubber wheels it is more likely Ralstoy (RAV014)	NPF	NPF	NPF
Large Gun Truck, "US Army Anti-aircraft Unit," three axle carrier, AA gun, searchlight and crew of three; 5-5/8" long (RAV006)	28	42	56
Large Transporter, "Ralstoy" International (?) sleeper cab w/two OW, vertical grille, steel semi-trailer w/No. 74 tank, No. 34 muzzle-loading cannon and No. 32 aircraft, olive drab color; Not known if Ralstoy issued them as a set; 9" long overall (RAV005) ...	20	45	60
Mayflower Moving Van, 8-1/2" long .	15	22	30
Phillips 66 Tanker.............................	37	56	75
Sedan, large, No. "2R," die-cast, Cadillac (?), marked "Ralstoy" and "Made in USA," four open vent windows, divided open windshield, three open rear windows, burnished white metal, long fenders, rear-wheel skirts, bumper guards, black rubber wheels, possibly an early postwar issue, 5-5/8" long (RAV012)	NPF	NPF	NPF

	C6	C8	C10
Tanker Truck, No. 102, "Ralstoy" International (?) sleeper cab w/two OW, vertical grille; trailer marked "Gasoline" and "No. 102," four tanks and four storage compartments; Ralstoy cab found in commercial finish or military olilve drab Trailer was Best Toy; entire length: 6-3/4", sleeper cab length: 3-3/8", semi-trailer length: 4" (RAV004)	14	21	28
Tractor, No. "48," Caterpillar tractor, marked "Whoopee," driver in different color, grooved wood-3/4" wheels w/rubber tracks on Kansas Toy body; 3" long (RAV002)	NPF	NPF	NPF

RANLITE

Whatever happened to Automobiles (Geographical) Limited of Halifax, Yorkshire, England? Except for the Ranlite Toys made from 1931 to 1932, there is no information about the company and what else it may have manufactured. The only advertising known is in the December 1931 issue of the *Meccano Magazine*. It is possible that the company was yet another Depression casualty. Ranlite's toys were quite expensive for their time, and it is unlikely that they were a marketing success. Certainly, very few have survived.

Complex in design these were quite different from other toys made in the 1930s. Bodies and wheels were molded in "Ranlite," which was similar to Bakelite, a hard and brittle plastic commonly used to make control knobs and radio cases. The chassis and fenders of the two cars were stamped out of heavy-gauge steel. The large clockwork motor powered the rear axle. The front wheels were steerable. At extra cost, a remote-cable control kit was available so that the vehicle could be wound up and steered around obstacles. Wheels could be removed and reinstalled with the small hub-nut wrench provided. The hollow Dunlop "Semi Pneumatic" tires were removable. The boxes were made of heavy cardboard, but the maroon paper covering tends to fade badly.

Two popular English saloons (sedans) were realistically modeled. Body and chassis of the Singer and the Austin are identical, but the radiator and hood are unique to each. The Austin has more wire spokes per wheel than the Singer. Both cars have a sliding sunroof. Upper and lower body sections were cast separately, which allowed for variations in color schemes. The Austin has a rear-mounted spare wheel and luggage rack, but no bumpers. The Austin name appears on a diagonal bar across the radiator, and the hood has vertical louvers. The Singer has a small letter "s" at the top front of the radiator, and the bonnet louvers are horizontal. The Singer has double-bar, spring-steel bumpers on the front and rear, resulting in a total length of 10-3/4 inches, whereas the bumperless Austin is ten inches long. Of the two cars, the Singer is scarcer. The fold-away key wind is permanently attached underneath so the body is not spoiled by having a visible key hole. No headlamps were fitted. The die-cast key wind, differential gears and front axle are subject to metal fatigue, which has often destroyed them.

The Golden Arrow racing car is 16-1/2 inches long and it is a beautifully proportioned model of the famous Seagrave Record Car. Except for the tires, it does not share parts with the two passenger cars. The key is separate and not attached to the motor. It has steerable front wheels and a remote-control cable was also available at extra cost.

The petrol (gasoline) pump is made of Bakelite. It has a flexible hose made of a tightly coiled spring and is a gold model of a contemporary English Hammond pump. There is no value guide to (or for) Ranlite toys, since few are changing hands in the 1990s and not enough data exists to develop a reliable and useful listing of values.

Ranlite Golden Arrow Racing Car with original box, key and advertising brochure. Photo from Gates Willard. Photo by E.W. Willard.

Ranlite Austin with original box, sunroof is in open position. Photo from Gates Willard. Photo by E.W. Willard.

RANLITE SERIES

A.G.L. PRODUCTIONS—SEASON 1931.

GOLDEN ARROW RACING CAR.—A replica in Ranlite material of this world-famous Racing Car, 16½ in long, operated by strong clockwork mechanism, having semi-pneumatic tyres, detachable wheels and stub axles may be obtained ready assembled or as a Constructional Set, comprising a complete set of components with fully illustrated assembly instructions for building the model. No special tools required. Neatly boxed, price **27/6** for either type.

Made in three standard colours: Red, Mahogany and Walnut.

AUSTIN AND SINGER SALOON CARS. The only scale models of these renowned cars are in the Ranlite Series, and are by far the most attractive toy ever produced. The models are driven by strong clockwork mechanism, having machine cut gears, folding winding key, sliding sunshine roof, semi-pneumatic tyres, detachable wheels and stub axles, and are in appearance exactly like the real car. The body work being of Ranlite, the colours are both rich and permanent. The chassis is heavily enamelled, whilst metal fittings are plated. Austin models are provided with a folding luggage carrier; Singer models with front and rear bumpers. Models may be obtained either ready assembled or as Constructional Sets, comprising a complete set of components with fully illustrated assembly instructions for building your own model. No special tools required. Neatly boxed, priced **35/-** for either type.

Made in four standard colours: Black, Maroon, Green and Black, Yellow and Black.

RADIATORS. Separate Radiators of the Austin and Singer type conforming to the official designs may be obtained in any of the following colours: Black, Green, Maroon, and Yellow, ready for fitting to existing cars. Price **3/6** each.

WHEELS. Sets of five wheels, complete with semi-pneumatic tyres of the Austin and Singer types, may be obtained in any of the following colours: Black, Green, Maroon, and Yellow, ready for fitting to existing cars. Price **5/-** per set.

HAMMOND PETROL PUMP. RANLITE Models of Hammond Petrol Pumps are correct in detail and proportion, and are made in three standard colours: Red, Green, and Yellow. Price **2/6** each, boxed complete.

A.G.L. PATENT REMOTE CONTROL. A unique feature of Ranlite Toys is that they can be readily fitted with the A.G.L. Patent Remote Control thereby enabling the cars to be steered by hand when in motion, in any desired direction. The control in the form of Bowden Wire, has a cable 4 ft. 6 in. long, and is complete with moulded handle and heavily plated fitting. The controls can be easily fitted to existing cars without the aid of any special tools. Price complete with full instructions for fitting, **7/6** each. Please state whether Saloon or Racing Car Control is required.

BRITISH MANUFACTURE

A reprint of a Ranlite catalog page. Photo from Gates Willard.

Left to right: Rear view looks at the Ranlite Singer and Austin. Photo from Gates Willard. Photo by E.W. Willard.

Ranlite Singer with original box and closed sunroof. Photo from Gates Willard. Photo by E.W. Willard.

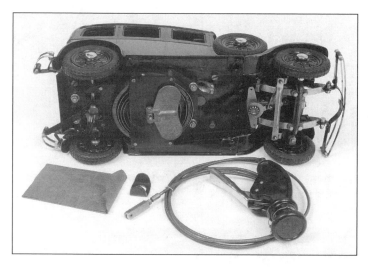

The underside of a Ranlite Singer with a hub nut wrench and envelope. Photo from Gates Willard. Photo by E.W. Willard.

REMCO

	C6	C8	C10
Barney's Auto Factory, builds convertible or sedan, w/box	160	240	320
Bulldog Tank	72	108	145
Electronic Mobile Loudspeaker and Signal System, 1955, 24" long	50	75	100
Flying Dutchman Antique Car	48	72	95
Movieland Drive-In Theatre, battery-operated, includes six small cars, ad cards, filmstrips, 1959, 14" long	80	120	160

	C6	C8	C10
Mr Kelly's Car Wash, 1960s	65	98	130
Old-Timer Convertible, 22" long	50	75	100
Shark Racer	75	100	125
Tiger Joe Tank, 1959	110	165	220
Tricky School Bus, 1968	35	52	70
Tru-Smoke Diesel Dump Truck, 1969	20	30	40
U-Drive Auto, w/driver	36	54	72

RENWAL

Accounts vary as to whether Renwal Manufacturing Company was founded in 1939 by Irving Rosenblum or Irving Lawner. What is indisputable is that Lawner spelled backward is Renwal. The firm seems to have begun as a manufacturer of a glass knife. A plastic knife replaced it and presumably led to the manufacture of plastic toys, which went on sale at least as early as August 1945. Its initial line consisted of WWII-era airplanes and dollhouse furniture. Vehicles were probably introduced in late 1946 or 1947 (the earliest known Renwal catalog is from 1948). The firm's early ads proclaimed it was "Famous for toys and houseware products."

In 1945, Renwal's showroom and factory were at 902 Broadway, New York City. An additional showroom at 200 Fifth Avenue seems to have been given up by 1946. In 1950, Renwal moved to Toyland Park, Mineola, New York. It seems to have remained there until the end (1970s). When it went out of business, its tooling was sold to Chein, which in turn sold it to Revell. (Years in parenthesis indicate the earliest known year of production.)

	C6	C8	C10
No. 0023 Motorcycle and Side Car w/Passenger, Handlebars steer, 1949, 5-1/4" long	50	75	100

	C6	C8	C10
No. 0039 Convertible Sedan w/Driver, doors open, top slides back, trunk opens, 1948, 6-1/2" long	30	45	60

Renwal Motorcycle and Side Car with Passenger, No. 23, handlebars steer, 1949, 5-1/4". Photo from Terry Sells.

Renwal Convertible Sedan with Driver, No. 39, doors open, top slides back, trunk opens, 1948, 6-1/2". Photo from Tery Sells.

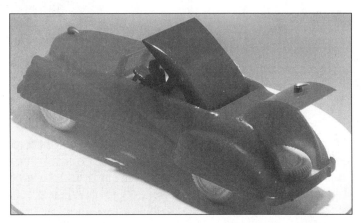

Another version the No. 39 Convertible Sedan with top up and opened trunk. Photo from Bob and Alice Wagner.

	C6	C8	C10
No. 0046 Coal Truck w/Driver, doors open, body raises, 1948, 7-1/2" long	50	75	100
No. 0048 Transport Truck w/Driver, doors open, body swings, 1948, 10-3/4" long	75	100	125
No. 0049 Gasoline Truck w/Driver, doors open, tank holds water, 1948, 7-3/4" long	50	75	100

Renwal Heavy Duty Coal Truck with Driver, No. 46, crank operates hoist, 1951, 10-3/4". Photo from Terry Sells.

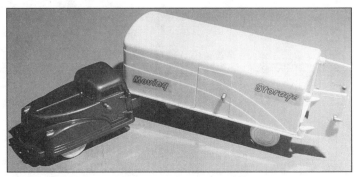

Renwal Transport Truck, No. 48, doors open, body swings, 1948, 10-3/4". Photo from Bob and Alice Wagner.

Renwal Gasoline Truck with Driver, No. 49, doors open, tank holds water, 1948, 7-3/4". Photo from Bob and Alice Wagner.

	C6	C8	C10
No. 0049 Gasoline Truck w/Driver, doors open, tank holds water, top reads "Super-X," working faucet inside rear door, 1950, 7-3/4" long	50	75	100
No. 0050 Dump Truck w/Driver, doors open, body raises, "Sand-Gravel," 1948, 7-1/2" long	62	93	125
No. 0056 Cement Mixer Truck, mixer revolves, rear cap comes off, tank raises, 1948, 7-1/4" long	75	112	150
No. 0057 Fire Truck w/Three Fireman, 1948, 7" long, 8" high when ladder extended	48	72	95

Renwal Gasoline Truck with Driver, No. 49, like other truck but with Super-X inscription, 1950. Photo from Bob and Alice Wagner.

Renwal Dump Truck with Driver, Sand-Gravel, No. 50, doors open, body raises, 1948, 7-1/2". Photo from Terry Sells.

Renwal Cement Mixer Truck, No. 56, 1948, 7-1/4". Photo from Terry Sells.

Back row: Renwal Racing Car, No. 58, 6-3/8". Front row, left to right: Racer, No. 150, 3-1/4"; Racer, No. 88, 4-3/8". Photo from Terry Sells.

Renwal Fire Truck with Three Fireman, No. 57, 1948, 7"—8" when ladder is extended. Photo from Bob and Alice Wagner.

Renwal Auto Carrier Truck, No. 79, four autos, cab turns, doors open, 1949, 13". Photo from Bob and Alice Wagner.

Renwal Steam Shovel Truck with Truck Driver and Steam Shovel Operator, No. 86, doors open, cab swings, shovel can be raised, 1949, 19". Photo from Terry Sells.

Renwal Two-door Sedan with Driver, No. 90, doors and trunk open, 1949, 6-1/2". Photo from Bob and Alice Wagner.

Renwal Plastic Garage, No. 92, 1949, 6-1/2". Photo from Dave Leopard.

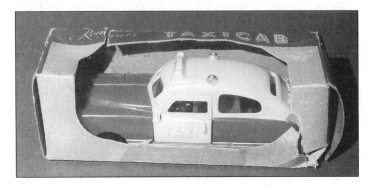

Renwal Taxicab with Driver, No. 91, 1949, doors and trunk open, 6-1/2". Photo from Bob and Alice Wagner.

Renwal Friction Motor Convertible with Driver, No. 106, 1950, 9-1/2". Photo from Bob and Alice Wagner.

	C6	C8	C10
No. 0058 Racing Car, marked "Speed King," 1948, 6-3/8" long ..	30	50	70
No. 0059 Sedan, 1948, 4-1/4" long..	6	9	13
No. 0060 Coupe, 1948, 4-1/4" long..	6	9	13
No. 0061 Racer, 1948, 4-3/16" long.	12	18	25
No. 0062 Truck (pick-up), 1948, 4-1/4" long..................................	5	8	10
No. 0079 Auto Carrier Truck w/Driver, four autos, cab turns, doors open, elevator raises cars for upper level, 1949, 13" long	50	100	175
No. 0086 Steam Shovel Truck w/Truck Driver and Steam Shovel Operator, doors open, cab swings, shovel can be raised, lowered, extended via handle on side of cab, 1949, 19" long	45	68	90
No. 0088 Racer, (1950), 4-3/8" long	20	30	40
No. 0090 Two-door Sedan w/Driver, doors and trunk open, 1949, 6-1/2" long...................................	45	60	95
No. 0091 Taxicab w/Driver, cab doors and trunk open, 1949, 6-1/2" long..................................	42	63	85
No. 0092 Plastic Garage, 1949, 6-1/2" long..................................	50	75	100

	C6	C8	C10
No. 0093 Panel Truck, "Delivery," 1949, 4-1/4" long	12	18	25
No. 0094 Gasoline Truck, "Gasoline," 1949, 4-1/4" long.......	12	18	25
No. 0099 Stake Wagon, gates removable, tongue hinged, 1950, 8-3/8" long	NPF	NPF	NPF
No. 0101 Stake Truck w/Driver, doors open, gates removable, 1950, 7-3/4" long	NPF	NPF	NPF
No. 0102 Coupe, 1950, 4-1/4" long..	8	10	15
No. 0103 Sedan, 1950, 4-1/4" long..	8	10	15
No. 0104 Convertible, 1950, 4-1/4" long..	10	15	20
No. 0105 Fire Engine, w/ladder, 1950, 4-1/4" long	10	12	20
No. 0106 Friction Motor Convertible w/Driver, 1950, 9-1/2" long	50	75	150
No. 0107 Speed King Friction Motor Racer w/Driver, 1950, 10-1/4" long..	NPF	NPF	NPF
No. 0110 Auto Jack, raises cars 1-1/2", 1950, base 3-3/4" long	5	8	10

	C6	C8	C10
No. 0113 Friction Motor Fire Truck w/Driver and two Firemen, w/water tank, pump, unwinding hose, nozzle w/water release, siren, gear-controlled ladder, 1950, 11-1/2" long, 16" high when ladder extended	NPF	NPF	NPF
No. 0123 School Bus, 4-7/16" long ..	7	11	15
No. 0124 City Bus, 4-7/16" long	14	21	28
No. 0126 Hook and Ladder Truck w/Drivers, cab turns, doors open, rear wheels turn, 1950, 15-3/4" long, 16" high when ladder extended	60	80	100
No. 0131 Cement Mixer, crank turns mixer, mixer revolves, tilts; can be filled and emptied, doors open, 1951, 9-7/8" long	50	70	90
No. 0132 Gasoline Truck, "Gas Oil," rear and cab doors open, tank can be filled and emptied through plastic hose, which folds up inside rear doors (1951), 12" long	NPF	NPF	NPF
No. 0133 Heavy Duty Tow Truck w/Driver, adjustable crane, windlass clicks, doors open, 1951, 11" long	50	70	90
No. 0134 Heavy Duty Dump Truck w/Driver, crank operates hoist, cab doors and tailgate open, 1951, 10-7/8" long	50	70	90

	C6	C8	C10
No. 0135 Heavy Duty Coal Truck w/Driver, crank operates hoist, load divider, unloading chute, cab doors open, 1951, 10-3/4" long ...	50	70	90
No. 0143 Sedan, 3-1/8" long	9	14	18
No. 0144 Coupe, 3-1/16" long, new in 1950	7	11	15
No. 0145 Fire Truck, 3-1/4" long, new in 1950	7	15	15
No. 0146 Hook and Ladder, 3-1/4" long	7	10	15
No. 0147 Convertible, 3-1/8" long	6	12	13
No. 0148 Gasoline Truck, 3-1/8" long	6	9	12
No. 0149 Pickup Truck, 3-3/16" long	7	10	15
No. 0150 Racer, 3-1/4" long	17	26	35
No. 0151 Fire Chief Coupe, 1950, 4-1/4" long	NPF	NPF	NPF
No. 0152 Police Coupe, 1950, 4-1/4" long	12	18	24
No. 0153 Taxi, 1950, 4-1/4" long	10	15	21
No. 0167 Fire Truck Builder Kit, w/ladder, hose reel, crank, firemen, driver, 1953, truck 7" long	NPF	NPF	NPF
No. 0168 Auto-Boat, auto on one side, boat on other, 1954, 6-1/2" long	20	30	50

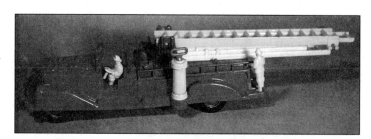

Renwal Friction Motor Fire Truck with Driver and two Firemen, No. 113, 1950, 11-1/2" and 16" with extended ladder. Photo from Terry Sells.

Renwal Gasoline Truck, No. 132, 1951, rear and cab doors open, 12". Photo from Terry Sells.

Renwal Hook & Ladder Truck with Drivers, No. 126, cab turns, doors open, rear wheels turn, 1950, 15-3/4" and 16" when ladder is extended. Photo from Terry Sells.

Renwal Cadillac Convertible with Driver, No. 174, top goes up and down, 1953, 5-1/2". Photo from Terry Sells.

Renwal Motorcycle Cop, No. 188, 1953, 9". Photo from Gary Linden.

Renwal Motorcycle Cop, No. 189, 1953, 3-3/4". Photo from Terry Sells.

Renwal Two-Car Garage with two Cars, No. 195, 1954. Photo from Dave Leopard.

Renwal Gasoline Truck, No. 8008, die-cast metal, 1955, 6". Photo from Terry Sells.

	C6	C8	C10
No. 0173 Speedway Racer w/Driver, 1953, 9-1/2" long	85	128	170
No. 0174 Cadillac Convertible with Driver, top goes up and down, 1953, 5-1/2" long	20	30	50
No. 0175 Motorcycle w/Sidecar Construction Kit, 1953, motorcycle 5-1/4" long	NPF	NPF	NPF
No. 0176 Two-door Sedan Construction Kit w/Driver, w/spare wheel, doors and trunk open, 1953, 6-1/2" long	NPF	NPF	NPF
No. 0177 Taxicab Construction Kit w/Driver, w/spare, doors and trunk open, 1953, cab 6-1/2" long	35	52	70
No. 0178 Fire Truck, w/two firemen, 1953, 15" long, ladder extends to 16"	NPF	NPF	NPF
No. 0179 Fire Truck, two firemen, 1953, 7-1/2" long, 8" high w/ladder extended	30	45	60
No. 0186 Tractor w/Driver, 1953, 5-1/4" long	NPF	NPF	NPF
No. 0187 Tractor and Trailer, 1953	NPF	NPF	NPF

	C6	C8	C10
No. 0188 Motorcycle Cop, 1953, 9" long	50	75	100
No. 0189 Motorcycle Cop, 1953, 3-3/4" long	NPF	NPF	NPF
No. 0191 Trailer Truck, w/two boats, 1953, 13-1/4" long	NPF	NPF	NPF
No. 0192 Trailer Truck, w/eight Logs, 1953, 13-1/4" long	NPF	NPF	NPF
No. 0195 Two-Car Garage, w/two cars, doors open, 1954, 4-1/8" x 3-5/8" x 2-1/4"	12	18	25
No. 0196 Pick-up Truck, 1953, 11" long	NPF	NPF	NPF
No. 0201 Old Fashioned Car w/Driver, open top, 1954, 8-1/2" long	NPF	NPF	NPF
No. 0206 Convertible, no motor, 1952, 9-1/2" long	NPF	NPF	NPF
No. 0207 Racer, no motor, 1952, 10-1/4" long	NPF	NPF	NPF
No. 0210 Take-Apart Hot Rod, 10-1/2" long, 1954	90	135	180
No. 0213 Fire Engine, w/water tank, pump, unwinding hose, nozzle w/water release, siren, gear-controlled ladder, no motor, 1952, 11-1/2" long, 16" high when ladder extended	NPF	NPF	NPF

HIGH GLOSS INFRA-RED BAKED ENAMEL

FINISHES...safe, non-toxic!

8007 Sedan.

8009 Racer

AN INFINITE CAPACITY FOR TAKING PAINS . . . that's what goes into your finished Renwal toy . . . from careful polishing of dies before they are hardened to the final application of enamel to a casting. Your customers will show their appreciation by buying the WORLD'S FINEST TOYS . . . toys by Renwal!

8015 Convertible

8013 Jeep

8012 Hot Rod

A page from a 1955 Renwal catalog.

	C6	C8	C10
No. 0216 Champion Racer, friction motor, dome over driver, siren, 1954, 10-3/8" long	NPF	NPF	NPF
No. 0218 Toytown Service Garage Set, w/five 3-1/4" cars, 1955, 7 x 5 x 2-7/8"	NPF	NPF	NPF
No. 0220 Take-Apart Racer, 1954, 10-1/2" long	NPF	NPF	NPF
No. 0221 Coal Truck Kit, 1954, truck 7-1/2" long	NPF	NPF	NPF
No. 0222 Dump Truck Kit, 1954, truck 7-1/2" long	NPF	NPF	NPF
No. 0223 Transport Kit, 1954, truck 10-3/4" long	NPF	NPF	NPF
No. 0224 Gasoline Truck Kit, 1954, truck 7-3/4" long	NPF	NPF	NPF
No. 0226 Cement Mixer Kit, 1954, truck 7-1/4" long	NPF	NPF	NPF
No. 0235 Motorized Fuel Truck, friction, driver, doors open, body raises, rear door opens to slide out chute, 1954, 7-1/2" long	NPF	NPF	NPF
No. 0236 Motorized Sand Truck, friction, doors open, body raises, rear gate opens, 1954, 7-1/2" long	NPF	NPF	NPF
No. 0237 Motorized Tank Truck, friction, doors open, tank cap opens for filling, rear door opens to faucet, 1954, 7-3/4" long	NPF	NPF	NPF
No. 0238 Motorized Ready-Mix Concrete Truck w/Driver, friction motor, doors open, mixer revolves as truck moves, raises, rear cap comes off, 1954, 7-1/8" long	NPF	NPF	NPF
No. 0239 Motorized Moving Van w/Driver, friction motor, cab, trailer doors open, 1954, 10-5/8" long	NPF	NPF	NPF
No. 0243 Racer w/Driver, 1954, 9-1/2" long	NPF	NPF	NPF
No. 0248 Motorized Fire Truck w/Siren, friction motor, driver, two firemen, 1955, 15" long, ladder extends to 16"	NPF	NPF	NPF
No. 0259 Engine Running Racer, transparent engine block shows action, 1955, 10-1/2" long	NPF	NPF	NPF
No. 0260 TV MobileTruck, camera, spotlight, microphone, cable "Renwal-TV" on side, 1956	75	112	150
No. 0270 Steam Shovel Construction Kit, 1953, truck 8-1/8" long	NPF	NPF	NPF
No. 0271 Hook and Ladder Construction Kit, w/two drivers, firemen, 1953, truck 15-3/4" long.	NPF	NPF	NPF

	C6	C8	C10
No. 0284 U.S Army Tank	3	5	7
No. 0301 Customized Service Truck, 1:32-scale, 1964	NPF	NPF	NPF
No. 0313 Motorized Pumper Fire Truck, w/driver and two firemen, w/siren and extension ladder friction, throws water through plastic hose, 1955, 11-1/2" long	NPF	NPF	NPF
No. 0329 Gasoline Truck, soft plastic, 6" long	8	12	16
No. 0621 Truck, same as No. 62, 1951, 4-1/4" long	NPF	NPF	NPF
No. 0813 Visible Auto Chassis, early 1960s, over three feet long	NPF	NPF	NPF
No. 2039 Convertible w/Driver, w/simulated chrome trim, 1952, 6-1/2" long	32	48	65
No. 2057 Fire Truck, w/simulated chrome trim, 1952	48	72	95
No. 2061 Racer, w/simulated chrome trim, 1952	NPF	NPF	NPF
No. 2088 Racer, but w/chrome trim, 1952	NPF	NPF	NPF
No. 2090 Sedan w/Driver, w/simulated chrome trim, 1952, 6-1/2" long	NPF	NPF	NPF
No. 2091 Taxicab, w/simulated chrome trim, 1952	60	90	120
No. 2093 Delivery Truck, w/chrome trim, 1952	10	15	20
No. 2094 Gasoline Truck, w/chrome trim, 1952	10	15	20
No. 2102 Coupe, w/chrome trim, 1952	10	15	20
No. 2103 Sedan, w/chrome trim, 1952	10	15	20
No. 2104 Convertible, w/chrome trim, 1952	10	15	20
No. 2621 Truck, w/chrome trim, 1952	10	15	20
No. 8001 Ferrari Racer, metal, motorized, 1955, 9-1/4" long	100	150	200
No. 8002 Maserati Racer, metal, motorized, 1955, 9-1/4" long	NPF	NPF	NPF
No. 8003 Pontiac Convertible, metal, motorized, 1955, 8-1/4" long	60	90	120
No. 8004 Plymouth Convertible, metal, motorized, 1955, 7-7/8" long	NPF	NPF	NPF
No. 8005 Chevrolet Sedan, metal motorized, 1955, 7-7/8" long	NPF	NPF	NPF
No. 8006 Ford Sedan, metal, motorized, 1955, 7-7/8" long	NPF	NPF	NPF
No. 8007 Sedan, metal, 1955, 6" long	NPF	NPF	NPF

	C6	C8	C10
No. 8008 Gasoline Truck, metal, 1955, 6" long	27	41	55
No. 8009 Racer, metal, 1955, 7" long	NPF	NPF	NPF
No. 8010 Delivery Truck, metal, 1955, 6" long	40	50	70
No. 8011 Pickup Truck, metal, 1955, 6" long	30	45	60
No. 8012 Hot Rod, metal, 1955, 6-1/2" long	NPF	NPF	NPF
No. 8013 Jeep, metal, 1955, 5-5/8" long	NPF	NPF	NPF
No. 8014 Fire Truck, metal, 1955, 6" long	NPF	NPF	NPF
No. 8015 Convertible, metal, 1955, 6" long	35	52	70
No. 8028 Citroen, metal, 1955, 6" long	NPF	NPF	NPF
No. 8029 Porsche, metal, 1955, 5-3/4" long	NPF	NPF	NPF
No. 8030 Pegasa, metal, 1955, 6" long	NPF	NPF	NPF

	C6	C8	C10
No. 8031 Lancia, metal, 1955, 6" long	NPF	NPF	NPF
No. 8032 Rolls Royce, metal, 1955, 6-1/8" long	NPF	NPF	NPF
No. 8033 Jaguar, metal, 1955, 6-1/8" long	NPF	NPF	NPF
No. 8034 MG, metal, 1955, 6" long..	NPF	NPF	NPF
No. 8035 Mercedes-Benz, metal, 1955, 5-7/8" long	NPF	NPF	NPF
No. 8036 Kaiser-Darrin, metal, 1955, 6-1/8" long	NPF	NPF	NPF
No. 8037 Austin-Healey, metal 1955, 6" long	NPF	NPF	NPF
No. 8853, 3-1/2" metal replicas of Renwal's plastic convertible, sedan, coupe, pick-up truck, gasoline truck, fire truck, hook and ladder, racer; 1955	NPF	NPF	NPF
No. 8854, 4-1/4" to 4-1/2" metal replicas of Renwal's plastic convertible, coupe gasoline truck, city bus; 1955	NPF	NPF	NPF

REPUBLIC TOOL PRODUCTS CO.
(DAYTON, OHIO 1922-32)

Charles Black received a patent for a unique cover to protect the friction mechanism between the rear wheels from dirt and moisture, and is stamped with the patent date, Nov. 1, 1921. Black had been employed at the Dayton Toy Works until 1922, when he left the company to form a partnership with Elijah Miller, another ex-Dayton employee. The company ceased making Republic Toys in 1932. Although Republic Toys were produced for a mere ten years, they have become an important part of American toy manufacturing history.

Contributor: Bob Smith, The Village Smith, 62 West Ave., Fairport, NY 14450-2102.

	C6	C8	C10
Bus, 1920s, 28" long	450	600	900
Cargo Truck, friction drive, green, c.1922, 13 " long	275	400	600

**Republic Cargo Truck, friction drive, green, 1920s, 13".
Photo from Bob Smith.**

	C6	C8	C10
Chemical Truck	170	255	340
Coupe	275	400	600
Dayton Racer, operates on large spring-wind motor cranked from front of car gray/blue/red, 1910 or 1922, 11" long	300	450	650
Ladder Truck, 17" long	250	350	475
Ladder Truck, friction, 24" long	250	375	500
Limousine, friction drive, blue, c.1922, 11" long	250	375	525
Momentum Dump Truck, w/driver, pat. 11/1/21, 20" long	300	450	600
Roadster, friction drive, red, 11" long, c.1922	225	350	500
Taxi Cab w/Driver, sheet-metal, friction, c.1926	275	400	550

Republic Cargo Truck, friction drive, green, 1920s, 13". Photo from Bob Smith.

Republic Limousine, friction drive, 11". Photo from Bob Smith.

Republic Roadster, friction drive, 1920s, 11". Photo from Bob Smith.

REUHL

Reuhl Prod. Toys were named after their founder, Andy Reul (the 'H' was added to the name to help in the pronunciation). Although Reul was working in his newly founded business before World War II, he didn't really get established until 1945. In the beginning, Reuhl made his models out of wood, Bakelite, Fiberglas and plastic. His work with plastic was outstanding. When he started getting large orders for scale models from Caterpillar Heavy Equipment Corp. and Massey-Harris Farm Equipment, Reul switched to die-cast metal. His castings were far superior to anything previously produced by other manufacturers. His attention to detail brought these 1:24-scale construction models to be miniature duplicates of the real thing. Most Massey-Harris models were done in 1:20-scale and had the same fine detail. Reuhl Products were too expensive for most retail stores. Because only a few retail outlets were able to sell the products successfully, they became almost exclusively sold at the Caterpillar and Massey-Harris dealer showrooms. Reuhl Products went out of business in 1958 after losing its two major customers—Caterpillar and Massey-Harris. Although some of today's products have great detail, Reuhl Products were the finest made farm and construction models in the industry, and they are highly sought after on today's market. Note: A clean, original box for any Reuhl model can double it's value.

	C6	C8	C10		C6	C8	C10
American Portable Material Elevator	NPF	NPF	NPF	Caterpillar No. 70 Four-wheel Scraper, die-cast, 1:24 scale	400	600	950
Caterpillar 1948 D7 Dozer, plastic kit, 1:24-scale, Reuhl/Curver, could also be purchased assembled	200	375	675	Caterpillar Ripper, die-cast w/plastic wheels, 1:24-scale	225	400	625
Caterpillar D7 Dozer, die-cast, 1:24-scale	300	475	750	Caterpillar Scraper 1948 No. 70, plastic kit, 1:24-scale, could also be purchased assembled	250	450	750
Caterpillar DW-10 Wheel Tractor, die-cast, 1:24-scale.....................	325	475	750	Caterpillar DW-10 Tractor with No. 10 Scraper, die-cast, 1:24-scale ..	700	1100	1800
Caterpillar No. 12 Grader, die-cast, 1:24 scale	650	900	1350	Caterpillar No. 10 Two-wheel Scraper, die-cast, 1:24-scale	350	500	800

Reuhl Caterpillar D7 Dozer. Photo from Bob Smith.

Reuhl Cedar Rapids Pitmaster Gravel Crusher. Photo from Bob Smith.

Reuhl Massey-Harris 44 Tractor. Photo from Bob Smith.

Reuhl Lorain Shovel. Photo from Bob Smith.

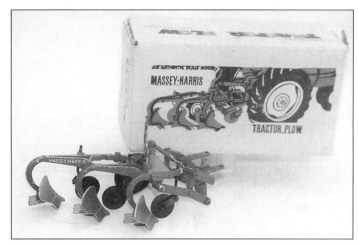

Reuhl Massey-Harris 3 Bottom Plow. Photo from Bob Smith.

	C6	C8	C10
Cedar Rapids Pitmaster Gravel Crusher, 221 parts	800	1450	2100
I.H. Farmall Cub Tractor, plastic kit, 1:16-scale, could also be purchased assembled	175	350	575
Cedar Rapids Pitmaster Gravel Crusher, 221 parts	800	1450	2100
I.H. Farmall Cub Tractor, plastic kit, 1:16-scale, could also be purchased assembled	175	350	575
Lorain Shovel	700	1250	1900
Massey-Harris Disc Harrow, die-cast, 1:20-scale, made to fit 44 tractor	175	300	575
Massey-Harris Loader, die-cast, 1:20-scale, made to fit 44 tractor	200	475	675
Massey-Harris Pull-type Combine, die-cast, 1:20-scale, made to fit 44 tractor	275	400	600
Massey-Harris Roadmaster Wagon, die-cast, 1:24-scale, made to fit 44 tractor	150	275	550

Reuhl Massey-Harris Disc Harrow. Photo from Bob Smith.

Reuhl Massey-Harris Loader. Photo from Bob Smith.

Reuhl Massey-Harris Roadmaster Wagon. Photo from Bob Smith.

	C6	C8	C10
Massey-Harris Self-propelled Combine, die-cast, 1:20-scale, made to fit 44 tractor	325	475	675
Model Race Car Type I, molded Fiberglas, 17" long	275	425	700

Reuhl Massey Harris Self-propelled Combine. Photo from Bob Smith.

	C6	C8	C10
Model Race Car Type II, molded Fiberglas	375	550	850

ROSS TOOL AND MANUFACTURING CO.

	C6	C8	C10		C6	C8	C10
Convertible, w/woman and dog, 3" long (RO008)	6	8	10	Mack Gasoline Truck, 4-5/8" long (RO004)	15	18	25
Hose Truck, plastic, 3" long (RO009)	6	8	10	Mack Moving Van, 4-5/8" long (RO003)	15	18	25
Hot Rod, plastic, 5" long (RO007)	15	20	30	Racer, plastic, 4" long (RO005)	15	18	25
Ladder Truck, plastic, 4-3/4" long (RO001)	12	15	20	Racer, several varieties, plastic, approx 3" long (RO006)	6	8	10
Mack Dump Truck, 4-1/4" long (RO002)	15	18	25				

Ross Convertible, woman and dog, 3". Photo from Dave Leopard.

Ross Hose Truck, plastic, 3". Photo from Dave Leopard.

Ross Racer, plastic, 4". Photo from Dave Leopard.

Ross Hot Rod, plastic, 5". Photo from Dave Leopard.

Ross Ladder Truck, plastic, 4-7/5". Photo from Dave Leopard.

Left to right: Ross Racers, several varieties, plastic, 3" each. Photo from Dave Leopard.

RUBBER VEHICLES UNKNOWN MANUFACTURERS

The following list, with its number codes, was compiled by Dave Leopard. Vehicles are broken down by types. The gaps in the numbering indicate vehicles that have been identified since the list was made up.

Contributor: Dave Leopard, 2507 Feather Run Trail, West Columbia, SC 29169-4915.

	C6	C8	C10
'34 Dodge Rack Truck, 4-7/8 " long (UT004)	NPF	NPF	NPF
'35 Chrysler Four-door Airflow Sedan, rear spare, ad on roof, 4-3/4" long (UA007)	NPF	NPF	NPF

	C6	C8	C10
'35 Chrysler Two-door Airflow Sedan, 5-1/8" long (UA008)	60	80	115
'35 DeSoto Four-door Airflow Sedan, 5" long (UA006)	60	80	115

	C6	C8	C10
'35 LaFayette (?) Sedan, fastback, solid, w/tires, 4" long (UA012)	30	40	50
'35 Plymouth Four-door Sedan, 4-7/8" long (UA008A)	NPF	NPF	NPF
'36 Plymouth Four-door Trunkback Sedan, 4-7/8" long (UA009)	75	112	150
'37 Plymouth Four-door Trunkback Sedan, 4-7/8" long (UA010)	75	112	150

	C6	C8	C10
'46 Nash Two-door Fastback Sedan, hollow, molded tires, 4" long (UA011)	12	18	25
Open Racer, left side header pipes, solid rubber, 3-1/2" long (UR001)	NPF	NPF	NPF
Open Racer, V-8, solid, large tires on wood hubs, 4" long (UR002) ..	NPF	NPF	NPF
Open Racer, solid, rubber tires on wood hubs, 6" long (UR003)	NPF	NPF	NPF

Rubber Vehicles, 1935 Chrysler Four-door Airflow Sedan, rear spare, ad on roof, spare, 4-3/4". Photo from Dave Leopard's book *Rubber Toy Vehicles*.

Rubber Vehicles, 1935 Chrysler Two-door Airflow Sedan, 5-1/8". Photo from Dave Leopard's book *Rubber Toy Vehicles*.

Rubber Vehicles, 1935 DeSoto Four-door Airflow Sedan, 5". Photo from Dave Leopard's book *Rubber Toy Vehicles*.

Rubber Vehicles, 1935 Sedan, possibly a LaFayette, 4". Photo from Dave Leopard's book *Rubber Toy Vehicles*.

Rubber Vehicles, 1935 Plymouth Four-door Sedan, 4-7/8". Photo from Dave Leopard's book *Rubber Toy Vehicles*.

Rubber Vehicles, 1946 Nash, Two-door Fastback Sedan, 4". Photo from Dave Leopard.

Rubber Vehicles, 1946 Nash, Two-door Fastback Sedan, 4". Photo from Dave Leopard.

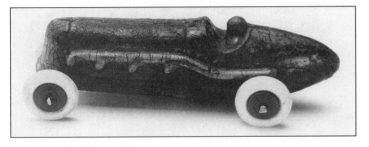

Rubber Vehicles, Open Racer, V-8, large tires on wood hubs, 4". Photo from Dave Leopard's book *Rubber Toy Vehicles*.

Rubber Vehicles, Open Racer, rubber tires on wood hubs, 6". Photo from Dave Leopard's book *Rubber Toy Vehicles*.

SAUNDERS TOOL & DIE CO.

	C6	C8	C10
Bump and Dump Truck, 10-3/4" long	40	60	80
Convertible, plastic wind-up, 10-1/4" long	48	72	95
Fire Chief Car, wind-up, 10" long	42	63	85
Fire Truck, wind-up, plastic, 12" long	45	68	90
Frazer Convertible, plastic wind-up	75	112	150
Hot Rod, friction, 7" long	34	51	68
Jaguar, 8" long	40	100	150

	C6	C8	C10
Ladder Truck	55	80	110
Marvelous Mike, battery-operated, four actions, 1950s, 17" long	118	177	235
Military Police Car, friction, 9" long	NPF	NPF	NPF
Nu-Style Sportster Convertible	50	75	100
Packard Convertible, 1947, 10-1/2" long	62	93	125
Police Car	27	41	55
Police Rescue Car	48	72	95
Race Car, wind-up, 8" long	42	63	85
Race Car	16	24	32
Sand Dump Truck	55	82	110
Searchlight Truck	85	128	170
Sedan, wind-up	42	63	85
Semi Trailer, 1960s, 16" long	88	132	175
Semi Van	32	48	65

Saunders Convertible, plastic windup, 10-3/4". Photo from Ron Fink.

Saunders Fire Chief, car windup, 10". Photo from Dave Leopard.

A look at the Saunders Fire Chief with its original box. Photo from Continental Hobby House.

Left to right: Saunders Hot Rod, friction, 7"; Stock Car Racer with removable hood, friction, 8". Photo from Bob and Alice Wagner.

Saunders Marvelous Mike, 1950s, battery-operated, 17". Photo from Don Hultzman.

	C6	C8	C10
Stock Car Racer, w/removable hood, friction, 8" long	60	125	175
Super Battle Tank, 8" long	27	41	55
Super Motor Bus	55	82	110
Super Searchlight Fire Truck, battery, bulb, on/off switch, 12" long	NPF	NPF	NPF

SAVOYE PEWTER TOY COMPANY

Savoye was incorporated August 1930. In 1931, Savoye Pewter Toy Co., manufacturer of pewter toys (pewter was often the word used for lead alloy or pot metal) was listed in a directory at 69 Paterson Plank Road in North Bergen, New Jersey, with six male and three female employees. The names of the owners may have been Selma and Joseph Wigh. In 1934, at the same address, the workforce was seven males and two females. Slush-mold toys were probably its only product. Savoye was in the 1936 phone book yet not in the February 1937 directory. Collectors identify vehicle toys as Savoye if they have a somewhat coarse appearance, heavy slush-mold body, and white rubber tires on oversized red wooden hubs that are smooth on the outside surface (no axle showing); but whether this is simply lore is not known at present. The son of one of the owners of Tommy Toy Co. thinks some Savoye-looking vehicles were made by Tommy Toy. If so, it's possible Savoye sold its molds to nearby Tommy Toy.

Contributor: Fred Maxwell, 4722 N. 33 St., Arlington, VA 22207. **Perry R. Eichor,** 703 North Almond Drive, Simpsonville, SC, 29681.

Left to right: Savoye Ambulance; Van, Police Patrol, 4"; Van, Police Patrol, 4", with Barclay wheels. Photo from Ferd Zegel.

Bus marked "Motor Coach," 7-1/2". Photo from Ferd Zegel.

Left to right: Savoye Bus, heavy 5th Ave. sightseeing bus, 4-3/4"; Tractor, Caterpillar (?), 4-3/4"; Oil car from Savoye's Tank Car Set. Photo from Craig A. Clark.

Savoye Cross-country Bus, partial upper deck, with window variation. Photo from Al Lane.

Left to right: Savoye Dump Truck, 4-3/8"; Coal Truck, with open windshield, driver and steering wheel, 4-3/8". Photo from Ferd Zegel.

Savoye Fire Engine, steam pumper, driver and fireman, 3-3/4". Photo from Fred Maxwell.

	C6	C8	C10
Ambulance, same as the Tommy Toy ambulance (SA025)	16	24	32
Bus, tour bus, two OW, reads "Motor Coach," dual-axle semi-trailer, twelve OW, gilt trim, also came w/single axle; 7-1/2" long (SA009)	NPF	NPF	NPF
Bus, heavy 5th Ave. sight-seeing bus, open overhanging upper deck, twelve OW, gilt or silver trim; 4-3/4" long (SA7)	62	93	125
Bus, cross-country bus, partial upper deck, twelve OW, rear-mount spare; 3-3/8" long (SA8)	20	30	40
Coal Truck, dump body on chassis, driver and steering wheel, open windshield, 4-3/8" long (SA27)	NPF	NPF	NPF
Coupe, two OW, silver VG (Graham like), VL, 3-3/8" long (SA003)	20	30	40
Coupe, slanted louvers, fantasy grille and large black rubber wheels (possibly not original), 3-3/8" long (SA004)	14	21	28
Dump Truck, 4-3/8" long (SA10A)	NPF	NPF	NPF

	C6	C8	C10
Fire Engine, Steam pumper, driver and fireman w/high style gilt helmets, large ten-spoke metal wheels, possibly an early Savoye, 3-3/4" long (SA17 ?)	NPF	NPF	NPF
Fire Truck, driver and steersman w/high style gilt helmets, bell on hood, two ladders (glued on), oversized wheel wells, oversized tires, 4-1/4" long (SA15)	NPF	NPF	NPF
Fire Truck, driver and fireman w/high style gilt helmets, two detachable ladders on high rack, oversized wheel wells, oversized tires, 3-3/4" long (SA16)	NPF	NPF	NPF

	C6	C8	C10
Gun Truck, Army, driver and gunner (smooth gear under gun barrel distinguishes it from similar gun trucks); 3-1/4" long (SA21)	NPF	NPF	NPF
Moving Van, six wheels, 3-7/8" long (SA023)	105	158	210
Open Convertible, w/driver in Cap (SA026)	10	15	20
Pickup Truck (SA022)	20	30	40
Racer, w/driver, 4-1/4" long (SA024)	NPF	NPF	NPF
Racer, w/driver and co-pilot, 4-1/4" long (SA24A)	NPF	NPF	NPF

	C6	C8	C10
Roadster, driver, open rumble seat, silver VG, (reminiscent of Tootsietoy Graham), VL, 3-1/2" long (SA001)	NPF	NPF	NPF
Roadster, 3-1/2" long (SA002)	NPF	NPF	NPF
Tank Car Set, marked "Oil," "Cap 80000," not known whether Savoye sold these as a set; 10-1/4" long overall, 3-1/4"-long cab, 3-1/2"-long tank car (SA20)	40	60	80
Tow Truck, coupe cab, chain and hook on crane, 4" long (SA013) ..	NPF	NPF	NPF
Tow Truck, w/oversized crane, wire hook, 5-3/4" long (SA014)	NPF	NPF	NPF
Tractor, caterpillar (?), w/large ten-spoke metal wheels, possibly an early Savoye (?), 3" long; same casting as Tommy Toy but longer wheelbase than Barclay No. 7 (SA019)	NPF	NPF	NPF

Left to right: Savoye Fire Truck, driver and steersman, 4-1/4"; Fire Truck, driver and fireman, two detachable ladders, 3-3/4".

Savoye Convertible, open. Photo from Al Lane.

Savoye Gun Truck, Army, driver and gunner, 3-1/4". Photo from Bill Conover.

Savoye Pickup Truck.

Savoye Moving Van, six wheels, 3-7/8" (this model was repainted).

Savoye Racer, driver and co-pilot, 4-1/4".

Top row, left to right: Savoye Roadster, 3-1/2"; Savoye Roadster, 3-1/2". Bottom row, left to right: Bus, 4-3/4"; Coupe, two open windows, 3-3/8". Photo from Fred Maxwell.

Savoye Truck with stake body, 5-3/4". Photo from Perry Eichor.

Savoye Tow Truck. Photo from Craig A. Clark.

Savoye Van, milk grade, sidemounts, 3-1/4". Photo from Al Lane.

Left to right: A Barclay tractor compared to Savoye Tractor, 2-3/4". Photo from Bill Conover.

	C6	C8	C10
Tractor, Caterpillar (?) tractor w/stack, 2-3/4" long (SA18)	10	15	20
Truck, heavy "Beer Truck," six wood barrels set in cast depressions, 4-3/8" long (SA010)	40	60	80
Truck, stake body, 4-1/2" long (SA011)	12	18	24
Truck, stake body, hinged tailgate w/chains, 5-3/4" long (SA012)	NPF	NPF	NPF
Van, reads "Milk Grade A," two OW, SM; 3-1/4" long (SA005)	20	30	40

	C6	C8	C10
Van, reads "Police Patrol," policeman on rear step, six OW, gilt trim, solid windows; 4" long (SA006A)	24	36	48
Van, marked "Police Patrol," policeman on rear step, six OW, gilt trim, SM; 4" long (SA6)	24	36	48

SCHIEBLE TOY & NOVELTY CO.

William E. Schieble was a partner in D.P. Clark & Co. for nearly ten years. In 1909, after some disagreements with Clark, he broke up the partnership and became the sole owner. At this time, Schieble changed the name of the company to Schieble Toy & Novelty. Things went well during the 1920s, but, as did many manufacturing companies, Schieble declared bankruptcy, in 1931.

Contributor: Bob Smith, The Village Smith, 62 West Ave., Fairport, NY 14450-2102.

	C6	C8	C10
Armored Car	300	450	600
Bus, No.110, 1920s	375	575	750
Cannon Truck	400	600	800
Coupe, 18" long	350	500	775
Delivery Truck	382	573	765
Fire Engine Pumper, flywheel drive, red/gold, c.1917, 11-3/4" long	300	475	725
Fire Engine Pumper, light works, 1920s, 20" long	375	550	725
Fire Ladder Truck, large driver, flywheel drive, white/red, c.1909, 21-1/2" long	400	600	800
Fire Ladder Truck, 1920s, 20" long	325	475	650
Fire Ladder Truck, w/small driver, flywheel drive, white/red, c.1909, 21-1/2" long	375	525	750
Fire Truck, flywheel drive, red/gold, c.1917, 11-1/2" long	300	450	650
Mack Semi Dump Truck, (Chein lookalike) c.1925, 22" long	425	700	900
Packard Express Truck	400	600	800
Pickup Truck	350	550	800
Roadster, 13" long	225	375	650
Roadster, spare tire on back, 18-1/4" long	400	600	850

	C6	C8	C10
Sedan, 17" long	500	775	850
Tank, WWI type	300	450	700
Touring Car, c.1909, 14" long	375	575	725
Wrecker	500	850	1300

**Schieble Fire Truck, flywheel drive, circa 1917, 11-1/2".
Photo from Bob Smith.**

Savoye Pickup Truck.

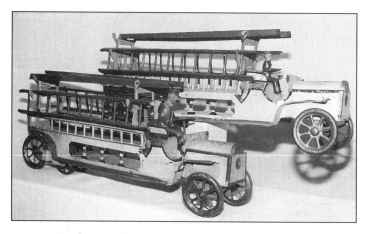

Left to right Schieble Fire Ladder Truck with flywheel drive and large driver, 21-1/2"; Fire Ladder Truck with flywheel drive, small driver, 21-1/2". Photo from Bob Smith.

Schieble Mack Semi Dump Truck, 1920s, 22". Photo from Bob Smith.

SCHUCO

Schuco was founded in 1912 by Heinrich Muller and Herr Schreyer. They later called Schreyer and Co., and adopted the name "Schuco" as its trademark. Schuco toys, noted for their ingenious mechanisms, were produced in the 1930s into the 1950s, and marked either "Germany" or "U.S. Zone Germany." Toy with other markings are reissues.

	C6	C8	C10
Akustico 2002, 1940s, 5-1/2" long ...	87	130	175
Anno 2000, 1940s, 5-1/2" long.........	80	120	160
Buick, No. 5311, 9" long..................	200	300	400
Cadillac DeVille Convertible 5505, plastic, 1960s, 11" long...............	80	120	160
Dalli 1011, tin car and plastic driver, 1950s, 6-1/2" long.......................	112	168	225
Elektro Ingenico 5311, remote control, 1950s, 8-1/2" long...........	250	382	510
Examico 4001, five-speed BMW, 1950s, 6" long...........................	165	248	330
Fernlenk, Auto No. 3000	92	138	185
Fex 1111, 1950s, 6" long	90	135	180
Fx-Atmos, almost 2" long, late 1950s-early 1960s	NPF	NPF	NPF
Gas Station 3054, 1950s, 8" long	60	90	120
Grand Prix Racer 1070, 1950s, 6" long..	80	120	160

	C6	C8	C10
Jaguar 1250, 1940s, 5-1/2" long......	160	240	320
Lasto 3042, 1950s, 4-1/2" long truck	60	90	120
Magico Auto 2008, 1950s, 5-1/2" long, responds to blowing............	300	450	600
Magico Car and Garage, 1950s, 6" long...	120	180	240
Mercedes 190SL 2095, 1950s, 8" long...	170	255	340
Mercedes TYP SSK 1928, 1950s, 4" long...	100	150	200
Mercer Auto 1225, 1950s, 7-1/2" long...	75	112	150
Micro Racer - Mercedes Benz 1038, 1950s, 4" long.............................	100	150	200
Micro Racer - Mercedes Benz 1044, 1950s, 4" long.............................	110	165	220
Micro Racer 101, Porsche style, 1950s, 3-1/2" long.......................	90	135	180
Micro Racer 102, Indy style, 1950s, 3-1/2" long	90	135	180

Schuco Examico, 1950s, 6".

Schuco Mercer Auto, 1950s, 7-1/2".

Schuco Micro Racer, 1950s, 4". Photo from Don Hultzman.

Schuco Studio Racer, 1950s, 5-1/2". Photo from Don Hultzman.

	C6	C8	C10
Micro Racer 1036, 1950s, 4-1/2" long	100	150	200
Micro Racer 104, Indy style, 1950s, 3-1/2" long	90	135	180
Micro Racer 1040, 1950s, 4" long	75	105	145
Micro Racer 1041, 1950s, 4" long	72	112	150
Micro Racer 1042, 1950s, 4" long	100	150	200
Micro Racer 1043, 1950s, 4" long	75	112	150
Micro Racer '57 Ford 1045, 1950s, 4" long	80	120	160
Micro Racer Alpha Romeo 1048, 1950s, 4" long	90	135	180
Micro Racer Go Kart 1035, 1950s, 4" long	100	150	200
Micro Racer Hotrod 1036, 1950s, 4" long	90	135	180
Micro Racer Mercer 1036/1, 1950s, 4" long	100	150	200
Micro Racer Porsche 1047, 1950s, 4" long	110	165	220
Micro Racer Rally 1034, eight three lane tracks, 1950s, 10' 6" long	60	90	120
Micro Racer Stake Truck 1049, 1950s, 4" long	90	135	180
Micro Racer Volkswagen 1046, 1950s, 4" long	90	135	180
Micro Racer Volkswagen Polizei 1039, 1950s, 4" long	100	150	200
Mirakocar 1001, non-fall action, 1950s, 4-1/2" long	72	108	145

	C6	C8	C10
Monkey Car, orange-black, smiling monkey, 1930s, 6" long	1400	2100	2800
Motodrill Clown 1007, composition head, 1950s, 5" long motorcycle	1000	1500	2000
Mystery Car 1010, non-fall action, 1950s, 5-1/2" long	90	135	180
Radio 4012, musical car, 1950s, 6" long	238	355	475
Station Car 3118, 1950s, 4-1/2" long	60	90	120
Studio Racer 1050, includes tools, 1950s, 5-1/2" long	125	188	250
Synchromatic 5700, resembles Packard Hawk, 1950s, 11" long	500	750	1000
Telesteering 3000 Limo, 1950s, 4" long	72	105	145
Varianto 3010, two tin car playset, 1950s, cars are 4-1/2" long	100	150	200
Varianto 3010 Super, service station w/two cars, 1950s, 4-1/2"-long cars	170	225	340
Varianto 3041 Limo, 1950s, 4" long	50	75	100
Varianto 3064, all plastic, 1950s, 8" long	30	45	60
Varianto Box 3010/30, tin garage and 3041 Limo, 1950s, 4-1/2" long	110	165	220
Varianto Bus 3044, 1950s, 4" long	70	105	140
Varianto Electro 3112, 1950s, 4" long truck	60	90	120
Varianto Electro 3112u, 1950s, 4-1/2" long truck	60	90	120
Varianto Lasto, No. 3042, 1950s, 4-1/4" long truck	80	120	160

SHARON

Schuco was founded in 1912 by Heinrich Muller and Herr Schreyer. They later called Schreyer and Co., and adopted the name "Schuco" as its trademark. Schuco toys, noted for their ingenious mechanisms, were produced in the 1930s into the 1950s, and marked either "Germany" or "U.S. Zone Germany." Toy with other markings are reissues.

	C6	C8	C10		C6	C8	C10
Dump truck, Mack, side-dump, No. 13SD, 4" long	100	175	250	Racer, unnumbered, spring loaded, 12" long	NPF	NPF	NPF
Open Racer, 6" long (SV003)	80	100	130	Racer, two-man, twelve cylinder, No. 11R, 5-3/4" long	75	145	225
Pierce Arrow-type Sedan, No. 10S	50	100	150	Rohr, 5" long, 1934 (SV002)	100	150	200
Pierce Arrow-type Sedan, No. 20S, 6-1/2" long	75	135	200	Trolley Car (SV4)	NPF	NPF	NPF
Pierce-Arrow Silver Arrow, 6" long, 1933 (SV001)	125	175	225				

Sharon No. 13SD Mack Side Dump Truck. Photo from Perry Eichor.

Another look at Sharon's No. 10S Pierce Arrow-Sedan (back) and the No. 20S Pierce Arrow-type Sedan. Photo from Perry Eichor.

Sharon 1934 Rohr, 5". Photo from Perry Eichor.

Sharon's No. 10S Pierce Arrow with it's original tag. Photo from Perry Eichor.

Clockwise from top: Sharon No. 11R Twelve-cylinder Racer; No. 20S Pierce Arrow-type Sedan; two versions of No. 10S Pierce Arrow-type Sedan; No. 13SD Makc Side Dump Truck; Another version of No. 11R Racer; Another version of No. 20S Pierce Arrow-type Sedan. Photo from Perry Eichor.

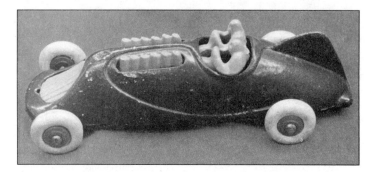

Sharon No. 11R Twelve-cylinder, two-man Racer. Photo from Perry Eichor.

Sharon match plate. Photo from Perry Eichor.

SMITH-MILLER

Smith Miller trucks entered an already competitive market in 1945. These cast-metal and aluminum trucks, produced in Santa Monica, California, should have failed—who would've thought that a new toy vehicle company could compete with such toy giants as Buddy "L," Structo, Marx and Hubley. Despite the stiff competition, Smith-Miller Toys stayed on the market for a full ten years outclassing virtually all toy trucks.

Their first trucks had two different classes, expensive replicas or smaller, no-name trucks that looked like half-breed Fords. During their last year they changed their profile from Mack Trucks to Auto-Car diesels with opening doors and working steering wheels.

Smith-Miller is once again in operation using original and new parts.

Contributors: John Taylor, P.O. Box 63, Nolensville, TN 37135-0063. Randy Prasse, 916 Hayes Ave., Racine, WI 53405

	C6	C8	C10		C6	C8	C10
B Mack Associated Truck Lines, fourteen wheels	NPF	NPF	NPF	Chevy Milk Truck, four wheels, plain tires, hubcaps, early, 1945-46	300	500	950
B Mack Jr Fire Truck, warning light, battery-operated, four wheels, rare	1400	2650	3950	Ford Bekins Van, fourteen wheeler, plain tires, hubs, one of the earliest Smith-Millers (?), 1944	350	450	650
B Mack Orange Dump, ten wheels, rare	950	1850	2800	Ford Coca-Cola, four wheels, wood soda cases, 1944	600	1000	1400
B Mack P.I.E., eighteen wheels	400	625	850	GMC Be Mac T-Trailer, fourteen wheel, 1949	265	350	650
Chevy Coca-Cola, four wheels, plain tires, early	425	638	850	GMC Coca-Cola Truck, twenty-four plastic bottles in six cases, four wheels, 1954-55	425	875	1925
Chevy Flatbed Tractor-Trailer, fourteen wheels, unpainted wood trailer, plain tires, hubcaps, early .	200	300	450	GMC Drive-O Steerable Dump, six wheels, cable w/hand control, 1949...	325	550	925
Chevy Ice Truck, c.1945	350	575	800	GMC Dump Truck, 1950-53, six wheels	185	280	470
				GMC Furniture Mart Pickup, four wheels, 1953 Truck	250	350	500
				GMC Machinery Hauler, ten wheels	200	300	450
				GMC Marshall Field & Company Tractor-Trailer, ten wheel T-Trailer	400	650	1000

Smith-Miller B Mack Orange Dump, ten wheels. Photo from Tim Oei.

Smith-Miller GMC Searchlight Truck with trailer. Photo from Bob Smith.

Smith-Miller GMC Drive-O Steerable Dump, six wheels, 1949. Photo from Bob Smith.

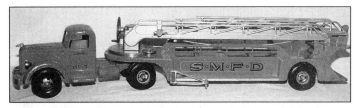

Smith-Miller L Mack Aerial Ladder Truck, eight wheels. Photo from Bob Smith.

Smith-Miller L Mack Army Materials Truck seven-piece cargo load, ten wheels. Photo from Bob Smith.

Smith-Miller L Mack Personnel Carrier, ten wheels. Photo from Bob Smith.

Smith-Miller L Mack Material Truck, minus two barrels and four timbers. Photo from R.F. Sapita.

Smith-Miller L Mack Merchandise Van, six wheels. Photo from Ray Funk.

Smith-Miller L Mack Merchandise Van and Trailer, twelve wheels. Photo from Bob Smith.

	C6	C8	C10
GMC Mu Grocery	250	350	500
GMC Peoples First National Bank and Trust Company Armored Truck, lock and key, 1951	225	400	525
GMC Rexall Drug, four wheels, rare	475	815	1550
GMC Searchlight Truck, Hollywood Film Ad w/trailer, 1953	550	900	1600
GMC U.S Treasury Armored Truck, w/lock and key, 1952	250	375	500
L Mack Aerial Ladder, SMFD, eight wheels	440	660	880
L Mack Army Materials Truck, three barrels, two boards, one large crate, one small, ten wheels	460	690	925
L Mack Army Personnel Carrier, ten wheels	460	690	925
L Mack Bekins Van, all white, ten wheels	750	1200	1800
L Mack Blue Diamond Dump, ten wheels	800	1300	1800
L Mack International Paper Co., ten wheels, rare	700	1000	2100
L Mack Lyon Van, six wheels	550	875	1200

	C6	C8	C10
L Mack Material Truck, two barrels, six timbers, six wheels	350	550	750
L Mack Merchandise Van, six wheels	475	775	1200
L Mack Merchandise Van and Trailer, twelve wheels	850	1400	2500
L Mack Mobile Tandem Tanker, twelve wheels	800	1300	1800
L Mack Orange Hydraulic Dump, ten wheels, rare	750	1650	2950
L Mack Orange Material Truck, ten wheels, three barrels, two boards, one large crate, one small	650	950	1200
L Mack P.I.E., fourteen wheel	450	800	1050
L Mack Sibley's Van, six wheels (rare)	600	900	1500

	C6	C8	C10
L Mack Tandem Timber, six wheel, eighteen or twenty-four timbers (varies)	420	630	950
L Mack Telephone Truck, six wheels	600	1000	1400
L Mack West Coast Transport, six wheel	800	1300	1800
MIC Aerial Ladder	375	565	750
MIC Fruehauf Road Star Tractor-Trailer, fourteen wheels	400	600	950
MIC House Trailer	380	550	750
MIC Hydraulic Dump, ten wheels	500	850	1250
MIC Lift Gate Truck, six wheels, two barrels	500	800	1100
MIC Lincoln Capri (for MIC House Trailer), steerable	425	700	950
MIC P.I.E. Tractor-Trailer, fourteen wheels	600	1000	1400
MIC Teamsters Hydraulic Dump, ten wheels	650	1000	1500
MIC Teamsters Tow Truck, six wheels	800	1400	1800
MIC Teamsters Tractor-Trailer, fourteen wheels	750	1100	1700
MIC Tow Truck, Official Tow Car, six wheels	500	800	1200
MIC Tow Truck, six wheels, unpainted, polished	400	775	1025

	C6	C8	C10
MIC Tractor-Trailer, polished aluminum trailer, No. decals, fourteen wheels	375	600	850
NEC Lumber Truck, six wheels, nine timbers	600	1000	1450
No. 201-L Lumber Truck, sixty boards, six wheel, 14" long	300	400	550
No. 202-M Material Truck, three barrels, three cases, eighteen boards, four wheels, 14" long	450	675	900
No. 203-H Heinz Grocery Truck, six wheels, 14" long	250	400	675
No. 204-A Arden Milk Truck, twelve milk cans, four cases, four wheels, 14" long	350	550	800
No. 205-P Oil Truck, four drums, six wheels, 14" long	275	415	550
No. 206-C Coca-Cola Truck, sixteen Coca-Cola cases, four wheels, 14" long	450	675	900
No. 208-B Bekins Vanliner, fourteen wheels, 22-1/2" long	325	500	850
No. 209-T Timber Giant, three logs, fourteen wheels, 23-1/2" long	260	350	550

Smith-Miller MIC Aerial Ladder. Photo from Ray Funk.

Smith-Miller MIC Tow Truck, six wheels. Photo from Tim Oei.

Smith-Miller MIC Lift Gate Truck, six wheels, two barrels. Photo from Bob Smith.

Smith-Miller Coca-Cola Truck, No. 206-C, sixteen Coca-Cola cases, four wheels, 14". Photo from Richard MacNary.

A look at the cover of a 1954 Smith-Miller catalog. Photo from Ray Funk.

Smith-Miller GMC Silver Streak Express Tractor Trailer, No. 311-E, fourteen wheels. Photo from Bob Smith.

Smith-Miller GMC Silver Streak Express Tractor Trailer, No. 311-E, fourteen wheels. Photo from Bob Smith.

Smith-Miller Tow Truck, No. 401, 15". Photo from Calvin L. Chausee.

	C6	C8	C10
No. 210-S Stake Truck, fourteen wheels, 23-1/2" long	250	375	500
No. 211-L Sunkist Special, fourteen wheels, 23-1/2" long	250	350	500
No. 212-R Red Ball, fourteen wheels, 23-1/2" long	250	350	500
No. 301-W GMC Wrecker, four wheeler	250	350	500
No. 302-M GMC Materials Truck, four barrels, three timbers	250	350	500
No. 303-R GMC Rack Truck, six wheels	250	350	500
No. 304-K GMC Kraft Foods, four wheels	275	475	550
No. 305-T GMC Triton Oil, three drums	175	263	350
No. 306-C GMC Coca-Cola, four wheels, sixteen Coke cases	450	675	900
No. 307-L GMC Redwood Logger Tractor-Trailer, thtree logs	500	800	1100
No. 308-V GMC Lyon Van Lines Tractor-Trailer, fourteen wheels	375	575	800
No. 309-S GMC Super Cargo Tractor-Trailer, fourteen wheels, ten barrels	250	350	500
No. 310-H GMC Hi-Way Freighter Tractor-Trailer, fourteen wheels	250	350	500
No. 311-E GMC Silver Streak Express Tractor Trailer, fourteen wheels	212	318	425

	C6	C8	C10
No. 312-P GMC Pacific Intermountain Express (P.I.E.) Tractor Trailer	300	450	600
No. 401 Tow Truck, 15" long	350	550	800
No. 401-W GMC Wrecker, six-wheels	350	525	700
No. 402 Dump Truck, 11-1/2" long	250	350	500
No. 402-M GMC Material Truck, four barrels, two timbers	250	350	500
No. 403 Scoop Dump, 14" long	275	325	550
No. 403-R GMC Rack Truck, six-wheels	225	380	550
No. 404 Lumber Truck, 19" long	375	560	750
No. 404-B GMC Bank of America, lock and key, four wheels	200	400	500
No. 404T Lumber Trailer, 17" long	200	300	400
No. 405 Silver Streak Six-wheel Tractor, 28" long	170	255	440
No. 405-T GMC Triton Oil, six wheels, three drums	250	400	500
No. 406 Bekins Van, six-wheel tractor and four-wheel trailer, 29" long	325	495	750
No. 406-L GMC Lumber Tractor-Trailer, fourteen wheels, eight timbers	250	350	500
No. 407 Searchlight Truck, marked "Hollywood Film ad," 18-1/2" long	800	1500	2500
No. 407-V GMC Lyon Van Tractor-Trailer, ten wheels	350	500	700
No. 408 Blue Diamond Ten-wheel Dump Truck, 18-1/2" long	650	1100	1600
No. 408-H GMC Machinery Hauler, thirteen wheels, marked "Fruehauf"	300	450	600
No. 409 Pacific IntermountainExpress (P.I.E.) Six-wheel Tractor Semi, w/eight wheel aluminum trailer, 29" long	500	750	1000

This Smith-Miller catalog illustrates the No. 402 Dump truck and the No. 401 Tow Truck. Photo from Ray Funk.

Smith-Miller GMC Material Truck, No. 402-M, four barrels, two timbers. Photo from Calvin L. Chaussee.

This Smith-Miller catalog illustrates a No. 404 Lumber Truck, No. 408 Blue Diamond and a No. 404T Lumber Trailer. Photo from Ray Funk.

Smith-Miller GMC Bank of America, No. 404-B, four wheels. Photo from Calvin L. Chaussee.

Smith-Miller B Mack Lumber Truck and Trailer, No. 404-T, twelve wheels. Photo from Bob and Alice Wagner.

	C6	C8	C10
No. 409-G GMC Mobilgas Tanker, fourteen wheels, two hoses	270	400	750
No. 410 Aerial Ladder Semi, six-wheel tractor and four-wheel trailer, 36" long, "SMFD	450	850	1500
No. 410-F GMC Trans-Continental Tractor-Trailer, fourteen wheels, marked "Trans-Continental Freighter"	250	350	550

	C6	C8	C10
No. 411-E GMC Silver Streak Tractor-Trailer, fourteen wheels...	185	350	475
No. 412-P GMC P.I.E, fourteen wheels	250	375	500

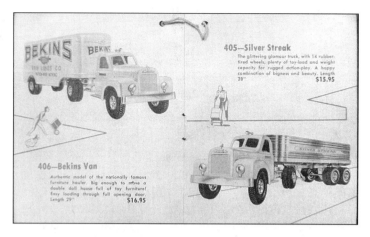

This Smith-Miller catalog illustrates the No. 406 Bekins Van and the No. 405 Silver Streak. Photo from Ray Funk.

Smith-Miller GMC Lyon Van Tractor-Trailer, No. 407-V, ten wheels. Photo from Bob Smith.

Smith-Miller GMC Mobilgas Tanker, No. 409G, fourteen wheels, two hoses. Photo from Tim Oei.

This Smith-Miller catalog illustrates a No. 407 Searchlight Truck, No. 403 Scoop Dump and a No. 409 P.I.E. truck. Photo from Ray Funk.

SOLIDO

Solido's military line seems to sell for between $45 to $65, in Mint condition. The following list is of their civilian line, as sold Mint in Box (C10) condition.

	C6	C8	C10		C6	C8	C10
12 Peugeot 104	n/a	n/a	20	28 BMW 2002	n/a	n/a	35
14 Matra Simco	n/a	n/a	35	29 Citroen CX2200	n/a	n/a	25
15 Lola T820	n/a	n/a	30	30 Renault 30	n/a	n/a	35
16 Ferrari Daytona	n/a	n/a	30	31 Delage D8 120'39	n/a	n/a	20
17 Gulf Mirage	n/a	n/a	30	35 Duesenberg '31 Convertible	n/a	n/a	25
18 Porsche Can Am	n/a	n/a	50	37 Renault 17TS Rally du Maros	n/a	n/a	25
20 Alpine Renault A441	n/a	n/a	20	38 Gulf LeMans	n/a	n/a	35
22 Renault 12 Station Wagon	n/a	n/a	20	39 Simca 1308 Hatchback	n/a	n/a	20
24 Porsche Carrera RS	n/a	n/a	25	40 Peugeot 604 Sedan	n/a	n/a	25
25 BMW 2.0 CSL	n/a	n/a	35	40th Anniversary Gift Set, includes Tiger Tank, M3 Halftrack, M20 Scout Car, M10 Halftrack, M20 Scout Car, M10 Tank Destroyer, 1984	75	1n/a	200
26 Ford Capri Rallye	n/a	n/a	30				
27 Lancia Startos	n/a	n/a	30				

Solido's 40th Anniversary Gift Set from 1984 consisted of a Tigre Tank, M3 Halftrack, M20 Scout Car and an M10 Tank Destroyer. Photo from Harvey K. Rainess.

Back row, left to right: No. 200 Combat Car M20; No. 202 Patton Tank; No. 203 Renault 4x4 Truck; No. 204 Antiaircraft Gun. front row, left to right: No. 205 105mm Howitzer; No. 206 250mm Howitzer; No. 207 Russian Pt-76 Tank. Starlux 30mm soldier and Britains 54mm Gunner included for scale. Photo from Ed Poole.

	C6	C8	C10
M-20 U.S. Armored Car	30	45	65
No. 200 Combat Car M20	30	45	65
No. 202 Patton Tank	30	45	65
No. 203 Renault 4x4 Truck	30	45	65
No. 204 Antiaircraft Gun	30	45	65
No. 205 105mm Howitzer	30	45	65
No. 207 Russian PT-76 Tank	30	45	65
No. 222 Tiger Tank	30	45	65
No. 226 German Armored Car	30	45	65

Back row, Left to right: No. 222 Tiger Tank; 226 German Armored Car; 231 Sherman Tank; 232 M10 Tank Destroyer. Front row, left to right: Renault R35 Tank; 234 Somua S35 Tank; 237 Panzer IV Tank; 241 German Half-Track. Photo from Ed Poole.

Left to right: Solido No. 253 General Lee U.S. Tank; No. 245 GMC 6x6 U.S. Truck. Decals were supplied and left to the buyers' imagination to apply. Toy soldier is a French Stralux and was added for scale. Photo from Ed Poole.

	C6	C8	C10
No. 231 Sherman Tank	30	45	65
No. 232 M10 Tank Destroyer	30	45	65
No. 234 Somua S35 Tank	30	45	65
No. 237 Panzer IV Tank	30	45	65
No. 241 German Half-track	30	45	65
No. 242 Dodge 6x6 Truck	30	45	65
No. 244 Half-Track M-3	30	45	65
No. 245 GMC 6x6 M-34 Truck	30	45	65
No. 245 GMC 6x6 U.S. Truck	30	45	65
No. 252 M7BI Priest Assault Gun	30	45	65
No. 253 General lee U.S. Tank	30	45	65
No. 253 Jeap and Trailer	30	45	65
Renault R35 Tank	30	45	65

STEELCRAFT

	C6	C8	C10		C6	C8	C10
Army Truck, Mack, c.1930, 22" long	650	1000	1450	Dump Truck, Mack, 26" long............	450	700	1000
Army Truck, Mack, c.1930, 26" long	375	562	750	Dump Truck, Mack, 1930s, 20" long	150	225	300
Bloomingdale's Delivery Truck, 25" long	450	650	900	Dump Truck, early 1934, 23" long....	275	425	575
Buick Pedal Car, early 1930s, 46" long	2000	4500	8000	Dump Truck Pedal Car, 62" long	2000	4000	6600
Cadillac Pedal Car, 38" long	2500	4500	9000	Fire Hook and Ladder Airflow Pedal Truck.........................	1600	2700	3800
Cadillac Pedal Car, 1926	1500	2500	5000	Fire Truck, 25" long.........................	750	1100	1500
City Delivery Truck, 19" long	287	421	575	Ford Pedal Car, 1930, 30" long........	650	1100	1650
City Fire Dept. Ladder Truck, early ..	500	800	1200	Fro-Joy Ice Cream Truck, c.1933	400	600	800
City Ice Co. Mack Truck, 24" long....	375	562	750	GMC Scissor Dump Truck, 26" long	550	850	1400
City Ice Cream Co...........................	250	375	500	GMC Trailer Truck	1200	2000	2800
City Milk Co., 18" long....................	400	600	800	Hydrox Ice Cream Truck, 1933, 22".	400	600	800
Coca-Cola Truck, twelve bottles on side	400	600	800	Inter City, 24" long..........................	500	800	1100
Cream Crest Truck, 18" long...........	270	405	540	Lincoln Pedal Car, 46" long.............	1500	2500	4000
Dump Truck, early 1930s, 24" long..	135	203	270				
Dump Truck, Airflow.......................	1500	2500	3500				

Steelcraft Cream Crest Truck, 18". Photo from Bob Smith.

Steelcraft Bloomingdale's Delivery Truck, 25". Photo from Bob Smith.

Steelcraft City Fire Dept. Ladder Truck. Photo from Tim Oei.

Steelcraft Lincoln Pedal Car, 46". Photo from Sotheby's.

Steelcraft Little Jim Mack Dump Truck, late 1920s. Photo from Bob Smith.

Steelcraft New York Trucking Co., headlights work, 1930s, 23-1/4". Photo from John Gibson.

Steelcraft Mack Moving Van, 1920s. Photo from Tim Oei.

Steelcraft Pontiac pedal car, 1935, 36".

	C6	C8	C10
Lincoln Zephyr Pedal Car, 1941.......	1400	2500	4000
Little Jim Fire Truck..........................	600	900	1200
Little Jim Mack Dump Truck, red/black, c.1928 (Little Jims were sold by J.C Penney's)	600	900	1400
Mack Ladder Truck, 26" long	450	675	900
Mack Moving Van, 1920s.................	NPF	NPF	NPF
Mack Pedal Car Dump Truck, 44" long	700	1100	1500
Mack Police Patrol, 25" long	1400	2500	4000
Mandrel Bus Van..............................	1100	1800	2400
Marion Steam Shovel.......................	200	300	400
Model T Roadster Pedal Car, license No. 65-287, 50" long........	450	675	900
New York Trucking Co., headlights work, 1930s, 23-1/4" long	800	1100	1400
Pedal Car, Pontiac, 1935, 36" long ..	NPF	NPF	NPF
Racer Pedal Car, 1941....................	800	1300	1800
Railway Express Truck, 26" long	1100	1600	2600
Richfield Oil Tanker..........................	800	1300	1800
Road Roller, 16-1/2" long.................	238	357	475

Steelcraft Sheffield Farms Truck, 1930s, 21". Photo from Bill Bertoia Auctions.

	C6	C8	C10
Roadster Pedal Car, 38" long	1800	2900	4500
Sheffield Farms Truck, 1930s, 21" long..	500	800	1300
Shell Motor Oil Truck, w/oil barrels ..	300	450	600
Steam Shovel, 26" long....................	225	338	450
Tank Truck, sheet metal, 25-1/2" long..	650	1100	1500
U.S Mail, c.1928, 27-1/4" long	1150	1725	2300
Van..	450	700	1000

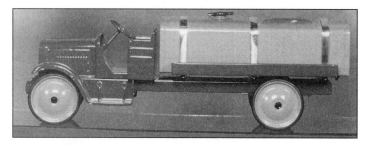

Steelcraft Tank Truck, sheet metal, 25-1/2". Photo from Bill Bertoia Auctions.

Steelcraft U.S. Mail, late 1920s, 27-1/4". Photo from Calvin L. Chaussee.

STRAUSS

Ferdinand Strauss, born in Bavaria in the late 1800s, immigrated to the United States where he became a toy importer in the early 1900s. By 1914, he had four New York toy shops. When war disrupted the importing of toys, he began manufacturing them. In 1918, he was located in East Rutherford, New Jersey, with fifty employees. Eventually Strauss was known as "The Founder of the Mechanical Toy Industry in America." Strauss seems to have been wholly or partially out of business in the late 1920s, and then resumed, turning out wind-ups and other toys until at least 1941-1942. He is also famous for having given employment to the very young Louis Marx.

	C6	C8	C10
Big Show Circus Truck......................	1500	2250	3000
Big-Show Circus, tin wind-up, containing lion and tamer, more in cage, no engine compartment, c.1925, 9" long............................	800	1500	2100
Bus Deluxe, 1920s, 12" long............	1000	1800	2500

	C6	C8	C10
Check-A-Cab	450	675	900
Circus Wagon, containing lion and tamer, 8-1/2" long, no engine compartment..............................	800	1500	2100
Circus Wagon, 10" long, has engine compartment..............................	1250	1875	2500
Green Racer, wind-up, 8-1/2" long...	200	300	550
Haul Away Truck, dump body, No. 22..	240	360	480
Hooligans Hack..............................	300	450	600
Interstate Bus Double Decker, tin wind-up, 10-1/2" long..................	375	600	850

Strauss Big Show Circus, lion and tamer, tin windup, 1920s, 9". Photo from Sotheby's.

Strauss Green Racer, 1920s, 8-1/2". Photo from Bob Smith.

Strauss Interstate Bus, tin windup, 10-1/2". Photo from Sotheby's.

Strauss Jitney Bus, tin windup, 1920s, 10". Photo from Bob Smith.

Strauss Leaping Lena, tin windup, 8". Photo from Bob Smith.

Strauss Racer, No. 21, tin windup, 1920s. Photo from Bob Smith.

Strauss Red Flash Racer, tin windup, 9-1/2". Photo from Bob Smith.

Strauss Yell-O-Taxi, 8-1/2". Photo from Bob Smith.

	C6	C8	C10
Jitney Bus, No. 66, tin wind-up, c.1921, 10" long	300	550	750
Kraka Jack Car, 1920s, 5-1/2" long	150	225	300
Leaping Lena, tin wind-up, 8" long	400	600	800
Long Haulage Truck	350	525	700
Old Jalopy, The, w/four college kids	100	150	200

	C6	C8	C10
Racer, No. 2 1, tin wind-up, c.1923	200	350	550
Racer, Red Flash Racer, windshield, tin wind-up, c.1919, 9-1/2" long	250	400	600
Red Star Van	400	600	800

	C6	C8	C10		C6	C8	C10
Reo Racer, tin wind-up.....................	225	338	450	Water Sprinkler Truck	450	675	900
Standard Oil Truck 73	325	488	650	What's It? Car, No. 53, 1925, 9-1/2"			
Timber King Log Truck, w/driver,				long...	600	900	1200
wind-up, 1920s, 18" long	235	355	470	Yell-o Taxi, No. 59, 8-1/2" long	425	750	950
Trikauto, No. 53...............................	188	282	375				

STROMBECKER

Strombecker Truck Hauler. Photo from Perry Eichor.

The Strombecker Truck Hauler's cab was used as a wrecker. Photo from Perry Eichor.

STRUCTO

Structo, of Freeport, Illinois, was founded in 1908 by three men: brothers Louis and Edward Strohacker and C.C. Thompson. They initially manufactured Erector Construction Kits. About 1919, they started making toy vehicles. In 1935, J.G. Cokey bought a majority of the business. When he died in 1975, the toy patents and designs were taken over by the Ertl Company.

Many of Structo's cast cabs were painted and these trucks almost always had solid black rubber wheels. Most of the wheels were finished with a plated disk over the wheel's center, which gave the appearance of a bright metal hubcap; although, some of the early trucks were issued with plain rubber wheels, without the plated disk hubcaps. For the most part the trucks with painted cabs were issued from around 1951-1954. Series No. 600 and No. 700 models represented this style.

In the early 1950s, Structo offered another group of cast cab-overs that were equipped with powerful wind-up motors and front axles that could be positioned for steering. All windups were made with distinct headlights. Rather than simply being cast into the cab detail, the headlights had a clear plastic lens with a metal rim. Series No. 800 models represented this style.

In 1955, Structo improved their cast cab-over design in several ways. The cabs were given a bright "chrome" finish and running lights were added to the roof of the cab's detail. The all rubber wheels were replaced with wheels consisting of cast metal "mag-like" rims with solid rubber tires. Series No. 600 and No. 700 models represented this style.

Late in the cast cab-over period, around 1958, Structo introduced a few tractor-trailer models with cast cabs and steel frames, not aluminum. These new but limited designs featured a good fifth wheel detail and saddlebag gas tanks.

Contributor: Randy Prasse, 916 Hayes Avenue, Racine, WI 53405, 414-637-0620, e-mail: prasse-photo@racineweb.net

	C6	C8	C10		C6	C8	C10
50th Anniversary Gold Cadillac, No. 20, 1958, rare, gold plated, given to executives and clients, gold plated, 6-3/4" long	150	200	275	Army Truck, w/canvas top, 17" long.	200	300	400
				Army Van, No. 415, pressed steel and canvas, 17-1/2" long	170	255	340
Aerial Ladder Truck, 33" long	175	282	375	Auto Transport, No. 706, 1954, trailer w/four metal cars and ramp, white cab w/red body, 27" long	115	175	250
Aerial Ladder Truck, No. 902	100	150	200				
American Airlines Sky Chief Box Van	75	138	185	Ballantine Beer and Ale Truck, 1950s	500	750	1100
Army Ambulance, No. 416, 17" long	175	263	350	Barrel Truck, No. 811, 1951-53, wind-up, included "Save w/Structo" oil can bank, red cab w/blue body, 12-3/4" long	115	175	225
Army Searchlight Cannon	75	125	175				
Army Tank, winds up, lights work, 13" long	150	225	300	Barrel Truck, No. 609, 1954, rare, same as early No. 811 but w/o wind-up, white cab w/red body, 12-3/4" long	115	170	225
Army Tank, No. 4120	60	90	120				
Army Truck, w/canvas top, 18" long, 1920s	350	525	700	Bearcat Speedster, No. 10, 1919	400	600	800
Army Truck, w/canvas top, 21" long.	125	200	300				

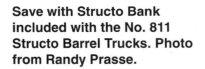

Save with Structo Bank included with the No. 811 Structo Barrel Trucks. Photo from Randy Prasse.

Structo 50th Anniversary Gold Cadillac, No. 201958, 6-3/4" long. Photo from Randy Prasse.

Structo Auto Transport, No. 706, 1954, 27" long. Photo from Randy Prasse.

Structo Barrel Truck, No. 811, 1951-53, 12-3/4" long. Photo from Randy Prasse.

Structo Caterpillar Tractor and Disk, No. 44, 1920-21, 11" long. Photo from Randy Prasse.

Structo Deluxe Cattle Transport, No. 712, 1955-56, 24" long. Photo from Randy Prasse.

Structo Freeport Motor Express, No. 601, 1951-52, a.k.a. Motor Express Truck, 12-3/4" long. Photo from Randy Prasse.

Structo Freeport Motor Express, No. 601, 1953, a.k.a. Motor Express Truck, 12-3/4" long. Photo from Randy Prasse.

	C6	C8	C10
Cadillac, metal, 6-1/2" long	25	38	50
Camper, w/cloth top, 12" long	55	82	110
Caterpillar Tractor, w/trailer, heavy spring clockwork motor, steel treads, No. 46	200	300	400
Caterpillar Tractor, No. 46, w/trailer, heavy pring clockwork motor, steel threads	175	250	350
Caterpillar Tractor and Disk, No. 44, 1920-21, early wind-up w/metal tracks and disc harrow, green cab w/red body, 11" long	175	250	350
Cement Mixer, 20" long, 1950s	90	140	200
City of Toyland Garbage Truck, 1948, 21" long..............................	100	135	200
City of Toyland Utility Truck	120	180	240
Cletrac Crawler, wind-up..................	212	318	425
Communications Center Truck, 21" long	175	263	350
Corvair Pickup.................................	30	45	95
Coupe, convertible, 1920s	160	240	320
Delivery Truck, tin electric lights.......	150	225	300
Deluxe Auto Transport, No. 706, 1956, trailer w/four metal cars and ramp, chrome cab w/yellow body, 27" long	115	175	250

	C6	C8	C10
Deluxe Cattle Transport, No. 712, 1955-56, large, double-deck trailer w/ramp, chrome cab w/green body, 24" long	125	175	225
Diamond T Hook and Ladder...........	190	285	425
Diamond T Machinery Hauler and Shovel, c.1940............................	188	282	375
Diamond T Semi, 1940s	265	398	530
Dump Truck, 1959, 14" long	50	75	100
Dump Truck, 21" long	200	300	400
Dump Truck, 1930s, 20" long...........	150	225	400
Dump Truck, open cab, 1920s, levers on each side of cab, No. 405, 18" long..............................	250	375	500
Dump Truck, No. 811, black and orange, 23" long	275	550	900
Dump Truck, 1940s, 19" long..........	125	225	300
Earth Mover	60	90	120
End Loader, No. 340......................	95	143	190
Fire Dept Emergency Patrol Truck, red bubble light, 1950s, 12" long .	55	82	110

	C6	C8	C10
Freeport Motor Express, No. 601, 1951-52, a.k.a. Motor Express Truck, orange cab w/gray body, 12-3/4" long	115	170	225
Freeport Motor Express, No. 601, 1953, a.k.a. Motor Express Truck, white cab w/red body, 12-3/4" long	95	150	200
Garbage Truck, 21" long	75	112	150
Gasoline Truck, No. 912, 1950s, 13" long	75	112	150
Gasoline Truck, No. 866, 1951-54, wind-up steerable front axle-Structo 66 decals, red cab w/red body, 13-1/2" long	150	200	300
Grader, 18" long	75	112	150
Grain Trailer, No. 704, 1953-55, same trailer as No. 702 but w/rear sliding door, white cab w/orange body, 20-3/4" long	115	175	225
Guided Missile Launcher, No. 906, w/wood and vinyl missiles, 13" long	70	105	140
Hi-Lift Bulldozer	40	60	80
Hi-Way Maintenance Truck	70	105	140
Hi-Way Transport, two trailers, 1940	325	488	650
Hi-Way Transport Tandem, 1920s	412	618	825
Hook and Ladder Fire Truck, early	262	394	525
Hook and Ladder Fire Truck, No. 251, 1939	185	278	370
Horse Van, 1966, 22" long	65	98	130

	C6	C8	C10
Hydraulic Dump Truck, 1960s	48	72	95
Ladder Truck, 1938	450	675	900
Ladder Truck, 1950s	95	150	225
Livestock Truck, 1960s	32	48	65
Loboy and Shovel, 1950s, 30" long	200	350	475
Log Truck, No. 940	120	180	240
Log Truck, 1950s, 11" long	70	105	140
Machinery Hauling Truck, No. 607, 1953, winch truck w/ramp, white cab w/blue body, 13" long	125	195	250
Machinery Hauling Truck, No. 607, 1951, winch truck w/ramp, orange cab w/blue body, 13" long	125	195	250
Mail Truck, 1928	288	432	575
Mechanical Dumper, late 1940s, 19-1/2" long	100	175	225
Mobile Communication Center	150	225	300
Mobile Crane, Ford Cabover	88	132	175
Motor Dispatch Tandem, 1929	450	675	900
Motor Dispatch Trailer Truck, early 1930s, 24" long	475	900	1200
Moving Van, No. 427, open cab, c.1929, 16" long	175	265	350
North American Van Lines	100	150	200
Overland Freight Hauler, No. 704, 1951-52, open rear stake trailer w/o ramp, white cab w/orange body, 20-3/4" long	100	150	200

Structo Gasoline Truck, No. 866, 1951-54, 13-1/2" long. Photo from Randy Prasse.

Structo Machinery Hauling Truck, No. 607, 1953, 13" long. Photo from Randy Prasse.

Structo Grain Trailer, No. 704, 1953-55, 20-3/4" long. Photo from Randy Prasse.

Structo Machinery Hauling Truck with original box, No. 607, 1951, 13" long. Photo from Randy Prasse.

Structo Package Delivery Truck with original box, No. 603, 1954, 13" long. Photo from Randy Prasse.

Structo Steel Cargo Company, No. 702, 20-3/4" long. Photo from Randy Prasse.

	C6	C8	C10
Package Delivery Truck, No. 603, 1954, enclosed box w/tailgate, white cab w/orange body, 13" long	95	150	200
Package Delivery Truck, No. 603, 1951-53, enclosed box w/tailgate, orange cab w/gray body, 13" long	115	170	225
Parcel Service, late 1950s-early 1960s, 12" long	85	150	200
Pickup Truck, 1940s, 17" long	100	150	225
Pickup Truck, metal, 6" long	32	48	65
Piledriver, 13" high	175	263	350
Police Patrol Truck, No. 426, 17" long	250	375	500
Popeye Truck, early	1700	2800	4200
Pumper, 1920s, 22" long	500	800	1200
Pumper, 1938	265	398	530
Pumper, 1950s, 19" long	106	159	212
Ramp Truck	90	135	180
Ready-Mix Cement Truck, 14" long	50	100	150
Ready-Mix Concrete Truck, 1960s	50	100	150
Renault Tank, clockwork, green w/red turret	260	390	520
Road Builder Set, 1950s	100	150	200
Roadster, 1920s, clockwork, 16" long	600	1000	1400
Rocker, 23-1/2" long	90	135	180
Sand Loader, c.1962	40	60	80
Sand Loader, c.1928, 12" high	100	150	200
Sanitation Dept. Garbage Truck, 17" long	105	158	200
Searchlight Truck, truck metal, light- and generator plastic, uses batteries, has rubber tires	62	93	125
Speed Wagon, No. 805, 23-1/2" long	275	550	900
Speedster, 1920s	400	600	800
Stake Truck, lights work, 1930s, 21" long	250	600	900

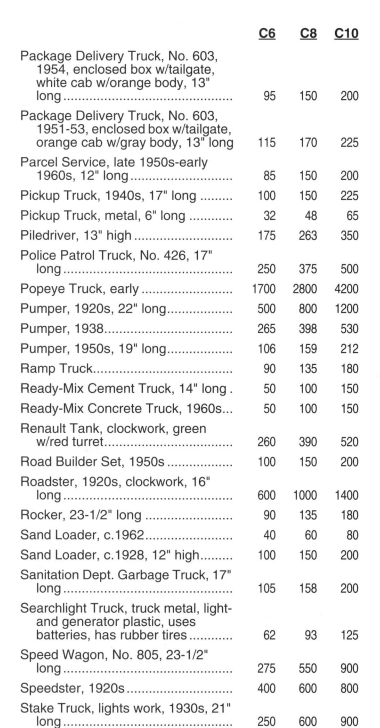

Structo Excavating Company, No. 605, 1951-54, a.k.a. Shovel Dump, 12-3/4" long. Photo from Randy Prasse.

	C6	C8	C10
Stake Wagon, No. 810, 21-1/2" long	275	550	900
Steam Shovel, 1920s, 9-1/2" long	200	300	400
Steam Shovel, 14" x 11"	45	68	90
Steam Shovel, 16" long	58	88	115
Steam Shovel, 21" x 18"	95	138	190
Steel Cargo Company, No. 702, 1951-55, blue or white cab, blue cab w/red body, 20-3/4" long	95	135	175
Steel Hauler, cast cab	110	165	220
Steer-O-Matic Turbine Wrecker	75	100	150
Structo Cattle Farms, No. 708, 1955-56, same as early No. 708 w/chrome cab, chrome cab w/orange body, 21-1/2" long	100	150	200
Structo Cattle Farms, No. 708, 1953-54, small trailer, early painted cab, white cab w/red body, 21-1/2" long	100	150	200
Structo Construction Co., No. 644, 1955-56, same as No. 844 but w/chrome cab and no wind up, chrome cab w/green body, 12-1/2" long	100	135	195
Structo Excavating Company, No. 605, 1951-54, a.k.a. Shovel Dump, orange cab w/blue body, 12-3/4" long	125	175	235

	C6	C8	C10
Structo Excavating Company, No. 606, 1955-56, rare paint variation of Deluxe Shovel Dump, chrome cab w/orange body, 12-3/4" long .	125	195	250
Structo Excavating Company, No. 606, 1955-56, a.k.a. Deluxe Shovel Dump, green cab w/yellow body, 12-3/4" long	115	160	225
Structo Steel Company, No. 705, 1956, same as No. 702 except w/ramp and chrome cab, chrome cab w/red body, 24-1/2" long	100	135	200
Structo Transcontinental Express, No. 710, 1957, late 1956-57 blue trailer; replaced yellow trailer, chrome cab w/blue body, 24" long	110	135	175
Structo Transport, No. 700, 1951-54, blue or white cab, white cab w/red body, 21-1/2" long	95	135	175
StructoTranscontinental Express, No. 710, 1956, early 1956 yellow trailer; discontinued mid-year, chrome cab w/yellow body, 24" long	125	175	250
Tank, No. 48, 11" long	225	338	450
Tank, olive drab w/orange turret, ten metal wheels, 12-1/2" long..........	300	450	600

	C6	C8	C10
Telephone Co., c.1948, 12" long......	67	101	135
Texaco Tanker, 25" long	50	75	100
Timber Toter, No. 714, 1955-57, trailer in green or blue, five or six logs w/chains, chrome cab w/green body, 21" long	90	125	175
Tow Truck, early	200	300	400
Toyland Construction Co., No. 844, 1953-54, wind-up steerable front axle and scissors lift dump box, white cab w/red body, 12-1/2" long..	125	175	225
Toyland Construction Co., No. 844, 1951-52, wind-up steerable front axle and scissors lift dump box, red cab w/blue body, 12-1/2" long	125	175	225
Toyland Construction Company Elevated Dump, 12" long	65	100	150
Toyland Garage Wrecker, No. 822, 1951-52, wind-up steerable front axle and winch chain w/hook, red cab w/gray body, 12-1/4" long	100	135	200
Toyland Garage Wrecker.................	50	75	125
Toyland Garage Wrecker, No. 822, 1953-54, wind-up steerable front axle and winch chain w/hook, white cab w/orange body, 12-1/4" long..	100	135	200

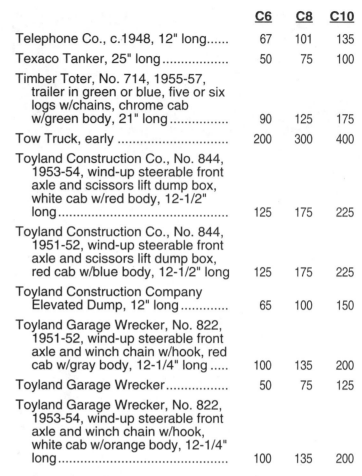

Structo Excavating Company, No. 606, 1955-56, a.k.a. Deluxe Shovel Dump, 12-3/4" long. Photo from Randy Prasse.

Structo Transcontinental Express, No. 710, 1957, late 1956-57, blue trailer, 24" long. Photo from Randy Prasse.

Structo Steel Company, No. 705, 1956, 24-1/2" long. Photo from Randy Prasse.

Structo Transport, No. 700, 1951-54, 21-1/2" long. Photo from Randy Prasse.

**Structo Transcontinental Express, No. 710, 1956, 24"
long. Photo from Randy Prasse.**

**Structo Timber Toter, No. 714, 1955-57, 21" long. Photo
from Randy Prasse.**

**Structo Toyland Construction Co., No. 844, 1953-54,
12-1/2" long. Photo from Randy Prasse.**

**Structo Toyland Construction Co., No. 844, 1951-52,
12-1/2" long. Photo from Randy Prasse.**

**Structo Toyland Garage Wrecker, No. 822, 1951-52, 12-
1/4" long. Photo from Randy Prasse.**

	C6	C8	C10
Toyland Oil Co.	125	200	275
Toyland Tow Truck.........................	50	75	100
Track Loader.................................	37	56	75
Tractor, early wind-up, two trailers, overall 20" long	162	243	325
Tractor, caterpillar type, w/cast iron driver, early, 8-1/2" long..............	275	415	550
Trailer Truck, early, 24" long	600	1000	1400
Transcontinental Express, plastic and metal, 1950s	120	180	240

	C6	C8	C10
Truck Assortment, No. 317: Dump Truck, blue; Stake truck; Lumber truck; heavy gauge metal, rubber wheels, original box folds to form garage; 1920s, each 9" long, 3-1/2" wide, 3-1/2" tall; price per set	175	250	400
U.S Air Force Jeep, Ride 'em, 26" long......................................	110	165	220
U.S Air Force Truck	50	100	150
U.S Army Road Grader....................	45	68	90
U.S Hi-Way Maintenance Service Truck..	100	150	200
U.S Mail Delivery Truck, No. 428, 17" long..	225	338	450
Van Lines, 1960s, 20" long	45	68	90
Vista Horse Van, four horses, 1966, 22" long....................................	50	75	100
Whippet Tank, heavy spring clockwork motor, enameled green, red and black, may read "Patented 1920," on sale in 1929, No. 48, 12" long	200	300	400
Wrecker, No. 4124, 21-1/4" long......	275	500	750
Yuba Tractor, copyright 1924...........	450	675	900

STURDITOY

The Sturdy Corporation of Providence and Pawtucket, Rhode Island, manufactured its steel toy trucks from about 1929 to 1933.

	C6	C8	C10
Ambulance, open cab, c.1926, 26" long	2000	3500	5000
American LaFrance Water Tower Fire Truck, 34" long	1000	1800	2750
American Railway Express Truck, 26" long	1000	1500	2200
Armored Truck, 24" long	2200	3700	5500
Coal Dump Truck, 1920s, 25" long	1200	2000	2900
Coal Truck, 26" long	1400	2300	3200
Coal Truck, high-sided, 27" long	1400	2350	3300
Dairy Truck, 34" long	1700	3000	4200
Dairy Truck, 25" long	600	1000	1400
Delivery Truck, 1920s, 26" long	1200	2000	3500
Dump Truck, 1920s, 25" long	800	1300	1800
Dump Truck, 1920s, 26-1/2" long	500	800	1200
Huckster Truck, 27" long	450	700	1000
Oil Company Tanker, 27" long	1100	1800	2500

	C6	C8	C10
Oil Tanker, "Gulf," 27" long	NPF	NPF	NPF
Police Patrol, 26" long	1100	1800	2500
Pumper, c.1930, 26" long	1100	1800	2500
Sand and Gravel Truck	900	1600	2000
Side Dump, 26-1/2" long	1100	1800	2530
Steam Shovel, 26" long	162	243	325
Tanker, 15" long	2000	3500	7500
Traveling Store, 26" long	1800	2900	4200
Trucking Co., 24" long	1150	1800	2600
U.S Army Truck, 26" long	550	850	1300
U.S Mail Screenside Truck	1200	2000	2725
Water Tower	1500	2500	3500
Wells Fargo Armored Truck, 24" long, c.1927	900	1700	2500
Wrecker, 30" long	1000	1650	2750

Sturditoy Coal Dump Truck, 1920s, 25". Photo from Tim Oei.

Sturditoy Dairy Truck, 34". Photo from Bill Bertoia Auctions.

Sturditoy Oil Company Tanker, 27". Photo from Tim Oei.

Sturditoy Oil Tanker, 27". Photo from Bill Bertoia Auctions.

Sturditoy Pumper, 1930s, 26". Photo from Bill Bertoia Auctions.

Sturditoy Traveling Store, 26". Photo from Bill Bertoia Auctions.

Sturditoy U.S. Army Truck, 26". Photo from Tim Oei.

Sturditoy Wrecker, 30". Photo from Bill Bertoia Auctions.

SUN RUBBER

Sun Rubber of Barberton, Ohio, was founded in 1923. Toy making started in 1924 and vehicles were introduced in April 1935. The owner was Tom W. Smith Jr.

Contributor: Dave Leopard, 2507 Feather Run Trail, West Columbia, SC 29169-4915.

	C6	C8	C10		C6	C8	C10
'34 DeSoto Airflow Four-door Sedan, No. 500, 4" long (SA002)	25	35	50	Open Master Truck, futuristic, No. 12111, 5-5/8" long (ST005)	25	35	55
'40 Dodge Four-door Sedan, c.1936, No. 12001, 4-1/2" long (SA003) ..	25	35	50	Open Racer, two drivers, No. 505, 1936, 4-3/8" long (SR001)	25	35	50
Ambulance, late 1930s, No. 12006, 3-3/4" long (ST007)	25	35	50	Open Racer, full fenders on rear, No. 1000, 1936, 6-1/2" long (SR002)	35	50	70
Art Deco Housetrailer, fits Teardrop Sedan, No. 1025, 4-3/8" long (SA005)	NPF	NPF	NPF	Open Racer, boat tail, "Super" racer, No. 12012, 6-3/4" long (SR003) .	30	45	60
Coupe, external exhaust pipes, from 1936, No. 5154" long (SA001)	25	35	50	Open Truck, stake sides, streamlined, No. 1005, 5-1/4" long (ST002)	35	45	55
Donald Duck Roadster w/Pluto (SD004)	80	100	150	Open Truck, futuristic, No. 12003, 4-1/2" long (ST004)	25	35	50
Donald Duck Tractor (SD008)	75	90	120	Pickup Truck, stake sides, streamlined, No. 510, 4-1/2" long (ST001)	25	35	50
Mickey Mouse and Donald Duck Fire Truck, No. 12017 (SD002) ...	75	90	120	Scout Car, four gunners, No. 12014, 1946, w/or without front winch, 6-3/4" long (SM002)	50	75	100
Mickey Mouse Tractor, No. 12020 (SD001)	75	90	120				

Sun Rubber 1934 DeSoto Airflow, four-door sedan, 4". Photo from Dave Leopard's *Rubber Toy Vehicles*.

Left to right: Sun Rubber Ambulance; Ambulance with military paint. Photo from Dave Leopard's book *Rubber Toy Vehicles*.

Sun Rubber Art Deco Housetrailer, 4-3/8". Photo from Dave Leopard's book *Rubber Toy Vehicles*.

Sun Rubber Mickey Mouse and Donald Duck Fire Truck.

Sun Rubber Coupe, external exhaust pipes, 1936, 4". Photo from Dave Leopard.

Left to right: Sun Rubber Coupe in two-toned color scheme; solid-colored Coupe. Photo from Dave Leopard's *Rubber Toy Vehicles*.

Sun Rubber Donald Duck Roadster. Photo from Dave Leopard.

Two different Sun Rubber Open Racers with two drivers. Photo from Dave Leopard's book *Rubber Toy Vehicles*.

Sun Rubber Mickey Mouse Tractor.

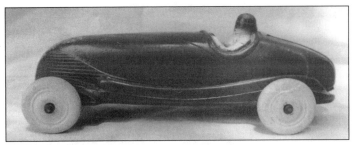

Sun Rubber Open Racer, boat tail, 6-3/4". Photo from Dave Leopard.

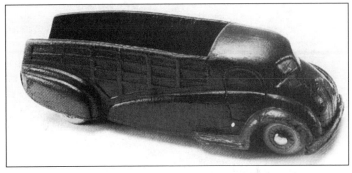

Sun Rubber Open Truck, stake sides, sreamlined, 5-1/4". Photo from Dave Leopard's book *Rubber Toy Vehicles*.

Sun Rubber Open Racer, 1936, 6-1/2". Photo from Dave Leopard's book *Rubber Toy Vehicles*.

Sun Rubber Pickup Truck, stake sides, streamlined, 4-1/2". Photo from Dave Leopard's book *Rubber Toy Vehicles*.

	C6	C8	C10
Station Wagon, woody, mid-1930s, No. 12007, 3-3/4" long (SA007) ..	25	35	50
Tank, revolving turret and gunner, No. 12015, 1946, 6" long (SM001)	50	75	100
Teardrop Sedan, 1936, No. 1010 , 5-1/2" long (SA004)	30	40	60
Town Car, brewster-type limo, exposed driver, No. 1015, 5-3/8" long (SA006)	35	50	80
Tractor/trailer, one-piece, three axles, futuristic, No. 12013, 5-1/8" long (ST003)	25	35	50
White Bus, streamlined, No. 520, 1936, 4-1/4" long (ST006)	25	35	50

Sun Rubber Scout Car, four gunners, 1946, with or without winch, 6-3/4". Photo from Ed Poole.

Pictured is an F.W. Woolworth catalog page of Sun Rubber toys from 1952—note the original prices!

Sun Rubber Town Car, Brewster-type limo, exposed driver, 5-3/8". Photo from K. Warren Mitchell.

Left to right: Sun Rubber Staion Wagon, woody, 1930s, 3-3/4"; military version of same vehicle. Photo from Dave Leopard's book *Rubber Toy Vehicles*.

Sun Rubber Tank with revolving turret and gunner, 6".

Sun Rubber Tractor/trailer, one piece, futuristic, 5-1/8". Photo from Dave Leopard's book *Rubber Toy Vehicles*.

Sun Rubber 1936 Teardrop Sedan, 1936, 5-1/2". Photo from Dave Leopard's book *Rubber Toy Vehicles*.

Sun Rubber White Bus, streamlined, 1936, 4-1/4". Photo from Dave Leopard's book *Rubber Toy Vehicles*.

No. 12008 Racing Plane

No. 12004 Coupe

No. 12002 Racer

No 12001 Sedan

No. 12006 Ambulance

No. 12013 Trailer Truck

No. 12005 Bus

No. 12007 Station Wagon

Sunruco
RUBBER TOYS
ARE "TOPS" IN
EYE APPEAL AND
SALES APPEAL!

No. 12017 Fire Truck

No. 12019
Mickey Mouse Aeroplane

No. 12018
Donald Duck Roadster

© WALT DISNEY
PRODUCTIONS

No. 12020
Mickey Mouse Tractor

THE SUN RUBBER COMPANY • BARBERTON, OHIO.

A catalog page of Sun Rubber vehicles.

THOMAS TOYS

Thomas Toys was owned by Islyn Thomas, who founded the company in 1944 after leaving his position as general manager of the Ideal Toy Company. According to Thomas, its first toys—jeeps, planes, and vinyl dolls—were produced that year. The firm was located at 80 Clinton St., Newark, New Jersey. It made only toys, and at its peak had 350 employees. Thomas Toys was tied to Acme Plastics, since Acme's Ben Shapiro was a partner. Toy made by acme from 1945 to 1950 were clearly marked "Acme." Some order sheets submitted by Thomas were printed in Acme's name. Thomas indicated that these toys were also Thomas Toys. Sometimes, but not always, Acme And Thomas Toys used the same order numbers.

The company's molds, and perhaps some of its sculpting, were provided by Richard Koegl (perhaps Koegel), whose Koegl stampworks were in Newark. Sculpting of some of Thomas' finer-detailed toys, such as its lines of small babies, dolls, and civilians, were done by a Mr. Kaiser. In 1960. Thomas, aware of the impending impact of new, low-priced Japanese imports, sold out to Banner Plastics. Thomas then became an international plastics consultant.

Thomas was made a member of the Plastics Hall of Fame in 1977. Originally from South Wales, he was made an Officer of the British Empire by Queen Elizabeth. He had served as chief engineer for the plastic parts in the Spitfire's Merline engine (which was made in the United States). n the immediate postwar period, heading Thomas Engineering Company, he had helped restore the ravaged European community by setting up a number of companies in England and Continental Europe. One of these companies was the toy company Popular Playthings in Wales, of which he was half-owner for a while. Founded in 1945, it continues in business today. Thomas is also the author of several books, including *Our Welsh Heritage* and *Injection Molding of Plastics* (Reinhold Publishing Corp.) and many technical articles.

Thomas Toys had at least three different numbering systems over the years, with the same items having their numbers changed as time went on. The items with an alphabetical code preceding the number appear to be the earliest, those with a "T" next, and those without a code the latest.

	C6	C8	C10
No 189 Maintenance Truck, w/detachable ladders, 5-1/2" long	NPF	NPF	NPF
No 222 Mobile Searchlight Unit, uses batteries, 15-1/2" overall length	100	120	140
No 222 Mobile Searchlight Unit, w/friction motor, uses batteries, 1954 overall length 15-1/2"	55	65	75
No. 018 Same as TMC-9, listed in 1955 as No. 18			
No. 019 Jeep and Trailer, w/yellow driver in GI helmet, 1954, 8-3/8" long	14	16	18
No. 019 Jeep and Trailer, yellow civilian driver, 8-3/8" long	14	16	18

	C6	C8	C10
No. 024 Sport Convertible & Sedan, set consists of numbers 77 and 77S, 1955, each 4-1/4" long	20	24	28
No. 026 Truck Wrecker, 5" long	35	40	45
No. 030 Coupe and House Trailer, 8-1/4" long	20	22	24
No. 040 Texaco Gas Truck, 4" long	15	20	25
No. 041 Delivery Truck, 4" long	15	18	20
No. 067 Police-Fire Chief Radio Car, each 4-1/2" long, price per each	15	20	27
No. 072 Plastic Motorcycle and Rider, 4" long	35	45	55
No. 074 Merry-Go-Round Truck, 4-3/4" long	20	25	30
No. 077 Convertible Coupe and Driver, 1953, 1954, 4-1/2" long	9	11	13
No. 077C Convertible Coupe and Driver, 1953, 1954, 4-1/2" long	9	11	13
No. 077S Streamlined Sedan, 4-1/2" long	11	13	15
No. 107 Military Policeman and Motorcycle, w/detachable policeman, 4" long	20	25	30
No. 125 Motorcycle, plated, 4" long	NPF	NPF	NPF
No. 126 Same as T-114			
No. 128 Taxi, 1953, 4-1/2" long	22	33	45

Thomas Toy Jeep with trailer, with driver, No. 019, 1954, 8-3/8".

	C6	C8	C10
No. 131 Car and House Trailer, overall length 9-1/2"	25	30	35
No. 132 Truck and Racer, 4" long	NPF	NPF	NPF
No. 134 Same as No. 257			
No. 135 Repair Truck with detachable ladder, 1953, 4" long	15	20	27
No. 139 Same as T-148			
No. 148 Truck and Air Compressor, 8-1/2" long	14	16	18
No. 160 International Race, 5" long (1955), sold w/ and w/o driver, same number	30	35	40
No. 162 Servi-Car (driver not included), 4-1/2" long	25	30	35
No. 168 Motorcycle, 4" long	20	25	30
No. 170 Motorcycle and Sidecar w/passenger, yellow girl passenger, no driver, 4" long	NPF	NPF	NPF
No. 175-6 Police & Fire Chief Radio Cars, each 4-1/2" long, price per each	11	13	15
No. 177 Large Tow Truck, 5-1/2" long	12	14	16
No. 183 Army Jeep and Trailer w/Driver, 8-3/4" long	14	16	18
No. 184-5 Army Radar and Tow Trucks, each 4" long (may be the same as T-192/3) price per each	16	20	24
No. 188 Military Police Jeep w/three MPs, 1955, 1956, 4-1/4" long	11	13	15
No. 196 Army Road Roller, self-winding, 4-1/2" long	NPF	NPF	NPF
No. 212 Plated Two-Tone Racer w/Driver, 5" long (same No. 160 except top half is Special Silver Metal Plated)	NPF	NPF	NPF
No. 234 Gas and Delivery Trucks w/Traders, overall length 6-1/4", per each	14	16	18
No. 237 Motorcycle and Sidecar, w/o passenger, 1955, 4" long	NPF	NPF	NPF
No. 245 Limousine and Trailer, w/luggage and rack, assembly kit (1955)	NPF	NPF	NPF
No. 25 Sedan w/Canoe and Polyethylene House Trailer, 1955, overall length 9-1/2"	30	35	40
No. 254 Polyethylene TV Truck, w/ladder, 1955, 4" long	NPF	NPF	NPF
No. 257 Polyethylene Sound Truck, 1955, 4" long	30	35	40
No. 261 Vespa Motor Scooter, 1955, 4" long	NPF	NPF	NPF
No. 267 Truck and Polyethylene Trailer, 1955, 6-1/4" long overall	NPF	NPF	NPF

Thomas Toys Motorcycle & Sidecar, No. 237, 1955, no passenger, 4".

	C6	C8	C10
No. 289 Jet Hot Rod, 1955, 5-1/2" long	NPF	NPF	NPF
No. 299 Searchlight Truck w/Friction Motor Assembly Kit, 1955	NPF	NPF	NPF
No. 303 Ferguson Tractor Assembly Kit, 1955	NPF	NPF	NPF
No. 334 Electronic Airport Traffic Control Set, contains plane, "flash" truck w/signal light, "radar" truck w/signal buzzer, remote control Morse Code Unit, 1956	NPF	NPF	NPF
No. 360 Indianapolis Speed Race, two racers w/drivers, spring-action mechanism, 1956	NPF	NPF	NPF
No. 369 Radar Signal Set, four radar vehicles, 1956	NPF	NPF	NPF
No. 449 Lumberyard Express, trailer has retractable wheels	NPF	NPF	NPF
No. 457 Jet Car	NPF	NPF	NPF
No. 519 Sport Car Transport, four sports cars included from Thomas Toys: Jaguar, Mercedes-Benz, Thunderbird, Alfa Romeo, Talbot, Corvette; 23-1/2" long when boxed	NPF	NPF	NPF
No. 520 Overland Express Van, 21-5/8" when boxed	NPF	NPF	NPF
No. 521 Cabin Cruiser and Trailer, fifty-six put-together parts, 22-7/8" long when boxed	NPF	NPF	NPF
No. 522 Jeep and Horse Trailer Set, includes doll family, pet, table, and bench, 18-7/8" long when boxed	NPF	NPF	NPF
No. 524 Animal Transport, No animals included, 21-1/8" long when boxed	NPF	NPF	NPF
No. 545 Speed Boat, Jeep and Trailer, w/boat driver outboard motor is rubber-band propelled	NPF	NPF	NPF

	C6	C8	C10
No. 558 Auto and Horse Trailer, 7-1/2" long bagged......	NPF	NPF	NPF
No. 566 Military Set Jeep, Howitzer, four soldiers	NPF	NPF	NPF
No. 572 Assorted Six Sport Cars Pkg, 5-1/8" x 9"	NPF	NPF	NPF
No. 576 International Sport Cars, same as No. 581, except packed three dozen in plain box			
No. 579 Authentic 8 Jeep Spare Tire, moveable windshield, w/o driver............	NPF	NPF	NPF
No. 580 8 Jeep and Driver, moveable windshield, spare tire ..	NPF	NPF	NPF
No. 581 Chest of Sport Cars, contains six Dozen "All-Poly Cars" in six different styles: Jaguar, Mercedes-Benz, Thunderbird, Talbot, Corvette, Alfa Romeo	NPF	NPF	NPF

	C6	C8	C10
No. 592 Stake Trailer Truck, 24-1/2" long when bagged (probably the same as No. 524)	NPF	NPF	NPF
No. 597 Van Trailer Truck, 24-1/2" long when bagged	NPF	NPF	NPF
No. 604 Same as T- 114			
No. 607 Auto Transport, Trailer loaded w/any four of these Sports Cars; Jaguar, Mercedes-Benz, Thunderbird, Alfa Romeo, Talbot, Corvette; 24-1/2" long when bagged......	NPF	NPF	NPF
No. 614 Assortment of 8 Authentic All-Poly Ack-Ack and Searchlight Jeeps, price per each	8	10	12
No. 635 Sight-Seeing Bus.........	NPF	NPF	NPF
No. 638 Same as No. 25, but in blister pack	NPF	NPF	NPF
T-110 No. 168 Motorcycle, plated, 4" long......	NPF	NPF	NPF
T-114 Road Roller, w/ivory driver, self winding, 1953, 4-1/2" long.....	NPF	NPF	NPF
T-140 Same as 131			
T-141 Same as No. 132			
T-144 Same as No. 257			
T-145 Same as No. 135 (both 1953)			
T-148 Tow Truck, 4" long, 1953.......	8	10	12
T-152 (1953) Same as No. 148			
T-171 Same as No. 162			
T-174 Large Tow Truck, 5-1/2" long	12	14	16
T-179 Motorcycle, 4" long	20	25	30
T-18 Wrecker, 5" long	25	35	45
T-192/3 Army Radar & Tow Trucks, each 4" long, olive drab (may be the same as No. 184-5)	NPF	NPF	NPF
T-205 Army Jeep and Driver, khaki .	NPF	NPF	NPF

Thomas Toy Jet Car, No. 457.

Thomas Toys Jeep & Driver, No. 580, khaki soldier, jeep in red, blue or green.

	C6	C8	C10
T-209 Army Maintenance Truck w/detachable ladders, olive drab, 5-1/2" long...............................	NPF	NPF	NPF
T-209 Same as No. 189 (1953)			
T-215 Army Road Roller (same as No. 196)			
T-223 Same as No. 77 (both in 1953)			
T-242 Same as non-friction-motor No. 222			
T-66 Same as No. 67			
T-79 Convertible Coupe (or Sedan), 4-1/2" long (Same as No. 77 and No. 77S)...............................	NPF	NPF	NPF
T-89 Same as No. 74			
TMC-10 Jeep, 1949, 4-1/4" long......	15	20	27
TMC-10 Jeep and Driver, driver is khaki soldier, jeep red, blue or green...........................	12	14	16

	C6	C8	C10
TMC-13 Trailer, for jeep, 1949, 4" long..................................	4	6	8
TMC-17 Streamlined Buick Sedan, 4-5/16" long	16	19	22
TMC-19 Airline Limousine, 1949, 4-1/2" long	15	20	27
TMC-25 Limousine and Trailer, 1949, 6-3/4" long	25	30	36
TMC-32 Dump Truck, 5" long (also in 1947 Acme order sheet)	12	14	16
TMC-40 Utility Trailer, 1949, 2-1/2" long..................................	6	8	10
TMC-51 Jeep and Trailer, 1949, 8-1/2" long	14	16	18
TMC-53 Truck and Trailer, 1949, 9" long overall	14	16	18
TMC-9 Streamlined Truck, 1949, 5" long..................................	10	12	14

TIPP AND CO. (TIPPCO)

Tipp's history is interesting. Founded in 1912 and named after an early director/employee (?), Miss Tipp, its ultimate owner, Phillip Ullman, was forced to flee from Germany in 1933. He went to England, where he founded Mettoy, eventually returning to Germany and recovering his company following the war. Tipp's military vehicles and overall production are clearly not up to the quality standards of Lineol and Elastolin and current prices reflect that fact. However, some of its pieces are particularly well-crafted, such as the Hitler Mercedes car. In the United States, Tipp tinplate pieces turn up at shows far more often, with its small Prime Mover being the most popular. Tipp military pieces sell for about a third that of Lineol and Hausser. Prices for Tipp military vehicles can be found as part of their photo captions.

Contributor: Jack Matthews, 13 Bufflehead Dr., Kiawah Island, SC 29455, e-mail: meriam@concentric.net.

	C6	C8	C10
Aerial Ladder Fire Truck, early.........	350	525	700
Bus, marked "Provincial Omnibus Co."..	1500	2900	4500
Club Sedan, tin lithographed, electric head lights, clockwork motor, rear trunk opens, 1933, 17" long..	500	800	11
Motorcycle and Rider, 6-1/2" high....	285	418	570
Police Motorcycle, battery headlight and friction, 11" long	550	950	1300
Santa Driving Roadster, tin wind-up, tree lights up, approx. 13" long	3500	5500	9500
Sedan, eight Cylinder, c.1930, 12" long..	550	900	1300
Silver Racer motorcycle, wind-up, 7-1/2" long..................................	500	750	1000
Stake Truck, wind-up, c.1930, 10" long..	135	198	270

Tipp Club Sedan, 1933, electric headlights, 17". Photo from Bill Bertoia Auction.

Tipp Santa Driving Roadster, tin windup, tree lights up, 13". Photo from Bill Bertoia Auction.

Tipp Silver Racer windup motorcycle, 7-1/2". Photo from Kent M. Comstock.

A large scenic Tipp box that held various toys.

Tipp Military Sedan, value as shown $600. Jack Mathews collection.

Tipp Armored Car, early and very rare, value as shown $1,500. Jack Mathews collection.

Tipp Command Car, value as shown $1,200. Jack Mathews collection.

Tipp Electric Tank, camouflaged, value as shown $2,000. Jack Mathews collection.

Tipp No. 162 with baggage cart, value as show $450. Jack Mathews Collection.

Tipp No. 162/167 Field Kitchen, value as shown $450. Jack Mathews collection.

Tipp No. 162/175, value as shown $500. Jack Mathews collection.

Tipp No. 162/174, value as shown $450. Jack Mathews collection.

Tipp No. 164 early large Sedan with British crew, rare, value as shown &1,750. Jack Mathews collection.

Tipp No. 164, rare, value as shown $550. Jack Mathews collection.

Tipp No. 169/240 Towing 88mm, value as shown $650. Jack Mathews collection.

Tipp No. 169/71, value as shown $600. Jack Mathews collection.

Tipp No. 169/72/171 with cleated cannon wheels, value a shown $600. Jack Mathews collection.

Tipp No. 169/274, value as shown $700. Jack Mathews collection.

Tipp No. 170/175 Wheeled Mortar, value as shown $600. Jack Mathews collection.

Tipp No. 176 Anti-Aircraft Truck, value as shown $950. Jack Mathews collection.

Tipp No. 184 Military Lastwagon, early camouflage and top, rare, value as shown $1,800. Jack Mathews collection.

Tipp No. 181/4 Pioneer Auto, rare, value as shown $950. Jack Mathews collection.

Tipp No. 181/4 Military Pioneer Auto, value as shown $600. Jack Mathews collection.

Tipp No. 194 Panzer Spahwagen, rare, value as shown $175. Jack Mathews collection.

Tipp No. 197, early, An accurate shot at the sheild stops the clockwork mechanism, value as shown $175. Jack Mathews collection.

Tipp No. 204 early tank, rare, value as shown $650. Jack Mathews collection.

Tipp No. 209 Tank, value as shown $750.

Tipp No. 217 Tracked Prime Mover, value as shown $990. Jack Mathews collection.

Tipp No. 934 Fuhrer Wagon, same as other version but in tan, value as shown $4,000. Jack Mathews collection.

Tipp No. 217 Tracked Prime Mover, camouflaged, British crew, value as shown $1,050. Jack Mathews collection.

Tipp No. 934 Fuhrer Wagon, very rare, value as shown $3,500. Jack Mathews collection.

TIP-TOP TOYS

Tip-Top toys were realistic, crisply detailed, and often unique. Wheels were either metal disks or Tootsietoy-like with lugbolts, metal hubs with rubber tires and rubber wheels. This progression helps to date the issues. Windshields and windows were open. Except where noted, cars and trucks were without bumpers.

Contributors: Fred Maxwell, 4722 N. 33 St., Arlington, VA 22207. **Perry R. Eichor,** 703 North Almond Drive, Simpsonville, SC, 29681.

	C6	C8	C10
Airflow Sedan, six windows, w/bumpers (TTTV014)	NPF	NPF	NPF
Coupe, Dodge (?) sidemounts, four windows, 1923, 3-1/8" long (TTTV001)	40	60	80
Coupe, die-cast, rearmount tire, 3-3/16" long (TTTV006)	25	50	75
Coupe, die-cast, streamlined, 1935 Huppmobile (?) w/realistic front end (forward fenders, setback grille, large louvers, bumpers, rearmount, tow loop), 3-1/4" long (TTTV007A)	50	75	100

	C6	C8	C10
Coupe, die-cast, cast rearmount; looks like Tootsietoy copy, 3-1/4" long (TTTV018)	NPF	NPF	NPF
Midget racer, die-cast, easily confused w/slush Barclay No. 53, 1-7/8" long (TTTV020)	NPF	NPF	NPF
Overland Bus, die-cast, thirteen windows, 3-3/8" (TTTV005)	25	40	60
Panel Truck, "Parcel Delivery," 2-1/8" long (TTTV010)	NPF	NPF	NPF
Pickup Truck, die-cast, "Tow Car," openwork handrails, 3-1/4" long (TTTV003A)	50	75	100
Pickup Truck, hinged tailgate, 3-1/4" long (TTTV004)	30	45	60
Pickup Truck, die-cast, "Tow Car," w/solid-cast handrails, 3-1/4" long (TTTV3b)	NPF	NPF	NPF
Racer, die-cast, slanted vee grille, round V8 ports, driver, 3" long (TTTV021)	NPF	NPF	NPF

Tip-Top Coupe, 1923, four windows, 3-1/8". Photo from Ferd Zegel.

Left to right: Tip-Top Sport Coupe, No. 145, 2-1/8"; Coupe, die-cast, 3-1/4" (similar to Tootsietoy). Photo from Ferd Zegel.

Left to right: Tip-Top Coupe, streamlined, 1935, 3-1/4"; Travel Trailer, Airstream-type, eight windows, 3-5/8". Photo from Ferd Zegel.

Tip-Top Overland Bus, thirteen windows, 3-3/8".

Left to right: Tip-Top Pickup Truck, hinged tailgate, 3-1/4"; Panel Truck, "Parcel Delivery," 2-1/8".

Left to right: Tip-Top Racer, rouded grille, strapped hood, short tail, 3-1/2"; Racer, slanted vee grille, driver, 3". Photo from Ferd Zegel.

Left to right: Tip-Top Racer, Miller-like, driver, 3"; Midget Racer, 1-7/8". Photo from Ferd Zegel.

Left to right: Tip-Top Racer, slanted vee grille, strapped hood, 4"; Racer, squarish grille, strapped hood, 3-1/4"; Record Racer, Bluebird, 4". Photo from Ferd Zegel.

Tip-Top Stake Truck, six-wheel version, 4-5/8". Photo from Ferd Zegel.

Left to right: Tip-Top Tanker Truck, "Gasoline," 3-1/2"; Pickup Truck, "Tow Car," 3-1/4". Photo from Dave Leopard.

	C6	C8	C10
Racer, die-cast, rounded grille, strapped hood, short tail, 3-1/2" long (TTTV022)	NPF	NPF	NPF
Racer, die-cast, strapped "16" hood, right exhaust, 4" long (TTTV023)	NPF	NPF	NPF
Racer, die-cast, Miller-like, driver, torpedo tail, six cylinder right exhaust, 3" long (TTTV024)	NPF	NPF	NPF
Racer, die-cast, squarish grille, left exhaust, driver, boattail, 3-1/4"long (TTTV026)	NPF	NPF	NPF
Racer, die-cast, slanted vee grille, strapped hood, left exhaust, boattail, 4" long (TTV025)	NPF	NPF	NPF
Record Racer, die-cast, Bluebird, rear fin, 4" long (TTTV027)	NPF	NPF	NPF
Small Sedan, 1933 Studebaker (?), 2-1/4" long (TTTV012)	NPF	NPF	NPF
Sport coupe, No. 145, die-cast, marked "TipTop Toy," under dash ventilator door, landau irons; shows parting-line and lower edge flash, 2-1/8" long (TTTV011)	60	80	100

	C6	C8	C10
Stake Truck, four- or six-wheel versions, body separately cast and fastened to chassis, 4-5/8" long (TTTV013)	75	100	125
Stake Truck, six-wheel versions, body separately cast and fastened to chassis, 5-1/4" long (TTTV013B)	NPF	NPF	NPF
Tanker Truck, die-cast, reads "Gasoline," two filler caps, 3-1/2" long (TTTV002)	40	60	80
Tanker Truck, die-cast, three fillers, 2-11/16" long (TTTV008)	NPF	NPF	NPF
Tanker Truck, die-cast, three filler caps, 3-1/4" long (TTTV019)	50	75	100
Trailer for above, two wheel dolly w/shaft, 2" long (TTTV3C)	30	45	60
Travel Trailer for Coupe, die-cast, "Airstream" type, eight windows, right-side door, 3-5/8" long (TTTV007B)	75	100	125

"Bull Dog" Indestructible Toy Auto Trucks

Exact reproductions of the large trucks after which they are patterned. These
Toy Auto Trucks afford children unlimited pleasure and amusement. Every
detail of construction and finish is faithfully carried out in miniature.

No. 45
"Bull Dog" Truck

Length Overall—26 inches.
Body—14½ x 7½ inches. Depth—2½ inches.
Frame—Heavy, deep channel steel.
Wheels—4¼ x ¾ inches, double disc. Heavy
 duty balloon tires.
Steering Gear—Knuckle joint.
Finish—Chassis, body and wheels Indian red
 baked enamel.
Equipment—Nickel-plated hub caps. Ratchet
 crank noise maker.
Packing—One in a carton. Weight per carton
 11 lbs.

No. 46
"Bull Dog" Dump Truck

Length Overall—26½ inches.
Body—14½ x 7½ inches. Depth—2½ inches.
Frame—Heavy deep channel steel.
Wheels—4¼ x ¾ inch double disc. Heavy duty
 balloon tires.
Steering Gear—Knuckle joint.
Finish—Chassis and hood black baked enamel.
 Body and wheels. Indian red.
Equipment—Nickel-plated hub caps. Ratchet
 crank noise maker.
Packing—One in a carton. Weight 14 lbs.

An advertisement showing Toledo's Bull Dog Truck and its Bull Dog Dump Truck.

TOLEDO METAL WHEEL COMPANY

The Toledo Metal Wheel Company was located in Toledo, Ohio, during the early and late 1920s. It manufactured a large range of pedal cars, as well as toy trucks. Its trade name for its products was "Blue Streak."

	C6	C8	C10		C6	C8	C10
Coal Truck, No. 50, "Bull Dog," 25" long	800	1350	1875	Pedal Car, 46" long	1200	2200	3300
Dump Truck, "Bull Dog," No. 46, 26-1/2" long	600	1000	1475	Pedal Car, "De Luxe," 54" long	2500	5000	7500
Fire Chief Pedal Car	3000	6000	10,000	Sprinkler Truck, "Bull Dog," No. 47, 27-1/2" long	600	1100	1510
Fire Pumper Car, red, 59" long	1250	1875	2500	Truck, "Bull Dog," open cab, No. 45, 26" long	500	1000	1500
Moving Van, "Bull Dog," No. 48, 26" long	550	1050	1550	White Dump Truck Pedal Car, 68" long	5000	9000	14,750

TOMMY TOY

Tommy Toy, 131 Palisade Ave., Union City, New Jersey, had its first sale on Nov. 13, 1935. Its principal owners were Dr. Albert Greene and Charles E. Weldon. It seems to have gone out of business between August 1938 and May 1939.

The following vehicles have been identified by Charles E. Weldon Jr., son of one of the owners of Tommy Toy. The Cannon Truck, aside from the hubs, looks just like Barclay's, which was produced in the same years. Some others resemble Metal Cast, Savoye, and other makers' vehicles. However, since slush molds did tend to change hands, production of a vehicle by one company would not preclude later manufacture of the same toy by another company. American Alloy is known to have produced copies of Tommy Toy's soldiers, using new molds. The only vehicle known to bear the Tommy Toy trademark is the No. 810 Cord.

	C6	C8	C10		C6	C8	C10
Aerial Ladder Truck, late 1920s-type (TTV001)	20	30	40	Double-Decker Bus, open top, no hood, like Barclay, late 1930s (TTV012)	16	24	32
Airflow-type Auto, like Savoye, c.1935 (TTV002)	32	48	65	Dump Truck, late 1930s, resembles Kansas Toy, Best Toy, Manhattan Toys (TTV013)	16	24	32
Ambulance, like Kansas Toy, late 1920s-early 1930s (TTV003)	16	24	32	General Trucking, late 1930s (TTV014)	12	18	25
Beer Truck, w/wooden barrels, late 1930s (TTV004)	14	21	28	Ladder Truck, mid 1930s (TTV015)	20	30	40
Cannon Truck, like Barclay, mid-1930s (TTV005)	17	25	34	Milk Truck, late 1930s (TTV016)	20	30	40
Convertible, no driver, mid-late 1930s (TTV006)	8	12	16	Milk Truck, grilled window, late 1930s (TTV017)	20	30	40
Convertible w/driver, 1935 Oldsmobile, mid-late 1930s (TTV007)	10	15	20	Milk Truck, smooth window, late 30s (TTV018)	20	30	40
Cord, 810, 1935 (TTV008)	40	60	80	Motorcoach, mid-1930s, like Savoye (TTV19)	NPF	NPF	NPF
Delivery Truck, "Delivery Deluxe," like Savoye, late 1930s (TTV009)	18	27	36	Oil Tanker, marked "Cap 80,000," like Metal Cast, which has different capacity number, 1930s, attaches to Tommy Toy Towing Car Coupe (TTV020)	8	12	16
Double-Decker Bus, closed top, early 1930s (TTV010)	16	24	32				
Double-Decker Bus, open top, extended hood, like Savoye, late 1920s (TTV011)	35	52	70	Packard Coupe, mid-1930s (TTV021)	17	26	35

No. 47
"Bull Dog" Sprinkler Truck

Length Overall—27½ inches.

Tank—14½ x 6 inches. Height 5 inches. Capacity of tank—1⅛ gallons. Fitted with filler cap, faucet and sprinkler attachment.

Frame—Heavy deep channel steel.

Wheels—4¼ x ¾ inches double disc. Heavy duty balloon tires.

Steering Gear—Knuckle joint.

Finish—Chassis and hood, black enamel. Tank and wheels, Indian red.

Equipment—Nickel-plated hub caps. Ratchet crank noise maker.

Packing—One in a carton. Weight—15 lbs.

No. 48
"Bull Dog" Moving Van

Length Overall—26 inches.

Body—14 x 7½ inches. Height—7¼ inches. Swinging rear doors.

Frame—Heavy deep channel steel.

Wheels—4¼ x ¾ inches, double disc. Heavy duty balloon tires.

Steering Gear—Knuckle joint.

Finish—Chassis and hood, black enamel. Body, Nile green. Wheels—red.

Equipment—Nickel-plated hub caps. Ratchet crank noise maker.

Packing—One in a carton. Weight 16 lbs.

No. 50
"Bull Dog" Coal Truck

Length Overall—25 inches.

Body—13 x 7½ inches. Depth—4¾ inches. Delivery chute on side of body with extra extension chute.

Frame—Heavy deep channel steel.

Wheels—4¼ x ¾ inch double disc. Heavy duty balloon tires.

Steering Gear—Knuckle joint.

Finish—Chassis and hood, Indian red enamel. Body, black enamel.

Equipment—Nickel-plated hub caps. Ratchet crank noise maker.

Packing—One in a carton. Weight—13 lbs.

Another Toledo advertisement showing the Bull Dog Sprinkler Truck , Moving Van, and Coal Truck.

	C6	C8	C10		C6	C8	C10
Police Patrol, open windows, late 1920s-early 1930s type (TTV022)	70	105	140	Racing Car, large, mid 1930s (TTV027)	16	24	32
Police Patrol, solid windows, late 1920s-early 1930s type (TTV023)	35	52	70	Racing Car, small, mid 1930s (TTV028)	12	18	25
				Sedan, four door, c.1935 (TTV029)	17	26	35
Pumper, mid 1930s (TTV024)	12	18	25	Sedan Towing Touring Trailer, 1936-1937 (TTV030)	20	30	40
Pumper, large, red hubs, late 1930s (TTV025)	11	16	22	Towing Car Coupe, early 1930s-type, like Savoye (TTV031)	16	24	32
Pumper, small, late 1930s (TTV026)	8	12	16	Tractor (TTV032)	12	18	25
				Wrecker, late 1930s (TTV033)	10	15	20

TONKA

In 1946, in the basement of a small schoolhouse in Mound, Minnesota, Lynn E. Baker, Avery Crounse and Alvin Tesch founded Mound Metalcraft Co. The company was incorporated September 18, 1946. The primary production was a major output of hoes, rakes, shovels, along with tie, hat and shoe racks—toy production was merely a sideline. During the first year, the company purchased tooling from the L.E. Streeter Co. for a toy steam shovel. The tooling was refined, and Mound produced their first two toys—a steam shovel and crane. After a successful debut at the International Toy Fair in 1946, Mound Metalcraft manufactured a total of 37,000 pieces of the two metal toys—the No. 100 Steam Shovel and the No. 150 Crane and Clam. Tonka Toys, named after Lake Minnetonka, enjoyed the first of what would be many years of successful sales in the toy truck business. A resident of Mound, Minnesota, Ering W. Eklof, was asked to design the first Tonka logo. In three days, the logo was designed to represent the lake area in which the plant was located. The waves reflected the waters of Lake Minnetonka and three birds were added along with a distinctive swash-type font. The logo remained unchanged from 1947 until 1955. The first Tonka catalog was printed in 1949.

The founding premise of Tonka was to provide consumers with a toy that was durable, reasonably priced and, of course, fun. Tonka devoted much time and resource designing and testing each truck. Three decades after its initial founding, the company grew from the original small schoolhouse with a half-dozen employees, to an expansive plant covering nearly one-third of a mile along the shores of Lake Minnetonka employing over 1,300 people that produced approximately 400,000 toys per week.

The production of Tonka Toys followed many of the same techniques used in the mass production of trucks and cars in Detroit, Michigan. A new toy would begin as a sketch. If the sketch received favorable reviews from consumers, it was then transformed into a three-dimensional clay model. A positive reaction to a clay model meant it would be produced in Fiberglas or metal to be reviewed by those involved with child supervision and early childhood development. If the toy passed this round of inspections, detailed drawings and blueprints were prepared and manufacturing specifications were developed. When trail production samples were completed, they were sent out for the toughest test of all—the children.

Tonka's production and management staff would observe the reaction of children as they played with the toys. This tests judged the play value of the toy, and safety and durability of the toy. If the toy passed this final test, it was sent into production.

Since the initial production in 1947, Tonka has become a world-wide operation. Late in 1955, Mound Metalcraft changed its name to Tonka Toys, Inc. In 1991, Tonka became part of Hasbro, Inc., and Tonka trucks continue to be the No. 1 brand in the non-powered toy truck category. Each year Hasbro introduces a dynamic line of fun, innovative state of the art trucks for children of all ages.

Contributors: . **John Taylor,** P.O. Box 63, Nolensville, TN 37135-0063. **Don Desalle, 5106 Knollwood, Anderson, IN 46011, 800-392-8697.** Desalle and his wife, Barb, are nationally-known authorities and collectors of Tonka trucks. The DeSalles are the authors of the Hasbro-licensed book, *Collector's Guide to Tonka Trucks 1947-1963.* Through the knowledge they have acquired at the antique shows the promote and attend, the DeSalles have an excellent knowledge base for the market value of Tonka trucks.

The DeSalles are licensed to reproduce replacement parts for antique Tonka Trucks. These parts are available through Julian Thomas, Thomas Toy Parts, Fenton, Michigan. Please see the Collectors and Dealers section for more information.

Don DeSalle, a native of Toledo, Ohio, attended Indiana University on a football scholarship where he obtained a B.A. and M.A. in chemistry and geology and was named All-American football player. DeSalle played in the Rose Bowl, Senior Bowl and the North and South game. His football continued as he played briefly with the Buffalo Bills.

Barb DeSalle, a native of Daleville, Indiana, obtained a B.S. and M.S. and an Ed.S. She has completed the coursework on her doctorate and is doing research on Satellite Communications at Ball State University.

Busy with DeSalle Promotions, Inc., promoting antique toys shows across the country, they have three college-age children

	C6	C8	C10
1947			
No. 100 Steam Shovel, 20-3/4" long	135	200	350
No. 150 Crane and Clam, 24" long ..	135	200	350
1948			
No. 200 Power Lift Truck and Trailer	200	350	600
1949			
No. 100 Stearn Shovel Deluxe, 22" long	100	250	400
No. 120 Tractor and Carry-All Trailer, w/No. 50 Steam Shovel...	155	280	475
No. 125 Tractor & Carry-All Trailer, w/No. 100 Steam Shovel	150	250	550

Tonka 1948 Power Lift Truck and Trailer. Photo From Don and Barb DeSalle.

	C6	C8	C10
No. 130 Tractor-Carry-All Trailer, 30-1/2" long	100	150	350
No. 140 Tonka Toy Transport Van, 22-1/4" long	150	300	500
No. 170 Tractor & Carry-All Trailer, w/No. 150 Crane and Clam	200	300	525
No. 180 Dump Truck, 12" long	100	175	375
No. 190 Loading Tractor, 10-1/2" long	NPF	NPF	NPF
No. 250 Wrecker Truck, 12-1/2" long	125	250	375
1950			
No. 145 Steel Carrier Semi, 22" long	125	200	350
No. 175 Utility Hauler, 12" long	100	150	300
No. 185 Express Truck, 13-1/2" long	200	450	900
No. 400 Allied Van Lines Semi, 23-1/2" long	175	260	400
1952			
No. 500 Livestock Hauler Semi, 22-1/4" long	100	150	350
No. 550 Grain Hauler Semi, 22-1/4" long	125	180	350
1953			
No. 575 Logger Semi, wood flat bed	125	180	350
No. 575 Logger Semi, 22-1/4" long..	125	180	350
No. 600 Road Grader, 17" long	50	75	100
No. 650 Green Giant Transport Semi, 22-1/4" long	150	300	500
No. 675 Trailer Fleet Set, two tractors (five interchangeable trailers), per set	450	680	975
Wrecker	125	200	350
1954			
No. 145 Steel Carrier Truck	100	185	380
No. 700 Aerial Ladder Semi Fire Truck, 32-1/2" long	175	260	450
No. 725 Star Kist Van, 14-1/2" long .	250	575	950
No. 750 Carnation Milk Step Van, 11-3/4" long	200	400	600

Tonka 1954 Utility Truck. Photo From Don and Barb DeSalle.

Tonka 1955 Stake Truck, six wheel. Photo From Don and Barb DeSalle.

Tonka 1955 Minute Maid Orange Juice Van. Photo From Don and Barb DeSalle.

Tonka 1955 Stake Truck, six wheel. Photo From Don and Barb DeSalle.

	C6	C8	C10
No. 750 Parcel Delivery Van, 11-3/4" long..............................	200	300	500
No. 775 Road Builder Set, Road Grader, Semi T&T Crane and Dump Truck, five pieces	350	525	900
Utility Truck	110	275	425
Wrecker...	100	300	500

1955

	C6	C8	C10
Allied Van Lines	150	275	500
Dump...	100	150	350
Freighter...	90	135	280
Hook and Ladder..............................	100	300	450
Livestock Truck	110	200	350
Loboy and Shovel	150	300	450
No. 065 Trailer, stake side	30	45	60
No. 600 Grader	75	125	200
No. 725 Minute Maid Orange Juice Van	275	650	950
No. 750 Carnation Milk Delivery Van	200	400	600
No. 850 Lumber Truck, six-wheel	175	260	400

	C6	C8	C10
No. 860 Stake Truck, six-wheel	175	360	500
No. 880 Pick-up Truck	125	280	450
No. 992 Aerial Sand Loader Set, Loader and Dump Truck	275	425	875
Rescue Van	200	450	800

1956

	C6	C8	C10
Green Giant Semi Reefer	155	350	600
No. 120 Shovel and Carry-All (Loboy), 33" long total..................	188	280	475
No. 180 Dump Truck, 13" long.........	100	150	350
No. 600 Road Grader, 17" long........	75	125	200
No. 700 Aerial Ladder, 32-1/2" long.	150	300	450
No. 880 Pickup Truck, 13-3/4" long .	150	350	650
No. 950 Pumper, 17" long................	150	275	450
No. 960 Wrecker	100	300	600
No. 980 Hi-Way Dump Truck, 13" long..	130	280	395
No. 991 Farm Stake Truck, 13" long.	150	250	460
No. 996 Wrecker, white, 12" long, rare	390	525	800
No. 998 Lumber Truck, 18-3/4" long	130	225	360
Rescue Squad Van, 11-3/4" long.....	225	400	850

	C6	C8	C10

1957

	C6	C8	C10
3-in-1Hi-way Service Truck, w/two snowblades, 13" long	275	400	700
Aerial Ladder Truck	200	300	500
Big Mike Dual Hydraulic Dump Truck, 14" long	325	595	1000
Farm Stake Truck	190	375	480
Gasoline Truck, 15" long	350	525	1000
Parcel Delivery Van, 12" long	200	350	500
Pickup with Stake Trailer, 20-1/2" long	150	250	400
Stake Trailer	30	45	75
Stock Rack Truck with Animals, 16-1/4" long	175	365	650
Thunderbird Express Semi, 24" long	150	400	600
Wrecker	100	300	500

1958 Next Generation Cars

	C6	C8	C10
No. 02 Pickup Truck	100	150	300
No. 03 Utility Truck	100	150	300

	C6	C8	C10
No. 04 Farm Stake Truck	100	150	300
No. 05 Sportsman Pickup w/Topper, 12-3/4" long	150	225	450
No. 06 Dump Truck	100	150	300
No. 12 Road Grader	75	112	150
No. 18 Wrecker Truck	100	250	450
No. 20 Hydraulic Dump Truck	125	175	275
No. 28 Pickup with Stake Trailer and Animal	125	175	350
No. 29 Sportsman Truck w/Box Trailer	150	225	400
No. 32 Stock Rack Truck	175	300	500
No. 33 Gasoline Truck, hinged back door, hose and nozzle	350	500	900
No. 34 Deluxe Sportsman with Boat Trailer, 22-3/4" long	150	325	750
No. 35 Farm Stake, w/two-horse trailer, 21-3/4" long	125	250	450
No. 36 Livestock Van	175	250	450
No. 37 Thunderbird Express	150	300	600
No. 39 Nationwide Moving Van, 24-1/4" long	250	475	800
No. 41 Hi-Way Service Truck	100	200	400

Tonka 1956 Dump Truck, 13". Photo from Don and Barb DeSalle.

Tonka 1957 Gasoline Truck, 15". Photo from Don and Barb DeSalle.

Tonka 1956 Pumper, 17". Photo From Don and Barb DeSalle.

Tonka 1957 Thunderbird Express Semi, 24". Photo From Don and Barb DeSalle.

	C6	C8	C10
Shovel & Carry-All Trailer	200	300	500
No. 45 Big Mike Dual Hydraulic Dump Truck, w/snow plow	375	675	1000
No. 46 Suburban Pumper	175	225	450
No. 48 Hydraulic Aerial Ladder	100	250	450

1959

	C6	C8	C10
No. 01 Service Truck, 12-3/4" long ..	100	150	350
No. 05 Sportsman	100	175	350
No. 14 Dragline, 20" long	100	175	375
No. 16 Air Express	350	425	700
No. 22 Deluxe Sportsman	150	325	500
No. 30 Tandem Platform Stake, 28-1/4" long.................................	240	450	800
No. 44 Dragline & Trailer, 26-1/4" long	150	275	400
Sanitary Truck, square back	450	700	1000
Tandem No. 36 Tandem Air Express, w/trailer, 24" long	325	650	1000
Tandem No. 40 Car Carrier..............	100	300	500
Tandem No. 41 Boat Transport, 38" long	250	350	700
Tandem No. 42 Hydraulic Land Rover, 15" long	550	825	1700

1960

	C6	C8	C10
Jolly Green Giant Special, white, green stake racks	375	450	850
No. 001 Service Truck....................	100	150	350
No. 002 Pickup.............................	100	200	375
No. 004 Farm Stake Truck	100	200	325
No. 005 Sportsman	100	275	400
No. 006 Dump Truck	75	125	290
No. 008 Logger	150	225	300
No. 018 Wrecker, white sidewalls	100	150	375
No. 020 Hydraulic Dump	75	150	300
No. 022 Deluxe Sportsman	100	250	400
No. 028 Pickup & Trailer	100	150	300
No. 035 Farm Stake and Horse Trailer..	125	180	350
No. 037 Thunderbird Express	150	350	550
No. 040 Car Carrier.......................	100	225	450
No. 041 Boat Transport, 38" long.....	250	450	850
No. 046 Suburban Pumper	100	250	350
No. 048 Aerial Ladder	125	250	350
No. 100 Bulldozer, 8-7/8" long, plated roller wheels only in 1960 .	75	125	200
No. 105 Rescue Squad, 13-3/4" long	100	250	450
No. 110 Fisherman Pick-up, w/sportsman, cover, 14" long.......	100	175	375

Tonka 1961 Dump Truck. Photo from Don and Barb DeSalle.

	C6	C8	C10
No. 115 Power Boom Loader, 1960 only, 18-1/2" long.....................	300	650	1000
No. 120 Cement Mixer, 15-1/2" long	100	150	300
No. 125 Lowboy and Bulldozer, 26-1/4" long	190	375	675
No. 130 Deluxe Fisherman, also new boat and trailer	150	350	550
No. 135 Mobile Dragline	100	250	450
No. 140 Sanitary Truck	350	550	900
No. 145 Tanker, first Tonka w/major use of plastic, 28" long................	100	250	450
Standard Oil Company Wrecker Special...	400	600	1200

1961

	C6	C8	C10
No. 002 Pickup..............................	100	190	320
No. 004 Farm Stake........................	85	175	370
No. 005 Sportsman	100	150	375
No. 006 Dump...............................	75	100	250
No. 012 Road Truck Grader, yellow.	75	100	200
No. 014 Dragline, yellow	100	150	250
No. 018 Wrecker............................	100	250	400
No. 020 Hydraulic Dump.................	75	110	250
No. 022 Deluxe Sportman...............	100	200	450
No. 035 Farm Stake Truck and Horse Trailer............................	100	180	350
No. 039 Allied Van	120	250	450
No. 040 Car Carrier........................	100	250	450
No. 041 Boat Transport Truck...........	150	300	650
No. 048 Aerial Ladder	125	200	450
No. 116 Dump Truck with Sandloader, 23-1/4" long	100	175	395
No. 117 Boat Service Truck, 1961 only	100	250	450
No. 118 Giant Dozer, 12-1/2" long...	70	100	250
No. 120 Cement Mixer	100	150	300

	C6	C8	C10
No. 130 Deluxe Fisherman	150	350	550
No. 134 Grading Service Truck, Trailer and Bulldozer, 25-1/2" long total	100	150	350
No. 135 Mobile Dragline..................	100	250	450
No. 136 Houseboat Set, 29" long total	200	400	800
No. 140 Sanitary Truck	400	700	1500
No. 142 Mobile Clam, 27-1/4" long ..	100	250	450
No. 145 Tanker	100	250	350

1962

	C6	C8	C10
No. 0200 Jeep Dispatcher, 9-3/4" long	50	75	100
No. 0201 Serv-I-Car,, 9-1/8" long......	75	125	200
No. 0249 Jeep Universal..................	75	125	175
No. 0250 Tractor, 8-5/8" long..........	50	75	100
No. 0300 Bulldozer..........................	50	75	100
No. 0301 Utility Dump, 12-1/2" long, revised Golf Club Tractor, 1961 only	100	150	300
No. 0302 Pickup.............................	95	150	250
No. 0308 Stake Pickup, 12-5/8" long	50	100	200
No. 0350 Jeep Surrey, fringe top, 10-1/2" long..............	75	125	200
No. 0402 Loader, yellow and green .	40	60	80
No. 0404 Farm Stake Truck.............	50	95	150
No. 0405 Sportsman	75	100	200
No. 0406 Dump Truck......................	75	150	275
No. 0410 Jet Delivery Truck, 14" long, 1962 only	200	350	850
No. 0420 Airlines Luggage Service, 16-5/8 long..............	100	250	400
No. 0512 Road Grader.....................	45	68	90
No. 0514 Dragline	150	225	300
No. 0516 Jeep Runabout, trailer, boat, 25-5/8" long total.................	75	175	350
No. 0518 Wrecker	75	175	325
No. 0520 Hydraulic Dump	75	100	220
No. 0524 Dozer Packer, 18-1/4" long total, Packer has eleven tires, sold only in 1962	100	250	400
No. 0528 Pickup & Trailer	50	75	150
No. 0530 Camper, 14" long.............	75	150	250
No. 0616 Dump Truck and Sand Loader..............	75	125	240
No. 0618 Giant Dozer	100	150	200
No. 0620 Cement Mixer	85	150	300
No. 0735 Farm Stake and Horse Trailer..............	75	125	225

	C6	C8	C10
No. 0739 Allied Van	125	250	350
No. 0834 Grading Service Truck......	70	100	150
No. 0840 Car Carrier.......................	100	150	300
No. 0926 Pumper Truck	100	150	300
No. 0942 Mobile Clam	100	150	320
No. 1348 Aerial Ladder	100	150	350

1963

	C6	C8	C10
No. 0050 Mini-Tonka Jeep pickup, 9-1/4" long	35	52	70
No. 0056 Mini-Tonka Stake Truck, 9-1/4" long	35	52	70
No. 0060 Mini-Tonka Dump, 9-3/4" long..............	30	50	75
No. 0068 Mini-Tonka Wrecker, 9-1/2" long	30	50	75
No. 0070 Mini-Tonka Camper, 9-5/8" long	75	112	150
No. 0200 Jeep Dispatcher	30	50	75
No. 0201 Servi-I-Cae	55	82	110
No. 0250 Tractor, yellow w/red seat	75	112	150
No. 0251 Military Jeep Universal, 10-1/2" long	25	38	50
No. 0300 Bulldozer	55	82	110
No. 0302 Pickup.............................	35	52	70
No. 0308 Stake Pickup	50	95	150
No. 0350 Jeep Surrey	50	75	100
No. 0352 Loader	40	60	80
No. 0354 Style-Side Pickup, 14" long..............	40	60	125
No. 0404 Farm Stake Truck.............	60	90	150
No. 0406 Dump Truck......................	45	68	90
No. 0422 Back Hoe, 17-1/8" long.....	100	175	350
No. 0425 Jeep Pumper, 10-3/4" long	100	175	400
No. 0512 Road Grader, red clearance lights..............	80	120	160

Tonka 1962 Cement Mixer. Photo From Don and Barb DeSalle.

	C6	C8	C10
No. 0514 Drag..................................	60	90	120
No. 0516 Jeep Runabout, trailer and boat..	75	150	300
No. 0518 Wrecker	45	75	150
No. 0520 Hydraulic Dump Truck......	45	68	90
No. 0522 Style-Side Pickup & Stake Trailer, 22-3/4" long total..............	75	125	250
No. 0524 Dozer Packer, yellow........	200	300	400
No. 0530 Camper.............................	25	38	50
No. 0534 Trencher, 18-1/4" long......	40	75	150
No. 0536 Giant Dozer	110	160	225
No. 0616 Dump Truck & Sand Loader, yellow...............................	100	150	235
No. 0620 Cement Mixer	75	125	250
No. 0625 Stake Pickup & Horse Trailer, 21-3/4" long overall..........	75	125	175
No. 0640 Ramp Hoist, 19-1/4" long, red and white	175	350	550
No. 0720 Terminal Train, 33-5/8" long, total, fifteen suitcases	105	175	300
No. 0739 Allied Van	118	175	235
No. 0840 Car Carrier........................	42	63	85
No. 0926 Pumper..............................	60	90	120
No. 0942 Mobile Clam......................	75	112	150
No. 1001 Trencher & LoBoy, 28-1/2" long total	75	112	150
No. 1348 Aerial Ladder Truck	100	150	200
No. 2100 Airport Service Set............	150	225	300

1964

	C6	C8	C10
No. 077 Mini-Tonka Mixer, 9" long...	30	50	75
No. 086 Mini-Tonka Van, 16" long ...	36	54	72
No. 090 Mini-Tonka Livestock Van, 16" long..	50	75	100
No. 096 Mini-Tonka Carrier, 18-1/2" long, two cars	50	75	150
No. 250 Military Tractor, black seat .	55	70	100
No. 251 Military Jeep Universal	35	55	75
No. 304 Jeep Commander, canvas top, 10-1/2" long	30	50	75
No. 315 Dump Truck, 13-1/2" long...	40	60	90
No. 375 Jeep Wrecker, 11" long	75	130	200
No. 380 Troop Carrier, 14" long.......	70	100	150
No. 384 Military Jeep & Box Trailer, 19-3/8" overall.............................	50	75	150
No. 404 Stake Truck, red	70	120	170
No. 425 Jeep Pumper, black steering wheel	100	150	275
No. 504 Stake Pickup & Trailer, 21-5/8" long	50	75	185
No. 525 Jeep & Horse Trailer, 19-1/4" long total, two horses	45	68	135

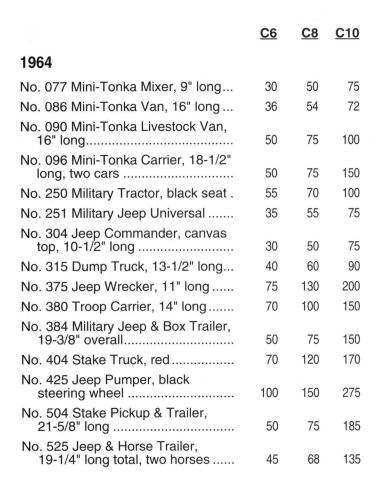

Tonka 1963 Dump Truck & Sand Loader. Photo From Don and Barb DeSalle.

Tonka 1963 Camper with original box. Photo From Don and Barb DeSalle.

Tonka 1964 Jeep Pumper. Photo From Don and Barb DeSalle.

	C6	C8	C10
No. 616 Dump Truck & Sandloader, orange and yellow........................	75	125	175
No. 640 Ramp Hoist, park green and white, very rare	300	650	900
No. 739 Allied Van Lines, black knob on door.......................................	75	125	175
No. 900 Mighty Tonka Dump Truck, one of the most popular Tonka vehicles ever made; there were 9,655,000 sold between 1964 and 1983......................................	65	100	230
No. 942 Mobile Clam, yellow............	50	75	100
No. 998 Aerial Ladder, two auxiliary ladders	50	75	100

Tonka 1964 Ramp Hoist, green, very rare. Photo From Don and Barb DeSalle.

TOOTSIETOY

Tootsietoy is one of the best-known names in the world of the toy collecting, and for good reason.

The toys, products of a Chicago concern that now has a century of manufacturing behind it, have long appealed to parents because of their cheap price, and to kids because of their high play value. The Tootsietoy line through the years has included toy cars, trucks, trains, dollhouse furniture, airplanes and toy soldiers. During the company's heyday, roughly from the 1930s through 1960s, a person would have had to search long and hard to find a child with no knowledge of the trademark.

Dowst and Company started in 1876 in the publishing trade, and moved into manufacturing after the 1893 Columbian World Exposition in Chicago, where the new die-casting technology was introduced to the public. By then named Dowst Brothers, the company released its first die-cast-body, free-axle toy car in 1911, the generic Limousine. The first specific-model car, the Model T Ford touring car, followed in 1914. The name Tootsietoy was adopted in the early 1920s and was registered in 1924 as the company's trademark. Theodore Dowst, who joined the firm in 1906, is generally seen as the guiding force behind the growth of toy production at Dowst Brothers. He remained with the company even after its purchase by Nathan Shure in 1926, until 1945. For most collectors, the toys of the Ted Dowst period are the most noteworthy.

High points in the world of Tootsietoy collecting include the 1933 Graham series, notable for its use of three-piece construction, with separately die-cast bodies, chassis and radiator grilles, and the 1935 LaSalles, which used four-piece construction, adding a casting for the rear bumpers. Collectors also avidly seek the 1932-33 Funnies series cars, which featured such comic figures as Andy Gump, Uncle Walt and Moon Mullins.

Interest seems to be growing in the various advertising toys Tootsietoy produced through the years, ranging from the 1932 Wrigley's Railroad Express truck to more recent U-Haul and Coast-to-Coast vehicles. Collector demand for post-war toys remains stable at a fairly low level; and it may not grow stronger any time soon, given the heavy contemporary interest in detailed scale models as opposed to made-for-play toys. On the other hand, interest in the post-Vietnam toys is inching upward, reflecting the maturing of the later Baby Boomers.

Contributors: John Gibson, 9713 Pleasant Gate Lane Potomac, Maryland 20854. Gibson has always been a collector of sorts, from Winchester Firearms to the Arts and Crafts Movement, art glass, art deco, art nouveau, vintage posters, pin up art, tobacco tin advertising and stained glass. While antique hunting in 1989, he discovered a mint, boxed set of Deluxe Tootsietoy Grahams and has been actively involved with collecting and writing about them ever since. He currently serves as the Corporate Historian for the Strombecker Corporation in Chicago, Illinois, home of Tootsietoy. Gibson is currently employed in the Washington, D.C. area in the specialized field of decorative painting. After years of research, he is now writing a definitive book on pre-war Tootsietoys and has branched into Civil War collecting. **Mark Rich,** P.O. Box 971, Stevens Point, WI, 54481-0971.

Miniature Vehicles

	C6	C8	C10
0510 Midget Assortment Boxed Set, ten-piece	150	200	250
0510 Midget Assortment Boxed Set, eight-piece	105	140	175
0610 Midget Assortment Boxed Set, twelve-piece	160	210	265
1628 Bus	6	9	12
1629 Wrecker	7	10	14
1630 Racer	5	7	10
1631 DeSoto Airflow Sedan	5	7	10
1632 Zephyr Railcar	7	10	14
1634 Fire Truck	7	10	14
1635 Delivery Van	6	9	12
1635 Delivery Van (Ambulance)	7	10	14
1666 Army Tank	4	6	8
1667 Armored Car	5	7	10

Prewar Tootsietoys

	C6	C8	C10
--- 1935 Ford V8 Roadster Fire Chief's Car	105	140	175
--- Box Trailer and Roadscraper Raker, sold only in boxed set farm tractor No. 7003	81	108	595
--- Ford Model A Van, marked "U.S Mail," sold only in sets	51	68	85
--- Graham Commercial Tire & Supply	165	220	275
--- Graham Coupe, four-wheel, Bild-A-Car	65	98	130
--- Graham Roadster, four-wheel, Bild-A-Car	117	156	195
--- Graham Sedan, four-wheel, Bild-A-Car	65	98	130
--- TransAmerica Bus, sold only in sets	165	220	275
0023 Racer, w/driver intact	45	68	90
0101 Buick Coupe	10	15	20
0102 Buick Roadster	13	19	25

	C6	C8	C10
0103 Buick Sedan	10	15	20
0104 Mack Insurance Patrol	33	44	55
0105 Mack Tank Truck	36	48	60
0108 Caterpillar Tractor, original treads only	42	56	70
0109 Ford Pickup Truck	20	30	40
0110 Bluebird Daytona record Car	51	68	85
0111 1934 Ford V8 Sedan	51	68	85
0111 1935 Ford V8 Sedan	24	32	40
0112 1934 Ford V8 Coupe	51	68	85
0112 1935 Ford V8 Coupe	24	96	120
0113 1934 Ford V8 Wrecker	72	96	120
0113 1935 Ford V8 Wrecker	45	60	75
0114 1934 Ford V8 Convertible Coupe	54	72	90
0114 1935 Ford V8 Convertible Coupe	39	52	65
0115 1934 Ford V8 Convertible Sedan	54	72	90
0115 1935 Ford V8 Convertible Sedan	39	52	65

Tootsietoy Graham Commercial Tire & Supply Co. Van, 1935. Photo from John Gibson.

Tootsietoy Buick No. 103 Sedan in No. 4657 tinplate garage.

Tootsietoy made various prewar Graham Sedans.

Tankers were among the vehicles featured in this reproduction of a Tootsietoy catalog page that originally ran in 1933.

Tootsietoy 1935 Ford Wrecker, No. 113.

Mack Tootsietoy Dairy, No. 192, one-piece cab, three trailers. Photo from Phillips.

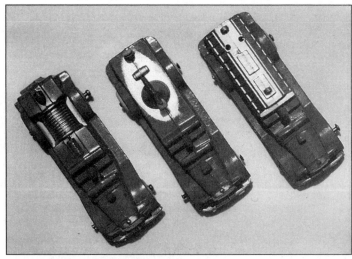

Left to right: Tootsietoy Insurance Patrol, No. 238; Hose Wagon, 236; Hook & Ladder, No. 236. Photo from John Gibson.

Tootsietoy Graham Town Car, No. 0516, 1930s.

	C6	C8	C10
0116 Ford V8 Roadster....................	23	34	45
0117 Zephyr Railcar.........................	51	68	85
0118 DeSoto Airflow Sedan.............	33	44	55
0120 Oil Tank Truck.........................	23	34	45
0121 Ford Pickup Truck..................	18	26	35
0123 Ford Lewis's Camelback Van..	195	260	325
0123 Ford McLeans Camelback Van	280	380	475
0123 Ford Miller & Rhoads Camelback Van	300	400	500
0123 Ford Shepards Camelback Van	285	380	475
0123 Ford Special Delivery Camelback Van	25	38	50
0123 Ford Wieboldt's Camelback Van	285	380	475
0180 Lincoln Zephyr & Roamer House Trailer, w/wind-up motor...	660	880	1100
0180 Lincoln Zephyr & Roamer House Trailer, w/o wind-up motor	435	655	875
0187 Mack Auto Transport, w/up-tilted trailer and three vehicles	360	480	600
0190 Mack auto transport, w/three Buicks	135	180	225
0190 Mack auto transport, w/four Buicks	165	220	275
0191 Contractors tipper set..............	133	180	225
0192 Mack Tootsie Toy Dairy, two-piece cab, three trailers	156	208	260
0192 Mack Tootsietoy Dairy, one-piece cab, three trailers	126	168	210
0198 Mack Auto Transport, one-piece cab, three 1935 Fords	195	260	325
0198 Mack Auto Transport, yellow, two-piece cab, three '34 Fords.....	360	480	600

	C6	C8	C10
0230 LaSalle Sedan........................	15	20	30
0231 Coupe	15	20	30
0232 Open Touring Coupe	15	20	30
0233 Boattail Roadster	15	20	30
0234 Box Van	15	20	30
0235 Oil Tank Truck.......................	13	18	25
0236 Fire Engine, Hook and Ladder	20	30	40
0237 Fire Engine, Insurance Patrol .	15	25	35
0238 Fire Engine, Hose Wagon.......	20	30	40
0239 Station Wagon	20	30	40
0511 Graham Roadster, five-wheel .	117	156	195
0512 Graham Coupe, five-wheel	72	110	145
0513 Graham Sedan, five-wheel	72	110	145
0514 Graham Convertible Coupe, five-wheel	80	120	160
0515 Graham Convertible Sedan, five-wheel	80	120	160
0516 Graham Town Car, five-wheel	88	130	175
0611 Graham Roadster, six-wheel ...	117	156	195
0612 Graham Coupe, six-wheel	72	110	145

	C6	C8	C10
0613 Graham Sedan, six-wheel.......	72	110	145
0614 Graham Convertible Coupe, six-wheel..............................	80	120	160
0615 Graham Convertible Sedan, six-wheel..............................	80	120	160
0616 Graham Towncar, six-wheel ...	75	113	150
0712 LaSalle Coupe.........................	180	240	300
0713 LaSalle Sedan.........................	180	240	300
0714 LaSalle Convertible Coupe	195	260	325
0715 LaSalle Convertible Sedan......	195	260	325
0716 Briggs Lincoln prototype, "Doodlebug"	60	90	125
0801 Mack Express Stake Semi-trailer, one-piece cab	78	104	130
0801 Mack Express Stake Semi-trailer, two-piece cab...................	96	128	160
0802 Mack Domaco Tank Semi-trailer, two-piece cab...................	111	148	185

	C6	C8	C10
0802 Mack Domaco Tank Semi-trailer, one-piece cab	87	116	145
0803 Mack Long Distance Hauling Semi-trailer	150	200	250
0804 Mack City Fuel Coal Truck, ten-wheel	165	220	275
0804 Mack City Fuel Coal Truck, four-wheel	240	320	400
0805 Mack Tootsietoy Dairy Semi-trailer Truck.............................	105	140	175
0806 Graham Wrecker....................	75	113	150
0807 Delivery Motorcycle, adapted from 5103	175	260	350
0808 Graham Tootsietoy Dairy	99	132	165
0809 Graham Ambulance	99	132	165

Tootsietoy Mack Domaco Tank Semi-trailer, No. 802, two-piece cab. Photo from John Gibson.

Mack tootsietoy Dairy Semi-trailer Truck.

Tootsietoy Mack Long Distance Hauling Semi-trailer, No. 803. Photo from John Gibson.

Tootsietoy Doodlebug, Briggs Lincoln prototype,1935, No. 716. Photo from John Gibson.

Tootsietoy Mack Express Stake Semi-trailer, No. 801, two-piece cab. Photo from John Gibson.

Tootsietoy Mack City Fuel Coal Truck, No. 804. Photo from The Graham Works.

Character vehicles are among those featured on this reproduction page from a 1933 Tootsietoy catalog.

Tootsietoy Shell Oil Truck, No. 1009. Photo from John Gibson.

Tootsietoy Fire Engine, Hook & Ladder, No. 1040. Photo from John Gibson.

Tootsietoy Wrigley Box Van, No. 1010. Photo from John Gibson.

Tootsietoy Roamer House Trailer, No. 1044, with door and tin bottom. Photo from John Gibson.

Tootsietoy Massey-Ferguson Farm Tractors, No. 1011, in red-and-silver and green-and-silver color schemes. Photo from John Gibson.

	C6	C8	C10
0810 Mack Railway Express Co. Truck, w/"Wrigley's Gum" ad, two-piece cab	111	148	185
0810 Mack Railway Express Co. Truck, w/"Wrigley's Gum" ad, one-piece cab	105	140	175
1006 Standard Oil Truck	87	116	145
1007 Sinclair Oil Truck	87	116	145
1008 Texaco Oil Truck	87	116	145
1009 Shell Oil Truck	90	120	150
1010 Wrigley Box Van	55	80	110
1011 Massey-Ferguson Farm Tractor	200	300	400
1016 Auburn Roadster, jumbo torpedo-single color	23	34	45

	C6	C8	C10
1016 Auburn Roadster, jumbo torpedo-two tone	36	48	60
1017 Coupe, jumbo torpedo-single color	20	30	40
1017 Coupe, jumbo torpedo-two tone	30	40	50
1018 Sedan, jumbo torpedo-single color	23	34	45
1019 Pickup Truck, jumbo torpedo-single color	23	34	45
1019 Pickup Truck, jumbo torpedo-two tone	23	34	45
1026 Cross Country Bus, jumbo torpedo, fully skirted	45	60	75
1027 Wrecker, jumbo torpedo, single color	23	34	45
1027 Wrecker, jumbo torpedo, two tone	36	48	60
1040 Fire Engine, hook and ladder	35	50	70
1041 Fire Engine, hose Car	35	55	75
1042 Fire Engine, insurance patrol w/single ladder and rear fireman	38	56	75
1042 Fire Engine, insurance patrol, open end	30	45	60
1043 No. 111 Ford Sedan and Small House Trailer	51	68	85
1044 Roamer House Trailer, w/door and tin bottom	297	396	495
1045 Greyhound Deluxe Bus, open front fenders and tin bottom	55	83	110

	C6	C8	C10
1045 Greyhound Deluxe Bus, open front fenders	35	50	70
1046 Station Wagon	43	64	85
4528 Limousine	27	36	45
4570 Ford, Model T, Open Tourer	33	50	65
4610 Ford Model T Pickup Truck	30	50	70
4629 (Yellow Cab) Sedan	19	26	32
4630 (Federal) Grocery Delivery Van	66	88	110
4631 (Federal) Bakery Delivery Van	75	100	125
4632 (Federal) Market Delivery Van	66	88	110
4633 (Federal) Laundry Delivery Van	66	88	110
4634 (Federal) Milk Delivery Van	51	68	85
4634 Army Supply Truck	45	60	75
4635 (Federal) Florist Delivery Van	165	220	275

	C6	C8	C10
4635 Armored Car	33	49	65
4636 Buick Coupe	23	34	45
4638 Mack Stake Truck	30	40	50
4639 Mack Coal Truck	30	40	50
4640 Mack Tank Truck	30	40	50
4641 Buick Touring Car	28	42	55
4642 Long Range Cannon	18	24	30
4643 Mack Anti-Aircraft Gun	25	38	50
4644 Mack Searchlight Truck	27	41	55
4645 Mack US Mail - Airmail Service	57	76	95
4646 Caterpillar tractor, original treads only	39	52	65
4647 Renault tank, original treads only	23	34	45
4648 Steamroller	99	132	165
4651 Fageol safety coach	28	38	48
4652 Fire Engine, hook and ladder	45	60	75
4653 Fire Engine, water tower	51	68	85
4654 Farm Tractor	48	64	80
4654 Farm Tractor for Army Field Battery Set, No. 5071	58	86	115
4655 Ford, Model A Coupe	27	36	45
4656 Buick Coupe in tinplate garage	60	90	150
4657 Buick Sedan in tinplate garage	60	90	150
4658 Mack Insurance Patrol, in tinplate garage	156	208	260

Left to right: Tootsietoy Station Wagon, No. 1046, 1940; reissued postwar Station Wagon. Photo from John Gibson.

Tootsietoy Ford Model T, Open Tourer. Photo from David Richter.

Tootsietoy Florist Delivery Van, No. 4635, 1924. Photo from John Gibson.

Tootsietoy Federal Milk Delivery Vans.

A pair of prewar Tootsietoy Ford Model A Coupes.

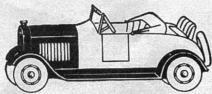

6-01 Roadster

This colorful assortment of popular Roadsters immediately recommends this package of twelve pieces, consisting of three Buicks, with blue chassis and yellow body; three Cadillacs, with grey chassis and blue body; three Oldsmobiles, with red chassis and grey body; three Chevrolets with yellow chassis and red body.

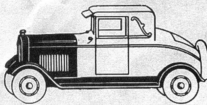

6-02 Coupe

Stylish and substantial Coupes are truly portrayed in this package of twelve. It is made up of three Cadillacs, three Buicks, three Chevrolets, and three Oldsmobiles. (See Roadster for color combinations.)

6-03 Brougham

See how perfectly the pleasing contours of the Brougham are reproduced in this package of twelve. The assortment has three Buicks, three Cadillacs, three Oldsmobiles, and three Chevrolets. (See Roadster for color combinations.)

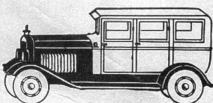

6-04 Sedan

The baby Sedan with all its fine appointments is displayed in this mixed box of three Buicks, three Cadillacs, three Oldsmobiles, and three Chevrolets. (See Roadster for color combinations.)

6-05 Touring Car

A box of surprising brilliance is this package of twelve Touring Cars with three Buicks, three Cadillacs, three Oldsmobiles, and three Chevrolets. (See Roadster for color combinations.)

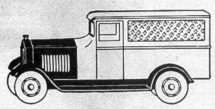

6-06 Delivery Truck

A pleasure and a study are the details of harmony and perfect reproduction combined in this box of twelve Delivery Trucks. Three Buicks, three Cadillacs, three Chevrolets, three Oldsmobiles. (See Roadster for color combinations.)

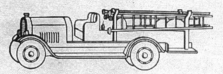

No. 4652—Hook and Ladder

Three detachable gilt ladders are set on a blue body, which in turn is mounted on a red chassis with gilt disc wheels. Weight, 25 pounds to the gross. Packed one dozen to the box.

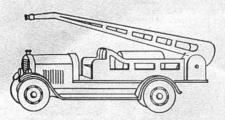

No. 4653—Water Tower

This attractive toy is completed with yellow body, red adjustable tower mounted on red chassis with gilt disc wheels. Length, three and seven-eighths inches; weight, twenty-seven pounds to the gross. Packed one dozen to the box.

A catalog ad depicting various Tootsietoy vehicles.

Tootsietoy Mack A&P Trailer Truck, No. 4670, 1929. Photo from John Gibson.

Tootsietoy Moon Mullins Police Wagon, No. 5104, non-articulated, from the 1932 Funnies series. Photo from John Gibson.

Tootsietoy Overland Bus Lines, No. 4680.

Tootsietoy Kayo Ice Wagon, No. 5105, articulated version, from 1932 Tootsietoy Funnies Series. Photo from John Gibson.

	C6	C8	C10
4665 Ford Model A Sedan	20	30	40
4666 Bluebird I Daytona Record Car	36	48	60
4670 Mack Tractor and two Semi-trailers, "A&P," "American Express"..	180	240	300
4680 Overland Bus Lines.................	54	72	90
5101 Andy Gump Roadster, standard......................................	175	265	350
5101 Andy Gump Roadster, articulated	225	340	450
5102 Uncle Walt Roadster, standard	175	265	350
5102 Uncle Walt Roadster, articulated	225	340	450
5103 Smitty Motorcycle, articulated .	225	340	450
5103 Smitty Motorcycle, standard....	175	265	350
5104 Moon Mullins Police Wagon, articulated	225	340	450
5104 Moon Mullins Police Wagon, standard......................................	175	265	350
5105 Kayo Ice Wagon, standard......	150	225	300
5105 Kayo Ice Wagon, articulated ...	240	320	400
5106 Uncle Willie Rowboat, standard......................................	135	210	275
5106 Uncle Willie Rowboat, articulated	240	320	400
6001 Buick Roadster, GM series	45	60	75
6002 Buick Coupe, GM series	45	60	75
6003 Buick Brougham, GM series ...	45	60	75

	C6	C8	C10
6004 Buick Sedan, GM series	45	60	75
6005 Buick Touring Car, GM series .	66	88	110
6006 Buick Screenside Delivery Truck, GM series	60	80	100
6015 Lincoln Zephyr, wind-up..........	450	600	750
6015 Lincoln Zephyr, plain version ..	270	360	450
6016 Lincoln Wrecker, plain version	450	600	750
6016 Lincoln Wrecker, wind-up........	570	760	950
6-01 No Name Roadster, GM series.	72	96	120
6-02 No Name Coupe, GM series....	72	96	120
6-03 No Name Brougham, GM series	72	96	120
6-04 No Name Sedan, GM series....	72	96	120
6-05 No Name Touring Car, GM series	93	124	155
6-06 No Name Screenside Delivery Truck, GM series	90	120	150
6101 Cadillac Roadster, GM series ..	57	76	95

	C6	C8	C10
6102 Cadillac Coupe, GM series	57	76	95
6103 Cadillac Brougham, GM series	57	76	95
6104 Cadillac Sedan, GM series......	57	76	95
6105 Cadillac Touring Car, GM series	78	104	130
6106 Cadillac Screenside Delivery Truck, GM series	66	88	110
6201 Chevrolet Roadster, GM series	57	76	95

Tootsietoy No Name Touring Car, No. 6-05, 1933, GM series.

Tootsietoy No Name Screenside Delivery Truck, No. 6-06, GM series. Photo from John Gibson.

Tootsietoy Cadillac Touring Car, No. 6105, GM series. Photo from John Gibson.

	C6	C8	C10
6202 Chevrolet Coupe, GM series...	57	76	95
6203 Chevrolet Brougham, GM series	57	76	95
6204 Chevrolet Sedan, GM series...	57	76	95
6205 Chevrolet Touring Car, GM series	78	104	130
6206 Chevrolet Screenside Delivery Truck, GM series	66	88	110
6301 Oldsmobile Roadster, GM series	57	76	95
6302 Oldsmobile Coupe, GM series	57	76	95
6303 Oldsmobile Brougham, GM series	57	76	95
6304 Oldsmobile Sedan, GM series	57	76	95
6305 Oldsmobile Touring Car, GM series	78	104	130
6306 Oldsmobile Screenside Delivery Truck, GM series	66	88	110
6665 Ford Model A Sedan	25	38	50

Postwar

	C6	C8	C10
1040 Hook and Ladder, 4" long	51	68	85
1041 Hose Car, 4" long...................	51	68	85
1931 Ford B Hot Rod, 3"..................	8	11	15
1940 Ford Special Deluxe Convertible, 6" long	28	41	55
1940 Ford V8 Hot Rod, 6" long	18	26	35
1941 Chrysler Windsor Convertible, 4" long...	14	21	28
1941 Chrysler Windsor Convertible, 4" long...	14	21	28
1941 International K1 Panel Truck, 4" long...	20	30	40
1941 White Army Half Track, 4" long	18	26	35
1942 Chrysler Thunderbolt Experimental Roadster, 6" long ...	23	34	45
1946 International K11 Oil Tanker, 6" long...	18	26	35
1947 Chevrolet Coupe, 4" long	13	19	25
1947 Futuristic-Looking Pickup Truck, commonly called Hudson..	37	56	75
1947 Jeepster, 3" long	9	14	18

Tootsietoy Chrysler Thunderbolt experimental roadsters. Photo from Gerald F. Slack.

Tootsietoy 1947 Futuristic-looking Pickup Truck, commonly called the Hudson, sold only in boxed sets. Photo from John Gibson.

Tootsietoy Pontiac Safari Station Wagon, 9".

Tootsietoy 1948 Buick Super Estate Wagon, open grille, postwar. Photo from John Gibson.

	C6	C8	C10
1947 Kaiser Sedan, 6" long	20	30	40
1947 Mack L Line Closed Side Stake, 6" long	20	30	40
1947 Mack L Line Dump Truck, 6" long	18	26	35
1947 Mack L Line Fire (ladder) Trailer, 6" long	43	64	85
1947 Mack L Line Fire Pumper, 6" long	43	64	85
1947 Mack L Line Log Truck, 6" long	43	64	85
1947 Mack L Line Moving Van, 6" long	25	38	50
1947 Mack L Line Stake Trailer, 6" long	63	94	125
1947 Mack L Line Tootsietoys Coast to Coast, 6" long	43	64	85
1947 Mack L Line Tow Truck, 6" long	20	30	40
1947 Offenhauser Hill Climber Racer, 3" long	9	13	18
1947 Studebaker Champion, five-window coupe, 3" long	39	52	65
1948 Buick Estate Wagon, yellow and maroon w/black wheels, 6" long	20	30	50
1948 GMC 3751 Greyhound Bus, 6" long	23	34	45

	C6	C8	C10
1949 Buick Roadmaster, four-door sedan, 6" long	25	38	50
1949 Ford Custom, four-door sedan, 3" long	11	16	22
1949 Ford Custom Convertible, 3" long	11	16	22
1949 Ford F6 Oil Tanker, 4" long	10	15	20
1949 Ford F6 Oil Tanker, 6" long	30	45	60
1949 Ford F6 Stake Truck (pickup), 4" long	13	19	25
1949 Ford Ft Pickup, 3" long	8	11	15
1949 Mercury Fire Chief Car, 4" long	14	21	28
1949 Mercury Sedan, four-door, 4" long	13	19	25
1949 Oldsmobile 88 Convertible, 4" long	15	23	30
1950 Chevrolet Ambulance, 4" long	13	19	25
1950 Chevrolet Deluxe Panel Truck, 3" long	10	15	20
1950 Chevrolet Deluxe Panel Truck, 4" long	13	19	25
1950 Chevrolet Fleetline, two-door fastback; sedan, 3" long	10	15	20
1950 Chrysler Windsor Convertible, 6" long	66	88	110
1950 Chrysler Windsor Convertible, 6" long	66	88	110
1950 Dodge Pickup Truck, 4" long	13	19	25
1950 Jeep CJ3, Army version, 4" long	13	19	25
1950 Jeep CJ3, Army version, 3" long	8	11	15
1950 Jeep CJ3, Civilian version, 3" long	8	11	15
1950 Jeep CJ3, Civilian version, 4" long	13	19	25
1950 Plymouth Special Deluxe, four-door sedan, 3" long	8	11	15
1950 Pontiac Chieftan Deluxe Coupe Sedan, 4" long	13	19	25

	C6	C8	C10
1950 Pontiac Chieftan Fire Chief Coupe Sedan, 4" long	18	26	35
1950 Twin Coach Bus, 3" long	23	34	45
1951 Buick LeSabre Experimental Roadster, 6" long	23	34	45
1952 Ford Mainline, four-door sedan, 3" long	8	11	15
1952 Lincoln Capri, two-door hardtop, 6" long	18	26	35
1952 Mercury Custom Sedan, four-door, 4" long	13	19	25
1953 Chrysler New Yorker, four-door sedan, 6" long	18	26	35
1953 Chrysler New Yorker, four-door sedan, 6" long	30	40	50
1954 American LaFrance Pumper, 3" long	10	15	20
1954 Buick Century Estate Wagon, 6" long	27	36	45
1954 Ford Ranch Wagon, 4" long	13	19	25
1954 Ford Ranch Wagon, 3" long	8	11	15
1954 Jaguar XK120 Roadster, 3" long	10	15	20
1954 MG TF Roadster, 3" long	10	15	20
1954 MG TF Roadster, 6" long	21	32	42
1954 Nash Metropolitan Convertible, 3" long	75	100	125
1954-55 Corvette Roadster, 4" long.	13	19	25
1955 Austin Healy 100-6, unassembled kit, 6" long	150	225	300
1955 Chevrolet BelAir, four-door sedan, 3" long	10	15	20
1955 Ford Customline V8, two-door sedan, 3 " long	11	16	22
1955 Ford F600 Stake Truck w/tin cover, 6" long	60	90	120
1955 International RC180, w/grain trailer	30	50	65
1955 International RC180, w/oil tanker, no decals	30	50	65
1955 International RC180, 6" long w/rocket launcher, Army version..	120	180	200
1955 International RC180, w/moving van	30	50	65
1955 International RC180, w/boat transport	30	45	60
1955 International RC180, w/car transport	30	45	60
1955 International RC180, w/gooseneck trailer	25	38	50
1955 Mack B Line Cement Mixer, 6" long	20	30	40

	C6	C8	C10
1955 Mack B Line Hook & Ladder, 6" long	38	56	75
1955 Mack B Line Log Trailer, 6" long	43	64	85
1955 Mack B Line Moving Van, w/o doors, 6" long	60	80	100
1955 Mack B Line Moving Van, w/doors, 6" long	90	120	150
1955 Mack B Line Oil Tanker, 6" long	23	34	45
1955 Mack B Line Open Stake Truck, 6" long	63	94	125
1955 Mercedes 300SL Gullwing (doors intact), 9" long	150	225	300
1955 Oldsmobile 98 Holiday, four-door hardtop, Army version, 4" long	13	19	25
1955 Oldsmobile 98 Holiday, two-door hardtop, 4" long	13	19	25
1955 Pontiac Safari Station Wagon, No. 895, 9" long	180	240	300
1955 Thunderbird Coupe, 3" long	8	11	15
1955 Thunderbird Coupe, 4" long	18	24	30
1956 Austin Healy 100-6, four-passenger roadster, 6" long	30	40	50
1956 Caterpillar Roadscraper, 6" long	18	26	35
1956 Chevrolet Cameo Pickup, 4" long	13	19	25
1956 Dodge D100 Panel Truck, 6" long	20	30	40
1956 Ferrari Racer, 6" long	28	41	55
1956 Ford F600 Army Gun Truck, 6" long	18	26	35
1956 Ford Farm Tractor, 6" long	25	38	50
1956 Jaguar XK140 Coupe, 6" long.	18	26	35
1956 Lancia Racer, 6" long	38	56	75
1956 Mercedes 190SL, 6" long	18	26	35
1956 Packard Patrician, four-door sedan, 6" long	18	26	35
1956 Porsche Spyder Roadster, 6" long	18	26	35
1956 Triumph TR3 Roadster, 3" long	9	14	18
1957 Ford F100 Styleside Pick-up w/o rear window, 3" long	8	11	15
1957 Ford F100 Styleside Pickup w/rear window, 3" long	8	11	15
1957 Ford Fairlane 500 Convertible, 3" long	8	11	15
1957 Greyhound Sceni-Cruiser Bus, 6" long	23	34	45
1957 Jaguar type D, 3" long	8	11	15

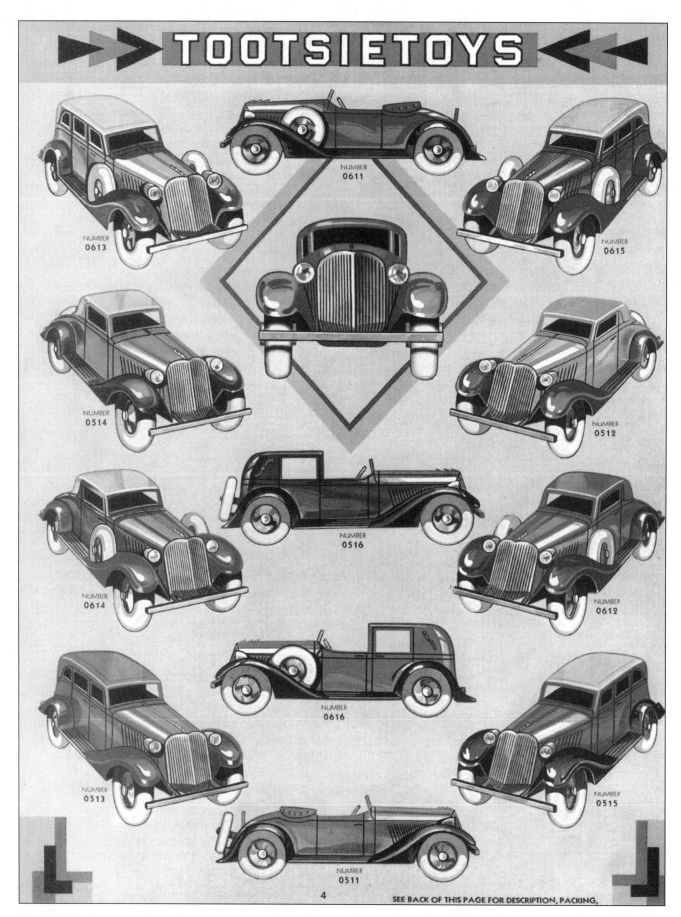

A reproduction of a Tootsietoy catalog page. The reprint is from 1989, the original ad ran in 1933.

	C6	C8	C10		C6	C8	C10
1957 Plymouth Belvedere, two-door hardtop, 3" long	8	11	15	1960 Chrysler Windsor Convertible, 4" long	13	19	25
1959 Chevrolet Semi Cab, w/three car transport	180	240	300	1960 Ford Falcon, two-door sedan, 3" long	8	11	15
1959 Chevrolet Semi Cab, w/Army flatbed	180	240	300	1960 Ford LTD, two-door hardtop, 4" long	13	19	25
1959 Chevrolet Semi Cab, w/three boat trailer	180	240	300	1960 International Metro Step Van, 6" long	126	168	210
1959 Chevrolet Semi Cab, w/dean van lines	180	240	300	1960 Jeep CJ5, Army version, 6" long	18	26	35
1959 Chevrolet Semi Cab, w/hook and ladder	180	240	300	1960 Jeep CJ5, Civilian version, 6" long	18	26	35
1959 Chevrolet Semi Cab, w/mobile trailer	180	240	300	1960 Jeep CJ5, Snowplow version, 6" long	38	56	75
1959 Chevrolet Semi Cab, w/log trailer	180	240	300	1960 Rambler Super Cross Country Station Wagon, 4" long	15	23	30
1959 Chevrolet Semi Cab only	105	140	175	1960 Studebaker Lark Convertible, 3" long	8	11	15
1959 Oldsmobile Dynamic 88 Convertible, 6" long	13	19	25	1960 Volkswagen Beetle, 6" long	27	36	45
1959 Pontiac Star Chief, four-door sedan, 4" long	13	19	25	1960 Volkswagen Beetle, 3" long	5	8	10
1960 Chevrolet El Camino, 6" long	18	26	35	1962 Ford Econoline Pickup, 6" long	15	23	30
1960 Chevrolet El Camino w/camper/boat, 6" long	50	75	100	Atomic Cannon/155mm Howitzer, 5-1/4" long	100	150	200
1960 Chrysler Windsor Convertible, 4" long	13	19	25	Metro Van, HO Series	21	28	35
				School Bus, HO series	10	15	20

TRU-SCALE INTERNATIONAL TRUCKS

Early in the 1940s, Joseph Carter founded the Carter Machine Company. Following World War II, Carter began to manufacture a line of toys. At first, Carter's toy line mainly consisted of International and John Deere farm tractors and implements. In the 1950s, Carter began his new line of 1:16-scale trucks under the Tru-Scale trademark. He felt that the International truck model would be the best choice, because International had been building trucks since 1907. The first Tru-Scale model was in the "S" series. This was the model then in production by the International Truck Company. The models marked with the "I.H." logo on the doors were sold by International Harvester outlets only. Any models marked "Tru-Scale" on the doors would have been sold through other retail outlets.

As the International Truck Co. redesigned its body style, Carter would follow this design with its comparable model. While thought of as a toy, one must consider the fine detail and workmanship that went into the Tru-Scale models. Its paint colors were correct, the grille styling and fender lines followed the real truck body lines, and they were very well detailed for a pressed-steel toy.

After the "S" series, the "A" series, "B" series, and "C" series trucks followed, in respective order. The models were made as pick-up trucks, service trucks with tool boxes, dump trucks with single or dual axle, semi-tractor trailer trucks with open or enclosed trailers, and also as grain trucks. The dump trucks came with either a hydraulic cylinder or manual control, depending on which model or year it was produced. The later "C" series came with plastic windows and whitewall tires with full hubcaps. Another feature was the finger-tip steering that worked by applying pressure on the front of the cab to steer the front wheels. Tru-Scale also produced some Private Label trucks, such as Ryerson Steel and Yale Trucking.

In 1971, Carter Tru-Scale sold the business to Ertl, which used parts of the Tru-Scale line for the new Ertl diecast International "Loadster" series. Ertl discontinue the Tru-Scale line of International trucks.

Contributor: Bob Smith, The Village Smith, 62 West Ave., Fairport, NY 14450-2102.

Tru-Scale International Service Truck, No. 1, green and white, circa 1953. Photo from Bob Smith.

Tru-Scale International Service Truck, No. 3, red and white, circa 1959. Photo from Bob Smith.

Top to bottom: Tru-Scale International Service Truck, No. 2, red and white, circa 1957; International Pickup Truck, No. 2A, light blue and white, circa 1953. Photo from Bob Smith.

Tru-Scale International Service Truck, No. 4, orange and white with white tires, 1960s. Photo from Bob Smith.

Tru-Scale International Pickup Truck, No. 5, red and cream, circa 1957. Photo from Bob Smith.

	C6	C8	C10
No. 01 Tru-Scale S series International Service Truck, green/white, c.1953	175	300	450
No. 2 Tru-Scale A series International Service Truck, red/white, c.1957	175	300	450
No. 2a Tru-Scale S series International Pickup Truck, light blue/white, c.1953	125	225	350
No. 3 Tru-Scale B series International Service Truck, red/white, c.1959	125	250	375
No. 4 Tru-Scale C series International Service Truck, orange/white, whitewall tires, windshield, c.1961	150	250	375

	C6	C8	C10
No. 5 Tru-Scale A series International Pickup Truck, red/cream, c.1957	150	250	375
No. 6 Tru-Scale C series International Pickup Truck, red/white, T/S decal, c.961	150	250	375

	C6	C8	C10
No. 6a Tru-Scale C series International Pickup Truck, blue/white, I/H decal, c.1961........	100	175	275
No. 7 Tru-Scale A series Internati6nal Grain Truck, blue, I/H decal, c.1957	150	250	375
No. 7a Tru-Scale B series International Grain Truck, green, I/H decal, c.1959.........................	100	175	275
No. 8 Tru-Scale S series International Ten-wheel Hydraulic Dump Truck, orange/white, c.1953	175	275	400
No. 9 Tru-Scale A series International Ten-wheel Hydraulic Dump Truck, orange, c.1957	175	275	400

	C6	C8	C10
No. 10 Tru-Scale B series Six-wheel Manual Dump Truck, orange, c.1959	150	250	375
No. 11 Tru-Scale B series Ten-wheel Hydraulic Dump Truck, orange, c.1959..........................	125	200	300
No. 12 Tru-Scale C series Six-wheel International Dump Truck, red/white, c.1961	125	200	300
No. 13 Tru-Scale B series Semi-Tractor and Van Trailer, red/white, c.1959	250	350	500
No. 14 Tru-Scale C series Semi-Tractor and Van Trailer, green/white, "Yale Trucking," c.1961	275	400	550
No. 15 Tru-Scale B series Semi-Tractor Hydraulic Dump Truck, dark red, c.1959..........................	125	225	350
No. 15a Tru-Scale C series Semi-Tractor Stake Truck, red/yellow, "Ryerson Steel, " c.1961	150	250	375
No. 16 Tru-Scale/Ertl, Ertl Int'l. Fleetstar Cab w/Tru-Scale Dump Trailer, white/green, c.1971, "Anderson Payload"....................	150	275	400
No. 16a Tru-Scale International C series Semi-Tractor Hydraulic Dump Truck, orange/yellow, c.1961	125	225	350

Top to bottom: Tru-Scale International Pickup Truck, No. 6, red and white, TS decal, circa 1961; International Pickup Truck, No. 6A, blue and white, circa 1961. Photo from Bob Smith.

Tru-Scale International Grain Truck, No. 7A, green, I/H decal, circa 1959. Photo from Bob Smith.

Tru-Scale International Grain Truck, No. 7, blue, I/H decal, circa 1957. Photo from Bob Smith.

Tru-Scale International Ten-wheel Hydraulic Dump Truck, No. 9, circa 1957. Photo from Bob Smith.

TURNER, JOHN C.

John Turner began in the trade working first with D.P. Clark and later with the Schieble Toy Co. He went off on his own in 1915. Within two years, he was producing a line of friction cars. In 1925, he was issued a patent for a new flywheel design made of metal disks, giving the appearance of large flat washers fitted together. The Turner flywheel is noticeably different from other manufacturers' mechanisms. Turner was located in Dayton and Wapkoneta, Ohio, from about 1915 into the 1940s.

Contributor: Bob Smith, The Village Smith, 62 West Ave., Fairport, NY 14450-2102.

	C6	C8	C10
Ahrens Fox Ladder Truck, 1920, 15" long	500	750	1080
Ahrens Fox Pumper, 16" long	650	1100	1600
Bulldog Mack Closed Cab Dump Truck, red and green steel, 23" long	325	600	875
Car Hauler	225	338	450
Crane Truck, 22" long	300	450	600
Delivery Van, 1920s, 12-1/2" long	900	1500	2200
Dump, 1930s, 17" long	200	300	400
Dump, 28" long, Dodge	175	250	325
Dump, C-Cab, 22" long	400	600	800
Dump, friction, early 1930s, 15-1/2" long	250	375	500
Dump, 26" long	250	375	500
Dump Truck, 1940s, 21"	200	350	475

	C6	C8	C10
Dump Truck, 1940s, 15-1/2"	200	325	450
Fire Engine Pumper, 15" long	750	1400	1800
Fire Engine Pumper, early, 26" long	550	800	1200
Garage, pressed steel, 21" long, 15" wide	150	225	300
Hook and Ladder, 15" long	225	338	450
Intercity Bus	500	750	1000
Ladder Truck, 1940s, 22"	250	375	500
Limousine	2000	3500	5000
Lincoln Sedan, 26" long	2000	3500	5000

Turner Crane Truck, 22". Photo from Calvin L. Chaussee.

Turner Ahrens Fox Ladder Truck, 15". Photo from Rodney A. Heesacker.

Turner Bulldog Mack, closed cab, 1930s, 23". Photo from John Taylor.

Turner Dump, friction, early 1930s, 15-1/2". Photo from Calvin L. Chaussee.

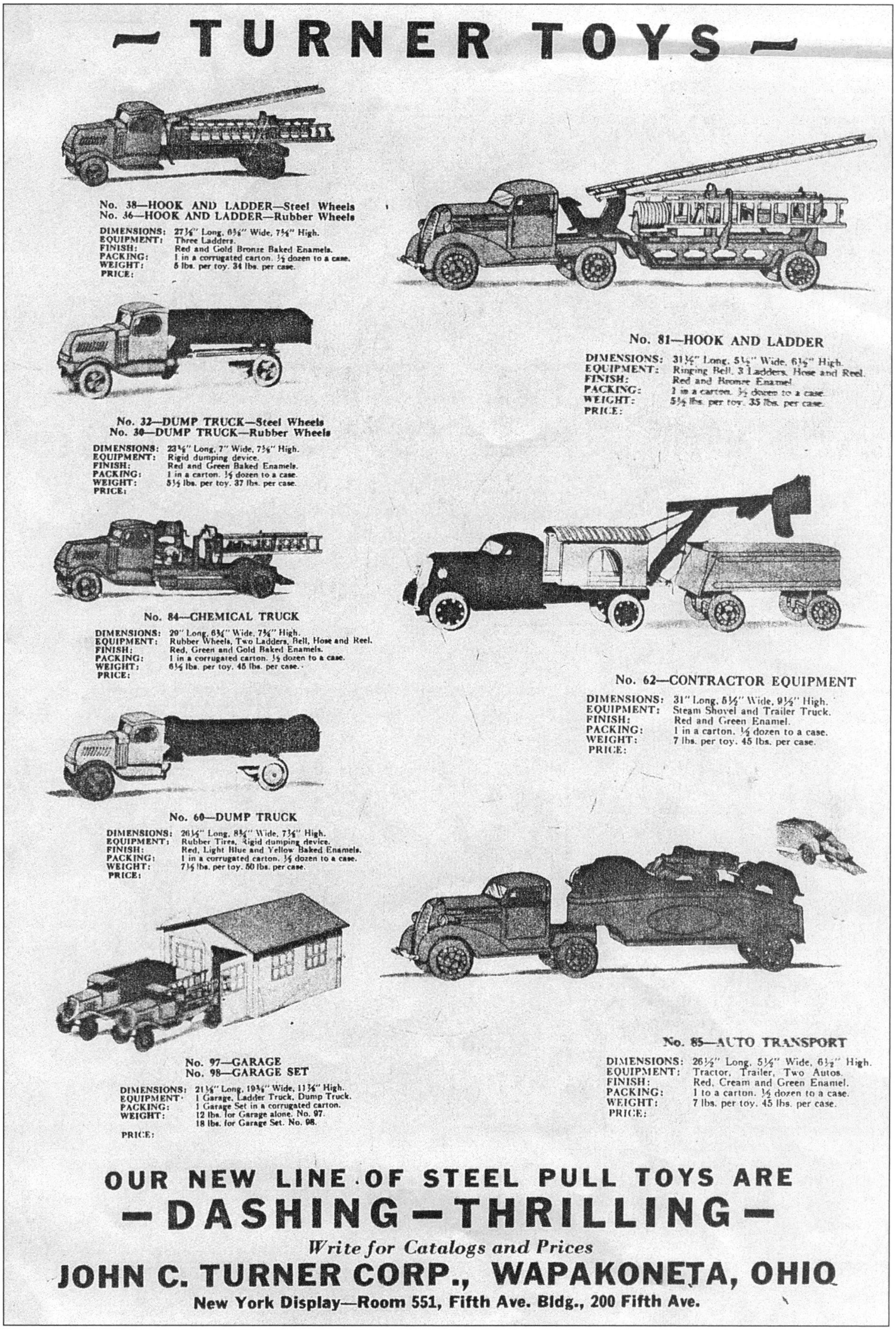
—TURNER TOYS—
No. 38—HOOK AND LADDER—Steel Wheels
No. 36—HOOK AND LADDER—Rubber Wheels
DIMENSIONS: 27⅛" Long, 6⅝" Wide, 7⅝" High.
EQUIPMENT: Three Ladders.
FINISH: Red and Gold Bronze Baked Enamels.
PACKING: 1 in a corrugated carton. ½ dozen to a case.
WEIGHT: 5 lbs. per toy. 34 lbs. per case.
PRICE:
No. 81—HOOK AND LADDER
DIMENSIONS: 31½" Long, 5½" Wide, 6½" High.
EQUIPMENT: Ringing Bell, 3 Ladders, Hose and Reel.
FINISH: Red and Bronze Enamel.
PACKING: 1 in a carton. ½ dozen to a case.
WEIGHT: 5½ lbs. per toy. 35 lbs. per case.
PRICE:
No. 32—DUMP TRUCK—Steel Wheels
No. 30—DUMP TRUCK—Rubber Wheels
DIMENSIONS: 23⅝" Long, 7" Wide, 7⅝" High.
EQUIPMENT: Rigid dumping device.
FINISH: Red and Green Baked Enamels.
PACKING: 1 in a carton. ½ dozen to a case.
WEIGHT: 5½ lbs. per toy. 37 lbs. per case.
PRICE:
No. 84—CHEMICAL TRUCK
DIMENSIONS: 20" Long, 6¾" Wide, 7¾" High.
EQUIPMENT: Rubber Wheels, Two Ladders, Bell, Hose and Reel.
FINISH: Red, Green and Gold Baked Enamels.
PACKING: 1 in a corrugated carton. ½ dozen to a case.
WEIGHT: 6½ lbs. per toy. 45 lbs. per case.
PRICE:
No. 62—CONTRACTOR EQUIPMENT
DIMENSIONS: 31" Long, 5½" Wide, 9½" High.
EQUIPMENT: Steam Shovel and Trailer Truck.
FINISH: Red and Green Enamel.
PACKING: 1 in a carton. ½ dozen to a case.
WEIGHT: 7 lbs. per toy. 45 lbs. per case.
PRICE:
No. 60—DUMP TRUCK
DIMENSIONS: 26½" Long, 8¾" Wide, 7⅞" High.
EQUIPMENT: Rubber Tires, Rigid dumping device.
FINISH: Red, Light Blue and Yellow Baked Enamels.
PACKING: 1 in a corrugated carton. ½ dozen to a case.
WEIGHT: 7½ lbs. per toy. 50 lbs. per case.
PRICE:
No. 97—GARAGE
No. 98—GARAGE SET
DIMENSIONS: 21⅛" Long, 19¾" Wide, 11¾" High.
EQUIPMENT: 1 Garage, Ladder Truck, Dump Truck.
PACKING: 1 Garage Set in a corrugated carton.
WEIGHT: 12 lbs. for Garage alone. No. 97.
18 lbs. for Garage Set. No. 98.
PRICE:
No. 85—AUTO TRANSPORT
DIMENSIONS: 26½" Long, 5½" Wide, 6½" High.
EQUIPMENT: Tractor, Trailer, Two Autos.
FINISH: Red, Cream and Green Enamel.
PACKING: 1 to a carton. ½ dozen to a case.
WEIGHT: 7 lbs. per toy. 45 lbs. per case.
PRICE:
OUR NEW LINE OF STEEL PULL TOYS ARE
—DASHING—THRILLING—
Write for Catalogs and Prices
JOHN C. TURNER CORP., WAPAKONETA, OHIO
New York Display—Room 551, Fifth Ave. Bldg., 200 Fifth Ave.

Turner trucks, as shown in a catalog advertisement.

No. 217—SPECIAL DELIVERY TRUCK with end gate, 24" long. Finest ever produced to retail at a dollar.

Just off the press . . . the Turner Catalog for 1937 showing 28 fast-selling numbers in actual colors. Your copy is ready. Write!

Colorful, Realistic Pull Toys to Retail Profitably at a Dollar

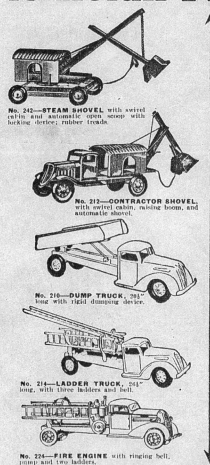

No. 242—STEAM SHOVEL with swivel cabin and automatic open scoop with locking device; rubber treads.

No. 212—CONTRACTOR SHOVEL, with swivel cabin, raising boom, and automatic shovel.

No. 210—DUMP TRUCK, 20½" long with rigid dumping device.

No. 214—LADDER TRUCK, 26½" long, with three ladders and bell.

No. 224—FIRE ENGINE with ringing bell, pump and two ladders.

Action alone won't sell toys in volume. It takes more than that! It takes what Turner Toys have this year in a higher degree than ever before . . . brilliant colors, realism, fine workmanship, a resale price within the reach of the mass pocket book. Plus a mark up that will be entirely satisfactory to you!

No better evidence of the qualities can be cited than the beautifully decorated numbers pictured on this page. They are made from the same quality and thickness of sheet steel as is used in the automotive industry. The joints are electrically welded. Edges are turned to protect hands and clothes. The lustrous enamel colors are **baked on**. And yet **you can sell them profitably for a dollar!**

Feature Turner Toys this year. They have the eye-appeal, dash and action it takes to insure quick turnover and big profits. Priced to retail from 60c to $4.00. Write today for quotations and our latest catalog showing all numbers in actual colors.

THE JOHN C. TURNER CORPORATION
Wapakoneta, Ohio   •   200 5th Ave., New York City

TURNER TOYS

Turner trucks, as shown in the August, 1937 issue of *Toys and Bicycles*.

Turner Dump, Dodge, 28". Photo from John Taylor.

Turner Overland bus, pressed steel. Photo from James Apthorpe.

Turner Dump, friction, early 1930s, 15-1/2". Photo from John Taylor.

Turner Speed Truck, 1930s, 22".

	C6	C8	C10
Mack Dump, 23" long	350	525	700
Mack Ladder Truck	250	375	500
Overland Bus, pressed steel	NPF	NPF	NPF
Packard (?) Roadster, 26" long, friction	900	1500	2200
Packard Racer, 1924, 26" long	800	1400	2000
Packard Roadster, 1920s, 16-1/2" long	600	950	1300
Panel Truck, early, 13" long	250	375	500

	C6	C8	C10
Speed Truck, C-cab, No. 40, c.1930, 22"	325	600	875
Speedster, 1920s, 17 " long	500	750	1000
Stake Truck, C-Cab, 22" long	188	282	375
Stake Truck, 1940s, 22"	175	275	400
Stake Truck, deco style	130	195	260
Steam Shovel, 14" long	68	102	135
Tow Truck, electric lights, 20" long	130	195	260
Water Truck, copper tank	150	225	300
Yellow Taxicab, flywheel drive, orange/black, four riders, c.1927, 9-3/4" long	312	468	625

UNIQUE ART MFG. CO.

Unique Art Mfg. Co. was in business from 1916, when it introduced its Merry Juggler and Charlie Chaplin. In 1931, it was located at Waverly and Peshine Avenues in Newark, New Jersey. Its president was Wm. Marbe, and there were twenty-eight employees. By 1934, there were 275 employees.

	C6	C8	C10
Artie the Clown in his Crazy Car	300	450	600
Capitol Hill Racer, w/2" tin racing car, 1930s, 17-1/2" long	100	150	200
Daredevil Motor Cop, 1940s, 8-1/2" long	500	750	1000
G.I Joe and His Jouncing Jeep, post WWII, 7" long	165	247	330

	C6	C8	C10
Krazy Kar, new in 1921	300	450	600
Lincoln Tunnel, moving vehicles, cop, 1935, 24" long	275	363	550
Motorcycle Cop, 1930s, 9" long	220	330	440
Rodeo Joe Crazy Car	158	235	315
Rollover Motorcycle Cop, 1935	200	300	400

Unique Art G.I. Joe and his Jouncing Jeep, 7". Photo from Mapes Auctioneers and Appraisers.

Unique Art Rodeo Joe Crazy Car.

VINDEX

Vindex was a division of National Sewing machine Co. of Belvidere, Illinois from 1928 to 1932. The sturdy, high-quality toys were more expensive than the competition which probably led to their demise during the Depression. Best known for its farm toys, Farm Mechanics Magazine often offered Vindex toys as premium. The Motorcycles, which feature the Henderson logo, ceased production after 1931.

Contributor: Kent M. Comstock, 532 Pleasant St., Ashland Ohio 44805, 419-289-3308, 800-443-TOYS.

	C6	C8	C10
Case Hay Loader, 9" long	3000	4500	5200
Case Manure Spreader, 12" long	500	1250	2000
Case Model L Tractor, 6-1/2" long	500	750	1030
Case Three Bottom Tractor Plow, 10-1/4" long	1000	2500	3700
Coast to Coast Bus, cast iron, c.1930, 12" long	1250	1875	2500
Combine	850	1500	2300
John Deere 3-bottom Tractor Plow, 9" long,	900	1400	2400
John Deere Manure Spreader, horse drawn	500	1100	1800
John Deere Thresher, 15" long	1500	2800	3900
John Deere Tractor, Model D, 6-1/2" long	950	1700	2600
John Deere Van Brunt Drill, 9-3/4" long	1000	1800	2900
Model L Tractor, 7" long	500	1000	1500
Oldsmobile Sedan	3000	5500	10,000

Vindex Hay Loader, Case, 9". Photo from Bill Bertoia Auctions.

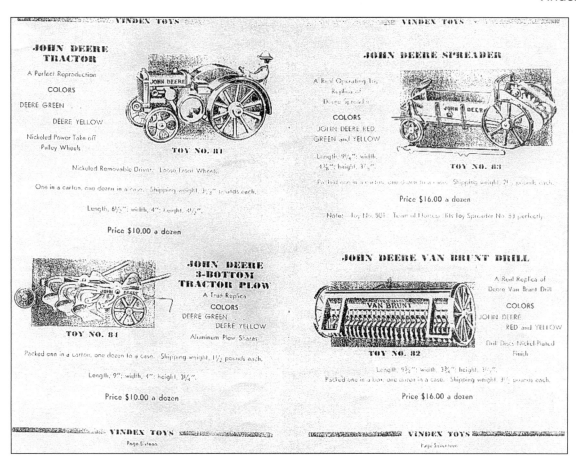

A look at some of the farm toys offered by Vindex.

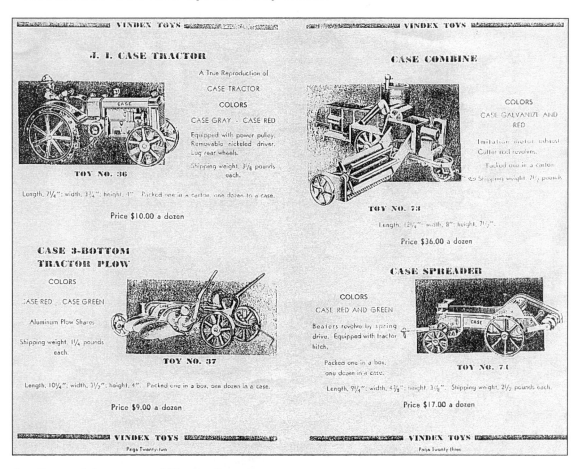

Another catalog page of Vindex farm toys.

Vindex Case Three-Bottom Tractor Plow, 9". Photo from Bill Bertoia Auctions.

Vindex Coast to Coast Bus, 1930s, 12". Photo from Bill Bertoia Auctions.

Vindex P&H power shovel, 12" and 17" when extended. Photo from Bill Bertoia Auctions.

Vindex Case 3-Bottom Tractor Plow, 10-1/4". Photo from Bill Bertoia Auctions.

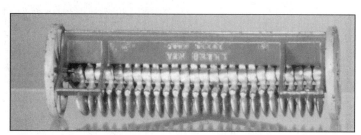

Vindex John Deere Van Brunt Drill, 9-3/4". Photo from Bill Bertoia Auctions.

Vindex Motorcycle with removable cop, red or green, 9". Photo from Kent M. Comstock.

	C6	C8	C10
P&H power shovel, cast-iron, wheels in Caterpillar base, handle revolves rig, 12" (17" extended)...	2500	5500	8000
Packard Club Sedan, 1929	10000	15000	26000
Pickup Truck, cast-iron, 7-1/2" long .	300	450	600
Pontiac Coupe, 7-3/4"	800	1400	1900
Racer, cast-iron, "2," 11-1/2" long....	900	1400	2100

Motorcycles

	C6	C8	C10
Motorcycle w/removable policeman, marked "Henderson," red or green, 9" long (VM001)	1000	1500	2500
Motorcycle w/Package Truck, "Henderson PDQ Delivery" w/removable blue rider, red or green, 9" long (VM003)	1800	2500	3500
Motorcycle w/sidecar, w/two removable policemen, red or green, marked "Henderson," 9" long (VM002)	1200	1800	3000

WANNATOY

Wannatoy was among the first toy makers off the starting block at the end of World War II. Of the millions of children born during the war, and the millions more who arrived soon afterward, a good percentage played with Wannatoys.

What seems to have been the company's first offering, the twenty-five-cent futuristic Coupe, was a hit toy for Christmas of 1945, selling a million units that season. With streamlined, Deco-influenced body and bubble top, the Coupe continued to sell well into the 1950s.

By 1950, the company had a modest but diverse line, sold through dimestores, that included toy semi-trailers, construction trucks, cars, airplanes, and ships. For at least one season the company offered toy assortments in see-through mesh Christmas stockings, ready to hang from the mantle.

Wannatoy was the trademark of Dillon Beck Manufacturing Co., based in New Jersey. Dillon Beck made toys of acetate, a hard plastic with a tendency to warp and lose form through time. Toward the end of its life as a toy maker, probably in the mid to late 1950s, the company produced soft plastic toys.

Contributor: Mark Rich, P.O. Box 971, Stevens Point, WI 54481-0971.

Trucks

	C6	C8	C10
Dump Truck, 1946 to mid 1950s, 3-1/2" long	6	9	12
Earth Hauler, 1949 to mid-1950s, 4-1/4" long	10	15	20
Hauling Truck, tractor-trailer, 1950s, 5" long	7	11	14
Ladder Truck, closed cab, white ladder, 1947 to mid-1950s, 6" long	11	16	22
Ladder Truck, open cab, white ladder, 1946 to mid-1950s, 4-1/2" long	9	14	18
Oil Tanker, tractor-trailer, 1950s, 5" long	7	11	14
Service Truck, mid-1950s, 5" long	11	16	22
Stake Truck, tractor-trailer, 1950s, 5" long	7	11	14
Steam Shovel, 1949 to mid 1950s, 4" long	12	17	25
Tank, revolving turret, 1950s, 3-3/4" long	10	15	10

	C6	C8	C10
Tractor, w/front scoop, 1948 to mid-1950s, 4" long	11	16	22
Van Truck, soft plastic, 5" long	4	6	8
Van Truck, tractor-trailer, 1950s, 5" long	7	11	14

Miscellaneous Vehicles

	C6	C8	C10
Cadillac, 9" long	8	12	16
Cement Mixer, 1948 to mid 1950s, 3-1/4" long	9	14	18
Convertible, 6" long	7	11	15
Coupe, futuristic, bubble top, 3-1/2"	11	16	22
Jaguar, mid-1950s, 6" long	10	15	20
Jet Auto, bubble top, 1948 to mid-1950s, 3-1/2" long	18	26	35
MG, clear windshield, mid-1950s, 4-12" long	11	16	22
Race Car, tail fin, late 1940s through early 1950s, 2-1/2" long	6	8	11
Sedan, early 1950s, 9-1/2" long	18	26	35
Woodie Jeep, 3-1/2" long	14	21	28

WILKINS TOY COMPANY

Wilkins, of Keene, New Hampshire, was begun by James S. Wilkins as the Triumph Wringer Company. But the tiny model Wilkins produced to promote his product proved so intriguing to prospective customers and their children, that requests for them poured in. The real thing was quickly forgotten as Wilkins turned to toy making. Its toys were generally cast iron and steel. The firm was acquired in 1894 by Kingsbury, which is still in business, though now as a tool and die maker.

Wilkins Aerial Ladder Truck, windup, 1910, 18". Photo from Phillips.

Wilkins Auto Surrey, 1911, light pressed steel with cast-iron wheels, windup, 7-1/2". Photo from Phillips.

Wilkins Automobile Racer, silver, light stamped steel, 10". Photo from Bob Smith.

	C6	C8	C10
Aerial Ladder Truck, wind-up, 1910, 18" long	300	450	600
Auto Surrey, wind-up, pressed steel, 1911, 7-1/2"	NPF	NPF	NPF
Automobile Racer, silver, clock-work motor, light stamped steel, 10" long, c.1905	750	1100	1700
Dray, driver, barrels, tiller	400	600	800
Fire Pumper, c.1924, driver, clock-work, 9-1/2" long	225	338	450
Fire Pumper, c.1924, driver, 11" long	550	850	1200

Wilkins Fire Station, 1911, opening doors, ringing bell, which released engine from house.

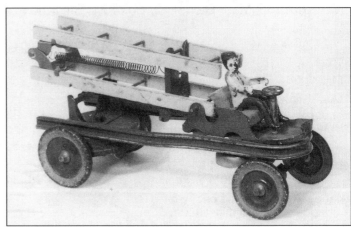

Wilkins Hook and Ladder Open Truck, steel, 9-1/4". Photo from Phillips.

	C6	C8	C10
Fire Station, c.1911, 13" long	NPF	NPF	NPF
Hook and Ladder, early, 26" long	NPF	NPF	NPF
Hook and Ladder, early, 14-1/2" long	600	900	1250
Hook and Ladder Open Truck, steel, wind-up motor, 9-1/4" long	175	250	325
Ladder Truck, wind-up, early, 15" long	450	695	925
Motor Truck Wagon, eighteen barrels, driver, 13" long	300	450	600
Panama Dump Truck, gray, light stamped steel, clock-work motor, c.1919, 14" long (also made as Kingsbury in 1923, different wheels, same value)	400	600	800
Runabout, 1911, w/driver	650	1000	1500
Tractor, 8-1/2" long	165	248	330
Tractor & Trailer, 17" long	225	338	450
Truck, open cab, very early, clockwork, 11" long,	450	675	900
Truck Wagon, w/cast-iron driver, clockwork, 190ss, 7"	NPF	NPF	NPF

WOLVERINE

Wolverine, of Pittsburgh, Pennsylvania was founded in 1903 by B.F. Bain. The company got its name from Bain's Michigan hometown. In later years, Wolverine became a subsidiary of Spang Industries. In 1970, it moved to Boonville, Arkansas. The "Sandy Andy," in all its variations, was probably Wolverine's most successful and famous toy.

	C6	C8	C10
Autolift, includes 2-1/2" tin car and four sections of track, 1930s, 10-1/4" high	150	225	300
Caterpillar Tractor w/Trailer, c.1930, wind-up, 20" long	305	458	610
Coke Coal Truck	88	132	175
Dump Truck, white, 12" long	55	82	110
Fire Dept. Truck	90	135	180
Loop-A-Loop, includes small car No. 30, 1930s, 19" long	125	188	250
Magic Auto Race, two cars, 1940s	50	150	200
Motor Race, two spinner, six cars	150	200	250
Motor Race, one spinner, four cars	50	100	150
Motorcycle Rabbit, 9-1/2" long, 1930s	90	135	180
Mystery Car, 13" long	138	205	275
Mystery Car and Trailer, press down to make car move, c.1953	218	327	435
Mystery Taxi, No. 33	200	300	400
Sky View Taxi	115	172	230
Speeding Bus, tin lithographed, driver and occupants, press down on rear to move, marked "5 Via Main St." and "19302," 14" long	105	158	210
Sunny Andy Tank, 14" long	130	195	260
Taxi, tin, 13" long	180	270	360

	C6	C8	C10
U.S Army Staff Car, 12" long	130	195	260
U.S.A Transport Army Truck	150	225	300
White Mustang Dump Truck, 14" long	75	112	150
White Stake Truck	102	153	205
Wolverine Express Bus, "Mystery Motor," 14" long	100	150	200

Wolverine Mysery Car and Trailer, 1950s. Photo from Calvin L. Chaussee.

Wolverine Mystery Taxi.

Wolverine Dump Truck, 12".

Wolverine U.S.A. Transport Army Truck. Photo from Ken Butler.

WYANDOTTE

Wyandotte Toys began in the fall of 1921, when William Schmidt and George Stallings decided that instead of making steel parts for the automobile industry, they would make toys. All Metal Products initially became well known for its large line of toy guns, rifles, and water pistols, but also would be increasingly known for pressed-steel vehicles and airplanes, mechanical toys and games, target sets, musical tops, doll carriages, and other sturdy toys for boys and girls.

Arthur Edwards bought into the growing company and became its president and general manager, running the company until his death in 1932. He was succeeded by his son C. Lee Edwards. By the mid 1930s, Wyandotte Toys was a major mid-price contender in the toy business. It was not unusual for Wyandotte to issue different sizes of the same toy. One might find the same stake truck in four sizes, ranging from 4-1/2 inches to fifteen inches. Additionally, the baked enamel toys came in many colors and color combinations, with special color runs for the Easter holiday. Lithographed toys also figured prominently, and with the Wyandotte Circus No. 503 truck and trailer of 1936, it reached the pinnacle of lithography.

During World War II, Wyandotte made clips for the M-1 rifle and was able to offer a reduced toy line of all-wood toys, but it would not be until after the war that it would get back to major toy production.

In April 1947 long-time employee William Wenner was elected president. In 1950, Wyandotte bought Hafner Manufacturing Company, with the thought of increasing market penetration by marketing its toy train line. In 1951, C. Lee Edwards, Mary Reberdy, and the estate of his late father, sold their interests to a new set of owners. The new directors hoped to reorganize the company successfully. It was during this time that one plant was moved to Martin's Ferry, Ohio, another to Pequa, Ohio, and one to the McCord Corporation for its gasket division.

The year 1955 saw both C. Lee Edwards and William Wenner retiring and selling their stock that was acquired as part of the 1951 reorganization. The company was also undergoing financial problems at the time. It has been reported that Louis Marx, of Marx Toys, to assume a larger market share for his own company, purchased some of the Wyandotte and Haffner toy lines and sent them to his Mexican operations. All Metal Products (Wyandotte Toys) filed for bankruptcy Nov. 6, 1956, thereby closing this chapter in toy history.

Values listed are estimates only and should be used ONLY as a guide Prices vary due to availability and condition of toys As to pricing, the West Coast is usually higher than the East Coast, while the Midwest is usually lower than the East Coast What you, the collector, offer to pay and eventually pay, is the true value. Offer or pay only what you feel a piece is worth.

Contributor: John Taylor, P.O. Box 63, Nolensville, TN 37135-0063. **Brian Seligman,** 11004 S. W. 37th Manor, Davie, Florida. Seligman was introduced to collecting by his mother, an antique dealer/collector in Vermont. He thought nothing was better than going to an old farm or estate auction. That is until 1989 when he picked up his first toy, a Steelcraft Road Roller. He was hooked from that day on. Originally, he started with large pressed steel pieces such as Buddy "L" and Keystone. As he was drawn deeper and deeper into the hobby and it became apparent that sending large toys from northern toy shows to Florida was getting expensive. He then began to pick up many of the more reasonably priced and colorful examples of pressed steel such as Marx, Girard and especially Wyandotte. What has transpired is a growing collection of Wyandotte vehicles, airplanes, games and other products. Seligman is trying to fill the spaces in his collection as well as acquiring as much research material to further his knowledge of the extent of Wyandotte toy production through the years. He has written a series of articles entitled "Why Not Wyandotte?" that has appeared in *U. S. Toy Collector Magazine*. Seligman is a General Contractor in South Florida, has a wife, three children and one dog.

Body Abbreviations

AS/FG: Air Speed / flat grille	**FN:** Flat Nose	**RC:** Rooster Comb
AS/CG: Air Speed / convex grille	**LS:** La Salle	**SW:** Shaded Windshield
AW: All Wood	**LS/T:** La Salle & Trailer	**SN:** Shark Nose
BT: Boat Tail Racer	**LN:** Long Nose	**SE:** Sleepy Eye
CO: Cab Over	**LN/T:** Long Nose & Trailer	**SB:** Soap Box Racer
CB: Checker Board	**OC:** Open Cab	**SP:** Speedster
CE: Construction Equipment:	**OE:** Open Eye	**SPC:** Sportsman's Convertible
CV: Convertible	**PV:** Panel Van	**SC:** Square Cab
CD: Cord	**PL:** Plastic	**TT:** Toy Town
CD/T: Cord & Trailer	**RR:** Rocket Racer	**WF:** Wide Face
FM: Farm Equipment	**RW:** Rounded Windshield	

Equipment Variations

brt: black rubber tire
bwmw: black & white metal wheels
bww: black wood wheels
e/l: electric lights
eww: embossed wood wheel
lmw: litho metal wheels
pmw: pressed steel wheels
rpw: red plastic wheels

trk: truck
wmw: white metal wheels
wpw: white plastic wheels
wrt: white rubber tires
www: white wood wheels
ymw: yellow metal wheels
yww: yellow wood wheels

Cars

	C6	C8	C10
Advertising Car, LN, www; red car w/display board on roof reads "Take a ride w/Sophie," "Sophie Tucker and her ROI; TAN show on the radio / C.B.S. Mon. Wed. Fri." on one side and "Roi-Tan Cigars / An auto a day is given away / a brand new 1939 Chevrolet" on the other side, 1936/40, 4-3/8" long....................	85	125	220
Air Speed Coupe, AS / FG, wrt; No. 309, 1934/37, 6" long..................	70	85	110

	C6	C8	C10
Air Speed Coupe, AS / CG, wrt; No. 309, 1934/37, 6" long...................	70	85	110
Air Speed Coupe and Trailer, AS / FG (and CG); wrt/brt, No. 341, 1934, 11-1/4" long	130	170	225
Ambulance, LN, bww; w/"Ambulance" and "Wyandotte Toys" decals, opening rear hatch, No. 340, 1936/38, 11-1/4" long....	65	85	125
Ambulance, LN, bww; marked "Ambulance" stamped on side, opening rear hatch, 1939, 11-1/4" long...	65	85	125
Ambulance, LN, brt; white plastic body / metal chassis, friction motor and siren, marked "Ambulance" and "Red Cross," stretcher, opening rear doors; No. 817, 1952/53, 9-1/2" long	35	50	120

Wyandotte Advertising Car, 1936/40, 4-3/8" long. Photo

Two examples of Wyandottes No. 341 Air Speed Coupe and Trailer. Photo from Brian Seligman.

Wyandotte Garage Set, plastic single door garage with two plastic cars, No. 4000, 1952, 2-3/4" x 2-1/2". Photo from Brian Seligman.

Wyandotte Ambulance, No. 340, 1936/38, 11-1/4" long. Photo from Brian Seligman.

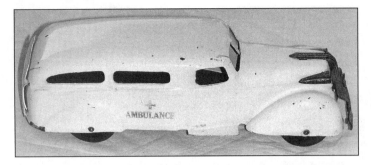

Wyandotte Ambulance, 1939, 11-1/4" long. Photo from Brian Seligman.

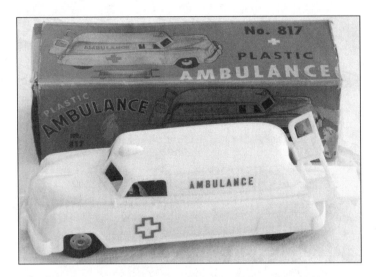

Wyandotte Ambulance with original box, No. 817, 1952/53, 9-1/2" long. Photo from Brian Seligman.

Wyandotte Ambulance, No. 224, 1939, 6-3/8" long. Photo from Brian Seligman.

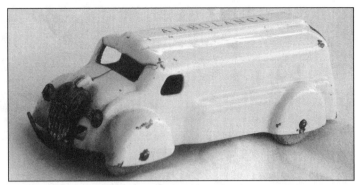

Wyandotte Ambulance, No. 379, 1938, 6-3/8" long. Photo from Brian Seligman.

Wyandotte Cadillac, 1952/54, 5-5/8" long. Photo from Brian Seligman.

Wyandotte Cadillac, No. 3100, 1955, 8-3/4" long. Photo from Brian Seligman.

	C6	C8	C10
Ambulance, LN, brt; friction, "Ambulance and Red Cross," stretcher, 1952, 6-1/2" long..........	70	85	105
Ambulance, FN, bww; side ports, inset front grille, No. 224, 1939, 6-3/8" long..................................	35	50	105
Ambulance, RC, wrt; four side ports, "Ambulance" stamped on top, surface mounted grille, No. 379, 1938, 6-3/8" long......................	40	65	110

	C6	C8	C10
Army Jeep, AW, bww; marked "Jeep," No. 368, 1942, 9" long.....	20	40	90
Cadillac, PL, pw; plastic, many colors, 1954, 3" long	30	50	95
Cadillac, PL, pw; plastic, many colors, used on auto transports, 1952/54, 5-5/8" long	30	50	95

	C6	C8	C10
Cadillac, "true scale," brt/white hubs; plastic, friction motor, many colors; No. 3100; 1955, 8-3/4" long	95	120	150
Convertible, SPC, brt; sportsman convertible, retractable top, woody look sides, license plate "WY650," No. 650 (No. 651 w/wind-up motor) 1947/48, 12" long	165	190	235
Convertible, CD, bww; "Fire Dept.," wind-up motor w/attached key, hood mounted brass bell, 1937, 13-3/8" long................................	125	300	475
Convertible, CD, brt; "Fire Dept.," brass bell, wind-up motor w/attached key, No. 384, 1939; 17-3/8" long................................	125	325	575
Convertible, CD, brt; "Fire Dept.," brass bell, Zephyr motor, No. 601, 1938/39, 17-1/4" long..........	100	300	525
Convertible, CD, brt; marked "Fire Dept.," Zephyr motor, hood mounted brass bell, 1938, 13-3/8" long	125	300	425

	C6	C8	C10
Convertible, CD, bww; 1938/39, 13-3/8" long	75	275	425
Convertible, SPC, brt; non-woody, plastic driver and windshield, attached key wind-up, license plate "WY 652," No. 652, 1947/48, 12" long........................	150	200	250
Convertible, CV, wrt/www; also part of the garage set (1938/40), No. 102, 1936/40; 4-3/8" long	10	45	65
Convertible, CD, brt on wood hubs; marked "Zephyr," pull back wind-up motor; No. 600, 1936/37, 13-3/8" long	125	350	550
Cord and Trailer Set, CD/T, bww; rear door opens in trailer, No. 363, 1938/39, 23-1/2" long	100	300	575
Coupe, two-door, SW, wrt; electric lights, 1933, 8-1/4" long	55	100	135
Coupe, two-door, SW, wrt/red hubs; no light; 1933, 8-1/4" long............	45	90	135

Wyandotte Convertible, 1947/48, 12" long. Photo from Brian Seligman.

Wyandotte Convertible, No. 652, 1947/48, 12" long. Photo from Brian Seligman.

Wyandotte Convertible, 1937, 13-3/8" long. Photo from Brian Seligman.

Two examples of Wyandotte's No. 102 Convertible, 1936/40, 4-3/8" long. Photo from Brian Seligman.

Wyandotte Cord and Trailer Set, No. 363, 1938/39, 23-1/2" long. Photo from Brian Seligman.

Wyandotte Coupe, two-door, 1933, 8-1/4" long. Photo from Brian Seligman.

Wyandotte Coupe, two-door, 1933, 8-1/4" long. Photo from Brian Seligman.

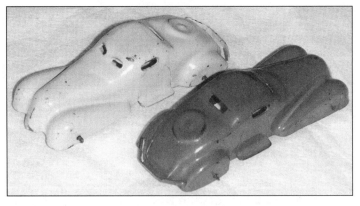

Two views of Wyandotte's No. 103 two-door coupe with yellow wood wheels from 1936/40. Photo from Brian Seligman.

Left to right: Wyandotte Coupes, two door with grille, No. 312, 1934/36, 4-1/2" long; Wyandotte Coupes, two door without grille, No. 312, 1934/36, 4-1/2" long. Photo from Brian Seligman.

Wyandotte Coupe, two-door, 1932, 4-7/8" long. Photo from Brian Seligman.

	C6	C8	C10
Coupe, two-door, LN; wrt or www; car also came w/two car garage set, No. 103, 1936/40; 4-3/8" long	10	45	75
Coupe, two-door, RW, wrt; w/out grille, trunk mounted spare tire; No. 312, 4-1/2" long, 1934/36	35	55	75
Coupe, two-door, RW, wrt; w/grille, trunk mounted spare tire, No. 312, 1934/36, 4-1/2" long	35	55	75

	C6	C8	C10
Coupe, two-door, SW, yww; 1932; 4-7/8" long	60	75	95
Coupe, two-door, RW, eww; circus type, 1934, 6-3/8" long	35	50	75
Coupe, two-door, RW, wrt; 1934, 6-3/8" long	35	50	75
Coupe, two-door, SW, yww; rumble seat, 1932, 8-1/4" long	55	95	135

	C6	C8	C10
Garage Set, metal lithographed double door garage w/a 4-3/8" coupe and convertible, marked "Two Car Garage," No. 501, 1938/39; 3-3/4" x 4-3/4"	50	75	115
Garage Set, metal lithographed single door garage, "Super Service," vehicles included varied, No. 754, 1952, 8-1/2" x 8-1/2"	50	75	115
Garage Set, plastic single door garage w/two 2-3/16" plastic cars, on back of each is imprinted; No. 4000, 1952, 2-3/4" x 2-1/2"	50	75	135
Garage Set, metal lithographed single door fire station garage w/one or two 6" fire trucks, "Toytown Fire Dept," No. 4003, 1952, 8" x 6"	50	75	115
La Salle (land cruiser), LS, wrt; No. 357, 1936/39, 15" long................	65	125	190

	C6	C8	C10
La Salle (land cruiser), LS, wrt; hood opens, electric lights, No. 385, 1939, 15" long.............................	75	130	210
La Salle (land cruiser), LS, brt or wd hubs; hood opens, no electric lights, 1939, 15" long	65	110	190
La Salle (land cruiser), LS, brt; key attached spring motor, No. 383, 1938, 15-3/4" long	75	150	190
La Salle w/Travel Trailer, LS/T, wrt; opening rear trailer door, No. 358, 1936/38, 26-1/2" long	145	275	525
Racer, boattail, BT, wrt; green/red, electric lights, No. 333, 1934, 8-5/8" long	60	105	155

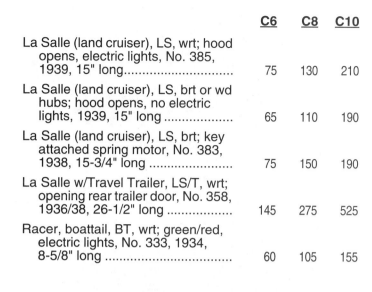

The front of Wyandotte's No. 501 Two-Car Garage Set. Photo from Brian Seligman.

Two examples of Wyandotte's Two-door roadster. Both are from 1934 and measure 6-3/8" long. Notice the circus wheels on the car on the right. Photo from Brian Seligman.

Wyandotte Coupe, two-door, rumble seat, 1932, 8-1/4" long. Photo from Brian Seligman.

The back of Wyandotte's No. 501 Two-car Garage Set. Photo from Brian Seligman.

The front of Wyandotte's No. 754 Super Service Garage Set. Photo from Brian Seligman.

The back of Wyandotte's No. 754 Super Service Garage Set. Photo from Brian Seligman.

Wyandotte Garage Set with plastic door and two 2-3/4" cars, No. 4000, 1952.

Wyandotte La Salle (land cruiser), No. 357, 1936/39, 15" long. Photo from Brian Seligman.

The front of Wyandotte's No. 4003 Toytown Fire Dept Garage Set. Photo from Brian Seligman.

The back of Wyandotte's No. 4003 Toytown Fire Dept Garage Set. Photo from Brian Seligman.

Wyandotte La Salle (land cruiser), 1939, 15" long. Photo from Brian Seligman.

Wyandotte La Salle with Travel Trailer, No. 358, 1936/38, 26-1/2" long. Photo from Brian Seligman.

Top to bottom: Wyandotte Racer, boattail, 10-1/4"; Racer, boattail, No. 333, 8-5/8"; Racer, boattail, No. 310, 5-7/8". Photo from Brian Seligman.

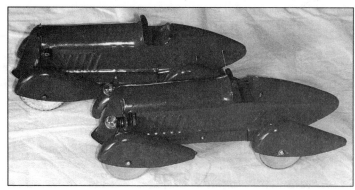

Top to bottom: Wyandotte Racer, boattail, white rubber tires, 8-5/8"; Racer, boattail, yellow wood wheels, 8-5/8". Photo from Brian Seligman.

Wyandotte Racer, Indy style, 7" long. Photo from Brian Seligman.

	C6	C8	C10
Racer, Indy style, brt; lithographed body w/attached head of driver, marked "Wyandotte" and "7," also "Jet Streak" version; 7" long	45	65	125
Rocket Racer, rr, wrt or bww; wood rear wheel, No. 319, 1935/36, 6-1/4" long	60	75	135
Sedan w/Travel Trailer, LN/T, wrt or bww; opening rear trailer door, No. 346, 1938, 11-3/4" long	60	140	225
Sedan, four door, CO, pmw; touring sedan (Nash style), No. 425, 1939, 11" long.............................	65	105	205
Sedan, four door, LN; wood wheels, 1938, 9-1/8" long	65	80	120
Sedan, four door, RW, wrt; 1934, 6-1/4" long	30	50	85
Sedan, four door, RC, wrt; electric lights; No. 334 (No. 339 w/o lights), 1934/35, 9" long	65	80	120

	C6	C8	C10
Racer, boattail, BT, wrt; green/red, No. 310, 1933/34, 5-7/8" long	40	60	110
Racer, boattail, BT, bww; red w/electric lights, 1934, 10-1/4" long	95	120	225
Racer, boattail, BT, yww; red w/electric lights, 1933; 8-5/8" long	75	105	195

	C6	C8	C10
Sedan, four door, CO, bpw; touring sedan (Nash style), No. 220, 1939/41, 6" long	30	60	95
Sedan, four door, LN, wrt; No. 316, 1938, 6" long	30	50	85
Sedan, four door, RC, wrt; No. 316, 1934/35; 6" long	30	50	80
Sedan, four door, SW, bww; sometimes included w/auto transport; 1934, 5" long	45	60	80
Sedan, four door, RW, wrt; w/grille, trunk mounted rear spare, No. 311, 1934/37, 4-1/2" long	35	60	95
Sedan, four door, RW, wrt; w/out grille, trunk mounted rear spare, No. 311, 1934/37, 4-1/2" long	35	60	95
Sedan, four door, PL; no tires, embossed at license plate is "yand," used on small car carriers, No. 311, 1950s, 2-1/4" long	35	50	70

	C6	C8	C10
Sedan, four door, LN, imw/brt; enclosed chassis; No. 344, 1938, 9" long	65	80	120
Sedan, four door, RW, eww; 1934, 6-1/4" long	30	50	85
Soap Box Derby Racer, SB; early red version w/red wd wheels and attached driver helmet, "Soap Box Derby" and "Thunderbird 226," 1941, 6" long	90	195	260
Soap Box Derby Racer, SB; red version w/red wd wheels and blue version w/black wd wheels, marked "Soap Box Derby" and "Thunderbird 226," No. 226, 1941, 6" long	75	150	195

Two versions of Wyandotte's No. 220 Sedan. Photo from Brian Seligman.

Two views of Wyandotte's No. 319 Rocket Racer. Photo from Brian Seligman.

Wyandotte Sedan with Travel Trailer, No. 346, 1938, 11-3/4" long. Photo from Brian Seligman.

Wyandotte Sedan, four door, No. 316, 1938, 6" long. Photo from Brian Seligman.

Wyandotte Sedan, four door, No. 425, 1939, 11" long. Photo from Brian Seligman.

Two versions of Wyandotte's No. 316, Sedan. Photo from Brian Seligman.

Left to right: Wyandotte Sedan, four door, without grille, No. 311, 4-1/2"; Sedan, four door, with grille, No. 311, 4-1/2". Photo from Brian Seligman.

Left to right: Wyandotte Sedan, four door, embossed wooden wheels, 1934, 6-1/4"; Wyandotte Sedan, four door, white rubber tires, 1934, 6-1/4". Photo from Brian Seligman.

Two versions of Wyandotte's No. 266 Soap Box Derby Racer. The car on the left has red tires, while the model on the right has black. Photo from Brian Seligman.

Two versions of Wyandotte's No. 334 four-door Sedan. Photo from Brian Seligman.

Wyandotte Sedan, four door, No. 311, 1934/37, 4-1/2" long. Photo from Brian Seligman.

Wyandotte Sedan, four door, No. 344, 1938, 9" long. Photo from Brian Seligman.

Wyandotte Sedan, four door, plastic, No. 311, 1950s, 2-1/4" long. Photo from Brian Seligman.

Left to right: Wyandotte Speedster, No. 378, 6-3/4" long; Wyandotte Speedster, No. 603, 10"; Wyandotte Speedster, with top, 10". Photo from Brian Seligman.

Wyandotte Earth Mover, No. 1602, 1952/55, 20-1/2" long. Photo from Brian Seligman.

Wyandotte Toy Town, large scale, No. 1009, 1941, 21" long. Photo from Brian Seligman.

	C6	C8	C10
Speedster, SP, bww; w/out lithographed driver and passenger, No. 378, 1937/38, 6-3/4" long	40	80	150
Speedster, SP, bww; pull back spring motor, No. 603, 1937, 10" long	60	100	165
Speedster, SP, bww; pull back spring motor, cord-like roof over cockpit, 1938, 10" long	65	105	175
Speedster, SP, bww; w/lithographed driver and passenger, No. 378, 1937/38, 6-3/4" long	50	100	200
Town Car (mistaken for Wyandotte but is Marx)			
Toy Town, large scale, TT, brt on wood hubs; delivery wagon, "Toytown Delivery," license plate "WY___," lithograph of driver in window, rear doors open, No. 1008, 1941, 21" long	70	125	225

	C6	C8	C10
Toy Town, large scale, TT; brt on wood hubs; w/out roof rack, estate station wagon, marked "Toytown Estate," w/woodie-like sides, license plate "WY1007," lithograph of family in widows, rear doors open, No. 1007, 1941, 21" long	70	175	275
Toy Town, large scale, TT, brt on wood hubs; w/roof rack, estate station wagon, marked "Toytown Estate," w/woodie-like sides, license plate "WY1009," lithograph of family in widows, rear doors open, No. 1009, 1941, 21" long	70	200	325
Toy Town, large scale, TT, brt on wood hubs; grocer wagon marked "Meats and Groceries," license plate "WY1008"; lithograph of driver in window, rear doors open, No. 1008, 1941, 21" long	70	125	225

Construction

	C6	C8	C10
Caterpilar Grader, CE; all plastic construction except for metal blade, black and yellow, 1952, 12" long	50	70	110
Caterpilar Scraper, CE; all plastic construction except for metal blade, black and yellow, 1952, 12" long	50	70	110
Caterpilar Wagon, CE; all plastic construction, black and yellow, 1952; 12" long	50	70	110
Earth Mover, CE, brt; orange, "Heavy Duty," operable rear dump, plastic engine and smoke stack, "Highway Engineers," No. 1602, 1952/55, 20-1/2" long	55	85	105
Earth Mover, CE, brt; orange, "Heavy Duty," operable rear dump, front scoop, plastic engine and smoke stack, "Highway Engineers," 1952/55, 20-1/2" long	55	85	105

	C6	C8	C10
Electric Conveyor, CE, brt; color?; No. 402, 1955, 14-1/2" long	40	65	190
Road Grader, CE; brt; orange, steerable front wheels and adjustable grading blade, "Power Grader"; No. 1603, 1952/55, 19" long	55	85	105
Road Roller, CE; plastic and tin, multi color, friction motor, "Construction," No. 905, 1952, 6-1/2" long..................................	20	40	85
Sand Loader and Dump Truck, CO/CB, brt; sand loader w/string operated dump hoist, "Wyandotte" on side of truck and "Wyandotte Construction Company" on side of sand loader, No. 401, 1954/56, 10-3/4" truck, 10-5/8" tall sand loader ..	85	125	195

	C6	C8	C10
Sand Loader and Hopper, CE bww; red and green super scoop shovel; No. 401, 7" high, 5-1/2" square; sand hopper No. 347; 1938; N/A; when 11-1/4" dump truck was added it was known as the "Highway Construction Set," No. 402, 5-1/2" high, 3-3/4" base, 20" reach	50	80	125
Steam Shovel, CE, brt; "Wyandotte Construction Company," also came w/lithographed body and "Sturdy Construction" on side, early 1950s, 7" x 4" body, 12" boom, 6 1/2" x 3-7/8" chassis	35	55	95
Truck Mounted Digging Combination, CO, brt; plastic cab w/lithographed grille and dash, steel chassis, clam shell bucket, "Sturdy Construction," No. 1012, 1952; 14-1/2" long	185	225	275

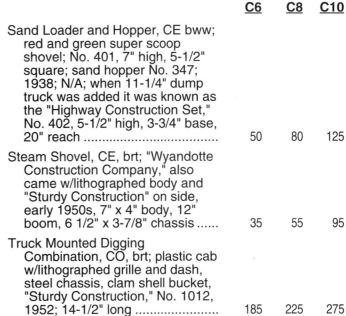

Wyandotte Road Grader, No. 1603, 1952/55, 19" long. Photo from Brian Seligman.

Wyandotte Sand Loader and Hopper, No. 402, 5-1/2" high, 3-3/4" base, 20" reach. Photo from Brian Seligman.

Wyandotte Sand Loader and Dump Truck, No. 401, 1954/56, 10-3/4" truck, 10-5/8" tall sand loader. Photo from Brian Seligman.

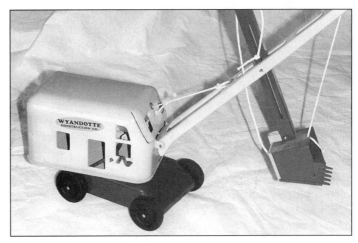

Wyandotte Steam Shovel, early 1950s, 7" x 4" body, 12" boom, 6 1/2" x 3-7/8" chassis. Photo from Brian Seligman.

Wyandotte Truck Mounted Digging Combination, 1952, 16-1/4" long. Photo from Brian Seligman.

Wyandotte Truck Mounted Digging Combination, No. 236, 1952; 5"long, 8-1/4" with boom. Photo from Brian Seligman.

Wyandotte Winch Truck, 1949/53, 23" long. Photo from Brian Seligman.

Wyandotte Winch Truck with Removable Steam Shovel, 1953, 19-1/2" long. Photo from Brian Seligman.

Wyandotte Winch Truck with Removable Steam Shovel, No. 1201, 1952, 22" long. Photo from Brian Seligman.

	C6	C8	C10
Truck Mounted Digging Combination, CO, brt (four rear tires); lithographed cab w/"Wyandotte" on side, lithographed crane body "Sturdy Construction Co," "Diesel," w/clamshell bucket, steel chassis "Wyandotte, Construction, Engineering" decal, 1952, 16-1/4" long	185	225	275
Truck Mounted Digging Combination, CE/PL, brt/dual rear; plastic, "Scooper," No. 236, 1952; 5" long, 8-1/4" w/boom	10	30	75
Winch Truck w/Removable Steam Shovel, WF, brt; "Wyandotte Construction Co." on side of removable crane, 1949/53, 23" long	85	105	145
Winch Truck w/Removable Steam Shovel, CO, brt; late 1940s/50, 7" long	65	80	100
Winch Truck w/Removable Steam Shovel, CO, brt; No. 236, 1952, 8-3/4" long	65	80	100

	C6	C8	C10
Winch Truck w/Removable Steam Shovel, CO, brt; all plastic; No. 238, 1952, 10" long	60	75	100
Winch Truck w/Removable Steam Shovel, CO, brt; steam shovel on wood wheels w/"Wyandotte Construction Co" decal; 1953; 19-1/2" long	80	100	145
Winch Truck w/Removable Steam Shovel, CO/OE, brt; steam shovel on tracks, No. 1201, 1952, 22" long	80	100	140

	C6	C8	C10
Winch Truck w/Removable Steam Shovel, CO, brt; plastic motor, rubber exhaust pipe, sliding rear ramp, removable crane, 1953, 22" long...	80	100	145
Winch Truck w/Removable Steam Shovel, OE, brt; on red plastic hubs, tractor and flatbed w/treaded steam shovel, tool box w/tools behind cab, 1954, 22-1/2" long..	50	75	145

Farm Equiptment

	C6	C8	C10
Farm Set, tractor w/stake trailer "Valley Farms Produce," harrow, spreader and coupler, 1955.........	NPF	NPF	NPF
Tractor, FM; plastic; brt; No. 603/602, 1954, 5" long.................	40	65	95

Wyandotte Winch Truck, 1953, 22" long. Photo from Brian Seligman.

Wyandotte Tractor, No. 603/602, 1954, 5" long. Photo from Brian Seligman.

Trucks

	C6	C8	C10
Army Truck, LN; brt; marked "Army Supply Corp.," canvas cloth top; No. 433, 1941, 11-3/4" long........	45	75	125
Army Truck, LN, brt; "Army Engineer Corp. No. 42," canvas cloth top; 1941; 17-1/2" long	60	90	140
Army Truck, LN, brt; "Army Engineers Corps," canvas cloth top; No. 1006; 1940-41, 21" long.	65	95	155
Army Truck, bww; marked "Army Supply," all wood construction; No. 214; 1941/42; 9-1/2" long......	35	55	95
Auto Transport, CO, brt; plastic cab, marked "Wyandotte" or "Auto Transport" on the side, 1952, 10-1/4" long	50	70	145
Auto Transport, CO, SC, brt; w/four "Cadillacs; No. 611; 1955; 42" long..	45	70	125
Auto Transport, OE; brt w/red plastic hubs; lithographed cab w/rear toolbox and five tools, four cars w/ramp, marked "Car o van," 1954, 23" long.............................	50	65	125
Auto Transport, CO, brt; lithographed cab and trailer, marked "Car a van Lines" and "Automotive Transport"; three 5-1/2" Cadillacs, loading ramp, 1956/57, 22-1/2" long	45	70	115

Wyandotte Army Truck, 1941, 17-1/2" long. Photo from Brian Seligman.

Wyandotte Auto Transport, 1956/57, 22-1/2" long. Photo from Brian Seligman.

Wyandotte Auto Transport, 1932, 21-5/8" long. Photo from Brian Seligman.

Wyandotte Auto Transport, 1940s/50s, 9-1/2" long. Photo from Brian Seligman.

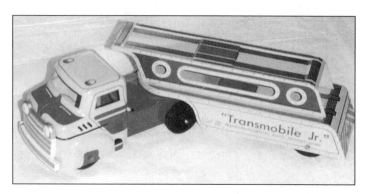

Wyandotte Auto Transport, No. 130, 1953, 12-5/8" long. Photo from Brian Seligman.

Wyandotte Auto Transport, No. 130, 1953, 12-5/8" long. Photo from Brian Seligman.

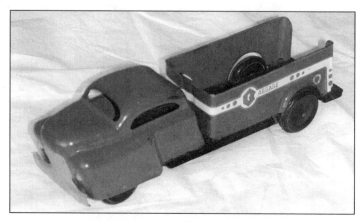

Wyandotte Baggage Truck, 1953, 11-1/2" long. Photo from Brian Seligman.

	C6	C8	C10
Auto Transport, CO, brt; plastic cab and lithographed trailer; marked "#455" "Auto Transport," "Wt.714," "Cap.4," and "Tires. 90-20"; No. 455, 1952; 10" long...	35	50	95
Auto Transport, CO, red cab, w/four plastic cars; 1940s/50s, 9-1/2" long	30	40	85
Auto Transport, CO; brt; plastic cab w/metal trailer, "Haul A Car," four plastic cars; No. 482; 1950s, 8-3/4" long	20	45	85
Auto Transport, SW, yww; orange cab and trailer w/three vehicles, 1932, 19" long	65	150	250
Baggage Truck, SN, bmw; marked "Baggage," 1953; 11-1/2" long....	40	70	135
Baggage Truck, LN, brt; marked "Baggage," w/freight cart, 1941, 11-3/4" long	45	75	115
Bank Truck (also called Bus Bank), RC, bww; green/red/orange, four portholes on each side, rear hatch w/coin slot and key, sealed chassis, No. 375, 1936-40, 6-3/8" long	40	65	115
Bread Truck, PV, wpw; red plastic body and metal red frame, marked "Silvercup Bread," friction, 1952, 4-7/8" long	45	75	105

	C6	C8	C10
Auto Transport, CO, pmw; red/yellow lithographed cab w/red and yellow trailer and four "Cadillac" cars, ramp for upper cars and tailgate lowers for lower cars, "AUTO TRANSPORT," No. 1104, 1952/53, 22" long	55	75	155
Auto Transport, SW, yww; green cab and black trailer w/four vehicles, electric lights, 1932, 21-5/8" long...	85	175	300
Auto Transport, SW, yww; orange cab and trailer w/four vehicles, 1932, 21-5/8" long	75	160	260
Auto Transport, OE, CB, brt; lithographed cab and trailer, four cars, marked "Transmobile Jr.," "Transcontinental Auto Freight Lines," and "I.C.C. 2034 / LT.WT. 6800 / CAPY 9000," No. 130, 1953; 12-5/8" long	50	70	145

	C6	C8	C10
Bus, CO, brt; no roof rack or decal, rear door, No. 1002 1941, 21" long	90	135	220
Bus, RC, bww or wrt; green/red/orange/yellow, eight windows on each side and rear panel w/two windows and embossed spare tire, sealed chassis; No 377, 1936-40; 6-3/8" long	40	70	115
Bus, CO, bww; blue; same window and rear panel design as No. 377, but different nose w/inset grille design, open chassis, No. 233, 1939, 6-3/8" long	40	70	115
Bus, CO, bww; roof rack and rear door, No. 1002, 1938, 21" long	90	135	220
Bus, CO, bww; no roof rack, rear door, "Coast to Coast Bus Line," No. 1002 (Heavy Duty Motor Bus), 1939-40, 21" long	90	135	220
Bus, CO; brt; no roof rack, rear door, "Coast to Coast Bus Line," No. 1002, 1941, 21" long	90	135	220

	C6	C8	C10
Cement Truck, CO, brt; plastic cab, attached mixer No. 239, 1952, 8-1/2" long	20	40	55
Cement Truck, CO, brt; "Cement Mixer / Sell / Rent," may have had attached mixer; 1940/50, 5" long	20	40	65
Circus Truck, RC, eww; two-piece, red cab and lithographed double trailers w/swing down rear ramps, reads "Greatest Show On Earth," cardboard animals on metal stands; No. 503, 1936, 19-1/4" long	200	750	1200
Circus Truck, LN, 1941; two-piece, red cab and lithographed double trailers w/swing down rear ramps, reads "Greatest Show On Earth," cardboard animals on metal stands, w/long nose-style cab, scarce, 19-1/4" long	250	850	1300
Coal Truck, SN, ymw; front scoop, lithographed dump bed w/tailgate, marked "COAL," "FUEL and SUPPLY CO.," and "444," No. 444, 1949, 13" long	50	130	225

Wyandotte Bank Truck (also called Bus Bank), No. 375, 1936-40, 6-3/8" long (front and back view). Photo from Brian Seligman.

Wyandotte Bus, No 377, 1936-40, 6-3/8" long (front and back view). Photo from Brian Seligman.

Wyandotte Bus, No. 1002, 1941, 21" long. Photo from Brian Seligman.

Wyandotte Bus, No. 233, 1939, 6-3/8" long. Photo from Brian Seligman.

Wyandotte Circus Truck, No. 503, 1936, 19-1/4" long. Photo from Brian Seligman.

Wyandotte Circus Truck, 1941, 19-1/4" long. Photo from Brian Seligman.

Wyandotte Dairy/Milk Truck, 1949, 12" long. Photo from Brian Seligman.

Wyandotte Dairy/Milk Truck, No. 4002, 1952, 7-1/2" long. Photo from Brian Seligman.

Wyandotte Dairy/Milk Truck, No. 805, 1952, 4-7/8" long. Photo from Brian Seligman.

	C6	C8	C10
Contractor Truck, LN, bww; "Contractor Truck," No. 434c, 1941, 11-1/4" long......................	45	70	105
Dairy/Milk Truck, SN, ymw; "Sunshine Dairy Farms," "Milk," and "Cream," w/one milk bottle, 1949, 12" long.............................	50	90	110
Dairy/Milk Truck, PL, rpw; w/two crates of milk, marked "Sunshine Dairy," "Milk," and "Cream," box reads "Early Bird Milk Wagon and Horse," No. 4002, 1952, 7-1/2" long..	50	80	115

	C6	C8	C10
Dairy/Milk Truck, LN, brt/brt on hubs, No. 362; 1937/38, 17-3/8" long......	55	80	115
Dairy/Milk Truck, PV, brt; plastic yellow body and metal red frame, "Sunshine Dairy," friction, No. 805, 1952, 4-7/8" long	20	35	95
Dairy/Milk Truck, LN, bww; w/two milk bottles, No. 349, 1939, 11-1/2" long	50	80	115
Dairy/Milk Truck, LN, brt; w/one milk bottle "Drink More Milk," No. 431, 1941, 11-3/4" long	60	85	120

	C6	C8	C10
Delivery Truck, LN, bww; opening rear door; green / red / grey / yellow, "City Delivery" stamped on side, same body as No. 340 ambulance, No. 345, 1938-39, 11-3/8" long	60	75	120
Delivery Truck, PV, brt; red plastic body/metal chassis, "Toy Town Delivery" and "Super Service," lithographed grille and dashboard, opening side and rear doors, No. 353, 1952, 11-1/2" long	50	75	110
Delivery Van, LN; wood wheels, 1938-39, 16-3/8" long	60	75	130
Delivery Van, LN, 1938; brt/ws hub, spring motor w/attached key, No. 382, No. 362 w/out motor, 16" long	80	95	150
Delivery Van, CO, wmw; lithographed cab and body, "Minitown Parcel Service," and "Courtesy Pays," w/white "w" in black circle, 1952, 12" long	55	125	190

	C6	C8	C10
Delivery Van, SE, brt; 1949, 12" long	30	55	85
Delivery Van, OE, brt; lithographed cab and body, cab w/rear van body, "Express Delivery Service," "Local," "National," and "I.C.C. 120/Cap. 4500/WT. 3250," No. 120, 1954, 9-7/8" long	35	60	95
Delivery Van, OE, brt; lithographed cab and body, cab w/rear van body, "Wyandotte Trucking," "Speedy Delivery," "New York Chicago San Francisco," 1954, 6" long	25	50	75
Diaper Delivery Truck, PV, brt; white plastic body and red metal frame, mark "Dy-Dee Wash," and "Stork," friction, No. 805, 1952, 4-7/8" long	20	35	95

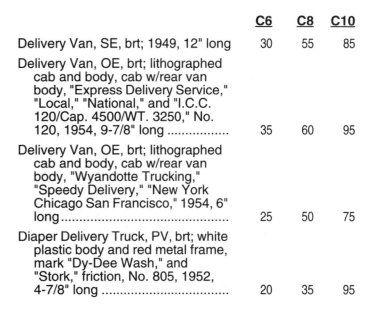

Wyandotte Delivery Truck, No. 345, 1938-39, 11-3/8" long. Photo from Brian Seligman.

Wyandotte Delivery Van, No. 120, 1954, 9-7/8" long. Photo from Brian Seligman.

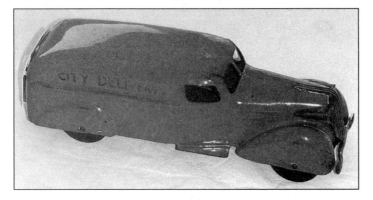

Wyandotte Delivery Truck, No. 353, 1952, 11-1/2" long. Photo from Brian Seligman.

Wyandotte Delivery Van, 1954, 6" long. Photo from Brian Seligman.

Wyandotte Diaper Delivery Truck, No. 805, 1952, 4-7/8" long. Photo from Brian Seligman.

Wyandotte Dump Truck, 1931/32, 15-1/4" long. Photo from Brian Seligman.

Wyandotte Dump Truck, No. 326 1931-32, 9-5/8" long. Photo from Brian Seligman.

Wyandotte Dump Truck, 1933-34, 15" long. Photo from Brian Seligman.

	C6	C8	C10
Dump Truck, SW, yww; side spring release mechanism, dual rear wood wheels, No. 326 (later version), 1931/32; 9-5/8" long......	60	80	105
Dump Truck, CO, mw; plastic cab and metal dump body, 1952, 20" long...	35	95	150
Dump Truck, CO, brt; marked "Automatic Loading," No. 331, 1955-56, 13" long........................	65	85	115
Dump Truck, AW, bww; marked "Highway Dept. Dump," all wood construction, No. 1009, 1942, 13-1/4" long...............................	20	40	90
Dump Truck, SW, wrt/red hubs; electric lights, 1933-34; 15" long..	55	95	165

	C6	C8	C10
Dump Truck, RC, brt/red hubs; w/lights working lights: No. 354, w/non-working headlights: No. 351, 1934-37, 15-1/4" long..........	65	95	135
Dump Truck, SW, wrt/red hubs; No. 328, 1934, 12-3/4" long...............	65	85	125
Dump Truck, LN, bww; mechanical, attached key, shovel, No. 381, 1938-39, 16" long.......................	65	95	135
Dump Truck, LN, bww; w/shovel, No. 361, 1938-39, 16" long..........	50	75	100
Dump Truck, CO, bww; side dump, No. 391, 1939/47, 17-3/8" long....	45	70	110
Dump Truck, CO, brt; lithographed cab, marked "Giant" on side of dump bed, w/11-3/4" shove, No. 1023, 1954/55, 20-1/2" long........	55	105	225

Wyandotte Dump Truck, No. 328, 1934, 12-3/4" long.
Photo from Brian Seligman.

Wyandotte Dump Truck, 1931/32, 15-1/4" long. Photo
from Brian Seligman.

Wyandotte Dump Truck, No. 326 (later version),
1931/32, 9-5/8" long. Photo from Brian Seligman.

Two versions of Wyandotte's, No. 318, Dump Truck.
Photo from Brian Seligman.

	C6	C8	C10
Dump Truck, CO, bww; w/shovel; Heavy Duty Dump Truck, No. 1001, 1938/41, 21" long	65	105	135
Dump Truck, CO, brt/wd hubs; 1941, 21" long	45	70	110
Dump Truck, CO, brt; red plastic cab, w/12" shovel, "Giant Construction Co." on side of dump body," No. 1014, 1953/54; 21" long	60	105	225
Dump Truck, CO, brt; side dump, No. 301, 1953-54, 21-1/2" long	60	75	115
Dump Truck, SW, yww; side lever w/slide track mechanism, dual rear wood wheels, No. 326 1931-32, 9-5/8" long	60	80	105
Dump Truck, CO, bww/mw; No. 426, 1940/45, 12-1/4" long	40	55	95

	C6	C8	C10
Dump Truck, SW, yww; side spring release mechanism, dual rear wood wheels, 1931/32, 15-1/4" long	75	150	225
Dump Truck, RC, bww; Easter Style, pink cab and purple dump body w/chicken stamped on sides, No. E318, 1937/38, 6" long	40	60	105
Dump Truck, RC, wrt; red/green/orange; No. 318, 1934-37, 6" long	40	65	70
Dump Truck, CO/SC, brt; hydraulic lift, opening tailgate, No. 300, 1955, 21-3/4" long	60	75	115
Dump Truck, CO, brt; late 1940s/50, 5" long	25	45	65
Dump Truck, SW, wrt; w/o grille, green or red, No. 315, 1934/36, 4-7/8" long	40	65	85
Dump Truck, CO, bpw; No. 222, 1939/41, 6" long	20	35	70
Dump Truck, SW, wrt; w/grille, green or red; No. 315, 1934/36, 5-1/4" long	40	65	85

	C6	C8	C10
...ruck, LN, bww; side level/rear dumping action, w/wheelbarrow, 1941, 12-1/4" long	45	60	95
Dump Truck, CO, brt; all plastic; No. 159, 1952, 5-1/2" long..................	20	35	65
Dump Truck, SW, yww; 1932, 5-5/8" long	20	35	75

	C6	C8	C10
Dump Truck, LN, bww; No. 318, 1938, 6" long..............................	35	55	85
Dump Truck, SW, eww; 1933, 7" long	50	70	100
Dump Truck, SW, wrt; larger version of 5-1/4" truck, 1934, 7" long	40	60	95
Dump Truck, SN, bww; marked "Sand Gravel Excavation," No. 1023, 1949, 12" long....................	60	80	110
Dump Truck, RC, brt; electric lites; No. 326, 1934, 10" long	40	60	95
Dump Truck, SN, ymw/bww; 1949, 12" long...	40	55	95
Dump Truck, CO, brt; marked "Giant," No. 1023, 1950s, 11-1/4" long	60	80	110
Dump Truck, LN, bww; w/5-1/4"; wheelbarrow, No. 343c, 1938/41, 11-1/4" long	60	80	110

Wyandotte Dump Truck, No. 222, 1939/41, 6" long. Photo from Brian Seligman.

Two versions of Wyandotte's No. 315 Dump Truck. The truck on the right is slightly longer because it has a grille. Photo from Brian Seligman.

Wyandotte Dump Truck, 1932, 5-5/8" long. Photo from Brian Seligman.

Wyandotte Dump Truck, 1941, 12-1/4" long. Photo from Brian Seligman.

Wyandotte Dump Truck, No. 318, 1934-37, 6" long. Photo from Brian Seligman.

	C6	C8	C10
Dump Truck, CO, ymw; plastic cab, tailgate, No. 352, 1952; 11" long..	50	65	105
Dump Truck, CO, mw; front end loader, lever action rear dump, plastic cab and chassis, lithographed body, marked "Sand," No. 443, 1952, 12" long ..	30	45	95
Dump Truck, SE/CB, brt; marked "Wyandotte," front scoop; No. 122, 1953, 10" long.....................	50	65	105
Dump Truck, RC, brt; imitation lights, No. 324, 1934, 10" long.....	40	60	95
Dump Truck, OE/CB, brt/mw; No. 124, 1955, 12" long.....................	60	80	110
EXPRESS (see tractor-trailer)			
Fire Truck, CO, 1952; ymw, plastic cab and metal lithographed trailer, No. 382, 20-1/2" long........	65	95	135
Fire Truck, SC, wpw; red w/white ladders, all plastic, "W" on wheels, No. 150, 1952; 6-1/4" long.............	20	35	70
Fire Truck, CO, brt w/bright metal hubs; plastic and steel, friction, siren and red flashing light, lever release ladder, 1952, 11" long.....	35	50	100

	C6	C8	C10
Fire Truck, CO, brt; plastic cab and metal lithographed trailer, mechanical, crank to raise ladder, 1952, 20" long.............................	65	95	135
Fire Truck, LN, bww; bell, two ladders, No. 366, 1941, 17-1/2" long..	50	70	120
Fire Truck, SN, brt; bell, two or three ladders, "Engine Co. No. 4," No. 428, 1949, 12" long.....................	45	70	100
Fire Truck, LN, bww; lithographed grille and rear bed, bell, two 7-1/2" ladders, "Engine Co. No. 4," No. 428, 1941, 11-3/4" long.........	50	70	120
Fire Truck, CO, brt; hook and aerial ladder truck, plastic cab and metal lithographed trailer, marked either "Hook and Ladder CO. NO. 3" or "Wyandotte Fire Department," plastic rear driver; No. 457, 1952, 11" long..............	50	75	110
Fire Truck, CO, brt; attached green ladder, reads "Wyandotte Fire Department" and "Fire Chief Hook and Ladder Truck," late 1940s/50, 11" long.......................	30	45	100

Wyandotte Dump Truck, 1933, 7" long. Photo from Brian Seligman.

Wyandotte Dump Truck, 1949, 12" long. Photo from Brian Seligman.

Wyandotte Dump Truck, 1934, 7" long. Photo from Brian Seligman.

Wyandotte Dump Truck, No. 343c, 1938/41, 11-1/4" long. Photo from Brian Seligman.

Wyandotte Dump Truck, No. 122, 1953, 10" long. Photo from Brian Seligman.

Wyandotte Fire Truck, No. 329, 1932/34, 10" long. Photo from Brian Seligman.

Wyandotte Dump Truck, No. 324, 1934, 10" long. Photo from Brian Seligman.

Top to bottom: Wyandotte Fire Truck, No. 329, 1932/34, 10"; Wyandotte Fire Truck, No. 308R, 1932, 6". Photo from Brian Seligman.

Wyandotte Fire Truck, No. 428, 1949, 12" long. Photo from Brian Seligman.

Wyandotte Fire Truck, No. 308R, 1932, 6" long. Photo from Brian Seligman.

Wyandotte Fire Truck, No. 1004, 1940/41, 27-1/2" long. Photo from Brian Seligman.

Wyandotte Ice Truck, one ice cube and one pair of ice tongs, No. 123, 1954, 10-1/4" long. Photo from Brian Seligman.

Wyandotte Fire Truck, 1949, 24" long. Photo from Brian Seligman.

	C6	C8	C10
Fire Truck, SE, brt; lithographed cab and body, lithographed 'control panel' inside body, 1952, 10-1/2" long	65	90	110
Fire Truck, OC, wrt; red body w/three ladders, axle activated bell, No. 329, 1932/34, 10" long...	65	90	110
Fire Truck, LN, brt; friction, siren and ladder, No. 156, 1952, 7-1/2" long	30	45	60
Fire Truck, OC, wrt; red body w/three green ladders, No. 308R, 1932, 6" long	65	80	110
Fire Truck, CO, brt; all plastic, No. 157, 1952, 5-1/2" long	65	80	110
Fire Truck, CO, six bww; "Hook and Ladder No. 10," 29" expanding ladder, hood bell, No. 1004, 1940/41, 27-1/2" long	65	125	250
Fire Truck, CO, brt; lithographed trailer, toolbox w/tools, "Hook and Ladder" and "1," No. 1021, 1955/56, 24" long	60	110	225

	C6	C8	C10
Fire Truck, LN, brt; red plastic body w/metal chassis, friction motor and siren, marked "Fire Dept. Rescue Squad," stretcher, opening rear doors; No. 818, 1952/53, 9-1/2" long	35	50	105
Fire Truck, WF, 1949; brt, lithographed trailer, "Hook and Ladder" and "10," 24" long	65	125	225
Garbage Truck, CO/SC, brt; dump action and rear loading sliding gate, marked "Metropolitan Department of Public Service" and "Help Keep our City Clean," No. 332, 1956/57, 17" long	70	110	140
Gardener's Truck, CO/CB, mw/brt; marked "Gardening," "Ferry's Seeds," "Fill," "Dirt," "Trees," "Shrubs" decal, wheelbarrow and round nose shovel, No. 121; 1953; 10-1/4" long	50	75	110
Ice Cream Cart, PL; all plastic, sliding lid and bell, 1953, 4-1/2" long	30	50	100
Ice Truck, SE/CB, lmw; lithographed body, marked "Igloo Ice Company," one ice cube and one pair of ice tongs; No. 123, 1954, 10-1/4" long	50	75	110
Ice Truck, LN, bww; two ice cubes and one pair of ice tongs; No. 348; 1938/39, 11-1/2" long	45	70	120
Ice Truck, LN, brt; one ice cube and one pair ice tongs, ink stamped "Toy Town Ice Co.," No. 432, 1941, 11-3/4" long	45	70	120
Ice Truck, LN, wmt; lithographed body, marked "Toy Town Ice Co." and "Crystal Clear," No. 432, 1941, 11-3/4" long	45	70	120

Wyandotte Ice Truck, No. 432, 1941, 11-3/4" long. Photo from Brian Seligman.

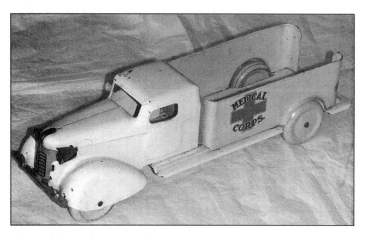

Wyandotte Medical Truck, No. 430, 1940/41, 11-3/4" long. Photo from Brian Seligman.

Wyandotte Ice Truck, No. 432, 1949, 12" long. Photo from Brian Seligman.

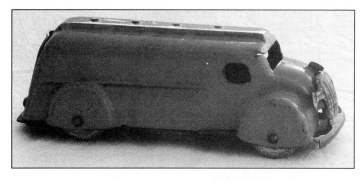

Wyandotte Oil/Gas Tanker, No. 376, 1936/38, 6-3/8" long. Photo from Brian Seligman.

Wyandotte Lumber Truck/Log Hauler, 1952, 10-1/4" long. Photo from Brian Seligman.

	C6	C8	C10
Ice Truck, SN, ymw; lithographed body, "Toy Town Ice Co.," "Crystal Clear" and "23"; No. 432, 1949; 12" long.............................	45	70	120
Lumber Truck/Log Hauler, SE, b/wmw; lithographed cab, flat bed has four plastic posts, marked "Lumber Supply," four logs included, 1952, 10-1/4" long........	45	60	105
Lumber Truck/Log Hauler, CO, brt; lithographed tractor, open log trailer, three logs included, 1956/57, 24" long.........................	50	75	145

	C6	C8	C10
Lumber Truck/Log Hauler, CO, brt; metal cab and trailer, three logs included, 1956/57, 11-1/2" long ...	50	75	135
Lumber Truck/Log Hauler, CO, brt; all plastic, six logs included, No. 176, 1952, 9-1/4" long	45	60	85
Lumber Truck/Log Hauler, CO, bmw; lithographed cab, "Timberland Lumber Supply," No. 426, 1950, 12" long......................	50	75	135
Medical Truck, LN, bww; reads "Medical Corps" w/a Red Cross on side of canvas cloth top, No. 430, 1940/41, 11-3/4" long	70	100	135
Oil/Gas Tanker, RC, wrt; four embossed top hatches and fold down rear hatch, sealed chassis, No. 376, 1936/38, 6-3/8" long......	30	55	110
Oil/Gas Tanker, RC, bww; four embossed top hatches and fold down rear hatch; sealed chassis, No. 225, 1939, 6-3/8" long...........	30	55	110
Oil/Gas Tanker, RC, wrt; four embossed portholes on each side, rear panel w/two windows and embossed tire (like bus), open chassis, 1939; 6-3/8" long ..	30	55	105

	C6	C8	C10
Oil/Gas Tanker, RC, wrt ('35-36), brt ('37); four imitation top hatches and fold down rear hatch, sealed chassis, No. 330, 1936/37, 10-1/2" long..................	65	90	125
Oil/Gas Tanker, CO, brt; rear fold down hatch; No. 1003 (Heavy Duty Gas Truck), 1939/40; 21" long.......	60	90	125
Painting Truck, SE, brt; "Jiffy Painting," "Decorating" and "Quick Service," w/two ladders, 1953, 10-1/4" long........................	50	75	110
Pickup Truck, PL, 1952; plastic, brt, No. 155, 5-1/2" long....................	10	40	65
Pickup Truck, PL, brt; plastic, 1950s, 7-7/8" long..................................	10	40	65
Railway Express Truck, CO, ymw; plastic cab and lithographed body, "Nation-Wide" "Air-Rail Service," late1940s/52, 11" long..	60	90	135
Railway Express Truck, CO, brt; REA lithographed, "Nation Wide," "Air; Rail Service" and "Railway Express Agency," late 1940s/52, 12-1/2" long.................................	60	90	135

	C6	C8	C10
Railway Express Truck, CO, brt; "Wyandotte Toys" and REA lithographed on each side, late 1940s, 6-1/2" long.......................	35	50	85
Riding Truck, RC, brt; No. 356, 1935/36; 16-1/4" long	50	85	155
Riding Truck, SC, brt; fire truck w/electric spot light and siren, No. 1704, 1952/56, 32-1/2" long	75	105	150

Wyandotte Oil/Gas Tanker, Two versions of Wyandotte's No. 330, Oil/Gas Tanker, 10-1/2" long. Photo from Brian Seligman.

Wyandotte Oil/Gas Tanker, Two versions of Wyandotte's No. 330, Oil/Gas Tanker, 10-1/2" long. Photo from Brian Seligman.

Front and back view of Wyandotte's Railway Express from the late 1940s, 6-1/2" long. Photo from Brian Seligman.

Wyandotte Oil/Gas Tanker, 1939, 6-3/8" long. Photo from Brian Seligman.

Wyandotte Pickup Truck, plastic, 1950s, 7-7/8" long. Photo from Brian Seligman.

Wyandotte Railway Express Truck, late1940s/52, 12-1/2" long. Photo from Brian Seligman.

Wyandotte Stake Truck, 1931/32, 15" long. Photo from Brian Seligman.

Wyandotte Riding Truck, No. 356, 1935/36, 16-1/4" long. Photo from Brian Seligman.

Wyandotte Stake Truck, 1940/41, 12-1/4" long. Photo from Brian Seligman.

	C6	C8	C10
Riding Truck, SC, brt on metal wheels; "Towing Service Car," wrecker boom w/chain operated winch, No. 1705, 1956/57, 32-1/2" long	75	105	145
Stake Truck, SW, yww; dual rear wood wheels, 1931/32; 15" long ..	60	85	125
Stake Truck, LN, bww; 1940/41, 12-1/4" long	50	75	105
Stake Truck, CO, mw; No. 426, 1940/45, 12-1/4" long	40	65	105
Stake Truck, SW, wd wheels; w/ and w/o electric lights, No. 352, 1933/34, 15" long	60	95	150

	C6	C8	C10
Stake Truck, RC, wrt brt mounted on red hubs; electric lights, No. 360, 1934/37, 15-1/4" long	75	105	150
Stake Truck, LN, wrt or brt mounted on red hubs; hand truck, No. 360, 1938/39, 16" long	60	95	135
Stake Truck, LN, wrt mounted on wood hubs; mechanical w/attached key, No. 380, 1938/39, 16" long	65	90	130
Stake Truck, CO, brt; lithographed cab, fourteen tires, rear opening door, steerable, 1955, 22-1/2" long	65	105	135
Stake Truck, CO, brt; mini hand truck, "Express," No. 1000, 1939/41, 21" long	65	105	135
Stake Truck, RC, wrt or brt; dual rear wood wheels, 1935/36, 10" long	55	80	120

Wyandotte Stake Truck, No. 352, 1933/34, 15" long. Photo from Brian Seligman.

Wyandotte Stake Truck, No. 360, 1938/39, 16" long. Photo from Brian Seligman.

Wyandotte Stake Truck, No. 360, 1934/37, 15-1/4" long. Photo from Brian Seligman.

Wyandotte Stake Truck, Easter, No. E325, 10" version (top) and No. E317, 6" version (left). Photo from Brian Seligman.

	C6	C8	C10
Stake Truck, RC, bww; Easter Style, pink cab w/light green bed, rabbit stamped on side, No. E317, 1937/38, 6" long	35	75	105
Stake Truck, RC, imw; Easter Style, pink cab w/light green bed, rabbit stamped on side, "Funny Bunny Wants to Stay," No. E325, 1937/38, 10" long	45	85	125
Stake Truck, LN, mw; Easter Style, pink cab w/light green bed, rabbit stamped on side, "Funny Bunny Wants To Stay," 1939/41, 11" long	45	85	125
Stake Truck, SW, wrt on red hubs, No. 327, 1934/35, 12-1/8" long	75	150	220
Stake Truck, SW, yww; dual rear wood wheels, No. 325, 1931/32, 9-3/8" long	50	75	115

	C6	C8	C10
Stake Truck, LN, wrt/bww; No. 317, 1932/37, 6" long	40	65	80
Stake Truck, SW, wrt; No. 327, 1934/35, 12-1/8" long	75	150	220
Stake Truck, SW, wrt; w/out grille, green or red, No. 314, 1933, 4-5/8" long	40	65	85
Stake Truck, SW, wrt; w/grille, green or red, No. 314, 1934, 5-1/4" long	40	65	85
Stake Truck, CO, brt; late 1940s/50s, 5" long	35	60	75
Stake Truck, CO, brt and bpw; "Wyandotte Toys" embossed on driver's side of cab; No. 221 1939/46, 6" long	20	45	70

Wyandotte Stake Truck, Easter, 1939/41, 11" long. Photo from Brian Seligman.

Wyandotte Stake Truck, No. 317, 1932 / 37, 6" long (two versions). Photo from Brian Seligman.

Wyandotte Stake Truck, No. 327, 1934/35, 12-1/8" long. Photo from Brian Seligman.

Wyandotte Stake Truck, No. 327, 1934/35, 12-1/8" long. Photo from Brian Seligman.

Wyandotte Stake Truck, No. 314, 1933, 4-5/8" long. Photo from Brian Seligman.

Wyandotte Stake Truck, No. 325, 1931/32, 9-3/8" long. Photo from Brian Seligman.

	C6	C8	C10
Stake Truck, SW, wrt; No. 317, 1934/35, 6-3/8" long.....................	50	75	85
Stake Truck, SW, eww; 1934/35, 6-7/8" long..........................	50	75	85
Stake Truck, SE/CB, brt/bmw; "Pickwick Pastures," "Livestock," "Dairy Cows" and "Wyandotte," No. 129, 1954, 11-3/4" long.........	35	60	110
Stake Truck, SN; bmw, 1949, 12" long	40	60	100
Stake Truck, RC, wrt, bww; No. 317, 1934/37; 5-5/8" long....................	40	55	75
Stake Truck, LN, bww; w/5-3/4" hand truck, No. 342c, 1938/39, 12" long......................................	65	75	105
Stake Truck, CO, six brt; plastic cab w/lithographed grille and metal trailer marked "Wyandotte Truck Lines," rear spare tire, 1952; 23" long...	90	135	175

	C6	C8	C10
Stake Truck, LN, mw; w/5-3/4" hand truck; No. 342c, 1938; 11-1/4" long..	65	80	105
Stake Truck, SW, brt; electric lights, No. 323, 1932, 9-5/8" long...........	60	85	175
Stake Truck, SW, yww or wrt on red hubs; No. 323, 1931, 9-5/8" long .	60	85	175
Stake Truck, SW, wrt or brt on metal spoke wheels, No. 325, No. 323 has non-spoke wheels, 1931, 9-5/8" long	60	85	175
Television Truck, PL, brt; red plastic body w/yellow metal frame, "Television Repair Service," friction, No. 803, 1954, 4-7/8" long...	35	50	95
Tow Truck, CO, brt; "Towing; Day and Nite," 1956/57, 13-7/8" long..	45	65	105

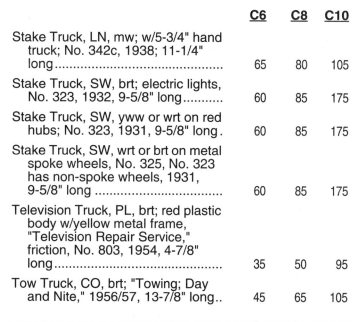

Wyandotte Stake Truck, No. 129, 1954, 11-3/4" long. Photo from Brian Seligman.

Wyandotte Stake Truck, No. 221, 1939/46, 6" long. Photo from Brian Seligman.

Wyandotte Stake Truck, 1949, 12" long. Photo from Brian Seligman.

Wyandotte Stake Truck, 1934/35, 6-7/8" long. Photo from Brian Seligman.

	C6	C8	C10
Tow Truck, LN, brt; lithographed grille, "Service + Wrecker," "Toy Town Only 24 hr Service," No. 365, 1941, 17-1/2" long	50	90	140
Tow Truck, LN, brt on wood hubs; "AAA Service," No. 1005, 1940, 22-1/2" long	50	90	140
Tow Truck, LN, bwt; lithographed grille, "Service + Wrecker," No. 365, 1938, 17-1/4" long	50	90	190
Tow Truck, CO, brt/red hubs; lithographed cab and body, "Towing Service," tools and two spare tires on boom, w/a "W" in red circle, roof mounted light; 1954/56, 15" long	65	105	145

	C6	C8	C10
Tow Truck, CO, brt on yellow plastic hubs; "Moto; Fix," "Toolkit," "Towcar," "Towing-Repairs," "Tire Change" and "Parts," w/tools and two spare tires, all metal construction, 1954, 15" long	105	135	150
Tow Truck, CO, brt; plastic cab, lithographed body, "24 hr," "Tire Change," "Towing Repairs," "Official Service Car," "We Have The Tools To Do The Job" and "Wyandotte," two spare tires on boom, tools, plastic cab No. 1015, 1953/54, 15" long	65	105	145
Tow Truck, SN, bmw/ymw; marked "Official Service Car" and w/a "W" in a circle, rear hoist, No. 429, 1949; 12" long	50	75	110

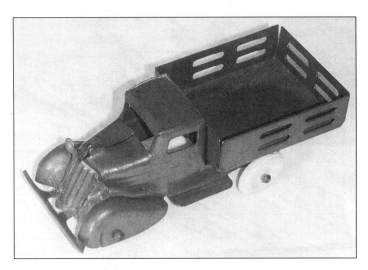

Wyandotte Stake Truck, No. 317, 1934/37, 5-5/8" long. Photo from Brian Seligman.

Two versions of Wyandotte's 1931 Stake Truck, 9-5/8" long. Photo from Brian Seligman.

Wyandotte Stake Truck, No. 323, 1932, 9-5/8" long. Photo from Brian Seligman.

Wyandotte Television Truck, No. 803, 1954, 4-7/8" long. Photo from Brian Seligman.

Wyandotte Tow Truck, 1956/57, 13-7/8" long. Photo from Brian Seligman.

Wyandotte Tow Truck, 1953, 9" long. Photo from Brian Seligman.

Wyandotte Tow Truck, No. 365, 1938, 17-1/4" long. Photo from Brian Seligman.

Wyandotte Tow Truck, late 1940s/50, 4-3/4" long. Photo from Brian Seligman.

Wyandotte Tow Truck, No. 429, 1949, 12" long. Photo from Brian Seligman.

Wyandotte Tractor Trailer (semi), No. 391, 1939/41, 17-3/8" long. Photo from Brian Seligman.

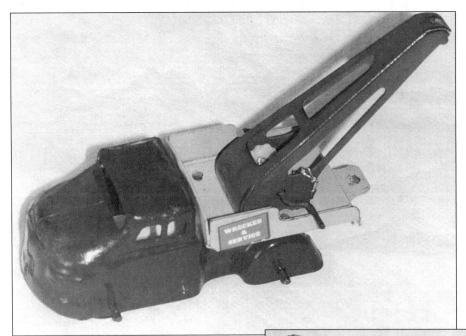

Wyandotte Tow Truck, late 1940s/50, 4-3/4" long. Photo from Brian Seligman.

Wyandotte Tow Truck, No. 429, 1949, 12" long. Photo from Brian Seligman.

Wyandotte Tractor Trailer (semi), No. 391, 1939/41, 17-3/8" long. Photo from Brian Seligman.

Wyandotte Tractor Trailer (semi), No. 390, 1939/41, 17-3/8" long. Photo from Brian Seligman.

Wyandotte Tractor Trailer (semi), 1956/57, 24" long. Photo from Brian Seligman.

	C6	C8	C10
Tow Truck, LN, bww; "Official Service Car," rear hoist, No. 429, 1940/41, 11-3/4" long..................	50	90	130
Tow Truck, SE, lmw; "Wyandotte Automobile Society," "Towing and Repairs" and "Towing Service Nite and Day," rear crank operated hoist, 1953, 9" long.......	45	70	110
Tow Truck, CO, brt; plastic No. 237, late 1952, 6" long.........................	45	60	75
Tow Truck, CO, brt; plastic, "Wrecker Service," late 1952, 5-1/4" long.................................	45	60	75
Tow Truck, CO, brt; late 1940s/50, 4-3/4" long.................................	45	60	75
Tow Truck, LN, brt on wood hubs; marked w/a "W," No. 1005, 1941, 22-1/2" long.................................	50	90	140
Tow Truck, CO, bww; rear hoist, 1940s, 12-1/4" long.....................	40	70	105
Tractor Trailer (semi), CO, fourteen brt on die-cast hubs; die-cast cab and aluminum trailer, "Grey Van Lines," "De Luxe Long Distance Moving," "Affiliated w/Greyhound Lines," also comes in "Chun King Orient Express" and Allied Van Lines versions; side and rear doors open, 1954, 24" long..........	90	150	225
Tractor Trailer (semi), CO, brt; side dump, "Wyandotte Construction Co.," No. 391, 1939/41, 17-3/8" long...............................	65	95	145
Tractor Trailer (semi), CO, brt; "Wyandotte Express Co," No. 390, 1939/41, 17-3/8" long..........	50	75	125
Tractor Trailer (semi), CO, brt; "Green Valley Stock Ranch," lithographed cab marked w/"Wyandotte" and "W" in a dot on cab; No. 390, 1950s, 17-1/2" long	80	95	165

	C6	C8	C10
Tractor Trailer (semi), CO, fourteen brt, lithographed cab, marked "Wyandotte Van Lines" on trailer, No. 1605, 1955, 22-1/2" long.......	95	130	175
Tractor Trailer (semi), CO, fourteen brt on red plastic hubs; "Wyandotte Van Lines" (also "Gambles"), retractable landing gear, double rear doors, No. 1850, 1952/54, 23" long...............	95	130	225
Tractor Trailer (semi), CO, brt; plastic cab, "Deluxe Highway Express," 1952, 23" long	65	80	115
Tractor Trailer (semi), CO, brt; "Highway Freight"; No. 392, 1939/41, 17-3/8" long	55	80	125
Tractor Trailer (semi), CO, brt /two sets rear dual wheels; plastic cab and metal open trailer, removable chains and side pieces, 1952, 23" long.................................	85	110	205
Tractor Trailer (semi), CO, six brt; baggage truck w/hand truck and baggage, No. 380, 1952, 17" long	70	90	120
Tractor Trailer (semi), CO, brt; lithographed cab, cattle truck, loading ramp, 1956/57, 24" long..	70	90	115
Tractor Trailer (semi), CO, brt on die-cast hubs; removable wooden stake panels, "Motor Freight Lines," No. 6001, 1953; 24-1/2" long.................................	75	100	125
Tractor Trailer (semi), CO, six brt w/wood hubs and metal inserts; rear door w/mounted spare tire, three front/two rear reflectors, marked "Van Truck," No. 1500, 1941; 25" long............................	60	105	175
Tractor Trailer (semi), CO, brt; plastic cab, "Coast to Coast Truck Lines," 1952, 23" long..................	85	110	145

Wyandotte Tractor Trailer (semi), 1953, 17" long. Photo from Brian Seligman.

Wyandotte Tractor Trailer (semi), 1952/53, 17" long. Photo from Brian Seligman.

Wyandotte Tractor Trailer (semi), 1953, 17" long. Photo from Brian Seligman.

Wyandotte Tractor Trailer (semi), 1952, 14-3/4" long. Photo from Brian Seligman.

	C6	C8	C10
Tractor Trailer (semi), OE, brt; lithographed cabmarked w/"Wyandotte Trucking" and "ICC W-1260" TARE 7000" and "GROSS 18000" on side, orange trailer w/"Shady Glen Stock Ranch" decal, 1953, 17" long	45	70	165
Tractor Trailer (semi), OE, brt; lithographed cab marked w/"Wyandotte" in bubble on side, red side dump body w/"Motor Fleet Hauling Service" and "W" decal, 1953, 17" long	45	70	165
Tractor Trailer (semi), OE, brt; lithographed cab w/"Wyandotte" in bubble on side, orange trailer w/"Shady Glen Stock Ranch" decal, 1954, 17" long	45	70	165

	C6	C8	C10
Tractor Trailer (semi), CO, pmw; side dump w/shovel, 1952/53, 17" long	45	70	145
Tractor Trailer (semi), SN, brt; "Wyandotte Van Lines," "National" and "Local"; No. 356, 1949, 15" long	65	80	110
Tractor Trailer (semi), CO, ymw; red plastic cab, lithographed trailer, "Wyandotte Van Lines," "National," "Local," 1952, 14-3/4" long	65	80	110

Wyandotte Tractor Trailer (semi), 1952, 9" long. Photo from Brian Seligman.

Wyandotte Tractor Trailer (semi), 1953, 7-3/4" long. Photo from Brian Seligman.

Wyandotte Tractor Trailer (semi), No. 456, 1952, 9" long. Photo from Brian Seligman.

	C6	C8	C10
Tractor Trailer (semi), CO; all plastic parts, removable side stake panels, No. 175, 1952, 9-1/4" long	50	65	100
Tractor Trailer (semi), CO, brt; grey or red plastic cab, lithographed trailer, "Freeway Van," 1952, 9" long	50	65	100
Tractor Trailer (semi), CO, brt; gray or red plastic cab, lithographed trailer, "Produce Van," "Refrigerated Cargo" and "Coast to Coast," 1952, 9" long	50	65	100

	C6	C8	C10
Tractor Trailer (semi), CO, brt; gray or red plastic cab, lithographed trailer, "Wyandotte Van Lines," "Coast to Coast" and "Moving-Packing-Storage," No. 456, 1952, 9" long	50	65	100
Tractor Trailer (semi), CO, brt; "Valley Farms Livestock Produce," 1953, 8-1/2" long	50	70	105
Tractor Trailer (semi), CO, brt; "Produce Van," "Refrigerated Cargo" and "Coast to Coast", 1953, 7-3/4" long	50	70	105
Tractor Trailer (semi), CO, brt; "Wyandotte Van Lines," "Coast to Coast" and "Moving Packing Storage," 1953, 7-3/4" long	50	70	105
Tractor Trailer (semi), CO; six brt w/wood hub and metal inserts; rear door w/mounted spare tire, mini tarpaulin, marked "Highway Freight," No. 1501, 1941, 25" long	60	105	175
Tractor Trailer (semi), CO, bww / brt; lithographed cab w/marked "Wyandotte" and "W Trucking," orange trailer w/"Shady Glen Stock Ranch" decal, 1952/53; 17" long	45	70	165

MISCELLANEOUS

	C6	C8	C10
Bus, "Twin Coach Buffalo, Niagara Lines," 15-1/2" long, aluminum	2500	3500	6000
Roberts Refuse Dump Truck, 1950s	68	102	135
Roberts U-Ride-It Fire Rescue Van, 21" long...	175	263	350
Robot Bus, see Woodhaven."Rocket" Pedal Car ..	450	675	900
Roi-Tan Cigars, promotional car w/pic of Sophie Tucker	130	195	260
Scientific Forklift.............................	100	135	67
Tractor, looks like Arcade, but has nickeled driver, 3" long................	NPF	NPF	NPF

A.C. Gilbert

Alfred Carlton Gilbert (1884-1961) is best known as the creator of the Erector set. However, Gilbert also produced some very attractive vehicles in the early 1920s.

	C6	C8	C10
Gilmortor Truck, wind-up, early, 10-1/2" long.................................	250	375	500
Racer, wind-up, 9" long....................	300	500	700
Stutz...	500	800	1200
U.S. Mail Truck, copyright 1920. 8" long..	375	565	750

A.S. Toy Company (Nuremberg, Germany)

Schumann made toys for approximately twenty years, and like many German toy companies, went out of business in the mid-1930s. Little is known about this small company, and its toys are considered rare. The A.S. trademark is usually on the door of the car.

Contributor: Bob Smith, The Village Smith, 62 West Ave., Fairport, NY 14450-2102. Smith began collecting toys in 1978 after being influenced by some friends who were members of the Genesee Valley Antique Toy Association (GVATA). Starting out with Dinky toys, he soon expanded to Tootsietoys, early hill-climber vehicles, pre war tin cars and early wind-up toys. Smith later joined the GVATA and became its president for ten years. He retired from the automobile sales business, and now devotes all of his time to his toy hobby and promotes his toy show. The Rochester Antique Toy Show (RATS) has grown to be one of the largest in the United States. Smith's articles about old toys an be seen in numerous magazines.

	C6	C8	C10
Racer, w/driver, tin lithographed, c.1908, marked "6", 7" long	600	850	1350
Touring Car, red and black, clockwork motor, glass windshield, c.1915, 9" long	1100	1500	2050

Acme

Acme produced only two toy vehicles, both in clockwork—a 1903 curved-dash Oldsmobile roadster and a delivery truck with a pressed-steel canopied roof. In 1905, Acme's owner, Jacob Lauth, began producing actual automobiles under the name Lauth-Juergens Co.

	C6	C8	C10
Curved Dash Olds, clockwork, c.1905, 11" long...........................	500	750	1000

Al Otto

	C6	C8	C10
Jeep Fire Truck	1000	1700	2500
Jeep Pickup Truck	400	750	1100
Jeepster	1100	1850	2700
Stock Car Racer, plastic, early, 4-1/2" long	4	10	25
Woody Station Wagon	600	950	1500

All American (Los Angeles)

	C6	C8	C10
Hot-Rod, c.1949, 9" long.................	210	315	420

All-American Hot Rod, red, 1949. Photo from Roger E. Canup.

AMF Pontiac Pedal Car, 37-1/2", cream, brown, red and yellow Pontiac insignia, 1930.

Left to Right: Barr Rubber Ford Army Truck; Ford Stake Body Truck, both 4-3/4". Photo from Dave Leopard's book *Rubber Toy Vehicles*.

American Metal Toy

This was essentially a toy soldier company, began business in Chicago in 1937, even though President Royce Reyff, along with C. Raymond Pierson incorporated the company in 1939. Because its toys were composed of lead zinc alloy, the lack of metal available during World War II forced the company out of business in 1942.

	C6	C8	C10
Tank, throwing flame, flame touching hull (AMV001)	40	60	80
Tank, throwing flame, flame not touching hull (AMV002)	45	68	90
Tank, throwing flame, marked "25" (AMV003)	60	90	120
Tank, marked "22" on side (AMV004)	50	75	100

American Precision Co.

	C6	C8	C10
Allis-Chalmers C Model Tractor, die-cast, 1950	150	225	300

AMF

	C6	C8	C10
Pontiac Pedal Car, 1930, 37-1/2" long..	1500	2500	3500
Rebel Racer Pedal Car, 1965	200	300	400

AMT

(Also, see "Promotionals")

	C6	C8	C10
Pontiac Pedal Car, 1930, 37-1/2" long..	1500	2500	3500
Rebel Racer Pedal Car, 1965	200	300	400

Aurora

	C6	C8	C10
T-Jet Mack Stake Truck, HO-scale ..	25	38	50
Vibrator 1962 Ford Sunliner, convertible or hardtop..................	40	60	80

Automatic Toy Company

Around the early 1950s, Automatic Toy Company was located at 77 Alaska St., Staten Island, New York.

	C6	C8	C10
Auto Speedway, two garages and three cars....................................	85	125	170
Auto Speedway, wind-up, one garage, two cars, c.1930	85	128	170
Cop 'N Car, plastic w/motor, siren, 4" long motorcycle, 8-1/2" car, c.1953..	NPF	NPF	NPF
Magic Crossroad Track, two wind-up cars, c.1950	85	125	170

Barr Rubber

Barr Rubber was located in Sandusky, Ohio. The following list and the code numbers in parenthesis, was compiled by Dave Leopard. Vehicles are broken down by type.

Contributor: Dave Leopard, 2507 Feather Run Trail, West Columbia, SC 29169-4915.

	C6	C8	C10
'35 Ford, two-door slantback sedan, 4" long (BA002)	30	40	60
'35 Ford Army Truck, 4-3/4" long (BT003)	35	45	70

	C6	C8	C10
'35 Ford Coupe, 4" long (BA001)	30	40	60
'35 Ford Panel Truck/Ambulance, 4-1/4" long (BT002)	30	40	60
'35 Ford Stake Body Truck, 4-3/4" long (BT001)	30	40	60

Beaut Mfg. Co.

Beaut Mfg. Co., North Bergen, New Jersey, was founded in 1946 by Eugene Buhler and Irving Reader (former machinist and salesman, respectively) for Barclay Mfg. Co. The company put out five toys—a taxi cab, a police car, a fire engine, a sedan and a child's wagon. The company was successful at first, selling to Woolworth's and many overseas buyers. Beaut eased toymaking activities around 1950 because of competition from plastic toys, although they continued until 1982 as a general machine shop.

	C6	C8	C10
Fire Car, No. 4, approx. 3-3/4"	10	15	20
Police Car, approx. 3-3/4"	10	15	20
Sedan, approx. 3-3/4"	10	15	20
Sedan Delivery, 3-3/4" long	20	30	40
Taxi, No. 1, approx. 3-3/4"	10	15	20
Wagon, No. 50	NPF	NPF	NPF

Benbros

	C6	C8	C10
Military Land Rover, 1950s, 1:64-scale	20	30	40

Bico

	C6	C8	C10
Bico Bus to Joyville, open double-decker, passengers, driver	2000	3500	5000

Big Bang

	C6	C8	C10
Army Tank, No. 5T, 8-1/8" long........	35	50	100
Motor Tank, No. 5T, c.1933, 9-1/2" long	100	200	350

Big Boy

See Kelmet

Bonnie Bilt

	C6	C8	C10
Armored Car, U.S. Army	11	16	22
Tank, plastic....................................	6	9	12

Left to Right: Barr Rubber 1935 Ford Slantback Sedan; 1935 Ford Coupe. Photo from Dave Leopard book *Rubber Toy Vehicles*.

Left to Right: Beaut Police Car; Beaut Taxi.

Barr Rubber Ford Panel Truck/Ambulance, 4-1/4". Photo from Dave Leopard's book *Rubber Toy Vehicles*.

Beaut Wagon, No. 50.

Boycraft Mack Dump Truck, 1920s, 22". Photo from Bill Bertoia Auctions.

Boycraft Steam Roller, 16". Photo from Joe and Sharon Freed.

Boycraft

Boycraft was the brand name used by Steelcraft for the toys it supplied to Sears-Roebuck in the late 1920s and early 1930s.

	C6	C8	C10
Mack Dump Truck, 22" long............	375	563	750
Steam Roller, 16" long	NPF	NPF	NPF

Breslin

Breslin Industries of Toronto made a number of lead-alloy toys, most or all of them copies, particularly of Barclay and Manoil. They can be easily distinguished from the originals because they usually read "Canada" or "Made in Canada."

	C6	C8	C10
Motorized Machine Gunner..............	30	40	50
Tank	30	40	50
Truck pulling Cannon	30	40	50

Left to Right: The Breslin Tank and Motorized Machine Gunner.

Breslin Truck Pulling Cannon.

Brimtoy Limousine, 1919, black, 11". Photo from Bill Bertoia Auctions.

Brimtoy (England)

	C6	C8	C10
Limousine, 1919, 11" long................	300	450	600

Brinks

	C6	C8	C10
Armored Car, 9" long	250	375	575
Truck Bank, aluminum, 8" long	40	60	80

Brio

	C6	C8	C10
Ladder Truck, red, yellow and black, red wheels, Brio stenciling on door..............................	NPF	NPF	NPF

Buckeye

	C6	C8	C10
Dump Truck.....................................	65	100	135
Livestock Truck	115	172	230
Pickup Truck	125	188	250
Red Star Express	200	325	475

Buffalo

	C6	C8	C10
Niagara Lines, 15-1/2" long, aluminum	2500	3500	6000

Brio ladder truck, red, yellow and black, red wheels, Brio stenciling on door. Photo from Perry Eichor.

Buckeye Semi Tractor, red. Photo from Calvin L. Chaussee.

Buffalo Toys

Buffalo Toys, of Buffalo, New York, began in 1924 and produced a number of lightweight steel toys until World War II. the firm ceased to exist in 1968.

	C6	C8	C10
Blue Bird Racer...............................	350	475	700
Bumper Car, wind-up, 10" long........	55	83	110
Mack Stake Truck, electric lights, circa 1928, 25" long	300	450	700
Red Streak Racer, 24" long	350	475	700
Silver Bullet Racer, 26" long	375	525	725
Silver Dash....................................	175	263	350
Silver Streak..................................	300	450	600

Burdette

	C6	C8	C10
Murray Express Truck......................	1600	2700	3800
Murray White Standard Bed Truck...	2000	3200	4600

Burnett

	C6	C8	C10
Cargo Truck, maroon and black, clockwork motor, driver, 8-1/2" long, c.1926	600	800	1200
Limousine, blue/black, clockwork motor, driver, 8" long, c.1925.......	600	800	1200
Roadster, green/black, clockwork motor, driver, folding windshield, c.1925, 7-1/2" long......................	600	800	1200
Toyland Bus, 14-1/2" long................	600	850	1250

Buffalo Toys Mack Stake Truck, 1920s, 25".

Burnett Cargo Truck, 1920s, maroon and black, 8-1/2"
(Coca-Cola bottles were not part of the original truck.).

Burnett Roadster, 1920s, green and black, 7-1/2".

Burnett Limousine, 1920s, blue and black, 8".

C.R. Dump Truck, 1930s, 16", green and yellow. Photo
from Bob Smith Collection. Photo by Len Rosenberg.

BW Molded Plastics

Little is known about BW Molded Plastics, except that in 1954, it was located at 1346 East Walnut Street in Pasadena, California. A mix of plastic toys were made, including musical instruments, teas set, ships and vehicles.

	C6	C8	C10
Auto Parade Set, pickup truck, convertible, coupe, ladder truck, racer, five piece (BW0873B)	NPF	NPF	NPF
Fire Truck, 3-1/2" long (BW0000) ...	13	20	27
Jaguar, 12-1/2" long (BW0888)	NPF	NPF	NPF
Jeep, 9-1/4" long (BW0886)	NPF	NPF	NPF
Race Car, 3-1/2" long (BW0000)	13	20	27
Roly The Steam Roller, "fully mechanized" (BW0879)	NPF	NPF	NPF
Tank, 10" long (BW0887)	NPF	NPF	NPF

C.R.

Rossignol began making toy vehicles in 1895. The company became best known for the toy trains it produced in the nearly 100 years it was in business. In 1920, C.R. came out with a line of toy buses that lasted until the company closed its doors in 1962.

Contributor: Bob Smith, The Village Smith, 62 West Ave., Fairport, NY 14450-2102.

	C6	C8	C10
Dump Truck, clockwork motor, green and yellow, head lamps, dual side mount wheels, c.1935, 16" long..........................	800	1300	2000
Large Bus..	1200	2000	2800
Rolls Royce, tin lithographed, clockwork motor, lights work, 14-1/2" long	1100	1900	2700
Streamline Sedan, wind-up, 14" long	550	700	900

Cass

	C6	C8	C10
Delivery Truck Ride 'em, wooden, 30" long	25	38	50
Dump Truck Ride 'em, wooden, 36" long	32	48	65
Station Wagon, wooden, 19" long	60	90	120
Streamlined Truck Ride 'em, 30" long	110	165	220
Tank, wooden, "General Lee," marked "224," 12" long	55	83	110
Truck Ride 'em, wooden, 40" long	150	225	300

Chad Valley

	C6	C8	C10
Aerial Repair Truck, clockwork, 4" long	175	262	350
Delivery Truck, marked "The Chad Valley Co. Ltd.," 10" long	650	1100	1500
Double Decker Bus, tin, marked "Chad Valley Toys," 6" long	65	98	130
Fordson Major Tractor, 6-1/2" long	100	150	200
Sedan, tin wind-up, rear luggage rack, 9-1/4" long	125	188	250

C.R. Rolls-Royce, tin lithographed, 14-1/2". Photo from Bill Bertoia Auctions.

C.R. Streamline Sedan, windup, 1930s, 14". Photo from Bill Bertoia Auctions.

CIJ

	C6	C8	C10
P2 Alfa Romeo, clockwork motor, handpainted, hinged filler caps, moveable steering wheel, 20-1/2" long	1200	2000	2700

Citroën

	C6	C8	C10
Fire Truck, clockwork, removable hose reel	650	1100	1600
Truck, open bed, wind-up, door opens, 16-1/2" long	550	850	1300

Cleveland Toy

	C6	C8	C10
Racer, aluminum, steel wheels, c.1935, 13" long	175	262	350

Cass Tank, General Lee, wooden, 12". Photo from Ron Fink.

Chad Valley Delivery Truck, 10". Photo from Bill Bertoia Auctions.

Cragstan G Men Car, tin friction, red, 6-1/2". Photo from Ron Fink.

Daytime Lines Semi-Stake Truck, cast aluminum, 18" 1940s.

Cohn

	C6	C8	C10
Fir Chief Pull Car, No. 34, 1940s, metal, 9" long	80	120	160
Superior Sales Service garage, tin...	150	225	300

Conway

	C6	C8	C10
Packard Convertible, clockwork, electric lights, 1948, 12" long	175	263	350

Cox

	C6	C8	C10
Adam 12, gas powered	90	135	180
Army Jeep, gas powered	72	112	150
Corvette, gas powered, 1966, 8"......	90	135	180
Ford GT-40, gas powered	112	168	225
Funny Car, plastic, 12" long	7	11	15
Gas Dune Buggy.............................	30	45	60
Matador, gas powered	NPF	90	135
Vega Funny Car, gas powered	37	56	75
Volkswagen, powered	37	56	75

Cragstan

	C6	C8	C10
Ambulance, friction...........................	70	105	140
Fire Chief Car, friction	82	123	165
G Men Car, tin friction, 6-1/2" long...	60	90	120
Greyhound Bus, friction, 9" long	35	52	70

D&L Plastics

	C6	C8	C10
Future Car, 1940s	20	30	40

Daisy

	C6	C8	C10
Tank-Daisymatic No. 64 Rapid Fire Tank, 1960s, battery-operated, four actions, 8" long	110	165	220
Tank-Daisymatic No. 80, 1965, battery-operated, five actions, w/darts, 8-1/2" long	100	150	200

Day Time Toys

	C6	C8	C10
Semi-Stake Truck, cast aluminum, 18" long..	300	425	600

Daytime Lines

	C6	C8	C10
Tractor Trailer	200	300	400

DeLuxe

	C6	C8	C10
DeLuxe Service Station, 1940s........	40	75	100

Distler

	C6	C8	C10
BMW Wanderer, wind-up................	250	375	500
Coupe, w/driver, clockwork motor....	600	1000	1400

Eccentric Saloon Car, wind-up, driver's head springs through roof, 8" long.......................... 500 800 1100

Electro Magic 7500 Porsche Cabriolet, battery-driven 450 675 900

Jaguar 340 510 680

Limousine, tin lithographed, battery headlights, chauffeur, clockwork motor, 12" long.......................... 900 1500 2200

Packard Convertible, 1950s 225 338 450

Uncle Wiggly Car 1500 2500 4000

Doll & Co.

	C6	C8	C10
Touring Car, open, live steam motor, hand painted tin, four-doors open, 19" long......................................	1500	2700	4000
Truck, open bed, live steam, chain driven, 19" long............................	2000	3700	6600

Dooling Brothers

The three brothers began their firm in 1939. There were seven different cars and one variation.

	C6	C8	C10
Arrow, 1948 to late 1950s	NPF	NPF	NPF
F Car, Hornet powered.....................	700	1100	1600
Mercury, "18," gasoline powered	1500	2000	2500

Deluxe DeLuxe Service Station, 1940s, with box. Photo from Ron Fink.

Mercury Midget .... NPF NPF NPF

Mercury Second Series, front drive.. NPF NPF NPF

Pee Wee, 12" long .... NPF NPF NPF

Streamliner, 16" long....................... NPF NPF NPF

Druge

Druge Bros. Mfg. Co. was located 888 92nd Avenue in Oakland. In 1948, its "Hyster" sold for the very high price of $9.75.

	C6	C8	C10
Cari-Car Lumber Carrier	100	150	200
Hyster Lumber Carrier	120	180	240

Dooling Brothers' Mercury "18" gasoline-powered racer brought at a 1993 auction. It was made in California in limited numbers between 1939 and 1945. Photo from Jeff Bub Auctions.

Druge Hyster Lumber Carrier. Photo from Tim Oei.

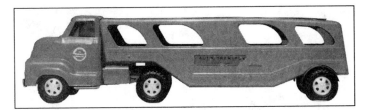

Dunwell Auto Transport. Photo from Roy Bonjour.

Dunwell Log Truck. Photo from Tim Oei.

Dunwell Grain Hauler. Photo from Tim Oei.

Dunwell Steel Carrier Co. Semi. Photo from Tim Oei.

Dunwell Livestock Transport. Photo from Tim Oei.

Dunwell Red Star Express Lines Truck.

Dunwell

Dunwell was the trade name given to its toys by Metal Products Co. of Clifton, New Jersey. Its trucks seem to have been sold from 1953-1958. Dunwell vehicles resemble the Tonka line, and are rare.

	C6	C8	C10
Auto Transport	95	150	225
Dump Truck	75	125	150
Grain Hauler	75	125	185
Land-o-Lakes Semi, 1956 mail offer, rare	250	400	500
Livestock Truck	125	200	300
Log Truck	125	200	350
Red Star Express Lines Truck, rare	300	500	650
Snowcrop Refrigerator Semi	300	400	500
Steel Carrier Co. Semi	75	125	185
Wrecker	125	200	300

Ebo

	C6	C8	C10
Delivery Truck, early, tin lithographed, clockwork motor, driver, 8" long	400	600	800

NEW!
#9318 — TOW TRUCK
St. Pk. — 6 ea. ctn. / Wt. 12 lbs.
Realistic with full action pulley-type tow arm.
Deep tread, molded whitewall tires with colored
hubs. Clear windshield; white and green cab, yellow truck body. 16" long; 5¾" high. Pilfer-proof
self-display shrink pack. Size: 16½" x 6½".

NEW!
#9216 — PICK-UP TRUCK
St. Pk. — 6 ea. ctn. / Wt. 9 lbs.
Detailed realism! Clear windshield, molded deep
tread whitewalls and colored hubs. Bright two-
tone blue color. 13½" long; 5¾" high. Attractive
pilfer-proof, self-display shrink pack. 14" long; 6"
high.

NEW!
#9316 — DUMP TRUCK
St. Pk. — 6 ea. ctn. / Wt. 12 lbs.
Looks like the real thing — 2 position lever tilts
dump bed. Deep tread, molded whitewall tires
with colored hubs. Clear windshield. 16" long x
6¼" high. Attractive pilfer-proof, self-display
shrink package. Package size: 16½" x 6¾".

This page from the 1964 Eldon catalog shows some of what was new that year.

Dan Gurney racing "Eldon Special" (Lotus 19B) Nassau, Jan. '64

"Tops in realism and excitement!"—
that's what world champion
race driver Dan Gurney says about
Eldon's 1964 road race sets!

Dan Gurney, world champion racing car driver, endorses Eldon Industries Inc.'s complete line of road race sets and accessories in 1964. His picture and endorsement appears on all packaging of Eldon's road race sets, and in addition, Gurney will be a spokesman for Eldon in their road race TV commercials.

Known in active world-wide racing as a "driver's driver" Dan Gurney has posted many important wins—the French Grand Prix in 1962—the Daytona Continental, Nassau, the Nuremburgring 1000 Kilometer—as well as many additional wins in American Stock Car racing events.

Dan Gurney's endorsement of Eldon road racing, as part of the promotional program for its model road race sets, will have a more significant meaning for the racing fan than would that of any other racing figure.

ROAD RACE SETS

Race car driver Dan Gurney endorsed all of Eldon's Road Race Sets. Photo from Eldon Fall 1964 catalog.

Eldon

	C6	C8	C10
Aerial Ladder Truck, 21" long..........	40	60	80
Concrete Truck, 17" long	44	66	85
Corvette, 14" long	44	66	85
Delivery Truck	40	60	80
Dump Truck, 18" long	30	45	60
Ford Lift Gate Truck, 18" long	30	45	60
Hot Rod, 18" long..........................	80	120	160
Hot Rod Kit, batttery operated, snap-together...........................	32	48	65
Mighty Tow Truck..........................	45	68	90
Road Race Slot Car Set, 1965.........	35	55	70
Stake Truck	40	60	80
Steam Shovel...............................	20	30	40
Tank Transport, military	48	72	95
Wrecker, plastic, 18" long	40	60	80

Elmar Products Company

	C6	C8	C10
Rocket Shooting Tank, 3-1/2" long ..	NPF	NPF	NPF

Empire Forces

	C6	C8	C10
Tank, composition (also in plaster) ..	NPF	NPF	NPF
Tank, composition (also in plaster) ..	NPF	NPF	NPF

Erwin

	C6	C8	C10
Ford, w/windshield wipers	40	60	80

Eldon Aerial Ladder Truck, 21".

	C6	C8	C10
Race Car......................................	55	82	110

Fallows Toys

	C6	C8	C10
Frederick & Henry, Horseless Carriage, w/driver, cast iron and tin, c.1905, 8" long	900	1350	1800

Firestone

The following list and the numbers in parenthesis, was compiled by David Leopard

	C6	C8	C10
'35 Ford Sedan, two-door humpback, 4-7/8" long (FA002) ..	50	60	75
'36 Ford Sedan, two-door humpback, 4-7/8" long (FA003) ..	70	105	140
'39 Mercury fastback Sedan, four-door, 4 3/4" long (FA001)	60	75	90

Two Empire tanks.

Fallows Toys Frederick & Henry Horseless Carriage with driver, 8".

Fischer Double-Deck Bus, tin clockwork, 7-1-2". Photo from Harvey K. Rainess.

Fischer Limousine, 9", green and black, back doors open.

Fischer Limousine, 7-1/2", circa 1918, green and black.

Fischer Limousine, c.1910.

Fischer, Heinrich & Co.

Fischer's easily recognized mark, a fish swimming through the letter A, is a unique trademark usually found on the rear of the car. The George Borgfeldt store of New York purchased many of the toys produced by Fischer for the American market. Not all of the Fischer toys carried his mark, however. Nifty toys, for example, was one of the trademarks used by the company. The great comic character tin toy, Toonerville Trolley, is one of the best known Fischer toys made under the Nifty trademark.

Contributor: Bob Smith, The Village Smith, 62 West Ave., Fairport, NY 14450-2102.

	C6	C8	C10
Automatic Dump Truck, clockwork motor, 10-1/2" long	550	825	1200
Double-Decker Bus, tin clockwork, c.1910, 7-1/2" long	680	1000	1500
Limousine, luggage rack, w/driver, 9" long	650	1000	1300
Limousine, green and black, clockwork motor head lamps, windshield, c.1918, 7-1/2" long	550	825	1175
Limousine, green and back, clockwork motor, back doors open, c.1915, 9" long	650	975	1275
Limousine, maroon, black stripes, w/driver, overhead rack, c.1910, 13" long	1700	2800	4500
Limousine, w/chauffeur, clockwork motor, 10" long	465	700	930
Torpedo, red and yellow tin lithographed, clockwork motor, c.1912, 8" long	700	1000	1375
Tourer, 8-1/2" long	NPF	NPF	NPF
Tourer, w/chauffeur and two women, 8 1/2" long	500	750	1000
Town Coupe, tin, clockwork motor, approx. 7" long	800	1300	2200
Vis-A-Vis, 6-1/2" long	NPF	NPF	NPF

Left to right: Fischer Vis-A-Vis, 6-1/2"; Tourer, 8-1/2". Photo from Bob Smith. Photo by Len Rosenberg.

Fischer Torpedo, 8", red and yellow, tin lithographed.

Futuristic

	C6	C8	C10
Car pulling house trailer, white tires, 6" long......................	NPF	NPF	NPF
Coupe, w/fin, black tires, 4-1/4" long	NPF	NPF	NPF
Oil Truck, black tires, reads "Super Oil," 3-3/4" long...........................	NPF	NPF	NPF

G&K

	C6	C8	C10
Delivery Truck, tin wind-up, w/driver, early, 5-1/2" long........................	475	715	950
Motorcycle, w/seat-like sidecar, tin wind-up, early, 6-1/2" long...........	800	1300	1800

Futuristic Car Pulling House Trailer, 6", white tires. Photo from Dave Leopard.

Futuristic Coupe with fin, 4-1/4", black tires. Photo from Dave Leopard.

Futuristic Oil Truck, 3-3/4". Photo from Dave Leopard.

Garland

	C6	C8	C10
Red Flyer Hydraulic Dump, Made in Detroit...........................	125	188	250

Garrett

Garrett Flexible Products of Garrett, Indiana, began in 1978. Its owner was F.H. Thurman, who designed Auburn Rubber's trucks, cars, etc., in the 1950s. He also designed the Garrett line, which was sometimes known as Rubber Toys Unique, with some toys marked "Unique."

	C6	C8	C10
Corvette Sting Ray, 7" long.............	15	22	30

Garton

	C6	C8	C10
Fire Department Ladder Aerial Car, 1949...	700	1100	1600
Ford Pedal Car, 1950s.....................	700	1100	1700
Hod Rod Pedal Car.........................	400	650	900
Woody Pedal Car, 1937..................	1300	2500	3900

Gay Plastics

	C6	C8	C10
Police, three wheeler, 8" long..........	35	52	70
Truck..	5	8	10

Gendron

	C6	C8	C10
Buick Pedal Car, 1920	5000	9500	18,000
Federal Knight Dump Truck.............	NPF	NPF	11,000

Garland Red Flyer Hydraulic Dump, 25".

Gendron Stearns pedal car, circa 1920, 41". Photo from Bill Bertoia Auction.

Globe Co. Roadster, cast-iron, 11-1/2". Photo from Bill Bertoia Auctions.

Gendron/Sampson Army Truck, 27" long	800	1300	2000
Gendron/Sampson Chemical Fire Truck, 28" long	1200	2000	2800
Gendron/Sampson Coal Truck, steel, 26" long	1000	1600	2500
Gendron/Sampson Dump Truck, pressed steel, 27" long	850	1350	1900
Gendron/Sampson Screen Side Express Truck, 27" long	650	1100	1500
Gendron/Sampson Stake Truck, 26" long	1500	2300	3500
Gendron/Sampson Tank Truck, 29" long	800	1400	2000
Racer Pedal Car, 38" long	1300	2000	3000
Sportster Pedal Car, 41" long	2000	3500	5300
Stearns Pedal Car, c.1920, 41" long	1000	1700	2640

General Toy of Canada

	C6	C8	C10
Racer, No. 3, tin wind-up, 4 3/4" long		75	112

Gibbs

	C6	C8	C10
Service Station	350	525	700
Truck, marked "Gibbs No. 701"	150	250	350

Giftcraft (possibly only the distributor)

	C6	C8	C10
Fastback Sedan, Nash, solid rubber, c.1946, 4" long	15	22	30

Gilmark

	C6	C8	C10
Esso Gasoline Truck	12	18	25
Rocket Car, driver, 1950s, 4" long	20	30	40
Sedan, w/opening hood	8	12	16
Tractor/Trailer Hi-Way Transporter	8	12	16

Glass

	C6	C8	C10
Gas Pump, 1930s	200	325	450
Motorcycle and Cop, 1930s	250	400	600

Globe Co.

	C6	C8	C10
Motorcycle w/Cop, 1930s, 8" long	650	1150	1675
Roadster, separate driver, kids in rumble seat, cast iron, 11-1/2" long	500	750	1000

Gong Bell

	C6	C8	C10
Mickey Mouse Bus Lines, Walt Disney Stars	250	375	500
Milk Truck, w/wooden bottles, 13" long	225	338	450
Racer, 20" long	150	225	300

Grey Iron

Founded as the Brady Machine Shop in Mount Joy, Pennsylvania in 1840, the company was organized as the Grey Iron Casting Company, Ltd. in 1881. As early as 1903 it was manufacturing toy banks and stoves, cap pistols, wheeled toys and trains, as well as a number of non-toy items. The firm's best known products are toy soldiers. It is still in business today as Donsco-John Wright, located in Wrightsville, though still casting in Mount Joy.

	C6	C8	C10
Convertible, Midget, 1-1/2" long.......	20	30	40
Coupe, Midget, 1-1/2" long	20	30	40
Ford Coupe, w/driver, 5-5/8" long	NPF	NPF	NPF
Ford coupe, w/driver, 8-3/8" long	475	515	950
Racer, Midget, 1-1/2" long	20	30	40
Sedan, 1927, 9" long........................	1000	1500	2000
Sedan, Older, Midget, 1-1/2" long....	20	30	40
Sedan, Airflow-type, Midget, 1-1/2" long..	20	30	40

Grimland (Marietta, GA)

Contributor: John Taylor, P.O. Box 63, Nolensville, TN 37135-0063.

	C6	C8	C10
Allied Vans, 7-1/2" long....................	55	85	115
Grey Van Lines, 7-1/2" long.............	55	85	115
Toys That Last Promo, 7-1/2" long, rare	75	135	200

Grimland "Toys That Last" salesman's promo, 7-1/2". Photo from John Taylor.

Grey Iron Midget vehicles, 1-1/2" each. Photo from Stan Alekna.

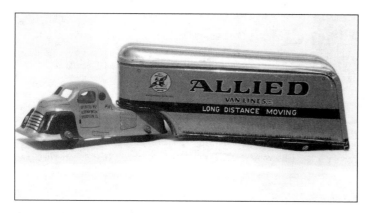

Grimland Allied Van Lines, 7-1/2". Photo from John Taylor.

Grimland Grey Van Lines, 7-1/2". Photo from John Taylor. Photo from John Taylor.

Gyro

Richard B. Munday became head of Dayton Friction Works in 1926, where he patented a horizontal flywheel and called his toys "Gyro" after the gyroscope. Gyro shut its doors in 1935.

	C6	C8	C10
Coal and Ice Dump Truck	250	275	500

Hafner

Chicago's Hafner began in 1900 as the Toy Auto Company, though it may not have produced its first model until the following year. By 1904, the firm's name became W.F. Hafner and eventually became the American Flyer company. Mr. Hafner set off on his own when he started the Hafner Manufacturing Company in 1914; his son joined him in 1918. Hafner manufactured wind-up trains until it was purchased in 1950 by Wyandotte.

	C6	C8	C10
Auto Express Co. Truck, clockwork, steel, 8-1/2" long	450	675	900
Runabout, w/upholstered driver's seat, steel clockwork, 7" long.......	450	675	900

Left to right: Hafner Auto Express Co. Truck, 8-1/2"; Hafner Runabout, 7".

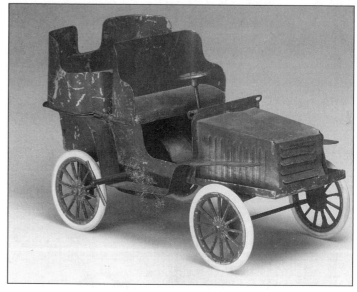

Hafner Touring Car without top. Photo from Bill Bertoia Auctions.

Hafner Touring Car, 10" pressed steel. Photo from Bill Bertoia Auctions.

	C6	C8	C10
Touring Car, pressed steel, clockwork, 10" long.....................	750	1125	1500
Transitional Phaeton, two figures, 9-1/2" long	1500	2500	3500

FRICTION TOYS

"GYRO" FRICTION STEEL TOYS

Sturdy....powerful....flashy steel toys....each equipped with friction motor (no springs to get out of order)....dependable, powerful, lasting. All BIG sizes for the money. Beautiful enamel finishes in two and three colors.

1F1219—12 pieces (no 2 alike) as follows:

	Retail Each
17 in. locomotive & tender	$1.25
13½ in. roadster	1.25
14½ in. dump truck	1.25
14½ in. coal & ice truck	1.25
18 in. hook & ladder	1.25
13½ in. roadster	1.25
13½ in. airplane	1.25
14½ in. delivery truck	1.25
20¼ in. dump truck	2.00
18½ in. coupe	2.00
18½ in. sport roadster	2.00
13½ in. coupe	1.25
Total Retail Value	**$17.25**
Your profit	6.00

Each in box. Asstd. 1 doz. in pkg.............Doz **$11.25**

1F1196—18 pieces asstd. as follows:

		Retail Each
2	13½ in. roadsters	$1.35
2	13½ in. roadsters with rubber tires	1.50
1	14 in. fire truck	1.35
1	14 in. fire truck with rubber tires	1.50
1	14 in. fire engine	1.35
1	14 in. fire engine with rubber tires	1.50
2	12½ in. coupes	1.35
1	12½ in. coupe with rubber tires	1.50
2	14 in. dump trucks	1.75
1	14 in. dump truck with rubber tires	2.00
1	18½ in. coupe with rubber tires and spare	2.50
1	18½ in. roadster with rubber tires and spare	2.50
1	25½ in. fire truck with 80 in. ext. ladder	4.00
1	26 in. bus with rubber tires	2.50
	Total Retail Value	**$32.60**
	Your Profit	13.60

Each in box. Asstd. 18 pcs. in pkg...... **$19.00**

1F2551—Trolley car, 21 in. long, 4-color enameled, steel trolley, long running friction motor. 1 in box.

Each **$1.50**

It's Easy to Buy from BUTLER BROTHERS

BUTLER BROTHERS ST. LOUIS

Gyro toys, as seen in a 1929 Butler Bros. Christmas catalog.

Handi-Craft Co.

	C6	C8	C10
Auto Casting Set, price w/box, No. 891, 1940s	72	105	145

Happy Sam

	C6	C8	C10
Driving Wood Truck, c.1920s, 8" long	80	120	160

Harris

Harris Toy Company of Toledo, Ohio, began production of cast iron toys in the late 1880s. The firm, which also jobbed for Dent, Hubley and Wilkins, stopped making toys in 1913.

	C6	C8	C10
Tiller Auto, w/driver	450	675	900

Hiller

	C6	C8	C10
Comet Race Car, non-powered, marked "4," 18" long	550	825	1200
Comet Race Car, fuel-powered, marked "3," c.1940-42	800	1300	1800

Hoge

	C6	C8	C10
Fire Chief Car, 15" long....................	250	450	650

Holgate

Holgate was founded by Cornelius Holgate in Philadelphia. About 1930 it began turning out educational wooden toys. It merged with Playskool in1958; now owned by Hasbro.

	C6	C8	C10
Army Tank, wooden, ten wheels, 12" long	65	82	130

Holmes Coal Co.

	C6	C8	C10
Delivery Truck, pressed steel, marked "Holmes Coal Co.," 17-1/2" long	4100	600	800

Ingap

	C6	C8	C10
Mouse Car, wind-up, Italian, 6" long	1650	2475	3300

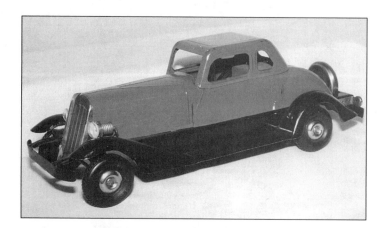

Hoge Fire Chief Car.

Hiller Comet Race Car, fuel-powered, 1940s, 3".

Ingap Mouse Car, 6", eccentric wheels, arms extend.

HOGE SIREN FIRE CHIEF WITH BELL

U. S. Patent 1962870

No. 267

A new and improved Fire Chief. Has all the great features of the No. 266 and in addition has a loud and clear ringing bell on the rear of the car. This bell works from a battery and is controlled by the same rheostat switch which operates the lights.

Dimensions: 14¼″ long; 5″ high; 5¼″ wide.
Packing: Each in corrugated carton. 1 dozen to shipping carton (without batteries).
Weight: 50 pounds.

(Page Ten)

The Hoge Siren Fire Chief car, as shown in a Hoge No. 35 catalog.

HOGE FIRE CHIEF

This Fire Chief is as popular as ever. Has a real automatic fire siren which starts low and becomes louder as auto picks up speed. Made of re-enforced heavy gauge full finished steel, with lustrous baked enamel finish and nickel plated trimmings. Special clutch mechanism which operates automatically, protecting the mechanism if car is pushed or pulled on the floor.

LIGHTING SYSTEM: Bright lights with rheostat control. Takes one battery.

All working parts accurately machined—a complete and finished job throughout.

Equipped with real non-skid rubber tires.

Dimensions: 14¼″ long; 5″ high; 5¼″ wide.

Packed in individual corrugated cartons, one dozen to shipping carton. Weight: 50 pounds. Without batteries.

Real Headlights- Dim and Bright   Rubber Tires   Automatic Fire Siren   No. 266

HOGE POLICE CHIEF

Real Headlights-   Rubber Tires   Automatic Siren   No. 265

An ideal toy for youngsters who want to pull or push toys along. Siren shrieks when car is either pushed or pulled. Has 2 real headlights operated on single flashlight battery—controlled by switch located inside of car.

Substantially constructed to stand up under abuse usually inflicted by vigorous children.

Beautifully finished in 2 tone green with nickel plated trimmings and real rubber tired wheels.

Car: 14¼″ long; 5″ high; 5¼″ wide.

Packed: one to a carton—one dozen to a shipping carton.

Weight: 36 pounds. Without batteries.

(Page Eleven)

Hoge Fire and Police Chief cars, as shown in a Hoge catalog.

JEP Delage Limousine, green and black, late 1920s, 13-1/2".

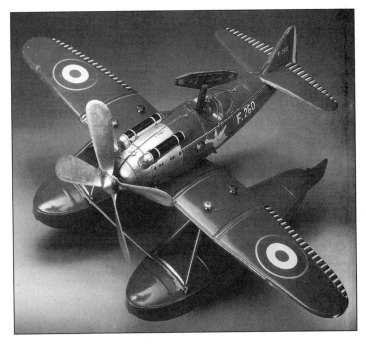

JEP Seaplane, tin wind-up, 13-1/2". Photo from Christie's East.

J&S

	C6	C8	C10
Hudson, die-cast, w/suspension	68	102	135

JEP (J de P)

J de P was founded in 1899 as the *Societe Industrielle de Ferblanterie*. The name was changed to *Jouets de Paris* (J de P) in 1928, as the company introduced a new line of toy cars. Four years later, the name was again changed to *Jouets en Paris* (JEP). This name stayed until 1965, when the company went out of business.

Contributor: Bob Smith, The Village Smith, 62 West Ave., Fairport, NY 14450-2102.

Jones & Bixler Express J&B Truck, 15-1/2".

	C6	C8	C10
Autobus, six-wheel, green/cream, clockwork motor, front/rear wheel steering, marked "Madeline-Bastille," c.1928, 10-1/4" long	1200	1600	2100
Bugatti Racer, tin lithographed, clockwork motor, "2," 8-1/2" long .	500	700	950
Bus, wind-up, 10-1/2" long	500	750	1100
Delage Limousine, green and black, clockwork motor, horn, battery-operated spot light, full steering, c.1929, 13-1/2" long	1300	2450	3600
Hispano Suiza, clockwork motor, lights work, 20" long	2000	4000	6600
Peugeot Coupe, clockwork, pre-WWII	300	500	600
Plymouth, wind-up, door opens, 13" long	400	600	800
Rolls Royce Open Phaeton, clockwork motor, steel, electric headlights, 19-1/2" long	2000	3500	5000
Seaplane, tin wind-up, 13-1/2" long .	NPF	NPF	NPF

Jones & Bixler

	C6	C8	C10
Auto, cast iron, driver, rider	1200	2000	3200
Express J & B Truck, 15-1/2" long ...	900	1350	1800
Peerless Racer, cast iron, 5" long....	500	800	1100
Red Devil Touring Car, cast iron, driver, 8-1/2" long	550	850	1200

Judy Company, The

The Judy Company of Minneapolis made educational toys, including a farm set called "Happy's Farm Family" (patented in 1945) which included a solid rubber car, pickup truck, and tractor, along with human and animal figures.

Contributor: Dave Leopard, 2507 Feather Run Trail, West Columbia, SC 29169-4915.

	C6	C8	C10
Farm Tractor, two-dimensional (part of set), solid rubber, 3-1/2" long (JF001)	15	20	25
Pickup Truck, two-dimensional (part of set), solid rubber, 5-1/4" long (JT0001)	15	20	25
Sedan, two-dimensional, (part of set), solid rubber, 5-1/4" long (JA001)	15	20	25

Kahn

	C6	C8	C10
Cadillac and Trailer, w/furniture, bushes, plastic, 1950	NPF	NPF	NPF

Kingston Producers

	C6	C8	C10
Duesenberg, w/transformer and steel track, 12" long	1500	2700	3700
Dump Truck	150	225	300
Electric Truck	150	225	300
Electricar, the Red Arrow, 1930s, 15" long	150	225	300
Electricar Set, racer and truck	500	750	1000
Ice Truck	150	225	300
Wrecker	150	225	300

Knapp

	C6	C8	C10
Electric Automobile, battery-activated, pressed steel, c.1903, 11" long	1500	2400	4000

Laketoy

	C6	C8	C10
John Wanamaker Delivery Van, wooden, 10-1/2" long	180	270	360

Lapin 1939 Hudson Coupe. Photo from Dave Leopard.

Lapin

Contributor: Dave Leopard, 2507 Feather Run Trail, West Columbia, SC 29169-4915.

	C6	C8	C10
1939 City Bus, 4" long	20	30	40
1939 Four-door Sedan, 4" long	17	26	35
1939 Hudson Coupe, 4" long	17	26	35
1949 Cadillac Convertible, 9" long	20	30	40
1949 Cadillac Convertible, 6" long	15	20	30
1949 Cadillac Sedan, 9" long	20	30	40
1949 Cadillac Sedan, 6" long	15	20	30
1949 Chevrolet Stake Truck, 5" long	12	18	25

Lee Stokes Industries

Lee Stokes started his firm in 1945 in New Oxford, Pennsylvania. Except for the first three, he created all his own models. Thirty-one different types were sold; six in O-gauge, the rest in HO, to take advantage of the postwar interest in HO-gauge trains and accessories. The cars were made of a very tough compound of plaster and urea formaldehyde, so that they stand up. The firm, with eight employees, sold internationally, as well as in the United States. It moved to Bel Air, Maryland, in 1950 and closed in 1955. Stokes died in 1991. Prices average $30; up to $50 for the Rolls-Royce.

Contributor: Dave Leopard, 2507 Feather Run Trail, West Columbia, SC 29169-4915.

	C6	C8	C10
1949 Chevrolet Coupe, 2-1/2" long (LV02)	10	15	20
Tractor/Trailer, modern decal, c.1948 Reo, 5-1/2" long (LV01)	20	25	30

Lapin 1939 Four-door Sedans. Photo from Bob and Alice Wagner.

Several Lapin 1939 Coupes. Photo from Bob and Alice Wagner.

An assortment of Lapin 6" Cadillacs. Photo from Bob and Alice Wagner.

An assortment of Lapin Chevrolet Stake Trucks. Photo from Bob and Alice Wagner.

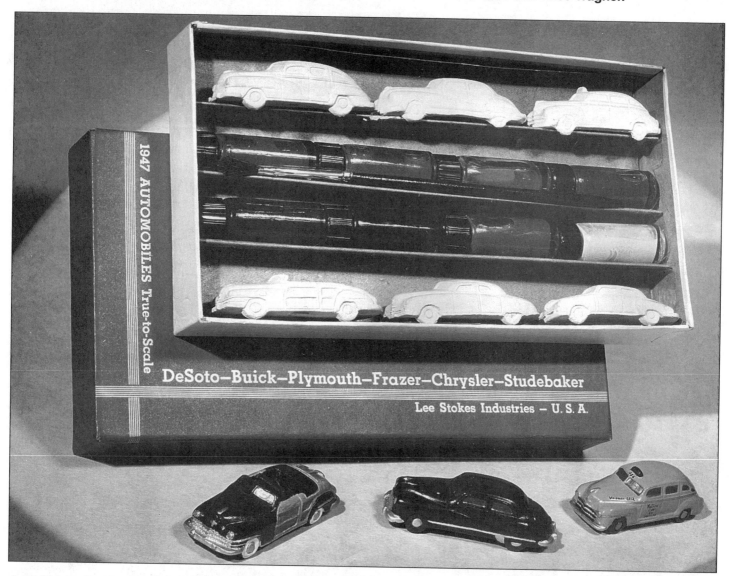

A 1948 Lee Stokes kit that included DeSoto, Buick, Plymouth, Frazer, Chrysler and Studebaker models. Photo from Lee Stokes Industries. B. Richmond, photographer.

Lido Auto, trailer, hitch, plastic, 9-1/2". Photo from Ron Fink.

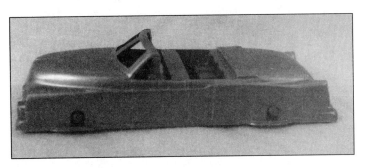

Lido Convertible, 1950s. Photo from Dave Leopard.

Lehigh Bitsi-Toys

These heavy die-cast toys with black rubber tires were produced around 1950.

Contributor: Dave Leopard, 2507 Feather Run Trail, West Columbia, SC 29169-4915.

	C6	C8	C10
Chevrolet Coupe, 2-/2" long (LV002)	10	15	20
Tractor Trailer, "Modern" decal, c.1948, 5-1/2" long (LV001)	20	25	30

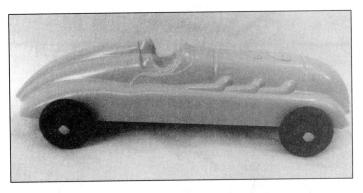

Lido Racer, 3". Photo from Dave Leopard.

Lido

Lido was founded in October 1947 by brothers Seymour and Effram Arenstein, with the purchase of Elite Toy Co. from David Krotman. Krotman made plastic bubble pipes, scissors and a horn. Located in Brox, New York, the firm was near the Lido Country Club, hence the name. For $6,800, the Arensteins bought the molds and the name. Lido's toys were small and always plastic. Eventually, the Arensteins were known as the "Louis Marxes of low-end" toys. At its peak, Lido employed close to 1,000 people. In the years after the 1950s, they employed several thousand indirectly in Hong Kong, Japan and Taiwan. They sold out, due to disagreements, to Bala Corporation of Philadelphia, which liquidated a year later. What was left was eventually bought by Gabriel Industries. From 1973-1990, Seymour Arentstein owned Joy Toy.

	C6	C8	C10
Auto, w/trailer hitch, 9-1/2" long	15	22	30
Convertible, 1950s	8	12	17
Fire Truck, 3" long	4	6	8
Jeep and Trailer	5	8	10
Limousine, tin wind-up, license plate reads "N.Y. 1918," lithographed, approx. 6" long	140	210	280
Racer, 3" long	4	6	8
Service Truck, 3-1/2" long	8	12	17

Lindstrom

The Lindstrom Tool & Toy Company made wind-up toys of light pressed steel, as well as tin. Located in Bridgeport, Connecticut, and Lindstrom began making toy cars about 1913. It seems to have ceased production in the 1940s.

	C6	C8	C10
Bumper Car, tin wind-up, 6-1/2" long	60	90	120
Ladder Truck, Mack type	138	247	275
Long Distance Moving Van, trailer only	75	112	150
Lumber Truck, steerable front wheels, tin, w/driver, No. 160, 10" long	125	187	250
Parcel Post Truck, tin wind-up, No. 2	200	300	400
Racing Car, tin wind-up, 1930s, 6" long	90	135	185
Skeeter Bug, tin wind-up, bumper car, 1930s, 7" long	120	180	240
Steam Roller, mechanical, No. 181, 12" long	50	75	100
U.S. Mail Truck, No. 1, early, 7" long	500	800	1200

Lineol (Trains)

	C6	C8	C10
Electric Racing Automobile Set........	1600	2500	3750

Lupor Metal Products

	C6	C8	C10
Ambulance, friction, 7" long	52	78	105
Army Ambulance, friction, 7" long	50	75	0
Fire Chief Car, No. 57	58	72	95
Lupor Citrus Fruit Trailer Truck	42	63	85
Police Car, friction, 1949 Ford, 7" long..	44	66	88
Race Master, tin wind-up, 11" long ..	100	150	200
Racer, no wind-up, 12" long.............	30	45	60
Racer, tin wind-up, No. 8, 1930s......	138	205	275
Seafood Transport Tailer Truck	42	63	85
Sedan, friction, 7" long	38	57	75
Tailer Truck	25	38	50

M&L Toy Co. Inc.

M&L was incorporated Oct. 21, 1947. It was located on Paterson Plank Road in Union City, New Jersey, and got its name from the two brothers (or father and son) who owned it, Morris and Louis (last name unknown). The company may have begun in 1946, and lasted until at least 1948. It made vehicles, trains, jeweled swords, water guns, mechanical toys and plastic horns. Most—or—all of its vehicles seem to have been sold unpainted and with plastic wheels. The alloy used in the vehicles was more than ninety-nine-percent zinc, with a smidgen of aluminum added. Most its toys were copies. There were about thirty employees. By 1948, it was at 123-33rd Street in Union City. Many, and perhaps all of their vehicles, were copies of discontinued Barclays.

Top to bottom: Compare this M&L Cabin Racer to this Barclay prototype. Photo from Perry Eichor.

	C6	C8	C10
Cabin Racer (2)	12	18	25
Coupe, spare tire post, 1930s (5) ...	12	18	25
Fire Ladder Truck (4)	12	18	25
Fire Pumper (3)	12	18	25
Racer, 2-3/4" long (1)	20	35	50
Sedan, streamlined (6)	12	18	25

Mason & Parker

	C6	C8	C10
Baby Auto, 1907, 7" long	450	700	1000
Truck, w/log load, wooden, c.WWII..	20	30	40
Truck, w/cloth top, wooden, c.WWII.	20	30	40

M&L Coupe, 1930s. Photo from Bill Conover.

M&L Fire Pumper. Photo from Craig A. Clark.

M&L Sedan, streamlined. Photo from Bill Conover.

Mason & Parker Truck with log load, wooden. Photo from Jack Mathews.

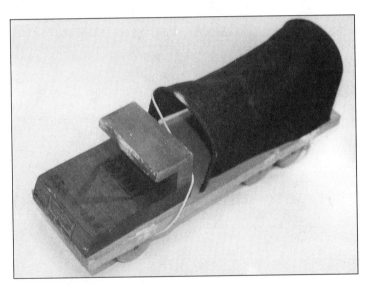

Mason & Parker Truck with cloth top, wooden. Photo from Jack Mathews.

Metalgraf Company

Metalgraf Company manufactured toys from 1920 until 1939. It is still in business today, but has not produced toys for many years. A Metalgraf car is seldom found offered for sale. They are considered rare and are especially hard to find in the United States.

Contributor: Bob Smith, The Village Smith, 62 West Ave., Fairport, NY 14450-2102.

	C6	C8	C10
Touring Car, gray/black lithographed, clockwork motor, steering,10" long, c.1922	1300	1900	3000

Metalgraf Touring Car, 1920s, 10". Photo from Bob Smith.

Modern Toys Tin Lizzie. Photo from Tim Oei.

Mitten

	C6	C8	C10
Dunlop Stake Truck, 16" long	100	150	200

Modern Toys (MT)

	C6	C8	C10
Convertible, 9" long.........................	125	188	250
Mobilgas Tanker	80	120	160
Stunt Car, No. 27, battery-op	35	52	70
Tin Lizzie, wind-up	NPF	NPF	NPF

Mohawk Toy

	C6	C8	C10
Blue Bird Taxi, wind-up, 6" long	188	282	375
Metropolitan Groceries, tin wind-up, 6" long.............................	170	255	340

	C6	C8	C10
Racer, No. 13, wind-up, driver, front window, 6-3/4" long	125	250	375
Yellow Taxi	275	363	550

Moko

Moses Kohnstam not only manufactured toys, he also ran a large wholesale house and had his toys made to order by toy companies such as Guntermann, Distler and Fischer. He became a distributor for Gama, Tippco, Levy, Carette and other companies. Most special-order toys carried the "MOKO" logo. Kohnstam died in 1912, leaving the business to his sons, Willi and Emil. His other son, Julius, had opened a branch office in England before 1900. The company closed in 1933, as were many other Jewish businesses in Germany prior to World War II. Emil fled to England, while Willi stayed in Germany. Willi died one year later. Emil joined his brother Julius to help run the English firm. Julius died in 1935. The MOKO Company survived, however, and is still in business today.

Contributor: Bob Smith, The Village Smith, 62 West Ave., Fairport, NY 14450-2102.

	C6	C8	C10
Flying Police Squad, clockwork motor battery searchlight, 10" long	1100	2000	2700
Kohnstam Sedan, four-cylinder, green/black, c.1928, 8" long	500	750	1150
Limousine, six-cylinder, green/black, 9-1/2" long, clockwork motor runs car in forward and reverse while pistons on top of engine move up and down; doors and hood open; c.1927, 9-1/2" long	800	1100	1800
Motorcycle w/rider, spring action, 7-1/2" long	1200	2100	2800
Motorcycle w/rider, tin clockwork, 8-1/2" long	1500	2700	4000

Moko Six-Cylinder Limousine, green and black, late 1920s, 9-1/2".

Mormac

	C6	C8	C10
Convertible, plastic, 9-3/4" long	30	45	60

Moxie

	C6	C8	C10
Horse Car, based on the actual promotional vehicle, tin lithographed, 8" long	338	507	675

**Moko Motorcycle and Rider, spring action, 7-1/2".
Photo from Bill Bertoia Auctions.**

**Moko Motorcycle and Rider, tin clockwork, 8-1/2".
Photo from Bill Bertoia Auctions.**

Mormac Convertible, plastic, 9-3/4". Photo from Ron Fink.

Nifty Speedy Felix the Cat car.

Nifty Skiddodle. Photo from PB Eighty-four.

MPC

	C6	C8	C10
Dump Truck, 7-1/4" long	11	16	22
Firewagon, three figures, ten accessories....................	12	18	25

Nifty

	C6	C8	C10
Bus, double decker, tin wind-up, 9" long	800	1400	2200
Felix the Cat Car, "Speedy Felix"	425	635	850

Noma Tank, wooden with a 4" wood peg sticking out at the top for reasons unknown. Photo from Jack Mathews.

North & Judd Semi-Trailer Stake Truck. Photo from Terry Sells.

Skidoodle, tin wind-up	1800	2900	4000
Truck, automatic tilter, w/driver, 9-1/2" long	600	950	1350

Noma

	C6	C8	C10
Car and Trailer, 1940s	65	98	130
Low Boy, wooden.............................	100	150	200
Steam Shovel, wooden	90	135	180
Tank, wooden, WWII......................	30	45	60
Truck, wooden, 1940s.....................	45	68	90

North & Judd

North & Judd, located in New Britain, Connecticut, made cast-iron toys for S.H. Kress during the year of 1930. Its original designs appear to have been marked with the company's name, but, for the most part, its toys are unmarked. The company currently makes quality hardware.

	C6	C8	C10
Austin Convertible, open top, marked "North & Judd"	NPF	NPF	NPF

Austin Sedan, two-door, marked "North & Judd" .... NPF NPF NPF

Bus, looks like Dent, 4-2/3" long ...... NPF NPF NPF

Ford Model A Coupe, looks like Arcade, has driver in window, trunk at rear, left cab 1-1/2" long.. NPF NPF NPF

Ford Model T Stake Truck, like Arcade's, but marked "Anchor Truck Co." (an anchor is North & Judd's trademark), 8-3/4" long..... 1500 2500 4200

Motorcycle Cop, Hubley's "Cop," separate nickeled driver is held by mushrooms at front of handlebars and on driver's feet .... NPF NPF NPF

Semi-Trailer Stake Truck, marked "North & Judd............................. NPF NPF NPF

Nosco Plastics

Nosco Plastics was located in Erie, Pennsylvania, and made a variety of plastic toys, including several planes and trains. Some of its toys appear in a 1952-53 *Toy Year Book*. In 1954 its address in Erie was 17th and Cascade Street.

	C6	C8	C10
Ace Racer, No. 6390, 8" long...........	60	100	160
Bus, marked "Nosco Lines"	NPF	NPF	NPF
Cop-Cycle, friction. No. 6357, 5-1/2" long...	75	125	225
Doodle-Bug, No. 6381, wind-up, 9-1/2" long	88	132	175
Fire Truck, No. 6386, 7-1/2" long	NPF	NPF	NPF
Hot See Hot Rod, friction, No. 6490, 10-1/4" long	80	120	160
Pokey Joe Fire-Pumper, No. 6430, 10-1/2" long	NPF	NPF	NPF

Nosco Doodle-Bug, 9-1/2". Photo from Terry Sells.

Nosco Hot See Hot Rod, friction, 10-1/4". Photo from Terry Sells.

Nosco Cop-Cycle, friction, 5-1/2". Photo from Terry Sells.

Nosco Vizy Vee Stockar Racer, 9-1/4". Photo from Terry Sells.

NOSCO PLASTICS
ERIE, PENNSYLVANIA · U.S.A.

VIZY VEE   No. 6564   Ind. pkg.
SIZE: 9¼'' long, 3½'' wide, 3¾'' high.
SHIP. WT. 1 doz. ass'td. colors 11½ lbs.

CLOUD HOPPER   No. 6530   Ind. pkg.
SIZE: 9⅜'' long, 7⅝'' wide, 3⅜'' high.
SHIP. WT. 1 doz. ass'td. colors 9½ lbs.

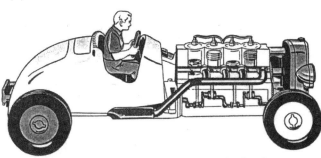

HOT'SEE ROD   No. 6490   Ind. pkg.
SIZE: 10¼'' long, 5'' wide, 4¼'' high.
SHIP. WT. 1 doz. ass'td. colors 15 lbs.

4 SHOOTER   No. 6595   Ind. pkg.
SIZE: 8⅛'' long, 4⅜'' wide, 3⅜'' high.
SHIP. WT. 2 doz. ass'td. colors 12 lbs.

JETGO   No. 6470   Bulk.
SIZE: 8¾'' long, 7½'' wide, 2'' high.
SHIP. WT. 2 doz. ass'td. colors 7½ lbs.

POOCHY   No. 6450   Ind. pkg.
SIZE: 18½'' long, 4¼'' wide, 5'' high.
SHIP. WT. 1 doz. ass'td. colors 15½ lbs.

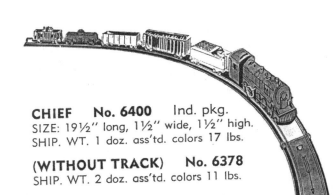

CHIEF   No. 6400   Ind. pkg.
SIZE: 19½'' long, 1½'' wide, 1½'' high.
SHIP. WT. 1 doz. ass'td. colors 17 lbs.

(WITHOUT TRACK)   No. 6378
SHIP. WT. 2 doz. ass'td. colors 11 lbs.

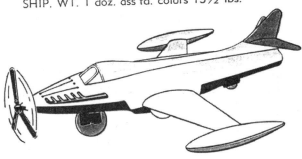

JETWIRL   No. 6550   Bulk.
SIZE: 8½'' long, 7½'' wide, 2'' high.
SHIP. WT. 2 doz. ass'td. colors 8½ lbs.

The Vizy Vee and the Hot See Hot Rod were among the vehicles pictured in this Nosco advertisement.

Roaring Roadster, 8" long	90	135	180
Station Wagon........................	NPF	NPF	NPF
Vizy Vee Stockar Racer, No. 6565, 9-1/4" long.............................	70	110	180

Ohio Art

Ohio Art was started in October 1908, by a dentist, H.S. Winzeler. Originally, its intent was to make metal picture frames (thus, its name). But in 1917, the firm bought C.E. Carter (Erie Toy Plant) and began producing metal toys, including a climbing monkey on a string for Ferdinand Strauss. Winzeler later sold the plant to Louis Marx, but continued making tin toys, while Marx, according to Ohio Art history, used the former Carter plant as the foundation of his own company. Ohio Art is still making toys in Bryan, Ohio.

	C6	C8	C10
Tank Bank, No. 15, 1941	78	117	155
Traffic Control, tin wind-up cars, 1950s, 3-1/2" long, base 19x13"..	40	60	80

Ohlsson & Rice

	C6	C8	C10
Midget Racer, aluminum body, rubber tires, 1940s......................	260	375	575
No. 76 Racer, gas-powered	500	750	1075
Pusher Racer, 11" long	270	455	540

Pagco

	C6	C8	C10
Racer, w/motor, 11" long................	80	125	160

Parker Bros.

	C6	C8	C10
Toy Town Garage, three lithographed tin penny cars w/paper lithographed garage, c.1910......................................	600	900	1200

Paya

	C6	C8	C10
Chrysler Airflow Sedan, tin lithographed, clockwork motor, 13" long.................................	312	468	625
Coupe, handpainted and stenciled, clockwork motor, doors open, 13" long	1000	1750	2500

Limousine, handpainted and stenciled, lights work, clockwork motor, 19" long	750	1300	1750
Motorcycle and Rider, tin wind-up, 10-1/2" long	312	468	625
Sedan, steel, doors open, battery lights, 19" long	500	850	1200

Payton

	C6	C8	C10
Bulldozer, soft plastic	12	18	25
Cement Mixer...............................	12	18	25
Tiger Tank, No. 411	20	30	40
Tow Truck	12	18	25

Perfect Rubber Co.

	C6	C8	C10
1935 Slantback Sedan, 3-3/4" long..	35	52	70

Peter-Mar

Ralph Lohr was the owner of Peter Products Manufacturing in Muscatine, Iowa. He was an entrepreneur, artist, and musician. Lohr operated a music store in the early 1920s. In 1941, he started manufacturing wooden kitchen items, such as clothes racks, stools, ladders, and ironing boards. Lumber was limited to government contracts during World War II, and Lohr was faced with closing the business. It was at this time that he discovered scrap lumber could be purchased from government contractors, and he started to design toys. The first of these were military vehicles. Farm toys were also very popular, so he began making tractors, hay racks, trailers, and wagons. Other toys were Noah's Ark, Humpty Dumpty, Lucky Dog, Village Smitty, Old Woman in a Shoe, Trolley Cars, Carousel, and Ferris Wheel.

The company was named after Lohr's son Peter, and Mary, the daughter of his partner, Clifford Hakes.

After more than fifty years, these toys are still popular and sought-after. When these toys are found in antique stores, the prices for a Noah's ark in Mint condition are $300. The Village Smitty, a pound-a-peg-type toy, has been sold for as much as $65. These toys are well constructed and durable.

	C6	C8	C10
Hay Wagon	42	63	85
Jeep, wood	NPF	NPF	NPF
Milk Wagon	42	63	85
Tractor, wood	90	135	180
Trailer, wood	67	100	135

Pinard

	C6	C8	C10
Cannon Truck, searchlight on grill, WWI, 13" long	475	713	950

Plasticraft

	C6	C8	C10
Jeep, articulating driver, plastic, 4" long	5	8	10
Truck, plastic	6	9	12

Plasticville

	C6	C8	C10
Gas Station	4	6	8
Sedan	NPF	NPF	NPF

Playboy

	C6	C8	C10
Delivery Truck, "Playboy Trucking Co.," 21" long	225	338	450
Dump Truck, 22" long	150	225	300
Intercity Bus, cream color, 23-1/2" long	300	450	600
Tow Truck, marked "Playboy Trucking Co.," white, 22" long	250	400	650

Playwood Plastics

This was a World War II-era company that made items out of wood composition. It was a subsidiary of Transogram, and its factory was located at 133 Floyd St., Brooklyn, New York.

	C6	C8	C10
Dispatch Rider on Cycle, round base, head higher, No. 407a (?)	7	11	15
Dispatch Rider on Cycle, No. 407 (?)	7	11	15
Motorcyclist, leather-type helmet (probably post-WWII), Nos. 438 or 436	NPF	NPF	NPF

Precision Plastics Station

	C6	C8	C10
Wagon, plastic wind-up, 7" long	55	82	110

Premier

	C6	C8	C10
Heavy Tank, No. 144	30	45	60
No. 52 Station Wagon, plastic, 4-3/4" long	15	22	30

Pressman

	C6	C8	C10
Ambulance, plastic	45	68	90

Processed Plastic

	C6	C8	C10
Army Tank	37	56	75
Army Wrecker, 9" long	35	52	70
Wrecker, 9" long	25	38	50

Rainbow

Contributor: Dave Leopard, 2507 Feather Run Trail, West Columbia, SC 29169-4915.

	C6	C8	C10
'35 Oldsmobile Coupe, 3-3/4" long (RA001)	40	50	65
'35 Oldsmobile Sedan, four-door, 3-1/4" long (RA002)	40	50	65
'35 Oldsmobile Sedan, four-door, 5" long (RA003)	50	65	80
'35 Studebaker (?) Stake Side Pickup, 5-1/4" long (RT001)	40	50	65
Racer, open, tapered tail, 4" long (RR001)	40	50	65
Racer, open, tapered tail, 5" long (RR002)	NPF	NPF	NPF

Ranger Steel Co (Roslyn Hts., NY)

	C6	C8	C10
No. 450 Cross Country Turnpike, two wind-up racers, etc.	85	128	170

Realistic

Realistic toys were made by Freeport Toys Mfg. Co., in Freeport, Illinois, during the late 1940s and early 1950s. It used some original Arcade molds to produce cast-aluminum vehicles. Realistic seemed to specialize in buses and produced varieties of both Greyhound and Trailways buses. Its bus models were often sold as souvenirs at bus terminals.

Contributor: Dave Leopard, 2507 Feather Run Trail, West Columbia, SC 29169-4915.

	C6	C8	C10
1939 Yellow Cab, 8-1/4" long (RV001)	60	75	100

Left to right: Rainbow 1935 Oldsmobile Sedan, 5";
Rainbow 1935 Oldsmobile Sedan, 3-1/4". Photo from
From Dave Leopard's book *Rubber Toy Vehicles*.

Rainbow 1935 Studebaker Stake Side Pickup, 5-1/4".
Photo from From Dave Leopard's book *Rubber Toy
Vehicles*.

Two different looks at the Rainbow 1935 Oldsmobile
Coupe, 3-3/4". Photo from From Dave Leopard's book
Rubber Toy Vehicles.

Rainbow Open Racer, tapered tail, 4". Photo from
From Dave Leopard's book *Rubber Toy Vehicles*.

A Realstic ad in the August 1947 *Toys & Novelties* magazine.

Reliable Bus, plastic, 6-1/4". Photo from Terry Sells.

Reliable Lowboy with crane, plastic, 6-1/2". Photo from Terry Sells.

Reliable Super Deluxe Mechanical Sedan, plastic windup, 6". Photo from Terry Sells.

Reliable Tractor-Trailer, plastic, 6-1/4". Photo from Terry Sells.

Flex Clipper Bus, No. 201 (RV005) .	NPF	NPF	NPF
Greyhound Bus, No. 101, silver sides, 8-3/4" long (RV002)	60	75	100
Hook and Ladder Truck, No. 501, 8-1/2" long (RV007)	NPF	NPF	NPF
Racer, No. 401, 5-1/2" long (RV006)	NPF	NPF	NPF
Trailways Bus, No. 301, 9-1/4" long (RV003)	88	132	175
Trailways Bus, 8-3/4" long (RV004)	88	132	175

Rehrberger

	C6	C8	C10
David Moving Van, c.1924, 7-1/4" long..............	2000	3500	5000

Reliable

	C6	C8	C10
Bus, plastic, 6-1/4" long	NPF	NPF	NPF
Curbside Delivery Van, plastic, 10-3/4" long................................	62	93	125
Delivery Truck, plastic, 1950s, 4-1/2" long................................	25	38	50
Lowboy w/crane, plastic, 6-1/2" long	NPF	NPF	NPF

	C6	C8	C10
Pickup Truck, plastic, 1950s, 4-1/2" long..	25	38	50
Sedan, plastic, 1950s, 4-1/2" long ...	25	38	50
Super Deluxe Mechanical Sedan, wind-up, plastic, 6" long...............	50	75	100
Tow Truck, 10-1/2" long...................	31	46	62
Tractor-Trailer, plastic, 6-1/4" long...	NPF	NPF	NPF

Reliance Molded Plastics, Inc.

	C6	C8	C10
Indian Scout Motorcycle, movable handlebars, revolving wheels, plastic, c.1948.............................	NPF	NPF	NPF

Revell

Revell was founded in 1951 by Lewis H. glasser and was located in Venice, California.

	C6	C8	C10
Backfiring Hot Rod	42	63	85
Caterpillar Tractor and Wagon.........	60	90	120

Richard Appel Victory Tank. Photo from Jack Mathews.

Richmond Dump Truck, 12". Photo from John Taylor.

Richmond Tow Truck, 13". Photo from John Taylor.

Grader, 12" long	45	68	90
Jr. Mechanic Gift Set	NPF	NPF	NPF
Maxwell Auto, 1950-51	37	56	75
Plumbing Service Truck, w/tools	67	100	135
Police Motorcycle, w/sirens	17	26	35
Prestige Auto Carrier, two cars	135	202	270

Rich Toy

	C6	C8	C10
National Biscuit Company Truck, w/two trailers, wood, w/wooden Nabisco boxes	800	1400	2200
Texaco Gas Station, 16" x 22"	205	308	410

Richard Appel (New York)

	C6	C8	C10
Victory Tank, wooden, WWII	22	33	45

Richard Toys

	C6	C8	C10
Heavy Transport Rid 'em, steel 32" long	225	338	450

Richmond

	C6	C8	C10
Dump Truck, steel, 12" long	50	85	125
Tow Truck, 13" long, scarce	75	125	195

Rico Co.

	C6	C8	C10
BMW, 1930s, 13" long	800	1400	2200
Bonnet Bus, tin wind-up, 6-1/4" long	262	393	525
Silver Bullet Racer, driver, wind-up, 11" long	300	450	600
Streamline Car, c.1935 tin wind-up, 7-3/4" long	262	393	525
Tom and Jerry Car, battery-operated, three actions, 1960s, 13" long	262	393	525

RSA

	C6	C8	C10
Motorcycle, sidecar, driver, rider, tin wind-up, 10" long	1200	2000	3400
Motorcycle, driver, rider, tin wind-up, 9" long	700	1100	1500
Motorcycle, driver, 6-1/2" long	225	338	450

Schoenhut

	C6	C8	C10
Every Boy Auto Build 5 in 1 Toy, wood set to build, boxed	45	67	90
Stutz Racer, 10" long	150	250	350

Seiberling Rubber

'35 Ford Two-door Slantback Sedan, 5" long (GA01)	40	50	65
'35 Ford Two-door Slantback Sedan, 4" long (GA02)	30	40	50

Sherwood Toy Co.

	C6	C8	C10
Roy Rogers Nellybelle Pedal Car, 1954	800	1400	2000

Skippy

	C6	C8	C10
Pedal Car, (American National ?), Chrysler Airflow, 1936, 54" long...	9000	15,000	25,000

Skoglund & Olson

	C6	C8	C10
Bugatti Racer, cast-iron, 1929-30, 7-1/2" long..................................	2000	3500	5500
Bus, 10-1/2" long..............................	850	1400	2200
Central Garage Wrecker, 11-1/4" long	800	1350	2000
Tank Truck, 10-1/2" long..................	1000	1900	2600

Sonicon

	C6	C8	C10
Sonicon Bus, battery-operated, Japanese, 13" long	288	432	575

Sonny

	C6	C8	C10
Army Truck, open cab, 27" long.......	500	850	1250
Dump, 26-1/2" long	600	900	1400
Moving Van	400	700	1000
Parcel Post Van	700	1200	1900
Police Patrol Paddy Wagon	600	900	1400
Railway Express Co. Truck, 26" long...	800	1200	2000
US 1120 Artillery Truck, 26" long.....	325	480	650
USA 1120 Anti-Aircraft Truck, 24" long	600	925	1450

Stanley & Cox

	C6	C8	C10
Tank, wooden, WWII........................	32	48	65

Stanley Works

	C6	C8	C10
Stanlo Coupe, build-it, 5-1/2" long, 1920s..................................	85	128	170

Star Band

	C6	C8	C10
Star Brand Shoes Are Better Racing Car, The Winner, tin lithographed, 8-1/2" long	650	1050	1500

Steer O Toys

	C6	C8	C10
Convertible, Kaiser-Nash type, plastic, push down to operate, 12" long..	300	450	600

Left to right: RSA Motorcycle, sidecar, 10" and Motorcycle, driver, 9". Photo from Bill Bertoia Auctions.

Steer O Toys Convertible, 1950s, Kaiser-Nash type, 12". Photo from Tim Oei.

Sturdibilt

	C6	C8	C10
Logging Truck, (Oregon)	325	510	650

Superior

	C6	C8	C10
Circus Truck	88	132	175
Dump Truck.............................	40	60	80
Fire Chief Car, w/driver	32	48	65
Service Station, metal, 1950s	188	282	375

TCO

	C6	C8	C10
Policeman on Motorcycle, tin lithographed wind-up, 11" long	185	278	370

Technofix

	C6	C8	C10
Grand Prix, No. 302, tin wind-up, three cars, built-in key................	125	200	275
Racer Motorcycle, tin wind-up, No. 15, 7" long...........................	125	175	250
Racer Motorcycle, tin wind-up, No. 4, 7" long............................	125	175	250
Racetrack, tin, mutli-color, w/two tin wind-up cars	150	225	300
Ralleye 65, No. 311, racing hill, tin wind-up, three attached cars, built-in key................................	150	225	300

Ted Toys

	C6	C8	C10
Racer Pull Toy, wood, two riders	125	188	250

Thimble Drome (Roy Cox)

	C6	C8	C10
Champion Racer	288	432	575
No. 81..................................	225	338	450
Prop Rod................................	68	102	135
Racer, w/engine	275	363	550
Racer, No. 25...........................	188	282	375
Racer, pusher...........................	170	255	340
Special, No. 28, w/motor	275	413	550

Technofix Racer Motorcycles, tin windups, 7" each. Photo from Kent M. Comstock.

Ted Toys Racer, wood, two riders, pull toy. Photo from Perry Eichor.

	C6	C8	C10
Special, No. 2 Pusher, 8" long	138	205	275
Special, wind-up..........................	400	600	800

Timmee

	C6	C8	C10
Army Tow Truck, hard plastic, 9" long...	12	18	25

Timpo

	C6	C8	C10
Delivery Van, friction, 4" long..........	100	150	200

Tipper

	C6	C8	C10
Fire Ladder Truck...........................	400	600	800

Toy Founders

	C6	C8	C10
Kaiser Convertible, 1947, windup, 11" long...............................	175	263	350
Kar Kit, clockwork, car 11" long, makes three types	175	263	350

Trailer Co.

	C6	C8	C10
Traveleer Land Coach Traveler, 1927	180	270	360

Tru-Toy

	C6	C8	C10
Tru-Toy Steer-O-Car, 13" long	112	168	225

Varney Scale Models

	C6	C8	C10
No. 2473 Ford Sedan, HO scale	NPF	NPF	NPF
No. 2474 Ford Pickup	NPF	NPF	NPF
No. 2475 Ford Panel Truck, HO Scale	NPF	NPF	NPF

Viceroy

(Canada)

Viceroy had several locations and specialized in rubber and vinyl toys and dolls. Some were authorized versions of Sun Rubber Toys.

	C6	C8	C10
Donald Duck Roadster, 6/2/03 (VD002)	62	93	125
Donald Duck Tractor, 4/3/04 (VD006)	62	93	125
Open Racer, Sun Rubber type, 6-1/2" long (VR001)	30	45	60
Open Racer, 4/1/02 (VR002)	22	33	45

Viking

	C6	C8	C10
Dump Truck, 27" long	550	850	1300

A pair of Viceroy 4-1/2", Open Racers. Photo from Dave Leopard's book *Rubber Toy Vehicles*.

Viceroy Open Racer, Sun Rubber type, 6-1/2". Photo from Dave Leopard's book *Rubber Toy Vehicles*.

Viceroy Donald Duck Tractor, 4-3/4". Photo from Dave Leopard's book *Rubber Toy Vehicles*.

Viceroy Donald Duck Roadster, 6-2/3". Photo from Dave Leopard's book *Rubber Toy Vehicles*.

Weeden Auto, live steam, 8-3/4".

Left to right: Wellmade composition jeep, 7-1/2"; 3-1/2" jeep that appears to be by M.A. Henry—which also made an 8" composition jeep. Photo from Ed Poole.

A variation of the 7-1/2" composition Jeep made either by Wellmade or M.A. Henry. Photo from Ed Poole.

Walker & Stewart

	C6	C8	C10
Mack Box Van, cast-iron, 5-1/2" long	95	153	190
Mack Open Bed Truck, cast-iron, 5-1/2" long	95	153	190

Warren

Warren, of New York City, was a toy soldier company, owned by John Warren Jr., from about 1936 to 1939. Its two vehicles were conversions of toys made by Kenton and are of particular interest to toy soldier collectors.

	C6	C8	C10
Scout Car (W173)	300	450	600
Staff Car (W174)	300	450	600

Weeden

Weeden was founded in 1882 by William N. Weeden, in New Bedford, Massachusetts. In 1884, he made his first toy steam engine. His toys included engines, vehicles, and boats. Weeden toys were produced into at least the 1940s.

	C6	C8	C10
Steam Auto, early, 8-3/4" long	1500	3000	4500
Steam Fire Pumper	1200	2000	3000
Steam Road Roller, brass, tin, cast iron, steam toy fired by alcohol, 1920s, 7" long	250	375	500
Steam Tractor, 9" long	250	375	500

Wellmade Doll & Toy Co.

	C6	C8	C10
Jeep, composition, 3-1/2" long	NPF	NPF	NPF
Jeep, composition, 7-1/2" long	37	56	75

Wells (England)

	C6	C8	C10
Automite Racer, plastic, 9" long	60	90	120
Dump Truck, 1930s, tin wind-up, 12" long	275	415	550
Go Cart, gas operated	90	135	180
Mustang, 13" long	75	112	150
Racer, tin wind-up, No. 77, 11-1/4"	300	400	500
Rolls Royce limo, 9" long	130	195	260
Texaco, Tanker	42	64	85
Texaco, Fire Pumper	60	90	120
Touring Sedan, tin wind-up, 11" long	312	468	625

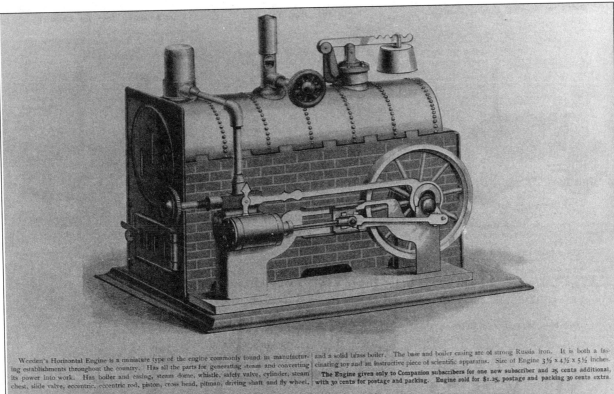

Weeden's Horizontal Engine is a miniature type of the engine commonly found in manufacturing establishments throughout the country. Has all the parts for generating steam and converting its power into work. Has boiler and casing, steam dome, whistle, safety valve, cylinder, steam chest, slide valve, eccentric, eccentric rod, piston, cross head, pitman, driving shaft and fly wheel, and a solid brass boiler. The base and boiler casing are of strong Russia iron. It is both a fascinating toy and an instructive piece of scientific apparatus. Size of Engine 3½ x 4½ x 5½ inches.

The Engine given only to Companion subscribers for one new subscriber and 25 cents additional, with 30 cents for postage and packing. Engine sold for $1.25, postage and packing 30 cents extra.

Electric Motor and Battery, Complete.

This Motor is run by an electric current generated in its base. It develops a high rate of speed, and can be used for running light toy machinery. We give with the Motor sufficient chemicals for running it a number of times. The 4-inch Aluminum Fan is not given with the Electric Motor, but will be sent for 25 cents extra. Notice "Village Blacksmith" offer below. Why not order it?

Given only to Companion subscribers for one new subscriber and 15 cents additional, with 40 cents for postage and packing. Motor and Battery sold for $1.00, postage and packing 40 cents extra.

The Leclanche Electric Bell Outfit.

All modern houses are supplied with electric door bells and call bells. They are easily put up, and not expensive in use.

The Outfit consists of a large Leclanché Battery, with Chemicals, a nickel-plated Electric Bell, mounted on a maple base and having a maple cover; a Push Button with porcelain knob; 50 feet insulated Copper Wire, Clamp Tacks, and full Directions for putting up.

Given, complete, only to Companion subscribers for two new subscribers; or for one new subscriber and 50 cents additional. See Conditions, page 522. Sold for $1.50. Sent by express, charges paid by receiver. Shipping weight of the Outfit 10 lbs.

Model Motor.

This Motor is 2½ inches high, has a 3-pole armature with no dead-centres, adjustable brushes, small pulley for running toys. We furnish all the parts for putting the motor together, including the castings, wire and explicit directions for winding.

Materials only given to Companion subscribers for one new subscriber and 15 cents for postage. Sold for $1.00, postage and packing 15 cents extra. The Motor wound, and ready to run, for one new subscriber and 25 cents additional, with 15 cents for postage. Price, $1.50, postage and packing 15 cents extra. Carbon, zinc and package of salts for battery, by mail for 25 cents.

Locomotive, with Tender, Car, Track and Station.

Description.

This is a perfect steam Locomotive. The Train, 22 inches in length, is made entirely of metal, and very handsome in appearance. The Engine alone is 7½ inches long, and uses alcohol for fuel. The Car has swivelled trucks. The Track, when put together, forms a 12-foot circular railroad. The Station, Truckmen, etc., are lithographed in colors on paper for pasting on wood.

This Locomotive, together with a Tender, Car, Track and Station, given only to Companion subscribers for four new subscribers; or for one new subscriber and $1.50 additional. See Conditions, page 522. Sold for $2.75. Sent by express, charges paid by receiver. Shipping weight 5 lbs.

"Village Blacksmith."

This toy is designed to be set in motion by an electric motor or steam engine. This is easily done by simply connecting the two with a belt or cord. When in motion the "Village Blacksmith" hammers away at his anvil, while a boy at his side operates the bellows, as natural as life. We will include the "Village Blacksmith" with a motor or steam engine for 50 cents extra, post-paid.

Price-List of Steam Toys. We can supply an Illustrated Price-List of Steam Toys which range in price from $1.00 to $10.00. These Toys are made by the well-known Weeden Manufacturing Co. This Price-List will be sent to any address on receipt of a two-cent stamp.

Weeden's steam-operated toys were big sellers for years. Toys pictured here are from the October 31, 1895 issue of *The Youth's Companion* magazine.

Wood Commodities Jeep, wooden. Photo from Jack Mathews.

Another version of Wood Commodities' Jeep. Photo from Perry Eichor.

Western Toy Co.

	C6	C8	C10
Jeep Pedal Car, aluminum...............	375	562	750

Wilco Promotional Toys

	C6	C8	C10
1967 Tanker, split window w/blue body and white trim....................	n/a	n/a	550
1968 Oil Tanker Ship, green body ...	n/a	n/a	1200
1985 Semi Tanker Truck, bank, blue body, white trim and red letters....	n/a	n/a	95
1986, 1933 Chevy tanker, bank, blue body, white trim and red letters	n/a	n/a	485
1988 Semi Box Truck, no barrels, white body, blue trim w/red and blue letters	n/a	n/a	25
1989 Race Car Transporter, white body, blue trim, red and blue letters	n/a	n/a	35
1990 Aerial Ladder Fire Truck, white body, blue trim w/red letters........	n/a	n/a	30
1991, semi-tanker truck, white body, blue trim, red letters	n/a	n/a	25
1992, race car transporter...............	n/a	n/a	25

Wood Commodities Corp. (New York)

	C6	C8	C10
Jeep, wooden, WWII	40	60	80
Tank, wooden, WWII......................	25	38	50

Wood Products Corp.

	C6	C8	C10
Jeep, steel, 10-1/2" long	60	80	100

Wood Products Jeep, steel, 10-1/2". Photo from Richard Jansen.

Woodhaven Animate Climbing Tractor, tin windup. Photo from John Monteleone.

Woodhaven

Research by John Monteleone has established that in the 1930s. Herman Joerger bought Animate Toy and, about the same time, Ranger Toys. He sold the business to his son, Herman Joerger Jr., who, in turn, sold it to his son, Kurt, the present owner. The firm made toys until at least 1939. It was located in Woodhaven, New York. Now called Woodhaven Telesis Corporation, it makes sheet-metal parts to order.

	C6	C8	C10
Animate Climbing Tractor, tin windup	125	188	250
Robot Bus, tin litho, 14" long............	58	87	115

Yone

	C6	C8	C10
Ford Falcon, wipers work.................	45	68	90
Monster Car, tin wind-up, monsters at windows, 1960s	48	72	95

Auction Houses

Bill Bertoia Auctions
2413 Madison Ave.
Vineland, NJ 08360

Brooks
81 Westside
London SWA 9AY, Great Britain

Butterfield & Butterfield
220 San Bruno Ave.
San Francisco, CA 90046

Chicago Antique Toy Auctions by Just Right, Inc.
6582 R.F.D.
Long Grove, IL 60047
708-949-0059

Christie's
502 Park Ave.
New Tork, NY 10022
212-548-1119

Continental Hobby House
PO Box 193
Sheboygan, WI 53082
920-693-3371

Garth's Auctions
2690 Stratford Rd.
Deleware, OH 43015
616-362-4771

Hake's Americana & Collectibles Auctions
P.O. Box 1444
York, PA 17405-1444
717-848-1333

International Toy Collectors Association
804 West Anthony Dr.
Champaign, IL 61822
217-351-9437

James Julia
P.O. Box 830
Fairfield, ME 04937
207-453-7125

Lloyd Ralston Toys
400 Long Beach Rd.
Norwalk, CT 06615
203-386-9399

Mapes Auctioneers & Appraisers
1729 Vestal Parkway West
Vestal, NY 13850
607-754-9193

Noel Barrett Antiques and Auctions
P.O. Box 300
Carversville, PA 18913
215-297-5109

Phillips
406 East 79th St.
New York, NY 10021
212-570-4830

Randy Inman Auctions
P.O. Box 726
Waterville, ME 04903
217-762-9706

Richard Opfer Auctioneering, Inc.
1919 Greenspring Dr.
Timonium, MD 21093-4113
410-252-5035

Skinner
357 Main St.
Bolton, MA 01740
508-779-6241

Sotheby's
1334 York Ave.
New York, NY 10021
212-606-7424

Ted Maurer Auctioneer
1003 Brookwood Dr.
Pottstown, PA 19646
215-32-31573

Clubs

American-International Matchbox Collectors & Exchange Club
Bob Fellows
532 Chesnut St.
Lynn, MA 01904-2717

Appraisers Association of America
386 Park Avenue South, Suite 2000
New York, NY 10016
212-889-5503
aal@rcn.com

Canadian Toy Collectors Society
91 Rylander Blvd., Unit 7, Ste. 245
Scarborough, ONT M1B 5M5
905-389-8047
ctcsweb@hotmail.com

Corgi Collectors Club
14 Industrial Rd.
Pequannock, NJ 07440
973-694-5006

National Automotive and Truck Museum of the United States
1000 Gordon M. Buehrig Place
Auburn, IN 46706
219-925-9100
Includes a museum of toy and model cars and trucks.

Collectors & Dealers

All American Toy Company
Bill Hellie
540 Lancaster, SE
Salem, OR 97301
503-399-8609
American Toy Company parts and limited editions

Bill Lango
127 74th St.
North Bergen, NJ 07047
Send an SASE for flyer

Brian Seligman
11004 SW 37th Mannor
Davie, FL 33328
DurangoBri@aol.com

Bylstone's
Bill and Sue Blystone
2132 Delaware Ave.
Brunswick, OH 44212
412-371-3511,
412-244-8028
Leading dealer in out-of-print collector books

Dave Leopard
2507 Feather Run Trail
West Columbia, SC 29619-4915
Rubber vehicles, old toy cars and trucks

Don and Barb DeSalle
5106 Knollwood
Anderson, IN 45011
800-392-8697
Collector of Tonka; promotes toy shows

Don Coviello
Box 283
Purchase, NY 10577
Collector; manufactures die-cast replicas of police cars

Edward Poole
926 Terrace Mt. Drive
Austin, TX 78746
1:36-scale ID vehicles and old wooden military vehicles

Fred Maxwell
4722 N. 33 Street
Arlington, VA 22207
Collector/researcher of slushmold vehicles

George Pravda
Spring Lake, MI
616-935-1392
Pedal cars

Heritage America Company
Michael Curran
P.O. Box 545
Hampton, IL 61256
309-496-9426
Toy vehicles

Iain C. Baillee
Town Mill
191 High Street
Old Amersham, Bucks HP7 0EQ

Illinois Antiques
Michael Curran
P.O. Box 545
Hampton, IL 61256
309-496-9426
Buddy "L" and Arcade

Jack Mathews
13 Bufflehead Dr.
Kiawah Island, NC 29455

Jeff Bub
1658 Barbara Dr.
Brunswick, OH 44212
216-225-1110
Auctioneer, appraisals

John Gibson
9713 Pleasant Lane
Potomac, MD 20854
grayghost@olg.com

Kent Comstock
532 Pleasant St.
Ashland, OH 44805
419-289-3308
Motorcycles of all type.

Lloyd L. Laumann
6980 C. Rd. 10, North
Waconia, MN 55387-9643
Tonka

Mark Rich
P. O. Box 971
Stevens point, WI 54481
mark.rich@sff.net

Model Cars & Trains Unlimited
Vincent Rosa
28 Arthur Ave.
Blue Point, NY 11715
516-363-2134

Oei Enterprises, Ltd.
Tim Oei
241 Rowayton Ave.
Rowayton, CT 06853-1227
203-866-2470
Buys, sells, trades and restores old toys.

Paul M. Provencher
Spring Garden House 20115 Woodfield Rd
Gaithersburg, MD 20882-1229
301-948-2858
ppro@compuserve.com
specializes in die-cast vehicles

Pedal Car Graphics
Bob Ellsworth
1207 Charter Oak Drive
Taylors, SC 29687
864-244-4308
Graphics for pedal cars

Perry R. Eichor
703 N. Almond Dr.
Simpsonville, SC 29681
kpmflyn@earthlink.net
Collector of vehicles, aircraft

Randy Prasse
916 Hayes Ave.
Racine, WI 53405
prasseephoto@racineweb.net
Structo

RATS Toy Shows
Bob Smith
62 West Ave.
Fairport, NY 14450
716-377-8394
oldtoys@frontiernet.net

Reid Covey
Box 2D
Highmarket Rd.
Constableville, NY 13325
sullivan@northnet.org

Richard Jansen
6420 Weber Rd.
Denmark, WI 54208-9438
Pressed steel toys

Richard MacNary
4727 Alpine Dr.
Lilburn, GA 30247
Coca-Cola vehicles

Robert and Alice Wagner
58 S. Main St.
Wharton, NJ 07885
Toy vehicles of all types

Rod Carnahan
541 El Paso St.
Jacksonville, TX 75766
Classic cast-iron toys

Ron Smith
33005 Arlesford
Solon, OH 44139
440-248-7066

Scott Smiles
848 S. Atlantic Dr., E
Lantana, FL 33462
Tin wind-ups

Smith-Miller
Fred Thomspon
P.O. Box 139
Canoga Park, CA 91305
Limited edition Smith-Miller trucks

Taylor's Toy
John Taylor
P.O. Box 63
Nolensville, TN 37135-0063
615-776-3104
taylortoys@midspring.com

Texas Car Peddler
Jay Dorsey
Fort Worth, TX
817-238-8363
Pedal cars

Rely on the EXPERTS for your Collecting Information

Stock Car Model Kit Encyclopedia and Price Guide
by Bill Coulter
This book lists and values more than 800 stock car models (nearly every one ever produced) and pictures over 300 models, from 1:43 to 1:24 scale and larger. It also contains valuable insights and tips for modelers and collectors.
Softcover • 8-1/2 x 11 • 208 pages
400 b&w photos • 40 color photos
STMK • $19.95

Die Cast Price Guide
Post-War: 1946-Present
by Douglas R.Kelly
From Hot Wheels to Franklin Mint, this guide provides three critical pieces of information every collector needs for buying, selling, or trading these ever popular toys: an index of the items made by each manufacturer, a brief historical outline of the manufacturer, and current values.
Softcover • 8-1/2 x 11 • 272 pages
250 color photos
AT5277 • $26.95

2000 Toys & Prices
7th Edition
Edited by Sharon Korbeck and Elizabeth Stephan
As always, rely on the accurate pricing of more than 19,500 items, each with up to three condition grades. That's over 55,000 values! Included is a directory of toy manufacturers and auction houses. Toys featured include banks, lunch boxes, games, PEZ dispensers, space toys, character toys, Fisher-Price, Hot Wheels, Star Wars, GI Joe, cast-iron vehicles, fast food toys and many more!
Softcover • 6 x 9 • 934 pages
500 b&w photos • 8-page color section
TE07 • $18.95

The Bean Family Pocket Guide
Fall/Winter 1999, Values & Trends
by Shawn Brecka
Features updates on new releases and recent retirements, as well as all-new sections on the most current trends in bean bag plush. Easy to read charts track changes in Beanie Baby values from Spring 1998 to Fall 2000. Also included are new "Fraud Alerts" to keep you informed of counterfeits and knockoffs.
Softcover • 4 x 8-1/2 • 272 pages
450 color photos
AT0136 • $12.95

Ultimate Price Guide to Fast Food Collectibles
Edited by Elizabeth A. Stephan
Ultimate Guide to Fast Food Collectibles features premiums from Arby's to White Castle and provides readers with the most up-to-date pricing. With over 1800 values and 500 photographs, this book is sure to become a standard in the hobby.
Softcover • 8-1/2 x 11 • 272 pages
500 b&w photos • 16-page color section
FASFD • $24.95

The Encyclopedia of Marx Action Figures
A Price & Identification Guide
by Tom Heaton
This book is a complete guide to the over 230 Marx action figures produced, with detailed photos that show the boxes and accessories, allowing you to identify and value your figures. Values are given in three grades: mint in box/carded; poor box and most accessories; loose with some accessories.
Softcover • 8-1/2 x 11 • 192 pages
425 color photos
MARX • $24.95

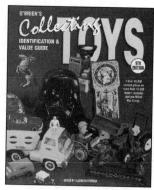

O'Brien's Collecting Toys
9th Edition
Edited by Elizabeth Stephan
This is the best encyclopedic, photo-intensive price guide and reference book for more than 16,000 vintage and obscure toys from the late 1880s to today. All of the 45,000 prices have been reviewed and updated from the eighth edition, with many increasing.
Softcover • 8-1/2 x 11 • 768 pages
3,500 b&w photos
16-page color section
CTY09 • $28.95

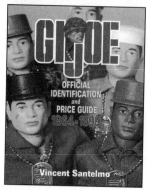

GI Joe Identification & Price Guide 1964-1999
by Vincent Santelmo
This guide is a comprehensive look at nearly every GI Joe figure produced from 1964-1999. Each figure has values for the doll itself, along with every accessory it came with. Because this guide is comprehensive, superbly illustrated in full color, and each item is individually valued, so you will be able to identify and value your items easily and quickly.
Softcover • 8-1/2 x 11 • 208 pages
1,000 color photos
JOID • $25.95

For a FREE catalog or to place a credit card order call
800-258-0929 Dept. TYBR
M-F, 7 am - 8 pm • Sat, 8 am - 2 pm, CST
Krause Publications, 700 E State St, Iola, WI 54990
www.krausebooks.com

Shipping and Handling: $3.25 1st book; $2 ea. add'l. Call for UPS rates. Foreign orders $15 per shipment plus $5.95 per book.
Sales tax: CA 7.25%, IA 6%, IL 6.25%, PA 6%, TN 8.25%, VA 4.5%, WA 8.2%, WI 5.5%
Satisfaction Guarantee: If for any reason you are not completely satisfied with your purchase, simply return it within 14 days and receive a full refund, less shipping.

Dealers call toll-free 888-457-2873 ext 880, M-F, 8 am - 5 pm

EXCITING REFERENCES FOR TODAY'S COLLECTORS

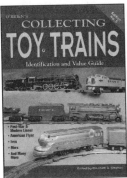

O' Brien's Collecting Toy Trains
5th Edition
Edited by Elizabeth A. Stephan
Experts and collectors provide insight into the ever-popular and always expanding world of train collecting. With more than 2,200 photographs, 6,000 items, 18,000 prices and 16 pages of color, collectors are sure to find the item they're looking for. The new alphabetized format will make this edition easy to use.
Softcover • 8-1/2 x 11 • 448 pages
2,200 b&w photos • 16-page color section
CTT5 • $24.95

Fun With Toy Trains
by Robert Schleicher
In addition to 24 exciting track plans, you will learn many facts on topics such as multiple train operation and how to use operating accessories to move logs, barrels, coal, and other commodities.
Softcover • 8-1/2 x 11 • 224 pages
160 b&w photos • 8-page color section
CMTH • $23.95

Standard Guide to Athearn Model Trains
by Tim Blaisdell and Ed Urmston Sr.
This book features more than 4,000 different models and a handy checklist format that will help you catalog your collection. Designed for both novices and professional collectors/dealers, this reliable guide will help you on your journey into this hot collectible field.
Softcover • 8-1/2 x 11 • 288 pages
420 b&w photos • 80 color photos
ACB1 • $24.95

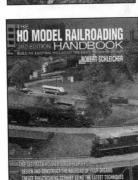
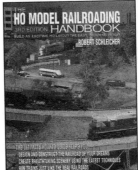

Scenery for Model Railroads, Dioramas & Miniatures
3rd Edition
by Robert Schleicher
Transform setups from miniature to magnificent with these expert-proven techniques. You'll learn the easiest and most effective methods for recreating the splendor of nature-but in miniature! Foolproof techniques are explained with easy-to-follow directions, step-by-step photographs and handy Reference Cards.
Softcover • 8-1/2 x 11 • 160 pages
120 b&w photos • 16-page color section
MRDM3 • $22.95

America's Standard Gauge Electric Trains
by Peter H. Riddle
This complete book covers the history of the Standard Gauge train, describes and values all makes of original Standard Gauge models and their contemporary counterparts, and includes plans for constructing a fully operational layout.
Softcover • 8-1/2 x 11 • 192 pages
50 b&w photos • 200 color photos
AT5226 • $26.95

The HO Model Railroading Handbook
3rd Edition
by Robert Schleicher
Learn to build exciting model railroad layouts with hot ideas, trends and products presented in an easy-to-follow, how-to style. The most well-respected and knowledgeable author in the field supplies all modelers, from beginners to experts, with the latest tips, tricks and techniques for building a new layout or refreshing an existing setup.
Softcover • 8-1/2 x 11 • 224 pages
250 b&w photos • 50 color photos
HOMR3 • $19.95

NEW EDITION

The Large-Scale Model Railroading Handbook
2nd Edition
by Robert Schleicher
Does your garden need a little magic? Are you interested in starting or expanding your large-scale collection? The completely updated 2nd edition of this best-selling book is loaded with technical tips to help make your G-scale railroading layouts a reality. New to this edition are an additional 16-page color section and information on simplified wiring systems for two or more trains using DCC, new locomotives, cars, and power supplies. Whether you are a novice and expert railroader, you will benefit from this book.
Softcover • 8-1/2 x 11 • 224 pages
300 b&w photos • 32-page color section
LSMRH2 • $23.95

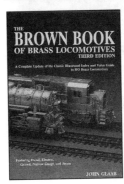

The Brown Book Of Brass Locomotives
3rd Edition
by John Glaab
Market prices for model brass locomotives of all types are yours in this updated third edition. You'll find models by class and type, manufacturer, and importer. Plus, you'll learn production runs as well as the original selling price. Illustrations help you identify numerous brass locomotives.
Softcover • 8-1/4 x 10-7/8 • 288 pages
BBBL3 • $24.95

For a FREE catalog or to place a credit card order call
800-258-0929 Dept. TYBR
M-F, 7 am - 8 pm • Sat, 8 am - 2 pm, CST
Krause Publications, 700 E State St, Iola, WI 54990
www.krausebooks.com

Shipping and Handling: $3.25 1st book; $2 ea. add'l. Call for UPS rates. Foreign orders $15 per shipment plus $5.95 per book.
Sales tax: CA 7.25%, IA 6%, IL 6.25%, PA 6%, TN 8.25%, VA 4.5%, WA 8.2%, WI 5.5%
Satisfaction Guarantee: If for any reason you are not completely satisfied with your purchase, simply return it within 14 days and receive a full refund, less shipping.

Dealers call toll-free 888-457-2873 ext 880, M-F, 8 am - 5 pm

TOY CARS & VEHICLES

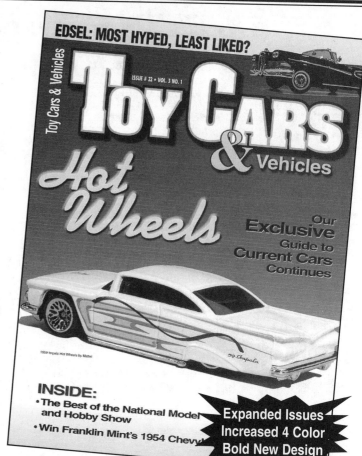

EDSEL: MOST HYPED, LEAST LIKED?

Toy Cars & Vehicles

ISSUE # 22 • VOL. 3 NO. 1

TOY CARS & Vehicles

Hot Wheels

Our Exclusive Guide to Current Cars Continues

1959 Impala Hot Wheels By Mattel

INSIDE:
- The Best of the National Model and Hobby Show
- Win Franklin Mint's 1954 Chevy

Expanded Issues
Increased 4 Color
Bold New Design

Save $5.00

Subscribe Today
1 year (12 issues)
for only $19.98

Fueled by premium editorial coverage including
**Racing Champions/Ertl • Brooklin • Minichamps
Hot Wheels • Matchbox • Revell-Monogram**

YOUR GUIDE TO TOY SHOWS IN Y2K

THOUSANDS OF TOYS FOR SALE!

ToyShop

The Toy Collector's Marketplace

ISSUE #219 • VOL. 13 NO. 1

January 14, 2000

Win
Over $200 Worth
of Toys in our
Huge Holiday
Giveaway!

The Best Toys of 1999

This issue was mailed December 20, 1999

$5.50 - Canada

Darth Maul book by Thinkway.
H.R. Pufnstuf by Living Toys.

Your Complete Buy and Sell Marketplace

ToyShop

Save $5.00

Order Today
1 year (26 Issues)
for only $28.98

The Complete Marketplace for buyers and sellers of toys, models, figures and dolls. Thousands of easy-to-read, categorized classified ads, display ads and a complete editorial package.

Credit Card Customers Call Toll-Free
800-258-0929
Dept. ABAX18

Monday-Friday, 7a.m. - 8p.m. • Saturday, 8 a.m. - 2 p.m., CST

Visit and order from our web site:
www.krause.com
Krause Publications • Dept. ABAX18
700 E. State Street • Iola, WI 54990-0001